THERION

Spelar på Ultra i Handen den:7 Maj
Start kl 19:30 BE THERE BAJSVÄCK

ENTOMBED

(STOCKHOLM - LP AKTUELLA)

GRAVE
(GOTLAND)

XYSMA
(FINLAND)

Crematory
(STOCKHOLM)

ABHOTH
(VÄSTERÅS)

MEGAROCK PROD. PRESENTS:

"A night of Metallic Mayhen med

CANDLEMASS
AGONY MANINNYA
ICCAGO

STOCKHOLM, LÖR 12/3
KOLINGSBORG KL.18.00
(T-SLUSSEN)

PRIS FÖRKÖP 50 KR
SAMMA KVÄ...
BILJETTER...
STOCKHOLM...
PER TEL. 08...

(STRÄNGNÄS)

SALA
FREDAG:
29/6
O.B.S !!!
18.00
BRAKAR DET LÖST
FOLKETS HUS
30:-

GRAVE
Första fastlandsspelninger.
för dessa VISBY grabbar

SATANIC
SLAUGHTER
(LINKÖPING)
RCHRISTE
(LINGHEM)

16 JUNI KL. 19.00
0 KR

ARR
POWER
HOUR

CW00970779

Third printing 2011. This edition first published in
the United States in 2008 by

BAZILLION POINTS BOOKS
61 Greenpoint Ave. #504
Brooklyn, NY 11222
United States
www.bazillionpoints.com

SWEDISH DEATH METAL
Copyright © 2006 by Daniel Ekeroth

Written by Daniel Ekeroth
Cover painting by Nicke Andersson
Scans by Chrille Svensson
Graphic design by Smile Studio,
Hans Eidseflot & Andreas Norrefjord
Winged skull design by Erik Sahlström

The text has been supervised by Stefan Pettersson, Orvar Säfström,
Victoria Klesty, Patric Cronberg, Tobias Pettersson, Fredrik
Karlén, Nicke Andersson, Fred Estby, Tomas Lindberg, Ola
Lindgren, and Anders Schultz.
Revised for Bazillion Points by Ian Christe
Edited by Polly Watson

The photos used in this book, promo photos aside, are from the
personal archives of Patric Cronberg, Anders Schultz, Nicke
Andersson, Orvar Säfström, and Jesper Thorsson.

Interviews were done by the author and on his behalf between
spring 2006 and spring 2008, if not otherwise indicated.

ISBN 978 0 9796163 1 0

Printed in China

Swedish Death Metal

Daniel Ekeroth

BAZILLION POINTS BOOKS

Contents Swedish Death Metal

ACKNOWLEDGEMENTS

Without the support of the following people, I would never have been able to complete this work. I am in endless debt to you, and I hope I can pay you back in some way in the future. May the left hand path be with you eternally!

Thanks and hello to:
Anders Björler, Fredrik Karlén, Fred Estby, David Blomqvist, Matti Kärki, Uffe Cederlund, Tomas Lindberg, Jesper Thorsson, Johnny Hedlund, Christoffer Jonsson, Johan Edlund, Kristian Wåhlin, Tomas Nyqvist, Fredrik Holmgren, Ola Lindgren, Daniel Vala, Jörgen Lindhe, Jan Johansson, Peter Ahlqvist, Dan Swanö, Mattias Kennhed, Totte Martini, Åke Henriksson, Mats Svensson, Roger Svensson, Lennart Larsson, Martin Schulman, Erik Strandberg, Jörgen Sigfridsson, Digby Pearson, Tobias Forge, Dennis Röndum, Peter Tägtgren, Lars-Göran Petrov, Mattias Kling, Tommy Carlsson

Special thanks to:
Nicke Andersson, Anders Schultz, Johan Jansson , Orvar Säfström Stefan Pettersson, Victoria Klesty, Christian Svensson, Robban Becirovic, Heval Bozarslan, Ronny Bengtsson, Oscar Szabo-Fekete Patric "Cronis" Cronberg

This book is dedicated to the memories of:
Tomas "Quorthon" Forsberg
Leif Cuzner
Stefan "Dark" Karlsson
Mieszko Talarcyk

The ones I have forgot
I'm completely aware of the fact that I have missed a lot of bands in this volume, and to all it may concern I am sorry for being too uninformed. If you spot any errors, or know about bands that you think should have been included, feel free to share your wisdom with the author for future pressings!

tamaraproductions@gmail.com

Preface

"Don't believe me what I tell you, not a word of this is true,"
—Thin Lizzy

The Phil Lynott quote above pretty much explains the mixed feelings I had while researching this book, as I realized I was doomed to propagate countless errors. Still, I decided to go ahead and make the journey anyway. After all, this isn't rocket science—this is Death Metal!

The main problem in dealing with a teenage-driven underground phenomenon like death metal is the unreliable sources. The few existing books on extreme metal generally just scratch the surface, making vague approximations. Minor bands are forgotten, and bigger bands are stripped of their uniqueness to fit a bigger context. So rather than rummaging through metal books I have scoured the massive corpus of fan-made 'zines, where the actual history of the genre is hidden. Still, fanzines hardly give the undisputed truth, since the core of these publications is teenage energy rather than scientific accuracy. Many things reported in their pages are outright falsehoods, sometimes even purposely! I have tried to compare the "facts" presented in different 'zines to a great length, but even this proved risky, since they frequently tended to steal information from one another.

So next I could go directly to the bands and ask the members themselves about their stories. To a large extent, I have done that. Even this proved to be a shaky foundation for correct information. Most band members don't seem to remember when line-ups changed, where demos were recorded, or when they played certain gigs. (Admittedly, I'm not entirely sure about these things when it comes to my own bands). The Swedish death metal movement generally took little interest in documenting its actions. People just did what they did for the sake of the moment—never mind the future. So much of the information in this book is based on fallible memories.

I began my work by sweeping my apartment and cellar in search of old demos and fanzines, and I became a real menace to some of my friends as I forced them to do the same. I rummaged countless cupboards and boxes in search of rare stuff, consuming everything eagerly in the darkness of my living room during hundreds of intense evenings. It was great to once again hear all the fantastic bands that never made it, and I also discovered a few that passed me by back in the days. For a while, I almost lost touch with reality, as my mind was completely occupied with the bygone death metal scene of my youth.

After about two years of dedicated listening and reading (and occasionally writing), I started to seek out band members and other prominent figures of the

Swedish death metal scene. It seemed an easy task at first. After all, everybody was enthusiastic about the project and shared their recollections freely. I also knew many of the key people personally. One guy answered while on tour in Japan, and another found time on the very same day he returned from a vacation in France.

A few guys just couldn't be found at all, but faith would be on my side. As it happened, a member from a forgotten band worked with one of my friends. I got in touch with a few other obscure bands through the horror movie trading community. The strangest episode of all was when a lost figure of the scene (he has no address or phone number!) turned up at a party in the middle of nowhere, and I shook him down on the spot for some wild anecdotes. At that moment, it felt that someone below really wanted this book to be made.

About the content, I'm very aware that this is not the definite survey on the subject. I have missed a lot of bands which should be in here, especially concerning the later part of the scene. During research I discovered new bands on a weekly basis, and was perpetually amazed at how massive the whole thing really has become. While reading, you must remember that this is *my* history of the early years of Swedish death metal. Like any other researcher, I can only be objective to a certain degree. I'm fully aware that much of the content of this book is based upon my own memories, my own taste, and my own knowledge. Many bands have naturally passed me by over the years, and it is just impossible to seek them all out.

I have also left out a lot of bands on purpose that others might think should qualify for this volume. Since I decided to concentrate on pure death metal, and the early scene in particular, the majority of Swedish black metal bands have been omitted. On the other hand, the focus on the early scene has urged me to include many thrash metal bands that some of you might feel are misplaced. But I have decided otherwise. In my opinion, there was no clear distinction between death metal and thrash metal during the early days of the movement—both kinds of bands were generally regarded as a part of the same scene. As you might see, I do favor pure death metal bands at the expense of all kinds of hybrids though. After all, this is a book about death metal!

I have also been forced to leave virtually everything that happened after 1993 out of the historical discussion. This was totally necessary to keep this book to a reasonable length. In my eyes, the early demo scene and the groundbreaking debut albums are the most important and interesting parts of the movement. I would rather discuss the early key bands and events than where they eventually led.

I have chosen to keep some of my personal taste visible throughout this book, which I believe is the only honest strategy and surely the most entertaining one. In keeping with the ruthless style of the good old 'zines, I think that my honesty captures more of the true spirit of death metal.

I would also like to make it clear right away that this book will focus on something which is pretty rare within rock journalism: music. My experience is that most books about music tend to focus on the sensational aspects of rock culture such as booze, sex, and drugs. When it comes to extreme genres such as death metal, writers often reduce everything to cheap exploitation as they revel in offensive lyrical contents and the image rather the actual music. I think such strategies are rather shallow and disrespectful, and I will not fall for such a simple and cheap approach. Instead, my focus will be on the greatest achievement of Swedish death metal—the incredible music. I will try to treat the subject with the respect it rightly deserves.

On a sad note, three irreplaceable pioneers of the extreme Swedish metal scene passed away during my work on this book: Tomas "Quorthon" Forsberg of Bathory, Stefan "Dark" Karlsson of Satanic Slaughter, and Leif Cuzner of Nihilist. Forsberg and Karlsson actually died a matter of weeks before I was supposed to interview them. I felt a little like the project was damned, but only grew more stubbornly convinced that it is time someone documented the movement which these giants actively created. This volume is dedicated to the memory of these legends.

I sure hope that you enjoy reading this guide as much as I enjoyed writing it. I also hope most of it is true, after all, and that you get some information about all the great bands Sweden has produced over the years. If something is terribly wrong, I urge you to contact me and share your wisdom. At last, I would like to make clear that even if my criticism against some artists seems harsh at times, I truly love every single band in this volume. Metal music—and death metal in particular—made my life worth living during my troubled teens of the late 80's. It kept me alive in this fucked-up world.

And it still does today.

Daniel Ekeroth

Foreward

Gather 'round death metal children. Gather 'round death metal oldsters. Gather 'round curious souls questing for the truth behind the brutality. Gather 'round posers. Remember that term? Posers? Still applies today, maybe more than ever. So all posers please exit this book immediately and proceed to the next cyanide handout. You'll be welcome there, at least by me. Heh heh. Okay, enough introductory rambling—let's get right to the intermediate ramblings, what do you say?

What is Swedish death metal? It's a distinct sound, it's a feel, it's a way of life through death. It's Swedish-fucking-death-metal and it's alive today to be sure, thank hell! Gather 'round hell-bent zomboids and let's give praise to some true (let's overlook the Swedish thing for two seconds) DEATH METAL originators. When this thing was new, a gutload of adrenalized death freaks were way on top of it all—great bands like Nihilist, Obscurity, Tribulation, Morbid, Grave, Dismember, Therion, and more. All this shit blew my mind!

If I may participate in a bit of self-indulgent time-warping, I'll tell you about being exposed to Swedish heaviness as a greasy aspiring metaller devouring all metal albums, demos, and 'zines that came my way. I stumbled upon Silver Mountain's *Shakin' Brains* LP when it hit the stores in 1983. I was 14, in case you're wondering, and was blown away by the musicianship and heaviness of this band. I still love that damn album. Soon after, Overdrive made its way through my stereo speakers. Hell yes! What intrigued me at the time was not only how great these bands were, but also where they came from.

Then something insane happened. The first Bathory album exploded onto my turntable and took me by complete surprise. I'll admit that when I first heard that devil goat of an album, I didn't care where it came from—I knew this was pure sickness in vinyl form! Open the floodgates, motherfuckers! Next thing I knew, Nihilist came and went, and holy hell what killer shit! Fortunately Nihilist morphed into Entombed and Unleashed. When Entombed's *Left Hand Path* came out, all felt right in this sick world. But I also have to contend with Carbonized, Macabre End, General Surgery, Comecon, and damn if Nifelheim and Maze of Torment don't crush skulls and other assorted bones! For a time it seemed that there was no end in sight to offshoots, side projects, and general death metal band inbreeding, and the world was better off for it. Death metal really seemed to be taking over.

Now if I may, I think it's time for some concluding ramblings before I'm out of here. What a kick-ass moment when Dismember crossed paths with Autopsy in Los Angeles in 1993 and a crazy freakin' show went down in a Chinese restaurant/underground club, complete with feet grazing the ceiling and all.

Great times, great friends. Another honorable and intense experience came when I got invited to Stockholm to record with Murder Squad on their second album. It was awesome to be surrounded by beer, whiskey, mind chocolate, old friends, new friends, and of course metal! At one point, I remember laying down a guitar track on the album and telling myself: *"Holy fuck, I'm playing guitar on a record with that classic Swedish Death Metal tone. Shit yeah!"*

What else can I say without saying too much? Thanks for the opportunity to be a part of this slab of death metal history—cheers to all who have molded this music into what it is today, and a toast to all who keep the beast alive and rotting!

Take it sleazy, sickos!

Chris Reifert
DEATH/AUTOPSY/ABSCESS

Introduction: Why Sweden?

"I've heard about this strange thing called death metal. Apparently it's only popular in Florida, where it's hot as hell, and here in Stockholm, where it's cold as hell. I personally don't get much about it, but it goes something like this: Aaaaaaargh!"—THURSTON MOORE, SONIC YOUTH, ONSTAGE IN STOCKHOLM IN 1991

When death metal established itself as a genre during the early 90's, two places stood out as the extreme metal centers of the world. One was the USA, especially Florida, from where bands like Morbid Angel, Death, Massacre, and Deicide hailed. This might come as no surprise, since the U.S. has been the center of popular culture for the last century, including a massive tradition of extreme music. But the other death metal center was Sweden and its capital city Stockholm, which spawned great bands such as Entombed, Tiamat, Therion, Unleashed, Afflicted, and Dismember. How could such a small country in the freezing north become so dominant in a genre so extreme? I don't have any perfect answers, but let me try to give you a bit of guidance anyway.

Since the 1980's, Sweden has been one of the countries in the world with the most metal bands per capita. I don't think metal music is more popular in Sweden than in other countries, rather the phenomenon probably has something to do with our social structure. Since Sweden is a wealthy country (it used to be, anyway), everybody who ever wanted to play in a band is able to do so. Instruments and rehearsal rooms have historically been provided by the municipalities to a large extent, and in certain places you could actually even get paid by certain associations to rehearse and make recordings. Many cities in Sweden still have large buildings with rehearsal rooms that you can rent for practically nothing.

Sweden is generally made up of extremely small and boring towns. Gothenburg is the second-biggest town, and it has less than 500,000 inhabitants. Most towns host about 25,000 people. There is simply not much else for youngsters to do than take up sports or start a band. So bands have emerged everywhere in large quantities. Since most of us started bands out of boredom and frustration, I think metal and punk were natural ways to go. In the small and worthless town of Avesta where I grew up, there were metal bands in every garage, school, and youth center. Metal was just everywhere. It was very hard to find gigs, since pubs are few in Sweden and most of those would never allow a metal band to play. Further, they don't allow anyone inside under 18 years of age, or more frequently, 20. Apart from occasional appearances at youth centers and school dances, there was no live scene to speak of for a long time. Most kids from my school fell into lives without meaning, or took up sports (among them Niklas Lidström, of massive ice hockey fame, and Tony Rickardsson, speedway motorcycle racing world champion).

Not until the death metal scene of the late 80's did Swedish metal really produce a dedicated movement, or anything to cause a stir internationally. Before death metal, only the radio-friendly hair band Europe and the guitar virtuoso Yngwie J. Malmsteen had any great success abroad. But in the mid-80's, something more extreme and original started to happen, with the groundbreaking black metal band Bathory and doom metal pioneers Candlemass. The unexpected success of these two groups probably galvanized youngsters in Sweden to be more dedicated in their own bands. Bathory and Candlemass were living proof that extreme music of superior quality could be produced in Sweden. They provided that example that Swedish metal could also be pretty successful—even in extreme forms.

Into the waiting rehearsal rooms went the few talented and hyperactive teenagers who kick-started a whole new movement. It began as a whisper, but eventually many of the bands (Entombed, Dismember, Tiamat, etc.) became leading forces of the international metal scene. They inspired others to continue, spawning countless new bands. Soon Sweden produced new influential leaders, such as At the Gates and Dissection. The favored studio of the early death metal scene, Studio Sunlight, gained a reputation of being one of the best in the world, encouraging youngsters to start their own studios. Sweden became synonymous with quality and originality, as the Swedish bands presented a different style than the U.S. or the rest of Europe. Everything quickly grew into a massive movement that is still here with us today.

In this book, I will examine the origins and development of this scene. I hope you enjoy the ride.

"NOW WE TAKE OVER, AND
RULE BY DEATH METAL
ENJOY OUR LONG-WAITED REIGN
BLOOD'S WHAT WE WANT"
—Possessed, "death metal"

Chapter One:
Dawn of the Dead

Death demo. Check out the fantastic artwork!

efore we begin this examination of the Swedish death metal scene, here is a brief overview of how the genre developed internationally. This is in no way a complete guide to the early death metal movement, but just a brief summary describing the most influential bands. If you are already familiar with the genre and impatient to get to Sweden, go ahead and skip this section and go straight to the next, "The Punk Connection" (page 18).

The development of extreme metal follows a simple bloodline. Metal started with Black Sabbath's heavy down-tuned riffs and occult imagery, developed via Judas Priest's precision riffs and speed, and finally arrived at Motörhead's high-charged mix of metal and punk. When the 70's turned into the 80's, these three venerable bands spawned the groundbreaking Newcastle, England, trio Venom, whose importance simply cannot be overestimated. Their first two albums, *Welcome to Hell* in 1981 and *Black Metal* in 1982, revealed how far you could take an extreme image, raw music, and harsh vocals. Venom paved the way for all three main genres of extreme metal: thrash metal—which was hardly ever called thrash metal back in the 80's, but rather speed metal; black metal, named after Venom's second album; and death metal.

Venom: Godfathers of death

Thrash metal started in the United States with bands like Metallica, Exodus, Anthrax and Slayer. The San Francisco Bay Area became the center of the movement, and the traditional style of thrash metal is generally referred to as Bay Area thrash. This genre was basically sped-up heavy metal, with riff orgies and steady "two-beat" drum patterns. The genre basically didn't have an image, and the lyrics often dealt with social topics. The big exception in the U.S. was Slayer, who initially wore primitive black and white corpse paint and sang about violence, death, and the occult. Slayer was the most brutal of the original thrash bands, and the only one that anticipated death metal to any great extent. Their 1986 album *Reign in Blood* was so intense that it probably would have been regarded as death metal, even by today's standards, if not for Tom Araya's high-pitched and fairly clean vocals. Later U.S. thrash bands such as Dark Angel and Sadus presented similar aggression.

Thrash metal was really brutalized and bastardized in Europe. One of the earliest and most important European bands following Venom's path was Switzerland's Hellhammer. This band reveled in self-styled occult trappings, and initially used stage names as well as corpse paint. They showed a more brutal approach than the American bands—especially the low-end guitar buzz and deep grunted vocals of Tom Warrior, which surely inspired the death metal genre to come. Hellhammer also participated in launching the term "death metal," as the members edited a metal fanzine called *Death Metal* in 1983. This 'zine probably also inspired the German label Noise Records, which released a compilation album titled *Death Metal* in 1984, featuring Hellhammer, along with the pretty un-deadly bands Running Wild, Dark Avenger, and Helloween. This album was notorious for its gory original sleeve, which anticipated the later covers of bands like Cannibal Corpse. After just one influential EP, Hellhammer transformed into Celtic Frost, who initially followed the brutal path but later lost it in a blur of glam.

Early Sodom demo tape

Around the same time, the German trinity of Sodom, Destruction, and Kreator also pushed the boundaries of extreme metal. Just like Hellhammer, these bands created a much rawer take on thrash metal than the one in the U.S. The guitars were a bit more down-tuned, the sound was rougher, the vocals grunted, and they went fully for violent and occult imagery. The arrangements and riffs of records like Sodom's *In the Sign of Evil* in 1985, Kreator's *Endless Pain* in 1985, and Destruction's *Sentence of Death* in 1984 stuck to the speed metal vein of Exodus and Slayer, but their raw aggression and blasphemous attitude surely pointed at something new. Hellhammer, Sodom, Kreator, and Destruction would all inspire the genre later known as death metal.

The term "death metal" was also used to describe the violent music of the incredible new Swedish band Bathory. Bathory's second album especially, *The Return*, in 1985 stepped beyond virtually everything else with its crude production, screaming vocals, and insane paces. Still, the thin production, simple riffs, and overall imagery didn't possess much of what would eventually be called death metal. Some European bands that would later play death metal were also formed around this time—Poland's Vader and Czechoslovakia's Krabathor both began in 1983—but they were yet little more than speed metal cover bands with a limited influence. To find the first musical expressions of today's death metal, we have to look again to the United States.

The first band to develop this new genre was probably San Francisco's Possessed. Influenced by the punkish Venom, Possessed was formed in 1982 by

Possessed
circa 1985

junior high school friends Mike Torrao and Mike Sus, who immediately set out to create aggressive music with an overly satanic image. In 1983, Jeff Becerra replaced original singer Barry Fisk when the latter committed suicide. With Becerra, Possessed's music rapidly turned more brutal. Becerra started using the term "death metal" to describe their music on a whim:

"I came up with that during an English class in high school. I figured speed metal and black metal were already taken, so what the fuck? So I said death metal, because that word wasn't associated with Venom or anybody else. I wasn't even about redefining it. We were playing this music and we were trying to be the heaviest thing on the face of the planet. We wanted just to piss people off and send everybody home. And that can't be, like, 'flower metal.'"
—Jeff Becerra, Possessed, from Choosing Death

So death metal it was. Another band that would be one of the main forces of the original death metal scene, simply known as Death, began as Mantas in Orlando in 1983. The band was started by young friends Barney "Kam" Lee and Frederick "Rick Rozz" DeLillo, and within weeks guitarist Chuck Schuldiner joined during a teen party. As the name indicates, Mantas were heavily inspired by Venom—Mantas was, after all, the stage name of Venom's guitarist. But Mantas' mission to combine the most brutal riffs and guitar tone imaginable soon went beyond Venom.

Other American bands that started during 1983 and 1984 were Chicago's Deathstrike, who became Master; Flint, MI's Tempter, who became Genocide and then Repulsion; Florida's Executioner, who became Obituary; and, most important of all, Tampa, FL's Heretic, who later became Morbid Angel. None of these bands had yet developed a style different from Venom's. They might have been a bit faster, with down-tuned instruments and harsher vocals—but they all still needed to mature. All would have eventually have a huge impact under their new names.

In October 1984, Mantas recorded their first proper demo, *Reign of Terror*. Though the music wasn't much more than crude speed metal, they felt that a name change was necessary to fit their violent music. So, just before Christmas, Mantas changed their name to Death. They added the slogan "corpse grinding death metal," an important factor in christening the new genre. On New Year's Eve, Death played their first gig, on a bill with Nasty Savage. The performance was recorded and the resulting tape found heavy circulation in the underground tape trading community. At this turning point, Chuck Schuldiner assumed creative control of the band, and would weather loads of lineup turbulence over the years to come.

Possessed further developed and cemented death metal with the classic *Death Metal* demo in 1984. This recording was groundbreaking. Unlike virtually all other contemporary bands, Possessed left most of the Venom/ Motörhead touches behind, creating "symphonic" tunes, and combining loads of complex riffs and drum patterns with the rawest sounds and fastest paces imaginable. Also, Becerra took his vocal style one step beyond anything the world had heard before, as he seemed to scream and grunt at the same time. All these ideas would later be considered trademarks of death metal, and Possessed's demo has since generally been considered the first pure death metal recording.

The *Death Metal* demo was extremely well received in the underground. Before the end of 1984, Possessed secured a deal with Combat Records. The band was strengthened by adding second guitarist Larry LaLonde, and on their spring break from high school in 1985, they recorded their debut album, *Seven Churches*. In my opinion this is without a doubt the first death metal album. The raw guitar sound, the harsh inhuman vocals, the complex songs, the satanic lyrics, and the pure aggression of this recording simply went beyond anything previously heard. The massive sound, numerous tempo changes, and unorthodox riff patterns are just startling, and in many ways Possessed left traditional speed metal formulas behind. Though few recognized it at the time, death metal had been born.

Back in Florida, the super-talented guitarist Trey Azagthoth developed his band Heretic during 1984 into the soon-to-be-gigantic death metal band Morbid Angel. Unlike most other extreme bands of the time, Morbid Angel didn't rely much on Venom for inspiration. Instead, they developed a more complex style by combining elements from Slayer and Mercyful Fate. They also concentrated on imagery, creating a trademark logo that helped cast an aura of mystique. In 1986 they recorded what was supposed to be their first album for the new label Goreque Records, run by David Vincent. The result became

Morbid Angel—the kings of death metal

known as *Abominations of Desolation*, and has subsequently been released by Earache Records. However, Trey Azagthoth felt the songs didn't reach their potential. He shelved the project and sacked everybody in the band but guitarist Richard Brunelle, feeling they couldn't match his standards. Before long, Morbid Angel would perfect a complex and advanced style of death metal that would become legendary.

At the same time, Chuck Schuldiner found a suitable drummer for Death in Chris Reifert, and together they put together the *Mutilation* demo. This demo was intense enough to earn the band a deal with Combat Records, already home to Possessed. The resulting *Scream Bloody Gore* was an extreme assault on the senses, and still possesses enough power to blow most extreme bands to the

Milky Way with its inhuman vocals, gory lyrics, raw guitar sound, hammering drums, and evil riffs. The album was hailed as an innovative masterpiece, and the band seemed to be heading for a bright future. However, Chris Reifert didn't want to move to Florida with Chuck, so the duo simply split up in 1987. Chuck once again had to search for new members, and Chris launched the primitive Autopsy—a band that would have a huge impact on the Swedish death metal scene of the late 80's.

During 1985 Tempter became Genocide, and gradually turned up the speed in search of fresh brutality. Their late 1985 demo *Violent Death* showed insane velocity. By 1986 they were probably, together with England's Napalm Death, the fastest band in the world. Genocide's *The Stench of Burning Flesh* demo had an immense impact on the underground scene. In June they rechristened themselves Repulsion, and financed a proper recording themselves, since no labels were interested. The resulting *Slaughter of the Innocent* was a revelation in fast brutality. However, the band was probably too extreme for its time. In November 1987, Repulsion officially folded. Nevertheless, they had introduced the next cornerstone of death metal: the exreme hyper-speed.

One of the few bands rivaling Repulsion's lust for velocity was Terrorizer from Los Angeles, formed in 1985 by teenage metalheads Oscar Garcia and Jesse Pintado. Terrorizer were initially inspired by bands like Death and Deathstrike/Master, but the major change came when Jesse got a demo from Napalm Death. The tape was faster than anything he and Oscar had ever heard, and they set out to play equally fast. Their new standard for speed clearly required a skilled drummer, and they soon found the incredible Pete Sandoval. With Sandoval aboard, Terrorizer recorded several furious rehearsals. However, the band was far too extreme for its hometown of Los Angeles. Terrorizer had a hard time finding shows, and the band soon faltered. Pete Sandoval was invited to join Morbid Angel in the summer of 1988, and Terrorizer called it quits.

At this point, Napalm Death was swaying the entire American scene. Napalm Death had actually started out in 1981, but up until late 1985 they had played more traditional (if fast and brutal) hardcore punk. The change came in November 1985, when ultra-fast drummer Mick Harris joined the group. Harris is said to have invented two crucial terms: "blast beat," to describe his insanely fast kick/snare drumbeat; and "grindcore," to describe the resulting ultra-fast music. Harris' hyperactive nature drove the band toward insane speed, leading to equally rapid changes in the lineup. After a couple of brutal demos, the band attracted the attention of upstart Earache Records, which released the debut LP *Scum* in 1987. This was probably the fastest record ever made to this point, and Napalm Death's influence on the entire metal world was to be massive.

Just as *Scum* transformed Napalm Death from an underground punk act into one of the most acclaimed extreme bands in the world, it also propelled Earache towards almost unimaginable success. The obscure underground operation rapidly sailed forward as the world's first death metal label. In the years to come, Earache signed most of the best death metal bands. Among the first was Carcass.

Carcass was formed in 1985 by drummer Ken Owen and guitarist Bill Steer, who also played in Napalm Death from 1987 to 1989. In 1987,

Napalm Death demo, punk style

Carcass teamed up with singer/bassist Jeff Walker, and soon recorded the *Flesh Ripping Sonic Torment* demo. The band distinguished themselves with ultra-down-tuned guitars and brutally fast paces. Further, their lyrics and imagery focused on gore and deformed body parts, traits that would later spawn an entire subgenre of gore-grind bands. Carcass soon attracted Earache Records, and they released their unrelenting debut, *Reek of Putrefaction*, in June 1988. The raw album sold unexpectedly well, and revered BBC radio host John Peel named it his favorite album of 1988.

Swedish Carcass poster

Earache—the world's first pure death metal label

Still, the record that caused the greatest stir that year was Napalm Death's *From Enslavement to Obliteration*, released in September 1988. It sold massively, knocking Sonic Youth from the first position of the UK independent chart. Napalm Death became a phenomenon, inspiring loads of bands to play harder and faster.

One of those bands, Morbid Angel, spent 1987 perfecting their own style. By this time David Vincent, who was supposed to release the band's shelved debut, had joined as bass player and singer. Morbid Angel practically lived in a Charlotte, NC, studio for months, and the resulting *Thy Kingdom Come* demo showed tremendous progress. The band had become tighter, faster, and more evil-sounding. But Trey Azagthoth wasn't satisfied. Hearing Napalm Death, he realized that they also needed a super-fast drummer to go further. In 1988, Morbid Angel returned home to Florida, and that summer they convinced Terrorizer drummer Pete Sandoval to join them. Ready for anything, they signed a deal with Earache.

As Morbid Angel were creating their majestic style, fellow Florida band Executioner changed their name to Xecutioner and started to act more serious. Xecutioner were in fact the first metal band to record a demo at the soon-to-be-famous Morrisound studio in Tampa. The demo was produced by Scott Burns, whose name would become synonymous with death metal. The tape immediately landed the band a deal with Roadrunner Records. After another name change to Obituary, the band returned to Morrisound to record their first album, *Slowly We Rot*.

Another Florida band attracting attention was Amon, soon to be Deicide. Founded in July 1987, within a month the band had recorded their first demo, *Feasting the Beast*. The band struggled through a proper demo, *Sacrificial*, and shortly afterwards signed to Roadrunner Records.

Simultaneously, former Death drummer Chris Reifert's new band Autopsy signed a deal with Peaceville. The year 1986 brought the release of *Beyond the Gates*, the second album by forerunners Possessed, and in 1988 the revitalized Death answered with their second effort, *Leprosy*. Death's album showed a new and more complex approach. Something insanely extreme was definitely coming over the metal world.

Death metal finally established itself as a full-fledged genre in 1989. That spring, strong debuts like *Slowly We Rot* by Obituary, *Severed Survival* by Autopsy, and *Altars of Madness* by Morbid Angel showcased all the fully assembled elements. Morbid Angel especially demonstrated how precise and aggressive death metal could be, and became leaders of the nascent style.

"'Infernal Death' with Death was like the whole essence of death metal in one riff, and that was quite easy to do. But when Morbid Angel came along, things got more complicated. You had to learn a bit more in order to play those songs."—MIKAEL ÅKERFELDT, OPETH/BLOODBATH

The second Carcass album, *Symphonies of Sickness*, was also a massive success, and soon record labels lined up to sign new bands. Immolation and Cannibal Corpse were quickly snapped up, along with Swedish bands Entombed and Carnage. Death metal was no longer just an obscure and undefined underground phenomenon.

In essence, death metal can be described by the following characteristics:

- Unpronounced, deep, growling vocals;
- Down-tuned, heavily distorted guitars;
- Fast drumming, with heavy use of double kick-drums;
- Complex song compositions with numerous breaks, stops, and tempo changes;
- Unorthodox and twisted riff patterns;
- Lyrics about death, gore, violence, the occult, and horror; and
- Imagery with trademark logos, but seldom any actual image or dress code.

This list is of course simplified, and any of the characteristics can be left out without disqualifying a band as death metal.

By 1989, the Swedish scene was about to break through. Now that the main influences are out of the way, I guess the time has come to end this summary of the international development of death metal. Once the Swedish scene got going, it tended to look to itself for inspiration rather than abroad.

The Punk Connection

As in the case of Napalm Death, extreme metal often evolved from extreme punk rather than heavy metal. This is particularly true for the early Swedish death metal scene, which didn't really develop from any tradition of Swedish metal at all. When the earliest Swedish hard rock bands, such as November, started out around 1969, they were in fact more like heavy blues/rock bands with some psychedelic elements, rather than actual metal groups. As the 70's moved on, the Swedish hard rock bands grew increasingly progressive. November probably remained the hardest of them. Further, Swedish heavy metal never really caused any commotion, with perhaps the exception of Heavy Load. The bands that were called metal in Sweden were mostly cheesy bands like Europe of "The Final Countdown" fame, so there wasn't much to build a new metal scene upon.

Instead, the Swedish death metal pioneers took their inspiration from the international speed metal scene, especially the punkish German bands, the death metal pioneers operating under the "speed metal" tag, and extreme punk. Even though there were times of fiendish and narrow-minded hostility between the metal scene and the punk scene, there are of course broad similarities between the two genres. The speed, the distortion, the heaviness, and the aggression—basically, the same ingredients make up the foundations of extreme punk and extreme metal.

Nobody remotely sensible can deny that the punk movement is where music originally started to get really fast and aggressive. Bands like Discharge and Black Flag were the most violent acts in the world in the late 70's and early 80's. When metal music started to get more brutal, it took aggression and speed from punk—from Motörhead via Venom and Slayer to Morbid Angel. Of course, the same development was happening in Sweden.

The first Swedish band that approached a more aggressive kind of punk was probably Rude Kids from Stockholm. Even though their debut album, *Safe Society* from 1979, is basically a traditional punk recording, hints of what was to come can be heard on the closing song, "Marquee."

This might have been the first time that a Swedish band used the stompy "D-beat" drum pattern that has been closely associated with crust punk since the success of the UK band Discharge. I think that "D-beat" was originally a Swedish term, used in the 80's, but I have seen it used since in international magazines. I think the *D* in "D-beat" originally referred to Discharge, but nobody seems to remember anymore. Another name for the beat is the "crust beat," or simply the "Discharge beat." Motörhead probably introduced this beat to extreme music, but Discharge perfected it.

As Swedish punk was becoming more aggressive, Rude Kids did not continue on a brutal path, but other guys around the country were ready to go further. One such guy was the notorious Rolf Revolt from Hudiksvall, who since 1976 played in countless obscure punk bands such as The Källare and The Turf. In 1980, The Turf was restructured as Missbrukarna, and Rolf got down to business creating aggressive hardcore. Even though Missbrukarna didn't release anything in their first years, they attracted attention by playing live quite a lot. However, by the time they finally released the tape *Krigets Gentlemän* in 1983, and then a split 7" with the band Panik in 1984, they had already been surpassed in brutality.

Perhaps the most important new brutal hardcore band was Anti

From top: First Anti Cimex 7" (the original pressing is worth a fortune); apocalyptic war-punk

Cimex from Gothenburg, formed in 1981. After a few rehearsals they recorded the crude *Anarkist Attack* 7", which was basically standard punk rock. The important change came in 1982 when they kicked out singer Nille, and their notorious bass player Tomas Jonsson took over the microphone. Anti Cimex's *Raped Ass* 7", released later in 1982, showed real progress, and is one of the rawest and most violent hardcore releases ever. Anti Cimex followed this classic record with the *Victims of a Bomb Raid* 7" in 1984, and the *Criminal Trap* 12" in 1986. Then they split up.

In 1990, Anti Cimex made a brief comeback, joined by Cliff from Moderat Likvidation and Black Uniforms, but those early years were what made Anti

From left: Åke of Mob 47
bashing away in the mid-80's;
Mob 47/ Protes Bengt comp CD

Cimex the most legendary Swedish hardcore band. The aggression of their first records is still vital, and Jonsson is one of the best hardcore singers ever.

While in Anti Cimex, Jonsson also played in the equally brutal Gothenburg band Skitslickers, known abroad as Shitlickers. The only record Skitslickers produced during their short existence, the *Spräckta Snutskallar* 7", is as intense as anything by Anti Cimex, cementing Jonsson's position as Sweden's number one hardcore maniac. Another important band of the first phase of Swedish hardcore was Moderat Likvidation from Malmö. Moderat Likvidation's sole 7", *Nitad* from 1983, has one of the rawest productions in hardcore history—the guitar sound remains unsurpassed.

Things also started to happen in Stockholm by 1983, as a hardcore scene gradually spawned bands like Agoni and The Sun. But the best and most intense of the Stockholm bands was the incredible Mob 47 from the northern suburb of Täby. Springing to life in 1981 as the primitive metal/punk band Speedy Snails, the band soon grew brutal.

"Chrille, Jögge, and I started out with two other guys during the summer of 1981. Back then we played some kind of mix between heavy metal and punk, but we soon transformed into a trio and started to bash out aggressive punk as Censur. We quickly got inspired by bands such as Discharge, Dead Kennedys, Poison Idea,

and Crucifix, but also Swedish bands such as Skitslickers and Anti Cimex."—ÅKE HENRIKSSON, MOB 47

With such influences, Mob 47 quickly turned super-aggressive and very tight. In 1983, they released the relentless *Hardcore Attack* demo, followed in 1984 by the *Kärnvapen Attack* EP. These recordings were packed with ultra-brutal hardcore at its best, winning the band attention overseas. The legendary punk magazine *Maximumrocknroll* hailed the EP as one of the best hardcore releases ever. Mob 47 was one of the most intense bands in the world.

"*We recorded everything on a four-channel tape recorder in our rehearsal room, which was in fact an office in the bowling hall where my father was working. It's been known as the 'Bowling Studio' ever since. We just wanted to play insanely fast D-beat punk, and deliver it as tight as possible.*"—ÅKE HENRIKSSON, MOB 47

Though one of Sweden's very best hardcore bands, Mob 47 didn't last long. Their final recording was the *Stockholmsmangel* demo in 1985, and a few gigs later it was all over. There just wasn't a big scene for Swedish hardcore, and the bands had virtually no places to play.

"*Around 1984 there were not many people in Stockholm who appreciated really extreme music. If they liked anything harder it was heavy metal or '77-style punk. The few gigs we did were cool, though, despite never attracting much people. We were probably ahead of our time.*"—ÅKE HENRIKSSON, MOB 47

They were ahead of their time, all right. The few times they managed to get to play live, they got extremely worthless terms.

"*We got a gig in Falun, and had to rent the PA when we got there. Then we were allowed onstage half an hour after the curfew, and given no money whatsoever. Our next show was in Norrköping, and three people paid to see us. We got 20 kroner [$3] for that show. It was a 120-mile drive back and forth.*"—JÖRGEN ÖSTGÅRD, MOB 47

As you might understand, hardly anybody was yet interested in really extreme music. Mob 47 eventually got fed up and quit—not until 2006 reforming and again playing some cool shows. Yet after the original break-up, Åke continued playing even more extreme music for a while.

"*During the mid-80's I also listened to extreme metal such as Possessed, Venom, and Slayer. Eventually I discovered Heresy, which was one of the first bands that combined punk and metal in a really extreme way. We became influenced by them in Protes Bengt, a project I had with Per and Ola from Filthy Christians. We wanted to play as fast as possible, but honestly, that 'battle' in Sweden had already been won by Asocial. Their demo was sick.*"—ÅKE HENRIKSSON, MOB 47

Asocial from Hedemora truly took hardcore punk to the next level. They started out as a more traditional hardcore band, and recorded loads of crude

*From top: Asocial, the godfathers of grind;
Religion Sucks—that fact eventually made
crust punk and black metal best buddies!*

rehearsals between 1980 and 1982. Although among Sweden's fastest and most intense bands, they never released anything during these years.

"I really can't remember when we formed the band, but I guess it was early in 1980. We were just a bunch of children that wanted to bash out punk. Some early influences were American bands like Jerry's Kids, MDC, and DRI, but we soon got into English bands such as Discharge and Exploited as well." —MATS SVENSSON, ASOCIAL

Asocial are key to any survey of extreme music, due to their first official release, the 1982 demo *How Could Hardcore Be Any Worse?* The guys obviously got the idea that they should play as fast as possible on this recording, and they really got sick with it. The intense drumbeat was unheard of—they called it the "one-beat" because the snare drum was hit constantly. This one-beat was basically what would later be called the "blast beat," but back in 1982 nobody knew anything about that. The sound of the recording is as brutal as anything at the time, just a wall of distortion and noise. Tommy screams angrily and the songs are short and intense. To my ears, Asocial invented grindcore with this demo.

"Originally the songs were written for a regular two-beat, but along the way someone figured out that it could sound more violent if you hit the snare on every beat instead. That was something unheard of back then, but we were young and angry and just did it. Tommy's vocals were also very harsh for the time [almost like the later growl style of death metal], but that mainly had to do with the fact that he was heavily hung over and hoarse during the recording. We didn't know what we were doing at all."—MATS SVENSSON, ASOCIAL

At least to my knowledge, at the time of the release of *How Could Hardcore Be Any Worse?* Asocial were the fastest and most extreme band in the world. It would be years before someone attempted a similar style again. At this point in time, bands like Napalm Death would have been slaughtered by Asocial!

"We sure didn't know about anyone who played as fast as we did back then. It was only later that bands like DRI, Siege, and Napalm Death started to get sick with speed. In fact, we heard a rumor early on that the guys of Napalm Death had heard our demo and decided to change style. I don't know if it's true, but if it is, that's a great honor!"—MATS SVENSSON, ASOCIAL

Asocial never really got the attention they rightly deserved for their ground-breaking development of extreme music, which may be one of the reasons why they never went back to this furious style. In any case, they had made their point—they were the fastest band in the world and couldn't go any further.

"When we did a gig up here in Hedemora together with Mob 47, they had obviously talked about showing those 'farmer boys' up north how brutal punk should be handled. Then we went up and fucking annihilated them with our set! Mob 47 were actually almost too intimidated to walk onstage after us, and nearly wanted to cancel. I guess we had made our point after that."—MATS SVENSSON, ASOCIAL

After bassist Tompa left Asocial in 1983 to form Svart Parad, the others continued as a straight crust band. Asocial's 1984 *Det Bittra Slutet 7"* is also one of Sweden's best punk releases, forming the corpus of traditional Swedish hardcore alongside Anti Cimex, Skitslickers, Moderat Likvidation, Svart Parad, and newer bands like Avskum, Totalitär, No Security, and Bombanfall.

"We never got much attention during our active years. We gigged a bit but nobody cared. As we tried to change our style later on, the thing that we had initially been doing became incredibly popular with bands like Napalm Death. I guess we were way ahead of our time."—MATS SVENSSON, ASOCIAL

Near the end of 1983, a young punk shaped the extreme ideas of crust into metallic form. He was Tomas Forsberg, better known as Quorthon of the band Bathory. Years later many punk bands made similar transitions into metal. The crust band Agoni transformed into the speed metal band Agony. Members from Asocial started superior thrash band Hatred. During the latter half of the 80's, bands like Filthy Christians and G-Anx developed a grind style similar to that invented by Asocial in 1982.

In 1988, the crust band Disaccord transformed into the death metal band Carnage, and in 1991; a young member of the punk band Moses formed the notorious black metal band Marduk. All these extreme bands developed through punk, and took it into metal territory.

"Disaccord was not strictly punk when I played with them, it was a Discharge-meets-Venom-and-Motörhead kind of thing—very fast and aggressive, just the way I liked it, and that's why I joined that band. I brought a more metallic edge to the Disaccord sound, with my solos and

MOSES
UTE NU!!!
DEMO #2
"HÅRDA BUD"
5 låtar för 15 pix
Melodiöst Punkgnöl!

MOSES
Mogge Håkansson
Bigatan 93
60361 NORRKÖPING

7

Moses flyer. After this demo, everything went black for Morgan Håkansson, who started the ultra-brutal Marduk

down-picking rhythm style. I really enjoyed my time with Disaccord. In the end, though, I became too engulfed in the murky swamps of death metal to be able to focus on anything else. I quit Disaccord and started Carnage the very next day with my friend Johan Liiva on bass and vocals."—MICHAEL AMOTT, CARNAGE/CARCASS/ARCH ENEMY

Digby Pearson of Earache Records recalls the wave of transformation:

"Like most guys from the old days, I started out as a massive fan of UK crust punk and American hardcore. Sweden was famous for their many crust bands early on, and I got every tape with every band from Fredda Holmgren at CBR. When I started to promote gigs, it was natural for me to bring over a couple Swedish bands. So I did a UK tour with Anti Cimex and the somewhat thrashier Agoni.

"Within the early tape trading scene there was also a small circle of punks that appreciated some heavy metal like Motörhead and Venom. Then came thrash metal, and the first Metallica demo, especially, was a coveted trade item on many punks' lists. And when I first heard a demo by Death, I realized that there was something even more extreme around. The metal of bands like Death and Vomit seemed to be the next extension of the extremity of the hardcore punk and thrash metal scenes. It was way more extreme."— DIGBY PEARSON, EARACHE RECORDS

"*The first band I was into was Kiss. Then my friend Kenny and I discovered some punk records in his father's collection, and we became punks. One day some guy played Venom for us, and we thought that was pretty cool as well. But it wasn't until I met Fred Estby at the age of thirteen that I really got into metal. He was a metalhead and showed me Metallica and Slayer. I was a punk and showed him Discharge and GBH. For some time, the rule was the fastest band wins. We didn't care if it was metal or hardcore.*"—NICKE ANDERSSON, NIHILIST/ENTOMBED

"*Punk was the beginning for me, and that led to death metal. When I discovered Possessed's first demo I was hooked, and since then extreme metal has been my main love in life. Today I listen almost exclusively to intense death metal, and it's great to see that Sweden has produced such quality bands as Visceral Bleeding, Insision, and Spawn of Possession.*"—MATS SVENSSON, ASOCIAL

There you have it. To a large extent, extreme metal was born out of extreme punk. Keep that in mind as we leave punk behind and examine how Swedish metal became brutalized.

"SUDDENLY POWERS COME FROM WITHIN
MUSCLES AND MIND ARE FILLED WITH WRATH
I BURST OUT IN FRENZY POWERS OF HELL
AND BREAK UP THE TOMB AND THE DARK
RAISE THE DEAD"   —BATHORY, "RAISE THE DEAD"

Chapter Two:
Swedish Metal
Gets Brutalized

BATHORY

In 1983, Sweden was basically a nice, quiet place for music. The charts were ruled by moronic pop bands like Freestyle, Noice, and Gyllene Tider—whose Per Gessle went on to international fame with Roxette. The few metal acts were weak hairspray bands like Europe and Treat, or marginalized heavy metal groups such as Heavy Load and Gotham City. The most extreme music Sweden produced—crust punk bands like Asocial, Anti Cimex, and Mob 47—were completely unknown to most people, even to fans of extreme music. Out of this environment of nothingness, the mighty Bathory emerged.

Bathory are without a shadow of a doubt the most important and influential of all extreme Swedish bands. Over their career, Bathory would change the face of metal. They were a cornerstone for the entire Swedish scene, and probably the biggest inspiration for the Norwegian black metal movement of the early nineties. Still, no Norwegian band would ever create music that came near the pure evil darkness of Bathory. In my opinion, no one has yet done that. Bathory are the proverbial masters of evil black metal, and always will be. Period.

Bathory was basically the one-man project of mythical singer/guitarist "Quorthon." His real name was never revealed during Bathory's career. Though the inner core of the extreme Swedish metal scene knew it, they kept it a secret. Quorthon himself gladly spread all kinds of invented names in interviews—like Runka Snorkråka, Pär Vers, Fjärt Bengrot, and Folke Ostkuksgrissla. (Learn Swedish and get the point!) Since his unexpected demise in June 2004, it's known that he was born Tomas Forsberg, but I'll still refer to him as Quorthon.

In the beginning, Quorthon was another marginalized kid saved by the punk movement of the late 70's.

"If I hadn't started to play in punk bands around '79–80 I could have ended up on the streets, with a needle in my arm. Luckily, I didn't have any such friends, so I got involved with the punk movement, and was inspired by bands like Exploited and GBH."—QUORTHON, BATHORY, FROM BACKSTAGE #2, 1996, MY TRANSLATION

Quorthon spent the early 80's in various Oi! and punk bands, the most notable being Stridskuk (Swedish for "War Cock"). The metal scene in Sweden was almost nonexistent at this point, but the young punk got more and more into bands like Black Sabbath and Motörhead. Quorthon soon combined his influences from GBH, Black Sabbath, and Motörhead, aiming to be more brutal than any of them. Eventually he put an ad in a music magazine searching for a bass player and a fast drummer who could play double kick-drums.

At the end of February 1983 he found drummer Jonas Åkerlund and bass player Fredrick Hanoi to play along with his ideas. Both had previously been in the traditional metal band Die Cast.

On March 16, 1983, Bathory was officially born as the trio met at Musikbörsen on Kungsholmen and walked to their first rehearsal in a small

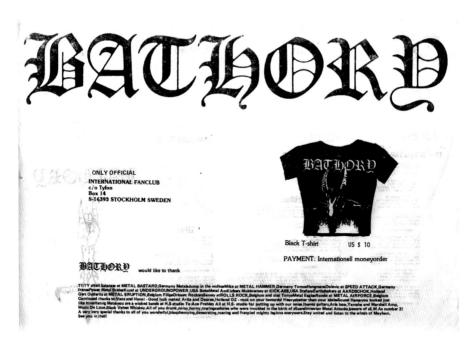

Bathory insert for the first album

room at Sigtunagatan, close to S:t Eriksplan in Stockholm. (This date was given in the box set *In Memory of Quorthon*. However, in what I feel is a very honest 1996 interview with Quorthon by Petra Aho in *Heathendoom* magazine #1, the birth date for Bathory is set to be March 3.)

"The first song we ever finished was called 'Satan Is My Master,' and it sounded like 'Symptom of the Universe' by Black Sabbath. The lyrics were ridiculous. The same week we did 'Witchcraft,' and shortly after 'Sacrifice.' The other two guys were more into Whitesnake, Iron Maiden, and Saxon. They actually wanted me to write such stuff instead..."—QUORTHON, BATHORY, FROM BACKSTAGE #2, 1996, MY TRANSLATION

During their very first rehearsal, the youngsters started to fool around with stage names, partly just to mock the famous Swedish band Europe, whose members had ridiculous names like "Tempest." This means the stage names of black metal were all a joke from the beginning, at least in Sweden. After a while, Bathory's young singer chose Quorthon as his pseudonym, having toyed with names like "Satan," "Black Spade," and "Ace Shoot." I guess we're all happy that he changed it to Quorthon.

The name Bathory had stuck in Quorthon's mind about a year earlier, as he visited the London Dungeon. He was intrigued by the figure of Elizabeth Bathory, sitting naked in a bathtub filled with blood—it wasn't the medieval horror story that fascinated him; it was tits and blood!

During this early period, Bathory supposedly made their only live appearances. They allegedly played six to eight gigs, all in front of about thirty people in places like youth centers. Though Bathory's few live appearances during 1983 have been confirmed by Quorthon in several interviews for Swedish fanzines, the booklet for the *In Memory of Quorthon* box set insinuates no such gigs ever occurred.

Anyway, the guys were hardly skilled enough to do gigs. Besides, their musical disagreements probably made it hard to choose which covers to play. Jonas and Fredrick were more into bands like Iron Maiden and Judas Priest, and Quorthon wanted to be more extreme than any band around. Complications were cemented within the band from the beginning.

"Well, we did play a little in Alvik a few times, around Nockeby by Smedslätten at a cinema theater. At the most we had a hundred people watching, and at least thirty bands playing. Everybody was drunk and everybody knew each other and everybody traded girlfriends backstage after the gig. It was just for fun, and it probably sounded awful."—QUORTHON, BATHORY, FROM BACKSTAGE #1, 1996, MY TRANSLATION

As you might guess, this early lineup wasn't very steady. During the summer of 1983, Jonas and Fredrick went on a trip to London. In the meantime, Quorthon kept Bathory going with Rickard Bergman on bass and Johan Elvén on drums from his old Oi band Stridskuk. This temporary version of Bathory recorded four songs live in the rehearsal room: "Sacrifice," "Live in Sin," "Die in Fire," and "You Don't Move Me." The two latter tracks survive, and serve as a good example of how Bathory sounded during its first months.

When Jonas and Fredrick returned from London they also got back in the band. During the months to come, the three guys changed rehearsal rooms several times, shuttling around Vasastan, Vikinghill, Västberga, and Solna. They were apparently more interested in drinking beer and having fun than actually playing music. Soon they felt that the band was stagnating due to musical differences, and they came close to splitting up in late 1983. But something unexpected happened that kept them together for at least one more month.

As the legend goes, Quorthon had been working part time in Tyfon's recording studio since 1982, courtesy of some kind of rehabilitation program at school. (He was a hell-raiser, you know.) The main reason he was allowed into the studio was probably that his father, Börje "The Boss" Forsberg, worked there. Strangely, neither Quorthon nor Börje Forsberg ever admitted to being family, but their relationship is common knowledge in the Swedish metal scene.

Under his father's command, Quorthon made coffee and sorted papers, leading to a regular part-time job in late 1983. At this point, Tyfon was compiling a record with Scandinavian metal bands. The label hoped to cash in on metal's popularity boom in Scandinavia following the band Europe's unexpected victory in the important Swedish music competition Rock SM. A bunch of mediocre Swedish bands, along with a few Finnish ones, including the decent Oz, were snapped up for the compilation.

Then a miracle happened. Just before the album was completed in January 1984, one of the Finnish bands backed out. Now the heads of Tyfon were desperate to find a replacement, but there simply were no bands around. Without much hesitation, Quorthon stepped forward and told them that he had a band. Bathory. The world of extreme music would soon be shaken to its foundations. Tyfon agreed to put the youngster's band on the record—even though they still hadn't heard a single chord. Blood was thicker than water, and in the future, father and son would lead Bathory into glory.

"*I made damn sure to do my very best in convincing Tyfon how well we would fill that spot. When they asked me what sort of music we played, I think I said something stupid along the lines 'very brutal' or 'rough and demonic stuff'. It was all very innocent.*"—QUORTHON, BATHORY, FROM THE <u>IN MEMORY OF QUORTHON</u> BOOKLET, 2006

A few days later, on January 23, Bathory rushed to the studio through a frozen and snowy Stockholm to do their first proper recording. At this point, even Quorthon didn't really know what they were supposed to sound like. It all just happened. Once in the studio, they played a slow version of "The Return of Darkness and Evil" for the bosses. Surprisingly, they kind of liked it, and Bathory were allowed to do two songs for the album. The second song they recorded was "Sacrifice." Within months the young Quorthon proudly saw Bathory's name on vinyl, as *Scandinavian Metal Attack* was released in March. During this time Bathory had virtually ceased to exist. Jonas and Fredrick both moved away, leaving Quorthon alone with his creation. (An interesting aside— Jonas Åkerlund today enjoys international fame as an acclaimed director of music videos for Prodigy, Madonna, and Metallica.)

To everybody's surprise, Bathory proved to be the most appreciated band on *Scandinavian Metal Attack*. In fact, over 95 percent of the fan mail the label received after the release was dedicated to this raw new band. Tyfon decided right away that Bathory had to make an album, and a startled Quorthon realized that he needed to revitalize the band with new members. Naturally, he again thought of his old friends from Stridskuk. Rickard Bergman accepted, but Johan Elvén turned the offer down. Quorthon had to find a new drummer quickly, as the recording was to be done in June. He managed to get hold of a guy named Stefan Larsson, and on May 22 the new version of Bathory recorded a rehearsal. As it turned out, this was the only time all three of them rehearsed before entering the studio.

On June 14, the unrehearsed trio entered Heavenshore Studio to put together Bathory's first album. The place was actually an old garage turned into a place to record demos. Tyfon only wanted to spend 5,000 SEK ($700) on the young band, so this was as good as it was going to get. Armed with a cherry-red Ibanez Destroyer guitar, a ridiculously small drum kit with one cymbal, and a 20-watt Yamaha amplifier (no distortion pedals used), Bathory went to work with the homemade eight-channel tape recorder at the studio. Due to the limited budget, they ran the recorder at half-speed to fit everything on one master tape, which created a "humming" sound on the finished product. The guys also had to work very quickly to stay within budget—the recording and mixing were subsequently done in somewhere between 32 and 56 hours.

"With the exception of the strange lack of oxygen and the problems we had controlling the sound, I remember almost nothing from the procedures or how we went about recording a lot of those Heavenshore albums. And yet, in addition to the smell of old dried grease all over those car parts and gadgets, my most vivid memory of recording the debut album is still the smell of decades of tobacco smoke accumulated in the carpets and walls—which was okay with me, because I was still smoking in those days."—Quorthon, Bathory, from the In Memory of Quorthon booklet, 2006

Bathory was released by Tyfon in autumn 1984, and was a total assault to the ears in the mediocre Swedish metal scene. This album sounds very much like early Venom, though the production is even rawer. The song "War," especially, is incredibly violent, and anticipates the brutality of later Bathory albums. Though the music is faster than anything in the metal scene at that time, some hardcore bands, like Asocial, were faster. It was still basically a mix of the satanic party rock of Venom and the energy of San Francisco thrash metal.

The vocals are in essence an extension of the vocal style of Venom's Cronos. Even though Quorthon maintained until his death that he had never heard Venom before making Bathory's first album, that's very hard to believe. We all heard that first Venom record, and the similarities between the two bands are just too obvious. In fact, Jonas Åkerlund has admitted to Erik Qvick of Nirvana 2002 that Bathory were exclusively inspired by Venom during these days.

Not only was the music similar to that of Venom, the album cover is also based on a "goat concept" similar to the first Venom sleeve. What Quorthon did was simply cut out a nose, a mouth, and a couple of eyes from various horror comic books, and paste them together to form a collage resembling a goat. He used loads of Tipp-Ex correction fluid and ink to cover up the cuts, and by hand drew the torso, the ears, the fur, and the horns. Though the result might look ridiculous to some, it has since become the trademark of Bathory, and the symbol has an undeniable evil feeling to it.

Also like the cover of Venom's debut, the picture was planned to be printed in gold. That was too expensive a color to use, though, so Quorthon asked the printer to do it as close to gold as possible. It turned out canary yellow. Quorthon thought it looked just awful—and truthfully, it does. The color was changed to white after the initial pressing of 1,000 copies. The first pressing of *Bathory* has become notorious as Gula Geten—"The Yellow Goat"—and has become one of the most valuable collectibles of extreme metal.

The story about the flip side of the sleeve is equally amusing. In true punk fashion, Quorthon bought a set of rub-on letters of the Old English font to lay out the band name and song titles. As it turned out, he was soon short one letter *c*. Figuring that *s* sounds enough like *c*, he rubbed the song "Necromancy" on as "Necromansy." The song/intro "Storm of Damnation" faced an even worse fate, as Quorthon simply neglected to put it on the track list.

There are no band photos on the sleeve simply because Quorthon didn't have any. Later, the refusal to include photos on Bathory's first three albums was one of the aspects that made the band so mystical and scary—but it originally happened by coincidence. In a similar way, no names were written on Bathory's first album, since two of the members had left the band. Quorthon never intended to create a mystique around the band; he just didn't want to confuse people with names that would never be associated with Bathory again. The only "names" appearing on the album are those of Quorthon, the pseudonym he had now settled for, and Boss—both credited as producers.

Since Bathory was far more extreme than any other band on Tyfon, Quorthon also had to come up with a name for an imaginary imprint. Initially he went for Noise, but upon learning that name was already taken by some German label, he settled for "Black Mark." Not until seven years later did Börje Forsberg start an actual label called Black Mark. Until then, it was just a fake name to separate Bathory from Tyfon's other releases.

They need not have worried. *Bathory* sold out its initial pressing of 1,000 in less than two weeks, and during the autumn the album continued to sell. Quorthon realized that Bathory could actually get serious, and he dedicated himself entirely to the project.

"[After the recording of the debut] I thought, 'That's it, I have actually experienced something.' Then it got some kind of cult status and Kerrang! *started to write a lot. So then it was time to make another album, and for the first time we thought: 'Wow, this is the big one!'"*—QUORTHON, BATHORY, FROM <u>HEATHENDOOM</u> #1, 1996, MY TRANSLATION

Now Bathory was on the move, and Quorthon started promoting his music around the world. He even claimed to have invented the term "death metal" in an interview in October 1984. It's probably true that he started to use the term around then, and it might even be true that he had never seen the term used before that. But, as I have explained, the term had already been used by others: Possessed, the fanzine of the Hellhammer guys, and the compilation album from Noise Records. But let's not argue over who was first—the important thing is that something new and exciting was about to happen. There were no fixed death metal or black metal genres at this point, just a still-unlabeled corpus of new, violent music. Börje Forsberg at Tyfon/Black Mark is sure that Bathory (and himself) were important for the birth of the genre:

"I was involved in the creation of death metal. I had the first death metal band in the world [on my label], since Bathory was the first to be called that in the U.S. I was one of the first death metal producers in the world."—Börje Forsberg, Tyfon/ Black Mark, from Close Up #1, 1991, my translation

He doesn't suffer from a lack of confidence, you have to give him that.

The return of darkness and evil...

If *Bathory* attracted attention within the metal scene, it was nothing compared to what the group's next album, *The Return*, would do. A planned 7" was shelved in late 1984 since the label didn't think it showed any progression. As a consequence, Stefan and Rickard soon exited the band. From then on Bathory was definitely Quorthon's one-man project, with various musicians by his side.

Unlike the other three of Bathory's classic first four albums, *The Return* was actually recorded in the professional Elektra Studio. By this point Quorthon had realized that an extreme "scene" had evolved around bands like Hellhammer/Celtic Frost and Sodom, and he knew he had to compete. So Bathory went beyond them all. Tyfon unleashed the album in 1985, and it hit the world like an A-bomb.

The music on *The Return* was so fast, so aggressive, and so extreme that people almost couldn't believe their ears. (I sure couldn't!) The production was colder and more disturbing than before, complete with grunted inhuman vocals. The lyrics had also stepped much further into the dark side. In many ways this is Bathory's most extreme record, and one of the most evil albums ever. Everything from the clouded full moon on the cover to the monotonic and relentless music and the satanic lyrics fits perfectly. Forget Venom, Mercyful Fate, and Hellhammer—*The Return* was the prototype for most of what would later be called black metal. Early Mayhem and Burzum, especially, owe a lot of debt to this phase of Bathory: the vocals, the songs, the production, the lyrics... it's all here. Bathory were soon hailed the world over as one of the most extreme forces of metal, and this was just the beginning.

"That album was recorded in Elektra's big, professional, and expensive studio. To have twenty-four channels and more than five microphones was just

incredible for us [...]. I can reveal that we tried to get the same drum sound as on Exciter's Heavy Metal Maniac. *They had such a brutal drum sound."*
—Quorthon, Bathory, from Backstage #30, 1996, my translation

Even though *The Return* sounded evil as hell, Bathory returned to the garage of Heavenshore for the next two albums. I guess the primitive equipment actually suited Bathory's music and budget better. But if a great black metal album has ever been made in a flashy studio, this is the one. Following *The Return*, Bathory started to get popular, and making live appearances became urgent—not least for the heads at Tyfon, who wanted to promote their product. But no drummers in Sweden were considered capable of performing the violent music, so Quorthon sought a suitable drummer in other countries. In early 1986 he approached Carsten Nielsen from great Danish thrash band Artillery, but Nielsen turned him down. Shortly after, Quorthon contacted Sodom's Witchhunter, who proved much more receptive to the idea. Witchhunter actually came up to Stockholm for rehearsals, but nothing came of it.

"*We only rehearsed for a couple of days and nights. We mostly watched a lot of videos, stuffed ourselves with junk food and that was it. We didn't get anywhere with that.*"—Quorthon, Bathory, from the In Memory of Quorthon booklet, 2006

Eventually Quorthon abandoned the idea of performing live, and he concentrated on producing studio albums. This relaxed the situation, and Bathory soon went on to great things. Throughout 1986 Bathory were inactive. It was up to other bands to hold the banner for extreme Swedish metal.

Sweden Loses Its Innocence

Nineteen eighty-six often described as the year Sweden lost its innocence, after the murder of Prime Minister Olof Palme, who was shot to death on the evening of February 28. The nation suddenly found itself in a state of shock from which it never really recovered. The investigation into the murder never came up with a conclusion. Sweden suddenly seemed a dark and creepy place. I guess the gates for extreme metal opened as the darkness embraced the nation. Relentless albums such as Slayer's *Reign in Blood* and Metallica's *Master of Puppets* provided a perfect soundtrack during cold winter nights.

Sadly, the death count in Sweden soon also included one of the most beloved and respected musicians in thrash metal—Metallica's Cliff Burton. On the morning of September 27, Burton was crushed to death under Metallica's tour bus in a tragic accident on the E4 highway outside Ljungby in southern Sweden. The concert in Stockholm the night before was to be Metallica's last with its classic lineup. Metallica and the thrash metal scene as a whole would never be the same. In retrospect, one can almost say that thrash metal started to die that day. Within a few years it was just gone.

In Sweden we got the terrible news on the metal radio show Rockbox the same night, when the startled host, Pär Fontander, informed us about what had happened. The show turned into a Metallica tribute, and many of their songs were aired that night. Metallica was already one of the most popular metal bands in Sweden—they were the favorite band of virtually everyone I knew. After this radio broadcast the admiration of Metallica took on almost religious proportions. In fact, a guy I knew tried to commit suicide after hearing the news that Cliff was gone. Extreme music was that important for so many of us.

That same night, Rockbox introduced another band to its listeners, and their music really fitted the sad program. The band was Candlemass, who had just released their groundbreaking album *Epicus Doomicus Metallicus* on Black Dragon Records. The majestic sadness of the song "Solitude" struck a nerve in all of us. At that precise moment a lot of us decided to start bands ourselves. I know I did. The legacy of extreme metal had to be conserved. We all picked up our guitars and started to mix the speed and energy of Metallica with the heaviness of Candlemass.

And Candlemass sure was heavy. The riffs are thicker than anything this side of Black Sabbath, and the lyrics more depressing than anything heard in Sweden before—especially the sinister "Solitude." The impaled skull on the cover still send chills down my spine. The production was almost perfect: clear, heavy and big. *Epicus Doomicus Metallicus* remains one of the best doom metal album ever released, no doubt about that. Though Candlemass could never live up to the quality of this first album, their seed was already planted. Within a few years, Swedish youngsters would infect the world of metal with sick new ideas of musical expression.

The importance of the radio show Rockbox should not be underestimated. For a few years this show introduced almost all the new exciting music. Personally, I heard not just Candlemass but S.O.D., Dark Angel, Death Angel, Heathen, Testament, and Overkill for the first time on Rockbox. The show probably started the craving for extreme music in Sweden. You listened to the broadcast, heard new bands, and the next day looked for their records. The show's host, Pär Fontander, played a more important role than has been recognized in creating the extreme Swedish metal underground. Five years before, Jonas Almqvist and Håkan Persson had an immense impact on the Swedish punk scene with their Ny Våg program—radio was important in the 80's!

"I listened to Rockbox with an almost religious dedication. For a couple of years, that's where you got to know about exciting music." —PATRIK JENSEN, ORCHRISTE/SEANCE/THE HAUNTED

"First there was a program called Hårdrock, and I taped every show and listened to it about ten times. Then came Rockbox, and Pär Fontander did such

Poster for one of Candlemass' first gigs, topping an all-star Swedish bill

a great work in spreading metal across Sweden. I can't imagine growing up without it."—TOMAS LINDBERG, GROTESQUE/AT THE GATES/DISFEAR

"Rockbox was something you listened to every week. Even though they didn't play much extreme metal, it was those few songs you waited for." —NICKE ANDERSSON, NIHILIST/ ENTOMBED

"You listened carefully to Rockbox because you knew they were going to play one or two really extreme songs. Then you wrote down the names of those bands and ordered them from the record store the next day. Rockbox was the only channel to discover new brutal music. It was only later that you got into tape trading and got information from magazines such as Metal Forces." —OLA LINDGREN, GRAVE

Bathory Enters the Eternal Fire

Returning to music actually produced in Sweden, as 1986 turned into 1987, an album appeared that instantly became an underground favorite. I am talking about the mighty Bathory, and their third album, *Under the Sign of the Black Mark*. The two earlier albums by Bathory had been great, but they were nothing compared to this almost perfect lesson in extreme metal. Countless fans of black metal still hail this as the best album of the genre. And its power is unquestionable. This is the stuff that nightmares are made of.

Even with less shock value than the two preceding records, this album really showed Bathory's potential. The songs are so much better, and every single composition has a dark soul of its own. The riffs and arrangements are a lot more elaborate, and there are a lot of tempo changes—something that would later be developed much further in death metal. "Woman of Dark Desires" and "Equimanthorn," especially, take considerable power from slowed-down choruses.

Under the Sign of the Black Mark is also a lot more varied than either *Bathory* or *The Return*. Fast tracks like "Massacre" alternate with slower numbers like the majestic "Enter the Eternal Fire" to great effect.

"The influence is real big. Quorthon was one of those who started the extreme black metal. Not like Venom or anything, but when it comes to tempo, listening to The Return *it was so fast you couldn't get your mind around it. Burzum or whatever—fuck you, ten years later! Quorthon was the shit. That's not only why I respect him, but also for the songs—*Under the Sign of the Black Mark *has everything. That was 1985, before anyone started blasting. Everyone was playing two-beats, and he already started blasting. He knew what was going on."*—Peter Tägtgren, Hypocrisy/Pain/Bloodbath/Abyss Studio

Furthermore, the album is one of the most atmospheric records ever released. Bathory's previous efforts sound dry and flat in comparison. *Under the Sign of the Black Mark* is drenched in big reverb, rendering a unique and disturbing touch to all. This exaggerated use of reverb wasn't originally planned as a source of atmosphere, though.

"If you listen to albums like Under the Sign... *and* Blood Fire Death, *we use an extreme amount of reverb—for example, ten-second reverb on a lot of things. No bands do that today since it just makes a mess. The reason we did it was because we recorded in a garage with filthy instruments, piss poor mixing*

Don't mess with these guys

Under the Sign of
the Black Mark—
*arguably the best
black metal album
ever*

*board, and such. It was so cheap and so bad that we had to obscure all the cuts
and such with a lot of echoes."*—QUORTHON, BATHORY, FROM <u>HEATHENDOOM</u>
#1, 1996, MY TRANSLATION

So almost by chance, Bathory invented the creepy black metal sound that
has inspired so many bands. When it comes to lyrics, *Under the Sign of the Black
Mark* is a bit more advanced than its precursors. There isn't as much satanism
or hell-raising, but rather dark visions about death and destruction. The song
"Call From the Grave" is a disturbing tale of what's going on in the head of a
person who is about to die. The topic of death would soon be developed into
absurdity by the forthcoming death metal bands. One final distinguishing point
about the third Bathory album is about Quorthon's vocals. On this record he
perfected his trademark screams to almost artistic levels. The Cronos-like grunts
of the previous albums are long gone, replaced by highly personal howls of agony.
These tormented screams would be copied by almost all black metal bands in the
90's.

Curiously, Quorthon always hated *Under the Sign of the Black Mark*.

"There isn't a record that I hate as much as Under the Sign… *There isn't
a second in the songs that I like. The sound is terrible, I sing like a crow, make
solos like a pig, the feeling is dreadful, and there's nothing good about this
album. Absolutely nothing!"*—QUORTHON, BATHORY, FROM <u>HEATHENDOOM</u>
#1, 1996, MY TRANSLATION

It's really strange to hear him say this, since the power of the album is so obvious. Apparently he wasn't trying to make the record the way it turned out, and was haunted by his initial vision. It's highly plausible that he never intended Bathory to sound anything like they did, and the result was a product of his limited capacity as a musician. However, it might be in this that the secret of Bathory dwells. The music almost created itself, with Quorthon as its instrument. His inability to control the music helped make it great and unique. This might also be why nobody has been able to master Bathory's style. Though Mayhem and Burzum tried, they never came close. Their problem was that they aspired to sound like Bathory, something Quorthon never sought himself.

An alternative view on Quorthon's negative attitude to this album is that it must have been frustrating for him to see that he could never live up to its success. Even though he became a better musician, got into better studios, and worked much harder on his songs, nobody ever liked his later stuff nearly as much as they liked *Under the Sign of the Black Mark* (along with, perhaps, the next album *Blood, Fire, Death*). This happens to a lot of bands—how many bands don't you think got worse after their first record, or even demo?—so it wouldn't be strange for this to be the case with Bathory, too.

After the fantastic *Under the Sign of the Black Mark*, Bathory made at least two exceptionally influential records. But by now things had already started happening in Sweden. Young kids armed with guitars and drums were continuing on the path paved by Bathory. Deep down in the underground, a monster started to crawl, and nothing could stop what had already begun.

Obscurity and Mefisto: The Rise of the Underground

One of the first Swedish bands to continue in Bathory's footsteps was Obscurity from Malmö. This evil band was started by Daniel Vala and Jan Johansson in 1985, but really began when Jörgen Lindhe of the ultra-obscure Vulcania arrived to complete the trio.

"The reason we formed Obscurity was that we were extremely fascinated by the rising black metal style. After Venom, Slayer, and Bathory's first albums there was no return; we were completely hooked."—DANIEL VALA/JÖRGEN LINDHE/JAN JOHANSSON, OBSCURITY

The following year Obscurity released two demos that would become cult classics in the Swedish underground, *Ovations of Death* and *Damnations Pride*. The first was a pretty crude affair, recorded before they were really ready. But it's still a great example of early violent speed metal.

"We had an idea of a simple, dark, and fucking brutal metal, so we started

OBSCURITY (R.I.P.!)

to learn how to play. When we had six songs, we turned them into a demo. Since we couldn't find a drummer who wanted to play fast, our guitarists had to record the kicks—and the drums were recorded last! The studio man just stared at us and wondered if we understood anything about music at all. We did everything backwards."—DANIEL VALA/JÖRGEN LINDHE/JAN JOHANSSON, OBSCURITY

They sure were eager to make some evil music. This first demo is so primitive that it almost turns into crust punk. But the guys improved their playing skills. Eventually they found an actual drummer, and their music grew more structured. When they went into the studio to record the follow-up, *Damnations Pride*, all the pieces had fallen into place.

"*We had a real drummer, much better songs, used a better studio, and had become much better musicians. The response when we released* Damnations Pride *was just overwhelming. We sold all the tapes quickly and started to get fan mail from all over the world. Greatest of all was to receive letters from Brazil, Japan, and Australia. It was just incredible!*"—DANIEL VALA/JÖRGEN LINDHE/ JAN JOHANSSON, OBSCURITY

The *Damnations Pride* demo truly sounded powerful. Some inspiration obviously came from Bathory, but probably more came from German thrash metal acts like Sodom, Kreator, and particularly Destruction. Daniel Vala's vocals almost sound as stunningly German as those of Schmier of Destruction himself! Listening to Obscurity today, they still sound amazingly fresh and vital. Obscurity was probably one of the fastest bands in the world; the song "Demented," especially, is just insane. At such moments, they directly anticipated the style that would later make Merciless the kings of the Swedish underground. Even though Obscurity were truly great and praised in the underground, they never got the attention they deserved. They were probably ahead of their time.

"*There were simply no places for us to play, so we never played live. Then we got thrown out of our rehearsal room. We also got tired of the fact that no label seemed to be interested in us at all. If we could have held out into the 90's everything would of course have been sorted out, but back in 1987 it all seemed completely hopeless. We didn't know there would soon be a massive second wave of extreme metal that would like old farts like us!*"—DANIEL VALA/ JÖRGEN LINDHE/JAN JOHANSSON, OBSCURITY

"*Obscurity was a great band. They never got anywhere because there was no scene back then. They never played live and nobody knew them. But their music made a huge impression on me.*"—KRISTIAN "NECROLORD" WÅHLIN, GROTESQUE/LIERS IN WAIT/DECOLLATION

While Obscurity threatened the streets of Malmö, a young group from Stockholm also started to explore the darker side of extreme metal. The classic Mefisto, rather than Obscurity, got the most attention in the extreme Swedish

*Clockwise from top left:
Megalomania—this demo
started the underground;
The Puzzle;
Mefisto circa 1987*

metal underground during 1986. This aggressive trio consisted of talented
teenagers Omar Ahmed on guitar, Sandro Cajander on bass and vocals, and
Roberto Granath on drums. Together they composed some of the most brutal
music yet heard in Sweden, and they quickly built up a cult status.

Mefisto was formed back in 1984 under the name Torment. Initially the
band wasn't very serious, and it wasn't until 1986 that they started to have an
impact. That year they made two classic demos, *Megalomania* and *The Puzzle*.
Both showed intense and evil quality, following the path of Bathory. As with
Obscurity, the thrash metal influence is obvious in Mefisto's music. The riffs and
the sound were heavily inspired by Sodom, Kreator, Destruction, and Slayer.
And Mefisto sound quite good. The drums are mainly hammered down in a
violent backbeat, and the riffs are dark and tight. Furthermore, the vocals differ
a lot from Quorthon's screams, as Sandro spits out the deadly lyrics in a harsh
and deep way. His vocals actually anticipate the dark growling vocal style of
later singers like Lars-Göran Petrov of Nihilist/Entombed and Jörgen Sandström
of Grave. All the musicians really knew how to handle their instruments, and
Mefisto were soon celebrated in the underground press as one of the future
hopes of extreme metal.

"*I was into tape trading, and the singer who formed Opeth, David, gave
me Mefisto's* The Puzzle *demo. Up until then I was interested in death metal,*

but I wasn't really blown away. Death metal like Hellhammer was just brutal, and I liked the brutality but I was missing something. Mefisto had a guitar player who played classical guitar intros, and the solos were great, but it still had that brutality which I was looking for. I was just completely floored. For me The Puzzle *is the Scandinavian death metal super classic."*—Mikael Åkerfeldt, Opeth/Bloodbath

Sadly, Mefisto never made it out of the underground. Like Obscurity they simply vanished after a couple of demos. They were probably too extreme and strange for the Swedish market at this stage. Another thing that held up the band was Sandro's being diagnosed with cancer in 1985, preventing him from concentrating fully on the band. Furthermore, there were apparently some disputes within the band. Sandro and Roberto wanted to continue on the dark and raw path, while Omar wished to explore his amazing guitar skills rather than to create primitive metal. This antagonism can be heard on Mefisto's second demo, *The Puzzle*, where the guitar solos take a far bigger role.

"Musically, we drifted in different directions, which you might be able to hear on the two demos. Omar's guitar solos started to take over, like seven-minute Malmsteen solos. He became very egoistic. Sure he was skilled, but Roberto and I wanted to play rawer and more straightforward, like on Megalomania. Roberto and Omar never really got along, which resulted in a tooth being kicked out during the demo recording. [Omar has a plastic tooth now]."—Sandro Cajander, Mefisto, from <u>Septic Zine</u> #5

Mefisto and Obscurity evaporated, and the Swedish underground had to rest for a while. The fact that neither of them ever played live didn't help. But neither are forgotten by the death metal bands that followed.

"Those Mefisto guys were pretty strange and obscure, even when they were active. Nobody knew them. The feeling about them was cloudy, a bit like Bathory. In fact, I don't know anybody that knew them to this day."—Fredrik Karlén, Merciless

"Mefisto were in the thank-you credits on a Bathory record, so I figured that they had cred. I had a mental image of these really heavy, cool-looking dudes, but they looked like 'kickers'—guys who beat people in the street. They had like Adidas sweatpants, and one of the dudes had a top hat. I was like, 'What the fuck is that all about?'"—Mikael Åkerfeldt, Opeth/Bloodbath

"If they had played live I think the scene would have gotten bigger more rapidly. But sadly, they never did."—Fred Estby, Dismember/Carnage

"Mefisto was important. I got their demo very early on. Obscurity was more clandestine for us up here in Stockholm, and I could never get hold of their stuff. Nobody here knew who they were, but we were curious since we read a bit about them in fanzines. The fact that these early bands never played live only proves how difficult it was to get gigs in the mid-80's. Extreme metal

bands really had to struggle against an environment that basically hated them."—NICKE ANDERSSON, NIHILIST/ENTOMBED

"You should never forget Mefisto; they were very early with demos. I liked them. Today they might sound pretty lame, but they had some great riffs. For me, they have a big sentimental value."—MATTI KÄRKI, CARNAGE/DISMEMBER

"I thought Mefisto were incredibly good. Their first demo is fantastic, especially since they were so young when they recorded it."—LENNART LARSSON, HEAVY METAL MASSACRE/BACKSTAGE MAGAZINE

Apart from Obscurity and Mefisto, only a few Swedish bands started to experiment with violent speed metal around this time. One was Satanic Slaughter, formed in Linköping around 1985 by the notorious Stefan "Dark" Karlsson. But Satanic Slaughter were pretty primitive and incompetent at this point, definitely not in shape to make a demo. In 1986 two members of Satanic Slaughter left to form their own band, the much better Total Death. Still, to my knowledge, Total Death never made a demo.

The early extreme Swedish metal scene as a whole was very unproductive. Among bands that would later be a part of the death metal scene, only Chronic Decay, Legion (originally and later known as Cranium), and Corpse (later Grave) were active. Chronic Decay and Legion at least released demos in 1986, but these are a far cry from what they would eventually produce. None of these bands had the power of Mefisto or Obscurity.

A few ultra-obscure bands made tapes around this time, such as Melissa (who would go on to play straight thrash), Greffwe, Virgin Sin, and the mysterious hooded and cloaked black metal unit Natas Forewop Eht, apparently formed back in 1984. Actually, I haven't seen the Greffwe or Natas Forewop Eht demos firsthand, but I have read reviews, and confirmed them with two guys who claim to have heard about them back in the 80's. Still, these bands could turn out to be just myths, which of course would only be cool! At least a 1986 rehearsal videotape exists of Eskilstuna's incredible Death Ripper, an ultra-necro thrash/death outfit decked out in corpse paint and spikes.

The Swedish record industry didn't show interest in extreme metal, which is actually pretty strange since Bathory did so well. Instead of trying to push artists that incorporated the ideas of Quorthon and the German speed metal scene, the labels desperately tried to find radio-friendly bands like Europe. Even when thrash metal caught their attention, they searched for polished bands in the Bay Area tradition. The problem was that Sweden had hardly anything worth signing.

𝕾𝖜𝖊𝖉𝖎𝖘𝖍 𝕿𝖍𝖗𝖆𝖘𝖍 𝕸𝖊𝖙𝖆𝖑

There were a few exceptions to the rule of mediocre Swedish thrash. One of the very first Swedish bands that could be labeled thrash metal was Maninnya

Clockwise from top left:
Maninniya Blade—dressed to kill;
probably the first vinyl with
"attempted" Swedish thrash metal;
Melissa—the boys your parents
warned you about

Blade from Boden. These guys started out as early as 1980, and four years and countless obscure demos later they presented the *The Barbarian/Ripper Attack* 7" single on Platina Records. Two years later they secured a deal with Killerwatt and made an album. Maninnya Blade were never really aggressive—they sounded more like a sloppy Motörhead than a thrash metal band. Eventually that changed, though, as the band transformed into Hexenhaus.

A better and much thrashier band of the period was Damien from Uppsala. Damien formed way back in 1982, but didn't produced demos until 1986. The first tape was the rather primitive *Hammer of the Gods*, rapidly followed by *Onslaught Without Mercy* in 1986, *Chapter I* in 1987, and *Chapter II*, also in 1987. By the time of their third demo, Damien had gotten it together to produce high-octane thrash metal with great potential. The songs were great, as were the vocals and the musicianship. Still, Damien's aggressive style of thrash didn't impress any labels. In 1988 they simply started their own Gothic Records to get their material out. Damien also played a few live shows during this time. Though sparsely attended, one of the shows would impact the fledgling death metal scene.

"Damien at Nya Strömmen in Norrköping in 1987 was the first thrash metal gig I ever attended. Since I had recently seen Anthrax's 'Gung Ho' video, I expected hordes of moshing maniacs. Instead I met four kids eating candy when I arrived at the venue. No one else was there except the band! But Damien's gig was cool anyway, complete with Hellhammer-style corpse paint. I was hooked. The experience urged me to arrange gigs myself about a year later, and eventually start a fanzine. After the gig I also became a close friend to one of the candy-eaters. His name was Morgan Håkansson, and in a few years he formed the black metal band Marduk."—ROBBAN BECIROVIC, CLOSE-UP MAGAZINE

One of the best Swedish thrash metal demos was Agony's *Execution of Mankind*, recorded in August 1986. Like Mefisto, Agony came from Stockholm. Originally they were a crust punk band called Agoni. Inspired by the thrash metal boom in San Francisco, they changed some members and transformed their music considerably. Even though Agony was pretty primitive and brutal, they brought a commercial polish to their music that Mefisto had lacked. The riffs and production are clearer and the songs are more thrash-oriented, with tempo changes, melodies, and mosh parts. Their music mixes Exodus vocals with some elements of Testament, Megadeth, and Slayer. Agony's qualities were apparent, and they soon secured a deal with Under One Flag.

One of the most intense and chaotic early Swedish thrash metal bands was Hyste'Riah from Landskrona. Their hysterical debut demo, *Attempt the Life,* was recorded November 26, 1987, in the ABF Studio in their hometown. The riffs and patterns actually smelled a bit of Destruction, even though they were obviously also inspired by the U.S. thrash scene. Despite receiving scant attention, the guys continued, and on May 10 they recorded their second demo in AssBangFreak Studio. Sadly, the resulting *Jeremiad of the Living* was not as aggressive as the debut. I guess the guys had become better musicians, and they had started to peek more at U.S. bands. Though their violent debut sounds better to my ears, their second demo is pretty good as well.

Another decent Swedish thrash metal band was Fallen Angel from Örebro. They started out back in 1984, and made a name with a couple of good demos. Their brightest moment was the high-quality *Hang-Over*, recorded September 22 and 25, 1989, in Studio Eagle One. Great harmonic mid-tempo riffs join truly great vocals by Johan Bülow, a guy who would later help out as session guitarist in the death metal band Altar. Fallen Angel eventually released an album in the 90's, but by then they sounded awfully dated.

One of the most talked about thrash metal bands in Sweden during the late 80's was Kazjurol from Fagersta. This band formed in 1986, and immediately appeared on the split 7" *Breaking the Silence*. At this point they were a pretty primitive crossover band, but they got some attention. In 1987, the group released their *The Earlslaughter* demo and the *Messengers of Death* 7". They developed a style similar to Suicidal Tendencies, and got some attention abroad. Much of this probably had to do with the fact that Peter Ahlqvist of Uproar Records was managing them.

Sweden's finest thrash—Hatred, Welcome to Reality demo

"Kazjurol started out as a pure joke band and I kind of liked them. I started to work with them, and before I knew it they had turned much more serious and got some members that actually could play their instruments. Then I started to manage Kazjurol and got them a lot of gigs. Probably too many!"—PETER AHLQVIST, UPROAR/TID ÄR MUSIK/BURNING HEART

Kazjurol's acclaimed 1988 demo, *A Lesson in Love*, eventually got them an album deal with Active Records. At this point they had developed a pure thrash metal style, and they played countless gigs up until 1990. Listening to Kazjurol today, it's hard to understand why they got so much attention—but you have to remember, the world was a different place then.

On the contrary, the brilliant Hatred from Hedemora were in my eyes the very best of the Swedish thrash metal bands. Like Agony and Bathory, this great band had its roots in the punk scene. The lineup originally featured no less than three of the members of the ultra-brutal hardcore band Asocial—the pioneers

*Clockwise from top: Early Kazjurol
pose. Fuck, as I remember it these guys
were big and menacing back then...what
was I on?;
Kazjurol 7";
A Lesson in Love—a demo just about
everybody had in the late 80's*

of blast beats: Tomas Andersson, Tommy Berggren, and Kenneth Wilkund. Hatred's first demo, *Winds of Doom,* from 1987, may be a standard affair, but that would soon change.

Hatred's second demo, *Welcome to Reality,* recorded on January 7 and 8, 1989, at Musikstugan, showed tremendous development. This recording is a feast of fast tempos, raw sound, razor-sharp riffs, tight drumming, and extremely well structured songs. Further, Thomas Lundin is a brilliant thrash singer, even though his high-pitched screams seem a bit dated today. Unlike other Swedish bands, Hatred were able to blend the rawness of the German speed metal scene with the precision of the Bay Area thrash bands. If Hatred had been from San Francisco, they might have become huge.

Hatred's quality was confirmed when they were one of two thrash metal bands along with Mortality chosen to appear on a Swedish metal compilation LP supervised by the radio show Rockbox. To my ears, their contribution "Tempted by Violence" remains, together with Agony's "Deadly Legacy," the best Swedish thrash metal song ever written. Hatred capture everything great about thrash metal—it's a shame they never made an album.

"Hatred were such a good band. Unlike all other Swedish thrash metal bands, they knew how to write songs. Hatred deserved so much more. They were good on an international level."—ROBBAN BECIROVIC, <u>CLOSE-UP MAGAZINE</u>

A band that got a bit more attention, though they were not nearly as good as Hatred, was Nyköping's Mezzrow. This band recorded the decent *Frozen Soul* demo in Studio Svängrummet on February 20 and 21, 1988. The San Francisco influences are very obvious, with riff orgies and mosh parts to the limit. They had some nice riffs, in pure Exodus/Death Angel style, and a decent vocalist in Uffe Pettersson. Eventually Mezzrow secured a record deal with the English/Swedish label Active.

But the most well known and successful Swedish thrash metal band was Hexenhaus from Stockholm. Unlike most other Swedish thrash metal bands, Hexenhaus didn't emerge from punk. They were a continuation of the earlier metal band Maninnya Blade. Since the members were already known within the metal scene, the band vaulted ahead of any other thrash metal band around. Their lack of punk roots might also explain why they lacked the aggression of many other Swedish thrash metal bands.

Hexenhaus saw the passing of an endless line of new members, which might be why they never cut it as a live band. Still, they released three pretty successful LPs on Active, the same label that released Mezzrow's only album. None of the three were actually very good. They were definitely too lame to widely impact the Swedish scene. The most interesting thing I can say is that their debut, *A Tribute to Insanity,* from 1988, featured the same cover painting that Morbid Angel would use for the *Blessed are the Sick* album three years later.

Sweden's first extreme
metal fanzine

Uppsala's Midas Touch, Helsingborg's God B.C., and the all-female Ice Age
were also decent Swedish thrash metal bands. But that's about it. There was
never really anything that could be called a full-fledged Swedish thrash metal
scene. The bands were basically on their own, with hardly any places to play or
magazines featuring them. But a few fanzines that cared about thrash started to
turn up in the mid-80's, the first probably being *Heavy Metal Massacre*.

*"Me and a guy named Micke Jönsson, who I had got to know from tape
trading, decided to start a fanzine in the spring of 1983, and the result was*
Heavy Metal Massacre. *The first issue came out in October, and we did four
issues until we folded in September 1984. We were the first magazine in Sweden
that wrote about bands like Slayer, Metallica, and Exciter."*—LENNART LARSSON,
HEAVY METAL MASSACRE/BACKSTAGE MAGAZINE

Heavy Metal Massacre stood out for its intention to include the most violent
forms of metal available. Apart from heavy metal and thrash, they also hailed
black metal as an art form rather than speculative noise. This approach is exactly

Clockwise from top:
Typical poster for a
mid-80's thrash
metal gig;

Hexenhaus, billed as
Hexen Hause;

Nyköping thrash attack

the one that would later drive death metal and later black metal into domination. Witness the open editorial from the first issue:

"Are you evil? I love to be evil, be tortured in the hands of death and listen to black metal. There are two ways to go with metal—the slow path or the raw and aggressive path. I have chosen the latter. Anguish and pain is floating in the room, and I feel fear. Whatever happens, I have chosen my path. If god won't have you the devil must!"—MICKE JÖNSSON, FROM HEAVY METAL MASSACRE #1, 1983

As true today as it was when it was written! Though some people tried to get the ball rolling during the mid-80's, Swedish thrash metal would never become a big or successful movement. None of Sweden's Bay Area-inspired bands were of any great significance for the development of Swedish death metal. By the time of these thrash metal recordings, far more extreme stuff had already crawled up from the underground. In 1988, death metal demos had started surfacing, and the extreme Swedish metal scene was about to change irrevocably. So let's leave this brutalizing phase of Swedish metal and focus on the real deal: death metal.

HANG-OVER

JEREMIAD OF THE LIVING

Clockwise from top: hysterical thrash metal

classic metalhead position portrayed on Fallen Angel's demo;

still hysterical;

Damien—pioneers of Viking metal?;

Chapter 1—great music, great cover

Chapter Three: The Birth of Swedish Death Metal

"WINGS OF DEATH, WINDS OF FUNERAL
THE CURSE OF THE OLD CEMETERY
A MAGIC SO PURE, WINDS OF FUNERAL
...CURSE OF DEATH"
—MORBID, "WINGS OF FUNERAL"

ooking back on the mid-80's, the world was a very different place. There were no cell phones, no Internet, and no CDs. In Sweden, we had two TV channels, and neither broadcasted any kind of music except on rare occasions. You would be glued to the TV just to see a few songs with a band like Status Quo at a Live Aid concert. The weekly radio program Rockbox became the most important hour of the week for metal kids like me. Plus if you were interested in extreme music, it was very difficult to find the records that were released. Only a few stores held thrash metal titles, and an album like Slayer's *Reign in Blood* was only available as an import. This harsh climate required you to be resourceful if you wanted to get the things you searched for, and this creativity paved the way for death metal.

When thrash metal grew more popular, more commercial, and inevitably boring, some youngsters went looking for something new and fresh. Something more brutal. Since metalheads were used to searching for music on their own, the transition from ordering rare records to finding clandestine demo tapes came naturally. The underground tape trading movement that emerged during the late 80's was the igniting spark that set the Swedish death metal scene ablaze. The main influences for the genre almost all came from obscure metal tapes that a handful of youngsters were bringing into the country.

"You usually listened to Metallica, Slayer, Celtic Frost, Kreator, Bathory, Sodom, Destruction, and that stuff. Then you discovered tape trading, and exchanged demos with bands from all over the world. It was great to discover intense stuff like Morbid Angel, Oblivion, Sadus, and Autopsy. It was totally incredible for a while, since you received so many letters from all over the world, from weird places like South America."—FREDRIK KARLÉN, MERCILESS

"Initially you sought out all the extreme records out there. Fred Estby, Fredda Johansson, and I laid our hands on everything we could find. Then we discovered tape trading, and started to get obscure stuff from all over the world. Forsberg in Tribulation, especially, was very important for the Swedish tape trading community; he was first with everything. From him you got stuff such as Repulsion and Master. And once you discovered death metal, thrash metal wasn't interesting at all anymore. I used to run home on my lunch break in school to stalk the mailman and see if something had arrived. Those were intense times!"—NICKE ANDERSSON, NIHILIST/ENTOMBED

"I was a notorious tape trader and swallowed anything extreme eagerly. My parents were a bit puzzled when our mailbox was suddenly filled with letters containing tapes from all around the world. This was a long time before the Internet or MP3s were invented. This was the real shit, kids!"—JESPER THORSSON, AFFLICTED

"Everybody was trading to some extent, but the dominating ones were probably Nicke Andersson, Magnus Forsberg, Patric Cronberg, and Tomas

Lindberg."—Orvar Säfström, Nirvana 2002

"*For some time, the mailbox was the central part of my existence. I remember getting such a rush when those letters and tapes turned up from South America or from the U.S.*"—Kristian "Necrolord" Wåhlin, Grotesque/Liers in Wait/Decollation

"*When all those demos came from the U.S. and South America, everything just got more brutal.*"—Fred Estby, Dismember/Carnage

So through tape trading people in Sweden first got to know about the new violent kind of music developing around the world, especially in the U.S. But tape trading was also a social activity that gave you something meaningful to do in the boring Swedish metal climate. These kids were spending hours every day copying tapes and writing long personal letters to people from all over the world, something that seems incredible today.

"*Apart from parties and some punk gigs there was not much going on in Sweden during the mid-80's. Most of the good bands came from the USA, so at times I probably wrote 50 letters a week to get stuff. You traded tapes, T-shirts, and 'zines. I still have several hundred demos from the 80's.*"—Johnny Hedlund, Nihilist/Unleashed

Though tape trading was surely one of the most important precursors to the development of Swedish death metal, remember that only a very limited circle of people were involved in the happenings in the late 80's. The core of serious tape traders was probably only about 50 people. But many outside that inner circle—like me—also traded tapes to some extent, even though they never saw it as a serious way to explore the world. It was more a way of exchanging music that you liked with your friends.

"*I never dealt very much with tape trading. I kept in touch with a few people and traded a few tapes, but it was never ambitious to the point of sending long lists to each other. We just recorded things that we thought the other one would like. In fact, I discovered a lot of interesting bands that way.*" —Christoffer Johnsson, Therion

"*It was amazing how young kids like me were actually corresponding with people from all over the world. You know, we actually sat down for hours and wrote long letters in English. We used to send compilation tapes to each other, and there was such dedication and energy to it all. I remember that Tompa Lindberg got a tape from Brazil or something where the guy had actually recorded himself presenting each song with an 'evil' voice—you know: 'Sadus Death to Posers!' Those were great times.*"—Kristian "Necrolord" Wåhlin, Grotesque/Liers in Wait/Decollation

Still, most regular metalheads didn't know anything about the underground, including even future luminaries like Anders Björler, Ola Lindgren, Anders Schultz, and Tomas Nyqvist.

Heavy Sound

Regeringsgatan 89
S-111 39 Stockholm
SWEDEN
Tel. 08 - 10 45 35

Öppet tiderna är:
vardagar 11-17:30   VÄLKOMNA !!!!!
lördagar 11-13:30

Det finns också engros
försäljning till andra
skivaffärer.

SVERIGES BÄSTA SKIVAFFÄR NÄR
DET GÄLLER HÅRDROCK OCH HM.

Här finns allt Lp, Maxisinglar,
Singlar och Videos med alla
kända och okända Metalmonster.

Vi för importskivor från alla
möjliga länder t ex England,
Usa, Holland , Japan, Spanien,
Italien, Tyskland m m.

Skicka in 5:- så får du vår
nya katalog som innehåller
allt av intresse för dig !!

Heavy Sound—the store that nourished the Swedish death metal scene

"*I discovered death metal, tape trading, and fanzines through Tompa Lindberg in the summer of 1989. To enter his home was to enter a different, clandestine world. Posters, flyers, craniums, albums, empty beer cans, demos, 'zines, and wine bottles everywhere. All in a terrible mess. It was really exciting to discover a completely new genre. The most extreme band I had heard before I met Tompa was probably Slayer.*"—ANDERS BJÖRLER, AT THE GATES/THE HAUNTED

"*When I got Possessed's* Seven Churches *in 1988 it changed my soul forever. A new world was opened, and I became obsessed with finding new exciting bands. I dedicated my life to death metal: read all the magazines and traded demos like crazy. I got at least two demos a day and spent all my spare time in my room writing letters. It was like a drug. I could never get enough.*"
—TOMAS NYQVIST, PUTREFACTION MAG/NO FASHION/IRON FIST PRODUCTIONS

"I really understood the scope of death metal when I visited Johnny Hedlund for the first time. He had hundreds of demos with bands that I had barely heard of. After that, I threw myself into tape trading full speed ahead myself."—ANDERS SCHULTZ, UNLEASHED

"When we got to know the guys from Nihilist and Dismember, they got us into all these obscure American bands. We knew nothing about that scene until we met them."—OLA LINDGREN, GRAVE

In those days of tape trading, the most important place for the up-and-coming Swedish scene was a small record shop in Stockholm called Heavy Sound. The store was basically one small room on Regeringsgatan, one of the seedier streets in central Stockholm. Heavy Sound primarily sold heavy metal and hard rock, but, unlike other stores, they also imported very extreme stuff by Sarcofago, Sodom, and Possessed. Most importantly, the owners also sold the demos of the young Swedish death metal bands emerging at the time.

"You should not underestimate the extremely important part that Heavy Sound played for the Swedish death metal scene. It was there you went to buy all the cool thrash metal and Bathory records. Other stores for extreme music didn't exist at all back then. But the two cool older men at Heavy Sound sold everything that was extreme, and also dealt with demos."—MATTI KÄRKI, CARNAGE/DISMEMBER

"I realized that some kind of scene was going on was when I visited Heavy Sound for the first time. I will never forget that feeling! Thrash metal albums everywhere. Back in those days it was pretty hard for people from smaller towns to find those records. Holy shit, we were just amazed! I bought the first demo of Mefisto, the first extreme Swedish band after Bathory that I knew about. Then we left our demos there, and they sold them."—FREDRIK KARLÉN, MERCILESS

"Heavy Sound was one of the very few places where you could find brutal records. I used to travel the 300 kilometers from Edsbyn just to go there. It was also the most important meeting place for metalheads during the mid-80's. The very first person from the death metal scene that I got to know was Buffla [Mattias], who was in Nihilist at the time. Then I met Tompa Lindberg, and through him everyone else. Naturally, I met both Buffla and Tompa at Heavy Sound!"—ORVAR SÄFSTRÖM, NIRVANA 2002

"Heavy Sound was definitely one of the most important places for me in the late 80's. It was there I saw an ad from a band searching for a bass player (I read it wrong, though, and thought they wanted a guitarist), and got in touch with two guys named Lars-Göran Petrov and Ulf Cederlund. That's how I got to know them, and we started to hang out in Bredäng, where they lived. I also remember how stunned we were when we found tapes with Corpse/Grave at Heavy Sound, and realized that some guys on Gotland had developed a music

similar to ours. We were totally unaware of each other at that point, but Heavy Sound helped us get in touch and meet one another."—NICKE ANDERSSON, NIHILIST/ENTOMBED

"I got involved with the death metal scene through an ad at Heavy Sound, where two guys named Nicke Andersson and Uffe Cederlund were searching for a singer for some band. It must have been around 1987. We quickly made friends, and even had some kind of hardcore band for a couple of weeks. Through Nicke I also got to know the guys from Dismember."—JOHAN EDLUND, TREBLINKA/TIAMAT

"The first time I felt some kind of movement going on was when I and Grant [McWilliams of General Surgery] went to the signing session for Bathory's Under the Sign of the Black Mark *at Heavy Sound in 1987. I was just a kid of about 14 years old, and saw all of these cool guys with even cooler T-shirts. Most of the people who would make up the early death metal scene were there. Even though I didn't get to know many back then, at least I got to know they existed. Before that, I only knew Grant, and I think I actually got to know him on an earlier trip to Heavy Sound. I had no friends in school, because nobody liked you if you were into extreme metal. The world basically changed at that Bathory session, because I saw that there were many of us."*—ANDERS SCHULTZ, UNLEASHED

"Since my dad lived in Stockholm, I was there pretty often. And every time I went there I visited Heavy Sound. It was always crowded, and it was such a nice event just to go there. I remember that the guys from Afflicted Convulsion used to hang out outside the store, drinking beer, though they surely weren't even allowed to buy it, as young as they were! It was a meeting place, and Heavy Sound was probably the first place that gathered something that could be called a scene."—ROBBAN BECIROVIC, <u>CLOSE-UP MAGAZINE</u>

"In Visby it was very hard to find extreme records. At best, the only shop we had brought in big releases such as Metallica and Anthrax. When we first went up to Stockholm and discovered Heavy Sound, a whole new world was opened. Regeringsgatan—that street name still sends shivers down my spine."—OLA LINDGREN, GRAVE

"We never had any money to record proper demos, and that was almost the same as a record for me in those days, to have a three-track demo. There was a record store called Heavy Sound, where you'd buy just any random band, just by looking at the logo: 'I can't see what that says, it must be great, I have to buy that!' I still have my entire demo collection, and guys like Nihilist, Carnage, Dismember, and Mefisto. Those were like Kiss; you were like, 'Wow, those guys are heroes.'"—MIKAEL ÅKERFELDT, OPETH

"In Gothenburg I guess Dolores played the same part as Heavy Sound did in Stockholm, and I bought loads of cool records there. But, unlike Heavy Sound, Dolores never really became a meeting place. There simply was no

Lars-Göran Petrov blasting away with Morbid at Ultrahuset

scene down in Gothenburg. If you were into extreme metal, you were pretty much alone."—TOMAS LINDBERG, GROTESQUE/AT THE GATES/DISFEAR

Heavy Sound also sold fanzines that would influence the youngsters who sought extreme new music: especially the English magazine *Metal Forces*. Since it was filled with demo reviews, it soon turned into a bible for tape traders.

"Metal Forces was extremely important; it covered loads of bands that you had never heard of before."—NICKE ANDERSSON, NIHILIST/ENTOMBED

"Metal Forces was the best of the bigger 'zines. It covered the big bands of the scene such as Death and Dark Angel, but they always had a few cool bands on their demo pages as well."—TOMAS LINDBERG, GROTESQUE/AT THE GATES/DISFEAR

"When I discovered Metal Forces, it took over the position that Rockbox had previously held as the main source for discovering new bands."—ROBBAN BECIROVIC, CLOSE-UP MAGAZINE

When it comes to Swedish 'zines, a few punk fanzines actually first noticed the upcoming new death metal genre. A great example of how death metal snuck into the punk world is the following review of one of the few gigs by pioneering underground band Morbid. This show took place at Birkagården on October 23, 1987, with Morbid opening for Hatred and Tribulation.

"While Morbid were doing their soundcheck, the doors were opened, so they left the stage to put on a lot of makeup and fix their stage props. After

that the gig began. They had a lot of effects—lights, sound, smoke, and a black coffin. As for the music, I had thought that Morbid would be awful, but they weren't. They were really good live, but I can imagine that they would suck on record. The sound gradually improved, and the audience banged like crazy. Morbid plays metal, as you might expect. Good, but it's ridiculous to speak in English between the songs."—FROM <u>BANAN</u> #7, MY TRANSLATION

Apart from short reports like this there was basically no coverage of the Swedish scene in fanzines. If you weren't a punk rocker, you might have missed everything. In Norway the climate was basically the opposite of Sweden. There were hardly any extreme bands around, but the country had two great 'zines: *Slayer Mag* and *Morbid Mag.*

"I didn't know anything about Swedish fanzines during the early days of the scene, but Slayer Mag *was reigning at this point. Even though you read* Metal Forces *and some other 'zines from Europe, as well as the U.S.,* Slayer Mag *was number one."*—OLA LINDGREN, GRAVE

"The early Swedish 'zines were pretty unfocused, and mainly wrote about thrash metal and hardcore. Then we discovered Slayer Mag, *which was a whole different story. Unlike all other 'zines, it exclusively contained great bands, was very well written, and looked great. It was the bible during the late 80's, and it was totally respected all over the world. We started to correspond with [the editor] Metalion, and soon made trips to Norway to visit him and his friends. We spent a couple of drunken New Year's Eves there, and hung out with all the guys who would later be part of the black metal scene."*—JOHAN EDLUND, TREBLINKA/TIAMAT

"We got to know Metalion early on since his 'zine was way more professional and focused than anything else

Metalion during the days when metal was all about raising hell and having a good time

around. We spent New Year's Eve there along with Treblinka in 1989. It was wild, I can tell you, and at one point "Dead" was about to throw himself out of a window. There was not much going on in Norway at that point; it was basically just Metalion and the bands Vomit and Mayhem. But I remember that there were a bunch of extremely young kids hanging around while we were there, and I guess they were the ones who later started all of those black metal bands. But back then we just saw them as annoying hangers-on."—KRISTIAN "NECROLORD" WÄHLIN, GROTESQUE/LIERS IN WAIT/DECOLLATION

"Slayer Mag *from Norway was superior to everything else already back then. Respect Metalion!"*—FREDRIK KARLÉN, MERCILESS

"Slayer Mag *from Norway was without a shadow of a doubt the 'zine you respected the most back then, and I corresponded with Jon for a few years. Morbid Mag was one of few other 'zines that everybody knew about in the 80's."*— CHRISTOFFER JOHNSSON, THERION

"Personally, *I discovered two Danish 'zines first:* Metallic Beast *and* Blackthorn. *They reviewed Master's demo and interviewed bands like Possessed and Mefisto very early on. In hindsight such things had a huge impact on me. Then I found out about the superior Norwegian fanzines.* Slayer Mag *especially was extremely respected.* Morbid Mag *didn't have as much cred, probably since they wrote a lot about thrash metal as well. It's so childish when you think back, but that's the way it was."*— NICKE ANDERSSON, NIHILIST/ENTOMBED

Through such fanzines, Nicke realized how many cool demo tapes were out there, and how to get hold of them without paying.

"Through *reading those 'zines I got an urge to make one myself, so I decided to start* Chickenshit. *Eventually I also understood that*

Chickenshit!

NOT

At Dawn They Read

ISSUE 4

COOL!

Clockwise from top:
Flyer for Morbid Mag;

ad for Nicke Andersson's never-released Chickenshit;

At Dawn They Read—the first Swedish fanzine to address death metal;

NOT #4. The cover is typical for the crossover atmosphere of the mid-80's

you could get all the rare demos if you started your own fanzine. Since I never released one single issue of my 'zine, you might say it was all a big scam! But honestly, Nihilist started to take most of my time, so I could never find the time to finish it."—NICKE ANDERSSON, NIHILIST/ENTOMBED

Nicke's fanzine never came out, even though he wrote and designed a lot of material. For a long time, Sweden remained far behind its neighbors Denmark and Norway when it came to fanzines. There were only a few regular metal magazines such as *Hammer,* and a handful of thrash metal 'zines like the archetypical *Heavy Metal Massacre* and *Metal Guardians.* But around 1987, a few 'zines that focused on more extreme metal appeared.

"There were a couple of extremely crude fanzines even back in our days, and in hindsight we owe lot to NOT and To the Death. *But the Norwegians were way ahead of the Swedes when it comes to 'zines;* Slayer Mag, *especially, ruled."* —DANIEL VALA/JÖRGEN LINDHE/JAN JOHANSSON, OBSCURITY

The early Swedish 'zines were primitive and badly written, but they nevertheless showed that something was happening in the underground. Oddly enough, all the first really extreme metal fanzines seemed to emerge from the far southern region of Skåne. The scene down there basically consisted of the brutal Obscurity and Virgin Sin from Malmö, thrash metal act Hyste'Riah from Landskrona, and the equally thrashy God BC from Helsingborg.

In 1985, the drummer Tom Hallbäck of the last band started what was probably the first of these new fanzines, *At Dawn They Read*. This fanzine was initially preoccupied with heavy metal in general, and was actually pretty similar to Lennart "Phantom" Larsson's *Heavy Metal Massacre*. As time went by, *At Dawn They Read* grew more brutal. Hallbäck continued to edit the 'zine way into the 90's.

Around the same time Hallbäck released his first issue, three youngsters in the Malmö area decided to start a fanzine as well. Led by Johnny Christiansen, they named their creation *NOT*. Unlike *At Dawn They Read*, which mainly covered metal, *NOT* focused on all kinds of brutal music. You could read about Bathory and Bulldozer along with Minor Threat and Gang Green. The writers swept the underground in search of brutal bands, and found the likes of Mayhem, Obscurity, and Mefisto. Furthermore, *NOT* looked a lot better than *At Dawn They Read*, and served as a model for later death metal fanzines such as *Putrefaction Mag*.

Another guy in the region making fanzines during this time was Martin Carlsson from Ystad. In 1987 he released the first issue of *Megalomaniac*. Unlike *NOT*, *Megalomaniac* wasn't very explorative, and Carlsson was still stuck in the thrash metal field. In fact, he seemed to hate most bands that went beyond the Bay Area way of musical expression. Bands such as Overkill and Paradox were hailed, while more brutal acts like Napalm Death were laughed at. *"If I want death metal, I want it well played,"* Carlsson said, explaining his musical taste in a dismissive review of Tribulation. Martin Carlsson would later continue *Megalomaniac* under the name *Candour*, after which he joined the staff at *Close-Up* magazine. Nowadays he is also one of the permanent contributors of the daily Swedish tabloid *Expressen*.

More in line with the taste of *NOT* was Martin Carlsson's neighbor Patric "Cronis" Cronberg. His search for extreme music was apparent in the name of his fanzine, launched in 1987—*To the Death*. Though there was not much death metal to cover yet, his intentions were obvious. He advocated aggressive bands like Terrorizer, Morbid, Death, Massacre, Darkthrone, and Obscurity. Cronberg's fanzine also looked a lot more death metal than other contemporaries, thanks to a lot of cool zombie drawings by Nicke Andersson of Nihilist, who also later drew a logo for *To the Death*. Eventually, like Carlsson, Cronberg started writing for *Close-Up* magazine. At this point, though, even Patric Cronberg's fanzine was mostly filled with thrash metal and hardcore. But with *To the Death*, we got closer to pure death metal journalism.

From top : Megalomaniac #2;
To the Death #1—*probably
the first Swedish fanzine to go
strictly death metal;*
"Cronis"'*s second issue*

"I have no idea why the southern part of Sweden was the first to get some kind of fanzine scene—all of us just got going at about the same time. There was a great atmosphere between us, and we all helped distributing each other's 'zines. I wasn't very good at promoting my own 'zine though. I handed out lots of free copies of issue #3, telling people to send me their demos. Later I discovered that I had forgotten to include my address..."—PATRIC "CRONIS" CRONBERG, TO THE DEATH

Though there was nothing like a proper death metal scene in Sweden from 1985 to 1988, the small community of tape traders, fanzine readers, and editors had started to make something happen. Brutal demos snuck into the country, and before long, the new exciting music had prompted people to form their own bands.

Death metal ever so slightly started to become a movement. The first participants even created a kind of dress code: flannel shirts, denim vests, white sneakers, and band T-shirts. When it came to T-shirts, it was cool to have the newest ones possible, quite the opposite of the metal scene of today. To find T-shirts with death metal bands was very hard, though, as the few produced were only made in very limited editions. For example, only five copies of the first Nihilist logo T-shirt (the white one) were printed. For the second one, with the white "ghost" motif, the run was increased to twenty copies.

But the most important thing was new music by extreme bands. As the flannel shirt–wearing youngsters around the country finally picked up instruments, Swedish death metal was born at last.

Merciless

Up to this point, no Swedish band had really followed in Bathory's footsteps. The pioneers Obscurity and Mefisto faded after just a couple of demos. The first to break the ice were the soon-to-be classic Merciless, from the small and idyllic town of Strängnäs, sixty-five miles west of Stockholm.

Merciless was formed in 1986 by the very young metalheads Fredrik Karlén on bass, Stefan "Stipen" Karlsson on drums, and Erik Wallin on guitar. Fredrik had previously been in a punk band, while Stipen and Erik used to play heavy metal. Together they became a furious metal platoon. When Kåle joined in some months later on vocals, the band was complete, and things started to happen pretty fast. Like Obscurity and Mefisto, they were influenced by Bathory and German speed metal acts like Sodom and Destruction. Fueled by the intensity of these bands and their own drunken teenage energy, Merciless tried to create the most brutal music imaginable.

"It was basically Erik, Stipen, and me back in 1986. We used to sit in Stipen's room at his parents' place and listen to Sodom, Bathory, and Slayer. Soon we realized that we had to play that kind of music ourselves. I can't remember what went on in our banging heads, but that we should start a band was certain. We had played in a few punk and metal bands before, but it was this kind of thing that really got us hooked."—Fredrik Karlén, Merciless

Unlike Obscurity and Mefisto, Merciless also started to play live gigs very early in their career—probably one of the primary reasons why Merciless eventually succeeded where Obscurity and Mefisto had failed.

"I remember our first gig very well. It was during our first months of existence, when we attended some kind of rock band competition in school. We wore corpse paint and crushed the shit out of everybody! That is really what we did! I almost banged my fucking head off, and they switched the bass amplifier off after a while, since it was too intense. Fucking pigs! Ha ha."
—Fredrik Karlén, Merciless

All this wild teenage energy would soon show results in the recording studio. Merciless' classic first demo, *Behind the Black Door*, was recorded in Studio Svängrummet in their hometown on July 18, 1987. On this demo Merciless developed the ideas of Obscurity and Mefisto into something incredibly brutal for its time. The most striking thing about this demo is Kåle's vocals, more aggressive than anything yet heard in Sweden—with the possible exception of Quorthon and a few punk singers such as Jonsson of Anti Cimex. He approaches the growling style that would dominate the early Swedish death metal scene. Further, the overall production is better than that of any previous extreme Swedish metal demo.

"When we recorded the first demo, we were really amazed at just how incredibly brutal the vocals sounded in the studio. In the rehearsal room

you could only hear a yawp in the broken PA. The sound engineer probably wondered what kind of lunatics he had gotten in there, as we went around decorated with red paint for bloodstains and inverted crosses on our jeans-vests."—FREDRIK KARLÉN, MERCILESS

Merciless started to get noticed in the underground during 1987, and were hailed by fanzines like *Slayer Mag* and *Morbid Mag*. Unlike Mefisto and Obscurity, they continued when problems occurred within the band. When Kåle left in 1988 he was immediately replaced by Rogga Pettersson. The change only seemed to make the band stronger.

"*Rogga has the best voice imaginable for thrash! We were completely in awe. With him aboard we recorded the best thing we have ever done in my opinion,* Realm of the Dark.*"—FREDRIK KARLÉN, MERCILESS

On this 1988 demo, recorded at Tuna Studio in the nearby town of Eskilstuna, the development was obvious. The pace is much faster, and the songs are more structured, with a lot of tempo changes, something that would be developed much more by upcoming Swedish death metal bands. The production is even better than on the great *Behind the Black Door*. As Karlén has pointed out, Rogga Pettersson's voice is even more aggressive than his predecessor Kåle's. The demo is perfect in every sense. Through intense tape trading, Merciless were soon known worldwide in the underground.

"*We received about ten letters a day for several years. It got to the point were we had to take days off regularly, just to try to answer half of it. Sadly there were a lot of letters that we never took the time to answer, and I regret that today. But what the fuck, we were drunk almost all the time back then, so I guess we did the best we could!*"—FREDRIK KARLÉN, MERCILESS

Realm of the Dark also caused quite a stir in the local metal underground. Everybody had the demo, and everybody loved it. I remember it being played endlessly at parties. The demo attracted the notorious Øystein "Euronymous" Aarseth, who soon signed them to his Deathlike Silence Productions label.

"*Our friend Pelle [Per, aka Dead], singer in the cult band Morbid, moved to Norway and started to sing in Mayhem. I guess Øystein Aarseth got to hear us through Pelle. DSP wanted to release us and they got in touch.*"—FREDRIK KARLÉN, MERCILESS

So Merciless was the first really extreme Swedish metal band to get a recording deal after Bathory. They started to play numerous live gigs during this time, and were soon recognized as the leading Swedish underground metal force. They became probably as well known for their outrageous metal lifestyle as for their music. Fredrik Karlén, especially, had a wide reputation of being the madman of Swedish metal. His regular behavior included jumping between balconies, and climbing up on roofs during parties. I witnessed his building-climbing abilities first hand during an insane party in Avesta in 1990,

From top: *The madmen of Swedish death metal*;

Realm of the Dark—*one of the best demos ever*;

Merciless' classic debut demo

as he managed to get up on the roof of Johan Jansson's (of Interment and later Dellamorte) block of flats.

"*During their early years, Merciless were never really known for their music here in Strängnäs. I knew that they had a band, but that was about it. What they were notorious for was their wild drinking antics! When I finally got to know them in 1989 I was sucked into that way of life too, and those days were just fucking insane. Karlén in particular is utterly mad!*"—TOMAS NYQVIST, PUTREFACTION MAG/NO FASHION/IRON FIST PRODUCTIONS

With all due respect to their fantastic music, Merciless can't rightly be called a death metal band. Sure, they've got speed and aggression, but their simple riff structures are more connected to thrash metal and the simplistic black metal of a band like Bathory. The seed was planted, but in my opinion the first pure death metal band in Sweden was yet to come—the mighty Nihilist.

Morbid, Nihilist, and the Early Stockholm Scene

Nihilist came from a core of five developing young musicians—Nicke Andersson, Alex Hellid, Leif Cuzner, Uffe Cederlund, and Lars-Göran Petrov. In 1986, the fourteen-year-old Andersson met Hellid and Cuzner during a summer camp. Some sources state that this happened in 1985, but Nicke has straightened me out on this point. They realized that they all liked extreme music, and formed the band Sons of Satan together.

"*We made some logos and rehearsed a bit, but it was never really serious. But in the autumn I started to travel the long way from Vårberg to Kista, where they lived, to hang out.*"—NICKE ANDERSSON, NIHILIST/ENTOMBED

Simultaneously, the two youngsters Uffe Cederlund and Lars-Göran Petrov got to know each other at school in Bredäng.

"*We were both metalheads; he played drums and he knew that I played guitar, so naturally we started to jam together. We formed some punk bands, since nobody else in school was into metal. Eventually we put up an ad at Heavy Sound, searching for a bass player. That's how we got to know Nicke Andersson.*"
—UFFE CEDERLUND, MORBID/NIHILIST/ENTOMBED/DISFEAR

The three teenagers found each other and soon began to create music.

"*Since it was a much shorter ride to Bredäng than to Kista, I started to hang out a lot with L.G. and Uffe. We started loads of bands under thousands of names, and even recorded a song called 'Evil' at the studio [Studio Z] in the youth center in Sätra, where we also rehearsed. I think we called ourselves Blasphemy on that demo, but I'm not sure. I'm also not quite sure who actually played in that band.*"—NICKE ANDERSSON, NIHILIST/ENTOMBED

"It kind of took off from there. I think we called ourselves Blasphemy for some time, with me and Nicke on guitars, L.G. on drums, and Kenny Håkansson [later in The Hellacopters with Nicke] on bass."—UFFE CEDERLUND, MORBID/NIHILIST/ENTOMBED/DISFEAR

While Nicke Andersson, Lars-Göran Petrov, Uffe Cederlund, Leif Cuzner, and Alex Hellid were fooling around in trial bands, another group rose in the Stockholm underground. That band was Morbid, and was formed at the end of 1986 by the teenagers Per Yngve Ohlin on vocals and "Slator" on bass. Though Slator may never have rehearsed with Morbid according to Uffe Cederlund, he was still involved with forming the band.

Members, especially guitarists, came and went around the group's mastermind, Ohlin, for a while, before the group ended up as a quartet with John Hagström (aka "John Lennart," aka "Gehenna") and TG from the punk band The Sun on guitars, and Jens Näsström on bass. They searched for a drummer to fit their evil and dark music, and eventually Lars-Göran Petrov joined. Soon TG, who wrote most of the group's material, left as well, and his job was offered to Uffe Cederlund.

"L.G. went behind our backs and joined Morbid, after which Nicke started to play drums in the remains of Blasphemy. Since L.G. was my closest friend, I hung around Morbid a lot and saw all their first gigs. The guitarists came and went in the band, and eventually it was my turn to join. Anyway, the other guys of Morbid weren't satisfied with L.G. and wanted to try out another drummer. 'Dead' and I brought in Nicke and rehearsed some songs. Though it sounded good, he didn't get the job. I don't remember why."—UFFE CEDERLUND, MORBID/NIHILIST/ENTOMBED/DISFEAR

Nicke Andersson, however, has a completely different recollection:

"Uffe and L.G. knew these guys, and told me they needed a drummer. So I went to their rehearsal space to give it a go. The day I went there I had put on a white Wehrmacht T-shirt, and that would prove to be a fatal decision. Obviously this was all wrong according to the image they wanted to create for themselves, so I was basically rejected even before I started to play! They wanted to be evil, and my T-shirt obviously wasn't. At this point I was still of the opinion that the fastest band wins, and didn't fully grasp which bands were "true" or not. But once I too had buried myself deeply in the death metal underground, I myself became the most stubborn antagonist toward everything that wasn't hard enough. Thinking back, it's a little embarrassing, but it's cool at the same time, because it shows dedication."—NICKE ANDERSSON, NIHILIST/ENTOMBED

If Nicke had chosen a Bathory T-shirt for his one rehearsal with Morbid, things might have turned out very differently for the Swedish death metal scene. Whatever the true circumstances, Morbid's early lineup did briefly

Morbid's ultra-legendary debut demo.
They don't make layouts
like this anymore...

separate Uffe and L.G. from Nicke. Blasphemy folded when Uffe and L.G. focused on Morbid.

"*When I joined Morbid, we restructured the old songs and started to get slightly serious. We only did one gig during this time, with Hatred and Tribulation at Birkagården. I remember that L.G. sent an anonymous threatening letter to Hatred before the gig, complaining about their 'lame' vocals. They found out somehow that it was him sending it, and it was pretty embarrassing to play the gig after that. Pelle, Jens, and John were pretty upset with L.G. for that. They were in fact about to sack him.*"
—UFFE CEDERLUND, MORBID/ NIHILIST/ENTOMBED/DISFEAR

On December 5 and 6, 1987, Morbid recorded their debut demo, *December Moon*, at Thunderload Studios. Though Morbid have become probably more notorious than Obscurity, Mefisto or even Merciless, their music was not as strong as any of those bands. Ohlin's vocals, especially, are more "strange" than good. He would later achieve much greater things with Mayhem. Still, Morbid made a great impact on the scene.

"*L.G. and I met Sandro of Mefisto at the only kebab place that existed in Stockholm at that time, and he brought us to Thunderload Studio. He convinced us to record there, and we eventually saved up the money to afford it. I think it cost us 2,600 SEK [$350], a lot of* *money for a bunch of teenagers in those days. Anyway, I brought my small Peavey amplifier and we recorded it in no time. We were pretty satisfied with the result, although I thought the unmixed version sounded much rawer and better. But we were very young, and didn't dare tell the somewhat older guy in the studio that his mix just ruined things."*—Uffe Cederlund, Morbid/ Nihilist/Entombed/Disfear

After the recording of *December Moon*, guitarist John Hagström decided to leave. The group never really recovered from that loss, and eventually Ohlin decided to leave as well. He went to Norway and joined Mayhem. He believed that he could develop an even more shocking stage show within this new band, and indeed he did. Though Morbid were in ruins, they found the strength to make another demo.

Morbid's Last Supper...

"John left immediately after the recording, probably because he was sick of traveling from Åkersberga to Nacka, where we rehearsed. We tried a few guitarists after that, but it never worked out. We continued as a four-piece, and did a few gigs at punk places without the horror show. It worked pretty well, but I think all of us felt that the band had in reality already folded. Eventually Pelle left for Mayhem, and to me, Morbid was no more after that. Despite continuing with another singer and guitarist, the true Morbid was over."—Uffe Cederlund, Morbid/Nihilist/Entombed/Disfear

In place of Ohlin, Morbid brought in Johan Scarisbrick, a photographer who happened to live nearby a small studio called Sunlight. This coincidence might have been the only reason that in September 1988, *Last Supper* was recorded at this soon-to-be-famous location.

"Ironically, we were more focused when we did the second demo. We rehearsed a lot, and it was very cool to have Zoran as the second guitar player. He is in fact the only guitarist I have ever played with who has given anything back to me. I started to learn how to play scales and stuff, and he got me into thrash bands such as Testament. Anyway, we weren't Morbid anymore. We were just a bunch of guys who didn't know when to stop."—Uffe Cederlund, Morbid/Nihilist/Entombed/Disfear

Last Supper might be a bit more musically advanced than Morbid's first demo, but it sounds somewhat confused and unfocused. Since this was the first time an extreme metal band was in Sunlight, I guess engineer Tomas Skogsberg still didn't have a clue as to how to handle the music. The riffs approach death metal structures, but are still very indebted to thrash metal. Scarisbrick's vocals are also somewhat strangely spoken—rather than screamed. But the overall feeling is cool.

"Though I liked it when we recorded it, I soon realized that everything sucked on this demo. Today I can't even listen to it. After Last Supper *we kind of realized that it was time to quit. At our second-to-last gig ever, only L.G. and I turned up. It was just a mess."*—UFFE CEDERLUND, MORBID/NIHILIST/ ENTOMBED/DISFEAR

So Morbid's second demo became their swan song. Without the visionary Ohlin, they couldn't find the energy to continue. Uffe Cederlund and Lars-Göran Petrov had also already started to collaborate in the group that would soon shake the death metal underground in its foundations—Nihilist.

Let's take the Nihilist story from the beginning. Nineteen eighty-seven was a turbulent year for the young drummer Nicke Andersson, and he started loads of short-lasting bands. But eventually Nicke and his friends from Kista— Alex Hellid and Leif Cuzner—decided to start the band Brainwarp. Initially they were inspired by strange thrash bands like Voivod and Wehrmacht, but gradually they became aware of more brutal and intense things.

"I guess Nihilist was actually a combination of the gang from Kista and the gang from Bredäng/Skärholmen. Though L.G. and Uffe weren't official members from the start, they were always very closely linked to the band. In fact, I don't know why L.G. and Uffe are credited as session members on our first demo. As I remember it, they were as involved as the rest of us, and both played at our first gig, back in 1987."—NICKE ANDERSSON, NIHILIST/ ENTOMBED

The fact that both Uffe Cederlund and L.G. Petrov were members of Morbid at this point could explain why they were seen as session members. Both were certainly involved in making Nihilist's first demo, *Premature Autopsy*.

"I always get a bit pissed off when reading Nihilist/Entombed biographies, because they are all wrong. In fact, I was the original guitarist and singer in Nihilist. Since my vocals sucked, L.G. ended up singing on the first demo. Buffla, on the other hand, wasn't a part of Nihilist at all. I guess Nicke wanted the members to exclusively play in Nihilist, and since L.G. and I had Morbid we were credited as session musicians. That's just bullshit. I lost interest in Nihilist after that, and focused on Morbid and Infuriation."—UFFE CEDERLUND, MORBID/NIHILIST/ENTOMBED/DISFEAR

Premature Autopsy was recorded in March 1988 at Studio Z. And what a demo it was, full of energy, cool ideas, and raw aggression. Nihilist's style at this point was basically the same powerful thrash/death mixture with screamed vocals that Merciless had already put on tape. But even though Nihilist were as influenced by the likes of Sodom and Destruction as Merciless had been,

From top: Early Nihilist photo;

Nihilist logo—gore style (courtesy of Kristian Wåhlin);

arguably the first Swedish death metal demo

WRITE US AT:

Nicke Andersson · Kungsholmsgränd 16 nb · 127 42 Skärholmen· SWEDEN

· SENTENCED TO DEATH · SUPPOSED TO ROT
· CARNAL LEFTOVERS

Nihilist 'PREMATURE AUTOPSY' DEMO

Premature Autopsy

ALEX: LEAD GUITAR
LEFFE: BASS
NICKE: DRUMS
MATTIAS: VOCALS

(SESSION MEMBERS: L.G.-VOCALS & UFFE - GUITAR)

RECORDED AT 'STUDIO Z', STOCKHOLM, MARCH, 1988. PRODUCED BY NIHILIST ENGINEERED BY LEIF MARTINSON.

THANX ALOT AND HI THERE TO:

Magnus Forsberg of (mighty) TRIBULATION,Cronis and T.T.D. zine, Gylve Nagell, Tomas Lindberg, Mark Sawickis (UNIFORCE zine), Uffe and L.G., Metalion, Laurent Ramadier (D.O.D. zine), Erik and his band, Fred and CREMATOR, Kenny H. (you rule!!!), Bill of CARCASS (total GODS!), John McEntee and REVENANT (totaly SICK!), Johnny & Norpan, Karlèn and MERCILESS, David and Bubbel -Bad zine, Jesse and TERRORIZER, MORBID, RIGOR MORTIS (NY), Ronny Eide, Babs, Shane of UNSEEN TERROR & NAPALM DEATH (grindcore gods!!!!), Trey and MORBID ANGEL, Andrè & VIGILANT, Johan of RIVERS EDGE, Jon Steinar, Alberto & SCHIZO, Zoran, BLACK UNIFORMS, Matte (Aspudden), Nonoe of MUTILATED, Kent Andersson, Benny (anorexia) , Emmi (get your dreadlocks back!). Tomas and Splatter zine.
Hope we didn't forget anyone and if we did we`re very sorry.

COVER BY NICKE

From top: Nihilist practicing traditional grave-disturbance;

Only Shreds Remain *demo*

you could tell something new was going on here. The structures were a little bit more advanced, and the soon-to-be-classic Entombed sound could be heard through the primitive recording.

"We just felt that it was time to record something, and used the same small studio we had fooled around in before. We only wanted to make a demo that some people would find cool, and hopefully wind up on a playlist next to bands like Repulsion and Master. It never even crossed our minds that we one day would make an album."—NICKE ANDERSSON, NIHILIST/ENTOMBED

Though *Premature Autopsy* was undoubtedly a great demo, Nihilist still hadn't fully developed the style that would so sincerely impress us all. But in retrospect, this demo represents one of the most important moments of Swedish death metal. It is so intense, so brutal, and contains all four members who would later make up the core of Sweden's most well-known and, in my opinion, best death metal band—Entombed.

"I will never forget the first time I heard the first Nihilist demo: it was just so fucking great! They were simply the best band around. Without Nihilist there would never have been such a death metal boom in Sweden. They opened the gates for so many other bands."—TOMAS NYQVIST, PUTREFACTION MAG/ NO FASHION/IRON FIST PRODUCTIONS

"Nihilist were fucking awesome, and the best thing that came out of the whole Swedish death metal scene. Period. I followed them closely, I was a fan of what they were doing, for sure. Nicke Andersson and I tape traded, and he'd send me rehearsal recordings of their new songs and it was terrifying – they were constantly raising the bar."—MICHAEL AMOTT, CARNAGE/CARCASS/ARCH ENEMY

But let's not jump to conclusions. At this point Nihilist was just one of many promising young Swedish bands, along with Merciless, Grave, Dismember, Treblinka, etc. Things were soon to change, as Nihilist followed Morbid's lead and entered Sunlight Studios to record their second demo on December 8, 1988. The resulting *Only Shreds Remain* tape was a revolution.

On Nihilist's second demo, the lineup had been altered as Cuzner went on to guitar and their somewhat older friend Johnny Hedlund was recruited on bass. His involvement with the band happened casually.

"Nicke just asked me if I wanted to play bass in Nihilist, as simple as that. I don't remember how it happened, but we probably met during some crazy party. That's how everything happened back then."—JOHNNY HEDLUND, NIHILIST/UNLEASHED

"We became a real band when Johnny joined in, and when L.G. became a permanent member shortly after, things really started to flow."—NICKE ANDERSSON, NIHILIST/ENTOMBED

With their new lineup and improved material, Nihilist easily blew away their contemporaries and delivered what can be seen as probably the first 100 percent pure Swedish death metal recording. The precise riffing, the ghastly growls of Petrov—very unlike the screams delivered on the debut—and Andersson's drumming are all just incredible. This demo is also the first to feature the special ultra-thick Studio Sunlight guitar sound that would later become the trademark of Swedish death metal. However, Nicke Andersson was not too excited about the recording when it was finished.

"We used Sunlight only because Morbid had been there. But I was not pleased with the studio. I think the production on our second demo sucks. The drums, especially, sound awful. Skogsberg didn't know much about how to take care of death metal back then. The reason we got the great guitar sound was that Leif moved on to guitar, and came up with that fat sound. At that point, we didn't know how he did it—but we loved it!"—NICKE ANDERSSON, NIHILIST/ ENTOMBED

The most important thing about this demo is the songs. The structures had become much more advanced, and all the compositions are just brilliant. Now there was no turning back. In the following year, Sweden would see the uprising of a handful of new death metal bands. It's amazing what Nihilist achieved at this point, especially considering the minimal time they had in the studio.

"For that recording, we hardly had any time at all. You had to pay for each hour in the studio, and we didn't have any money. And back then you didn't rehearse much before a recording, so it was pretty stressful."—JOHNNY HEDLUND, NIHILIST/UNLEASHED

Now let's turn to one of the most revoltingly named bands of all time, Treblinka. Operating under the name of a German World War II concentration camp caused some problems. Before one of their first gigs, they were asked to explain that they were not Nazis before they would to be allowed to play. Once on stage, Johan Edlund began the gig by exclaiming: *"Our name is Treblinka, and we are fucking proud of it!"*

The origin of this group can be found in River's Edge, which included future Treblinka members Stefan Lagergren on guitar and Anders Holmberg on drums. This was a pretty intense thrash metal band with a clear German vibe. When River's Edge entered Soundstation Studio in June 1988 to record the *Mind the Edge* demo, the group was joined by Johan Edlund on vocals. His tormented screams added a ghastly touch.

"River's Edge was their band. I was only a session member who sang Stefan's lyrics. I guess they wanted it to be a bit more commercial, in the vein of Metallica and Megadeth. That style was something I neither wanted nor could do. I wanted to do something more extreme, and I also wanted to do my own thing. Compose songs, write lyrics, fold demo sheets, and the lot." —JOHAN EDLUND, TREBLINKA/TIAMAT

Johan Edlund had already started his own project, Treblinka, in March

1988. While he was hanging out with River's Edge, both Stefan Lagergren and Anders Holmberg from that band soon became in Treblinka. The band also included bass player Jörgen Thulberg, who previously played in the hardcore band The Clint Eastwood Experience. This quartet was the first incarnation of one of Sweden's biggest metal bands, Tiamat.

"We were just a couple of friends who started to play in a band since we had nothing else to do. We never had any thought at all of ever making a record or anything like that. There was no clear idea of what we should be about yet; we just tried to have some fun. When we made our first logo, we just filled it with everything that we thought was cool; spider webs, ice, fire, a demon, 666, a pentagram, and an inverted cross. It just looked silly, but I guess it was a great achievement to incorporate all those things into one word!"—JOHAN EDLUND, TREBLINKA/TIAMAT

Treblinka were pretty isolated from the rest of the early Stockholm bands, operating from the nice northern suburb of Täby rather than from the seedier suburbs such as Skärholmen and Kista. They also sounded different. Instead of striving for that fat Sunlight sound, they looked more to thrash metal and the likes of Bathory and Venom. In that way, they are more linked to bands like Merciless and Mefisto than to later bands like Nihilist and Dismember.

"We were quite outside the Stockholm scene. We were in a sense in the scene, because we knew all the guys and partied together and had the same musical taste, but we sounded a bit different. I always wanted to be a black metal band. I was never into that gore/splatter thing that most bands reveled in. In fact, I always wanted bands like Nihilist to get more into inverted crosses and the occult as well. So it wasn't like we tried to be different; we just did what we thought was right."—JOHAN EDLUND, TREBLINKA/TIAMAT

Treblinka's debut demo, *Crawling in Vomits*, was recorded in Sunlight Studios on November 18 and 19, 1988. It showed a simple approach, with semi-distorted guitars, strange melodies, and simplistic one-string riffs. The recording is topped with Johan Edlund's grim and harsh screams, and it all has an evil and cold feeling, which would make these Treblinka demos favorites among later black metal bands. Everything on this demo is crude and amateurish to the limit, but nevertheless powerful.

"It was hard back then. First, none of us had any money, so we had to save up everything we could get for a long time before we could afford to record a demo. The reason we chose Sunlight was that Morbid had recorded there, even though both Nicke Andersson and Uffe Cederlund thought the sound sucked on that demo. But we didn't know of any other studio, so we went in there anyway. Then there was the problem that we didn't know anything about how to record. We couldn't even distort our guitars enough."—JOHAN EDLUND, TREBLINKA/TIAMAT

Clockwise from top:
River's Edge demo;

flyer for a very early Treblinka gig. Note ultra-cool logo that includes anything "necro" and evil;

Treblinka's debut demo, in typical "horror-comic style";

Treblinka's second demo—new logo, new image

Expulsion circa 1988

Treblinka's second demo, *The Sign of the Pentagram*, followed the next year, and shows a somewhat more professional approach. Though still primitive and raw, the riffs are more thought-through, and the arrangements are better structured. Even though the music might be more thrash-oriented this time around, the lyrics are definitely more evil. Where the first demo dealt with gore and partying, the second goes straight for satanic stuff. I guess around this time the band decided to distinguish themselves from other Swedish bands with a more evil concept in the vein of Bathory. In 1989, a few evil lyrics and a touch of makeup made all the difference.

On the surface, Treblinka both sounded and looked evil—even though the atmosphere is ruined by a blues part in the middle of one of the songs. Curiously, Tiamat later repeated this "error" on its first album—the blues break reveals the fact that this is music made by teenagers basically just having a good time! Nonetheless, Treblinka's demos were important, and they remain respected to this day. In fact, I think they are as powerful as anything the band made after the name change to Tiamat.

"On our second demo we were much more focused. We had really decided to be a black metal band, and the lyrics were much more thought-through. We still didn't know how to record, or exactly how we were supposed to sound."
—JOHAN EDLUND, TREBLINKA/TIAMAT

Treblinka's Stefan Lagergren and Anders Holmberg simultaneously played in Expulsion, a continuation of their previous band River's Edge. In 1988 and 1989 they released the demos *Cerebral Cessation* and *Veiled in the Mist of Mystery*. Both of them sounded pretty much like Treblinka, small surprise. Johan Edlund even helped them out with guest vocals. Yet Expulsion were fated to cause no impact, despite making a couple CDs in the mid-90's. Edlund, on the other hand, would soon take on the world with Tiamat.

"I really don't remember singing on any Expulsion demo, but I guess I did. Back then we hung out with Tomas Skogsberg at Sunlight Studios whenever a band was recording, and I probably did loads of guest appearances that I have forgotten about. We were a small group of friends, and since we had no flats and couldn't get into the pubs, we just hung out wherever we could."—JOHAN EDLUND, TREBLINKA/TIAMAT

One of the most important bands of the earliest phase of the scene was Dismember, formed in April 1988 by Fred Estby on drums, David Blomqvist on guitar, and Robert Sennebäck on vocals. Fred was actually a guitarist, but when he couldn't find a drummer he got an old drum kit from his friend Nicke Andersson and taught himself to play drums.

Nicke initially had a great impact on Dismember—he also came up with the band name and designed their logo. His original idea was to call the band Dismemberizer, but he ran out of space while drawing the logo and so cut the name to Dismember. Fred Estby further explains the band's primitive origins.

"We were just three kids with skateboards, a few rotten guitars, a small room for rehearsals in my parents' basement, the worthless old drum kit of Nicke Andersson, and a thirty-watt amplifier. David didn't even own a guitar back then, so he borrowed some crap from me. Our influences were Death, Slayer, Autopsy, Possessed, Pentagram from Chile, Vulcano, Schizo, Sarcofago, and the first record by Sepultura."—FRED ESTBY, DISMEMBER/CARNAGE

So they were a bunch of friends who didn't know what to do except bash out metal as hard as possible. It comes as no surprise, then, that Dismember's first recording turned out to be such a disaster.

"The absolute first demo we recorded, one which we never released, was a terrible mess. We recorded it at the youth center in which we rehearsed, and the guy who recorded it didn't know anything about anything. He was just pretending. It turned out really disastrous. It sounded so awful that even we realized that it would be better if we didn't release it."—FRED ESTBY, DISMEMBER/CARNAGE

"We didn't even keep a copy for ourselves. He who recorded it was totally stupid."—DAVID BLOMQVIST, DISMEMBER/CARNAGE/ENTOMBED

"We didn't know much, either. But when we recorded our next demo it was already a lot better. We had rehearsed a bit more, and we managed to

*From left: Dismember's
debut demo, with artwork by
Nicke Andersson;*

Last Blasphemies. Classic
death metal!

get the sound guy who had recorded Nihilist."—FRED ESTBY, DISMEMBER/
CARNAGE

The sound guy wasn't the only thing they borrowed from Nihilist. Unlike
Treblinka, Dismember walked straight down the track set out by their friends,
with similar riffs and sound. In fact, Nihilist's Nicke Andersson also played bass
as Dismember entered the small Studio Z at the local youth center in December
1988 to make their first real tape. The resulting *Dismembered* demo showed
a group to be reckoned with. Sure it was rough and primitive in many ways,
but you can definitely sense that special Swedish death metal feeling. The riffs
and guitar sound are right on the spot. But the most striking thing about this demo
is Robert Sennebäck's insane vocals. I'm actually not sure if I like them or not, but
these twisted teenage screams have a very special feeling—more black metal than
death metal, in a restless teenage kind of fashion. A song like "Death Evocation"
sounds very different on later recordings.

"*Dismembered was recorded with the eight-channel tape recorder at the
youth center where we and Nihilist rehearsed. We were pretty satisfied with the
result, even thought the vocals weren't that great. After a few months Robert
learned to sing deeper, so we actually booked time to dub over the vocals and
guitars for a second release of the demo. This never happened, since I was so
stupid that I placed the master tape inside our Peavey amplifier on my way
to the studio—which of course erased the whole damn thing!*"—FRED ESTBY,
DISMEMBER/CARNAGE

Instead of a second version of the demo, Dismember had to write some
songs for a brand new recording. And the second demo really showed their
brilliance. *Last Blasphemies* from 1989 is classic Swedish death metal at its very
best. Fat sound, groovy riffs, hammering two-beats, and growling vocals to the
limit. It's a totally awesome tape, even though it sounds pretty primitive.

"*The second demo was recorded at Studio Kuben, and I think that was
a big mistake. The guy there didn't understand or care anything about us; he
just wanted to get paid. Apart from the vocals, the result wasn't that good to
my ears. The drums, especially, sounded horrible, and the fact that I played*

very sloppily didn't help much either."—FRED ESTBY, DISMEMBER/CARNAGE

In any case, Dismember should have dominated the scene, since they were definitely one of the best bands around. But, as we will see, the death metal movement works in mysterious ways. Dismember suddenly folded in October 1989, when drummer Fred Estby left to join Carnage, and guitarist David Blomqvist joined Entombed on bass.

"*Unlike David and Robert, I had quit school to concentrate fully on music. I realized that I had to get an album out as quick as possible, and when I met Mike Amott we kind of clicked in our determination to get things done. So I left Dismember to join Carnage.*"—FRED ESTBY, DISMEMBER/CARNAGE

"*I really don't think I was as determined as Fred Estby!*"—MICHAEL AMOTT, CARNAGE/CARCASS/ARCH ENEMY

As it turned out, Carnage would later split up and pave the way for a new version of Dismember. Though Dismember's first two demos had great qualities, they were very inspired by Nihilist, whose third and final demo really set the standard going forward. Nihilist's lineup had by now been altered, as guitarist Leif Cuzner had moved back to his native Canada with his parents. The obvious choice for a replacement was their previous guitarist Uffe Cederlund, as Morbid had called it quits and his new band Infuriation was going nowhere.

"*There was never any talk of who would replace 'Leffe' when he left the band. I was just in again, although I thought that we should change our name already at that point. Nicke thought that the name was too established to abandon, though, so we stuck to Nihilist.*"—UFFE CEDERLUND, MORBID/ NIHILIST/ENTOMBED/DISFEAR

L.G. was now the permanent singer of Nihilist, and with the two ex-Morbid guys aboard the band got busy. Nicke wrote some new material, and booked Studio Kuben for their third recording. The resulting *Drowned*, released in 1988, showed Nihilist in full force. Everybody knew that this band would make it big. The riffs and vocals are superb, and Nicke's drumming had reached new heights. What may be a bit of a disappointment is the guitar sound, which isn't as fat as on *Only Shreds Remain*.

"*We really wanted to capture that guitar sound that Leif had created, so Uffe borrowed his guitar to get it straight. We actually believed that the sound was in the guitar, but we were wrong. It wasn't until the demo was already done that Uffe realized that the sound was actually in the Boss Heavy Metal pedal, with basically all the switches set on ten. And since then, he has always used it.*" —NICKE ANDERSSON, NIHILIST/ENTOMBED

Although Uffe Cederlund made slight changes from Cuzner's initial settings, the important thing is that the midrange knob on the pedal is set on max.

"*I never tried to re-create Leif's guitar sound; I just borrowed his guitar. I don't even think that Nihilist or Entombed ever had a similar guitar sound*

From top: Nihilist looking grim and evil;

Nihilist live (note the trademark flannel shirt!);

Drowned *demo*

to that of Only Shreds Remain. *The good thing about Leif was that he was the first one who understood how to use the Boss Heavy Metal distortion pedal. We didn't know how to handle that pedal, so Drowned sounded pretty bad.*"—UFFE CEDERLUND, MORBID/NIHILIST/ENTOMBED/DISFEAR

As Nihilist developed, the band experienced some turmoil. Bassist Johnny Hedlund didn't want to take the same musical direction as the others. He was the oldest one in Nihilist, however, and the others were still very young. Nobody had the guts to fire him. Instead, they simply split up the band in the summer of 1989. One week later Nicke and Uffe resurrected the band as Entombed, originally as a duo.

"*Nicke didn't want to play with me in the band anymore, so he just said that Nihilist was no more. Then he started Entombed, and I started Unleashed. The rest is history, and I am very happy that things turned out the way they did. If I had stayed, we would not have been a good band. We had different ideas about everything.*"—JOHNNY HEDLUND, NIHILIST/UNLEASHED

"*During the summer of 1989, we and Johnny started to drift in different directions. He presented some song ideas that we thought sucked, and we were also getting annoyed with his fascination with Vikings. But it was a really stupid and childish decision to break up the band instead of talking to him or firing him. But we were only children, so we couldn't handle it.*"—NICKE ANDERSSON, NIHILIST/ENTOMBED

A few other death metal bands started to play in Stockholm in 1988, such as Afflicted Convulsion, Therion, and Crematory. Even though none of these were quite ready for demos yet, there was no doubt that something was going on in Stockholm at this point. But what about the rest of Sweden—was something happening out there as well?

Grave and Grotesque: Early Death Metal Around the Country

Most of the early Swedish death metal bands were based in Stockholm, but there were a few exceptions. In addition to the mighty Merciless from Strängnäs, another important band was Grave from Visby, a village on the semi-deserted island of Gotland in the Baltic Sea. In this isolated location, a bunch of guys who grew up in the name of metal got a band together.

"*We started to play together when we were thirteen years old. The only one who knew how to handle an instrument was our drummer, Jensa; the rest of us just grabbed one instrument each and banged our brains out. During our first years we played under loads of names, such as Destroyer, Rising Power, and Anguish. As Anguish we even recorded a 'demo,' but I will never play that to*

From top: *Grave's* Sick Disgust Eternal *demo;*

early Grave flyer

NEW ETERNAL DEMO OUT NOW

DEMO NO.1 "SICK DISGUST
ETERNAL" DEMO `88.
DEMO NO.2 THE NEW ONE
"SEXUAL MUTILATION"
DEMO `89.:::::::::::::::

GET IT NOW FOR ONLY
30 SKR.OR 5 US.DOLLARS
EACH. CASH ONLY.........
ALSO AVAILABLE:POSTERS
WITH "S.D.E." DEMO MOTIV
OR THE "S.M." DEMO MOTIV
FOR ONLY 10 SKR.OR 2 U.S
DOLLARS EACH.ORDER FAST.

RAW BRUTAL DEATH METAL..
SEND MONEY TO:::::::::::
GRAVE c/o OLA LINDGREN
IRISDALSGATAN 80.
62142 VISBY, GOTLAND
SWEDEN

SPREAD IT SPREAD IT

anyone! We were just kids who wanted to play metal, even though we didn't know how to."—OLA LINDGREN, GRAVE

In 1986 the youngsters got serious and rechristened themselves Corpse. By then they had gotten into speed metal, and the German scene in particular inspired them to go down a more brutal path. The rather primitive demo *Black Dawn* was recorded during 1986, and the guys got more obsessed with extreme metal day by day. In 1988 Corpse changed their name to Grave, under circumstances typical of the early Swedish death metal movement.

"The reason for the name change was that we wanted to get rid of our bass player, since he sucked, but we were too cowardly to sack him. So we just changed our name to Grave when we got one of our first gigs—and never told him about it! Well, naturally he turned up at the gig to find out what this evil-sounding band was all about, and could see that the mysterious Grave was in fact his own band. Fuck, I get so embarrassed when I think about it..."—OLA LINDGREN, GRAVE

As you can see, Grave repeated the childish story of Nihilist! Anyway, as Grave things would really start to happen. On August 30, 1988, Ola Lindgren, Jörgen Sandström, and Jens Paulsson entered Yellow House "Studio" to record the *Sick Disgust Eternal* demo over three hectic days. The result is pretty brutal and straightforward, with simple riffs and screamed vocals. The production is crude, and the arrangements still smell of thrash. Even though the songs are good, this demo was only a sample of how great the band would eventually become. A song like "Into the Grave" sounds much more brutal on their debut album. Nevertheless, Grave were independently developing music similar to the bands in Stockholm.

"The band was actually not very organized at this point. We just wanted to be a brutal speed metal band, not much else. I really like our first demo, even today; it has a cool German feeling to it. Kreator and Sodom, you know?" —OLA LINDGREN, GRAVE

Another band starting in 1986 was Sandviken's Sorcery. At this point they were still basically a thrash metal band, proof of which can be heard on the early demos *The Arrival* from 1987 and *Ancient Creation* from 1988. This didn't matter much, since everything fairly brutal back then was accepted by the underground. Sorcery was a part of the scene. On their 1989 demo *Unholy Crusade* they showed more Death tendencies, something they would later develop further. Sorcery never became truly "deadly," but in the late 80's they were surely one of the hardest Swedish metal bands outside of Stockholm.

The same can be said about Surahammar's Tribulation, led by notorious tape trader and drummer Magnus Forsberg. This group started out in 1986 as Pentagram, and quickly released the crude *Infernal Return* demo. In February the next year they changed their name to Tribulation, and the *Pyretic*

Convulsions demo came in 1988. Their style was chaotic and strange thrash metal, and they had quite a reputation within the early Swedish underground. Magnus Forsberg especially was a central character for the whole scene. Still, their music could never really be considered death metal.

In addition to Grave, there was one band outside of Stockholm that actually produced true death metal in 1988—the amazing Grotesque from Gothenburg. The origin of Grotesque can be found in Conquest, formed by guitarist Kristian Wåhlin in 1986.

"I was basically inspired by German speed metal, and back then that was just about the most brutal music you could find. Apart from us there were three or four other speed metal bands in Gothenburg, but all of them were more into U.S. stuff such as Metallica. Obviously we were too extreme for people back then, and nobody liked us."—KRISTIAN "NECROLORD" WÅHLIN, GROTESQUE/LIERS IN WAIT/DECOLLATION

Though they never got any attention, Wåhlin struggled on with Conquest through endless lineup changes. The difficulty of finding suitable members led Kristian to try out every person who was into some kind of extreme metal, and in 1988 the band ended up with the eleven-year-old(!) drummer Johan Lager. The same year, Conquest's guitarist and later bass player David Hultén learned of a guy named Tomas Lindberg, who was into the same kind of music they were. Before long, he joined as vocalist.

"I was actually looking for a bass player for my hardcore band, and asked a guy that I knew played guitar if he wanted to join. He turned me down, since he thought that we couldn't play, but asked me to join his band Conquest as a singer instead. So I went to their rehearsal room and met Kristian. It was only the two of us there, and we did a couple of Bathory covers with only guitar and vocals. Then I was in. It felt right instantly."—TOMAS LINDBERG, GROTESQUE/AT THE GATES/DISFEAR

"I think it was our bass player who got to know that there was a guy in our neighborhood who was into extreme metal, and that was enough for us to ask him to join!"—KRISTIAN "NECROLORD" WÅHLIN, GROTESQUE/LIERS IN WAIT/DECOLLATION

After adding Tomas Lindberg, the band soon changed their name to Grotesque. Their style got increasingly brutal, mainly due to Lindberg's firm base in underground death metal.

"I guess we all got more into extreme music, and personally I was very much into Possessed and Bathory at this time. But it was Tomas who got us into the underground death metal scene and tape trading. After that, everything got extremely brutal, and we started to get serious with inverted crosses and corpse paint. People here thought we were insane. You have to remember that around 1988 the black metal thing was considered very

dated, and techno-thrash was the reigning trend."—KRISTIAN "NECROLORD" WÅHLIN, GROTESQUE/LIERS IN WAIT/DECOLLATION

As you might suspect, Grotesque soon sounded very different from the other bands in the area. Conquest had always been completely unknown even in the underground, but things were about to change. The brutalized band got their hands on a crude tape recorder, and produced the primitive tape *Ripped from the Cross* in late 1988.

"That was initially just a rehearsal tape, recorded because we wanted to hear the songs ourselves. Later we added new vocals and a second guitar, and that is the version of the recording that we traded."—TOMAS LINDBERG, GROTESQUE/AT THE GATES/DISFEAR

Though *Ripped from the Cross* was indeed crude, it definitely proved that Grotesque were to be reckoned with. They were already one of Sweden's most brutal bands, and Kristian's strange guitar riffs and Tomas' soulful screams would inspire many bands to come.

All in all, the earliest phase of the Swedish death metal scene remained almost entirely a Stockholm phenomenon. Among the few other death metal bands around the country before 1989 were Carnage from Växjö and Macrodex from Eskilstuna.

"There was a strong hardcore punk and skater scene in Vaxjo at the time, and we moved in those circles. Great people, although Carnage didn't fit into that scene very well—we were too heavy, too brutal, too new. The metal scene was lame, though. They were either rehearsing Metallica covers or trying to be Bon Jovi. We were much happier in the hardcore scene."—MICHAEL AMOTT, CARNAGE/CARCASS/ARCH ENEMY

Carnage and Macrodex both still had some maturing to do before they could produce demos—though the pre-Macrodex band Cruelty made a pretty intense demo called *Who Cares?* at the end of 1988.

One place with some kind of extreme metal scene was Linköping, with the bands Satanic Slaughter, Total Death, and Orchriste. The scene there basically stayed alive because bands had great opportunities to play live at a cultural project called Rockkarusellen—"The Rock Carousel." But these Linköping bands could hardly be labeled actual death metal, and none made demos until 1989. The national scene was still in its cradle during 1988. During the next year, however, Swedish death metal started to become much more visible.

Clockwise from right:
Sandviken's heaviest;

Tribulation/Pentagram. If you don't
remember it, this was what most death
metal pioneers looked like around 1986;

Sweden's number one tape trader
promoting his own band;

Tribulation's debut demo

Cold death! - SORCERY

PYRETIC CONVULSIONS

TRIBULATION

1. Encroached Visions
2. Pecuniary Aid
3. Where Nothing Remains
4. The Conjuring
5. Dogmother

TRIBULATION IS:

Toza   guitar, vocals
Hojas   bass
Neuman   guitar
Forsberg   drums

A FIVE TRACK DEMO WITH TRIBULATION

PYRETIC CONVULSIONS

NOW AVAILABLE FOR ONLY $5 or 30 SKR

PYRETIC CONVULSIONS

BAND CONTACT:
TRIBULATION
735 00 Surahammar
SWEDEN

Chapter Four:
The Scene Gets Going

"INTO ETERNAL DEATH,
    YOUR FAITH HAS DIED
INTO THE DARKNESS,
    INTO THE GRAVE"
—GRAVE, "INTO THE GRAVE"

Clockwise from top:

Poster for classic death metal gig in Stockholm. Anorexia was Anders Schultz of Unleashed's old hardcore band. Anders was sick on the day of the gig, so Anorexia never played—that didn't stop the youngster from attending the gig and banging his head like crazy!;

poster for seminal thrash metal gig in Stockholm (Death sadly never appeared);

poster for Grave's first gig outside of Gotland. Dismember are not billed

Before 1989 there was hardly a Swedish death metal scene worth talking about. All that existed were a few friends, playing in a couple of bands. They rehearsed, bought records, traded tapes, and wrote letters, but only occasionally met, spoke, or hung out with anyone outside their closest circle. Very few gigs took place—the most important happenings remained the few thrash metal concerts that found their way to Sweden.

"The early scene was so small, you knew about almost everybody who was into extreme metal, through tape trading or concerts. I mean, you didn't only know the bands, but also kids who were just into the music. In any given Swedish town, we would know if there was a dedicated metalhead or not. Here in Gothenburg we probably knew everybody who was into any kind of speed metal. You have to remember that the early death metal scene was built on sheer love of the music. Nobody ever thought that anyone would ever release an album, and it was almost impossible to get a gig. The music was just something that you had to do. Furthermore, it wasn't considered cool to be a death metaller. If you were into extreme music, you were considered strange and socially hopeless. A nerd, really. Everybody involved in the early scene was 'true' in every sense."—Kristian "Necrolord" Wåhlin, Grotesque/Liers in Wait/Decollation

"We were outcasts, and if you saw somebody with a flannel shirt and a

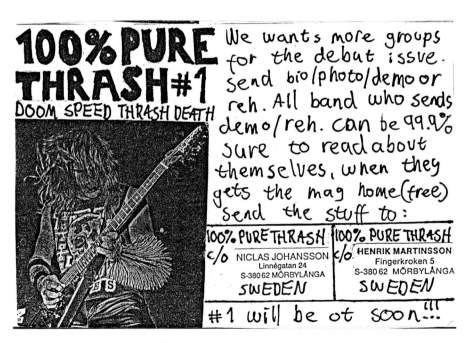

Thrash metal once ruled the earth

metal T-shirt, you immediately had a connection and could start to talk. The first gig I ever attended was Anthrax and Testament in 1987. I think I realized right there that this was where I belonged."—ANDERS SCHULTZ, UNLEASHED

"People don't get how small the scene was back then. If you saw somebody with a death metal T-shirt in town, you always knew that person by name. You met at thrash metal concerts, drank beer, and exchanged addresses. That was the beginning of the scene."—JESPER THORSSON, AFFLICTED

"I went to all the thrash gigs at Fryshuset in Stockholm. It was there you met all the people. I remember the guys from Kazjurol and Mortality walking around selling demos outside the Slayer gig in 1988."—PATRIK JENSEN, ORCHRISTE/SEANCE/THE HAUNTED

"We had to travel a long time by boat to catch those thrash metal gigs, but we all went for it. I think we got to know the guys from Nihilist and Dismember at the Slayer concert in 1988, but it might have been as early as Metallica in 1986. Uffe, Nicke, Fred, and all those great people. Eventually we started to trade demos, and we just knew that we had to get out of Gotland and move to Stockholm. Later you always brought loads of demos to those thrash gigs to sell. In fact, the stuff that was going on outside was more important than the gig itself! The concerts and Heavy Sound were the only public places we could meet. All of us were too young to go to the pub, and everybody lived with their parents."
—OLA LINDGREN, GRAVE

"Thrash metal gigs of the 80's were important occasions—it was so great to see these bands. I got to know a lot of people there, such as the guys from Täby in Treblinka and Expulsion."—NICKE ANDERSSON, NIHILIST/ENTOMBED

"There was no scene, just a few friends, a couple of metalheads and a couple of punks who partied together. The 'scene' was that small. Everybody who listened to extreme stuff, recorded demos, and wanted to play met at concerts like Anthrax, Slayer, Candlemass, and such stuff. It became a core of people who listened to extreme music. Morbid was pretty important back then. One of the first underground happenings was when they played in Bredäng."
—FRED ESTBY, DISMEMBER/CARNAGE

As the participants of the early Swedish death metal scene got older—remember, many were still only fourteen to seventeen years old—they began to crawl out of their parents' homes and hang out on the town. The first death metal bands started to get their acts together and began putting on shows. In the beginning, though, nobody really cared what these very young bands were doing, and very few metalheads actually attended these gigs.

"We did our first gig with Nihilist at Kista youth center late in 1987. Not a single person in the audience liked metal; the kids just stared and laughed. We were so young and so extreme. People thought we were a joke."—NICKE ANDERSSON, NIHILIST/ENTOMBED

Poster for one of the very first death metal gigs held in Stockholm

"*There were not many gigs at all back then, just a few. We did one north of Stockholm with Nihilist just after I had joined. It was basically us and forty friends that we brought along. After the gig I remember that we sat in a circle and puked in a bucket. A bit fucked up when you think about it; I guess it was Nicke's humor. Well, the scene was not much more than that in the old days!*"
—JOHNNY HEDLUND, NIHILIST/UNLEASHED

"*To get a gig back then was almost impossible, and you had to take whatever you could get. The first gig we ever did with Grotesque was at the Finnish Association in the suburb of Kortedala, really strange. But I really enjoyed those primitive days, and I guess that's why I love playing at punk venues with Disfear today. It's honest. It's true.*"—TOMAS LINDBERG, GROTESQUE/AT THE GATES/DISFEAR

As time went by, opportunities for underground metal bands to play live improved slightly. Still, the only places that would touch a death metal band were punk venues and youth centers.

"*On Gotland there were absolutely no places at all. Once in a while some youth center put on a show with everybody who had an instrument on the island. We played a couple of these strange shows—you know, twelve-year-olds with violins or whatever. There was no metal scene here at all. I think the first time we ever played outside of Gotland was as late as 1990, when we got to Sala together with Dismember and Entombed."*—OLA LINDGREN, GRAVE

"*Grotesque might have done about ten gigs all in all, most of them at youth centers. The biggest things we ever did were a gig with Carcass and a memorable night with Morbid and Nihilist. The only time we ever played outside of Gothenburg was when Jon Nödtveidt brought us to Strömstad. There weren't many possibilities back then; if you wanted to play, you had to make it happen yourself.*"—KRISTIAN "NECROLORD" WÅHLIN, GROTESQUE/LIERS IN WAIT/DECOLLATION

"*There were no metal venues for a long time. The only ones that had places with frequent gigs were the punks, who had venues like Ultrahuset, Hunddagis, and Vita Huset. At actual rock clubs they hated extreme metal. The biggest gig we did with Nihilist during that time was probably in Bredäng, in front of about 200 people. Not until later did the scene really start to move.*"—JOHNNY HEDLUND, NIHILIST/UNLEASHED

"*That gig in Bredäng was the first time a death metal gig actually attracted a lot of people. I was just amazed, and started to sense that something might be happening. You know, this was the first time people we didn't know came to see us—because they liked us!*"—NICKE ANDERSSON, NIHILIST/ENTOMBED

"*We rehearsed at a youth center called Runan, and eventually started to book gigs there with ourselves and our friends. They had a small stage and a PA, but before us hardly anyone ever played there. The staff at the place never liked what we did; they hated the music and despised the youngsters who came to those concerts—who were basically our friends in Nihilist and Dismember. Runan was also located next to a cemetery, which of course caused some problems…*"—JOHAN EDLUND, TREBLINKA/TIAMAT

"*Some youth centers hosted gigs because they felt like they had to. Runan in Täby, in which the guys from Treblinka were involved, was a great alternative— with good sound, smoke machines, and a light rig. Then there were the punk places, such as Hunddagis in Haninge. I saw Therion in a living room there! It's hard to imagine today.*"—JESPER THORSSON, AFFLICTED

"*Our first gig was at Hunddagis, and there couldn't have been more than forty people there—that's how many could fit into the small living room where the minimal stage was. We played three songs, and two of them once again as encores, if I remember it right. The small crowd was pretty wild. I was so nervous before the gig that my body was shaking. I was really shy back then. Our second gig was at a youth center in Husby where there was no stage. We played on the floor in front of five sitting, but still headbanging, death metallers, and fifteen shocked immigrant kids wondering what the hell was going on. I have no idea who booked us for that gig. Those were the only two gigs we ever did with Matti Kärki."*—CHRISTOFFER JOHNSSON, THERION

"The first gig we ever played in another town was in Värnamo, together with No Security. For us it was cool to be offered a gig outside of Stockholm, even though fewer than ten people turned up. Later I heard that No Security thought we had a rock star attitude, which sounds strange since we were just a bunch of teenagers who had only released two demos. I guess they just had to think that about us since we were a metal band, and they were punks. The greatest thing about this gig was that the guys from Carnage turned up, and we got to know them."—NICKE ANDERSSON, NIHILIST/ENTOMBED

"I don't think anyone who wasn't there in the late 80's can ever understand the feeling, the honesty, and the energy of the early death metal scene. You worked your ass off for nothing, and never complained about anything. It was pure love and dedication. As the 90's came, death metal turned into big business, and that initial feeling was lost forever."—TOMAS LINDBERG, GROTESQUE/AT THE GATES/DISFEAR

That the underground spirit disappeared from the death metal scene in the early 90's is very true. Today, even the smallest band can find a gig at a local rock festival, and record a pretty professional demo. Back then, everything was hard work and dedication.

Around 1988, some new fanzines appeared that focused on death metal. Previous 'zines like *Megalomaniac* and *At Dawn They Read* had basically been thrash metal 'zines with some death in them, but now things were getting more hardcore. The first wave of extreme metal fanzines had primarily been a phenomenon in the south of Sweden, but the second wave was created by prominent band members all over the country.

In Stockholm, Nihilist's Nicke Andersson was working on *Chickenshit*. Though never released, it probably inspired others to follow his example—everything he did back then inspired people. Both Alex Hellid and Uffe Cederlund in Nicke's band Nihilist started to make 'zines, and Hellid even released one issue of his *Dark Awakening*. Two other Stockholm guys who published a fanzine were Johan Edlund and Stefan Lagergren of Treblinka, who edited the wonderfully named *Poserkill*.

"The 'zine was started around the same time as Treblinka. Stefan actually made most of it; I just did a couple interviews. Nicke Andersson started out a long time before us, but unlike him we actually managed to release at least one issue!"—JOHAN EDLUND, TREBLINKA/TIAMAT

Apart from this hilarious fanzine, Edlund also started to distribute extreme music under the name Mould in Hell. He also released Treblinka's 7" under that name. The Swedish death metal scene was becoming dynamic. During the years to come, virtually everybody did something creative, as had been the case with the hardcore scene during the early 80's.

Clockwise from top left:
Johan Edlund and Stefan Lagergren's
one and only issue of Poserkill. *Great cover!;*

The chaotic cover of Cascade #1;

Ultra-rare first issue of Jon Nödtveidt's Mega Mag;

*Edsbyn's great contribution to journalism—*Hang 'Em High

Down in Billdal, Gothenburg, the two youngsters Tomas Lindberg and Johan Österberg unleashed the unrelenting fanzine *Cascade* during 1988.

"*The influences for our 'zine were taken from the thrash metal and hardcore scenes. I went through all the credits on records by bands like Voivod and Celtic Frost to discover new bands. I was mainly into smaller 'zines myself, and I loved the underground. The 'zine that made me realize that I could make one myself was Patric Cronberg's* To the Death. *His 'zine inspired me a lot, and before long Johan and I put together the first issue of* Cascade."—TOMAS LINDBERG, GROTESQUE/AT THE GATES/DISFEAR

The resulting fanzine is a whirlwind of everything brutal in music, with a layout that is chaotic to the brink of collapse. *Cascade* was at the very front of the extreme metal scene, and its first issue featured bands such as Nihilist, Morbid Angel, and Obscurity. A couple more issues followed before *Cascade* met a premature death. Tomas Lindberg joined the fantastic band Grotesque around the same time he started *Cascade*. Johan Österberg would soon form Decollation, and later Diabolique—both with Grotesque's Kristian Wåhlin.

"*In the end we had built up a great trading community with people from all over the world, and the demos and 'zines just kept flowing in. It was originally through the 'zine that I got in touch with Nicke Andersson, and through him, the entire Stockholm scene. The death metal scene there was way ahead of the rest of Sweden, so when you made a 'zine, Stockholm was the main focus. I had a really good time making it, but eventually I focused more on producing music.*"
—TOMAS LINDBERG, GROTESQUE/AT THE GATES/DISFEAR

The first issue of *Cascade* inspired two youngsters in the isolated northern town of Edsbyn—Orvar Säfström and Erik Qvick—to start the fanzine *Hang 'Em High*. These guys were totally dedicated to death metal, and at the same time they formed the band Prophet 2002, later rechristened Nirvana 2002.

"*Erik bought the first issue of* Cascade *at Heavy Sound, and we immediately felt that we had to do a 'zine ourselves. We were about fourteen years of age at the time, so it turned out pretty crude. But hey, it was just something you had to do. Death metal was a way of life.*"—ORVAR SÄFSTRÖM, NIRVANA 2002

Their dedicated work soon paid off; the first issue of *Hang 'Em High* appeared a couple months later. The 'zine included lots of thrash metal, but also aimed to include the most extreme bands around, like Grotesque, Death, Bathory, and Nihilist. After two cool issues, *Hang 'Em High* folded. The editors focused on their band—which soon folded as well, a loss on both accounts.

"*The best thing about making a fanzine was all the friends you made. We got in touch with great people such as Tompa from Grotesque, Johan Edlund from Treblinka, and all the guys in Dismember and Nihilist. We bonded instantly and started hanging out—despite living extremely far away from each other! Those were days of complete dedication, with a lot of traveling.*"—ORVAR SÄFSTRÖM,

In Strömstad, about fifty miles north of Gothenburg, things started to happen when Jon Nödtveidt from Rabbit's Carrot started up *Mega Mag* in 1989. The first issue was basically a crude thrash metal 'zine, but the second and final issue in 1990 was almost exclusively dedicated to death metal. Jon also left Rabbit's Carrot to form the fantastic band Dissection at this time. *Mega Mag* #2 really is the shit, with a wonderful layout and great interviews. The Swedish scene is well covered, and I can't find anything bad to say. It's a shame Nödtveidt didn't continue with *Mega Mag*, but I guess Dissection took all of his time.

"*Jon Nödtveidt was one of the guys who connected people from all around, and his fanzine was great. He was the one who brought Grotesque to play in Strömstad—our only gig outside Gothenburg ever.*"—TOMAS LINDBERG, GROTESQUE/AT THE GATES/DISFEAR

One of my personal favorite early Swedish fanzines was *Putrefaction Mag*,

Clockwise from top left: flyer for Mega Mag #2;

Putrefaction Mag—*one of the best Swedish fanzines ever made;*

grim flyer for Putrefaction Mag

edited by the hyperactive kid Tomas Nyqvist from Strängnäs. He never had a band, but after about a year as a dedicated tape trader, he decided in late 1988 to start a fanzine. A few months later, he released his first issue.

"I was just driven by my love for the underground. My favorite pastime was writing letters and getting to know people and bands, so Putrefaction Mag *was just a natural development of my correspondence. I never thought much about it; I just cut and pasted it together and had a blast!"*—TOMAS NYQVIST, PUTREFACTION MAG/NO FASHION/IRON FIST PRODUCTIONS

Unlike all previous extreme metal fanzines, *Putrefaction Mag* was almost entirely dedicated to death metal. When Nyqvist occasionally included thrash, it was generally Swedish underground bands like Tribulation and Suffer. He searched for unknown bands everywhere, and was one of the first to acknowledge the Norwegian black metal scene. Unlike most other editors, he also managed to publish on a regular basis during his first years. He produced fourteen issues until 1999, and during that time also started the legendary label No Fashion.

"I didn't have much else to do. I was fed up with school and lived in the middle of nowhere, so I worked with my fanzine. All my time was spent at the typewriter, and it paid off, since Putrefaction Mag *sold very well all over the world. Number 4 sold over 500 copies in Germany and Holland alone! It worked incredibly well, especially considering it was written in bad English by a young teenager!"*—TOMAS NYQVIST, PUTREFACTION MAG/NO FASHION/IRON FIST PRODUCTIONS

The most successful magazine editor of the Swedish metal scene, Robban Becirovic, also got going during these years. He didn't start out with a 'zine, however. Rather, Becirovic started Sweden's first local radio program entirely dedicated to extreme metal: Power Hour.

"I started Power Hour back in 1987, while I was still in school in Norrköping. I never thought much about it in the beginning; I just thought it would be fun to play my favorite records. I guess I started to realize that we could make something out of it all when Anthrax and Testament played at Fryshuset about a year later. I got the idea that we should make an interview, with them, and since we didn't know anything about how to book an interview we just snuck outside the tour bus in hope of catching one of the members. I was like a sports journalist who tries to get a comment from a player after a game!" —ROBBAN BECIROVIC, CLOSE-UP MAGAZINE

After this brief meeting with Anthrax, the young radio host realized he could probably get in touch with record labels to get free records and book proper interviews. Since no other media in Sweden cared about metal back then, it proved easy to arrange just about anything. Even the gigantic Metallica agreed to an exclusive interview on their ...*And Justice for All* tour. As the radio program continued, Robban Becirovic developed his connections and eventually started to think of promoting shows for the bands he knew.

"The first gig I arranged was Agony at a place called Strömsholmen on April 22, 1988, and that night just turned into a nightmare. We had to rent a new sound system at the last minute, which we had to carry to the venue by hand, since the money from the eight presold tickets wasn't enough to rent a car. Then we discovered that the stage couldn't hold the weight, and when everything looked the darkest, the police turned up, since we had stolen the material to build the stage.

"Eventually the gig was on, but only fifty people had turned up. The break-

Radio POWER HOUR - A Scandianvian radio show for the brave and open minded. Two hours weekly of Thrash/Death, Heavy Metal/Hard Rock and Hardcore/Punk. Send your stuff to:

Radio POWER HOUR
Box 1113
S-600 41 NORRKÖPING
SWEDEN

...and get dressed for success.

POWER HOUR PRODUCTIONS
Radio Show · Concerts · Management · Demo Distribution

Power Hour—a local radio show that actually delivered

even was 200. Only four of them were over eighteen and allowed admission. Finally we had to close the bar to get people in, and the owners of the place turned increasingly mad. In the end I owed them a lot of money, but I didn't have any. They were a bunch of scary-looking biker types, and I was just a kid of seventeen years. Finally, I had to call my mom to sort things out."—ROBBAN BECIROVIC, CLOSE-UP MAGAZINE

Though everything went completely wrong at his debut gig as a promoter, Becirovic decided to continue arranging concerts. Already he seemed to be "in it for life," and determined to work hard. In the autumn he initiated a series of concerts labeled Thrash Bash. The first Thrash Bash was held November 25, 1988, with Mezzrow, Total Death, and Brejn Dedd—one of future Edge of Sanity and Unisound studio man Dan Swanö's earliest bands. Brejn Dedd also included vocalist Tony "It" Särkkä, later notorious for his work in Abruptum.

"Robban was the king of the extreme metal scene in Östergötland in the late 80's. I mean, his radio program was lousy and his early gigs were very poorly arranged, but he had such energy and a genuine love for the music. He just called people up in cold blood to interview them and book shows. It was he alone who made sure local bands had somewhere to play, and his work kept the scene alive. Down here, he was the epitome of cool."—DAN SWANÖ, EDGE OF SANITY/UNISOUND

At this point, the scene was very small, and only a few people turned up at the sporadic gigs that were held. But Robban Becirovic endured, and eventually presented more than forty Thrash Bash nights. Even though he eventually put on a lot of death metal gigs, he mainly stuck to thrash metal during the early years. Death metal bands still had a hard time finding gigs and getting somebody to interview them in the late 80's.

"I don't think Robban liked us; he was more thrash metal–oriented. But the guy who really hated death metal back in those days was Martin Carlsson of Megalomaniac *and* Candour. *Whatever these guys say today, they didn't support us at all back then. We, on the other hand, thought that Robban and Martin were wimps when they hailed bands like Forbidden."*—NICKE ANDERSSON, NIHILIST/ENTOMBED

So antagonism between thrash metal and death metal did exist, although the climate was a lot friendlier than the hostility that later came to exist between death metal and black metal scenes. Another guy arranging gigs at this point was Jörgen Sigfridsson from Uppsala. Jörgen founded the magazine *Heavy Rock* in 1986, and initially was mainly occupied with traditional heavy metal. Soon he started to promote gigs under the Heavy Rock name, gradually focusing on more aggressive stuff.

"Personally, I felt that the extreme Swedish metal scene kicked off when I arranged the gig with Candlemass, Agony, and Damien at Brantingsgården in Uppsala on November 29, 1987. That was actually the first time a lot of people turned up at a gig with intense Swedish metal bands."—JÖRGEN SIGFRIDSSON, HEAVY ROCK/MUSIK MED MENING

"We knew Jörgen way before we even started to listen to death metal, and we actually stayed at his place when we went down to that early Candlemass gig in Uppsala. He was one of the first characters in the Swedish metal scene, as he started his 'zine Heavy Rock *in 1986."*—ORVAR SÄFSTRÖM, NIRVANA 2002

That gig was Candlemass' second show ever, definitely the first gig with extreme Swedish metal bands to draw people from across the country. Jörgen Sigfridsson later became a major promoter in the death metal movement. But the guy who dominated the field promoting extreme gigs in Sweden was Peter "Babs" Ahlqvist from the small industrial town of Fagersta. As a kid he got into punk, and, as is customary in the punk world, his creative pursuits began early.

"I started to make fanzines in 1981. First I was into classic English punk, but soon I also discovered American hardcore. Then I got involved with the Swedish scene and started to arrange gigs around 1982/1983. For many years we had no fixed venue. We cooperated with a place in Hedemora called Tonkällan, and did gigs wherever we could here in Fagersta. Hedemora was a great place back then, with bands like Asocial and Svart Parad."—PETER AHLQVIST, UPROAR/TID ÄR MUSIK/BURNING HEART

The concert business soon expanded, and Peter brought over classic UK

Posters from Thrash Bash concerts #1–4

Flyer for Thrash Bash 5. Note that all these shows featured Total Death, Mezzrow, or Merciless. It was a small scene!

Primitive flyer for Heavy Rock

Candlemass, Agony, and Damien in Uppsala —the gig that initiated the scene

punk bands such as Disorder, Subhumans, and Instigators. The hyperactive youngster also traveled all over Sweden to catch gigs with bands such as Mob 47 and Anti Cimex. In addition to this, Peter was a notorious tape trader and read every fanzine around in order to get to know bands from all over the world. After a while, Peter's name became known in the international scene. He began to contribute to the legendary American punk magazine *Maximumrocknroll*, and started his own hardcore fanzine *Uproar*. Along the way, he also started distributing records, and eventually got the idea of releasing music himself.

"*My fanzine* Uproar *gradually turned into a record label, and my very first release was a split-tape with Asocial and Bedrövlers. After that I went on to records, with the Crude SS 7".".*—PETER AHLQVIST, UPROAR/TID ÄR MUSIK/ BURNING HEART

After these initial releases, Uproar continued with several punk singles and the album *The Vikings are Coming*—a compilation of mainly hardcore bands from Fagersta. During the mid-80's, Peter got a bit more into metal, releasing the first 7" by local crossover act Kazjurol in 1987. The following year he released a second compilation album, *Hardcore for the Masses*, encompassing a variety of extreme bands from all over Sweden, such as grind maniacs Filthy Christians and G-Anx; crossover thrashers SLR, Tribulation, and Kazjurol; crust bands Totalitär, Asocial, and Disaccord (which soon transformed into Carnage); and punk bands Strebers and Happy Farm. In hindsight, the most important band on the album was beyond a doubt the young Nihilist, with the song "Sentenced to Death."

"*That song was in fact the first by a Swedish death metal band ever to be released on vinyl, so in a way it's a legendary album! Even though many of the bands on the album had started to flirt with extreme metal at this point, Nihilist was way ahead of them all. It was only after the release of* Hardcore for the Masses *that I realized that death metal was a growing phenomenon.".*—PETER AHLQVIST, UPROAR/TID ÄR MUSIK/BURNING HEART

Once Peter began exploring extreme metal, he soon got the idea of arranging more metal gigs, and tried to initiate a festival called Thrash 'Til Death. He also booked thrash metal acts like Hexenhaus and Agony around the country.

"*Someone told me that Hellhammer sounded like Crude SS. Our local shop didn't have their record, so I got the first one by Celtic Frost instead. And I loved it. I also went to the UK to see Napalm Death in 1987, and they had a huge impact on me. Around that time people stopped caring whether bands played punk or metal, as long as they were extreme. I gradually got more into speed metal, and started to arrange gigs with bands like Agony and Hatred. For some time I tried to put together a small metal festival as well, but it didn't really work out by then. I would get my revenge later, though!*"—PETER AHLQVIST, UPROAR/TID ÄR MUSIK/BURNING HEART

He sure did. During the late 80's and early 90's, Peter Ahlqvist would sail up as the number one promoter of extreme metal gigs in Sweden. In the following years, several promoters started booking gigs with extreme Swedish bands, and many new fanzines came out. Most importantly, new bands started to form, and the old ones got busy in the recording studios.

"When the gigs started to turn up, I went to every damn one of them. I went to all the Thrash Bashes, all the gigs in Fagersta, and everything I knew of in Stockholm. I bought the whole death metal thing, and I wanted to live it every minute of my life. It was wonderful to grow up like that."—DAN SWANÖ, EDGE OF SANITY/UNISOUND

Bajsligan: The "Army of Excrement"

As Dan Swanö says, during these times you could finally start to live death metal. Nobody lived it more intensely than the death metalers in Stockholm— the anecdotes of their daily adventures are innumerable. At the time, the scene was very limited, and consisted of a few people who hung out together regularly. They formed a kind of underground society, called Bajsligan—"The Shit League," or "Army of Excrement." Under this moniker, they partied endlessly and raised some good hell. Since all were teens, they usually had to hang around town while partying. None had their own apartment or could get into the pubs. In particular, subway stations became the scene of countless drinking and headbanging excesses in front of startled travelers.

Sit down and relax as I present a glimpse of Bajsligan's wild years in the words of the participants themselves. Our chief guide will be Anders Schultz of Unleashed, the man with a thousand drunken memories.

"I guess it all started, like so many other things back then, with the group around Nicke Andersson. You know, Nicke, Fred Estby, Uffe Cederlund, and those guys hung out at thrash metal gigs, and gradually a group of death metallers started to grow around them. After a while, the group started to meet every Friday and Saturday at 'the map' at the Central Station, and just hung around town as some kind of gang."—ANDERS SCHULTZ, UNLEASHED

"I used to hitchhike a lot to Stockholm during the late 80's, and whenever I got there I went straight to 'the map.' There were always people there. I mainly hung out with the guys in Nihilist, Treblinka, and Dismember—who were outside the actual Bajsligan. We usually looked for some party, but most of the time it ended up with us drinking outdoors. One time we were about to visit Jukk of Treblinka, but naturally he wasn't home. So we stood out in the cold for hours, drinking warm beers. That was the way it was back then."—ORVAR SÄFSTRÖM, NIRVANA 2002

"When I myself joined in somewhere in 1988/1989, the tag Bajsligan had already started to be used. By this point, the guys from Nihilist and Dismember

*were hardly the inner core anymore. Instead it was people from Carbonized, Crematory, and Afflicted Convulsion who raised the most hell. The one who introduced me to it all was my childhood friend Grant McWilliams, who was about to start General Surgery at the time."—*ANDERS SCHULTZ, UNLEASHED

"If I remember it straight, Bajsligan met every Friday and Saturday night at one of the stairs that connected the Central Station's two floors, just in front of the SL-center. You met at 'the map.' We were there at times, but Afflicted Convulsion were hardly the most notorious participants. Another cool name from back then was 'The Bredäng Mafia,' which basically consisted of Nihilist and Dismember." —JESPER THORSSON, AFFLICTED

*"When the gigs started to turn up, Bajsligan grew. We met the guys from Treblinka and Expulsion in Täby, and the guys from Therion in Upplands Väsby. We were all so happy to find like-minded people. Remember that it was not considered cool at all to be into extreme metal back then. Nobody liked you, especially not girls. So I guess we had to search the town to find friends. We went everywhere, and got to know everybody connected to the scene."—*ANDERS SCHULTZ, UNLEASHED

"Bajsligan drank beer and talked about Metal in a typical narrow-minded teenage style. The only thing that counted was brutal death metal. Even extreme thrash bands, such as Slayer, were despised by some, and everybody hated technical thrash metal. 'Fucking wimpy techno-thrash; it's better to tune down

Various members of Entombed, Carnage, etc., fooling around in the Stockholm suburbs

Treblinka and Nicke Andersson hanging out by "the map" before the Exodus/ Nuclear Assault gig in Stockholm, 1989. Note the lady-hat that Nicke was wearing in those days—he found it in the gutter and used it for a long time!

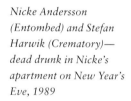

Nicke Andersson (Entombed) and Stefan Harwik (Crematory)— dead drunk in Nicke's apartment on New Year's Eve, 1989

Anders Schultz (Unleashed) and Mats Nordrup (Crematory) losing their minds in the apartment of Johnny Hedlund (Unleashed)

to Z and just destroy!' It was like that."—JESPER THORSSON, AFFLICTED

"Eventually there were always people at 'the map' at 7:30 every Friday and Saturday night. Some days there were ten people, and others there were forty. In the winter we drank at subway stations or on trains, and in the summer we drank outdoors wherever we found a place. Forests, parks, cemeteries, wherever. I met Johnny Hedlund at a party in the park at Gärdet, and we basically decided to start Unleashed right there."—ANDERS SCHULTZ, UNLEASHED

"I think Bajsligan was centered around bands like Carbonized; we were a bit outside of it. But naturally, we got a fair share of the action. We were too young to get in anywhere, so we had to meet outdoors. During the summer we often met in Täby and hung out in a park or forest with our beers and tape recorders. In the winter we got on the subway or a train, and traveled all day while drinking and listening to extreme bands. It was a very special time."
—JOHAN EDLUND, TREBLINKA/TIAMAT

"During the early days, we had problems finding alcohol, since few, if any, of us were the legal age to buy it. Our favored drink was Folköl [a special kind of Swedish beer with an alcohol level of about 3.5 percent available to eighteen-year-olds], but few of us were even allowed to buy that. We always found ways to get it, though, with fake IDs or whatever. If someone of legal age was with us, he bought hundreds of beers for the group. Johnny Hedlund was the only one who could buy booze, but he was rarely involved with Bajsligan. But when Filthy Christians were to appear on national television, he bought strong beer for us all and everything just went berserk!

"Gradually, Bajsligan started to draw people from other towns. The crazy guys in Merciless and their equally crazy friends, especially, were an integral part of Bajsligan early on. Naturally, they were much respected for their music— but probably even more respected for their insane drinking antics!"—ANDERS SCHULTZ, UNLEASHED

Besides "the map," Bajsligan congregated upstairs in the station around a large circular hole that looked down to the second floor. Known as Bögringen— "the gay circle"— the former cruising spot made an excellent vantage point.

"Bajsligan's gatherings by the notorious 'Bögringen' every Friday night at Stockholm Central Station were so important. Our bunch from Eskilstuna went there almost every weekend just to hang around, drinking beer at subway stations. Also, there were always rumors of gangs of kickers looking for us to beat us up. It was wicked!"—MATTIAS KENNHED, MACRODEX/HOUSE OF USHER

"I remember the meeting before the gig with Exodus and Nuclear Assault in 1989. The guys from Nihilist, Treblinka, and Nirvana 2002 hung around the map and drank beer as usual. Then the guys from Gothenburg arrived. Believe me, those guys were crazy. Tompa [from Grotesque] was so insanely drunk that he couldn't walk, and I think somebody actually locked

him into one of the lockers for a while. Later that night, he was sent lifeless to the hospital emergency room to get his stomach pumped. But, basically, that was just a regular night."—ORVAR SÄFSTRÖM, NIRVANA 2002

"I went to Stockholm as often as I could. Occasionally there was a gig, and if we found it, we went there. Often we wouldn't get in, since we were too drunk, but the important thing was to meet all these cool people and party!"— DAN SWANÖ, EDGE OF SANITY/UNISOUND

"When people from outside of Stockholm started to hang around, we also started to visit them in their hometowns. I especially remember an intense trip to Strängnäs to hang out with the guys in Merciless, and these guys really knew how to party! Then when all the gigs in Fagersta started to turn up, we went there as often as we could. It didn't matter if you missed the gig; the important thing was to party and raise hell. I remember one night we missed our train home and broke into some kind of warehouse with stoves and refrigerators. There we were, a bunch of drunken death metalers sleeping among all this new and shining equipment. It must have been a sight."—ANDERS SCHULTZ, UNLEASHED

"To be honest, I don't remember participating in anything called Bajsligan. I wasn't part of anything like that. I was probably at home alone, writing letters and songs. Bastards, they let me do all the work while they were partying!" —NICKE ANDERSSON, NIHILIST/ENTOMBED

"The most memorable night of all in Bajsligan's history must have been when the guys from [the New York bands] Immolation and Mortician came over in 1989. I think they were here to visit the guys from Nihilist, but they were soon drawn into the world of Bajsligan. That night we ended up at the subway station of Midsommarkransen, and just drank ourselves crazy while blasting out death metal on the tape recorder. They were just shocked to see how wild it was, and that we were getting away with it without being arrested and beaten up by the cops. Imagine it, about forty teenagers who were insanely drunk and noisy among horrified subway travelers!

"By 1991, Bajsligan's antics were so notorious that a photographer followed us around to document our habits. He actually did an exhibition about us at Kulturhuset later on. Isn't it great—drunk death metal teenagers as art?"—ANDERS SCHULTZ, UNLEASHED

Drunk death metal kids as art—can it get any weirder, or greater, than that? In my opinion, Bajsligan's wild years should be a regular exhibition at every art gallery in the world.

Anyway, despite what a great time these youngsters were having, the participants of Bajsligan eventually grew up and left the streets. Today "the map" no longer exists in Stockholm's Central Station. It was removed in the early 90's to make space for lockers. But Bögringen still remains, long after Bajsligan finally

Patric "Cronis" Cronberg (in Treblinka shirt) and the notorious Onkel (aka the Shit Man) on a chaotic train trip to Stockholm. Later that night, Tomas Lindberg (Grotesque) had to be taken to hospital due to excessive drinking

Jesper Thorsson (Afflicted) going crazy. Note his trademark Iron Maiden T-shirt

Anders Schultz and Chelsea Krook (later in Expulsion) on their way to New York. Bajsligan goes overseas

Ross Dolan (Immolation), Sharon Bascovsky (Derketa), Will Rahmer (Mortician) and Johnny Hedlund (Unleashed) taking it easy in a well-decorated bedroom

dissolved.

"*Eventually, Bajsligan attempted to enter the pubs. Few of us were legal age, but we found a couple of seedy places that would let us in anyway. The first places we discovered was Kloster Pub and Pinocchio on S:t Eriksgatan. After that we found Snövit on Ringvägen. When most of us had turned eighteen, we also started to hang out at Cityhallen on Drottninggatan. Snövit actually made us their core clientele, and started to play death metal in their basement.*

"*Although Bajsligan kind of stuck together into 1992, I guess it started to fall apart when we got old enough to enter the pubs. Many of the bands also got busy with tours and recordings, and we just grew apart. You know, to own flats and having obligations like jobs and girlfriends. Before that, we were just a bunch of kids with nothing better to do than hang around, raising hell. Those years with Bajsligan will always remain one of the best periods in my life. It was so intense, so full of energy and creativity. I can't imagine something like it ever happening again.*

"*If you think about it, I probably owe everything to death metal. If I hadn't gotten into the scene, I probably wouldn't have searched my way out of the stinking suburb I was living in. Death metal urged you to get out and find cool people to hang out with. If I had never discovered it, I would probably have been sitting rotting away at the same local pub as the guys I went to school with. Death metal kind of saved my life, even though I surely have lost a few brain cells while at it!*"—ANDERS SCHULTZ, UNLEASHED

The Movement Grows Nationally

With bands like Morbid, Nihilist, Treblinka, and Dismember, things had started to happen. The groundbreaking recordings of Nihilist in particular infected the whole Swedish scene, and shortly many bands around the country got ready to produce demos themselves. But in the rest of Sweden, the few death metallers around were pretty lonely and isolated.

"*Outside of Stockholm, the early death metal scene was extremely small. There were Sorcery in Sandviken, Merciless in Strängnäs, Grave on Gotland, Carnage in Växjö, Macrodex in Eskilstuna, and Grotesque in Gothenburg. You were lucky if you knew just one other guy in your hometown who liked extreme music.*"—TOMAS LINDBERG, GROTESQUE/AT THE GATES/DISFEAR

One of the few bands already playing death metal were Visby's unrelenting Grave. Their *Sexual Mutilation* demo was recorded during the first two days of 1989 at Graveyard Studios, and was a big step forward for the deadly trio. This recording contains great doomy riffs, deep growls, and an atmosphere of pure death. Although *Sexual Mutilation* was good, Grave still lacked the immense qualities of a band like Nihilist—but what band didn't? Some of the riffs and arrangements still smelled a bit of thrash, but it was heavy stuff nevertheless.

"I guess we gradually started to incorporate more extreme stuff in our music, but we never really knew what we were doing back then. We never sat down and decided to be a 'death metal' band or anything; it was just a natural development. When I look back on our demos, Sexual Mutilation *is my favorite one. It has a unique feeling to it."*—OLA LINDGREN, GRAVE

Grave continued their development the same year with the *Anatomia Corporis Humani* demo. They were becoming really brutal, and the music had touches of that special Swedish death metal feeling. The Stockholm style had infected Grave's sound, and the songs were now better structured. Fat groovy riffs, tight sound, and cool arrangements brought greatness from a great band.

"That last demo is pretty strange. It is very down-tuned, ultra-brutal, and there are a lot of effects on the vocals. I think we were going through a Carcass period at the time, since we were all extremely into the Symphonies of Sickness *album."*
—OLA LINDGREN, GRAVE

Another great band from this era never made it out of the underground—Macrodex from Eskilstuna. This town already had a crust punk scene with bands like No Security. Even Macrodex started out as the crossover band Cruelty, which released the pretty intense demo *Who Cares?* in 1988.

"Macrodex was born out of the brutal hardcore band Cruelty in 1988, and as we changed our name we went more for a metal sound. Originally we were influenced by established bands like Slayer and Bathory. But as we started to trade tapes, a whole new world opened, with things like Immolation and Morbid Angel. We gradually purified our death metal and tried to wash our thrash influences away."—MATTIAS KENNHED, MACRODEX/HOUSE OF USHER

As Macrodex, the group showed potential. Their debut demo, *Disgorged,* was recorded at a local studio in the early days of 1989, and offered furious and blistering death metal. Like many other bands of the period, they kept some thrash elements, and the sound is pretty clear, with a heavy bass in the bottom. Macrodex's furious metal was similar to Dark Angel's. The drummer really had an aggressive and in-your-face style. Very good stuff indeed! On June 22 and 23, Macrodex entered Studio Skyline to record the follow-up, *Infernal Excess.* This demo continued on the same path. Macrodex stood out as one of the most promising bands in the field of extreme metal. In spite of their qualities, they were almost ignored.

"I really liked them. If I had to name just one band that deserved more than they ever got, I would say Macrodex."—MATTI KÄRKI, CARNAGE/DISMEMBER

"Macrodex was one of the best bands of the late 80's, but they just couldn't keep it together."—ROBBAN BECIROVIC, <u>CLOSE-UP MAGAZINE</u>

Another band playing violent thrash during 1989 was Suffer from Fagersta, formed in February 1988. After almost two years of rehearsals, they

Side I

Intro:"The Desolation"
Granulate Sorcery
Intense Brainconvulsions

Side II
Cemetery Inhabitants
Reduced From Life

Recorded in StudioFragg 9-10 of
december 1989.

Thanx to Jukka Hietala, Coolman,
J.O., and Pontus. E.

Cover layout by Ronny Eide and
Suffer.

Death Is An Art

Clockwise from top left:
Macrodex demo;

Grave—Sexual
Mutilation;

Cemetery Inhabitants.
Evil stuff;

Mattias Kennhed
(Macrodex) during his
death metal days

Nirvana 2002

finally entered Studio Fragg on December 9 and 10, 1989. The resulting demo, *Cemetery Inhabitants*, was chaotic thrash metal somewhere between Exodus and Kreator, but intense enough to be associated with the death metal scene. Suffer would go on to release a couple of singles, and eventually a CD in 1994. But the increasing demand for brutality within the scene would always place them in the shadow of more extreme bands. Still, they were a good band and I remember being impressed by them at a drunken gig in 1990.

In 1988, the three young kids Orvar Säfström, Erik Qvick, and Lars Henriksson in the northern town of Edsbyn also got hooked on extreme metal and decided to start a band. Säfström and Quick had edited the earlier mentioned fanzine *Hang 'Em High*, and now it was time to put their ideas of music on tape. Initially they called their band Prophet 2002.

"Erik and I started the band around the same time we got our fanzine together. It was in connection to the Slayer gig at Fryshuset in 1988, so I guess it all happened in August. Apart from the three of us, there was only one person into death metal up here, and that was [future Hellacopters drummer] Robert Eriksson, who soon moved to Östersund and formed Celeborn. Most people were into metal in every small town in Sweden at that point, but we were the only ones here to go beyond thrash." —ORVAR SÄFSTRÖM, NIRVANA 2002

The group soon changed their name to Nirvana, but due to copyright issues they eventually had to combine it with their previous suffix 2002, and subsequently became Nirvana 2002 in 1989. (The reference to Nirvana in the credits of Entombed's *Left Hand Path* of course refers to Nirvana 2002.) Now the guys started producing crude recordings. First they did two tracks, "Truth & Beauty" and "Brutality," with a portable four-channel recorder. Despite sounding ultra-primitive, Nirvana 2002 distinguished themselves from other local bands with their sheer brutality. After this first recording they continued with two even more primitive rehearsals, *Watch the River Flow* and *Excursion in 2002*, both recorded with a regular tape recorder.

"*We just lived death metal. We did the fanzine, recorded some rehearsals, and hitchhiked down to Stockholm as often as we could to hang out with like-minded people. It was never very serious back then; it was just something you did.*"—ORVAR SÄFSTRÖM, NIRVANA 2002

A band that on the contrary had some impact during this period was the earlier mentioned Grotesque from Gothenburg. The band faced some problems early on in 1989, as drummer Johan Lager and bass player David Hultén left the band. Kristian Wåhlin and Tomas Lindberg decided to continue, and basically ran Grotesque as a duo for the rest of its existence, with various musicians helping them out. The two dedicated youngsters also continued to record obscure rehearsals. Notable among these are *Ascension of the Dead*, an early recording of "Incantation," with Tomas on drums; and the demo known as *4/7-89*. But Grotesque's next demo was the brilliant *Blood Run from the Altar*, later known as *The Black Gate Is Closed*. Grotesque had improved a lot, and their intense brutality put them light-years ahead of any other band in the Gothenburg area. Though this tape was very short, it made Grotesque's name known.

"*That tape is the one that most people have. Still, we never really did an official cover for it. We used it for trading, and copied more tapes and new covers whenever somebody wanted it. Our recordings were still mainly done for our own pleasure.*"—TOMAS LINDBERG, GROTESQUE/AT THE GATES/DISFEAR

Next in Grotesque's steady flow of rehearsal tapes was *Fallen to Decay*, apparently recorded in small doses before and after *Blood Run from the Altar*. Only a few tape covers were made. At this point, there was talk about doing a mini-LP, so in November 1989 Grotesque entered Ken's Pagan Studio to record these songs more professionally—titling the release *In the Embrace of Evil*.

"*Nothing came of the idea of a mini-LP back then. Later, two of the songs turned up on* Incantation, *and eventually the whole thing got out on CD with the song order corrected and an added intro.*"—TOMAS LINDBERG, GROTESQUE/ AT THE GATES/DISFEAR

Even though nothing much really happened for Grotesque, they built a national reputation. Grotesque had a unique style of brutality that made them different from virtually all other bands. They were unpolished, raw, and advanced to the limit. The riffs were technical yet straightforward, and the music had a very special feeling. On top of this, they had the truly original and

From left: Rare cover
for Grotesque's
The Black Gate Is Closed;

*Grotesque pose (yes, that's
my precious #1 copy of the
Grotesque mini album—
only played once!)*

emotional screams of singer Tomas Lindberg, and some satanic lyrics.

"*We never cared what others thought. I just wrote the kind of riffs I liked,
and Tompa delivered the kind of vocals and lyrics he liked. It was something
we had to do. We had to make those recordings, and I'm not sure if we even
considered them proper demos. We never sent them to labels and hardly
ever considered releasing an album.*"—KRISTIAN "NECROLORD" WÅHLIN,
GROTESQUE/LIERS IN WAIT/DECOLLATION

The band soon sailed up as Nihilist's closest rivals wasn't Grotesque, but
Carnage from Växjö. This band really knew how to play death metal. Carnage
was founded by the talented guitarist Mike Amott, as he left his former punk
band Disaccord in 1988. Since his father was from the UK, Amott spent a lot
of time in England in the mid-80's, becoming inspired by the extreme punk
scene there. He got to know Bill Steer from Napalm Death, and was heavily
influenced by Steer's musical ideas. No surprise then that Carnage's debut
demo, *The Day Man Lost,* sounded a lot like Steer's other band, Carcass. In
fact, everything reeks of Carcass on the recording—including the sound, the
riffs, and the vocals.

"*Bill Steer influenced a lot of people and bands. He was the first guitarist
to tune to low-B, and that is now a standard tuning in extreme metal. Someone
should write the guy a check! Of course he was an influence for Carnage, too.*"
—MICHAEL AMOTT, CARNAGE/CARCASS/ARCH ENEMY

During this time, Amott got offers to join Napalm Death as well as Carcass.

From left: Carnage demo; typical thrash show flyer—a dying breed

He decided to stick with his own band, though, apparently thinking that the first Carcass album sounded pretty dirty, and that Carnage could go further. While their first demo had been somewhat unoriginal, they adopted a more personal style with *Infestation of Evil*. This second demo lies somewhere in between the chaos of Carcass and the Swedish death metal sound established by Nihilist. The lineup issues had been straightened out by now, as Fred Estby from the folded Dismember replaced the inferior Jeppe Larsson. Dismember would soon supply even more blood for Carnage. However, the change from playing in Dismember was pretty shocking to Estby.

"It was really messy. I joined them and moved down to Växjö for a while, only to discover that they had even worse conditions than we did in Stockholm. With Dismember we had worked our way up, and had our own decent rehearsal space that we paid for. But they were still in the state where they rehearsed at a shitty youth center, where you couldn't play too loud, so it really didn't work. Then the demo I did with Carnage was recorded in Växjö at some guy's house. He had some synthesizer drums that I had to record on. Mike Amott and Carnage were not very coordinated at that point."—FRED ESTBY, DISMEMBER/CARNAGE

With more bands, death metal soon gripped places all around Sweden. The Östergötland region, especially, seems to have been a good breeding ground for extreme demos during 1989. From Motola came Metroz's *Brain Explosion* and Toxaemia's *Kaleidoscopic Lunacy*. From Linköping emerged Orchriste's *Necronomicon*. Söderköping gave birth to Allegiance's *Sick World*. Though none of these got any wide attention, they proved the underground was spreading.

The Stockholm Scene Reigns

The most exciting things were still happening in Stockholm—something Carnage obviously understood; they moved there in late 1989 and soon secured a record deal. Probably still too crude for a record deal, the promising Stockholm band Afflicted Convulsion was formed in 1988 by a gang of hell-raising teenagers.

"*We were basically just a gang that hung out in Örby/Älvsjö south of Stockholm. We had a few bands, but mainly we were practicing stage dives in the pool at Älvsjöbadet and moshing to Kreator in someone's room. First we called ourselves Reptile, then Defiance. But in 1988 we discovered more extreme stuff than thrash metal, and became Afflicted Convulsion. In 1989 it all turned into a serious band, as Joacim Carlsson and Yasin Hillborg joined.*" —JESPER THORSSON, AFFLICTED

During 1989 the group rehearsed extensively, and recorded a couple rehearsal tapes such as *Toxic Existence* and *Psychedelic Grindcore*. Though just crude Walkman recordings, the band's potential was apparent. They played psyched-out grindcore, with weird twists like a blast-beat version of the "Batman" theme. By the time they recorded *Psychedelic Grindcore* in December 1989, Afflicted Convulsion had advanced into being something like a death metal version of Voivod.

"*I would say that we were a pretty serious band; we rehearsed at least three times a week. First we rehearsed in Tyresö in a room we shared with Crematory. Then we moved to Alphyddan in Nacka, a room we shared with Dismember and Entombed. Our final rehearsal room was at Telefonplan, and we shared it with Grave.*"—JESPER THORSSON, AFFLICTED

Another band from Stockholm that had started to develop during the late 80's was Therion. This band was the brainchild of Christoffer Johnsson, and they started out playing thrash metal in 1987.

"*We began in 1987 under the name Blitzkrieg. Back then we were a trio, and I played bass. We were absolute beginners, and the music was some kind of mix between thrash metal à la early Metallica, Motörhead, and Venom. A year later we switched the name to Therion after a brief period as Megatherion. I started to play guitar, and we developed into a death metal band, even though we were still very inspired by Slayer.*"—CHRISTOFFER JOHNSSON, THERION

Therion recorded their debut demo, *Paroxysmal Holocaust*, in Studio Sveasträng during March and April 1989. Therion's first demo contained a lot of power and ideas, even though it was hardly as original or direct as the

new demo

THE NEW STUDIO DEMO IS FINALLY OUT!
It's called "BEYOND REDEMPTION"
and it contains 4 brutalizing
tracks in 20 minutes.....
Demo prices:
3$ (Europe)
4$ (Overseas)
15 SEK (Scand.)
Also available:
Black t-shirt
with white print
on both sides for:
8$ (Europe)
10$ (Overseas)
50 SEK (Scand.)
EXPERIENCE THE SICK PSYCHO
DEATH METAL GRIND AND FEEL
FREE TO ORDER A DEMO TODAY,
BASTARDOS!!!

JOACIM CARLSSON
Hägerstensvägen 177
126 53 HÄGERSTEN
SWEDEN

out now

PSYCHEDELIC
GRINDCORE
OFFICIAL REHEARSAL -89-

Clockwise from top left: Good old flyer;
Afflicted Convulsion's chaotic first demo;
Psychedelic Grindcore—*that's just what it is;*
Afflicted Convulsion circa 1988. As usual, they have
broken in somewhere just to hang out

recordings of Nihilist or Carnage.

"It was recorded in a free-of-charge studio called Sveasträng, which was located in a shelter in a school...I think. Afflicted Convulsion had already been there. The guy at the place didn't know very much about how a studio worked. Since we knew even less, the result could have been better. We recorded four songs, but one of them, 'Animal Mutilation,' turned out so sloppy that we couldn't release it. Everything was recorded and mixed in one afternoon."
—Christoffer Johnsson, Therion

Keeping this in mind, it's a miracle *Paroxysmal Holocaust* sounds as good as it does. On this recording Therion featured none other than future Dismember front man Matti Kärki on vocals, the first time he ever sang.

"A friend of mine tried out with them first, but he didn't get along with Christoffer Johnsson. So he encouraged me to go for it instead. When I tried to explain that I couldn't sing, he just said that he couldn't either; the only thing to do was to scream. So I tried some rehearsals with them to get to know the songs, and they liked what they heard. I was in, and since then I've been a death metal singer. I recorded one demo with Therion before I also got fed up with Johnsson and left. He is a strange man, he really is."—Matti Kärki, Carnage/Dismember

On Therion's next recording, Christoffer took over the vocals himself, something he never intended.

"Actually, it sucked to sing; I didn't want to do it. We really wanted another

Old Therion logo

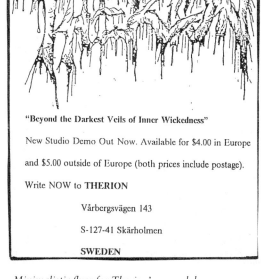

"Beyond the Darkest Veils of Inner Wickedness"

New Studio Demo Out Now. Available for $4.00 in Europe

and $5.00 outside of Europe (both prices include postage).

Write NOW to **THERION**

Vårbergsvägen 143

S-127-41 Skärholmen

SWEDEN

Minimalistic flyer for Therion's second demo

singer to replace Matti, but since we couldn't find anyone, we decided that I should try again. I had a terrible headache on the evening when the vocals were to be recorded—we allowed ourselves the luxury of two days in the studio this time—and the reason I sang so low was that it hurt too much to sing in higher frequencies! Ha ha. Since we were broke, we couldn't book another day. The others weren't very pleased with the results, so I barely got their approval to ever sing again."
—CHRISTOFFER JOHNSSON, THERION

I don't understand their doubts—I really think Christoffer's vocals sound good. It might have been too extreme for the period, as he supplied those ultra-deep grunts through a lot of reverb. Anyway, *Beyond the Darkest Veils of Inner Wickedness* showed progress, as they now combined brutality with atmospheric solos and great song compositions. The heavy parts are especially cool, in a Hellhammer kind of way. This demo really creates a lasting uncanny feeling. As with Therion's first demo, it's a miracle that it turned out as good as it did.

"It was recorded in a cheap, crappy studio, with an utterly uninterested technician who spent all his time on the phone instead of working. He really had no idea about anything. But back then no studio in Sweden knew anything about death metal, apart from Thunderload and Sunlight. It was the same story as with the first demo; we recorded four songs, but one turned out too bad to include." [The song, 'Genocidal Raids,' did appear on the debut album two years later.]

"When it came to the songs, we started to challenge the scene, something that we kept on doing over the years, and this has made Therion what it is today. We recorded an outro, a very melodic guitar piece with clean chords in the background, along with several unorthodox things we did in the beginning of the song 'Megalomania.'"—CHRISTOFFER JOHNSSON, THERION

Another original Stockholm death metal band was Carbonized, founded and commanded for many years by Lars Rosenberg, who was later in Entombed and Therion. Rosenberg was surely determined, because even though the band faced massive lineup changes early on, he didn't falter. In September 1989, Carbonized recorded their debut demo, *Au-To-Dafe*, at Studio Sveasträng—a facility frequently used by Swedish death metal bands, since it was basically free. In comparison to Carnage and Nihilist, this recording was crude and primitive. But the heart was definitely there, and the songs had great grinding intensity. The demo also benefits from vocals by Matti Kärki, who seemed to be everywhere during those early years of Swedish death metal.

"I joined Carbonized almost immediately after I left Therion. It was a serious band, but it wasn't really death metal in my eyes. Still, we were very inspired by Morbid Angel's first album."—MATTI KÄRKI, CARNAGE/DISMEMBER

The final death metal demo recorded in 1989 was made by one of the most underrated bands in the Swedish scene, the mighty Crematory. During the last days of the 80's they put *The Exordium* on tape at Studio Grottan—the first studio choice for death metal bands until Nihilist and Entombed's later successes in Studio Sunlight. To my ears, this is definitely one of the most brutal and best of all Swedish demos. Sure, they lacked the massive guitar sound of Nihilist and Dismember, and their songs might not have been as direct. But Crematory possessed a kind of raw heaviness that few other Swedish death metal bands came near. Everything is so twisted, the voice so guttural, the atmosphere so dark. Back then I loved them, and I thought they were heading for a glorious future. Time would prove me wrong.

Let's finish this exploration of 1989 demo cassettes with the most massive one of all, Entombed's *But Life Goes On*. This great release was recorded on September 23 and 24 at Studio Sunlight.

"The reason we went back to Sunlight was that we heard the Treblinka 7"recorded there, and it sounded great to our ears. So we gave Skogsberg a second chance."—NICKE ANDERSSON, NIHILIST/ENTOMBED

This time around, the restructured and rechristened band and their engineer Tomas Skogsberg knew exactly what they wanted to produce. Entombed created one of the most brilliant Swedish death metal demos.

"But Life Goes On was recorded very shortly after Nihilist had split up. Alex was busy with his studies at that time, so everything was made by me, Uffe and L.G. Uffe and I played all the guitars and bass."—NICKE ANDERSSON, NIHILIST/ENTOMBED

One of the reincarnations of Carbonized, relaxing at Ultrahuset

ENTOMBED
»But Life Goes On«

Clockwise from top left: Carbonized's great demo;
Crematory—one of the most underrated
Swedish death metal bands;
Entombed's debut demo;
one of the first photos of Entombed;
compilation tapes…don't you miss them?

ETERNAL DEATH

ETERNAL DEATH COMP TAPE 1990 IS OUT NOW.ON THE TAPE
IS MENY INTRESTING BANDS LIKE/GRAVE/CONVUSION/NUN
SLAUGHTER/CRYPTIC/PUTREFACTION/SACRED CRUCIFIX/
FUNEBRE/CARNAGE AND MENY MORE.
"IF YOU WILL HAVE THE TAPE SEND ME 4 US DOLLAR"
(IN CASH PLEASE)
TO: ETERNAL DEATH C/O TOBBE WALLSTRÖM TORSG.20
62145 Visby SWEDEN.......

"After Nihilist broke up, Nicke and I talked about forming a new band. The first version of Entombed was only me and him; all the other guys were out of the picture. We rehearsed once, did three songs, and then I went to work for a month to pay for a recording. It was only me and Nicke in the studio, but after a week we called L.G. and asked him if he wanted to sing. The original idea was him playing the bass as well, and Entombed being a three-piece."—UFFE CEDERLUND, MORBID/ NIHILIST/ENTOMBED/DISFEAR

So whatever the cover of *But Life Goes On* indicates, Alex and David were in no way part of Entombed at this point. Although the sound was definitely ultra-brutal, it's still clear and precise. Their trademark guitar sound is definitely cemented, as were complex song structures with a variety of fast beats, backbeats, D-beats, breaks, and slower parts. Even the solos sound

Producer Tomas Skogsberg

perfect this time, adding to the songs' qualities. Above all, I think Petrov pulls off one of his best vocal performances on this tape. Most of it consists of deep growls, but occasionally he slides into tormented screams in a completely natural way. Entombed couldn't be stopped at this point—it was only a matter of weeks before they earned a recording deal with Earache.

"Something had obviously happened with Skogsberg and Studio Sunlight, because everything sounded so much better on this recording. I guess he had started to realize what death metal was all about, and we got along well."—NICKE ANDERSSON, NIHILIST/ENTOMBED

Swedish death metal was about to hit the international scene, and Entombed would eventually become one of the most praised and original bands of the whole international movement. The lineup was soon completed with their old Nihilist partner Alex Hellid, plus David Blomqvist from the folded Dismember. The future seemed bright.

"I loved Entombed just as much as I had loved Nihilist, and I loved most of the other bands from Stockholm as well. There was no doubt that Stockholm was leading the scene in Sweden; everything that came out from there was superior.

And Entombed were the best of the lot."—Tomas Nyqvist, Putrefaction Mag/No Fashion/Iron Fist Productions

The Last Hour of Thrash Metal

Despite the mounting demos and adventures in fresh death metal, thrash metal had not yet lost its grip on young Swedish musicians. Another year would pass before the full-fledged death metal boom would wipe away virtually all the old school thrash bands. Let's look at some of the Swedish thrash metal bands soldiering onward in the wake of death metal.

The first thrash metal demo recorded in Sweden during 1989 was Mezzrow's *The Cross of Tormention*, put on tape in Studio Svängrummet on January 7 and 8. A traditional thrash affair in the vein of Testament and Exodus, this recording already sounded dated, with semi-spoken vocals, and typical backing vocals à la Anthrax.

A more refreshing form of thrash came from Tribulation's *Void of Compassion*, recorded almost a year later on December 29 and 30 at Musikstugan in Falun. On this recording, Tribulation desperately tried to bring some new blood to the fading thrash metal genre by incorporating breathtaking tempo changes, strange harmonies, and harsh and desperate vocals. Tribulation remained an integral part of the Swedish scene, playing live endlessly with bands like Carcass and Entombed, but their music couldn't stand up against the massive power of death metal.

The week after Tribulation left Musikstugan, Hatred entered the same studio to create *The Forthcoming Fall*. Where Tribulation tried to develop the concept of thrash, Hatred stayed with an old formula. The result is a blistering thrash metal attack, which might have gotten them worldwide attention a few years earlier. The riffs are crystal clear, catchy as hell, and reeking of quality. But no matter how good Hatred were, the days of thrash were simply over. Singer Tomas Lundin tried to extend his thrash career by joining Hexenhaus, but nothing much came out of it. The others realized that death metal was the real deal—Johan Jansson and Sonny Svedlund went on to form Interment, and Kenneth Wiklund joined Centinex.

Though Swedish thrash metal mainly operated on the demo tape level, a few bands had secured recording deals by the end of the 80's. Although Sweden never produced any thrash metal albums of great significance, a couple of records deserve to be analyzed. One of the best Swedish thrash metal albums of the 80's was Agony's *The First Defiance*, recorded at Silence studio during August and September 1987. *The First Defiance* was released by Under One Flag in 1988, and showed a competent and tight band. The production is fine, and many of the riffs are of superior quality. The only thing missing is some aggression. If

MEZZROW

"THE CROSS OF TORMENTIO

HARVEY
WALLBANGER

*Clockwise from top: Mezzrow—sticking with thrash metal; Harvey Wallbanger demo;
Thrash Bash 6 flyer; Tribulation—the "kings" of crossover*

they had kept more of their punkier past instead of cutting it to appear more metal, they would probably have been fantastic. Nevertheless, Agony's sole album is pretty good, especially the closing song, "Deadly Legacy."

Another band that shone pretty bright was Uppsala's Damien. In 1988 they recorded their only EP, *Requiem for the Dead*, which they released on their own Gothic Records. On this record they continued their powerful and effective thrash metal, with catchy riffs and some great screaming vocals. Their songwriting skills were way ahead of those of most other Swedish bands of the genre. In fact, Damien sounded far more evil than any other Swedish thrash band in 1988, and should have been able to survive into the death metal era. But time started to slip away for them, and they never got any attention. Death metal came along and wiped Damien away.

The aggressive Swedish band Maninnya Blade's debut *Merchants in Metal* came out on Killerwatt in 1986. Their music was, to be honest, more like punkish heavy metal than thrash metal. But in 1987 some members of the band morphed into Hexenhaus, one of the most successful Swedish thrash metal bands. Like Agony, Hexenhaus released their debut in 1988, as Active Records unleashed their *A Tribute to Insanity*. Also like Agony, Hexenhaus were very inspired by the Bay Area bands, but the overall result is weaker. The production is lame, especially the crappy-sounding guitars. What really makes this record rather boring are the uninspired song structures and substandard vocals. The riffs are decent, but it sounded pretty dated and unoriginal already. Active offered two more albums by Hexenhaus, *The Edge of Sanity* and *The Awakening*, but both failed to impress. Still, Hexenhaus was regarded as Sweden's prime thrash outing for many years—and they "stole" members from superior bands such as Hatred and Damien.

Active Records kept its faith in Swedish thrash metal, though, and went on to sign Mezzrow as well as Kazjurol before the end of the 80's. Mezzrow's sole album, *Then Came the Killing*, from 1990, is actually superior to the Hexenhaus albums, with great mid-tempo thrash full of mosh parts. Nothing could hide the fact that this kind of music had become awfully dated.

A funny anecdote—one of the members of Mezzrow actually appeared for a brief segment on the UK/European MTV Headbangers Ball shortly after the release of the album. At the suitable location of Heavy Sound store, hostess Vanessa Warwick asked the youngster from Mezzrow his opinion of metal, and he mumbled something about thrash metal being the most exciting music in the world. Behind him, however, another youngster, looking through a box of records, looked up when he heard that and exclaimed: "No! *That is death metal.*" That young intruder was Lars-Göran Petrov of Entombed.

The most dated-sounding Swedish thrash metal album of 1990 was Kazjurol's *Dance Tarantella*. Their earlier crossover style was now completely washed away, as the band attempted to play techno-thrash. Honestly, they were hardly skilled enough to pull it off. Their new songs felt uninspired and lame, and the old songs presented here had sounded better on previous recordings. The vocals are very weak, and so is the flat sound. *Dance Tarantella* also contains countless spelling errors on the sleeve, and worthless joke songs like "T-ban the Fastest." Everything just felt dated and boring. If you compare this album to all the death metal being developed at the same time, it's very obvious why the thrash metal scene would soon be wiped out. Even the bastion of thrash, Active Records, eventually faced reality and went for death metal.

Though some of these Swedish thrash metal bands were quite celebrated back then, their records caused no impact at all on the metal scene to come. Swedish thrash metal just didn't have what it took during the 80's, and by 1990 it was too late for the genre.

"There never was anything like a Swedish thrash metal scene. The problem with Swedish thrash metal was simply that the bands weren't good enough. They had one or two good songs on their albums, but that was it. When death metal came along, all of that was changed; these guys really knew how to make good songs."—ROBBAN BECIROVIC, <u>CLOSE-UP MAGAZINE</u>

"When we discovered death metal, we quickly started to get very stubborn opinions of what was okay and what was not. And thrash metal was not considered exciting. I remember that Hexenhaus used to laugh at the noise we made, and we just thought that they were wimps, posers, and nerds. Swedish thrash metal was definitely not considered cool in any way as death metal started to grow. We even smiled behind the back of guys like Robban Becirovic, and it's almost embarrassing when I think back on how hardcore death metal I was."—NICKE ANDERSSON, NIHILIST/ENTOMBED

Some bands persisted with the thrash metal formula into the 90's, though, refusing to lay the genre to rest. Among the thrash metal demos of 1990 were Harvey Wallbanger's *Abomination of the Universe* and Mortality's *The Prophecy*. Though both of these demos certainly possessed some quality, they simply sounded awfully behind the times. Despite some thrash bands who continued to struggle during the early 90's, thrash metal could be declared dead as death metal rose from the underground.

Blood, Fire...Death!

The future of Swedish metal had already been revealed in a release from 1988 that took us all by storm. Once again the legendary Bathory showed the way with the amazing *Blood Fire Death*. This album differed a lot from their previous three efforts, combining influences from thrash metal with atmospheric black metal mayhem in the same way Swedish death metal would do about a year later.

Bathory's Blood, Fire,Death

The production on *Blood Fire Death* immediately sounds bigger than before. Though still primitive and rough, the guitar sound is somewhat thicker, and the bass is clearly audible in the mix. The toms and kick-drums are fat and loud, and the overall impression is much heavier compared to Bathory's previous releases. More importantly, the drum pattern is often a two-beat adopted from thrash metal—and would soon form the basis for the early stage of Swedish death metal, as well. There are also lots of tempo changes and effective cymbal/kick stops, something later developed to great length in death metal.

Blood Fire Death remains a masterpiece, and was innovative at the time of its release, but the music on it can't be labeled as death metal by today's standards. However, its brutal fusion of black metal and thrash metal came really close. In 1990, though, death metal was ready at last. All the dedicated work by the young musicians in the Swedish death metal scene would finally pay off, and the underground broke through.

The Pioneers: A Summary

"People have a tendency to make the old death metal scene into something it never was. It was in reality just a very small group of kids between the ages fourteen and eighteen who played some music. Nobody cared about us back then. That it turned into a big movement was just some kind of 'freak accident,' even though there was some kind of talent involved as well."—UFFE CEDERLUND, MORBID/NIHILIST/ENTOMBED/DISFEAR

I think it would be a good idea to conclude the demo years of Swedish death metal with a brief summary of its central characters. If you take a closer look at these founding years, it's startling to realize how very few people were actually involved. We are talking about a handful of bands, a couple of fanzines and a few dozen people really. The majority of metalheads still didn't know what death metal was about. Most of us were still trapped within the thrash metal way of thinking. Sure, we knew about the first albums of Possessed and Death, but these bands were still regarded as rough thrash metal by many. Extreme thrash for sure, but still thrash.

But as you've seen, something new was in the air. A group of very dedicated, and very young, tape traders and musicians would change the face of Swedish metal forever. The fact that everybody involved with the creation of Swedish death metal was so young is remarkable—hardly anybody over twenty was involved at all. This could be true of other genres, such as crust punk and hardcore, but death metal is remarkable considering the obvious complexity of the music. It's highly advanced in many aspects—the speed, the unorthodox tuning and riffs, the many tempo changes and breaks—and yet it was all done by teenagers.

"I was completely into the death metal scene for two reasons. First, I loved the music, which had an honest, aggressive power to it. But I loved it even more since it was something that just grew up out of nowhere, driven by the energy of some creative teenagers. There were no commercial aspects, just an urge to create. It wasn't something calculated or planned; it just happened. And they did it all themselves. That deserves all the respect in the world."—FREDRIK HOLMGREN, CBR RECORDS

If you strip down this group of youngsters to its core members, you end up with a handful of bands and about ten central characters. If you exclude Obscurity and Mefisto, who were isolated and never really took part in any scene, the first band of importance was Merciless. Despite being from the small town of Strängnäs, Merciless managed to record demos and get them out to make their name and music known. Unlike all previous extreme Swedish metal bands, the members of Merciless worked hard at sending out tapes, writing letters, and traveling around the country in search of like-minded people. So they were the first Swedish underground band that aimed to be part of a movement. In fact, the four members of Merciless' classic lineup—Erik Wallin, Fredrik Karlén, Stefan Karlsson, and Rogga Pettersson—played an important part in launching the scene with their attitude, music, and dedication.

The energy of Merciless soon infected other parts of Sweden. In Stockholm, the two closely linked bands Morbid and Nihilist started making music never heard before. They were soon followed by Dismember, Therion, Afflicted Convulsion, and Treblinka, and Stockholm quickly became the creative center of extreme Swedish metal. Simultaneously, a few kindred spirits turned up around the country: Grave from Gotland, Carnage from Växjö, and Grotesque from Gothenburg. These bands made incredibly brutal exciting new music, creating Swedish death metal.

The underground movement would never have grown as big without the total dedication of a few key characters. Most important was probably Nicke Andersson. He not only created most of the material for Nihilist—he was also a leader of the tape trading scene, and worked on his fanzine, *Chickenshit*, even though it was never released. Nicke's hyper-creative nature influenced many of his close friends, and soon Alex Hellid of Nihilist, Uffe Cederlund of Morbid and Nihilist, and Johan Edlund and Stefan Lagergren of Treblinka were all working on 'zines as well. Though he never released a single issue, either, Cederlund must win the competition for coolest fanzine name: *Fucking Rotten Occult Zombie Death!*

Apart from Nicke Andersson, five other guys deserve equal credit for creating Swedish death metal. First, Tomas Lindberg and Johan Österberg in Gothenburg made the 'zine *Cascade* and were heavily involved with tape trading. Lindberg was also a creative force in Grotesque. Dedicated tape trader Patric Cronberg's groundbreaking fanzine *To the Death* inspired many others to start 'zines dedicated to extreme metal. And the most notorious tape trader of all, Magnus Forsberg, also the drummer in strange crossover band Tribulation, deserves a nod. He discovered most demos and bands first, and influenced the whole Swedish scene with his taste.

"*I guess not many people today have any idea who Magnus Forsberg is, but he had an enormous influence on the early Swedish death metal scene. His tape trading activity was extremely important, and he should not be forgotten. Nicke was also very important. If you sent him a tape, about fifty people would have it a week later.*"—ORVAR SÄFSTRÖM, NIRVANA 2002

Well, that's it basically. These few youngsters and bands are the true originators of what would become Swedish death metal. In addition, one must mention Fredda Holmgren, who took great part in pushing the movement by distributing records and organizing early gigs. The Norwegians Jon "Metalion" Kristiansen of *Slayer Mag* and Ronny Eide of *Morbid Mag* also had an influence, since they traded loads of tapes over the border. If you strip it all down to the core of creativity and originality, you can put the top five bands, tape traders, editors, and musicians of the earliest phase like this:

Bands: Merciless, Nihilist, Carnage, Grotesque, Treblinka

Tape traders: Magnus Forsberg, Nicke Andersson, Patric Cronberg, Johan Österberg, Tomas Lindberg

Fanzine editors: Patric Cronberg, Johan Österberg/Tomas Lindberg, Johan Edlund/Stefan Lagergren, Orvar Säfström/Erik Qvick

Musicians: Nicke Andersson, Erik Wallin, Kristian Wåhlin, Mike Amott, Uffe Cederlund

These catalysts were soon followed by loads of bands and a few fanzine writers such as Alex Hellid, Tomas Nyqvist, and Jon Nödtveidt. As the original

Nicke Andersson—the main character of Swedish death metal

masters soon secured recording deals, Swedish death metal finally broke through to the world. The following chapter will explore how the Swedish death metal scene developed during the year its first albums finally appeared.

> "IN THE SHRINES OF THE KINGLY DEAD
> DOWN UNLIT AND ILLIMITABLE TOMBS"
> —Tiamat, "In the Shrines of the Kingly Dead"

Chapter Five:
The Underground
Breaks Through

The final gig

NYA STRÖMMEN
NORRKÖPING

4 maj kl. 20.00
entre: 20 kr

*Clockwise from top left: cool poster; minimal poster;
CBR mail order form; CBR compilation 7"*

"EVILUTION" LP/CD
CBR 108/CBRCD 108
$10/$16

"ABSOLUT ANTI-CIMEX
COUNTRY OF SWEDEN LP/CD/VIDEO
CBR 121/CBRCD 121/CBRVID 901
$10/$16/$25

ABSOLUT
Country of Sweden
ANTI CIMEX

"HJÄLTERSKELTER" MLP
CBR 107
$8

MORE ANTI-CIMEX BACK-
CATALOGUE IS TO BE RE-
PRESSED IN THE NEAR
FUTURE

HJÄLTER
SKELTER

T-SHIRTS

OMNITRON

DESIGN A

ANTI-CIMEX

DESIGN A

Logo printed white
on black shirt
$14

LP cover printed
white on black
shirt
$14

"A KRIXMAS KAROL" 7"EP
CBR 116
$3

DESIGN B

DESIGN B

Front as design A
Backmotive are
"MASTER PEACE"
printed white on
black shirt
$15

Front are second 7"
cover
Back are LP cover
printed white on
black shirt
$15

CBR 108 AND CBR 107
ARE ALSO AVAIBLE
EXCLUSIVE FROM US
ON COL. VINYL. THE
SAME PRICE AS BLACK
VINYL.

BERGSLAGSROCKEN -90

ALL THAT JAZZ
DEATH (USA)
999 (UK)
SATOR

WILLIAM - PESTILENCE (NL)
PRESIDENT GAS - ANTI CIMEX
DAMBUILDERS (USA) - MEZZROW
Med reservation för ändringar

FOLKETS PARK FAGERSTA Lördag den 2 juni kl. 16.30
(start lilla scen 17.00 - stora 19.00)
Pris 130:- (+ förköp)

FÖRKÖP:

STOCKHOLM: Heavy Sound, House Of Kicks, CBR, Pet Sounds - GÖTEBORG: Dolores, Pet
Sounds, VÄXJÖ: Sin City Records - KARLSTAD: Riff Raff - UPPSALA: Jörgen S. 018/21 21 08
- KÖPING: Birdnest 0221/185 97 - VÄSTERÅS: Skivbörsen - ÖREBRO: Folk & Rock - NORR-
KÖPING: PowerHour 011/11 99 33 - BORLÄNGE: Folk & Rock - FAGERSTA: Playman
Dessutom pr. telefon/postförskott:
TID ÄR MUSIK
0223 - 165 88 /155 75/102 31
Arr. TID ÄR MUSIK, Studiefrämjandet, Fagersta Kommun, Folkets Park

Clockwise from top left: Original poster for Bergslagsrocken 1990, with Death atop the bill instead of Morbid Angel;

flyer for one of countless thrash metal concerts in Fagersta;

"Stipen" (Merciless), Richard Cabeza (Unanimated/Dismember), and Björn Gramell (Damnation) on their way to Fagersta

DEATH ANGEL

FORBIDDEN

ROCKBORGEN FAGERSTA
Fre. 18/5 Kl. 19.30
Pris: 90:-/80:(medlemmar - gäller ej förköp.)

FÖR STOCKHOLM: Heavy Sound, **KÖP**
House Of Kicks, CBR - UPPSALA: Jörgen S. 018/21 21 08 - VÄSTERÅS:
Skivbörsen - ÖREBRO: Folk & Rock - NORRKÖPING: Bobban B.
011/11 99 33 - FAGERSTA: Playman och pr. telefon och postförskott:
Ring 0223/165 88 /135 75
Arr. TID ÄR MUSIK/FAGERSTA KOMMUN/EROR

LUDVIKA-VÄSTERÅS

DRI

THRASH ZONE

WITH

CORROSION OF CONFORMITY

+ SUPPORT

KAZJUROL

ROCKBORGEN FAGERSTA
Fre. 11/5 Kl. 20.00
Pris: 90:-/80:(medlemmar - gäller ej förköp.)

FÖR
STOCKHOLM: Heavy Sound,
House Of Kicks, CBR - **UPPSALA**: Jörgen S. 018/21 21 08 - **VÄSTERÅS**:
Skivbörsen - **ÖREBRO**: Folk & Rock - **NORRKÖPING**: Robban B.
011/11 99 33 - **FAGERSTA**: Playman och pr. telefon och postförskott:
Babs 0223/165 88 / 155 75
KÖP

Arr: TID ÄR MUSIK/SATANIC SIDEBURNS

A HIGHER FORM OF

THRASHING !!

MORBID ANGEL   NAPALM DEATH

TREBLINKA   RDA

Rockborgen Fagersta lörd. 25/11
Förköp: Babs 0223-155 75, Robban 011-11 99 33   kl. 20.00
OBS! Förmodligen enbart förköp (risk för utsålt).
Arrangör: TID ÄR MUSIK/Fagersta Hardcore Crew   Pris: 90:-
THE HARDCORE UTOPIA TOUR

Clockwise from top left: Flyer for thrash metal gig in Fagersta;

early poster for Napalm Death's gig in Fagersta—as you can see Morbid Angel was actually supposed to have headlined;

a tape recorder on full volume was standard equipment on the travels to Fagersta. Note the flannel shirt inferno!

*A*s the 90's approached, the Swedish death metal scene was still a limited group of dedicated metalheads based in Stockholm, though spreading to other parts of Sweden as well. The entire movement was very innocent, and few involved had any thoughts about recording albums or touring. But the power of death metal was too immense to ignore. Before long, record labels and distributors realized the quality and potential of the music. Recording studios, most notably Studio Sunlight in Stockholm, even started to specialize in producing death metal.

The popularity and availability of death metal brought a steady release of albums in 1989. Suddenly, music that had previously been isolated within the tape trading community was available for a much larger group of people.

"During 1989 the scene started to grow immensely. Many extreme bands released albums that got distribution in Sweden, like Obituary, Autopsy, Morbid Angel, and Pestilence. Before that, there were of course a couple of death metal albums [Possessed and Death], but it wasn't until 1989 that the genre was established."—ANDERS BJÖRLER, AT THE GATES/THE HAUNTED

"If we should talk about one record, Morbid Angel's Altars of Madness *changed everything. Before that there was no clear distinction between death, speed, or thrash among regular metalheads. It was just brutal metal. But* Altars of Madness *opened people's eyes, and made us realize something new was going on. Everybody bought that record. Everybody. And thrash metal was executed by it—the whole genre just disappeared."*—ROBBAN BECIROVIC, CLOSE-UP MAGAZINE

"Back then, the release of a death metal album was material for weeks of partying. And since all of us were so young, we usually partied at cemeteries and in forests. I was one of the few guys who could actually have parties at my home occasionally, since my parents were often out of town. And whenever a new brutal album was released, we would party like crazy."—KRISTIAN "NECROLORD" WÅHLIN, GROTESQUE/LIERS IN WAIT/DECOLLATION

"A guy who definitely gets all the credit in the world for bringing death metal to Sweden is Fredda Holmgren, who used to run Chickenbrain Records. He was totally aware of exciting things going on in the underground, and he was the first to discover Earache and import their albums."—ROBBAN BECIROVIC, CLOSE-UP MAGAZINE

"Those Earache Records that Fredda Holmgren brought to Sweden influenced us all. A defining moment for me was Fredrik Karlén's eighteenth birthday party, which was held at the place of Micke Sjöstrand in Chronic Decay. Matti Kärki and Rickard Cabeza brought test pressings of Altars of Madness *and* Symphonies of Sickness *from CBR, and we played them constantly throughout the weekend. It was like a death metal festival!"*—MATTIAS KENNHED, MACRODEX/HOUSE OF USHER

The role of Fredrik Holmgren should not be underestimated. Back in 1983 he started the punk fanzine *Asocial*, and the following year he started Chickenbrain Records (CBR). In the early days Holmgren only distributed records, and was among the pioneers in bringing independent foreign releases to Sweden. In 1985 he started to release 7" singles himself, initially rereleases of punk bands like Ingron Hutlös and Raped Teenagers.

"I came from punk, and within that scene everybody wanted to do something. So I started a 'zine; then I distributed records and did my own releases. It was very down-to-earth, and you traded your own 7" singles for other people's releases. No money was ever involved in the beginning."— FREDRIK HOLMGREN, CBR RECORDS

In 1987 CBR released its first album, with the punk band Puke, and quickly became the biggest distributor in Sweden when it came to independent and underground releases. Most importantly for the death metal scene, Fredrik discovered Earache very early on and brought the records into the country.

*"The first thing I got from them was a flexi 7" with Heresy; then I discovered Napalm Death in 1987. I was still just trading at that point. Then I got Nuclear Blast, Peaceville, and the lot. I guess I got a lot of input from guys like Nicke Andersson and Johnny Hedlund, who kept on asking me about extreme metal albums. Since no other distributor in Sweden was into that kind of stuff in the late 80's, I just got in and distributed everything."—*FREDRIK HOLMGREN, CBR RECORDS

Since one of CBR's main goals was to spread Swedish underground music, before long they offered demo tapes by Dismember, Nihilist, and others.

*"I got to know these people since they bought a lot of stuff from me, and when they started to release demos, it was natural for me to distribute them. I loved the early death metal scene; it was so full of energy. People traded stuff, built up networks, and created everything themselves. The music was also very good and aggressive. It sold well too—I think the Nihilist demos sold about 3,000 copies each. Amazing when you think about it."—*FREDRIK HOLMGREN, CBR RECORDS

Beginning in late 1988, the first really extreme foreign bands made their first appearances in Sweden. The first of these highly influential concerts was Napalm Death's Scandinavian tour, November 17–27, 1988. And a certain Fredrik Holmgren at CBR made it happen—a reminder of how much ahead of everybody else he was at that point. He understood the extreme music scene and made it come alive. In my case, he practically delivered Napalm Death to my front door, as I lived close to Fagersta, where they played.

Napalm Death coming to Sweden was an event of some magnitude. We talked about them eagerly as we drank ridiculous amounts of beer on the train to Rockborgen in Fagersta, though we were only fifteen or sixteen years old.

As we understood it, this was the fastest speed metal band in the world, but we were still not prepared for Napalm Death. A notorious scene personality called "The Bolt" referred to Napalm Death as "the most famous band in the world," and gave them the nickname "Nappe Död."

Everyone was blown away by Napalm Death's incredibly fast and brutal performance—especially the bewildered sound technician. At this point, Napalm Death was one of the fastest, most extreme bands in the world, and we were all inspired. There were no limits anymore. The road to the Swedish death metal boom lay wide open.

"I guess that tour with Napalm Death was the first major death metal happening in Scandinavia. It was a pretty ambitious tour with many gigs, and people were just blown away everywhere—especially the sound guys! Then I brought Carcass over, which caused similar reactions."—FREDRIK HOLMGREN, CBR RECORDS

"The first and most important one was Napalm Death in 1988."—FRED ESTBY, DISMEMBER/CARNAGE

"First Napalm Death. Then Morbid Angel and Carcass."—ANDERS BJÖRLER, AT THE GATES/THE HAUNTED

The Napalm Death tour changed the future for one band in particular. The support act on the whole Scandinavian leg was Filthy Christians, but each venue could also put one local band on the bill. In Fagersta the rather uninteresting Kazjurol had the honor of opening, but in Stockholm a young band called Nihilist persuaded the promoter to put them on the bill.

"When we heard that Napalm Death was coming, we knew we had to play. We terrorized Fredda Holmgren with countless calls. He didn't take us seriously at all, and insisted that the piss-awful band Kazjurol would play in Stockholm as well. But finally he surrendered and allowed us on the bill."—NICKE ANDERSSON, NIHILIST/ENTOMBED

Digby Pearson of Earache Records was accompanying Napalm Death on the tour, and so got the opportunity to witness Sweden's most brilliant death metal band in action.

"I guess my introduction to the Swedish death metal scene was on that tour with Napalm Death, specifically at a gig in Stockholm where the support act was Nihilist. They totally blew me away! All I could think about was how talented they were; super tight, well-rehearsed, and extreme as hell. I had to sign them to Earache; the only problem was that they were still under eighteen and pretty inexperienced. So I waited until they were ready."—DIGBY PEARSON, EARACHE RECORDS

Earache was in fact the first international label to care for Swedish death metal. Since they were also the hottest label within the genre—with bands like Napalm Death, Carcass, and Morbid Angel—and had made an early signing of the Swedish

Poster for Napalm Death's legendary concert in Fagersta

grindcore band Filthy Christians, their office got flooded with Swedish demos. But no band managed to get a deal apart from Entombed.

"We had the chance to sign nearly every Swedish band after the success of Entombed. But since nothing could top them, we ignored the pack of Dismember, Unleashed, Grave, etc., who followed."—DIGBY PEARSON, EARACHE RECORDS

So one night with Napalm Death in Stockholm was a turning point in Nihilist's career. For the Swedish scene as a whole, the most important place for extreme gigs in the late 80's was doubtlessly Fagersta—a small town about 125 miles northwest of Stockholm. Everybody into extreme music in Sweden went there to see gigs. People were dedicated back then!

Fagersta was put on the metal map by Peter Ahlqvist, who booked gigs relentlessly during the late 80's. He virtually took over the local music organization Tid Är Musik, and in 1988 managed to get an old cinema building. Once it was at his disposal, he created the legendary venue Rockborgen.

"The place was ideal for arranging gigs. As soon as we got it we started to bring over every exciting band we could lay our hands on. The first gig at Rockborgen was Napalm Death in 1988, and after that it just rolled on for years."
—PETER AHLQVIST, UPROAR/TID ÄR MUSIK/BURNING HEART

After Napalm Death, Peter arranged a series of classic gigs at Rockborgen, which soon turned into the best venue in Sweden for extreme music. Week after week, great bands including Kreator, Sodom, Sepultura, Pestilence, Obituary, Benediction, Atheist, Death Angel, Carcass, and Forbidden came to this small town in the middle of nowhere. Rockborgen became a center for the death metal movement. These gigs were also crucial for the Swedish scene, since bands like Merciless and Entombed suddenly had a great place to play.

"The death metal movement was very similar to the hardcore punk movement, so I felt like a kid again when we started to arrange really brutal gigs. The scene had a very good atmosphere and I enjoyed it very much. I guess one of the best gigs we ever did was Sodom, Sepultura, and Merciless in 1989. The timing was just perfect, as Sepultura had a great underground following, Sodom's credibility was intact and Merciless were in their prime. Nights like that you'll never forget!"—PETER AHLQVIST, UPROAR/TID ÄR MUSIK/BURNING HEART

When the gigs proved successful and people kept coming, Peter Ahlqvist launched an annual festival called Bergslagsrocken. The bill of the first one in 1989 featured a variety of pop, punk, and metal bands. On the first festival the brutality was represented by German speed metal titans Kreator, but the next year's lineup sent shivers down the spine of all death metallers in Sweden. Apart from the great Dutch band Pestilence, a name appeared atop the bill that made strong men weak: Morbid Angel.

"The most important gig I ever arranged was definitely that one with Morbid Angel. I just had to get them over, since they were by far the most exciting band in the scene at that point. I found out the phone numbers to their homes and started to call them, and as it turned out they were excited about coming to Europe as well. So I sent them the money for airfare. It turned out to be a big success, and literally everyone in the scene turned up. That gig really made people come together, and nothing was the same after that night."—PETER AHLQVIST, UPROAR/TID ÄR MUSIK/BURNING HEART

Originally Death were supposed to headline the festival, which few remember since Morbid Angel could have substituted for any band at this point without anyone complaining. I was one of the excited youngsters who attended the gig, and the atmosphere was electrifying. This was one of the few nights in Fagersta when most people made sure to stay sober enough not to miss the headliners. And the gig blew us all away. Morbid Angel were simply gods. The impression couldn't be ruined, not by the bad sound, and not by T-ban of Kazjurol preparing for stage dives repeatedly stepping on guitarist Richard Brunelle's distortion pedal, thus cutting off the distortion.

"The most important gig of all was Morbid Angel's appearance at Bergslagsrocken in 1990. That took everything to a new level. After that show, everything went crazy."—JESPER THORSSON, AFFLICTED

BERGSLAGSROCKEN 90
FOLKETS PARK FAGERSTA Lör 2/6

Arr: TID ÄR MUSIK   Pris: 130:-

TID ÄR MUSIK Arr:

BERGSLAGSROCKEN 90

SATOR
999 (UK)
DEATH (USA)
ALL THAT JAZZ
WILLIAM
PESTILENCE (NL)
PRESIDENT GAS
ANTI CIMEX
DAMBUILDERS (USA)
MEZZROW

Pris: 130:- + förköp

FOLKETS PARK FAGERSTA Lör 2/6
Förköp & Info:
TID ÄR MUSIK tel. 0223-165 88/155 75/102 31

ROCKBORGEN
Fagersta
Övriga arrangemang våren - 90

20/4
PSYCHOTIC YOUTH,
23 TILL, HAPPY FARM, R.I.F.

5/5
D.O.A.
(Amerikansk kult-hardcore-rock),
STREBERS, IDENTITY

11/5
D.R.I., CORROSION OF
CONFORMITY, KAZJUROL

18/5
DEATH ANGEL,FORBIDDEN
+ ev. ett tredje band
(Obs! Enda Sveriges spelningen
för dessa förbandband!!!)

Walk Together
Rock Together

Förköp/Info: Tid Är Musik

CARCASS

SYMPHONIES OF SICKNESS

ROCKBORGEN FAGERSTA
Lörd. 10/2 Kl. 20.00

Förköp: Babs 0223-155 75. **Stockholm** Heavy Sound, CBR,
House of Kicks. **Västerås** Skivbörsen. **Norrköping** Robban 011-
11 99 33. **Uppsala** Jörgen Sigfridsson. **Fagersta** Playman.

Arr.: TID ÄR MUSIK/FAGERSTA GORE CORE CREW   75:—/65:— (Medl.)

*Clockwise from top: Typical partying
on the bus to Fagersta. Fredrik
Lindgren (Unleashed) is drinking in the
front. Beside him is "Burton-Matte,"
who tragically committed suicide. Rest
in peace;*

*flyer for another legendary gig.
(the first time I saw Entombed);*

*Fagersta gig ads and ticket for
Bergslagsrocken 1990*

"Napalm Death played the first important gig in Sweden, but it was nothing compared to Morbid Angel. That was an event of massive importance. People were excited for months before that gig, and it set new standards for everything. To point out the moment that really made death metal big in Sweden, that gig is it. It was insane."—FREDRIK HOLMGREN, CBR RECORDS

"For some time, Bergslagsrocken in Fagersta was the climax of each year. Fuck, I get very nostalgic when I think back about it. We went there by train, and it was completely full of drunk and crazy thrashers. We had such a good time! Extreme music from the tape recorder and a lot of booze. I think we used to be about one hundred metalheads on those trains to Fagersta. Some of us had to go straight to the police station at arrival because we were too drunk and missed the whole thing. Ha ha!"—FREDRIK KARLÉN, MERCILESS

"Rockborgen in Fagersta was the death metal center in Sweden. It was the place where everybody met, drank like hell, and just had a wonderful time. Sometimes you got too drunk and missed all the bands, but it didn't matter. The important thing was to meet people. Everybody was so friendly and cool, and you liked everyone else's band as much as your own. I wouldn't trade those times in Fagersta for anything in the world."—DAN SWANÖ, EDGE OF SANITY/UNISOUND

"Fagersta was absolutely the most vital and important place for extreme metal gigs during the years 1988 to 1992. It was such a good atmosphere there, just a big fucking party where everybody got to know each other. The gigs were great, totally packed and charged with frantic stage diving activity. I have never seen such wild action at gigs since. Everybody went there, and everybody was a hardcore fan. It was complete passion. It was in Fagersta that the scene really became alive."—ROBBAN BECIROVIC, CLOSE-UP MAGAZINE

"Fagersta was the place to be. Cool people, good gigs, and a great atmosphere. Connections were made, and the scene started to spread rapidly. We got out of the subway system in Stockholm, and people from smaller towns got out of their isolated hellholes. We got together, and the energy was immense."—ANDERS SCHULTZ, UNLEASHED

Apart from important appearances by international death metal titans, gigs by Swedish bands started happening more frequently. The concerts became a bit better attended, and bands soon had the opportunity to play outside of their hometowns. An exchange of gigs began, and soon the death metal scene was alive and kicking.

"Our third gig ever was our first proper show, right after our second demo during the summer of 1989. It was in Strömstad, organized by none other than Jon from Dissection—only back then he was in a thrash band called Rabbit's Carrot. The gig featured us, Jon's band, and Grotesque. An unforgettable night! Metalion from Slayer Mag was there, and on a video recording from the gig you can see Onkel [also known as the notorious "Shit Man"] banging in the audience. That night I learned what a real death metal concert should be like!"—CHRISTOFFER JOHNSSON, THERION

"I remember we put together a gig with Afflicted Convulsion, Unleashed, General Surgery, and Crematory at Axelsberg's youth center. Over 300 people showed up and it turned into chaos. The most memorable gig we did was in Esbjerg, Denmark, with Invocator. The audience just went crazy and knew all the songs, though we had only released demos at that point. Still, those demos had sold by the thousands—and that is probably more than most metal albums sell today here in Sweden!"—JESPER THORSSON, AFFLICTED

"The first gig Treblinka did that was actually attended by

General Surgery and Unanimated— Stockholm death metal double threat

people we didn't know, and who liked our music, was at Hunddagis, together with Morbid, Nihilist, and Dismember. I can't remember when it was, but it must have been one of Morbid's very last gigs. The last gigs we put up at Runan attracted a lot of people, the one with Disharmonic Orchestra and Pungent Stench was especially insane. There must have been about 350 people there, in a room suitable for about 150..."—JOHAN EDLUND, TREBLINKA/TIAMAT

"The first major death metal gig with only Swedish bands was when Entombed played their first gig ever, in Rinkeby on November 4, 1989. It was a huge bill with Carnage, Therion, Sorcerer, Crematory, Count Raven, and some other bands. We, Nirvana 2002, were supposed to play as well, but sadly it never happened. After the gig most of us got beaten up, since about 2,000 kickers were waiting for us outside. Nicke and I got away, though—we took a cab to his place straight after the gig!"—ORVAR SÄFSTRÖM, NIRVANA 2002

During 1989, Norrköping's Robban Becirovic also continued his Thrash Bash concerts, and his local radio program. Many of the bands that played in Fagersta also played at Thrash Bash in Norrköping while in Sweden, but somehow these gigs never attracted audiences like the ones in Fagersta. Peter Ahlqvist in Fagersta had been in the extreme music scene much longer, was older and more business-minded. Robban Becirovic was still basically a fan, in it because he loved the music.

"Peter Ahlqvist really knew what he was doing. All his gigs were well organized. My own shitty little gigs were nothing compared to what was going on at Rockborgen and Bergslagsrocken."—ROBBAN BECIROVIC, CLOSE-UP MAGAZINE

The Swedish death metal scene really started to move in 1989. Many classic demos were recorded, the gigs started flowing, and new bands and fanzines turned up on a regular basis. Some of the first Swedish death metal albums were also recorded during 1989, then released in 1990. And in 1990 Swedish death metal completely broke through. But before the albums in 1990 came a few singles released in 1989. Although these were all minor releases on small labels, they represent the first vinyl steps of Swedish death metal.

The easiest way to release a single was to find a label to press your demo cassette onto vinyl. Both Nihilist's *Drowned* demo and Carnage's *Torn Apart* demo were released—on the obscure labels Bloody Rude Defect Records and Distorted Harmony, respectively. The Nihilist 7" was in fact a bootleg made by Nicke Andersson and Fredda Holmgren at CBR.

"It was a 100 percent bootleg, and we mainly did it to make a few extra bucks for ourselves. I guess I was also excited about seeing something we had recorded on vinyl."—NICKE ANDERSSON, NIHILIST/ENTOMBED

A few new recordings also went onto vinyl in 1989. Most significantly, Treblinka put out the *Severe Abomination* 7" on Mould in Hell Records, the label they created for the sole purpose of releasing their own recordings. Singer/ guitarist Johan Edlund also distributed other releases under the same name, and along with guitarist Stefan Lagergren edited *Poserkill* 'zine—Edlund was the essence of DIY back then! This single pretty much followed the style of their demos, with primitive sound, raw riffs, and ghastly vocals from hell.

"When I turned eighteen my family gave me a bank account with about 10,000 SEK [$1,200], and I immediately put it all into that Treblinka 7", which naturally was pressed in 666 copies. They were pretty upset at first, but since it sold out in a matter of days, or rather hours, it was just incredible. I guess they changed their minds. In hindsight, it was the best thing I ever did. I made some money, could buy a new guitar, and eventually the 7" got us the recording deal. I could also afford to party more during weekends!

"The main reason I started to distribute records was that Nuclear Blast traded 200 copies of the 7" for a bunch of their records, so I had to sell them. After I had sold everything, Mould in Hell practically ceased to exist. When I think back, I probably should have continued. It was a great way to make connections, and it was fun as hell."—JOHAN EDLUND, TREBLINKA/TIAMAT

After recording the 7", Johan Edlund started to get more serious with the

The gigs started to get going for real, as international bands hit the youth centers

Later Thrash Bash ads. As you can see, death metal bands were taking over

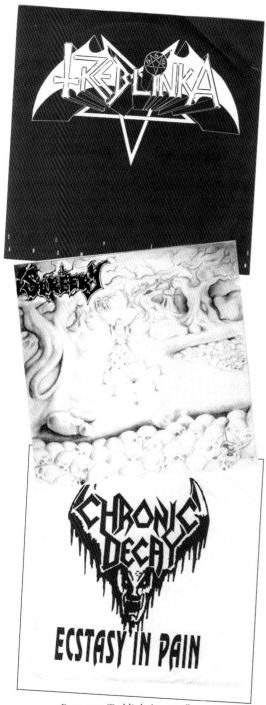

concept of the band. He eventually realized that the Treblinka name was too provocative, and didn't fit the band's philosophy very well. So in the autumn of 1989 the group was rechristened Tiamat. The group also fell apart during this time, as both Stefan Lagergren and Anders Holmberg left the band to focus on Expulsion. However, Tiamat only seemed to get stronger amid the turbulence.

Another band that managed a 7" during 1989 was Eskilstuna's Chronic Decay, who released their intense *Ecstasy in Pain* EP. This recording is in fact more brutal thrash metal with harsh hardcore vocals than actual death metal, but stands as a document from the time when the scene was discovering and moving into more extreme territories. During 1990, the French label Thrash also started to get in on the Swedish death metal scene, and released the 7" singles *No Canonisation* with Carbonized and *Rivers of the Dead* with Sorcery.

At this point in history, it remained hard to get a decent record deal. Many great bands were around, but only a few could release fully developed albums. Many releases that saw light during 1990, however, remain immortal classics to this day, marking the breakthrough of Swedish death metal.

From top: Treblinka's rare 7";
Sorcery—Rivers of the Dead;
Chronic Decay 7"

Mayhem's classic car. As you can see, it is actually an Audi

The Awakening

The first full-length Swedish death metal album was Merciless' blistering debut *The Awakening*. Recorded during the summer of 1989, it wasn't released until March 1990—things moved pretty slowly back then. Once again they chose Tuna Studio in Eskilstuna, where they had such great results with their second demo. Merciless' debut album was also the first release on Øystein Aarseth's Deathlike Silence Productions label, so it is a classic in many aspects. The recording was an insane happening, according to bassist Fredrik Karlén.

"*We recorded it within a week, if I'm not mistaken. We used the same studio in Eskilstuna where we had put* Realm of the Dark *on tape. The guys from Mayhem came over and head-banged in the studio during the recording, and it was really fun since we hadn't met them before. I will never forget it! We had only seen Mayhem in pictures before, so we kind of expected a couple of macho men two meters tall, heavily drunk with their weapons drawn. Well, that was* not *the case!*

"*First entered Pelle ['Dead'], with his long legs and long blond hair, and two other short guys with black hair lingered shyly behind him. It looked like Gandalf with the little hobbits from* Lord of the Rings! *Pelle kept on talking about a bunch of sick things he had experienced in his little cabin in Norway, as Øystein kept drinking Coke around the clock. He was also constantly talking about upcoming tours for Merciless across Eastern Europe. Necrobutcher, on the other hand, was a cool man who mainly wanted to drink whiskey.*

"I fooled these guys that I had a made a machine in which I burned feces, and they actually believed it! They ran around in my small apartment and screamed for me to show them my machine. Boy, were they disappointed when they didn't find anything. Mayhem were extremely great guys back then. They seemed happy when they went back to Norway with the master tape of The Awakening *in the trunk of their old yellow Volvo, with dice hanging from the rear mirror; it's true! Fuck, Pelle—we miss you! See you!"*—FREDRIK KARLÉN, MERCILESS

How did *The Awakening* rate after these crazy recording sessions? It's mainly hyper-aggressive speed metal in the vein of their demos. Occasionally they get closer to death metal structures, such as the double kick-drum and crushing guitar intro of the opener, "Pure Hate." The production is raw and crude, no big changes compared to their demos. But the sound suits their primitive music perfectly, and Rogga's angry screams really hit the mark. At this time, Merciless was at the top of their career. They ruled the underground.

Sadly, Merciless never got out on an Eastern European tour, since Mayhem wasted all of Deathlike Silence's money on bombs and blood on their own ill-fated tour. But at least in Sweden I remember watching them perform constantly at metal gigs—with my head banging like crazy.

"We played almost every weekend for a while, and we attended a lot of other bands' gigs as well. I have most fond memories of when we played with Sodom and Sepultura in Fagersta 1989. Holy shit! Tom Angelripper is standing there in sweatpants. With a semi-hard-on in my pants, I approached him with the stumbling phrase, 'Hello Ripper, we like your music.' Sepultura were great guys, so fucking cool and nice. You know, back in those days they were fucking gods to me. I met Max six or seven years later, when he jumped out of their tour bus here in Stockholm. I just said: 'Hello Max, do you remember me?' And he immediately replied, 'Yes, you're the bass player from Merciless.' I was overwhelmed. Respect, Max!"—FREDRIK KARLÉN, MERCILESS

The Awakening never sold many copies—the initial pressing was limited to 1,000. Though highly praised in the underground metal scene, Merciless never made it far outside that underground. They might have been a little too crude for the wider audience, and their Germanic thrash style might have been considered a bit dated already. The new hot things were the fat sound of Entombed, and the complex song structures of Morbid Angel. But I think the main reason for Merciless' commercial failure is that they were released by a very obscure underground label. Øystein Aarseth couldn't really promote them, plus he was probably very busy with his own master plan for black metal. Instead, a band from Stockholm took Swedish death metal to the next level, both artistically and commercially. Of course, I'm talking about Entombed.

Flyer for Merciless debut album

Left Hand Path

The core members of Entombed had made quite an impression in their earlier band Nihilist. Everybody who had heard or seen them knew it was only a matter of time before they made it big. When Nihilist transformed into Entombed, big things started happening instantly. Digby Pearson of Earache Records had actually called up Nicke Andersson to sign Nihilist, only to learn that they didn't exist any more. But given the chance instead to sign Nicke's new group, Entombed, Digby never hesitated.

"I was actually quite relieved that they had changed the name; there might have been problems otherwise, since an American band was also called Nihilist. It made no difference to me that Johnny was gone; what was important was that Nicke was involved. He was the major talent, the driving force, and the leader of the band."—DIGBY PEARSON, EARACHE RECORDS

Nicke Andersson has a slightly different recollection.

"They got in touch after we had released the Entombed demo. I remember that David Vincent of Morbid Angel called me up from the Earache office and said that they loved us, and then Digby got on the phone and offered us a deal. We had in fact gotten an offer from Nuclear Blast before that, but back then it was Earache or nothing. I thought Nuclear Blast had bad bands, ugly layouts, and a bad-smelling German touch to it all. Back then, Earache was the label for death metal."—NICKE ANDERSSON, NIHILIST/ENTOMBED

With the Earache contract in their eager hands, the youngsters in Entombed would soon bring Swedish death metal to international fame.

"I don't think we even signed the contract until after the album was released. And it obviously was a shitty contract. But we didn't know anything about that back then. All we wanted was to record an album for Earache. We were young, naïve—and got ripped off, basically."—NICKE ANDERSSON, NIHILIST/ENTOMBED

Entombed was on the way to the big leagues. On November 4, 1989, the band played their first show, in Rinkeby, drawing loads of people. A month later it was time to enter the studio to create one of the most innovative and stunning albums of all times. Right at this point, bassist David Blomqvist decided to leave the band.

"The main reason why I quit was that I was really a guitarist, and didn't feel comfortable playing the bass. Sure, I rehearsed all the songs for Left Hand Path, *but I thought it was honest to quit Entombed before the recording. Uffe or Alex—or Nicke, for that matter—could do the bass just as good, or better than me, so it felt okay to leave. So I left, and joined Carnage immediately. I*

Left Hand Path:
The album that finally broke Swedish death metal worldwide

also felt that I had played with Nicke for a couple of months, but with Fred all my life. It felt strange to play with another drummer."—DAVID BLOMQVIST, DISMEMBER/CARNAGE/ENTOMBED

After Blomqvist departed, *Left Hand Path* was recorded with producer Tomas Skogsberg in the soon-to-be-famous Studio Sunlight in December 1989. A few months later, Earache released the LP to an unprepared world.

"We wrote three new songs, entered the studio, and recorded it all during three or four weekends. It was done very quickly, and it all went smoothly, apart from the fact that I got badly beaten up one night before the recordings. I drank too much back then, and acted very stupid while drunk."—UFFE CEDERLUND, MORBID/NIHILIST/ENTOMBED/DISFEAR

The album hit the metal world like a hurricane, and Entombed were soon praised outside of Sweden. To most listeners, this album sounded completely new and fascinating. The ultra-crunching and down-tuned guitars were the fattest ever heard, and unlike on many of the earlier Swedish death metal demos, the clarity of the sound was preserved. The guitar sound on Entombed's debut remains the best example of the "Sunlight sound," named after the recording studio. To my ears, the sheer rawness and aggression has never been surpassed, not even by Entombed themselves. The guitar sound was described as the aural equivalent of a chainsaw through flesh.

"I give full credit for that immense guitar sound to Tomas Skogsberg. It was his production that made it so huge. I just used a worthless Ibanez guitar, a small Peavey combo amplifier, and a Boss Heavy Metal pedal. Basically,

there are two Boss Heavy Metal–distorted guitars, one in each speaker, and a DS1-distorted one in the middle. It got tight since I did all the rhythm parts, which I continued to do until To Ride, Shoot Straight and Speak the Truth.*"*
—UFFE CEDERLUND, MORBID/NIHILIST/ENTOMBED/DISFEAR

But there is so much more to *Left Hand Path* than the fantastic guitar sound. One thing that distinguished Entombed from many other death metal bands was the brilliant drumming of Nicke Andersson, who was only seventeen at the time. Unlike most drummers within the scene who played without fluid fills or a living flow, Andersson used a lot of feeling and dynamics. Though his style wasn't perfect yet, he was light-years ahead of anyone else in Sweden.

Furthermore, the vocals of Lars-Göran Petrov were undeniable. He growled his guts out in the traditional death metal way, but still possessed a personal and unique feeling. His vocals never fell into toneless grunts, but remained perfectly audible and clear. Petrov also varied his vocals slightly more than most Swedish death metal singers, and pulled off some incredible screams.

In addition to these advantages in sound and musicianship, Entombed also distinguished themselves through superior songwriting. Nicke Andersson wrote most of the riffs and arrangements on this record, so the credit goes almost entirely to him. He commercialized Swedish death metal in a positive sense, with catchy and

Entombed relaxing in the forest

memorable structures. Every single tune has some incredible details that give the song a unique life. There are so many cool fills and amazing breaks on this record, and these details owe a lot to progressive bands such as King Crimson. Nicke states that he had never even heard King Crimson or progressive rock back then—all the more impressive. Demo songs like "But Life Goes On" are taken to new heights, and new numbers like the title track reach almost divine quality. There isn't a dull moment on this album. It's flawless.

We were all stunned upon its release. Of course, some people argued that Nihilist had been better, but you know how it goes: the first recording will always be considered the best.

Entombed behind bars.

"I did see Nihilist perform a couple of times and it wasn't excellent, but still good. They were very young and inexperienced. They undoubtedly got better as a live band when they were called Entombed, but I always preferred the Nihilist material, though—it just hit me harder at the time."—MICHAEL AMOTT, CARNAGE/CARCASS/ARCH ENEMY

Regardless, we were all marked for life by Entombed—from Dismember and Grave in Sweden, who tried to copy *Left Hand Path*, to Mayhem and Burzum in Norway, who turned against it. This album changed everything in Scandinavia. Until this point, Swedish death metal had been almost exclusively an underground phenomenon, and not many people abroad had heard of the Swedish bands. *Left Hand Path* changed all that. Entombed perfected Swedish death metal, and the world stood amazed.

"The album received very good reviews, sold pretty well, and we were happy as hell. We also got out on our first small tour, which was done by train across Europe! Since we didn't know anything about touring, we thought this was the way every band traveled. It was stressful and very hard work, but we enjoyed it. We were just a bunch of guys from the suburbs, and we were on tour. To us, it was incredible."—NICKE ANDERSSON, NIHILIST/ENTOMBED

Though the flow of great Swedish death metal albums hasn't stopped since *Left Hand Path*, no record has ever surpassed its devastating quality. In my opinion, it remains the best Swedish death metal album ever made. It's also one of the most influential, and it set out the (left hand?) path for things to come for years. Everything on this album reeks of high class, from the massive sound to the fantastic cover painting by Dan Seagrave.

Entombed were on a roll. They soon recorded a video clip for the song "Left Hand Path"—the first ever for a Swedish death metal band. The clip was done in pure underground fashion. Notorious madman Kim Hansen of the underground film association ILEX asked the band if he could film a gig with them in Sandviken, and later they shot some additional footage at Skogskyrkogården—the famous "Forest Cemetery" designed by Gunnar Asplund.

"It was made just for fun. We never thought it would ever be broadcast, but I guess we were wrong! It was lousy, of course, but I actually like it more than that awful video we made for 'Stranger Aeons.'"—UFFE CEDERLUND, MORBID/NIHILIST/ENTOMBED/DISFEAR

The equipment was primitive, video cameras borrowed from the city government. The result was a crude-looking clip, with heavy use of old and cheap-looking filters and effects. Soon MTV asked Entombed for a video, and Kim Hansen had to transfer the poorly shot video to one-inch tape. Of course the result looked awful, but, true underground personality that he was, Kim convinced MTV that was the way they intended it to look. He later went on to be a comptroller at engineering firm Sandvik AB, and is probably the craziest person ever to enter the field of advanced economics.

"They got in touch with me and said they couldn't broadcast it due to the poor quality. I just bullshitted them and said that it was all intentional. After some negotiation, I convinced them that this was the way the clip was supposed to look. They didn't know anything about death metal, and swallowed everything I said. Anyway, I guess they had the last laugh, as I sold the rights to it for a few hundred bucks. Then Entombed skyrocketed, and the clip rolled endlessly..."—KIM HANSEN, ILEX

Entombed became the undisputed leaders of Swedish death metal. Loads of bands started to imitate them, while others turned against their style to distinguish themselves, probably due largely to envy. What *Altars of Madness* had been for international death metal, *Left Hand Path* was for Sweden.

"When Entombed got a recording deal, and their debut went so well, it ignited the whole Swedish scene. But it also created some envy. Personally I was a bit envious, even though I would never have admitted it back then. Their two-beat death metal was never my favorite style, but I was impressed since they were extremely tight. Nicke's melodic and hardcore-influenced riffs really impressed me as well, and had, in fact, since the days of Nihilist."—CHRISTOFFER JOHNSSON, THERION

"Entombed's debut album was probably the most important event

in the development of Swedish death metal—Entombed's music, the Sunlight sound, and Thomas Skogsberg's production."—JESPER THORSSON, AFFLICTED

"I still have the unmixed tape from the Left Hand Path *recording without the vocals. It is the rawest and most brutal thing ever."*—DIGBY PEARSON, EARACHE RECORDS

Mean grindcore.

Mean

To understand how fresh and brutal *Left Hand Path* felt, compare it to Earache's other release by a Swedish band in 1990: Filthy Christians' *Mean*. Though Filthy Christians can't be described as death metal in any way, they had been an integral part of the underground during the late 80's, and definitely contributed to the brutalization of Swedish music.

Mean was recorded on April 7–11, 1989, in Musikstugan in the band's hometown of Falun. To be honest, the material was already a bit dated. When the record was finally released a year later, Filthy Christians' time had definitely passed. They played traditional grindcore/crossover, with short fast songs and grunted vocals. The sound was thin, and the guitars appeared just a little bit out of tune. Further, the songs were somewhat boring, with stereotypical riffs and unexciting arrangements. Frankly, their earlier material was better.

To make things worse, Filthy Christians made the very unwise decision to start the album with a cover of Donna Summer's 1979 disco hit "Hot Stuff," a completely misplaced "joke" in the wake of death metal seriousness. Furthermore, their politically charged lyrics didn't help matters. If the album had been released in the mid-80's it might have worked, but in the early 90's death metal was already beginning to dominate.

*"*Mean *was not quite metal or extreme enough at the time; it was quite rooted in the old hardcore sound. It was okay, but I had one eye on the future of extreme music, which Earache gave birth to. As it happened, the coming death metal scene killed off the popularity of hardcore/metalcore bands like Filthy Christians. The sense of humor in their lyrics dated them quickly."*—DIGBY PEARSON, EARACHE RECORDS

Dark Recollections

At the same time that Entombed were working on their debut, the young guitarist Michael Amott was looking for a record company willing to sign his band Carnage. By now, the band's lineup had strengthened with the addition of former Dismember players Fred Estby and Matti Kärki, and they obviously had something great in them. When former Dismember guitar player David Blomqvist joined after his departure from Entombed, the group appeared

Dark Recollections cover

unstoppable. Soon Amott was offered a deal by his friends at the English label Necrosis, which had already signed Repulsion from Michigan and Cadaver from Norway. The young band went for it. In February 1990, Carnage entered Studio Sunlight to record what would become the second album of pure Swedish death metal.

"It was very easy—too easy I guess! Carnage was nowhere close to ready for an album, but we made one anyway!"—MICHAEL AMOTT, CARNAGE/CARCASS/ARCH ENEMY

"Mike moved up to Stockholm. Johan didn't want to move, so Matti joined us instead. Then David got in on it as well and the whole carousel was spinning like crazy. I hastily booked a studio, and we simply recorded every song we knew."
—FRED ESTBY, DISMEMBER/CARNAGE

Dark Recollections by Carnage was a minor classic in the style Entombed had introduced a couple months earlier. The Sunlight sound de by Tomas Skogsberg is in fact heavier than on the Entombed album, even though the guitar sound isn't as crushing or clear. There is more bass, and the overall feeling is almost as devastating. The riffs are also very similar to Entombed's—the heavy Carcass influence of Carnage's demos is almost gone, save for the gore-drenched lyrics.

There are a couple of weaknesses, like the obvious Entombed imitations done by Matti Kärki and Fred Estby. In fact, they sounded like a watered-down Petrov and Andersson, respectively. But both handle themselves pretty well, limiting the complaints. Carnage's sound may be a second-rate copy of the *Left Hand Path* sound to some extent. But to Carnage's credit, their arrangements are very original. Where Entombed focused on the two-beat,

Estby favoured the punkier D-beat and used a tiny bit more grind. Like the first Entombed album, *Dark Recollections* has a beautiful painting by Dan Seagrave on the cover.

More confusing was that some Dismember songs included on the album sounded much weaker than on the old demos. The sound is undeniably better, but a lot of the feeling is gone. This same problem plagued countless Swedish death metal albums. Within the scene, a common prejudice dictated that "*the first demo is their best work*" by nearly any band. Even though this is surely a cliché, based upon nostalgia, it is also true in many cases—like this one.

Though they surely had much more to offer, Carnage split up after this sole album when Michael Amott was invited to join Carcass. After the release of Carcass' fantastic *Symphonies of Sickness*, nobody in the world would have turned that offer down. So Amott went to the UK, leaving the others behind, bewildered in the ruins of Carnage.

"*Carnage was to a large degree my creation, but we had gone through so many line-up changes that I didn't really recognize what we had started just a couple of years earlier. Things moved very fast after Fred Estby joined, and that was all good, but I felt we'd lost something along the way. I was disappointed with the album recording. it didn't live up to my expectations, my own performance included. Then came the Carcass offer and it was a big deal for me. It was one of those opportunities that are very rare. I grabbed it with both hands and it changed my whole life.*"—MICHAEL AMOTT, CARNAGE/CARCASS/ARCH ENEMY

"*I wasn't really depressed about our split-up, but it was all just so strange. We were the first Swedish death metal band after Entombed to get an album out—and then the band just dies. It was strange.*"—FRED ESTBY, DISMEMBER/CARNAGE

The breakup of Carnage only brought out more energy in Matti Kärki, David Blomqvist, and Fred Estby. They went on to reform Dismember with more intensity than ever. In the years to come, they would produce some of the most brutal Swedish death metal. But the new version of Dismember was yet to come. In 1990, it was up to other bands to hold the banner of Swedish death metal high.

Sumerian Cry

One of the bands at the very front of the scene was Tiamat, the evolved version of Treblinka. They had recently signed to the English label C.M.F.T. to record the album *Sumerian Cry*. This debut had actually been recorded prior to the two massive records by Entombed and Carnage. And this groundbreaking album was in fact the first of the classic Studio Sunlight albums, since it was put on tape during October and November of 1989. But since it wasn't released until April 1990, *Sumerian Cry* might have been a bit overlooked.

"*We actually recorded and paid for the album ourselves; we never even sent out any of the Treblinka singles to labels. But eventually a couple of labels got in touch, since our name had started to be known. Back then, I guess it was actually more important to have some kind of credibility within the scene, rather than producing good music. And since we obviously had the credibility, we soon signed a deal that appeared out of nowhere in the mailbox. We actually got ripped off, since all they did was press and distribute the album. Nevertheless, it was a good way to get the band going.*"—Johan Edlund, Treblinka/Tiamat

Tiamat's album showed a different approach from that of most contemporary Swedish bands. They simply didn't sound anything like Entombed or Carnage —or Merciless, for that matter. Tiamat basically continued along Treblinka's path of dark and mysterious lyrics, retaining the primitive corpse paint and pseudonyms like "Hellslaughter." For

Sumerian Cry

Sumerian Cry inner.

a brief period, they labeled themselves black metal. But by the late 80's, you have to remember that black metal was not yet an established genre; it was just a tag you attached to any band that had satanic undertones in their lyrics.

For one thing, the use of corpse paint was not something new or unique in the Swedish metal scene—look at Damien, Merciless, Morbid, Third Storm, and Grotesque. It appears that when the Swedish death metal scene eventually got tired of this attribute, the Norwegian black metal scene simply picked it up.

"*Both Jörgen and I were very much into the black metal thing. We went to hardware stores to buy nails and black leather paint to construct our own stage props. The other two guys had never really been into that, so it actually felt better after they left.*"—Johan Edlund, Treblinka/Tiamat

The music itself was still obviously death metal, with a meaty sound and Edlund's deep growling vocals. Some people today could argue that the crude performances of the musicians create a weird atmosphere that links Tiamat to later black metal aesthetics. But to my ears any atmosphere that might have been created is ruined by the blues part and the ridiculous cartoon-sampling at the end of the record. In those days, metal was still all about fun.

"Even though our debut album was primitive, it displays very well what we were trying to conjure at that point—a total black metal image. It felt much better with our new band name, and the whole concept was more solid."— JOHAN EDLUND, TREBLINKA/TIAMAT

The crude performances, to be honest, display the band's limited talent. They simply couldn't play more precisely. Further, their song structures didn't feel really thought-through, and this was actually a fairly amateurish album. Today it sounds pretty dated. Still, we loved it, and Tiamat were definitely respected. In fact, I still get the shivers when I listen to their debut. Despite its shortcomings, *Sumerian Cry* is an album with a soul, which is something that most albums nowadays seem to lack. The cover of *Sumerian Cry* was painted by Grotesque's Kristian "Necrolord" Wåhlin, launching his career as a successful artist.

"It was actually by pure coincidence that he made that cover. We met him and Tompa Lindberg on a trip to Norway right after the recording, and we played them a tape of it. Kristian said that he wanted to try to paint something for it, since he had started to try to paint with oil and airbrush."—JOHAN EDLUND, TREBLINKA/TIAMAT

"Besides the lack of studios, there weren't many people who designed album covers at this point. The guys in Tiamat knew that I painted a little, and simply asked me if I wanted to do their cover. I did it with acrylic, and I guess it was the first time I ever painted in color. Too bad the photo of the painting that was used for the album is of awful quality—in reality the painting looked a bit better. The work I did with Tiamat opened the door for me to work with Therion, and after that the offers came in on a regular basis."—KRISTIAN "NECROLORD" WÅHLIN, GROTESQUE/LIERS IN WAIT/DECOLLATION

An album by Tiamat with a cover painting by a guy from Grotesque—it could hardly be more evil at this point in the Swedish scene. In time, Tiamat would become one of the most successful Swedish bands of all, and Wåhlin would be Sweden's most prominent cover artist. *Sumerian Cry* is a historical document of Swedish death metal. Though he did not appear on the album, a final credit is due Stefan Lagergren. To a large extent this album is his masterpiece, since he wrote most of the material. Very few people seem to know this, and it's a shame such a talented composer has fallen into oblivion.

Time Shall Tell

A more orthodox death metal recording from this time was Therion's mini-LP *Time Shall Tell*. This record was released on the local label House of Kicks, run by the guys from the like-named record shop, which had recently started to focus on extreme metal. Since death metal was getting hot, they started to distribute the records and eventually put out their own releases. The simple story of how Therion were signed illustrates the atmosphere of the late 80's:

"They sold our demo tapes in their store, got impressed, and offered to release our mini-LP."—CHRISTOFFER JOHNSSON, THERION

Sometimes it can be as straightforward as that. The recording was done at Studio Sunlight, and the sound is pure Swedish death metal. The music was also very typically Swedish scene, with hammering drums and catchy song structures. The creepy vocals are great, sending chills down the toughest of spines. The sound wasn't that clear, though, and *Time Shall Tell* actually sounded very much like Therion's demo tapes.

Therion mini-LP.

"We chose Sunlight this time, and if I remember it correctly, we had two days in the studio during the autumn of 1989. Tomas Skogsberg knew his business, but the recording was done as if it had been for a demo. Still, the vocals turned out great, and after that there was no more talk about finding another singer. We also printed a dozen tapes from the recording while we waited for the album to be released, which took almost six months. The deal was that they printed 1,000 copies, and we got nothing. But we reasoned that we would have a better chance at a proper contract if we could send records to the labels.

"House of Kicks pressed another 1,000 nevertheless, which led to some arguments when we got signed to Deaf/Peaceville. We didn't want them to sell more of Time Shall Tell, *especially since we didn't get a dime from it. I once threatened to press legal charges if we didn't get paid for the last 1,000 copies, but since House of Kicks was Peaceville's distributor, they threatened back to sabotage the distribution and promotion of our next album. So I had to swallow my pride. Today I see* Time Shall Tell *as our third demo."*—CHRISTOFFER JOHNSSON, THERION

For the Security

Another recording deal came to pass during 1990 when Carbonized attracted the French label Thrash. They began the year with a new demo simply titled *Re-Carbonized.* It followed the path of their first recordings, but in my view suffers from weaker vocals, as Matti Kärki had recently departed the group.

"It was a good band, but I had gotten an offer from Carnage. Carbonized were a bit messy at the time, and some members seemed to behave strangely, so

I just fucked it and went with Carnage. In Carnage things seemed to happen, with recordings and everything."—MATTI KÄRKI, CARNAGE/DISMEMBER

With Kärki out of the picture, Carbonized became a trio, with Lars Rosenberg of Entombed on bass and vocals, Christoffer Johnsson of Therion on guitar and vocals, and Piotr Wawrzeniuk on drums. All three would also eventually be in Therion together. In January 1991, these guys entered Studio Sunlight to record *For the Security*, an album of really intense death metal with loads of grind parts and a fat sound. Everything is tight as hell, and the vocals are really cool and aggressive. The songs themselves might fail to impress, but the intensity of the album is enough to make it successful. Sadly, Carbonized got a bit overlooked. Their small French label couldn't do enough to promote the band, and the members' duties in Entombed and Therion probably took too much of their time. Still, *For the Security* is an album that has withstood the test of time. The grind parts sound especially impressive today. Nevertheless, Carbonized soon faced even more member turmoil and eventually folded.

Incantation

One of the best records of 1990 came from Gothenburg's Grotesque. At the start of the year, the duo of Tomas Lindberg and Kristian Wåhlin found a second guitar player in Alf Svensson. Together with session drummer Thomas Eriksson, the strengthened Grotesque entered Studio Sunlight in August 1990 to record three new songs.

"It was very hard to find a suitable studio during the early years. Either you recorded with crappy equipment at some youth center, or you had to enter a regular studio. Those studios were way too expensive for us, and they also didn't have a clue as to how to handle death metal—just listen to the dreadful result on At the Gates' debut album. Finally, the only option was Sunlight. The price was fair, and Tomas Skogsberg had gradually learned how to deal with extreme metal."—KRISTIAN "NECROLORD" WÅHLIN, GROTESQUE/LIERS IN WAIT/DECOLLATION

The resulting recording was probably one of the best in the Swedish underground to date. Grotesque managed to combine technical skill with rough production, miraculously pleasing at the same time fans of unpolished death metal and fans of well-produced stuff. Unfortunately, problems had started to appear within the band.

"We were very young, and we all had strong opinions about our music. Initially I had been in total control of the music, but when Alf Svensson joined on guitar, things started to change. I thought our Possessed/Morbid Angel thing was getting lost, and that we were becoming a 'regular' death metal band. Not that I disliked Alf or anything; it just wasn't my creation anymore.

I guess the band couldn't take another creative mind, since both Tompa and I were very difficult to argue with. The situation became impossible, so I decided to fold the band."—KRISTIAN "NECROLORD" WÅHLIN, GROTESQUE/LIERS IN WAIT/DECOLLATION

"We were becoming more influenced by psychotic bands such as Atheist, and our ideas started to get strange. Eventually the songs didn't feel like Grotesque anymore, and we thought it would be more honest to split up. I had also started to sing with Infestation, and I guess Kristian didn't like that. Still, I remember the decision to fold Grotesque as mutual."—TOMAS LINDBERG, GROTESQUE/AT THE GATES/DISFEAR

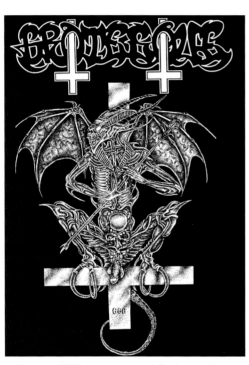

Kristian Wåhlin's great artwork for Incantation

As fate would have it, Grotesque became much more appreciated after their demise. Shortly after they split, the local label/record store Dolores asked if they could release some of their material. Nobody had any objections.

"We knew the guys at Dolores very well, since we bought all our records from them. In fact, their store was probably the main center of the Gothenburg scene, just like Heavy Sound had been in Stockholm. It was a place you hung out at and met people. Of course they could release our stuff if they wanted."—KRISTIAN "NECROLORD" WÅHLIN, GROTESQUE/ LIERS IN WAIT/DECOLLATION

The *Incantation* mini-LP contained three songs from their last demo, plus two tracks from 1989's unreleased *In the Embrace of Evil*. The new recording was obviously the most powerful. The title track "Incantation" stands out as one of the most complex and majestic Swedish death metal songs ever. The many tempo shifts, breaks, and brilliant riffs made Grotesque absolutely unique. They also differed from most other contemporary Swedish death metal bands by openly touting satanic lyrics and imagery—which attracted the growing black metal underground, though the music was definitely death metal.

As the story goes, Tomas Lindberg and Kristian Wåhlin initially both wanted the hilarious pseudonym "Virgin Taker." To avoid a serious fight, they settled for "Goatspell" and "Necrolord" instead. (Original bass player Per Nordgren did snag the name "Virgin Taker" twenty years later, when Grotesque reunited for the release party of the first edition of this book!)

"We were always interested in the imagery. Brazilian bands, especially, had a huge influence on me. I designed the logo with inverted crosses, and we adopted stage names early on. First I called myself 'Vomitlord,' but eventually settled for 'Necrolord.' During shows we wore corpse paint, and Tomas ran around with a big inverted cross.

"Our photo sessions were hilarious. First we needed to choose the right cemetery. Here in Gothenburg there was a particularly cool one with a big sign that said 'Think About Death' at the entrance. Then we borrowed cool clothes from friends—things like leather pants and coats were very hard to find in those days. When we did the photo shoot for the record, the police actually turned up, thinking we were grave desecrators. In one of the pictures you can actually see the police car in the background!"—KRISTIAN "NECROLORD" WÅHLIN, GROTESQUE/LIERS IN WAIT/DECOLLATION

"That fucking leather coat... I thought that was cool for about a week, and naturally we did the photos during this time. I was just a kid trying to express myself, and never realized how ridiculous I looked. Both Nicke Andersson and I were also into some kind of pointy shoes for a while, and of course both Entombed and Grotesque did photos in which they can be spotted. We looked like nerds."
—TOMAS LINDBERG, GROTESQUE/AT THE GATES/DISFEAR

Nevertheless, the leather coat actually started a trend within the scene, and you could see countless kids walking around in similar garb after the pictures of Grotesque were circulated. I'm happy to report that the legendary coat worn by Tomas Lindberg actually came into my possession during the work on this book, as I swept the wardrobe of a friend in search of old death metal memorabilia.

Grotesque differed when it came to production, something that later drew attention from the black metal movement. Most bands that recorded at Studio Sunlight went for that typical massive guitar wall, but Grotesque kept the rawness of the demo period. The primitive and grim sound really suits their music, and none of the clarity of the riffs is lost. The thing that really hits the spot is Tomas Lindberg's absolutely brilliant vocal performance. His voice contains so much feeling and soul that I get the shivers every time I listen to this record. In a way, he combines the cold brutality of David Vincent from Morbid Angel with the tormented screams of Quorthon from Bathory, and it sounds fantastic. *Incantation* remains one of my favorite records; it's completely unique and stunning even today.

"For me, Nihilist was the one in the Swedish scene. But my other choice would be Grotesque; they were unique as well."—DIGBY PEARSON, EARACHE RECORDS

It's a shame Grotesque couldn't keep it together. They were definitely one of the very best Swedish death metal bands and could have gone on to great

Wrath of the Unknown, *one of the best
Swedish demos ever made*

Beyond Redemption *demo*

things. Luckily, the split-up of Grotesque would soon spawn two new groups of
superior quality: Liers in Wait and At the Gates, the latter of which would turn
out to be one of the most innovative and best Swedish death metal bands.

So there are the Swedish death metal albums of 1990. Entombed, Merciless,
Carnage, and Tiamat proved that Swedish death metal was breaking through.
The following two years would be like an endless feast of great albums and
concerts. As a restless teenager, that was a wonderful climate to grow up in.
Almost every week there was a band playing, and you could actually live death
metal. But a lot of other things were going on during 1990, as the underground
saw the release of countless brilliant demos.

The Demo Boom: Stockholm

After these key records were released, new bands started to form everywhere,
while old ones that hadn't gotten a record deal yet continued to make great
demos. Death metal started to become a way of life for many restless teenagers,
and the atmosphere was creative and vital. As usual, most of the best demos of
1990 were made by bands from Stockholm.

Continuing their brutal path, Crematory once again entered Studio Grottan

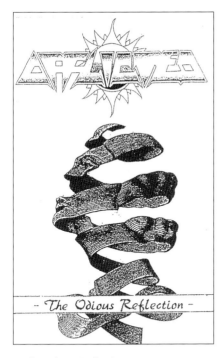

The Odious Reflection

The rebirth of Dismember

to record *Wrath from the Unknown* during the autumn. (They were one of the few bands from Stockholm who didn't switch to Sunlight.) The result is as blistering as their debut. By now they stood out as one of the most original and extreme Swedish death metal bands. Crematory were all about brilliant riffs, effective solos, heavily distorted bass, and great growling vocals. *Wrath of the Unknown* was a masterpiece of brutal and dark death metal.

Another highly original band from Stockholm was Afflicted Convulsion. A couple of months before Crematory went to Studio Grottan, Afflicted Convulsion recorded *Beyond Redemption* in the same studio. This demo tape is almost as brutal as Crematory's, with in-your-face sound and plenty of blast beats. Compared to other Stockholm bands, Afflicted Convulsion sounded pretty chaotic.

"Though it's a bit sloppy, I regard Beyond Redemption *as our first actual demo. It was on this recording that we started to get our ideas together."* —JESPER THORSSON, AFFLICTED

The slight sloppiness was sorted out before their next demo, *The Odious Reflection*. The band also shortened their name to Afflicted in the fall of 1990, and found a new singer in Joakim Bröms. They also chose to try out the famous Studio Sunlight, which resulted in a much more professional sound. They remained brutal, with growling vocals and massive blasts, but also included a lot of punkish D-beats and a more varied style. You could almost sense that the new singer had more than he showed on this recording, but that would come in the future.

"We weren't very satisfied with that demo. As I remember, we were working on our debut 7" at the same time, and I guess we cared a lot more about that recording. We tried to do too much at the same time, but we had used our allowances to pay for the recordings, and we were all about to graduate from school. What I liked about The Odious Reflection *was Joakim Bröms' vocals.*

"The fact is, we did one test recording just after he joined the band, and that recording sounded so much better than either the demo or the 7". The two songs on the test-recording, "Consumed in Flames" and "In Years to Come," were supposed to be released on a 7", but sadly, that never happened."—JOACIM CARLSSON, GENERAL SURGERY/AFFLICTED/FACE DOWN

Nineteen-ninety also saw the glorious comeback of Dismember, risen from the ashes of Carnage in a very hasty decision.

"Shortly after the break up of Carnage, we were supposed to do a radio interview with some guy in Rinkeby about Carnage. We went there and explained that we had reformed Dismember and that Carnage was no more. It was right outside the radio studio that we decided it. Fred simply asked us if we were in, and we didn't hesitate. Then we did the interview and went straight to work on new material."—MATTI KÄRKI, CARNAGE/DISMEMBER

Dismember's comeback demo, *Reborn in Blasphemy*, was soon recorded with Tomas Skogsberg at Studio Sunlight, and the result is just fantastic. The songs are so powerful and the sound is absolutely massive. Matti Kärki probably pulled off the best vocal performance of his career, which adds to the overall feeling of a masterpiece. It could be argued that Dismember sounded too much like Entombed, but I always thought that they had something unique. There was some kind of insane intensity to Dismember that Entombed in all their grace strangely seemed to lack. After this comeback demo, there was no doubt that Dismember would become one of the leading bands of the Swedish scene.

"Compared to the first two Dismember demos, this was a whole different affair. We got along very well with Tomas Skogsberg. Unlike all other engineers at the time, Skogsberg really tried to understand and improve the music, even though he was in no way a metalhead himself. He was a professional, and helped us to sound as good as possible."—FRED ESTBY, DISMEMBER/CARNAGE

Another band that would soon join the biggest names in Swedish death metal was Unleashed. The band was founded late in 1989 when Johnny Hedlund split with the rest of Nihilist and hooked up with former Dismember singer Robert Sennebäck. Unleashed could be seen as the last first-generation, or the first second-generation, death metal band in Sweden.

"We were just a bunch of pals who thought that we should start to play the meanest, darkest shit imaginable. We decided on the spot that we should record a demo, and just play as hard as possible. That's how it started. Anders, Fredrik,

Clockwise from top left: Unleashed's great debut demo;

... Revenge;

Exhumed—Obscurity;

flyer for General Surgery's first demo

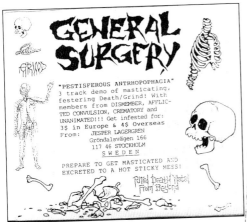

Robban, and I."—JOHNNY HEDLUND, NIHILIST/UNLEASHED

The new band's debut demo *The Utter Dark* was recorded on March 17 and 18 at Kuben Studios, and it was just great. The heavy sound was somewhat similar to Crematory and Therion, but Unleashed definitely had something of their own. One of the strongest points is the voice of Robert Sennebäck, who sang in the style he developed in Dismember. The straightforward death metal on their debut demo is a good lesson in intensity. The sound might be a bit muddy, but Unleashed was onto something great.

"*Compared to Nihilist, we worked a lot differently in the studio. We worked more like a group, and everybody was involved in decisions. That was not the case in Nihilist. I think band democracy is important to make everybody feel that there is a future in the band.*"—JOHNNY HEDLUND, NIHILIST/UNLEASHED

Unleashed entered Kuben Studios for a second time during the last two days of September 1990. Continuing on their speedy path, ...*Revenge* contained all the energy of the first demo, but the sound had been cleaned up since their last visit. The songs are generally hammered out in a furious two-beat, with some cool doomy parts added for good measure. Unleashed really didn't sound like other Swedish death metal bands, and they faced a bright future. Before long they found themselves on Century Media, a sign of how much attention Swedish death metal had gained.

"*They contacted us and wanted to send us material from their other bands to show what they could do for us. We had three other labels after us as well, but we settled on Century Media.*"—JOHNNY HEDLUND, NIHILIST/UNLEASHED

After these two demos, singer Robert Sennebäck quit Unleashed to rejoin his old comrades in Dismember as a guitarist. Unleashed quickly adapted to their new situation, with Johnny Hedlund taking over the vocals as the band headed toward greatness.

One of the most intense bands during this creative period of Swedish death metal was General Surgery. Although always kind of a side project involving members of various Stockholm bands, they delivered the goods. Their debut, *Pestisferous Antrhopophagia*, was recorded on April 24 and features wildly insane gore-grind in the vein of Carcass. During this early period of the band, the bass was handled by none other than Matti Kärki, singer of Carnage and Dismember. General Surgery might be a parenthesis in the Swedish death metal history, but a fucking cool one. They are still going today with a completely new lineup.

"*I started General Surgery out of pure love for Carcass. The band was only meant to copy Carcass 100 percent. The name of the band was taken from the book that Carcass used to get the obscene pictures for their first album cover. We were a tribute band. We just wanted to play like Carcass.*"—MATTI KÄRKI, CARNAGE/DISMEMBER

As General Surgery came into being, a second generation of death metal bands was incubating in the Swedish capital. Among the first of these Stockholm-based bands was Exhumed, who recorded their *Obscurity* demo on October 23. They followed the path of Crematory and Carbonized, spiced up with some guttural and heavily delayed vocals that sound pretty cool! The band was rather primitive at this stage, though, which shows in the faster parts, which aren't very tight. They tended to focus on mid-tempo parts, which can get a bit annoying in the end. But Exhumed had some talent, and would go on to greater things after they later transformed into Morpheus.

Another interesting band from Stockholm, Necrophobic, released a demo of considerable quality in 1990 titled *Slow Asphyxiation*. All in all, this is a pretty straightforward death metal recording, with relentlessly hammering two-beat drums and growling vocals. The structures are in the vein of Nihilist/Dismember, where "bee-swarm" riffs interact with open chord choruses. But some glimpses of guitarist David Parland's talent appear here and there through soulful melodies. His genius as a guitar player has been sadly neglected over the years. After he started Dark Funeral under the pseudonym Blackmoon, he received more notice for making extreme statements in the media than for his guitar work. Even though Necrophobic had immense power, their albums lacked something. But at one point they were one of the most promising newcomers of the Swedish death metal scene.

In the northern Stockholm suburb of Rönninge, Desultory began their journey in 1989. On June 3–4, 1990, they went into Studio Sunlight to record their debut demo, *From Beyond*. One might expect yet another typical fat death metal production, but Desultory actually tried to do something creative. Instead of looking at the likes of Entombed and Dismember, they took their inspirations from Bay Area thrash metal and spiced it up with harsh vocals. With their regularly tuned guitars and thrashy down-pick riffs, Desultory sounded like no other Swedish death metal band. They achieved a much clearer sound in Sunlight than any band produced there before.

Desultory were indeed active during their first year, and on August 8–10, 1990, they again entered Studio Sunlight. The *Death Unfolds* demo basically follows the style of their debut, even though the guitar sound might be a little more death metal–inspired. The songs are still basic thrash compositions, and to me the group's biggest disadvantage is the riffs. Though they might have felt a bit fresh back then, they are simply too basic and unexciting. Compared to what At the Gates did on their 1995 album *Slaughter of the Soul,* you see what I mean. Still, Desultory was welcomed as a fresh breeze of air in 1990.

A more traditional Stockholm death metal band, Lobotomy, was founded during 1990. The group emerged from the same Kista-gang that birthed Alex Hellid and Leif Cuzner. Founding member Daniel Strachal had actually been in the pre-Nihilist band Brainwarp together with Hellid, Cuzner, and Nicke

FROM BEYOND

Clockwise from top: Desultory—
From Beyond;
flyer for Desultory's second demo;
Excruciate demo;
When Death Draws Near

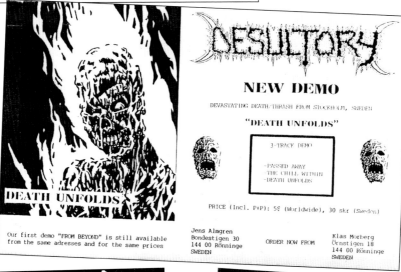

DESULTORY

NEW DEMO

DEVASTATING DEATH/THRASH FROM STOCKHOLM, SWEDEN

"DEATH UNFOLDS"

3-TRACK DEMO

-PASSED AWAY
-THE CHILL WITHIN
-DEATH UNFOLDS

PRICE (Incl. P+P): 5$ (Worldwide), 30 skr (Sweden)

Our first demo "FROM BEYOND" is still available
from the same adresses and for the same prices

Jens Almgren
Bondestigen 30
144 00 Rönninge   ORDER NOW FROM
SWEDEN

Klas Morberg
Örnstigen 18
144 00 Rönninge
SWEDEN

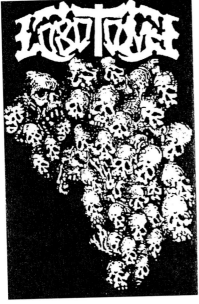

MUTILATION OF THE PAST

Andersson. Lobotomy's debut demo, *When Death Draws Near*, was recorded on November 24 and 25 at Studio Sunlight, and possessed that typical fat and clear Stockholm death metal sound—almost. On this demo you can actually hear how the Sunlight sound was becoming standardized, too clear, and starting to lack soul. But Lobotomy's main problem was that they were void of anything unique. The riffs and arrangements are like a watered-down Unleashed, and it all feels a bit halfhearted. On the plus side are Lars Jelleryd's deep vocals, but overall this demo hinted that the quality of Stockholm's death metal scene was stagnating. *When Death Draws Near* is a decent demo, nothing more.

Finally, Excruciate formed in Upplands Väsby in 1989. The group quickly rose to integral status within the Stockholm death metal scene, and in April 1990 they recorded a demo. Breaking with tradition, Excruciate traveled to You Are Studio in Lübeck, Germany, to produce *Mutilation of the Past*. The result is intense and tight, with several cool riffs, numerous tempo changes, and some good deep growls provided by session vocalist Christoffer Johnsson of Therion. All they lacked were good songs and originality. Compared to established bands they sounded pretty shallow. Though they eventually became lost in the competition, Excruciate had quite a reputation in the early 90's.

The Demo Boom: Nationally

Outside of Stockholm, many creative bands surfaced during 1990. Finspång's Pan-Thy-Monium recorded their debut demo ...*Dawn* at MAPS Studio in July. The demo combined atmospheric and melancholic death metal with ghostly guttural vocals, and soon attracted the French label Osmose Productions. The most interesting fact about Pan-Thy-Monium might be that the band featured Dan Swanö on guitar as well as Benny Larsson on drums. Both had already established another band that would later be one of Sweden's finest, Edge of Sanity.

"Edge of Sanity started out in November 1989 as one of countless 'weekend projects' in Finspång. Our first rehearsal ever was recorded as Euthanasia. The other guys in the band came from a punk background, and I was a metalhead. The only thing we had in common was that we were all very curious about playing death metal."—DAN SWANÖ, EDGE OF SANITY/ UNISOUND

Swanö sent one of their rehearsal tapes to the major UK metal magazine *Kerrang!*. After their review, suddenly letters started to appear from all around the world. Edge of Sanity didn't even exist as a regular band—it was just a bunch of beer-drinking kids fooling around on a few weekends.

"I realized that we should make a serious band out of Edge of Sanity when the letters started to drop in. Initially, that was a problem, since all of

us regarded other projects as our main bands. We sat down and set out some guidelines for our music, which was basically that it should be anti-thrash, melodic, and a bit complicated. Suddenly, we were a real band. "—DAN SWANÖ, EDGE OF SANITY/UNISOUND

In the summer of 1990, Edge of Sanity made a proper demo, *Kur-Nu-Gi-A*. Although the band developed a lot over the years, it was obvious from the start that they could deliver nicely structured and well-produced death metal, with powerful vocals, killer riffs, and a steady drummer. As it turned out, *Kur-Nu-Gi-A* was their only proper demo, as they earned a contract with Black Mark almost instantly.

"*We really tried to make that demo as professional as possible, with a color sleeve and proper printing. Further, we spread loads of demos and flyers to promote ourselves. All that work brought a massive response, and we sold loads of that tape. We also started to get a lot of contacts with other bands, and eventually Börje Forsberg called me up and signed us.*" —DAN SWANÖ, EDGE OF SANITY/UNISOUND

Within a few months, Edge of Sanity would be one of the leaders of the second generation of Swedish death metal. Another band that should have been among the leaders was Nirvana 2002. During 1990, this deadly trio from Edsbyn finally recorded a proper demo, as they entered Studio Sunlight and made *Mourning*. Expenses were covered by Studiofrämjandet—a municipal program that was supposed to help out youngsters with different projects, but between 1989 and 1991 they seemed mainly to finance death metal recordings!

"*Mourning contained all the classic ingredients of a Swedish death metal demo: it was recorded in Sunlight, Nicke and Uffe produced it, I used Uffe's guitar and amplifier—and Studiofrämjandet paid for it all!*"—ORVAR SÄFSTRÖM, NIRVANA 2002

Nirvana 2002 actually used the exact same equipment and settings as Entombed on *Left Hand Path*, as you can tell when listening to the result. In fact, not even Entombed ever managed to get this ultra-brutal sound again. Among the lost jewels of Swedish death metal, *Mourning* is definitely a sacred treasure.

Afterwards, Nirvana 2002 did a primitive recording of the song "The Awakening of..." with fills on the first riff instead of double kick-drum. Then the full-fledged follow-up to the great *Mourning* was *Disembodied Spirits*, recorded in Studio Edsbyn by Jasse Karsbo. With *Disembodied Spirits*, Nirvana 2002 continued their journey in the footsteps of Entombed and Dismember, with great death metal driven by Orvar Säfström's catchy riffs and massive vocals. *Disembodied Spirits* is probably the best-known Nirvana 2002 demo, partly since it is the only one with a cover. In fact, I still listen to it on a regular basis. Besides, Fredrik Holmgren of CBR officially released the tape. The last song, "The Awakening of...," also surfaced on Jörgen Sigfridsson's compilation 7" *Is*

This Heavy or What? II.

"*The recording we did in Edsbyn was very primitive compared to the one at Sunlight. The equipment was crap, and you couldn't even do a 'punch-in' overdub. I guess the demo turned out okay, anyway, keeping all the problems in mind.*"—ORVAR SÄFSTRÖM, NIRVANA 2002

After this, Nirvana 2002 recorded two more songs in Studio Sunlight for a boxset of 7" singles CBR planned to release, but nothing came of it. When drummer Erik Qvick moved to Uppsala to study his instrument, the band folded before they even made a live appearance. Nowadays Quick is a respected drum instructor in Reykjavík, Iceland—he is probably the most skilled musician ever to crawl out of the Swedish death metal scene.

Nirvana 2002 were one of the greatest bands of the Swedish death metal movement, and it's a shame that they never made it. Orvar Säfström would still get his fifteen minutes of death metal fame, though, as he joined Entombed as a session singer. Säfström later made a nice life for himself as a film critic, and until recently he hosted a film program on national Swedish television. (If you ever attended film festivals in Cannes or Venice and saw a guy with long hair and huge sideburns—it was probably him!)

"*The band just faded during 1991, and suddenly it was gone. We were actually dealing with a few labels, such as Necrosis, but nothing came of it. In hindsight I am glad—it would have been a disaster if we had signed a seven-album deal with Nuclear Blast or something like that.*"—ORVAR SÄFSTRÖM, NIRVANA 2002

Ending this incomplete survey of death metal demos released in Sweden until 1991, among many good demos I have left out are Obscene's *Grotesque Experience* and Suffer's *Manifestion of God*. There are just too many good ones to cover them all completely. Let us leave the demos and see how Fredrik Holmgren at CBR came to put some Swedish death metal out on 7" vinyl singles.

Singles of Death

By 1990, Fredrik Holmgren and CBR were at the forefront of Swedish record labels. After his many punk releases, Holmgren's first foray into metal came with the crossover band Krixhjälters. He released two albums with them before they transformed into the thrash band Omnitron in 1989. But Omnitron's debut album the following year offered only a taste of the brutality to come. CBR also released two pure death metal singles during 1990: Tiamat's *A Winter Shadow* and Unleashed's *...Revenge*. The Unleashed 7" was actually a vinyl release of their demo, but still showed CBR's intentions. Of course Holmgren couldn't keep a band like Unleashed, and the group was soon signed to Century Media, who immediately released the *And the Laughter Has Died* 7".

"I never intended to start releasing death metal albums; I was still mainly into hardcore at heart. The reason I did those 7" singles was basically that the bands wanted them, and since I had the distribution going, I was just glad to help them."
—FREDRIK HOLMGREN, CBR

Fredrik Holmgren seemed to be a restless person prone to exploring new things instead of sticking with what worked commercially. An early attempt to open a record store under the atrocious name Lollipop failed, and right behind him came others who stepped in and took advantage of the opportunity.

CBR soon lost its position as the number one distributor of extreme metal in Sweden to a guy named Calle von Scheven, who had started the distribution company House of Kicks back in 1986. He initially didn't seem to understand anything about extreme metal, but he picked up the ball when CBR fumbled.

"The guys at House of Kicks used to sell the records I distributed, but after a while they took over from me. They were older, smarter, and much more business-minded, while I was still mainly a punk. Their shop worked a hell of a lot better than mine. Eventually, I went to work for their distribution arm when they changed their name to Sound Pollution."—FREDRIK HOLMGREN, CBR

Unlike Holmgren, Calle von Scheven very successfully started a record store. Soon House of Kicks even took over Heavy Sound's position as the number one record store and meeting place for death metal youngsters in Stockholm. Following CBR's example, House of Kicks also started to release records in 1990, starting with Therion's mini-LP *Time Shall Tell*. The company soon sailed up as Sweden's number one distributor of extreme metal.

It's important to note that these guys were basically in it for commercial reasons. They never actually discovered or pushed anything themselves; they just distributed it and cashed in. Later, the very same guys would get their hands on No Fashion Records, under dubious circumstances.

By 1991, the Swedish death metal scene was alive and kicking in every aspect, and it continued to dominate and expand until 1993. During these two years, death metal came to everyone's attention in Sweden, and the whole phenomenon just exploded. These two years were also the end of my teens, and I couldn't have asked for a better, more intense climate to finish off my youth.

MAILORDER

| NIHILIST "DROWNED" 7" $5 | UNLEASHED "..REVENGE" 7"/DEMO (LTD AS 7") $5/$4 | ENTOMBED "DROWNED" DEMO $4 | DISMEMBER "REBORN IN BLASPHEMY" DEMO $4 |

POSTAGE: 1$ EACH ITEM

CBR

HARD RAW FAST

CBR RECORDS
BOX 6038
126 06 HÄGERSTEN
SWEDEN

Clockwise from top left:
Classic releases from CBR;
House of Kicks ad;
A Winter Shadow—7" cover;
A Winter Shadow—demo cover

Side A – A Winter Shadow
Side B – Ancient Entity

Tiamat are:
Hellslaughter – Guitar & Lead vocals
Juck – Bass
A.D. Lord – Lead Guitar
Oakbeach – Drums

Acoustic guitars by Hellslaughter,
A.D. Lord & Oakbeach.
Keyboard by Oakbeach & A.D. Lord.

Recorded and mixed at Sunlight Studio
the 9th & 10th of Nov. 90.
Produced and mixed by Tiamat.
Engineered by Thomas Skogsberg.
Cover art by Kristian Whålen.

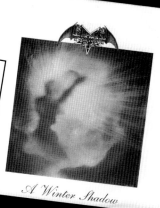

A Winter Shadow

This page, clockwise from top:
Pan-Thy-Monium demo;

flyer for Immortal Rehearsals;

Disembodied Spirits—the only Nirvana 2002
demo that actually has a cover

Facing page, clockwise from top:
Is This Heavy or What? II comp 7"
(with Nirvana 2002);

Suffer demo;

Obscene demo

-GROTESQUE EXPERIENCE-

Chapter Six:
The Reigning Years of
Swedish Death Metal

"I AM SUPREME – SPAWNED
BY THE STRONGEST FORCE
I AM UNCHALLENGED
I AM OVERLORD"

—LIERS IN WAIT, "OVERLORD"

From top: Entombed live;

Anders Schultz of Unleashed surrounded by Entombed in a drunken tour bus extravaganza;

Entombed, looking grim and evil

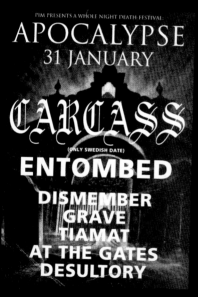

Clockwise from top left: Close-Up
magazine #1. Nice headline;

Poster for Bergslagsrocken 1993;

Signed poster for Sacred Reich's gig in
Fagersta;

Carcass performing with the elite of
Swedish death metal

he years 1991 to 1993 were massive for Swedish death metal. Great albums were released on a regular basis, an incredible number of new bands started to produce demos, and the production of fanzines just exploded. Several bands embarked on international tours, and opportunities to play in Sweden increased dramatically. An innocent teenage movement had suddenly become one of the most exciting and powerful musical genres around. The movement worked commercially, too, as records sold like crazy. The heyday of Swedish death metal had arrived.

"The scene got bigger with each year, and continued to do so until the second wave of black metal broke through somewhere in 1993. People started to get a good view of the scene. Since you traded demos at gigs, you got to know a lot of people, and discovered new bands. By 1991 there were easily hundreds of people who were really active within the scene with bands, fanzines, gig bookings, etc." —Jesper Thorsson, Afflicted

Fanzine editors were definitely busy in 1991. New 'zines like *Putrefaction Mag, Expository Mag, Hymen, Mould Mag, Fenzine, Hypnosia, Slimy Scum, Never Believe, Suffozine,* and many others turned up everywhere. It seemed virtually everybody had their own fanzine for a while, and naturally, most of them were not very carefully made. Personally, I enjoyed them all, but some guys started to get annoyed.

"I was getting pissed off at all the 'zines around. The editors couldn't spell, they couldn't write, the questions stank, and the layouts sucked. I wanted to show everybody that I could do it better. I also wanted to get the music I loved out to more people than I could with my radio program and concerts. So I started Close-Up *together with my friend Christian Carlquist."*—Robban Becirovic, Close-Up Magazine

Close-Up had already been initiated by Carlquist, who had been working on the fanzine *Inzinerator* with Dan Swanö since 1989. Their ambition was to make a Swedish fanzine that could match *Slayer Mag,* with color printing and a professional layout. But as with so many other 'zines, *Inzinerator* folded after just one issue. Becirovic's energy and dedication took the 'zine concept to the next level.

"The first issue was made when I was in military service, and I wrote most of it by hand. Luckily, we had a friend whose dad worked at a printing firm, so we snuck in there on weekends to transfer it to a computer. I guess we were the first Swedish 'zine that used a computer. We didn't know much about how to handle it, though. We printed out every article separately and pasted the fanzine together by hand."—Robban Becirovic, Close-Up Magazine

Close-Up quickly gained attention as one of Sweden's best and most professional fanzines. Before long everybody wanted to be featured in *Close-Up.* Many times it was also the first to cover new and exiting things. Its articles about Mayhem and Burzum in fact changed the whole Swedish scene. Since 1991, *Close-Up* has grown constantly, gradually recruiting the best writers from other 'zines, such as Martin Carlsson from *Megalomania/Candour*, Mikael Sörling from *Profitblaskan*, Patric Cronberg from *To the Death*, and Jonas Granvik from *Metal Wire*. Other fanzines came and went, but *Close-Up* eventually developed into a regular magazine.

During 1991, death metal started sneaking into television and the mainstream press. Entombed in particular were featured everywhere, as the hungry media sensationalized this crazy new genre. Sweden's biggest rock festival, Hultsfred, jumped on the bandwagon, incorporating extreme bands such as Entombed on their bill. But the concert organizer who really made death metal his main focus during 1991 was Peter Ahlqvist. Up until this year, Bergslagsrocken had been a festival of all kinds of alternative music, from indie pop to gore-grind. But the festival in 1991 featured exclusively death, thrash, and crust bands.

"Many times we had to book a bit more mainstream-oriented bands to satisfy the other participants in [the culture organization] Tid Är Musik, but it was always our extreme shows that worked best. So they pretty much let us do what we wanted after a while. In 1991, we only brought extreme bands to Bergslagsrocken. Death metal was finally hot and 'hip.' Entombed, especially, got a lot of attention, and they were actually acclaimed in the mainstream media by traditional music journalists."—PETER AHLQVIST, UPROAR/TID ÄR MUSIK/ BURNING HEART

Showcasing the musical health of the scene, CBR Records released the compilation album *Projections of a Stained Mind* in 1991. Fredrik Holmgren's label had been increasingly involved in the death metal scene, and now presented the most promising Swedish bands on vinyl. This allowed people everywhere to glimpse of the scene's quality and power. Apart from established bands like Entombed, Merciless, Therion, and Grotesque, the album also brought out upcoming titans Dismember and Unleashed, plus underground acts Nirvana 2002, House of Usher, Skull and Chronic Decay —not to mention the notorious Norwegian black metal band Mayhem.

"It was actually Jens Näsström [ex-Morbid, Skull] who put the record together; I just released it. I guess I was starting to drift away from death metal a bit already at this point."—FREDRIK HOLMGREN, CBR RECORDS

The album opens with Entombed's "Forsaken," definitely among the highlights of the compilation. It's one of Entombed's best tracks ever, so it's a shame they never recorded it under better circumstances. The sound is a muddy and grungy mess, but great anyway. Great performances are also delivered by Therion, Grotesque, and Merciless. Today it's especially refreshing to hear how brutal Therion were then. Among the bands that hadn't previously made any albums, Unleashed, Nirvana 2002, and Dismember impressed the most. In fact,

Dismember's "Sickening Art" and Nirvana 2002's "Mourning" are the only songs on the album that fully capture the massive Sunlight sound, as all the other tracks have demo-style productions.

Failing to impress to any great extent were the Eskilstuna bands House of Usher and Chronic Decay. Both were competent, but couldn't compete. The outsiders Mayhem, and especially Skull, also felt a bit out of place. Mayhem surely deliver some great stuff, and Ohlin's vocals are fantastic. But when you compare them to Grotesque, they simply fail. Grotesque sounded much more evil and raw. Skull, on the other hand, presented some strange form of thrash/death/punk that seemed completely misplaced. They caused no impact at all on the future, and were best regarded as an echo from the past. They were pretty respected within the scene at the time, though, as their bass player, Jens Näsström, used to play in Morbid.

This compilation presented most of the premier bands of the Swedish scene, but didn't offer much of the fat Sunlight sound that would be the trademark of Swedish death metal over the next years. As mentioned, Dismember and Nirvana 2002 were the only bands that didn't have a muddy, demo-like sound. Though the rawness of the album still sounds vital, some other releases did a better job of defining Swedish death metal in 1991.

Entombed and Earache

In late 1990, Entombed were on the verge of becoming international metal stars. Their debut album sold like crazy, and the band had gone on its first tours. Expectations for their second album were sky high, and Entombed were preparing to record an EP and start a new tour in early 1991. They had found a steady bass player in Lars Rosenberg, and everything looked great. Then the unexpected happened. During an unfortunate New Year's Eve party, Nicke Andersson got so upset with their singer L.G. Petrov that he called him the next morning and told him he was out of the band.

"L.G. was sacked because I thought he was hitting on my girlfriend at the time. It wasn't thought through at all, but I got mad as hell with him and simply told him to fuck off."—Nicke Andersson, Nihilist/Entombed

"I remember L.G. calling me on a Sunday evening in tears, explaining that he had been kicked out of the band. I didn't understand anything. I called Nicke to see what was going on, but he said that this was the way it was going to be. If we weren't cool with it, we could leave as well. It was a personal thing between them, and I don't think anyone else really know what happened. It was Nicke's band and his decision, but it was a stupid thing to do."—Uffe Cederlund, Morbid/Nihilist/Entombed/Disfear

As 1991 came along, Entombed had no lead singer. The upcoming studio recording and the tour were already booked, so the band really had to find a replacement within days. The guys thought instantly of their friend Orvar Säfström from Nirvana 2002, and he was offered the job temporarily.

"Uffe called me out of the blue and told me that they had to record an EP and do a tour across Europe in the spring, and asked me if I could stand in as vocalist. Since Entombed was the coolest band in the world at that point, it was impossible to turn that offer down. So, for half a year, I was in."—ORVAR SÄFSTRÖM, NIRVANA 2002

Orvar went down to Stockholm and started to rehearse with Entombed. In February the beleaguered band entered Studio Sunlight to record *Crawl*, also the first Entombed recording for bass player Lars Rosenberg.

"That recording was just horrible to do. Nicke was completely hung over and I didn't know how to sing the songs. Nicke actually stood next to me and gave me signs when I was supposed to sing. Awful."—ORVAR SÄFSTRÖM, NIRVANA 2002

The resulting EP has a crude, almost demo-like, sound and possesses none of the power of *Left Hand Path*. Still, it's a very brutal and dirty recording with a lot of atmosphere to it. Orvar Säfström sounds pretty soulful, even if you can tell that he was not too rehearsed. In retrospect, *Crawl* says a lot about the Swedish death metal scene in 1991. The song "Forsaken" remains one of Entombed's finest, and I would give anything to hear that with the *Left Hand Path* sound. After the recording of *Crawl*, Entombed hit the road for a two-week European tour, with Dutch act Asphyx opening.

Entombed—ready to take on the world

"Unlike the recording, the tour was a wonderful experience. It was packed everywhere, and the crowds just went crazy. I think we were one of the first death metal bands to play in East Germany, and people were just dying to see us. I also did a festival gig with Entombed in the summer, but then I focused on Nirvana 2002... though we soon folded."—ORVAR SÄFSTRÖM, NIRVANA 2002

Eventually, Entombed recruited former Carnage bass player Johnny Dordevic as their new singer. In the summer of 1991, it came time for the reigning kings of the scene to enter the studio—Sunlight, of course—to record their eagerly awaited second album, *Clandestine*. This time around, Entombed really concentrated on making a brutal yet clear-sounding album. The results are mixed. In its favor is the really massive, fat, and clean production. The clarity is obtained mainly by cranking the mid-range knobs to the max on all the guitars, and it really accents the riffs. But the mid-range sound is also a problem, because some aggression is obviously lost. Don't get me wrong, it sounds pretty good; it just wasn't as brutal. The lame vocal performance also really weakens the album. Johnny Dordevic didn't work out as a singer, so Nicke decided to grunt on the album himself—although they tried to keep it a secret at the time, and claimed that Dordevic was actually singing. This idea proved unwise, and gives the whole album a somewhat bitter flavor. (Though Johnny Dordevic actually sings one vocal line on *Clandestine*—can you spot it?)

"I brought Johnny into the band mainly because he was a good friend. In retrospect, I probably should have checked to see whether he could sing first. Or, better, I should never have sacked L.G. in the first place. I was just young and impulsive. That's all I can say."—NICKE ANDERSSON, NIHILIST/ENTOMBED

On the positive side are the songs, which are as great as ever. Fantastic riffs blend together in complex compositions that make you bang your head instinctively. The arrangements are also very cool and effective, with great breaks and stops here and there. But the best thing about *Clandestine* is the massive drum performance of Nicke Andersson. All his fills and patterns are amazing. He alone makes this record rock like nothing else in the world of death metal. If this album had been recorded with a slightly more brutal sound and L.G. Petrov on vocals, it might have been one of the best Swedish death metal albums of all time. As it turned out, it isn't—but it's greater than most!

"To me, the main flaw on Clandestine *is not my awful vocals or the sound, but the song structures. We were heavily influenced by Atheist at the time, and wanted to create something similar with complex and technical songs. Truthfully, we really couldn't play those songs very well. When I look back at all the Entombed records, I think this one and* Same Difference *are the two worst. With a different singer, a slightly slower tempo, and a few riffs cut out, it would probably have turned out much better."*—NICKE ANDERSSON, NIHILIST/ENTOMBED

"That album wasn't fun to record. I think Nicke was fed up with death metal already at that point, and he made the album too complicated and strange just to amuse himself. Some parts are cool, but it just isn't Entombed. And the vocals sucked."—UFFE CEDERLUND, MORBID/NIHILIST/ENTOMBED/DISFEAR

Despite the flaws of *Clandestine*, you have to remember that every Entombed release was a milestone for the Swedish death metal scene at this point. They were just one notch above every other band out there. After the recording of *Clandestine*, Entombed played at the big rock festival in Hultsfred, the first gig ever as a singer for Johnny Dordevic. That Hultsfred appearance was also Entombed's major break in Sweden. Up until this point they had been huge in the underground, but now they became the darlings of the mainstream press. Everybody was suddenly excited about this incredible and violent band, and for a long time they were all over the Swedish media. Entombed also toured in Sweden in 1991—the first Swedish tour for a homegrown death metal band. Peter Ahlqvist made it happen.

"Entombed had become huge, and it was such a good time hanging around with them on that tour. Apart from Örnsköldsvik [an utterly boring and worthless place in the north of Sweden, mostly known for breeding ice hockey players like Peter Forsberg], all gigs were very well attended and you could really feel that the Swedish scene had exploded. And Entombed ruled that scene."—PETER AHLQVIST, UPROAR/TID ÄR MUSIK/BURNING HEART

"Entombed were by far the most important band in the Swedish scene. Everything they did had a huge impact. A lot of copying and jealousy was going on."—FREDRIK HOLMGREN, CBR RECORDS

"Clandestine was our peak commercially, but the band was in a state of chaos during this time. I often had to sing during tours, since we really hadn't any singer. Strangely, hardly anyone seemed to notice or care."—UFFE CEDERLUND, MORBID/NIHILIST/ENTOMBED/DISFEAR

Dismember and Nuclear Blast

At this point, Earache was by far the leading death metal record label internationally, with a roster including Morbid Angel, Napalm Death, Carcass, and Bolt Thrower. After the release of Entombed's debut, *Left Hand Path*, Earache had the chance to sign just about any band out there. But as I have pointed out before, they didn't sign any other Swedish band during the early 90's. And where Earache hesitated, loads of other labels soon entered the market.

One growing label looking into death metal was Germany's Nuclear Blast, founded in Donzdorf by Markus Steiger in 1987. Initially Steiger focused on obscure and commercially hopeless hardcore punk releases, but by 1990 he had discovered death metal. For a long time the label remained far behind Earache, but eventually Nuclear Blast became one of the most successful metal labels in the world. Among their early key signings were Pungent Stench from Austria, Righteous Pigs from Las Vegas, and the young Swedish band Dismember. Dismember's debut, *Like an Ever Flowing Stream*, was probably the most important Swedish death metal album of 1991.

"*I was very happy when I first heard the first Dismember album. I loved it, and I was very relieved to see that Fred and company continued to make fantastic death metal, which in my opinion by far eclipsed what we had done together in Carnage.*" —MICHAEL AMOTT, CARNAGE/CARCASS/ARCH ENEMY

The circumstances around Dismember landing their record deal illustrate how eager Nuclear Blast was to get a piece of the death metal action.

"*It was a bit funny. We had just recorded* Reborn in Blasphemy *but didn't have any covers made yet. At the same time, we had a gig in Sala, so we brought a few demos with us. Present at the gig was a certain Dave Rotten from Spain, who bought one of them. Apparently he was on some trip around Europe at the time, and played the demo for Marcus Steiger at Nuclear Blast when he visited them. And they just went mad about it. Somehow they got my number from Uffe in Entombed, but when they called me I was just puzzled and gave them Fred's number instead so he could sort things out.*" —MATTI KÄRKI, CARNAGE/DISMEMBER

"*The funny thing was that we had written to Peaceville, Roadrunner, and Earache before we made the demo. We informed them that we were the continuation of Carnage, and that we could send them a demo. But none of them were interested. They didn't even want to listen to the demo!*" —FRED ESTBY, DISMEMBER/CARNAGE

Dismember's similarity to Entombed soon started to pay off. People who loved Entombed loved Dismember as well. But Dismember also had unique, over-the-top aggression that Entombed lacked after *Left Hand Path*. Dismember remained extremely brutal, with songs that were straightforward in an almost punk fashion. The guitar sound is as intense as Entombed's, and the production is one of the best examples of the Sunlight sound. This debut is probably one of the most brutal Swedish death metal albums. Some of us missed Matti Kärki's vocal style from Dismember's demo, and felt a bit let down by his new L.G.-inspired touches. Nevertheless, we all loved this piece of vinyl—it's just great.

"*After we completed the lineup with Rickard and Robban, we rehearsed about five days a week. We were very well prepared when we went into the studio in March 1991, so everything went smoothly during the twelve days we had. It all turned out great, and Nuclear Blast was as excited as we were with the result. After the release, everything just exploded.*" —FRED ESTBY, DISMEMBER/CARNAGE

The lyrical content of *Like an Ever Flowing Stream* proved very offensive, which soon gave Dismember an unimaginable media boost. The saga started when British customs opened a package from Nuclear Blast and discovered the naughty Dismember album inside. They were shocked by song titles like "Soon

Tjena morsan, jag har bara varit ute och lekt med grabbarna.

Blod, svett och...blod

DÖD ATT LEMLÄSTA är det sista jag skulle misstänka death-metal bandet **Dismember** för att göra. Men det är lemlästa deras namn betyder.

Dessa 17-19 åringar från "Stockholms uslaste förorter" poserar med grisblod på LP-omslaget till sin färska LP-debut "Like an everflowing stream" (se recension på skivsidorna) men kommer till Nöjesguidens fotografering med nytvättade hår.

– Det här är som svart-

vinbärssaft, sött! Men fan, det svider i ögonen. Stänk mer på **Mattis** hals, han ska se ut som en "butcher"!

Den här gången är det bara teaterblod de hällt över sig. Grisblodet var billigare på charkbutiken vid S:t Eriksplan men helst vill de inte använda sig av djurblod överhuvudtaget.

– Egentligen skulle vi haft människoblod, men det får man inte köpa från sjukhusen, säger trummisen och vegetarianen **Fred**. Människor är faktiskt mindre

försvarslösa än djur.

Fotografen undrar lite försynt varför de gör sånt där, vad det ska vara bra för.

– Vi vill mangla skiten ur folk, säger gitarristen **David**. Provocera och väcka alla dödskallar. Låtarna på MTV är så jävla glada och handlar bara om kärlek. Är de sorgsna så är det för att tjejen gjort slut. Det finns annat i världen också. Man blir inte glad när man tittar på Aktuellt till exempel.

Annat som upprör Dis-

member är hiphoparna. De slåss mycket mer än andra gäng och deras klädstil är skitful. Brallor som släpar två meter efter benen och FBI-kepsar får hela gruppen att skrika av vämjelse.

– Vi behöver inte investera pengar i kläder, säger sångaren Matti. Titta på den här bra och billiga tröjan med snyggt tryck (LP-omslaget till "Like an ever flowing stream"). Den här stilen har jag varit trogen i flera år.

C N

LIKE AN EVERFLOWING STREAM

From left: Dismember drenched in blood;

Dismember's blistering debut

to be Dead," "Dismembered," etc., and revolted by the back cover photo, which depicts the band covered in blood. The customs officials apparently felt they were on to some kind of scoop, and decided to investigate the record further. After reading the lyrics to "Skin Her Alive," the customs squad had seen enough. They decided to take legal action against the band. Enter into the disputed zone of what you can legally print in the UK, as I present the nasty lines of Matti Kärki:

> *Haunted by my conscious, living my life in hell*
> *Didn't hesitate, when I moved into the kill*
> *Screams echoed in the distance, and I cannot ignore*
> *Smiling at the memories, when I slaughtered the whore*
> *Skin her alive!*
> *Time has come to confess, I did it for the thrill*
> *I had never dreamt of, that it would be so nice to kill*
> *Blood colors my thoughts, slipping out of time*
> *Murder is my game, skin her fucking alive*

As you can see, the lyrics are just a bloody horror tale about a demented killer's twisted memories of one of his murders. As it turned out, the lyrics are based on an actual murder that happened close to Matti Kärki's home.

"It's no glorification of a murder—it was never that, just a description. That one lyric that they got obsessed over is in fact a description of an actual event. My neighbor killed his wife. So I wrote a lyric about it, from the killer's point of view. It's based on the truth, and I guess I thought that you couldn't censor the truth."—MATTI KÄRKI, CARNAGE/DISMEMBER

Anyway, the lyrics—based on a true story or not—were considered too much by some people in ye olde United Kingdom. On July 29, 1992, the group appeared in the court of Great Yarmounth. They were charged with spreading obscene material, and the future of death metal lyrics as well as free speech was really at stake. The aim

Den svenska death-metalgruppen Dismember åtalades i Storbritannien för spridande av obscen konst. Därför fick de spela sin låt i domstolen.

Britter åtalar svensk grupp

Av NILS HANSSON

Det blir allt svårare att provocera, det är något som inte minst dagens rockband får erfara. Det svenska death metal-bandet Dismember har dock lyckats.

När en sändning av bandets singel "Skin her alive" skickades till England nappade den brittiska tullen och beslagtog paketet, vilket ledde till en bannlysning av gruppens skivor och konserter i väntan på domstolsutslag.

I går stod gruppen och dess skivdistributör inför en domstol i London, åtalade för spridandet av obscen konst, vilket är olagligt i Storbritannien.

De fem medlemmarna spelade upp "Skin her alive" inför domstolsjuryn för att ge den möjlighet att avgöra musikens eventuella obscenitet.

Vid en eventuell fällande dom lär även de prejudicerande effekterna bli betydande.

Bandet beräknas dock vara tillbaka i Sverige i tid för sitt framträdande vid årets Hultsfredsfestival.   □

Article on the Dismember trial

of the prosecutors was to ban similar lyrics outright. So Dismember entered the court to defend us all in the name of death metal.

"At first I just thought it was all hilarious. We got a lot of attention, and could go to England for free. But after a while I realized it was all so fucked up, and the whole thing kind of scared me. I mean, what the fuck was going on?" —MATTI KÄRKI, CARNAGE/DISMEMBER

In court, the entire Dismember album was played to a crowd of puzzled lawmen. They probably couldn't believe their ears, and they doubtlessly found the lyrics completely inaudible. All this might sound very silly and unbelievable today, but these are the historic facts. Thankfully, the judge understood the absurdity of it all and released Dismember on all charges. Their album could be sold in the UK. Still, their video was banned from broadcast within the Queen's Empire, since it contained the most taboo thing of all—blood.

In the end, Dismember had just gotten some free publicity and gained a reputation as one of the most controversial bands in the world. More to the point, they were one of the best examples of awesome, primitive, and ultra-brutal old school Swedish death metal. *Like an Ever Flowing Stream* is an album everybody should have in their collection. Although I still think *Left Hand Path* remains the best of the classic Sunlight-produced death metal albums, Dismember's debut is probably the most aggressive and devastating.

Dismember rode a wave of success, and toured with bands like Obituary and Napalm Death. Their banner years, 1991 and 1992, represented the peak of the Swedish death metal scene. The movement snuck in everywhere, and good quality records appeared on a regular basis.

Therion and Deaf

Though Therion eventually wound up on Nuclear Blast, at this point they had a big problem finding the right label. They apparently disagreed totally with House of Kicks, and left for Peaceville's newly started Deaf imprint. Peaceville was originally started in 1987 by proprietor Paul "Hammy" Halmshaw as a cassette label, but after the success of Earache they went for grind and punk with bands like Doom and Electro Hippies. By the end of the 80's they had entered the death metal field, grabbing great bands like Autopsy and Darkthrone for their roster. Therion's full length debut, *Of Darkness*—recorded as early as September 1990, possibly that winter—wasn't released until 1991. This time, the recording was a bit more structured.

"*It was better, but for being a proper record we had very limited resources. We got about $700 from the label and put in another $700 ourselves. We recorded and mixed the whole album at Sunlight during six days in the winter of 1990. We weren't very pleased with the mix, so we redid it during an extra day. Since time was limited, we could never reach a satisfying result on the songs 'Dark Eternity' and 'Time Shall Tell,' so we just included the versions from the mini-LP instead. Strangely, very few seem to have noticed that.*"—CHRISTOFFER JOHNSSON, THERION

Even though *Of Darkness* can be regarded as a classic, Therion were already drifting away from their death metal roots. Though the recording had been done at Studio Sunlight, the pure death metal sound wasn't there. Also, the use of keyboards was rather unorthodox.

"*For this album, Peter got the idea that we should use keyboards on two songs. Mainly as an effect on 'The Return,' but also for a melody at the end of "Genocidal Raids." I think that Nocturnus was the only death metal band that had done that before.*"—CHRISTOFFER JOHNSSON, THERION

Personally, I think the biggest step away from death metal lies in the riffs. Instead of bee-swarms or chunky grooves, Therion used traditional heavy metal down-picks. The song structures are a bit stereotypical, and the record simply doesn't flow. Still, it has an undeniable dark feeling. Christoffer's voice, especially, is very powerful, which together with the occasional blast is enough to make this album into some good death metal, after all.

Enter Century Media

Deaf only kept Therion for that one record, but a label that would be able to stick with their bands for a long time was Century Media, founded in late 1988. The label boss Robert Kampf had played guitar in the German thrash band Despair, and he initially started the company only to release Despair's music. In the early days, Kampf was in

Therion's full-length debut.

fact helped out by his friend Markus Steiger of Nuclear Blast. Once Century Media began signing death metal bands, however, the label soon challenged Nuclear Blast, as well as Earache Records.

Kampf seemed especially attracted to Swedish bands in the early 90's, starting with Grave from Gotland. When Grave signed with Kampf, they had already released the Grave/Devolution split LP and the *Anatomia Corporis Humani* mini-LP—a vinyl release of their 1989 demo on Prophecy Records.

"We sent our third demo to just about every label there was. A lot of them kept in touch, such as Earache and Peaceville. But Century Media was working faster than any of them, so we just went with them without thinking too much about it. We were young and didn't understand a word of a contract anyway; we just wanted to record an album."—OLA LINDGREN, GRAVE

Once on Century Media, Grave released the *Tremendous Pain* 7", but it was their blistering full-length debut that would really reveal their potential. On June 17, 1991, Grave entered Studio Sunlight to record their powerful *Into the Grave*, which blew all their previous recordings onto oblivion. That alone was pretty unusual—most bands back then sounded more aggressive on their demos.

"Century Media invited us down to Germany to record that single, and it was only after that we started to discuss a deal. It felt amazing for us to go abroad, so in a way they lured us onto their roster! But it turned out well."—OLA LINDGREN, GRAVE

Into the Grave is one of the purest examples of the typical Swedish death metal sound of the early 90's. The production is thick as gravy, with a wall of crushing guitars, yet it's more primitive than the production of Entombed, Carnage, or Dismember. Grave's songs are also rougher. Simple yet effective riffs are either hammered out or rushed like a swarm of angry bees. Jörgen Sandström's voice, on the other hand, was one of darkest and deepest of the period, and suits the music perfectly. When it comes to arrangements, the drum pattern is usually in the form of a distinctive two-beat similar to Autopsy. All in all, this is probably the most straightforward of the classic Sunlight productions. There is no fancy bullshit here, just pure death metal. The similar song structures can make the album seem a bit monotonous, but it's still all great. This is death metal in its purest form.

"This was the first time we actually worked in a proper studio, so naturally it turned out a lot better than our self-produced demos. For us, Sunlight was the only option when we could finally choose a studio. On the other hand, we were really determined to sound different than Entombed or Dismember. I think we succeeded. The album also benefits from the fact that we had composed some really good new songs by then. It wasn't just a compilation of old demo songs; it was new and fresh and brutal as fuck."—OLA LINDGREN, GRAVE

Grave finally got some well-deserved attention for their blistering music. They were praised all over the world, and soon began their first tours.

"We got out on tours in Europe as well as the U.S. after that album, and it was all just a chaotic party. To let a bunch of young guys live out their dream like that is like asking for trouble! Never mind that the sound was crap every night, since nobody knew how to handle death metal live back then, and that the band usually was too drunk to perform well—it was all a blast! I would not trade those times for anything."—OLA LINDGREN, GRAVE

Another of the Swedish bands Century Media laid their hands on was Unleashed, already more than ready to record an album. Unlike most other Swedish bands up to this point, Unleashed left the country to record *Where No Life Dwells*, at Woodhouse Studios in Dortmund, Germany, in April 1991.

"We wanted a slightly different sound, and were probably a bit afraid to sound too much like Entombed. To choose another studio gave us some perspective. There was nothing wrong with Sunlight; we just wanted something different."—JOHNNY HEDLUND, NIHILIST/UNLEASHED

The result is somewhat different from what Studio Sunlight had previously done for them, with a cleaner sound and clearly separated instruments. Still, the sound is definitely heavy and raw in the trademark Swedish style. When it comes to song composition, Unleashed had a more basic approach than most other Swedish bands. The riffs are simple and catchy, the arrangements straight-on, and the breaks fairly plain. The album may not be as powerful as records by Entombed, Dismember, or Grave, but it comes right behind them. Personally, I think the weakest thing about Unleashed at this point were Johnny Hedlund's vocals. Even though he does a decent job, he hasn't got the power of a singer like L.G. Petrov, and Robert Sennebäck's vocals on Unleashed's demos were far

From top: Into the Grave;
Megatrends in Brutality —*not really brutal*;
Unleashed —Where No Life Dwells

Unleashed lined up in the Woodhouse Studio

Not so flashy sleeping conditions during Unleashed's first tour

stronger in my opinion. Nevertheless, this was a great album, and Unleashed would immediately become one of Sweden's dominant death metal bands.

"It all happened very fast after the first album. We went touring immediately, and that was simply a dream come true, to meet all the people you had been mail corresponding with for all those years. We sold incredible amounts of merchandise on the European tour with Morbid Angel in 1991, and it worked great on the U.S. tour as well. All the kids were into Unleashed, even though we were still pretty unknown. It was a wonderful time."—JOHNNY HEDLUND, NIHILIST/UNLEASHED

Although Unleashed and Grave were probably the best bands on Century Media during the first years of the 90's, it was Tiamat that eventually secured the cash flow and made the label into what it is today. Initially, the label didn't have much faith in the young Swedish band.

"Actually, Johnny Hedlund and Fredrik Lindgren of Unleashed got us signed. Robert Kampf of Century Media was very skeptical about us, but after constant nagging from Johnny and Fredrik they gave in and offered us a deal. They practically forced him to sign us."—JOHAN EDLUND, TREBLINKA/TIAMAT

Tiamat's *Sumerian Cry* had been well received, so expectations rose for their follow-up, *The Astral Sleep*. It was obvious that the band's creative leader, Johan Edlund, had new visions already. In order to broaden their perspective, they left Sweden to record their second album in the same Woodhouse Studio that Unleashed had used. The album alienated some of Tiamat's old fans, but also won them countless of new followers.

The Astral Sleep is in fact so different from *Sumerian Cry* that you wonder if it is the same band. Well, it wasn't—former main songwriter Stefan Lagergren was long gone. The only thing left of the original concept was the logo and some dark lyrical content. The music had drifted away from the dark and heavy death metal of the debut, replaced by two new types of songs. First came a couple of thrashy songs, with down-picks and steady two-beats. These songs sounded amateurish even then, and are very unconvincing. But the majority of the album shows another side of Tiamat, with slow songs accentuated with acoustic guitars and keyboards. This doomy approach works a lot better, and reminds me of bands like Paradise Lost and Celtic Frost. Edlund's vocals are harsh and soulful, and probably the band's strongest element. The songs are generally a bit too long, and the musicians still weren't very skilled. Today it all sounds dated as hell, but the album worked pretty well back then. Still, it was only a taste of how Tiamat eventually would drift far away from metal.

"I guess some of the changes had to do with the fact that the new members, Thomas and Niklas, brought in some new ideas. They were also a bit more skilled than us. Personally, I had gotten into gothic bands such as Fields of the Nephilim by then, and I guess that is reflected in the music. I still think

we managed to keep the dark atmosphere of the debut on The Astral Sleep.*"*
—JOHAN EDLUND, TREBLINKA/TIAMAT

By 1991 Century Media had also nabbed the band Comecon, which initially featured Entombed's former singer L.G. Petrov. Comecon were basically a continuation of the thrash/crossover bands Krixhjälters and Omnitron, and was probably their attempt to enter the new and exciting death metal scene. The band's debut, *Megatrends in Brutality*, was recorded at Studio Sunlight in May and June 1991, but sadly turned out to be pretty lame.

The album actually delivers some uninspired and stereotypical crust punk, spiced up with a few blasts and some guitar melodies. I guess they wanted to cash in on the death metal movement, but it was just too obvious that the band members were still rooted in their punk and thrash backgrounds. The use of a drum machine also gives the music a stiff and boring feeling, and the overall sound is weak. Some people still insist that a real drummer was used, but if that is the case, he must be the most machinelike and boring drummer within the whole death metal scene.

Comecon were living proof that Swedish death metal couldn't be handled by anyone born before the 70's. The only thing a bit deadly are L.G.'s vocals, yet even he delivers a pretty poor performance. But all in all, Century Media had built up an impressive roster. Grave, Unleashed, and Tiamat all sold pretty well, and the label gradually strengthened its position.

𝔇olores and the 𝔊othenburg 𝔅ands

While Stockholm held down the heart and core of Swedish death metal, things started happening elsewhere around the country. In particular, the Gothenburg area scene came into its own around 1991. When Grotesque split up, two new bands were spawned: At the Gates and Liers in Wait. The local label Dolores expected that the quality of Grotesque would continue through these new constellations, so they convinced both bands to release mini-albums for them—just as Grotesque had done. Indeed, both new bands were fantastic.

At the Gates' *Gardens of Grief*, recorded at Studio Sunlight in February, was one of the most convincing debuts of 1991. The band was the best possible synthesis of Tomas Lindberg and Alf Svensson from Grotesque, and the twins Anders and Jonas Björler from Infestation.

"It all started when Grotesque folded in the summer of 1990, after which Kristian Wåhlin, Tomas Lindberg, and Alf Svensson decided to form a new project. Since I knew Tomas, I was asked to play bass, and a guy named Hans Nilsson was recruited as drummer. We had no name at that point, but talked about names like At the Gates and Liers in Wait. At first we worked with music by Kristian and Alf, but Kristian soon left and took the drummer with him.

Then I switched to guitar, and my brother Jonas joined on drums."—ANDERS BJÖRLER, AT THE GATES/THE HAUNTED

"*As I recall, the first version of the new band was initially called Liers in Wait. It was me on vocals, Anders on bass, Kristian and Alf on guitars, and Hans on drums. Then Kristian and Hans left, and took the band name with them. I was a bit angry about that, because I thought it sounded much better than At the Gates.*"—TOMAS LINDBERG, GROTESQUE/AT THE GATES/DISFEAR

"*After a month Jonas switched to bass, and Tompa brought in a guy [Adrian Erlandsson] from Varberg, who he had met at Bergslagsrocken, to play the drums. He was a regular guy with short hair, and walked around with heavy medicine books in his backpack all the time. He didn't look metal at all, but boy could he play the drums! Now we felt that we had a band. I had only played guitar for about six moths at this point, so when At the Gates was officially formed in September 1990, we started to rehearse intensively.*"—ANDERS BJÖRLER, AT THE GATES/THE HAUNTED

Everybody knew in advance that this band would be great. At the Gates had a unique style, based on highly complex songs with expressive riffs and endless tempo changes. Originally they barely had any hooks at all, but every riff was so memorable that you got caught anyway.

"*We were very influenced by bands like Atheist in the beginning. Most of At the Gates' original material was created by Alf Svensson, so he is responsible for our unorthodox style. I think he is a very interesting musician even today.*"

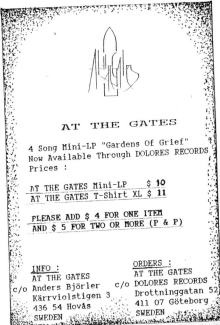

From left: flyer for At the Gates' mini-album; Liers in Wait—extremely brutal stuff

Originally, At the Gates' first recording was meant to be a demo, but since Dolores Records had previously released an album with Grotesque, they were very interested in Tomas and Alf's new band and wanted to release something immediately.

"We were lucky. The Grotesque mini-LP had done pretty well, so when we recorded the demo they wanted to release that too. We just thought about the recording as a demo, but when Dolores wanted to release it nobody objected. After that, everything went very well for us. Hard work combined with timing and luck paid off."—Anders Björler, At the Gates/The Haunted

You can hear all the hard work put into At the Gates' first record. The songs are very well structured, incredible when you think that Anders hadn't even touched a guitar one year earlier! My only objection to this mini-album is the vocals. For some reason, Lindberg traded his trademark screams for a deeper voice, and the result isn't as good as on the Grotesque album.

"I had to scream in Grotesque, since we had this black metal vibe. I wanted to explore my voice after that, so I used the same kind of growls as I did in Infestation when At the Gates started. I felt free to do whatever I wanted, but I realized that screams would suit At the Gates better after the mini-album."—Tomas Lindberg, Grotesque/At the Gates/Disfear

So Tomas brought back his old screams, and soon At the Gates rose to become one of the most influential and unique Swedish death metal bands.

"Alf made most of the decisions about the production. He pressed Tomas to sing hard and dark, and we even pitched some passages. The music was almost entirely Alf's; he mixed Swedish sadness with an almost classical atmosphere. Almost like a pompous soundtrack. We never said that we had to be different, but I guess we developed our own style. The reason for this was probably that we came from different backgrounds, and that everybody wanted to prove they had musical ability. But I still don't understand what made us sound like we did. It's a mess of folk music, death metal, and classical music."—Anders Björler, At the Gates/The Haunted

Long before their international success, though, Kristian Wåhlin and Hans Nilsson had left the embryonic At the Gates to form Liers in Wait.

"As I see it, we just did a couple of rehearsals together with Anders, Tomas, and Alf. There was never an actual band at that point; we just hung out and jammed a bit. I know there was some talking about band names like At the Gates and Liers in Wait back then, but nothing would materialize yet."—Kristian "Necrolord" Wåhlin, Grotesque/Liers in Wait/Decollation

During 1991, guitarist Kristian Wåhlin, drummer Hans Nilsson, and bassist Mattias Gustavsson developed into the intense Liers in Wait. In October 1991 the trio entered Studio Sunlight for their first recording session. Since they had no vocalist, Christoffer Johnsson from Therion volunteered to sing. Just like At the Gates, Liers in Wait lingered on Dolores Records on the merits of Grotesque, leading to the speedy release of *Spiritually Uncontrolled Art*.

"Just as in Grotesque, we hardly even considered our first recording as a demo; it was just something we had to do. Then the guys at Dolores heard it, and offered us to release it. There were never any contracts or anything like that; it was just something that happened."—Kristian "Necrolord" Wåhlin, Grotesque/Liers in Wait/Decollation

Liers in Wait might be among the most brutal stuff Sweden had yet produced. The album presents myriad complex and evil-sounding riffs, rushed out in complete anger. The drums are hammered out in an aggressive backbeat or steady blasts. Atop it all, Christoffer Johnsson delivers the vocal performance of his life. The combination assaults the senses, and the sheer intensity is amazing. Sparse keyboards create evil moods, and it all works well. The only down part of the record is the pretty thin sound. Apart from that, it is a masterpiece. More than At the Gates, Liers in Wait was the musical continuation of Grotesque—no surprise, since Kristian Wåhlin wrote all the material for both bands.

"I was in total control of Liers in Wait, and since I was very angry during this time, the record turned out insanely extreme. I also put a lot of strange passages in the songs, and doubled the intended speed as the work progressed. I was angry and wanted to create something brutal and sick. Kind of Necrovore on speed."—Kristian "Necrolord" Wåhlin, Grotesque/Liers in Wait/Decollation

Obviously Liers in Wait were very special, and offers arrived from many record labels. But as was the case with Grotesque, Kristian soon felt that Liers in Wait had lost their initial power. Instead of going full speed ahead, he decided to fold his band just as things started to happen.

"When we started to rehearse after our first recording, something had obviously changed. It wasn't as mad any longer, and we actually sounded more like Grotesque than Liers in Wait. I thought it sounded more tired, and I lost interest. I guess it had something to do with the fact that I wasn't as angry. I had also started to focus on my paintings, so the music became secondary. The only thing I regret in my career is that we didn't record more during those early years. I had so many ideas back then, but everything was held back by problems with the lineups and other shit. With Grotesque we often rehearsed as a trio with me, Tompa, and Tomas Eriksson. We should have recorded more stuff."—Kristian "Necrolord" Wåhlin, Grotesque/Liers in Wait/Decollation

"I think Liers in Wait had very bad luck with their timing. Their record came out a bit after At the Gates', and we were seen as the continuation of Grotesque instead of Liers in Wait. To me, they were the true continuation of Grotesque. Their mini-album was also way ahead of its time, extremely brutal and complex, with some Egyptian touches. They did then what Nile

did about ten years later. Spiritually Uncontrolled Art is a lost jewel of Swedish death metal. We had all the luck and they got nothing. It wasn't fair. It was cruel."—Tomas Lindberg, Grotesque/At the Gates/Disfear

Both Liers in Wait and At the Gates stood out with their progressive versions of extreme metal. But at the moment, straightforward death metal was still the most popular thing around.

Under the Sign of the Black Mark

The Swedish label Black Mark really tried to get in on the death metal market in the early 90's. The label was originally an extension of Tyfon, invented to release and promote the records of Bathory. But the death metal genre was simply too tempting, and before long, label manager Börje Forsberg started signing more bands, beginning with Edge of Sanity.

"I sent a demo to the newly started Black Mark label, and the next day Börje Forsberg himself called me and was eager to sign us. Within days, we became the first band to be contracted on the label since Bathory."—Dan Swanö, Edge of Sanity/Unisound

Edge of Sanity's debut, *Nothing but Death Remains*, was probably the first Swedish death metal album made in 1991, recorded in January at Montezuma Studios. The result is very death metal–sounding, with distinct two-beats and groovy slower parts. Dan Swanö provides his trademark vocals, with oceans of depth and power. The riffs and the songs are less convincing. This band was fairly obviously still under construction, and had yet to find a style of their own. When they did, boy, what great things they achieved.

"I thought the sound on the album turned out very bad, mainly because the guy in the studio didn't know anything about how to run things. Since I had worked a bit with recordings myself, I knew that everything could have turned out so much better."—Dan Swanö, Edge of Sanity/Unisound

By 1992, Black Mark also laid their hands on Cemetary from Borås, and later they would also sign the similar band Lake of Tears from the same town. Cemetary was basically the creation of guitarist and vocalist Matthias Lodmalm, and over the years he would lead his band into strange territories. Early during their career, though, they remained a traditional death metal band. They chose Studio Sunlight to record their debut album during February and March of 1992, and then chose Kristian Wåhlin to paint the cover.

Cemetary's debut, *An Evil Shade of Grey*, was basically a traditional Swedish death metal album with the fat Sunlight sound. Their songs and structures followed traditional formulas, with abundant two-beats, slow grind, screamed growls, chunky riffs, and numerous breaks and stops. But Cemetary also had some unorthodox ideas. Unlike most death metal bands, they were not

Edge of Sanity debut album

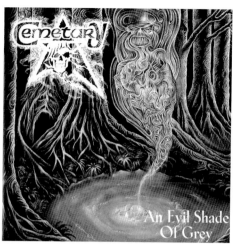

An Evil Shade of Grey—*not really
Kristian Wåhlin's greatest cover art*

Unorthodox—*a masterpiece
of classic death metal*

Seance's brutal debut album

afraid to use keyboards and clear melodies. Most songs on the album also have a considerably slower tempo than usual in Swedish death metal. Compared to contemporary Swedish bands, I guess Therion and Edge of Sanity might be the best references. But Cemetary would soon create far more original stuff, as they started to transform into an atmospheric doom metal band.

While Cemetary was heading for mellow stuff, other bands went in the opposite direction. One of the most brutal Swedish death metal bands in the early 90's was Linköping's Seance, whose 1991 demo *Levitised Spirit* already showed a U.S.-inspired brutality unusual in Sweden. It wouldn't be long until they got a recording contract through Black Mark.

"*Seance was formed out of Total Death and Orchriste in 1990, and this time we went for intense death metal full ahead. We spent a lot of money to make our demo professional, and since all of us worked at the Saab factory we could afford it. Luckily, many labels were interested. In the end we chose between Nuclear Blast and Black Mark. Or I guess we ended up on Black Mark since Börje Forsberg called Nuclear Blast and said that we had already signed for him! Such a liar!"*—PATRIK JENSEN, ORCHRISTE/SEANCE/THE HAUNTED

So Black Mark it was. Soon after the deal was closed, Seance entered Berno Studio in Malmö to make their debut album. The resulting *Fornever Laid to Rest* was definitely among the most brutal Swedish death metal albums of the time. Like Liers in Wait, Seance didn't look very much to other Swedish bands for inspiration. Instead, they owe a lot to the Americans in Deicide. Everything, including the songs, the riffs, and the vocals, reeked of Deicide. But it didn't matter, since their music was delivered with such precision. The riffs flow very well and the drums hammer without mercy. Loads of tempo changes and breaks make the album interesting throughout, and the vocals are as beastlike as Glen Benton's of Deicide ever were. I guess this was the album that gave previously unknown Berno Studio its niche within extreme metal. *Fornever Laid to Rest* was above all a triumph for guitarist Patrik Jensen, who made all the lyrics and most of the music. He showed that Sweden could also produce U.S.-style death metal of superior quality.

While Seance's debut was one of the most extreme Swedish death metal albums, the best and most successful thing Black Mark ever released was probably Edge of Sanity's second album, *Unorthodox*. Just like the debut, this album was recorded at Montezuma studio, starting in January 1992. Edge of Sanity were basically forced into the studio by Black Mark, who didn't care about their complaints about the last visit to Montezuma. Dan Swanö claims that Black Mark got a discount at Montezuma, and forced bands to use it since it was cheap for them. He also says Börje Forsberg had never even heard about Sunlight. Regardless, everything turned out great this time. The clear and in-your-face production showed that you could obtain that typically fat Swedish sound outside Studio Sunlight.

"The reason Unorthodox *sounds so incredibly superior to our debut is basically because I was involved in the production from the beginning. I was obsessed with making the album sound as good as I knew the studio was capable of. We brought all our own gear, and I was very active during the mix."*—DAN SWANÖ, EDGE OF SANITY/UNISOUND

The riffs and songs are of much higher quality than on the debut, and Edge of Sanity had greatly developed their trademark guitar melodies. The tightness is incredible, especially since most of the album was astonishingly recorded live. Best of all are the vocals of Dan Swanö and the drumming of Benny Larsson. Both could now be called masters of the genre. At the time of its release, we were quite amazed at Swanö supplying some clean vocals on a few parts. That was daring and unheard of on what was still basically a pure death metal album. *Unorthodox* is a perfect mix between melancholic melodies and brutality. The splendid result had a downside, though.

"The album turned out exactly the way I wanted it. It sounded so good, I was satisfied with the lyrics, and every riff was killer. In a way, I had accomplished everything I had ever wanted with death metal. So I guess that was the beginning of the end for Edge of Sanity. I felt that I could never match what we had done, so I gradually started to lose interest in the band. I started to focus on other projects and on my studio."—DAN SWANÖ, EDGE OF SANITY/UNISOUND

Though Black Mark successfully found new good bands, they didn't know how to break a band. They provided no tour support and hardly any promotion. Acts that released albums on Black Mark all feel disappointed in hindsight.

"Being on Black Mark, we found out the hard way how dirty the record business can be. Everything bad that can happen to you as a band happened to us; it was a mess."—DAN SWANÖ, EDGE OF SANITY/UNISOUND

"Hallelujah… I only sent our demo to Black Mark because I was such a huge Bathory fan. Then Börje Forsberg turned up at a gig we did with Immolation, Massacre and At the Gates in Uppsala, and he charmed us into signing like a used-car salesman. Later we realized nothing worked on that label. Nothing. If we had signed with Nuclear Blast instead, things would probably have turned out very differently."—PATRIK JENSEN, SEANCE/THE HAUNTED

At the Gates and Peaceville

At the Gates started to gain major attention during 1991. Their mini-album stirred the underground, and the scene was eager to hear what they could achieve on a full-length release. They attracted a lot of labels, among them Peaceville's imprint Deaf, which had previously signed Therion.

"We sent our mini-LP to Hammy at Peaceville, and he thought it sounded interesting. Many other labels contacted us as well, but we liked Peaceville. They had a great roster back then, with bands like Autopsy and Darkthrone, before they wimped out with worthless black metal. We went into ART Studio in Gothenburg before any contract was written."—ANDERS BJÖRLER, AT THE GATES/THE HAUNTED

At the Gates and Deaf seemed like a great partnership, a hungry new band and a hungry label. Unlike Therion, At the Gates later transferred to the regular label Peaceville when Deaf folded. In November 1991 the Gothenburg quintet entered ART Studio to record *The Red in the Sky Is Ours*. At the Gates really stood out by not using Studio Sunlight, and their album had a much cleaner sound than other death metal releases. Sadly, in this case cleaner meant weaker—the guitar sound is horrible.

"That album sounds the way it does for many reasons. Mainly because it was recorded by an absolute moron named Hans Hall, a guy who was allergic to electricity—he wore white gloves in the control room. Hall was completely incompetent and didn't know anything about metal at all. We should have brought our own amplifiers to the studio, but we couldn't afford the transportation. Instead we had to use a tired old Mesa Boogie combo, with some kind of old orange distortion pedal. The guitar sound didn't turn out very well. Kerrang! said it best: 'The guitars sound like wet cucumbers.' Then the recording turned out to be very expensive. When I talked to Hammy in 1997, he said that The Red in the Sky Is Ours *was still the most expensive recording they had ever done. Strange."*—ANDERS BJÖRLER, AT THE GATES/THE HAUNTED

The album Hans Hall ruined

Even a moron named Hans Hall couldn't hide the fact that the unique and complex style of At the Gates had developed to perfection. The supercharged interaction between Anders Björler and Alf Svensson is stunning, and all the musicians perform with great feeling. Fortunately, Lindberg also abandoned his death metal style of singing, and his screams contain so much feeling that it is painful.

"I still see that as a lost album. The songs were good, but everything was ruined by the atrocious production. It was not fun to record; I only wanted to get out of there as soon as possible. I can't even listen to it anymore." — TOMAS LINDBERG, GROTESQUE/AT THE GATES/DISFEAR

Despite the sound, *The Red in the Sky Is Ours* is an immortal classic of melodic and powerful death metal. I really can't say anything bad about the music. At the Gates clearly represented the future of Swedish death metal.

Active: From Thrash to Death

While Earache and Peaceville led the British death metal labels, a third UK outfit, Active Records, arrived on the scene in the early 90's. Starting off nicely with Atheist's acclaimed *Piece of Time*, Active soon looked to Sweden. Founder Dave Constable had in fact lived in the country for many years and ran the label together with a Swede, Lena Graaf. (Both Constable and Graaf also contributed to the

At the Gates relaxing backstage. Tomas Lindberg is missing—
he's probably passed out.

magazine *Metal Forces*—I guess the "Active" banner was pretty accurate.)
Initially they signed Swedish thrash metal bands Hexenhaus and Mezzrow, but they
soon turned to death metal acts like Therion, who had now left Deaf Records.

Therion's second full-length album, *Beyond Sanctorum*, was recorded at
Montezuma Studio in December 1991, right before Edge of Sanity were there. As
the New Year approached, Therion were ready to take on the world. To my ears,
Beyond Sanctorum has a better production than the debut, and it contains a
variety of cool sections. The sound is pretty intense, though it has nowhere near
the massive power of the Sunlight productions. At times, it sounds more like
thrash metal than death metal. Yet curiously, Christoffer Johnsson disagrees
entirely with Dan Swanö's assessment of producer Rex Gisslén.

"*The producer Rex Gisslén used to be the keyboard player in the Swedish
boy band Shanghai during the 80's! It is peculiar that he was the producer
who knew most about death metal when it came to song structures. Skogsberg
might be the one who could do the best sound, but he never knew when to
cut in guitars and things like that. Rex got most of it instantly, even quicker
than oneself. I'm a bit disappointed with the sound, though. We wanted to get
away from the Sunlight sound, but in retrospect I would have preferred it.*"
—Christoffer Johnsson, Therion

Therion's second album is quite varied, containing everything from insane blasts to melancholic frailty. And therein lies the flaw—the songs don't fit together very well. The epic structures feel confusing rather than innovative. In addition, some of the riffs are mediocre and tired in standard rock style. Nevertheless, this is definitely a death metal album, as the screaming growls leave no doubt. But as time would tell, Therion later drifted into even more obscure musical territories.

"*We had already started to use more keyboards—both Peter and I had acquired a taste for them. We also experimented a bit with strange drum patterns and guitar scales. A lot of the stuff that would later be trademarks of the band started to grow on this album. We also went out on our first tours during this time, with gigs in Holland and Belgium. We had to rent a minivan and fold the seats to fit in our gear. We could hardly fit into the bus ourselves, and literally sat on each other. We had a great time and a hard time simultaneously.*"
—CHRISTOFFER JOHNSSON, THERION

Active also signed the classic band Merciless during 1991, who were desperate for a decent label after their time on the dysfunctional Deathlike Silence Productions. In the turbulent rising death metal scene, Merciless also wanted to adopt a deadlier approach. In June 1991 they chose Studio Sunlight to record their second album. *The Treasures Within*, however, didn't see the light of day until late 1992. Though the songs kept the same aggressive and simple style as before, the new approach was apparent in the sound. The crunchy guitars and hammering drums mimicked the typical Swedish death metal style, which didn't

 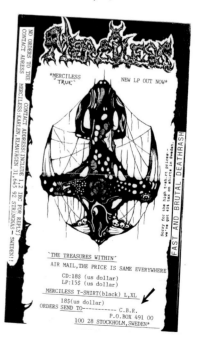

*From left: Therion—*Beyond Sanctorum;
Flyer for Merciless' second album

really suit Merciless' music too well. Their debut had sounded far more evil. Sure, it's a good record, but not as good as *The Awakening*. Merciless simply didn't sound fresh and intense anymore.

"*We never really got going. I guess the problem was the record labels, which didn't push us enough. Some of it probably had to do with the fact that we didn't have a decent promoter. We didn't know anything about such things back then. I am convinced that we would have become much bigger if we had released* The Awakening *on Kreator's label or something like that. The Germans were mad about our music back then. But fuck it all, I don't regret anything. Merciless will always remain an underground group. Flag of hate!*"—FREDRIK KARLÉN, MERCILESS

Century Media Reigns On

Century Media remained the major home for Swedish death metal bands in the early 90's. Unlike other labels, they managed to keep their bands, who in turn continued to produce successful albums. In 1992, Grave continued on their deadly path with *You'll Never See*, again displaying relentless death metal that strengthened their position as one of Sweden's leading bands. Grave's second album sounds a lot cleaner than their debut, but most of the brutality is intact. The guitars are meaty as hell, and Jörgen's vocals are incredibly deep and powerful. He was definitely one of the best singers in the scene at this time. The song structures were a little bit less brutal, with more slow parts. All in all, this was a very good album, though it couldn't match the band's relentless debut.

"*After the tours for* Into the Grave, *we went straight to songwriting again. We lived death metal, and soon we had enough material to go into the studio. We were starting to mature at this point, and the songs were more thought through. I guess our second album lies between the furious two-beat death metal of the debut and the groove of* Soulless. *It was just a natural step. After the recording it was straight back to touring again. Great times!*"—OLA LINDGREN, GRAVE

Likewise, Unleashed were obviously having a great time. In April 1992, exactly one year after Unleashed's debut album had been recorded, the group went back to Woodhouse Studios to begin *Shadows of the Deep*.

"*We were basically having the time of our lives at that point. We had made an album, been on tours with Bolt Thrower, Morbid Angel, and Paradise Lost, and had actually been making a few bucks while at it. Remember that I was a teenager who lived with my parents, and I felt like a kid getting paid to enter Disneyland! I bought a new TV and drank a lot of booze. Then it was back to the studio; it was incredible.*"—ANDERS SCHULTZ, UNLEASHED

This album stuck to the basic formula of Unleashed's debut, with some slight differences. First of all, the production isn't as good. The sound is a bit dry and powerless, though it still sounds like death metal. Worse than that, the songs felt a bit more stereotypical, with a couple of unconvincing riffs and too many stiff, slow tempos. Also, Hedlund's vocals are more screamed and hoarse. Although I kind of like it in small doses, nothing can hide that the vocals aren't that powerful. It's still a good album, but less convincing than Unleashed's debut.

"There were some problems with communication, since neither we nor the guys in the studio spoke very good English. It caused some frustration and stress. We weren't too fond of the sound of our two first albums back then, but today I like them both a lot. But the best thing about our second recording was all the drinking sessions. We lived at the home of Frank Albrecht from Rock Hard, *and totally thrashed his place!"*—ANDERS SCHULTZ, UNLEASHED

Century Media's main band was Tiamat, now increasingly popular around the world. The ever-changing group pushed the boundaries of what could be called death metal. As usual for Century Media bands, Tiamat went into Woodhouse Studio, pretty much the label's house studio, to record *Clouds*. Tiamat's third album continues the ideas from *The Astral Sleep*, with a majority of slow and mellow songs. Looking closer, the new songs smelled a bit of traditional 80's heavy metal. These guitar riff–oriented songs didn't fit the lyrics or Edlund's vocals very well, and the guitar solos seem completely misplaced.

"Personally, I think this album was fucked up because everyone involved wanted to do something different. It's a soup with too many chefs. I wanted to take a Celtic Frost direction, but a couple of the others wanted it to be something like Dokken, or Dio at best. The producer didn't believe in us at all, and it was very difficult to finish the album."—JOHAN EDLUND, TREBLINKA/TIAMAT

On a positive note, the sound is big and clear. The Celtic Frost–ish guitar sound is a nice touch. Some of the slower, atmospheric parts anticipate the style Tiamat would later perfect on *Wildhoney*. The problem is that this album is a compromise, with some factions in the band still trying to keep in touch with the extreme metal scene. The occasional two-beat drum pattern sounds terribly out of place, and Edlund's vocals actually sound weaker the harder he pushes his voice. It was apparent that Tiamat would never produce anything extreme again, and were drifting away from metal altogether. The mellower they became, the better they sounded. Tiamat's future direction was obvious, and would not be brutal. All in all, *Clouds* is a flawed album with contradictions and compromises. But it maintained Tiamat's popularity, which would explode after their next album.

"All the problems might have made the album special in some way, but when I think back on it or listen to it, all I can remember is the trouble. I can't judge it for what it is, but it definitely didn't turn out as I wanted it to. The band fell apart after that, and on the next album I really did what I had wanted to do on Clouds.*"* —JOHAN EDLUND, TREBLINKA/TIAMAT

Clockwise from top left:
Clouds—*death metal
meets Dokken;*

Unleashed—Shadows
in the Deep;

*Unleashed on tour with
Bolt Thrower*

Nuclear Blast Takes Command

As Century Media tightened their grip on the Swedish death metal scene, Nuclear Blast began breathing down their necks, chasing a bigger piece of the cake. Nuclear Blast's Swedish flagship, Dismember, only released an EP during 1992. But *Pieces* again showed that Dismember were among the most orthodox of classic Swedish death metal bands. They stayed with the established formula of ultra-thick guitars, hammering drums, bee-swarm riffs, and grunted screams. This is Swedish death metal in its purest form, full of aggression and violence, on one of the rawest recordings the movement would ever produce.

"We got so many tours during this time, so we had no time to record a second album. We had to do something to keep our name up, so we went into Sunlight for a couple of nights to record an EP. It wasn't as properly done as the album, but I guess it turned out pretty cool in its rawness. The guitar sound is just insane!"—FRED ESTBY, DISMEMBER/CARNAGE

Nuclear Blast had also signed Afflicted, and in 1992 this original Stockholm band finally entered Studio Sunlight to make their first album. The *Prodigal Sun* debut is a far step from their initial style. By now, Afflicted had developed a peculiar form of death metal with lots of strange harmonies and tempo changes. I guess Voivod would be a decent reference point. Of the Swedish bands, they were probably closest to At the Gates, with their many weird melodies. Some grind elements from their earlier days were preserved, leading to a pretty confused and strange album.

"The recording sessions were exhausting. We had different opinions in the band, and since we all were stubborn, we ended up with an album sounding worse than the Wanderland *demo. I guess we experimented too much and were too focused on creating something original. Sometimes it worked, but other times it turned out a mess."*—JOACIM CARLSSON, GENERAL SURGERY/AFFLICTED/FACE DOWN

I personally kind of like their unpredictable and chaotic nature, but not the sound. Even though *Prodigal Sun* had been recorded at Sunlight, it shows none of the fat heaviness usually associated with that studio. Instead the album sounds pretty thin, with loads of screeching treble. The vocals of Joakim Bröms are also fairly uneven. Some screams are great, but his growls tend to sound more hardcore than death metal. Overall, this was a decent debut, but surely couldn't match other releases from the same year—artistically or commercially.

"In the end I think it turned out to be a pretty unique album, but it could have been much better. In hindsight, I prefer the versions of the songs that you can find on our demos. In any case, no other band sounded like us at that point." —JOACIM CARLSSON, GENERAL SURGERY/AFFLICTED/FACE DOWN

By now, Nuclear Blast had also contracted Hypocrisy. The band's founder,

Pieces

Hypocrisy's debut album

Peter Tägtgren, had become increasingly inspired by the death metal genre. In the early 90's he spent some time in the United States, and tried to become a member of Malevolent Creation and Meltdown. When he moved back to Sweden, he started Hypocrisy as a solo project. Soon he had recruited some friends, and their *Rest in Pain* demo immediately secured them a deal with Nuclear Blast. The prolific Tägtgren understood that they needed to get an album out fast in order to get in on the popular death metal market, and the band rushed into Studio Rockshop to record their first album, *Penetralia*.

Hypocrisy's debut is very clear-sounding, with super-triggered drums and sharp guitars. The sound could be the most severe problem with *Penetralia*. It is simply not very brutal, but rather plastic and thin-sounding. Further, the riffs and song structures were a bit too basic to impress. Their music is somewhere in between the Swedish band Unleashed and U.S.-style death metal, and the overall impression is a bit impersonal. It's pretty obvious that this album was a bit rushed, and that the band should have waited before they recorded it. But in hindsight, Hypocrisy were wise to release the record quickly. They gained attention and got on the bandwagon before it was too late. They made their name known, and their later, superior albums did very well.

House of Kicks

House of Kicks in Stockholm tried to edge deeper into the record market as well. Calle von Scheven was determined to capitalize on this lucrative field of music, and he sought new bands to sign. Among the first signings were Desultory from Rönninge, who tried something new with the death metal formula. Just like Therion, they released a mini-LP on House of Kicks—a compilation of their acclaimed demos showing off their thrashy style, and a much cleaner sound than most other bands.

Though Desultory's debut album is tight and professional, they really couldn't cut it as a death metal band. The riffs are far too simple and stereotypical, and the heavy use of melodies just didn't fit. The brutal vocals of Klas Morberg were good, but the music was too dull to cause any impact. It remained up to At the Gates, a couple of years later, to show how thrash metal and death metal should be combined.

Entombed and the Rest

But what about Entombed in 1992? Well, their only release this year was the *Stranger Aeons* EP. The record was basically recorded for the upcoming Gods of Grind tour with Carcass, and contains just the title track and two hastily recorded songs—the new "Dusk" and a new recording of the old demo track "Shreds of Flesh." All in all, *Stranger Aeons* sounded very good, but was nothing exceptional by Entombed's standard.

"*It was recorded during one Friday evening in November 1991. It was only Nicke and I in the studio, and I think it turned out pretty cool.*"—UFFE CEDERLUND, MORBID/NIHILIST/ENTOMBED/DISFEAR

It was apparent that Entombed were at a turning point, a band without a singer and a stripped-down creative core consisting of just Nicke and Uffe. Soon talk circulated about L.G. returning to the band. This fortunately proved to be true, as he rejoined the old flock for the Gods of Grind tour in spring 1992.

"*It simply wasn't working out with Johnny, and one day Alex said that we should bring back L.G. So he was in again, and we did the tour with Carcass. That tour was the first one on which we actually sounded quite good. Before that we kind of sucked live. We could never get the sound we wanted, and we had problems finding a suitable singer while L.G. was out of the band.*"—UFFE CEDERLUND, MORBID/NIHILIST/ENTOMBED/DISFEAR

Entombed were back in their old fine form. But rumors started to spread that they would stop playing death metal and go for 70's hard rock on their next vinyl. But this just couldn't be true—or could it?

Bands like Stockholm's Katatonia were already trying hard to do something fresh with the death metal concept. After many years in the rehearsal room, they entered Dan Swanö's newly started Unisound studio in June 1992 to record *Jhva Elohim Meth...* They secured a deal with the up-and-coming Dutch label Vic Records, and soon the demo reemerged as a record titled *Jhva Elohim Meth...The Revival.*

The slow, melancholic riffs of Katatonia really were something else back

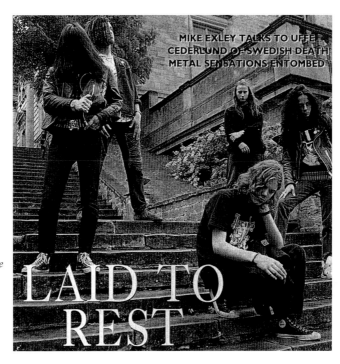

MIKE EXLEY TALKS TO UFFE CEDERLUND OF SWEDISH DEATH METAL SENSATIONS ENTOMBED

LAID TO REST

*Entombed at
the stairway to
international fame*

then, influenced by bands like Paradise Lost. The tormented voice and depressed lyrics of Jonas Renske add to the atmosphere and mood, as do the keyboards and acoustic guitars. Katatonia nodded to the rising black metal movement with a pentagram logo, and they even used corpse paint for a brief period. It seems laughable today, but back then it made all the difference. Though their debut was sloppy and crude, Katatonia definitely had a special feeling.

Among other important releases, 1992 brought Pan-Thy-Monium's *Dawn of Dreams* on Osmose, Centinex' *Subconscious Lobotomy* on Underground Records, and Authorize's *The Source of Dominion* on Putrefaction. All of these had limited significance. As you can see, Swedish death metal virtually exploded during 1992. New local death metal scenes erupted all around the country during the early 90's, making the death metal movement into something massive.

Chapter Seven: The Death Metal Explosion

EUCHARIST has now their "DEMO 1 -92" available. It contains three songs with good sound and quality copied cassettes. Get this masterpiece of brutality for just 30 sek (6 us $). Order from:

```
              EUCHARIST          EUCHARIST
          c/o Thomas Einarsson c/o Daniel Erlandsson
              Ejdervägen 4          Bräckestigen 2D
              430 20  VEDDIGE       430 20  VEDDIGE
              SWEDEN                SWEDEN

                       NO RIP OFFS!!!!!!
```

"TRAIL OF LIFE DECAYED"
DEMO-91

"TRAIL OF LIFE DECAYED"
DEMO-91

Clockwise from left: Eucharist flyer;
Dark Tranquillity flyer;
Trail of Life Decayed *demo*

From top: Inverted flyer;
Infanticide flyer;
local gig posters

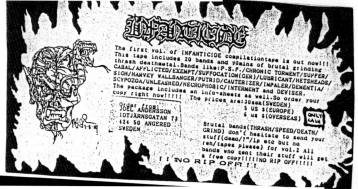

MARTIN G.:   MARTIN A.:   JOCKE:
VOCALS   GUITAR   DRUMS

Clockwise from top left: Total Death
and Orchriste on the bill with Carcass;
Edge of Sanity's Immortal Rehearsals;
Thrash Bash 10 flyer;
Darkified demo inlay

Until 1990, the nucleus of Swedish death metal remained in the Stockholm region, with only a few bands scattered around the rest of the country. But as the genre grew, fanzines and gigs spread the word, and the shit finally hit the fan. From 1990 to 1993, many interesting and productive local death metal scenes emerged—some in the weirdest places.

The Gothenburg Area

For a long time, the Gothenburg scene was far behind Stockholm's. During the mid-80's only a few thrash metal bands were based there, such as Intoxicate, Pagandom, and Ice Age. There was no metal scene to speak of until the underground speed metal band Conquest transformed into Grotesque late in 1988. The importance of Grotesque for Gothenburg cannot be overestimated. Not only did they produce some of the best Swedish death metal ever made, their members were also active in other fields. Singer Thomas Lindberg edited the classic fanzine *Cascade*, and guitarist Kristian Wåhlin would soon become famous for his album artwork.

Towards the end of Grotesque's career, Lindberg also played in the band Infestation with the twins Anders and Jonas Björler. Yet Infestation's 1990 demo *When Sanity Ends* never really got any attention. When Grotesque folded, Lindberg and the Björler brothers teamed up with Grotesque's guitarist Alf Svensson to form At the Gates. The melodic and melancholic death metal of At the Gates would inspire the whole Gothenburg region. With this great new band, Gothenburg metal musicians had started a distinguished style of their own. Many would follow in the footsteps of At the Gates.

Another Gothenburg band that started already back in 1989 was Eucharist, who quickly adopted the ideas of At the Gates and released their own acclaimed debut demo tape in 1992. In fact, they were almost as good as At the Gates, but their career never took off. Another band in the new melodic style was the heavy metal band Desecrator, renamed Ceremonial Oath as they started to get into brutal stuff. Their 1991 demo was followed by the *Lost Name of God* EP the following year. Ceremonial Oath's guitar player Anders Iwers simultaneously started In Flames, who were never productive and got no notice back then. Eventually they would become one of the biggest Swedish metal bands of all time, but that's another story.

Grotesque's other main man, Kristian Wåhlin, continued in the super-brutal Liers in Wait in the same violent vein as Grotesque. Sadly, their style never became popular among other Gothenburg bands. But Ceremonial Oath's Tomas Johansson teamed up with Liers in Wait's Kristian Wåhlin to form the project Decollation, and released the EP *Cursed Lands* on Listenable in 1992.

Another band launched in 1989, Septic Broiler, released the thrashy demo

Enfeebled Earth in 1990. Afterwards, they changed their rather corny name to Dark Tranquillity, and released the thrash attack *Trail of Life Decayed* demo tape, which also came out as a vinyl EP. Inspired by At the Gates, they grew increasingly melodic and mellow, but the early demos were pretty brutal.

"*To me, the second generation of Gothenburg death metal bands mainly consisted of Dark Tranquillity and Ceremonial Oath. They were based in the underground, and had been around at the Grotesque gigs. I also see Dissection as part of the Gothenburg scene; we hung out a lot and influenced each other. Apart from that, there was a strange gang of Finnish grind-alcoholics in the suburb of Angered. We got along great with these maniacs, and they were much more a part of the early 90's scene than the likes of Eucharist and In Flames.*"
—Tomas Lindberg, Grotesque/At the Gates/Disfear

This drunken group of maniac Finnish expatriates started loads of bands around the nicely named planned community of Angered: Evoked Curse, Exempt, Sacretomia, and Monkey Mush all made demos during 1990 and 1991. Other area bands that recorded demos during this period include Satanized, Segregation, and Runemagick. As you can see, Gothenburg had become a death metal town.

The happenings around the city also spawned regional scenes. Alingsås, north of Gothenburg, saw Mutilator and Inverted emerge, while the southern town of Halmstad produced Autopsy Torment and Pagan Rites. There was also a growing scene in Strömstad, about thirty miles north of Gothenburg. The central character there was definitely Jon Nödtveidt from the thrash band Rabbit's Carrot. He turned to more brutal stuff with Satanized, and famously Dissection. Jon also edited the great *Mega Mag* and arranged gigs during the early 90's. He would have a great influence in the years to come.

"*The early Gothenburg scene was pretty brutal. Most of the melodic stuff turned up later, and I guess we in At the Gates are to blame for that.*"—Tomas Lindberg, Grotesque/At the Gates/Disfear

Goth Town Boras

In tiny Borås, forty miles east of Gothenburg, a doom/goth scene started to reign. In 1989 a guy named Mathias Lodmalm was pretty alone with his ideas about death metal. He created the band Cemetary, which gradually gained attention with the 1992 album *An Evil Shade of Grey* on Black Mark. Though in essence death metal, the album also contained keyboards, melodies, and some very slow parts. Over the years, Cemetary became increasingly mellow, inspiring other kids in Borås to start similar bands.

The first bands Cemetary influenced were Forsaken Grief, Morbid Death, and Carnal Eruption, all formed in 1990. These bands soon split, however, and

Lake of Tears'
debut demo

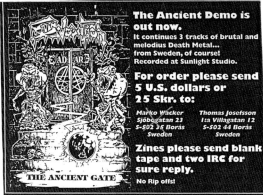

The Ancient Demo is out now.
It continues 3 tracks of brutal and melodius Death Metal... from Sweden, of course! Recorded at Sunlight Studio.

For order please send 5 U.S. dollars or 25 Skr. to:

Marko Wacker
Sjöbogatan 23
S-502 35 Borås
Sweden

Thomas Josefsson
I:a Villagatan 12
S-502 44 Borås
Sweden

Zines please send blank tape and two IRC for sure reply.
No Rip offs!

THE ANCIENT GATE

Evocation flyer

spawned the softer and far more successful Lake of Tears in 1992. After one demo tape, Lake of Tears signed to Black Mark and released a bunch of albums throughout the 90's. At this time of writing, they remain the second-best-selling band on Black Mark—next to Bathory, naturally. Nineteen ninety-two also saw the birth of goth/metal band Beseech, who would later make a slew of albums.

A rather brutal death metal band named Sickness emerged from the area. After two demos, they transformed into the much more laid-back Benighted. Their drummer Kristian Engqvist, one of the central characters of the local scene, also edited the 'zine *Undead*. With Cemetary, Lake of Tears, Beseech, and Benighted around, Borås became synonymous with mellow goth metal.

But Borås also produced one high-quality traditional death metal band during the early 90's, the great Evocation. The members had previously been in minor death metal bands such as Decomposed (the brothers Vesa and Janne Kenttäkumpo) and Morbid Death (Thomas Josefsson and Marko Wacker-Palmén, also members of the grindcore band Harrasmentation).

Evocation recorded their debut demo, *The Ancient Gate*, at Studio Sunlight in 1992—capturing great, fat-sounding, well-structured death metal to the max. After the demo, the group was completed by Cemetary's Christian Saarinen on bass. Evocation continued with the equally good *Promo 92*, and played a few gigs with bands like Dismember and Master.

The band rates among the finest examples of classic Sunlight death metal. In fact, producer Tomas Skogsberg states that Evocation is one of the best and most professional bands he ever worked with. Sadly, the band got lost in the massive flow of demos in 1992 and never made it. They were just a bit too late.

Death Center Finspang

Besides Stockholm, the tiny town of Finspång was the second real death metal center of Sweden. The area had some kind of scene in the late 80's, since Robban Becirovic in the nearby town of Norrköping had arranged gigs there since 1988. Thanks to the nearby venue, young bands had a reason to stay together. The most dedicated and talented of the young musicians in the area was Dan Swanö, and he would gradually become the leading character of the Finspång scene. He started a myriad of bands and opened the great Gorysound/Unisound studio, which soon became one of the death metal centers in Sweden.

"Finspång was definitely a center for extreme music in the early 90's, mostly thanks to Dan Swanö. He did so much for death metal with his bands and especially his studio. In Norrköping, almost nothing else was going on apart from Marduk."—ROGER SVENSSON, ALLEGIANCE/MARDUK

Among other bands, Swanö started Pan-Thy-Monium, Incision, and above all Edge of Sanity. He used the initial success of Edge of Sanity to promote his studio. When people heard his recordings of bands such as Marduk, groups from all over the country started visiting Finspång to record albums. Other bands in Finspång during the early 90's were the strange black metal act Abruptum, Ophthalamia, Darkified, and Grimorium. All of them recorded memorable demos, and the Finspång phenomenon created a nationwide buzz. For some time, Finspång was the hottest place for death metal in Sweden.

"It was incredible back in the early 90's. There was a circle of about fifteen people who played in loads of bands, such as Pan-Thy-Monium, Edge of Sanity, Ophthalamia, and Abruptum. I guess Edge of Sanity were the first to get noticed outside of Finspång, and I think most of it had to do with the fact that our demo was reviewed in Kerrang!*"*—DAN SWANÖ, EDGE OF SANITY/UNISOUND

The rest of the Östergötland region was far behind, even though some interesting bands turned up here and there. Norrköping had the black metal titans Marduk, Nyköping had the brutal act Gorement, and Linköping was already established, with underground bands such as Satanic Slaughter, Total Death, and Orchriste. But the band that really put Linköping on the map was Seance, who took Swedish death metal to new levels of brutality with their two albums *Fornever Laid to Rest* in 1992, and *Saltrubbed Eyes* in 1993.

The Strange Case of Mjölby

The death metal scene that rose in the godforsaken town of Mjölby is one of the strangest chapters in the history of the genre. Seemingly out of nowhere, the town started spewing out incredibly violent gore-grind bands, until the streets were crammed with them. The first was probably Traumatic, rising from the death/thrash band Crab Phobia in 1990. Their *The Process of Raping a Rancid Cadaver* demo was recorded at Art Serv Studio in Mjölby. The band soon gained attention with an unrelenting style, and inspired a streak of gore-grind bands with their two singles in 1991: *A Perfect Night to Masturbate* on CBR, and *The Morbid Act of a Sadistic Rape Incision* on Distorted Harmony. Don't you just love those titles?

"Actually, I have no idea if we were first or not. If you ask any member of any band, they will probably all say they were first. I guess most of it happened at the same time. Carcass were worshipped like gods here. In fact, I guess I was the only one who never really liked them!"—Totte Martini, Traumatic

At any rate, the Mjölby-based Salvation and Belsebub also released demos in 1990. Then all hell broke loose. During 1991 and 1992, relentless demos were unleashed by Funeral Feast, Mesentery, Nefarius, Midiam, and Lucifer (a continuation of Salvation). In 1993, the madness continued with Retaliation, Genetic Mutation, and Dominus, who later became Carcaroht. Most of them bashed out furious grind with lyrics that would make a pathologist sick.

A couple other bands turned up in Mjölby during 1992, such as Cerberus and Dawn. Cerberus would soon transform into the Viking metal band Mithotyn, who eventually had some success after releasing six demos and three albums in the late 90's. Dawn, on the other hand, ended up on Necropolis Records after three demos, and released three decent black/death albums between 1995 and 1998.

The central character of the Mjölby scene was probably Henrik Forss. Apart from playing in Dawn, Funeral Feast, Retaliation, and Nefarious, he also edited the 'zines *Brutal Mag* and *Dis-organ-ized*. Later he also coedited the classic *Septic Zine*. Among his other claims to fame, he sang on Carcaroht's first demo as well as In Flames' first mini-CD.

The Eskilstuna Scene

Eskilstuna has a fine history of brutal music. The legendary crust band No Security came from there, as did the cult label Finn Records. Eskilstuna also spawned the band Chronic Decay as far back as 1985, followed by the great Macrodex in 1988. Both were early pioneers of Swedish death metal.

"I guess the main reason for the growth of the Eskilstuna scene was that we

Clockwise from top:
Crab Phobia demo;

Traumatic demo;

Traumatic 7"

had two large buildings with rehearsal rooms provided by the municipality—
*Balsta Musikslott and TBV. These soon turned into places to party, and
spawned tons of project bands. For a long time there were no places to play
live, but eventually the venues Klubb Dolores (later Max 500), where At the
Gates did one of their first gigs, and K13, where Unleashed did one of their
first gigs, opened.*"—MATTIAS KENNHED, MACRODEX/HOUSE OF USHER

Apart from compilation appearances, the only vinyl from these two early
bands was Chronic Decay's *Ecstasy in Pain* 7" in 1991. However, Macrodex
were more talented, and their splitting up
in 1990 allowed the death metal boom to
happen in Eskilstuna. After their demise,
the members of Macrodex spread out in
three new bands: Crypt of Kerberos, House
of Usher, and Infester. Crypt of Kerberos
was the most active, releasing two demos
and the *Visions Beyond Darkness 7"*
during 1991. The band was quite slow and
doomy—very different from Macrodex.
They released the single *Cyclone of Insanity*
in 1992, and the album *World of Myths* in
1993, both on Adipocere Records.

The second band to rise out of
Macrodex, House of Usher, also released a
7" in 1991. *On the Very Verge* was a rather

experimental record, and showed some interesting patterns. The band definitely had some unique ideas, but they split up after two demos in 1993. However, the talented guitarist Martin Larsson was soon recruited by At the Gates.

"I thought House of Usher was one of the most underrated Swedish bands of all. Martin was the perfect guy for At the Gates, since we had similar ideas about music."—ANDERS BJÖRLER, AT THE GATES/THE HAUNTED

Macrodex also spawned Infester, but this band only made one demo in 1992 before calling it quits. However, once the Eskilstuna scene was on the move, bands like Ileus, Eternal Darkness, Exanthema, and Obscene all released demos between 1990 and 1992. Eternal Darkness was probably the most successful, and they released the *Doomed* 7" in 1992 as well as the *Twilight in the Wilderness* album in 1993. The same year also saw the release of the Exanthema/Chronic Decay split album, and the Eskilstuna scene seemed to be thriving.

Avesta and the Scene in Bergslagen

The gloomy industrial region of Bergslagen has always bred extreme music. As the death metal movement grew, the steel town of Avesta in particular started churning out good bands. The tradition of extreme music had its roots locally in neighboring Hedemora, home to groundbreaking crust punk bands Asocial and Svart Parad. Some members of Asocial also formed one of Sweden's best thrash metal bands, Hatred, which rehearsed in Avesta in the late 80's with Johan Jansson on guitar.

To a great extent, the dedicated Johan Jansson took the extreme music scene of the area to the next level by starting Beyond in 1988. Beyond was basically a Celtic Frost–inspired band that transformed into the much deadlier Interment after the guys became increasingly influenced by bands like Death and Possessed. The scene in Avesta was also fueled by Fagersta, just twenty miles away, where youngsters could attend all the brutal shows. Luckily, a youth center opened in Avesta that focused entirely on music, and soon sponsored the local compilation tape *Avesta Mangel*.

Recorded in Studio Fragg in June 1991, the Avesta comp featured punk legends Asocial, crust/grind band Uncurbed, Interment, and the new death metal band Entrails. Underscoring the community nature of the scene, the first three of those bands all included Johan Jansson! The local scene soon exploded, and during 1991 and 1992 lots of new extreme bands turned up: Fulmination, Uncanny, Sadistic Gang Rape, Regurgitate, and Headless. The youngsters also formed a community named Rundgång that organized gigs, drawing bands like Merciless, Suffer, and Dismember to town.

All the Avesta bands started to spew out demos. Among the best are Interment's *Where Death Will Increase* from 1991 and *Forward to the Unknown* from 1992; Uncanny's *Nyktalgia* from 1992; and Fulmination's *Through Fire* from 1993. A couple of new compilation tapes explored the scene further. Strangely, none of the bands released an album until Uncanny made a split with Ancient Rites in 1993, and then the full-length *Splenium for Nyktophobia* in 1994. The crust band Uncurbed also released their debut album, *The Strike of Mankind*, for the German label Lost and Found in 1993. Almost all these recordings were made at Dan Swanö's Gorysound/Unisound studio.

"I guess I was the house studio for that youth center in Avesta for some years. All of the bands from there were very cool guys, and it was a pleasure to work with them."—DAN SWANÖ, EDGE OF SANITY/UNISOUND

The first death metal band in the region to release an album was Centinex from Hedemora. After their *End of Life* demo in 1991, the hard-working bandleader Martin Schulman scored a deal with obscure label Underground, and the following year they debuted with *Subconcious Lobotomy*. Another band from the area, Wombbath from Sala, recorded the *Several Shapes* 7" for Thrash Records in 1992, followed by the album *Internal Caustic Torments* the next year. Undoubtedly, Avesta still had the best bands and most viable scene.

But the most successful death metal figure of the area lived about forty-five miles north, in the town of Ludvika. Here Peter Tägtgren got his project Hypocrisy together in 1992, and signed with the upstart German label Nuclear Blast. Over the years, Hypocrisy has become one of Sweden's biggest metal bands. Tägtgren also started his Abyss studio in the early 90's, and he eventually took over Dan Swanö's—to say nothing of Tomas Skogsberg's—role as Sweden's premier death metal producer.

"The first Abyss studio was a discarded bomb shelter. There was like a big fucking iron door, and when you closed it, just ventilation slits all around. It was a big concrete thing. Turn off the lights and it was pitch black. I said: 'This is like the abyss, and it was like cling—*this is what it's going to be called.' In the bunker I was using a 16-track Fostex recorder. I bought it very cheap, so tracks one and sixteen never worked. They would have cost more to fix than I paid for the whole thing. So it was a fourteen-channel studio. Quarter-inch tape. I had like one reverb, one echo, and a couple of compressors. If someone needed to compress something extra—sorry, we didn't have them! That was the answer then. We just tried to make the best of it. It was just about making things work for whatever you have. So I recorded a bunch of demos and stuff, and eventually I got signed to Nuclear Blast."*—PETER TÄGTGREN, HYPOCRISY/PAIN/BLOODBATH/ABYSS STUDIO

"One day one of the bands recording in my studio brought a tape that was done in Abyss, and said that they were looking for a sound like that. I was amazed when I heard it; everything sounded so good. I guess I realized that my days were over. I thought that I could never do anything as good as that."—DAN SWANÖ, EDGE OF SANITY/UNISOUND

*Clockwise from top left: No Security
on the bill with Unleashed;*

one of Cruelty's few gigs;

Beyond's ultra-rare rehearsal tape;

Crypt of Kerberos demo

230 THE DEATH METAL EXPLOSION

Clockwise from top left:
The Avesta Mangel *comp tape;*

Avesta Mangel II;

Interment *demo;*

Uncanny *demo*

Uppsala Bloodbath

Even though Uppsala was overshadowed by the nearby capital city of Stockholm when it came to extreme metal— and everything else, basically—they had always had a music scene. During the 80's, Uppsala was in fact something of a thrash metal center, with bands like Damien, Tradoore, Vivaldi's Disciples, and Midas Touch. Many of these bands produced records, setting an example for metal kids in Uppsala that it was possible to get somewhere with music.

Another perhaps even more important reason for the development of extreme metal in Uppsala was the small record store Expert. Just like Heavy Sound in Stockholm, Expert imported all sorts of extreme records during the mid-80's that other stores wouldn't touch, infecting countless record collections with bands like Sodom, Destruction, Bathory, Possessed, and Death.

One of the first really extreme Uppsala bands was the obscure black metal act Third Storm, formed by notorious metalhead Heval Bozarslan in 1986. Their aim was to be the most evil band imaginable, and their brutal views were way ahead of any other band from Uppsala. They probably surpassed even Bathory, at least in terms of brutality—but Third Storm's songs sucked and they could barely play. Bozarslan's vocals in particular were totally insane. They played their first gig in December 1986 wearing corpse paint on their faces, and they probably scared everybody to death with songs like "Thrash and Black" and "Sacrifice to Evil."

"We wanted to play blasphemous metal like Bathory, Sodom, and Hellhammer. We did a few gigs and eventually recorded a rehearsal demo, but it was very hard keeping the band together. I had to kick one guy out because he wanted to play 'gay metal.' In late 1988 I was the only one who wanted to continue, so I had to fold the band."—HEVAL BOZARSLAN, THIRD STORM/ SARCASM

Bozarslan didn't get very far, but he succeeded in planting the seed for extreme metal in Uppsala. Third Storm were followed by Necrotism, Convulsion, Codex Gigas, Crematorium, and the hilarious noise project Eternal Tormentor. The last released the *E.T Is Not a Nice Guy* demo back in 1988. Though not death metal, it was early proof of something brutal in the underground.

In March 1990, Necrotism changed their name to Embalmed and recorded the demo *Decomposed Desires*, perhaps Uppsala's first 100 percent death metal recording. The singer in both Eternal Torment and Embalmed was a dedicated guy named Stefan Pettersson, a driving force of the town's death metal scene in many ways.

Since the Uppsala youth center Ungdomens Hus held brutal metal concerts on a regular basis, bands from other areas came to Uppsala to play gigs. This kept the scene alive, even though none of the early local bands in town managed to get a recording deal. My old punk band Roof Rats played one of our first gigs there in

Grab 'em by the balls - MIDAS TOUCH

Clockwise from top left: Well...;
the ultra-evil logo of Third Storm;
information sheet for Musik Med Mening;
ultra-primitive advertisement for Heavy Rock

1988, together with Black Uniforms and Refuse. The place was crawling with skinheads as well as punks, and we all drank ourselves stupid. It was insane. Ungdomens Hus continued to be a great place with hardly any rules until Gwar played there in 1992. Afterwards, the city started to clean the place up.

Many of these early concerts were arranged by Jörgen Sigfridsson, who also ran the small record label Opinionate—originally named Is this Heavy or What?—and Step One Records. He had previously played drums with Third Storm for a brief period. The omnipresent Sigfridsson later started the booking group Musik Med Mening together with Stefan Pettersson—then in Eternal Torment and Embalmed, later in Diskonto, Sportlov, and Uncurbed. Aiming to bring as many death metal bands to Uppsala as possible, they impressively succeeded in luring Immolation, Massacre, Seance, Entombed, Master, Invocator, and Merciless.

Uppsala eventually produced two great extreme metal bands. First was Sarcasm, founded in late 1990 by Heval Bozarslan of Third Storm with Fredrik Wallenberg of Embalmed. Initially they blasted primitive Autopsy-style death metal, but over demos such as *In Hate* in 1992, *Dark* in 1993, and *A Touch of the Burning Red Sunset* in 1994, they transformed into an atmospheric band in the vein of Dissection. I saw this band live back in 1992, and they were just great. Sadly they never made an album, and Sarcasm fell apart after Wallenberg moved to Gothenburg and started the crust band Skitsystem with Tomas Lindberg and Adrian Erlandsson from At the Gates.

The more fortunate Defleshed was formed in 1991 by talented guitarist Lars Löfven. After a few straight death metal demos, the band became a relentless thrash/grind act with atomic bombs of destructive power. In 1993 they released the 7" single *Obsculum Obscenum* on Miscarriage, and shortly afterwards signed a deal with Invasion. In all, they produced seven intense albums until playing their final gig in 2005 at the legendary metal pub Fellini in their hometown.

The Stockholm Scene Gets Flooded

As the death metal scene exploded throughout Sweden, Stockholm remained the center of activity. Established bands including Entombed, Dismember, Therion, Unleashed, and Tiamat continued to make successful albums and grow huge on the international scene. Others like Katatonia, Afflicted, Necrophobic, Lobotomy, Hypocrite, and Desultory also strengthened their positions. And the Swedish capital also saw also loads of new death metal bands recording demos during this period. One reason for the massive production of Stockholm demo tapes was nearby Studio Sunlight. If you had a band, it was easy to get that special death metal sound. And many, many did—not just bands from Stockholm.

During 1991 the bands Unanimated, Epitaph (aka Dark Abbey), and

From left: Flyer for Is This Heavy or What? *compilation 7";*

Is This Heavy or What? *compilation sleeve*

Mastication debuted their demos. In 1992 the death metal explosion continued with demos by Incardine, Proboscis, Excretion, Unpure, Votary, Dispatched, Obscurity (aka Vicious Art, no relation to the legendary Obscurity from Malmö), and Scum—who later became Amon Amarth. Bands appeared everywhere, and most of them recorded at Studio Sunlight. This became problematic, leading to loads of similar-sounding demos. Since the songs on many of the tapes were of inferior quality, interest in the Sunlight sound waned. Instead of being a guarantee of quality, the Sunlight name soon indicated a lack of imagination.

Some of the bands were still of superior quality. One of the best of the second-generation Stockholm bands, Unanimated included young drummer Peter Stjärnvind, who later played with Merciless, Face Down, Murder Squad, Entombed, and Nifelheim. The promising Unanimated signed with upstart Swedish label No Fashion, and in 1993 they released the powerful debut *In the Forest of the Dreaming Red*. Another young band, Necrophobic were picked up by Black Mark, who released their debut, *The Nocturnal Silence*, in 1993. Necrophobic's guitarist David Parland, especially, showed immense talent in his playing and songwriting, and the band suffered a lot when he later left to concentrate on the black metal band Dark Funeral. A third album worth mentioning during 1993 was Morpheus' *Son of Hypnos*, but none of these bands ever reached international fame.

The most successful Stockholm band after the original scene has instead been Amon Amarth, which developed out of Scum in 1992. They gradually built up a slow and catchy form of death metal over demos, a single, and a mini-album before they secured a deal with Metal Blade in 1998. They are immensely popular around the world, even though they never got attention of the same magnitude in their hometown. All in all, none of the new bands that turned up in the early 90's could match any of the original bands. The average quality of death metal was already decreasing.

Up North and Down South

Strangely, death metal never hit the big time in the north or south of Sweden during the turbulent early 90's. Especially in the south, a bigger scene should have emerged. Malmö was one of the first towns to have an extreme metal band with Obscurity, and the region had spawned Sweden's first extreme metal fanzines: *At Dawn They Read, NOT,* and *To the Death.* The only important export during the early 90's was Deranged—a great band that has prevailed over the years with an unrelenting gore-grind version of death metal.

In a similar way, each major city in the north of Sweden only produced one or two bands during the early 90's. Piteå had Morgh, Sundsvall had Left Hand Solution, Bollnäs had Fantasmagoria, and Nordmaling had Mephitic. Umeå was the only city with some kind of scene with bands like Nocturnal Rites, Moral Decay, and Disgorge. All of these bands were of inferior quality compared to those from the southern part of Sweden, though. Only Umeå's brilliant thrash innovators Meshuggah made good on an international level, but they hardly fit into the death metal movement.

Death metal spread slowly from its most explosive centers in Stockholm, Gothenburg, Bergslagen, and Östergötland. If you lived far away from these areas, you weren't affected as much. Umeå was probably also held back by the city's massive hardcore scene, which virtually dominated the entire area. Bands like Refused were hailed worldwide for their aggressive and politically charged punk, and thrill-seeking kids went for that rather than death metal. It wasn't until the black metal movement that Umeå launched some extreme bands to be reckoned with, such as Naglfar.

That's briefly how death metal swept across the country and created local scenes during the early 90's. But as the corpus of death metal expanded drastically, the average quality sank proportionally. Many of the guys inspired by death metal simply were not ready to start bands or record demos. Unlike hardcore and punk, death metal is pretty complicated music that you just can't learn how to play in a few weeks. Soon enough, death metal got watered down, accepted, and eventually overrun by a countermovement: black metal.

FIRE STORM

DEATH-GRIND

THE BACK DOOR BAND

på DEN 26/1

KATARINAGÅRN 20.30

Ⓣ MEDBORGARPLATSEN

DERANGED
...THE CONFESSIONS OF A NECROPHILE

THE SICK AND BRUTAL FOUR TRACK DEMO
"CONFESSIONS OF A NECROPHILE" FINALLY
OUT. ZINES, BANDS, LABELS AND TRADERS-
GET IN TOUCH OR ORDER THE TAPE FOR
EITHER 5 DOLLARS (U.S) OR 20 KRONER
(SWE) WRITE TO:

PER GYLLENBÄCK
LÄRKVÄGEN 11B
245 62 HJÄRUP
SWEDEN

RIKARD WERMEN
C/O FRANSSON
ÅNGAVÄGEN 9
245 62 HJÄRUP
SWEDEN

STEP ONE PRESENTERAR:

CANCER
CEREBRAL FIX
MONOLITH
MORPHEUS

Inträde: 100:-
FREDAG 19 MARS KL. 19.00.
UNGDOMENS HUS-UPPSALA
SVARTBÄCKSGATAN 32
FÖRKÖP:
MUSIKÖRAT, EXPERT, SKIVBÖRSEN
(UPPSALA)
FAR OUT, HOUSE OF KICKS,
HEAVY SOUND (STOCKHOLM)

DROGFRITT

Death is just the beginning...

Clockwise from top left:
Unanimated demo;
typical primitive gig poster;
Morpheus on stage with Cancer;
Deranged flyer

Chapter Eight:
The End of the Original
Scene–Black Metal
Takes Over

"MEET THE CHAOS
ON THE OTHER SIDE
THE PAST IS HAUNTING YOU
DEATH IS JUST THE BEGINNING"

—MARDUK, "STILL FUCKING DEAD"

*Clockwise from top left: Euronymous
and Maniac of Mayhem in the
joke band Septic Cunts. Note
Euronymous' Gandalf-like hat;*

*Maniac (Mayhem) with chainsaw on
an old stove. Metal was all about fun
back in the mid-80's!;*

Euronymous in corpse paint;

Dead in corpse paint—no more fun!

ven though Swedish death metal was more active than ever in 1992, at this point something started to go wrong. Negative vibrations hung in the air after the two biggest concerts in Sweden during this period went totally wrong. First, Morbid Angel canceled a show with Entombed and Unleashed in Stockholm on December 1, 1991, because their gear didn't arrive at the venue in time, reportedly due to a road accident. Despite the Swedish bands' best efforts, the frustration of the expectant audience that night was only the beginning of a downward spiral.

In following months, Pestilence, Sepultura, Cancer, and Fudge Tunnel concerts were also canceled, and the death metal audience became increasingly pissed off. The biggest letdown of 1992 was probably the legendary Florida band Deicide's first appearance in Sweden. The entire scene was excited—Deicide was definitely one of the most controversial death metal groups in the world, and also one of the best. Their overly satanic image had given them a dark cult status. Notorious bandleader Glen Benton gained media attention with numerous shocking statements. Among the most "memorable," he claimed to like torturing animals, and boasted of plans to commit suicide at age thirty-three to mock the death of Jesus Christ.

On November 25 we gathered at Fryshuset in Stockholm to witness what should have been the most intense concert of the year. The bill was impressive. Apart from Deicide, the hyped Dutch band Gorefest were appearing with their respected drummer Ed Warby. Also on the bill: the brutal Germans Atrocity, along with Swedish bands Therion and Furbowl. The evening began badly when Furbowl weren't even allowed to play, since Deicide apparently didn't want too many opening acts. Therion had to go on first, and they hardly made a good impression. The sound was very bad, and they looked uninspired, probably due to the stressful atmosphere backstage. The part in which a couple of hooded and masked guys appeared onstage with torches simply didn't work at all.

Gorefest were somewhat better, but during the middle of their set a loud bang was heard. Everybody assumed the sound was a part of the show, and Gorefest finished their set as usual. But this was the beginning of the end of the unfortunate evening. After Gorefest's gig nothing happened for a long time, and rumors started to spread. Eventually Atrocity's singer arrived onstage and declared that a bomb had gone off, and an entire wall had been blown apart.

"That night was just a terrible mess. Deicide had gotten a lot of media coverage before that gig due to their satanic image and especially Glen Benton's statements about animal sacrifice. The entire day, Lili and Sussie [two very well known Swedish singers and animal rights activists] kept calling, wanting to get Benton on the phone so they could 'talk some sense' into him. I refused. Eventually Benton got fed up with these calls, and grabbed the phone out of my hand. Then he started to tell these two young blond girls that he was going

to 'put his big satanic cock up their tiny asses' and stuff like that. They got absolutely insane, but he just smiled and hung up.

"After that some TV show started to phone, wanting someone from Deicide to come to the studio for a live debate. They refused, so I asked Christoffer Johnsson of Therion to do it. He refused. Just when I had finally convinced Piotr [Wawrzeniuk, Therion's drummer] to do it, the bomb went off and everything turned into a nightmare. In the middle of everything, the TV station continued to call me. I was still trying to convince Deicide to play—which they didn't want to do—and to convince the security guards to let them—which they definitely *didn't want to do*. If Deicide hadn't taken the stage, I would have lost more money than I owned! And then the sisters started to call again!"—JÖRGEN SIGFRIDSSON, <u>HEAVY ROCK</u>/MUSIK MED MENING/STEP ONE RECORDS

Finally, Deicide agreed to walk onstage, and the guards stepped aside to avoid a riot. The band went into "Sacrificial Suicide" in big style, then the lights were switched on, and Deicide were ordered to leave the stage. They continued

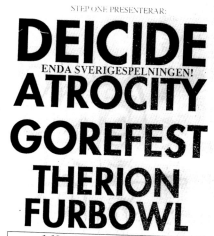

Clockwise from top left:
Flyer for Morbid Angel gig
that never happened;

poster for Decide's ill-fated
Stockholm concert;

gig flyer

with a couple of more songs in the fully lit venue before everything came to a sudden end. Everybody felt ripped off.

Speculation began about who had placed the bomb. One theory was that Norwegian satanists were behind it, attacking either Therion or Gorefest—considered too wimpy in their eyes—or their rivals in Deicide. This is highly improbable, however, since the members of the black metal scene are notorious for baseless bragging about their crimes. It's more reasonable to think that the attack was conducted by militant animal rights activists offended by Glen Benton's statements concerning animal sacrifice. The truth behind the bombing has never been revealed. In any case, the young audience felt frustrated and disappointed. Death metal couldn't seem to deliver anymore. Worse, almost no Swedish venues would dare book extreme bands after this dreadful night. In a way, this was the Altamont of Swedish death metal.

"That night was the end of the original death metal scene in Sweden. After that there were hardly any shows for a long time, and it all just faded. The great feeling that had been present at that Candlemass gig in 1987 was long gone. I got out of the scene shortly after. It was over."—JÖRGEN SIGFRIDSSON, HEAVY ROCK/MUSIK MED MENING/STEP ONE RECORDS

Though the past year had delivered so many good albums, 1992 was the beginning of the end of the original Swedish death metal movement. The massive amount of new bands and demos might have felt like a sign of health, but in reality the average quality of the music had decreased. Further, some of the very best demos that were released during this time got lost in the overpopulated market, and in many cases inferior bands got the attention. Brilliant bands like Crematory, Interment, and Evocation just vanished in the massive blur of death metal. People were beginning to get tired of it all. Even the good bands soon got trapped in old, stereotyped formulas.

The fact that virtually everybody played in a band at this point also affected the climate at live gigs. Since everybody had to focus on their own bands in the stiff competition of the times, people tended to be less enthusiastic about other people playing music, and they became less active at concerts. Where a stagediving culture had reigned previously, patrons began to act immovable and stiff. The fewer shows also drew fewer and fewer attendees. There was an obvious slow draining of energy in the original death metal scene. Frankly, the fun seemed to slip out of the genre by the end of 1992.

Furthermore, the media now wrote a great deal about death metal. The music could be read about in the mainstream magazines, and the underground fanzine corpus had expanded a lot. Death metal fans could hear about their favorite bands everywhere. It was just a matter of time before the thrill-seeking sector of the audience lost interest. Death metal had become accessible and accepted. The shock value was gone. Some of the people who had used death metal to distinguish themselves from others started to notice something terrifying: it had become trendy among average kids to like some death metal.

"Most of the Swedish bands kept on playing virtually the same song with the same sound and the same lyrics over and over again. Further, you got kind of turned off when you saw a band like Entombed in flashy magazines and on moronic TV programs. So I can understand why people started to search for something else."
—Dan Swanö, Edge of Sanity/Unisound

"When Entombed used a mainstream icon such as La Camilla [a disco diva in Army of Lovers] in their video, and Dismember were baking gingerbread in the major tabloids, death metal was doomed. It wasn't dangerous anymore, and something else could come take over."—Christoffer Jonsson, Therion

By the time death metal became socially acceptable in Sweden, the underground had already moved in a different direction. The success of Swedish death metal had created a countermovement, especially in the neighboring country of Norway. Apparently overnight the media, as well as hungry metal kids, would lose most interest in the previously exciting death metal scene to focus on something "new"—black metal.

The Birth and Development of Black Metal

It is common knowledge that black metal was born with the arrival of Newcastle, England, trio Venom in the autumn of 1979. They created a devilish image,

and adopted stage names like Cronos, Mantas, and Abaddon. In 1981 they released their classic debut, *Welcome to Hell*, on Neat Records. Though the album set out the satanic imagery and lyrics of the black metal genre, the music wasn't really well played or creative. Still, the rough and primitive Motörhead-like hard rock that Venom delivered sure sounded hellish at the time.

With their second album, *Black Metal*, Venom coined the term in 1982. The music was a little bit more advanced, anticipating the thrash metal scene that would emerge from San Francisco the following year. The media immediately picked up on the black metal tag, and desperately tried to create a genre from the more controversial bands around. However, not many bands could yet be incorporated in such a genre, so the determination point remained the image rather than the music.

The second band labeled black metal was probably Mercyful Fate from Denmark, led by the charismatic singer King Diamond. Their complex and majestic heavy metal was much more advanced than Venom's music. The lyrics were intensely satanic, however, as was the cover of their 1982 mini-LP, *Nuns Have No Fun*, on which shocked parents and delighted kids could see a girl being set on fire by a group of hooded figures. King Diamond also introduced the use of demonic face painting to the genre, something that would become a regular part of black metal imagery in the 90's.

Mercyful Fate's "Nuns Have No Fun" EP

Another band connected to the embryonic genre was Switzerland's Hellhammer, who later evolved into Celtic Frost. As Hellhammer, this corpse-painted trio made truly raw and brutal music that went along perfectly with their satanic lyrics. Their simple yet effective riffs and fat guitar sound were groundbreaking, anticipating the later trademark sound of early Swedish death metal. When the group transformed into Celtic Frost, the music explored more orchestral and experimental territories. The lyrics also became more personal, with topics about inner feelings and majestic stories. But for a couple of years, Celtic Frost was one of the world's most extreme and original metal bands, with a huge impact on the mid-90's black metal scene.

But the purest black metal band of the 80's was without a doubt Bathory from Sweden. As I have said before, no other band took lyrical and musical evil to a more perfect, atmospheric heights. Bathory's third album, especially, *Under the Sign of the Black Mark*, was almost the blueprint for all future black metal. The music contained all the things that would become essential for the genre—the speed, the atmospheric and primitive sound, the simple riffs, and the tormented screaming vocals. In retrospect, Bathory really created black metal.

Other bands in the 80's would occasionally be connected to the black metal corpus, even if they didn't actually belong there. Bands that at one time or another found themselves under the black metal umbrella include German speed metallers Sodom, Destruction, and Vectom; California thrashers Possessed and

Slayer; hilarious Canadian joke band Piledriver; and UK thrashers Onslaught. Some articles even desperately tried to label regular metal bands like Accept, Grave Digger, Anvil, Exciter, and Angel Witch as black metal. These bands only flirted with satanic lyrics at early stages of their careers, if at all.

During this turbulent time, Øystein "Euronymous" Aarseth started his band Mayhem in Oslo, Norway. The musical inspiration came from the likes of Venom and Bathory, as well as German speed metal—and, I would guess, extreme punk bands like Discharge and Disorder. In 1985 the young Norwegian band recorded their debut demo *Pure Fucking Armageddon*, and Mayhem started to attract a small underground following with their ultra-primitive and violent music. In 1987, Mayhem began earning a reputation as a very brutal underground band with the infamous *Deathcrush* mini-album on Aarseth's own Posercorpse label, later renamed Deathlike Silence. At this point, there was no talk whatsoever about black metal, and Mayhem called their music "total death metal." Later, Aarseth claimed to always have played black metal, but historical revisionism is a hallmark of the genre. Most of the satanic imagery was yet to come.

Aarseth seemed obsessed with any violent and strange underground metal he could find, anywhere in the world. He hailed groups like Sarcofago from Brazil, Sigh from Japan, Tormentor from Hungary, Monumentum from Italy, and the brutal Merciless from Sweden. Many of these bands would later schedule releases on Deathlike Silence. The atmosphere was open, and connections were made through tape trading. The ignorance, chauvinism, and nationalism of the forthcoming genre couldn't have been farther off. The situation was rather the opposite, where Aarseth felt Norway couldn't produce good music.

Even at this early stage, Aarseth's importance for the black metal scene really can't be overestimated. Unlike the organic development of Swedish death metal, the Norwegian black metal scene was in fact a calculated creation, planned and brought to life by Øystein Aarseth alone. He had a tremendous capacity to get people into his ideas and make them follow the path he had set for the future of extreme metal. He was originally the mastermind, even if he still never called his style black metal.

The first major development in Norwegian black metal was when Mayhem recruited the Swedish singer Per "Dead" Ohlin from Morbid in 1988. Ohlin and Aarseth had similar ideas about stage performance, and together they worked out the black metal image that would become the standard for the genre's followers. Among Ohlin's morbid onstage habits, he used to cut himself pretty badly, and inhale from a bag containing a dead bird. Anecdotes about Ohlin's strange antics are numerous. Among the weirder ones are that he used to bury his stage clothes underground to give them a grave-like touch, and that he clipped obituaries from newspapers and attached them to his jacket.

The two visionaries pushed each other further into darkness, and sometime

Hårdrockarna i Entombed tar avstånd från djävulsdyrkar.
Därför står de på de norska satanisternas dödslista.
Foto: JENS ASSUI

De står på djävuls-dyrkarnas dödslista

Av ANDERS FALLENIUS

Det kända svenska hårdrockbandet Entombed har tvingats ställa in sin konsert i Oslo.

Orsaken är att norska satanister hotar mörda gruppens medlemmar.

– Vi bedömer hotet som mycket allvarligt, säger Calle Schewen på gruppens skivbolag.

Entombed är Sveriges mest kända hårdrockband inom genren "death metal". Gruppen har genomfört framgångsrika turnéer utomlands och har dessutom fått ta emot flera utmärkelser. De utsågs bland annat till "årets bästa metal-grupp" 1991.

Senaste skivan, "Left Hand Path", har sålt i mer än 400 000 exemplar, varav 350 000 utomlands.

Död och mystik

I "death metal" handlar texterna ofta om död, mystik och satanism.

– Men det finns ingen satansdyrkan i Entombeds texter. Gruppen tar avstånd från allt som har med det att göra, säger Calle Schewen på skivbolaget House of Kicks Records.

Detta retar olika satanist-grupper, framför allt i Norge.

– Entombed hyllar inte döden. De spelar lite metal, har den kände norske satanisten Euronymus förklarat.

Den största sataniströrelsen i Norge, som också har förgreningar till Sverige, leds av en man som kallar sig Count Grishnackh. Han är även känd som "Greven" och leder själv en rockgrupp.

– Deras senaste skiva heter "Aska" och på omslaget finns en nedbränd kyrka. Den som köper skivan får också en tändare, säger Calle Schewen.

Brände kyrkor

"Greven" har nyligen avtjänat ett längre fängelsestraff för att han under rituella former tänt eld på åtta kyrkor.

Tillsammans med sina anhängare har han dessutom upprättat en dödslista över

olika fiender. På listan finns Entombeds medlemmar – Lars-Göran Petrov, Ulf Cederlund, Nicke Andersson, Lars Rosengren och Axel Hellid.

Hoten utreds nu av kriminalpolisen i Norge.

"De ska dödas"

Ema-Telstar, som sköter Entombeds turné, har ställt in den planerade spelningen i Oslo den 15 maj.

– De norska satanisterna har förklarat att Entombeds medlemmar ska dödas så fort de visar sig i Norge. Därför ställer vi in konserten, säger Calle Schewen.

Anhängarna runt "Greven" dra sig inte för att göra verklighet av sina hot.

Nyligen dömdes en ung kvinnlig svensk satanist till fängelse för mordbrand.

På order av norska djävulsdyrkare hade hon tänt eld på ett hus där en av medlemmarna i svenska "death metal"-bandet Therion bodde.

Orsaken var att Therion ansägs "ha ställt sig på det godas sida".

Tabloid story about death threats against Entombed

in 1990 they finally adopted the satanic image that would become so crucial for the genre. Before this, Aarseth was just obsessed with death and the occult the way teenagers can be. The music was now exclusively labeled black metal, and the journey into satanic mayhem had begun.

Aarseth's, and to some extent Ohlin's, version of black metal can be seen as a countermovement to the successful death metal genre. Aarseth turned against the clear and massive production quality of death metal bands, and instead advocated the rawer sounds of Bathory, Venom, and Hellhammer. Though I sincerely believe that Aarseth preferred these more primitive bands, I think there's more to the picture. It's well documented that Øystein initially was very into death metal and grindcore, even though he obviously didn't like the commercial success of the genres. He must have felt overrun by the whole movement, and that Mayhem was losing ground. Aarseth probably realized that Mayhem could not compete with bands like Entombed and Morbid Angel, so he had to turn against them to find unclaimed terrain to rule. He opposed the anti-image of death metal and Bay Area thrash metal, and created a total image of black metal. Much like a businessman, he manufactured his own trend in a very calculated way. Unlike the seemingly-random evolution of the early death metal scene, Aarseth's plan for black metal envisioned albums and world domination from the very beginning.

Among the first rules for this new version of black metal was that the lyrics had to deal with satanic and misanthropic topics. Any social commentary was completely forbidden. Secondly, the sound needed to be raw and primitive in the tradition of Bathory. Good sound was replaced with atmospheric noise. Further, the vocals should be more like tortured screams than deep growls, to separate black metal from death metal. Aarseth also advocated simpler riffs and song structures, and didn't tune guitars down very low. This yielded a thinner sound, further distinguishing the music from death metal.

Other important rules for black metal concerned how to dress. Only black clothes were accepted, and Aarseth loved spikes and bullet belts in the tradition of German speed metal. The last black metal ingredient was face paint. He took his ideas from King Diamond, Hellhammer, and Sarcofago, and developed them into a genre trademark. The so-called corpse paint would be used by hundreds of bands, and by the mid-90's was among the best selling tricks around. Hervé Harbaut of Osmose Productions once told me that every band wearing corpse paint in 1997 sold at least 10,000 albums.

Now the modern black metal genre was born, but Aarseth couldn't get as many people into his ideas as he wanted. However, an unexpected event soon gave him all the attention, shock value, and media coverage he could have wished for—though he lost his singer in the process. The strange and depressed Swedish singer of Mayhem, Per Yngve Ohlin, killed himself on April 8th, 1991. Controversially, Aarseth showed no emotion about the loss, but instead exploited the suicide to promote his band and record label. Now kids searching for kicks were enthralled by Aarseth. Within months of the suicide, Øystein opened the record shop Helvete in Oslo—a base from which to recruit young followers and promote Mayhem. The fact that his band didn't have a singer didn't seem to bother him.

Aarseth initially mostly attracted kids from Norway, but a fair share of Swedes hopped on board. Within just a few months, many young musicians had become obsessed with Aarseth and his ideas, and soon a lot of Norwegian death metal bands transformed into black metal bands. Amputation became Immortal, Thou Shalt Suffer turned into Emperor, and Darkthrone swapped their Swedish-inspired death metal for primitive black metal. Most notoriously, Old Funeral's guitar player Christian Vikernes had already left the band to form his own creation, Burzum.

Aarseth didn't realize that he wouldn't be able to control some of the more extreme youngsters that picked up his ideas. Some of the followers went further than he imagined, and their actions soon reached insane heights. Boasts of grave desecrations, arsons, and death threats started to be everyday ingredients of the scene. Aarseth's creation would soon strike back at him without remorse.

On August 10, 1993, Øystein Aarseth was stabbed to death by his former pupil Vikernes, and suddenly the black metal movement had lost its two most prominent members. Vikernes obviously didn't care much about the black metal scene anymore, as he had his own agenda. He considered signing to Earache at this point, demonstrating his independence from the black metal scene. The influences of Aarseth on his acolyte had been erased.

One could claim that the true black metal scene died in that moment, and that everything since has only approximated the original concept. But of course the violent and morbid act only boosted the genre to popularity. The media reveled in the gruesome deeds, and black metal got attention everywhere. Thrill-seeking teenagers around the world got into Norwegian black metal, too. In the following years, the black metal concept Aarseth had developed would grow into a massive trend. Black metal bands would completely flood the world of extreme metal. And though the general quality of these bands was questionable, they would take all the media attention from death metal. Even in Sweden, death metal was suddenly considered dated and old-fashioned.

A Blaze in the Swedish Sky

Many old death metallers were baffled by the sudden shift to black metal.

"I never understood what black metal was all about—why suddenly everybody wanted to be so angry and 'serious.'"—NICKE ANDERSSON, NIHILIST/ ENTOMBED

"That early-90's black metal thing seemed so faked when it came around. I remember when Darkthrone were here to record their first album, and Uffe of Entombed tried his best to help them. Then we had a barbecue. We acted as usual, drank beer and raised hell. The Norwegians acted like nerds, especially Gylve [Nagell, aka Fenriz], who walked around in a ridiculous cowboy hat and insisted on being called 'Hank Amarillo.' Some months later you could see the same guy with a new name and a new image, talking shit about us. What the fuck was that?"—ANDERS SCHULTZ, UNLEASHED

"I got to know Gylve early on, and had a great relationship with him and Darkthrone. They in fact stayed at my place when they recorded their first album. Then suddenly all the guys in Norway just turned their backs on us, and I have hardly spoken to any of them since. It's all just so strange."—UFFE CEDERLUND, MORBID/NIHILIST/ENTOMBED/DISFEAR

"I was through with extreme metal when black metal came around. That just seemed boring, with no gigs and hateful attitudes. I could feel nothing for that."

—FREDRIK HOLMGREN, CBR RECORDS

Despite the reluctance of some, Aarseth's ideas and the events in Norway of course infected the Swedish scene. Above all, one interview by Robban Becirovic with Mayhem's leader Euronymous caused an unimaginable impact.

"I guess to some extent I'm to blame for the black metal trend here in Sweden. That interview we did with Mayhem just changed everything. Black metal destroyed much of the buddy thing that was going on in the death metal scene. Everybody suddenly wanted to appear so fucking evil with an agenda of satanism, racism, fascism, and other stupid things. The slogans and views of Euronymous' were recycled over and over again by kids who tried to be cool."
—ROBBAN BECIROVIC, CLOSE-UP MAGAZINE

Ironically, Robban was forced to cancel his Power Hour radio show around the time black metal started to take over. He was simply thrown out of the studio, his slot soon occupied by a regular pop music program. Death metal apparently didn't interest the media like it used to. Now when the media wanted shock value, it turned to black metal rather than death metal.

These changes sank into the Swedish scene slowly. The second, post-Bathory generation of Swedish black metal basically consisted of three bands: Marduk, Abruptum, and Dissection. One might argue that bands like Treblinka and Grotesque could also be described as black metal, and before them Obscurity and Mefisto, but in my opinion they played primitive death metal. The three bands above really took things to the limit, and created something unique.

No Fashion

While black metal ascended, a guy named Tomas Nyqvist had launched the label No Fashion in the small town of Strängnäs. Nyqvist was already heavily involved in the scene as editor of the acclaimed fanzine *Putrefaction Mag*. Unlike most other 'zines, *Putrefaction Mag* was released on a regular basis, and it came as no surprise when the hyper-creative young Nyquist expanded his activities.

"It all started with Putrefaction Mag, *since the work with it gave me loads of connections and also some cash. Soon I got the idea to start an independent record label, and when I got an insanely brutal demo with the Dutch band Bestial Summoning I just asked them if I could release an album with them. They agreed and I quickly named my label No Fashion, since I felt that the death metal scene was getting commercialized and I wanted to go against that. I didn't know anything about releasing records; I was just a kid on adrenaline."*—
TOMAS NYQVIST, PUTREFACTION MAG/NO FASHION/IRON FIST PRODUCTIONS

This first release was pretty crude, but sold enough to encourage Nyqvist to continue. Next he released *Winter of Sin* by the Norwegian act Fester. This album came out right before the Norwegian black metal boom, and it sold

No Fashion advertisement

pretty well. Nyqvist realized that the label could actually work, and he went searching for the right bands. Unlike many other label managers, he knew exactly what was good and what was not. He quickly built up an impressive roster. His connections and knowledge of music soon made his small label the hottest in Sweden.

"*After Fester, I rapidly signed Marduk, Unanimated, Dissection, and Katatonia. Though I thought all these bands played death metal at that point, they all got associated with the upcoming black metal movement. My label skyrocketed after the release of Marduk's* Dark Endless. *Then I released Dissection's* The Somberlain *and everything just went insane. I couldn't believe it; my little underground project had suddenly become huge and the records sold by the tens of thousands!*"—

TOMAS NYQVIST, PUTREFACTION MAG/NO FASHION/IRON FIST PRODUCTIONS

Tomas Nyqvist's importance for launching the new Swedish black metal scene should not be underestimated. Though he didn't originally consider those bands black metal, he felt that their atmospheric and melodic music offered something new. As long as he ran No Fashion, the label was synonymous with quality, and he expanded his roster with Merciless and Throne of Ahaz.

Ironically, No Fashion would soon be the most fashionable metal label in Sweden. If Nyqvist had been able to keep it together, No Fashion could have become one of the dominant metal labels worldwide. But fate intervened, and Tomas Nyqvist lost his grip on his creation while still a teenager.

"*Everything went so fast and it slipped through my hands. I really could have used some help with the label; I was too enthusiastic and signed too many bands. Eventually I ran out of money. Then the guys at House of Kicks offered to press the albums and take care of the distribution. I was nineteen years old and swallowed everything they said, but the bastards ripped me off without mercy. They ruthlessly stole my label; that is what they did. I didn't even get any albums myself, and I never got a dime for any of the albums that I released.*"—
TOMAS NYQVIST, PUTREFACTION MAG/NO FASHION/IRON FIST PRODUCTIONS

After Nyqvist exited No Fashion, the label ceased to be important. The guys at House of Kicks knew more about running a label, but they just didn't have the same understanding of the scene. The best bands on the label, Marduk and Dissection, soon left—while bands that were about to sign, like Satyricon, refused to do so when they heard what had happened to Nyqvist. Among the later signings, only Dark Funeral has caused any musical or commercial impact.

Tomas Nyqvist was devastated for a long time after losing his creation, but eventually continued *Putrefaction Mag* with Rogga Pettersson from Merciless. In the 2000's he also built up the new label Iron Fist Productions, which now has contracts with Axis Powers, Skitsystem, Flesh, and Deceiver. Tomas Nyqvist's legacy rests with No Fashion and *Putrefaction Mag*, though, and we can largely thank him for the early Swedish black metal scene.

Dissection

The first of the second-generation black metal bands in Sweden was probably Strömstad's Dissection, who found their own musical path in a zone between black metal and death metal. Dissection formed in February 1990, when Jon Nödtveidt left his thrash metal band Rabbit's Carrot to voyage to a more intense constellation. He soon persuaded Rabbit's Carrot's drummer Ole Öhman to join him, together with their friend Peter Palmdahl, and the new band was born. They quickly made a rehearsal tape and the demo *The Grief Prophecy* in 1990. It was obvious that this band was dead serious.

Dissection's first vinyl appearance was their 1991 *Into Infinite Obscurity* 7", released by the obscure label Corpsegrinder. This recording sounds pretty much like a demo, but hints of what later made Dissection great were already apparent. All the musicians perform very well, the vocals are soulful, and the songs have a good flow. Glimpses of their trademark minor chord melodies were starting to show, though they had yet to perfect that style. For now, Dissection were a promising death metal band in the vein of Grotesque. For a couple of years, Dissection progressed rapidly over a series of rehearsal and demo tapes, until perfecting their unique style of extreme metal. They soon stood out as one of Sweden's most promising metal bands. By 1993 Dissection had secured a deal with No Fashion.

On March 1, 1993, Dissection entered Unisound studio to record *The Somberlain,* one of the most impressive and majestic debuts in Swedish metal history. Filled with brilliant riffs and inventive song structures, the album never loses its flow despite countless tempo changes. At this point Dissection had really found a unique style loaded with melancholic melodies and interesting patterns. Unlike other bands that used a lot of minor chords, Dissection didn't just bash them out as chords; they hit the strings separately to create unique moods. Dan Swanö's production is big and clear, and really fits the music.

From left: Dissection demo;
The Somberlain, *one of the*
masterpieces of Swedish death metal

"*Of all the recordings I have ever done, the first Dissection album is probably the one I am most proud of. Jon is a musical genius within his genre, and this is his greatest work. For me, this is a pure death metal album. There is not one second of black metal on it in my eyes.*"—DAN SWANÖ, EDGE OF SANITY/UNISOUND

"*The Somberlain is without a shadow of a doubt the best record I ever released on No Fashion. Its immense qualities are as apparent today as they were back then. It is a masterpiece.*"—TOMAS NYQVIST, PUTREFACTION MAG/ NO FASHION/IRON FIST PRODUCTIONS

Dissection didn't sound like any contemporary metal band. If you have to compare them, it should be to At the Gates. Jon's vocals especially remind me of Tompa's. The daring nature of the band was also evident in some unorthodox heavy metal screams à la King Diamond, clear choruses, and acoustic guitars. Some influences from Swedish folk music were also apparent, turned into something new in the hands of Dissection. *The Somberlain* was a fantastic record, and would influence countless bands.

Dissection were obviously not your average black metal band—in fact, they never called themselves black metal back then. Before long they upgraded to a deal with Nuclear Blast. On *Storm of the Lights Bane* from 1995, Dissection continued the path of their debut, but also showed more black metal tendencies. The bombastic drumming and the massive minor-chord swarms, especially, resembled Norwegian bands like Mayhem. But "Where Dead Angels Lie" and "Night's Blood" showed Dissection's own qualities. They didn't need traditional black metal attributes like corpse paint to make a statement. At this point, Dissection were as much death metal as black metal. They were unique.

From left: Cover of Dissection 7";
Dissection flyer

"*I would say Dissection were at least as important as At the Gates when it comes to the development of death metal. They had fantastic melodies and great melancholy. After we toured with Dissection and Morbid Angel across the States in 1996, loads of bands over there got inspired by the 'new' Swedish sound.*"
—ANDERS BJÖRLER, AT THE GATES/THE HAUNTED

Marduk

On the other hand, a band that fully embraced black metal aesthetics was Marduk from Norrköping. Their main creative force, Morgan Håkansson, had caught onto the movement from the beginning. In 1990, he abandoned his punk band Moses to focus on the darker side. Unlike Dissection, Marduk used corpse paint and quickly built up a hellish atmosphere. Among the original members was singer Andreas Axelsson, also a guitarist in Edge of Sanity.

"*With Marduk it was all or nothing. We wanted to be the most extreme in every way, both with our music and our image. We did everything—wore corpse paint, cut ourselves badly, and drank pig's blood. Everything we did was more violent than any band in Sweden at that time.*"—ROGER SVENSSON, ALLEGIANCE/MARDUK

In 1991, Marduk had material enough to enter Dan Swanö's Unisound studio (then named Gorysound) to record their *Fuck Me Jesus* demo, a very death metal–sounding recording with a heavy and fat sound. The song structures are basically death metal as well, combining heavy riffs with hammering two-beats. What makes a difference are some occasional grind parts, melodic guitars, and of course the hellish vocals of Andreas. All in all, it was a powerful recording, and Marduk quickly gained attention within the scene—still basically a death metal scene, anyway. Marduk obviously had great potential, and before long they secured a contract with No Fashion.

"During that recording there was not much talk about black metal. Instead, the idea was that it should have the feeling of the early recordings by Master, mixed with elements from Unleashed and Grave. The satanic stuff was just cosmetics on top of that."—DAN SWANÖ, EDGE OF SANITY/UNISOUND

In 1992, Marduk once again entered Dan Swanö's studio to record their debut album, *Dark Endless*. Though evil as hell, it lacks the atmospheric touch so crucial in black metal. In fact, this recording is very similar to the demo. All the corpse paint, satanic lyrics, and inverted crosses in the world couldn't hide the fact that the music reeked of death metal. In fact, the band sounded a lot like Edge of Sanity, hardly a surprise when you consider Dan Swanö recorded them. Marduk still had to find their style, and this record sounds pretty lame compared to some of their later material.

"The fact is that it doesn't sound like anything else but death metal, heavily inspired by bands like Autopsy."—ROGER SVENSSON, ALLEGIANCE/MARDUK

Still, *Dark Endless* was probably the first Swedish album of the 90's with the ambition to be black metal. True, Tiamat had used some attributes, but nowhere near as many as Marduk. The first Marduk album to really possess that black metal atmosphere was *Those of the Unlight* from 1993. By then,

Marduk—all made up and ready to go

Marduk had been added to Osmose Productions' crafty black metal roster, alongside bands like Immortal and Enslaved.

"Hervé [Herbaut, manager of Osmose Productions] just called one day and asked us if we were interested in a deal, and of course we were. It was a big step from the dysfunctional No Fashion. Osmose did a lot for us, got us out on good tours and did loads of promotion. Without Hervé, Marduk never would have become as successful as we did."—ROGER SVENSSON, ALLEGIANCE/MARDUK

Marduk's new recording had a much more lush sound, and a lot more atmosphere. The riffs are simple and driven on the grind parts, incorporating a great deal of melody on slower passages—some obviously inspired by Swedish folk music. The vocals are even more insane, now turned into tormented screams. *Those of the Unlight* is probably Marduk's most traditional black metal recording, and one of my personal favorites. Since Marduk's first album smelled so much of death metal, this was probably the first 100 percent Swedish black metal album since Bathory's *Under the Sign of the Black Mark*.

"Unlike Marduk's first record, Those of the Unlight *is pure black metal. I still like that record a lot, and it was fucking extreme for its time."*—ROGER SVENSSON, ALLEGIANCE/MARDUK

After *Those of the Unlight*, Marduk recruited the ultra-fast drummer Fredrik Andersson and their music quickly turned even more brutal. On the 1994 album *Opus Nocturne* they set new standards for speed within the black metal genre, and for as long as Fredrik was in the band they continued on that path. Marduk's masterpiece of sheer brutality must be *Panzer Division Marduk* from 1999, an album that basically consisted of blast beats (after that they had obviously made their point, and have mellowed out a bit). The band has occasionally been accused for being too simplistic and narrow-minded, but personally I just love their straightforward version of hyper-speed black metal.

Abruptum

Marduk's main creative force Morgan Håkansson was also heavily involved with the third of the second-generation Swedish black metal bands—Abruptum. Honestly, Abruptum's music is hard to label, since it is just so incredibly strange. But their image was definitely evil and mysterious to the max. The idea for the band dates as far back as 1987, when Tony "It" Särkkä planned to form the most evil band in the world. Abruptum didn't come to life until 1990, though, when Tony teamed up with equally minded Jim "All" Berger. Together they immediately created the vicious demos *Hextum Galaem Zelog* and *The Satanist Tunes*. (The first demo also included a bass player named "Ext," but he didn't last long in the band.)

Abruptum's early demos attracted Øystein Aarseth in Norway, and the twin pillars of evil corresponded frequently. In 1991, Abruptum released the *Evil* 7" on the Psychoslaughter label, making them the first of the second-generation Swedish black metal bands to be released on vinyl. The music on the demos and the single is primitive, slow, chaotic, and pretty rocking metal. In truth, their music actually resembles a band like Butthole Surfers more than any metal band. It's all spiced up with some ghastly guttural vocals. I guess the overall feeling of madness appealed to the black metal movement.

After the 7", Jim "All" Berger left the band, and was replaced by Morgan "Evil" Håkansson of Marduk. The duo quickly made the *Orchestra of the Dark* demo, which pretty much followed the ideas of the earlier recordings. Now they had such an impact on Øystein Aarseth that he signed them to Deathlike Silence. And when Abruptum got down to business in creating their debut album, they took their ideas one step further into darkness.

When *Obscuritatem Advoco Amplectere Me* was released in 1993, it simply sounded like no other extreme metal album in the world. The record consists of two twenty-five-minute compositions built on screeching distorted guitars, insane inhuman screams of torment, and horror film–style keyboards. The only thing that keeps it together at all is an occasional pattern of slow, heavy drums. To put in a nutshell: drums, screams, and noise. I guess it roughly compares to the most chaotic aspects of Butthole Surfers or Lydia Lunch. Abruptum weren't really music—they were all about atmosphere, darkness, and madness.

Even though the band was promoted by Euronymous as "the audial essence of pure black evil," the humor behind it was obvious. Reportedly, they recorded some "vocals" by putting Tony Särkkä under a sofa—with the others sitting on it as he moaned in pain into the microphone! Intentional or not, the humor reached perfection as they evoked the artwork of Spinal Tap's unfortunate *Smell the Glove* by using a plain black cover.

With their next album, *In Umbra Malitae Ambulado, In Aeternum in*

ABRUPTUM är ett av de äkta satanist band som finns. Jag vet att det är sant för jag känner folk som känner dom i bandet och dom är äkta! ABRUPTUM är latin och betyder "avgrund". Alla texter är på latin och musiken är någon slags brutal doom-death-metal med undantag för en grind del. Musiken är improviserad rätt in i studion men det låter trots det inte så illa. Lite för högt pris kanske, 25 kr + porto. Nu är det så att dom har gjort en ny demo som jag inte hört men den ska tydligen vara mer annorlunda. Dom vill också att äkta satanister skriver och berättar om sina erfarenheter, visioner m.m och även dom som vill fråga något om satanism kan skriva till dom på adress: Tony Särkää, Profilvägen 8 A, 612 35 FINSPÅNG.

Abruptum flyer

SONGS:
1. CORPUS IN - AS TRAHERE ABINCERE.
2. VIS SEMINA DIES HORA DEA-
            MEMBRA CORPORA.
3. FECI FACTUM SANGUINE GLADIOS MADE-
            FIERI FACTUS.
4. TORTUS TORQERO COLLA TUMENT-ES.
5. TURANNUM BELLUX EVENTUS ALCI EXEO-
            SIVIUM VITAE CARTHAGINIS INTEGRA.

·6·6·

THIS TAPE IS DEDICATED TO THE SUPERIOR
UNHOLY ANCIENT ONE-THY ONE WITHOUT
NAME OR SHAPE-THE ALL...
CONTACT:
ABRUPTUM-c/o TONY "IT" SÄRKKÄ.   NO
PROFILV.8a-612 35 FINSPÅNG.   USED
     · SWEDEN·   STAMPS......OK!

*Abruptum's evil
second demo*

Triumpho Tenebrarum from 1994, Tony Särkkä and Morgan Håkansson took the Abruptum concept another step forward. This album is actually just an hour-long "jam," with virtually no references to normal music. Okay, the pounding, slow drums remain, but the sounds and screams have even less substance than before. This is the kind of audio nightmare for which bands like Bathory, Burzum, or Samael were only a warm-up. Still, this had nothing to do with metal anymore. Abruptum had transitioned completely into the realms of horror film terror, or even distorted avant-garde music. There are no structures to guide you through the noise, and even Abruptum's demos sound like traditional rock in comparison. This is pure madness.

After these two insane albums, the duo of Särkkä and Håkansson produced yet one similar recording, 1996's *Vi Sonus Veris Nigrae Malitiaes.* After that, Särkkä obviously got fed up with the whole thing, and Håkansson was left to continue Abruptum as a solo project on the side of his main creation, Marduk. Even though Abruptum never played anything that can actually be labeled as black metal, the sounds they created reflect the atmosphere of the second-generation black metal movement better than any other band.

Exit Black Metal

From 1993 onwards, loads of Swedish youngsters got into black metal. Hundreds of bands imitated the music, lyrics, and image of Marduk, Dissection, and Abruptum (Abruptum's image, anyway!), along with the Norwegian originators. Among the bands that released albums in following years came Ophtalamia, Nifelheim (probably the best of the lot), Throne of Ahaz, Mörk

Gryning, The Abyss, and, best-known of all, Dark Funeral. Tons of demo bands also hailed the dark side and predictably despised death metal. Naturally, the strong imagery of black metal attracted teenagers, and before long it became a much more popular and fashion-oriented trend than the death metal scene had ever been. To me, this was only natural. Black metal is generally much more accessible music than death metal, since it mainly uses regular song patterns veiled in satanic imagery and distorted guitars. The songs are simpler and thus easier to follow, the screamed vocals aren't as demanding to listen to as deep growls, and the image made it easier to market. It was just a much more commercial genre.

Very few of these black metal bands survived into the 2000's. Apart from Marduk and Dissection, only Dark Funeral and Nifelheim have been able to maintain their credibility and popularity. Among newer bands, only Watain seems to have achieved any larger acceptance. A recent movement, suicide black metal, with bands like Shining and Silencer, has probably taken the original concept a bit too far. Few people seem to care anymore. In a very ironic paradox, black metal and crust punk have recently started to embrace one another. Members of Darkthrone and Satyricon have lately claimed that they love punk, while among crusties, black metal is the latest fashion. In fact, the latest album by crust punk band Skitsystem sounds very black metal—while the latest black metal opus by Darkthrone sounds very punk! This would have been unimaginable in the early 90's.

"There were so many shallow bullshit attitudes within the black metal scene, with a lot of unnecessary rules that you should follow. The most stupid of the rules was that you couldn't listen to death metal if you listened to black metal, and Marduk actually got a lot of shit for touring with bands like Deicide, Obituary, and Cannibal Corpse. What the fuck was all that about? Those are great bands! We should have stood united instead of fighting like a bunch of infants. Personally, I always just fucked all the rules. I have always liked and respected black metal, death metal, and crust punk equally. Fuck it, what was evil about following rules? Much of the black metal scene was so weak and childish."—ROGER SVENSSON, ALLEGIANCE/MARDUK

Though black metal overshadowed the death metal scene for many years, death metal is still here with us today. Death metal has survived as a genre, and is probably as vital today as it was back then. Meanwhile, the Swedish scene broadened, branching into many different subgenres, as we will soon see.

THRASH BASH 17

GORGUTS
(Kanada)

BLASPHEMY
(Kanada)

MARDUK

Ons. 31 mars Kl. 19.30

Kammaren, Tunnbindaregatan 37, Norrköping

Entré: 90:-

Arr: Power Hour

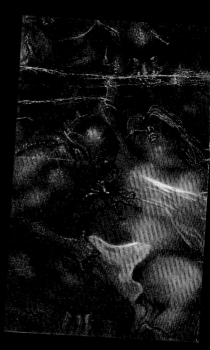

Clockwise from top left:
Marduk's first logo (I think designed by Dan Swanö);

Fuck Me Jesus *demo;*

Dark Endless;

Thrash Bash 17—everything went black!

"AT MY WORST I'M AT MY BEST
WIDE AWAKE BUT LET SANITY REST
I'M FULL OF HELL—ALL KINDS OF HELL"
—ENTOMBED, "FULL OF HELL"

Chapter Nine:
The Dead Live On...

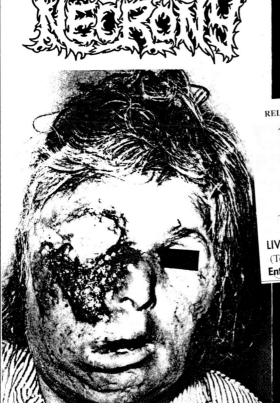

Clockwise from top left: Necrony demo; Furbowl flyer; Nasum—kings of Swedish grindcore; Deranged flyer

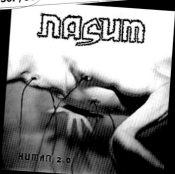

HAPPYS WEEKEND PRESENTERAR:
RELEASEPARTY FÖR <u>FURBOWL</u> "Those Shredded Dreams"

THERION
FURBOWL
MORPHEUS

LIVE PÅ TRE BACKAR - Fredag 13 November 20.00.
(Tegnérgatan 12-14.) - Lördag 14 November 20.00.
Entré: 50:-/60:-

NASUM

HUMAN 2.0

WITH THE DEMO "CONFESSIONS OF A NECROPHILE" DERANGED BRING
YOU FOUR SLICES OF INTENSE GRINDING DEATH-METAL WITH UNFO-
RGETTABLE VOCALS WHICH WILL BLOW YOUR MIND IN PIECES. THE
DEMO COMES WITH A COLOURED COVER, PRINTED CASSETTE AND A
LYRIC SHEET CONTAINING THE WORST PORNO-GORE LYRIX EVER MA-
DE. ALL THIS COULD BE YOURS IF YOU ONLY PULLED YOUR FIST
OUT OF YOUR ARSEHOLE, ORDER THE TAPE NOW FOR EITHER 5 $
OR 20 KRONOR, WRITE TO:

RIKARD WERMEN   PER GYLLENBÄCK
ÄNGAVÄGEN 2   LÄRKVÄGEN 118
245 62 HJÄRUP   245 62 HJÄRUP
SWEDEN   SWEDEN

"...BUT REMEMBER, STAY BIZARRE"

WE ARE
GOING TO
EAT YOU!

This brief history of Swedish death metal ends here. By 1993, the genre was ridiculously well established, and everything that followed has already been covered extensively in fanzines and magazines. Of course death metal didn't die—the superior bands kept going, and great new ones are still emerging. Death metal outlived the whole black metal movement. Unlike a genre such as hardcore, which quickly got locked into fixed patterns, death metal has been allowed to find new expressions. Especially in Sweden, death metal has exploded into a variety of different styles and subgenres since the mid-90's. Let me briefly summarize the most distinguished, along with some personal favorites.

Grind

The fastest and most basic of genres, grindcore has its roots in extreme punk. In Sweden, it began with a demo tape by Asocial back in 1982, *How Could Hardcore Be Any Worse?*. The style was later developed by bands like G-Anx and taken toward metal by Filthy Christians from Falun. When these guys signed to Earache in 1989 they proved that some kind of success was possible for a Swedish grindcore band—even if not for Filthy Christians themselves. The punk version of grindcore can be described as short songs played at maximum speed, with simple riffs on conventionally tuned guitars and screamed lyrics with political content.

G-Anx

Filthy Christians' politically charged grindcore was followed by bands like Arsedestroyer, but Nasum from Örebro would eventually become the reigning kings of Swedish grindcore. Nasum began in 1992 as a side project to Anders Jakobsson's main band Necrony. Unlike Necrony with their gore-drenched lyrics, Nasum dealt with political topics. When singer/guitarist Mieszko Talarczyk joined the lineup in 1993, the band released a strong bunch of 7" singles and secured a deal with the leading U.S. metal label Relapse.

With the albums *Inhale/Exhale* in 1998, *Human 2.0* in 2000, *Helvete* in 2002, and *Shift* in 2004, the band gradually took over. In late 2004, Nasum were one of the biggest grindcore bands in the world, but that ended when Mieszko was tragically killed in the tsunami disaster in Thailand just before the New Year. Nasum will most certainly continue to be an influence, but the title of Sweden's grind kings probably now belongs to Gadget from Gävle. Just like Nasum, they have contracted with Relapse, and will get all the necessary promotion. Musically, they are already as intense as Nasum ever were.

Apart from the punk-oriented side of grindcore, Sweden has produced a lot of gore-grind bands in the vein of Carcass. Unlike punk grind, this subgenre generally features very down-tuned guitars, somewhat more complex songs, and guttural vocals. And of course, the lyrical topics are blood and guts rather than politics. Sweden's pioneer in this style was General Surgery, and the genre became pretty widespread in the early 90's with bands like Traumatic, Monkey Mush, Nefarious, Necrony, and Regurgitate, the last of which developed out of the great Crematory. Necrony was probably the most gore-obsessed of all these bands, but their story ended as main member Anders Jakobsson focused on Nasum. Instead, Regurgitate has endured. They are still going today with their death metal–smelling grind, and so is the resurrected General Surgery.

The most successful and original Swedish gore-grind band has to be Deranged from Malmö. Their style of grind has the most links to death metal, especially the riffs and the guitar solos. Since 1990, Deranged has basically been the project of guitarist Johan Axelsson and drummer Rikard Wermén. Over several albums and line-up changes the band has consistently produced unrelenting death/grind. Their style hasn't changed much; it remains the same kind of steady, hammering madness.

"Why don't we conform to the groovy Swedish death metal sound? Just a matter of taste, I guess."—RIKARD WERMÉN, DERANGED

To me, their masterpiece is the ultra-brutal *High on Blood* from 1999, one of the most destructive Swedish albums of all time. Deranged have labored practically alone in their single-minded pursuit of pure death/grind, and their dedication has taken them on to far-off places like Japan. Though Axelsson is mainly occupied with his work at Berno Studio at the moment, Deranged have continued to sporadically produce high quality albums.

Death N' Roll

With Deranged grinding toward eternity, other bands developed more relaxed variations on death metal. One of the most notable mid-90's Swedish death metal styles has been called death n' roll. Though generally credited to Entombed, I honestly think a band called Furbowl came up with the idea first.

Furbowl was started in 1991 in Växjö by former Carnage member Johan Liiva-Axelsson—no relation to Johan Axelsson of Deranged. Their 1992 debut, *Those Shredded Dreams*, displayed a new take on death metal, combining the furious death sound with traditional rock riffs and structures. They developed

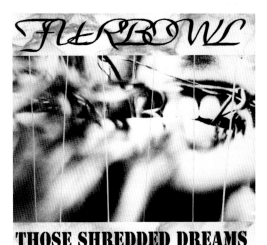

THOSE SHREDDED DREAMS

Furbowl's groundbreaking first album.

the style further on their second album, *The Autumn Years* in 1994, flattening the sound to make room for even more rock n' roll elements. But Furbowl never gained much recognition or success for their innovative music. Instead, Entombed became more widely associated with this new style.

What Entombed achieved on their third album, *Wolverine Blues*, was truly remarkable. In comparison to the pure death metal of their earlier recordings, Entombed now focused entirely on making catchy and groovy songs. Unlike Furbowl, they managed to do it without subtracting any of the death metal feeling. The sound is just perfect. Clean, big and brutal all at once. Every song has a soul of its own—as evidenced by the fast pace of "Eyemaster," the backbeat mayhem of "Out of Hand," the groove of "Wolverine Blues," and the heaviness of "Demon."

"For me, this album was actually the natural continuation of Left Hand Path. *But I guess in an environment as filled with musical rules as the death metal scene, every slight change is seen as a revolution. To me, it was still pure death metal."*—NICKE ANDERSSON, NIHILIST/ENTOMBED

"At that point, Nicke had loosened his grip on Entombed and allowed all of us to take part in the decisions. He had also given up his obsession of us being a pure death metal band, with long black hair and the right image. Everything felt good, even though I was drunk most of the time."—UFFE CEDERLUND, MORBID/NIHILIST/ENTOMBED/DISFEAR

Together with *Left Hand Path*, this is Entombed's masterpiece. Entombed later intensified their rocking tendencies before the great *To Ride, Shoot Straight*

Advertisement for the majestic Wolverine Blues

and *Speak the Truth* in 1997, until their development came to a halt after Nicke Andersson's unexpected departure. The following album, *Same Difference* in 1998, had none of the quality of Entombed's earlier records—but they recovered with *Uprising* in 2000 and especially the great *Morning Star* in 2001.

"*This might sound strange, but I actually think Entombed is the most underrated of all Swedish death metal bands. They deserved to get so much bigger in Europe, and especially in the U.S. They should have sold far more records. When they released* Wolverine Blues, *they should have become mega-stars.*"—Jesper Thorsson, Afflicted

Wolverine Blues even benefited from a short-lived agreement between Earache Records and Sony/Columbia that briefly made Entombed a major label band alongside labelmates Napalm Death and Carcass. But even with Entombed sharing an American publicity office with New Kids on the Block, it should have been obvious that it would never work. Death metal, even Entombed's novel grooved-down version, could not be marketed with mass-produced gloss.

How did other Swedish death metal bands relate to the death n' roll style? Surprisingly, few dared to follow in the path of the mighty Entombed. In the harsh black metal climate of the mid-90's, the most accepted form of death metal was oddly enough melodic stuff. I guess it was a bit like in 1990 again— bands understood that they could never become as good as Entombed, so they went another direction.

From left: Dark Tranquillity's
original logo;
Eucharist's debut album

A few bands did attempt the death n' roll formula. The most successful was surely Nine from Linköping, who started out in 1994. Nine immediately got a record deal for their Entombed-ish death rock, and have successfully continued on the path ever since. A more disastrous attempt at the death n' roll formula came from the old death metal band Vermin. In 1998 they released *Millennium Ride*, nothing more than a bunch of songs copied directly from Entombed's *To Ride, Shoot Straight and Speak the Truth*.

Another adaptation of death n' roll came from my old band Dellamorte from Avesta. Fully inspired by Entombed, we started in 1995 and subsequently released three albums: *Everything You Hate* in 1996, *Uglier and More Disgusting* in 1997, and *Home Sweet Hell* in 1999. Though Dellamorte sounded very much like Entombed, I guess we looked to Motörhead and Discharge, where Entombed had been more inspired by Black Sabbath and Kiss.

Dellamorte only hinted at crust punk, but a couple of pure punk bands incorporated the sound of Entombed. Most notably, Nyköping's Disfear used Studio Sunlight to apply the death metal sound to their albums *Soul Scars* in 1995 and *Everyday Slaughter* in 1997. Other bands using the death metal sound for the crust formula during this time were Skitsystem, Driller Killer, and Uncurbed. The popularity of fusions of crust punk and death metal was cemented when Osmose Productions started the imprint Kron-H, mainly for the primary purpose of signing Disfear, Loud Pipes, Dellamorte, and Driller Killer.

The Gothenburg Sound

Death n' roll never became massive—its commercial success was limited to Entombed. Instead, the "next big thing" developed on the west coast of Sweden.

Gothenburg, or Göteborg, became the center for a new style, soon labeled "the Gothenburg sound." Used in many ways over the years, the term was coined to distinguish the scene in Gothenburg from its counterpart in Stockholm.

"The Stockholm thing was a couple years before us. When I played with Dark Tranquillity, we started in 1989, and it was a reaction towards that music, really. In Stockholm they had more of a garage, death metal vibe going, and we were more into Iron Maiden and speed metal from Germany. And we were incorporating New Wave of British Heavy Metal like Priest and Saxon into death metal."—ANDERS FRIDÉN, DARK TRANQUILLITY/IN FLAMES

Where Stockholm offered mainly fat guitars, growling vocals, relentless production, and bass heaviness, Gothenburg went in the opposite direction. As originally defined in smaller Swedish metal 'zines, the Gothenburg sound included death metal with the following traits:

- More melodies and traditional verse/chorus structures;
- A clearer sound and less brutality. Studio Fredman was a factor here, as opposed to Stockholm's Studio Sunlight. The guitars aren't as crushing, and the drum work is usually more sterile;
- The vocals are screamed rather than grunted.

The originators of the Gothenburg sound include Intoxicate, Ceremonial Oath, and Eucharist. But these bands never got much attention. Instead, Dissection and At the Gates showed the world how to combine strong melodies with musical brutality. As Dissection discovered their own field of blackish death metal, At the Gates did more to pave the way for other melodic Gothenburg bands. Already on their two first records, At the Gates redefined death metal with atmospheric harmonies and complex guitar work. The interaction between Anders Björler and Alf Svensson was just amazing. Then on *With Fear I Kiss the Burning Darkness* in 1993 and *Terminal Spirit Disease* in 1994, they showed how melodic structures could be incorporated into catchy songs. *Terminal Spirit Disease*, especially, was a revelation that would influence hundreds of bands. At the Gates also benefited a lot from the soulful screams of Tomas Lindberg—in my opinion, no one has ever been able to match his vocal style.

"Up until 1994 we had a pretty unique style, but then Dissection and In Flames started to get more melodic. In Flames went for the 'happy' folk music thing, while Dissection peeked at traditional heavy metal like Thin Lizzy and Iron Maiden. It was some kind of symbiosis where we listened to our friends' bands. It was a creative environment with a quiet competition, where you wanted to outdo everyone else."—ANDERS BJÖRLER, AT THE GATES/THE HAUNTED

In 1993, Eucharist finally got its lineup together and released *A Velvet Creation*. This album contains some of the best Gothenburg death metal ever, but it never gained wider attention. This probably had a lot to do with the awful "plastic" production. Also, the band broke up during this period. In their place, two other bands from Gothenburg used ideas from At the Gates to find commercial success: Dark Tranquillity and In Flames.

"It all started out in this tiny club. If you were not playing, you were helping out, you were at the door, you were pushing people off stage, or you were selling or drinking beer. It was really cool. I think it held like 150 or 200 people tops, and we all started there. I mean, At the Gates started there, but they were not even At the Gates, they were another band, Grotesque. And Dark Tranquillity, Ceremonial Oath, and a bunch of thrash bands that turned into all kind of cool bands. A lot of the known Swedish bands from Gothenberg definitely started in that place, and we all know each other pretty well."—ANDERS FRIDÉN, DARK TRANQUILLITY/IN FLAMES

Dark Tranquillity started as a pure death metal band in 1989, but by 1993 they had been influenced by At the Gates to start playing melodic death metal. Although some of their riffs feel uninspired, they gained a lot of success with *Skydancer* in 1993 and *The Mind's I* in 1997. Eventually the band drifted away from the Gothenburg sound to explore electronic and ambient music.

Dark Tranquillity's success was nothing compared to the enormous popularity of townmates In Flames. Personally, I think that In Flames originally were far better than Dark Tranquillity, and they rightly got attention for *Lunar Strain* in 1994 and *The Jester Race* in 1996. Then something happened—they drifted away from their initial *very* melodic death metal. They signed to Nuclear Blast, and moved incrementally into mainstream territory with each release. By *Reroute to Remain* in 2002, they were among the most successful of all Swedish bands, but no longer had much to do with extreme metal. They began to appear in the U.S. *Billboard* album charts. Then in 2006 their economic contributions made In Flames the first metal band to win the Swedish Export Award from the national government—a strange honor for a band with a death metal past.

"It's something new and refreshing to hear that they're actually recognizing a metal band. I mean, really right now I don't know any other exports from Sweden, musically."—BJÖRN GELOTTE, IN FLAMES

Not surprisingly, the commercial success of In Flames spawned hundreds of imitators around the country, such as Ablaze my Sorrow, Sonic Syndicate, Avatar, and, most importantly, Soilwork. In the United States, the ravaging of the Gothenburg melodic death metal sound has more recently reached a crisis point in the mid-2000s metalcore scene.

"It's weird sometimes, when we have toured with a bunch of these bands from the metal/hardcore/whatever genre. The bands say they are influenced by us, and they know our history very well, but their fans don't--they have no clue who we are. To me, it's like, 'What? You don't know about Sweden? You don't

Slaughter of the Soul—*the masterpiece of retro thrash*

know about where we come from?"—ANDERS FRIDÉN, DARK TRANQUILLITY/IN FLAMES

"*There was never any hype until At the Gates had already split up. Bands like In Flames and Dark Tranquillity continued on in our style, and created a second wave with the likes of Gardenian and Soilwork. I guess the term 'Gothenburg sound' wasn't really established until the late 90's, when the sound started to spread.*"—ANDERS BJÖRLER, AT THE GATES/THE HAUNTED

"*People might think I am bitter about the success of In Flames, but that is not the case. These guys created something new out of death metal and worked their asses off to make it work. Okay, they have had a lot of luck, but I really think they deserve their success.*"—TOMAS LINDBERG, GROTESQUE/AT THE GATES/DISFEAR

𝕽𝖊𝖙𝖗𝖔 𝕿𝖍𝖗𝖆𝖘𝖍

Just as At the Gates kick-started the whole Gothenburg sound, they also paved the way for the next trend in extreme Swedish metal with their last album, *Slaughter of the Soul*. This album really took Sweden by storm when it was released in 1995, and eventually the world followed suit.

"*It was always Anders who had the feeling for riffs and melodies, as Alf brought in the complex structures. When Alf left, Anders just went berserk with his riffs, and that turned into* Slaughter of the Soul.*"*—TOMAS LINDBERG, GROTESQUE/AT THE GATES/DISFEAR

Not since Slayer's *Reign in Blood* had such a massive and unrelenting thrash attack been unleashed. Though the structures were basically thrash metal, the death metal sound and Tomas' screams created something new and fresh.

"It was natural for Jonas, Tompa, and I to go for more traditional song structures when Alf quit. We all had a thrash metal background. The thrash influences could be heard on previous recordings as well, but the production of Slaughter of the Soul *really made them obvious."*—ANDERS BJÖRLER, AT THE GATES/THE HAUNTED

At the Gates' riffs are brutal, simple, and catchy, and everything is so tight that you almost lose your breath. Unlike on their previous albums, the drum patterns are very simple, steady two-beats combined with double bass drum backbeats. Though we didn't realize it back then, At the Gates had again initiated an extreme metal subgenre, something I'll call retro thrash.

With *Slaughter of the Soul*, At the Gates were at the top of their career. It was quite a shock when they folded shortly after a U.S. tour with Napalm Death. Disagreements within the band were apparently the reason, and the members went in separate directions.

"Musical disagreements were definitely part of the split-up, but that could easily have been solved if we hadn't been so young and immature. All of us were too stubborn, and exhausted from endless touring. There was also a lot of pressure on Anders to come up with riffs to match those of Slaughter of the Soul. *In the end, it was impossible to continue. You have to understand that we never really got very popular during our existence. We toured under hard conditions, and the whole death metal scene was trapped in a downward spiral. It was only years after our split-up that people started to refer to our last album as a masterpiece."*—TOMAS LINDBERG, GROTESQUE/AT THE GATES/DISFEAR

As it turned out, the Björler brothers and drummer Adrian Erlandsson teamed up with guitarist Patrik Jensen, formerly of Seance, and singer Peter Dolving, formerly of the hardcore band Mary Beats Jane, to continue along At the Gates' thrashy path. The new band was called The Haunted, and with this constellation they built even further on the retro thrash of At the Gates' last days.

On The Haunted's self-titled debut album in 1998, most of the death metal sound and structures were washed away. Instead we faced precise and furious thrash metal to the limit. Over the years, The Haunted have continued to produce superior-quality retro thrash, and they have eventually and rightly been so successful that they can earn a living from their music, something very few Swedish bands ever achieved. Apart from the guys in In Flames, I guess only Nicke Andersson of Entombed and Johan Edlund of Tiamat ever made a good living out of death metal.

"Jensen's ideas made The Haunted what it has become. In the early days he already had a bunch of material to build on, so Jonas and I developed our riffs to work with that."—ANDERS BJÖRLER, AT THE GATES/THE HAUNTED

Imitators of late At the Gates and The Haunted are simply too many to list. Most are fairly unoriginal and uninteresting. Among the more successful followers are Corporation 187 from Linköping, Arise from Alingsås, and Construcdead from Stockholm. But the very best At the Gates/The Haunted clone was Carnal Forge from Sala. This was basically a continuation of the At the Gates–sounding band In Thy Dreams, with the addition of Dellamorte's singer Jonas Kjellgren. Carnal Forge rise above other bands due to tightness, insane speed, and the brilliant vocals of Kjellgren. Carnal Forge have rightly been successful, probably inspiring bands in their own right.

Extreme Death Metal

As usual, retro thrash and moreso the Gothenburg style spawned a countermovement. A lot of people simply didn't want to hear catchy and melodic versions of a musical genre that used to be all about aggression and brutality. Some bands looked to the U.S. for inspiration, home of brutal acts like Morbid Angel, Suffocation, Deicide, and Cannibal Corpse. The riffs and song structures of these bands are more advanced and complex than those of acts like Entombed or Dismember. Few Swedish acts had attempted such brutality before, save for Liers in Wait, Seance, and Karlstad's brutality platoon Vomitory.

One of the first of a new rise of brutal Swedish death metal bands in the late 90's was Throneaeon from Västerås. The members started out in 1991, but didn't find their style or even a band name until 1995. On their 1996 demo *Carnage* they hammered out precise brutality in the vein of Deicide. Sadly, Throneaeon never made it out of the underground. They attempted extreme death metal during a time when keyboard-driven black metal and melodic death metal prevailed. After a couple of overlooked albums, they changed their name to Godhate in 2004, and are continuing their brutal mission.

Nineteen ninety-five also brought Soils of Fate, a blasting death metal machine with a high level of precision. When Soils of Fate released their *Sandstorm* album in 2001, they sounded like nothing previously heard in Sweden, with ultra-guttural vocals, chunky riffs, and machine-gun drumming. But they didn't get very far, as disagreements within the band held them back.

One brutal new Swedish death metal band that actually attracted a bit of attention was Stockholm's Insision, which I myself joined in 1999. Much to my surprise, we secured a deal with the legendary Earache label in 2001, playing Suffocation-style death metal. Things were changing within the scene, and brutality was appreciated again. Our following albums, *Beneath the Folds of Flesh* in 2002 and *Revealed and Worshipped* in 2004, did well enough to allow tours in far-off places like Thailand and Australia. Other bands that walked the path of brutality are the great Immersed in Blood, Imperious, Stabwound,

Strangulation, and Deviant. Though these bands have mainly operated in the underground, Stabwound and Immersed in Blood have already toured the U.S.

The band that really took death metal to a new level was Spawn of Possession from Kalmar. Their style is probably the most complex and technically advanced death metal in the world, with endless sequences of complicated chord patterns. It's just amazing that Sweden has produced a band like Spawn of Possession, an international leader of hyper-complex death metal.

"I got into death metal around 1991, when I first heard Morbid Angel. After that I discovered Swedish bands such as Grave, Dismember, Entombed, and Hypocrisy. Initially I was a huge fan of Swedish death metal. But when we started the band we got more into U.S. bands like Suffocation, Death, and Monstrosity. Along the way we realized that we should use our technical abilities, rather than restrain them, to develop our music."—DENNIS RÖNDUM, SPAWN OF POSSESSION

Spawn of Possession's 2003 album *Cabinet* shows how far the death metal formula can be taken, and they have deservedly toured a lot. Drummer Dennis Röndum and bass player Niklas Dewerud also played in the similar band Visceral Bleeding, who could become as important as Spawn of Possession in the future. Dennis Röndum seems hopeful that a new Swedish death metal scene is growing.

"I guess our generation never really cared for black metal, melodic death metal, or any of the trends reigning in the mid-90's. We feel a great connection to bands like Aeon, Insision, Imperious, Immersed in Blood, Visceral Bleeding, and Godhate. All of these bands did their own thing from the beginning, and therefore they will prevail."—DENNIS RÖNDUM, SPAWN OF POSSESSION

Retro Death

Finally—what do you think happened in the late 90's when modern death metal became mainly about melody and technical prowess, while black metal had become a million times trendier, weaker, and more watered-down than death metal could ever be? Naturally, some guys started to look in the rearview mirror for inspiration. A project such as Bloodbath done by death metal "celebrities" like Dan Swanö from Edge of Sanity and Mikael Åkerfeldt from Opeth was all about old school Swedish death metal. Since 1999 they have occasionally continued on that dirty old road, accompanied by similar bands and projects such as Paganizer, Deceiver, Facebreaker, Flesh, and Ribspreader.

Nostalgia for the old days has also infected a new generation. Teen metalheads too young to participate back in the day have formed bands that cherish everything once at the heart and soul of death metal. Turning against the overproduced melodies and riff orgies of the modern scene, they look to older bands for inspiration. Ironically, in some ways this makes the retro movement the very opposite of the classic death metal scene. Instead of being adventurous and daring like the original movement, these guys are playing it safe and sticking to fixed patterns. If the members of Nihilist and Grotesque had ever had the same mentality, they would have sounded like Grand Funk Railroad. Still, this old school–loving movement sure feels like a fresh breeze. My personal favorite is without a shadow of a doubt Repugnant from Stockholm. As they started in 1998, they may have been the first of the retro death bands.

"When I was a kid around 1992 and 1993, death metal was already accessible, so I searched out rare black metal albums to get my kicks. Bands like Marduk and Mayhem looked, sounded, and felt obscure and dangerous, so of course I liked them. But around 1996, most black metal bands had become more accessible and unexciting than death metal ever were. By 1997 extreme metal had reached an all-time low, and I thought everything sucked. By then I almost exclusively listened to old death metal bands from Stockholm, and when I started Repugnant the following year it was natural for us to go for the classic style."—TOBIAS "MARY GOORE" FORGE, REPUGNANT

Their amazingly old school–sounding death metal is something you must hear to believe. They have succeeded with everything, including the sound, the riffs, the vocals, and even the artwork. Everything looks and sounds just like the late 80's. Repugnant's *Hecatomb* EP from 1999 is especially fantastic in every sense, and has itself inspired new bands.

Zombie Destruction

From left: Hecatomb—*the masterpiece of retro death;*

Katalysator—*young kids playing old music*

"To be honest, I guess it was pretty calculated to go for an old school approach. Nobody else was doing it in 1998, so the field was wide open. We just did some catchy songs with basic pop structures, but we used the most evil-sounding riffs imaginable."—Tobias "Mary Goore" Forge, Repugnant

Repugnant's career was shaky, however. After a few gigs with Macabre in Holland and Belgium, and a drunken Finnish tour with Centinex, it was all over. Their sole full-length wasn't released until 2006, almost four years after their demise. For a while, three members played in the pop/rock band Subvision, but drummer Tobias Daun later joined Dismember, rekindling the death metal flame.

"I guess we split up because we had to. Most extreme metal albums I have ever liked were created by teenagers. You simply need a naïve, adolescent aggression and passion to get it together. If you can't make it ugly, dirty, and mean, you should get out. My passion was gone. I was over twenty and searching for new ways of musical expression. So instead of watering Repugnant down, we decided to quit at our best."—Tobias "Mary Goore" Forge, Repugnant

Wise words from a young man. They weren't alone in the field of retro death metal, though. In 1998 the mighty Kaamos started out in Stockholm, charged by the addition of drummer Christoffer Barkensjö as he left the first version of Repugnant. As Repugnant slowly died, Kaamos gradually took over as the kings of Swedish old school death metal. Their music and sound may not be as sharp as Repugnant's, but Kaamos surely have been more successful. They have released two albums on the Candlelight label, *Kaamos* and *Lucifer Rising*, and both contain brilliant and simple death metal the way it once was. Unfortunately, they haven't succeeded with their studio sound. Their live performances were fantastic, but their albums don't contain the same evil atmosphere as those of Repugnant. The link between these two bands is strong—Repugnant's Tobias Forge and Kaamos' Karl Envall edited the very old school–looking *Outshitten Cunt Mag* in the late 90's. Karl also played bass on Repugnant's first demo. Sadly, Kaamos recently declared that they have quit. They will be missed.

This retro death metal trend was not a small movement in Stockholm within a group of friends. Around the country, another generation started to play death metal the old way during the 2000's—including Necrovation from Everöd, Morbid Insulter from Hönö, and Tribulation from Arvika (no relation to the classic Swedish thrash band). My favorite among these retro death bands is Katalysator from Uppsala, who are insanely old school in everything they do. Katalysator's first demo, *Zombie Destruction*, sounds amazingly like Grotesque. When I saw them live in 2005, they looked like dead ringers for Nihilist. To deepen the connection to the late 80's, singer Pelle Åhman also edits the primitive-looking *Torment Mag*.

With Katalysator the circle is closed, and we are back to the atmosphere that reigned when a young group called Nihilist began in 1987. Sure enough, Nicke

Andersson has started up a pure old school death metal project called Death Breath with a revolving cast including Scott Carlson of the Michigan masters Repulsion. The original way of the scene seems to be alive again.

I'm pleased to report that the earlier, Swedish edition of this book even helped bring back the bands Grotesque, Nirvana 2002, Interment, Treblinka, Obscurity, and Uncanny. The book release party has now become an annual event each January in Stockholm, celebrating the death metal era with gigs at Kafe 44—the only club left from the old days. After reuniting, Obscurity has even remained active, and they never played live at all during the pioneer era.

One more thought: Sound Pollution (continuing after House of Kicks) is still the major extreme metal store in Sweden, and also one of the biggest distributors of metal labels. But recently they have been challenged by the cool store Repulsive Records, who exclusively deal with ultra-brutal music. Whereas Sound Pollution is now basically a mainstream metal/punk/indie pop store, Repulsive is *definitely* the store for the new Swedish extreme metal scene, taking up the mantle where Heavy Sound and later House of Kicks left off. In fact, vocalist Pelle of Katalysator/Invidious even fulfilled his required work training program for school at the Repulsive store! It's like the late 80's all over again, and Katalysator/Invidious seems destined to lead the scene. Old geezers like me can just sit back and enjoy the ride.

If you want to get philosophical, it is almost like history repeating itself with this new scene of traditional Swedish death metal. Just like the kids of the late 80's got fed up with Swedish hair bands like Europe and a stagnating thrash metal scene, the kids of the 2000's got fed up with melodic Swedish bands like In Flames and a stagnating black metal scene. As the murder of prime minister Olof Palme in 1986 created a climate of horror and creativity, the murder of foreign minister Anna Lind in 2003 maybe had a similar impact.

I think it would be a good idea to end this survey of the origins and development of Swedish death metal on that note. Swedish death metal has developed, grown, and survived all metal trends of the last twenty years. The future of the heritage is secure with bands like Spawn of Possession, Godhate, and Visceral Bleeding, plus projects such as Bloodbath and Death Breath. In addition, several old bands, among them Interment and Evocation, have recently reformed and proven their ability to deliver music as brutal as ever.

Best of all, most of the initiators of the Swedish death metal scene are still active, still kicking serious ass. Impressively, the four Swedish horsemen Dismember, Entombed, Unleashed, and Grave are still blasting death metal, joining together for the "Masters of Death" tour of Europe in late 2006. Tiamat and Therion are still exploring new musical territories, while Merciless, General Surgery, and Necrophobic show vital signs of life now and then. After serving as inspiration for an entire wave of melodic metalcore bands during the 2000's, At the Gates plans a return and world tour in summer 2008. And most significantly, many bands with roots in the Swedish death metal scene have developed into international metal titans—among them Hypocrisy, In Flames, Dark Tranquillity, Arch Enemy, Soilwork, Meshuggah, Amon Amarth, In Flames, Opeth, and The Haunted.

As you might understand by now, death metal is unstoppable. The left hand path will be followed into eternity...

VOMITORY

DEMO

* Snabb, brutal Death-metal
* Skitbra ljud
* INTE inspelad i Sunlight
* Trettio kronor

Urban Gustafsson   Ulf Dalegren
Grossbolsgatan 2 B   Klarinettgatan 28
667 00 FÖRSHAGA   654 71 KARLSTAD

DOWNFALL RECORDS

PRESENTS:

price:
7 US$

If you can't find this at
your local records-shop
demand them to order it from
our distributors or directly
from Downfall Records!

5 tracks of FAST & BRUTAL
US-style bloody DEATH METAL

IMMERSED IN BLOOD (Swe)
'Relentless Retaliation'
MCD (FALL MCD 005)

Distributed by:
Sweden - Border Music,
Spain - Goi music,
Italy - Pulsar Light,
France - Ordealis,
UK & Eire - Pro Sonic/PHD!

Downfall Records, PO Box 12009, 402 41 GBG, Sweden
fax: +46-31-24 666 2
e-mail: downfall_records@hotmail.com

...ot, but
...SWEDISH
...METAL
...actually.

INSISION
Meant To Suffer

Demo 1 1998
Four songs for $6 eller 25:- inom landet

INSISION

c/o J. Ahonen
Kårsta Björknäs
186 96 Vallentuna
Sweden

...l@worshipper.com   http://metalstorm.hypermart.net

...ome let us see some blood...

Clockwise from top left: Vomitory flyer;
Death Breath posing with Nifelheim;
rare flyer for Insision's debut demo;
Insision's 2000 demo;
Immersed in Blood flyer

The A-Z of Swedish Death Metal Bands

TOTALBRUTAL MANGLARFEST
med:

Fredagen den 30 mars
Axelsbergs Ungdomsgård, T-bana Axelsberg
Insläpp kl.18.30   Entré 30 kr
OBS! DROGFRITT-ALKOTEST
Arr: Axelsbergsgården/Hövdingagården
+ovanstående band

NEW DEMO OUT NOW
FOREVER TO BE VANISHED THERE IN....
3 TRAX OF DEVASTATING DEATH
FOR 4$ OR 20 Swk + IRC

FOR INFO, WHRITE TO;
JÖRGEN KRISTIANSEN
KLOCKANTORPSG, 24b
72344 VÄSTERÅS SWEDEN
OR
THOMAS KRZYZOWSKI
RÅBYKORSET 45
72469 VÄSTERÅS SWEDEN

Abhoth flyer

Achromasia: Chanting for...

The debut demo, Lord of Chaos, is finally released! Six songs of vile
Necro Cyber Metal, which combines old-style Death with some more
modern influences, such as the inhuman sickness of a drum
machine...
Trades are cool with us. Zines, please write for review copies.
Distributors, write, fax, or email for more information on wholesale
prices.

$4.00 (USA) or $5.00 (World)
Send hidden cash, or make
checks/money orders out to: Ray Miller

ADVERSARY
P.O. Box 302
Elkhart, IN 46515-0302
USA

fax: 219 295-1501   email: rmiller2@sun1.iusb.indiana.edu

Adversary flyer

Afflicted: Wanderland

Afflicted: Rising to the Sun *(1992, 1000ex)*

ALLEGIANCE
C/O ROGER SVENSSON
HAMNGATAD 7
614 34 SÖDERKÖPING
SWEDEN

(Include 1 I.R.C for a sure reply)

Allegiance

Altar flyer

A Mind Confused:
Out of Chaos Spawn 7"

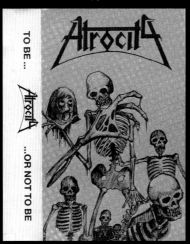

Atrocity: To Be… or Not to Be

At the Gates: Gardens of Grief 7"

At the Gates/Suffer/Lubricant gig-poster

Azatoth: The Dawn

World Domination Tour poster

Brejndedd: Born Ugly

Butchery: The Coming

Carbonized artwork

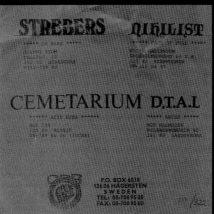
CBR Compilation (322ex)

Centinex flyer

CENTINEX IS A NEW GRIND/DEATH-CORE
BAND FROM SWEDEN. THEIR NEW DEMO
"END OF LIFE" IS OUT NOW. IT
INCLUDES 4 TRACKS WITH 2 VOCALISTS.

TO GET YOUR COPY SEND
25 SKR/5 $ (EUROPE) OR
6 $ (OVERSEAS)

ZINES,COMPILATION TAPES, RADIO-
STATIONS ETC SHOULD SEND BLANK
TAPE AND 2 I.R.C.'s.

CENTINEX
M.SCHULMAN
WINQVIST GATAN 6
77600 HEDEMORA
SWEDEN

Centinex cassette

Centinex: Live Devastation *(500ex)*

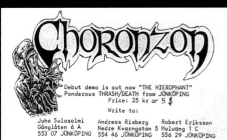

Debut demo is out now "THE HIEROPHANT"
Ponderous THRASH/DEATH from JÖNKÖPING
Price: 25 kr or 5 $

Write to:

Juha Sulasalmi   Andreas Risberg   Robert Eriksson
Gånglåten 6 A   Nedre Kvarngatan 5   Hulunig 1 C
553 07 JÖNKÖPING   554 46 JÖNKÖPING   556 29 JÖNKÖPING

Choronzon flyer

Crematory: Netherworlds of the Mind

DEBUT DEMO OUT NOW !!
20 min of BRUTAL Death Metal
Highquality sound & professionally
printed cassettes.
Recorded at EKO-Studio (16-ch)
Price:20 SEK+Postage
Overseas:4$
Contact: Marko Tervonen
          Soldatgatan 17
          461 62 Trollhättan
          SWEDEN

"Forever Heaven Gone"

Crown of Thorns flyer

Damnation: Divine Darkness

Damnation: Insulter of Jesus Christ!

Darkane/Hypnosia gig poster

Darkified: Dark

Dark Tranquillity flyer

Dawn of Decay flyer

Desultory flyer

Hellfest '97

Disorge flyer

Dispatched flyer

*Edge of Sanity/Dellamorte/
In Thy Dreams gig poster*

Entombed/Possessed split

Entombed/Sewer Grooves gig flyer

Epitaph/Exruciatz split-LP
Out now on INFEST REC.
Epitaph LP coming in spring

Send I.R.C for info or 12 $ to order the split-LP

EPITAPH
c/o Manne Svensson
Solv. 10 A
191 70 Sollentuna
SWEDEN

(info)

INFEST REC.
B.P. 197
75519 Paris C.X. 19
FRANCE

(order)

Epitaph flyer

Epitaph (Dark Abbey): Blasphemy

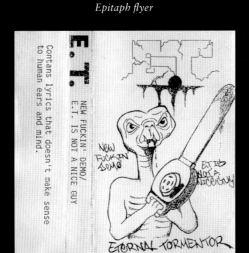

Eternal Tormentor: E.T is not a Nice Guy *demo*

Exempt flyer

Exhumed logo

Fallen Angel flyer

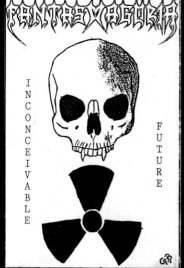

Fantasmagoria: Inconceivable Future

Fulmination: Through Fire *demo*

Gardens of Obscurity flyer

Formicide: Comatose *demo*

BIOGRAPHY

The band formed as late as early 1991, have already gained an enormous response from the death metal underground.
Referred to by some as the only new band who have the capacity to become one of the bigger deathbands.
You might think that **FURBOWL** are new to the scene, think again, frontman Johan Axelsson formed **CARNAGE** (R.I.P.) a band formed 1987, and forerunners of swedish death metal together with **NIHILIST** (now Entombed) and **GROTESQUE** (now At The Gates.)
In may 1991 they recorded their first and only demo "*The Nightfall Of Your Heart*", which led them to their contract with swedish label STEP ONE Records.
Produced and guested by Mike Amott (**CARCASS** guitarist) who also was a founding member of **CARNAGE**.
To get that special and raw sound, they prefered to enter a studio in the south of sweden, instead of the now overused Sunlight studio. As the band are far from the typical swedish deathband, they found their own sound and style.
The present lineup: Johan Axelsson - Vocals & Bass
Max Thornell - Drums
Anders Gyllensten - Guitar
Arild Karlsson - Guitar

The album:

THOSE SHREDDED DREAMS
For contact: STEP ONE, BOX 3019, 750 03 UPPSALA, SWEDEN. Phone: + 46-18-212108, Fax: +46-18-129215.

Furbowl biography

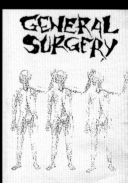

General Surgery:
Pestiferous Antrhopophagia

OUT MARCH 1991

GENERAL SURGERY

NECROLOGY EP

UNBELIEVABLY PUTRID AND GROTESQUE SONGS
OF SAVAGE SURGICAL BUTCHERY WHICH WILL
EASILY CARVE AND CONFOUND YOUR MIND!!!!

1000 pressed on colored vinyl !

Gx Tx Gx Px RECORDS
P.O. BOX 251
MILLERSVILLE, PA 17551

$ 4 (us)
$ 6 (world)

General Surgery flyer

God B.C.

HUMAN RELIC

Gorement: Human Relic

GOREMENT HAVE THEIR SECOND DEMO OUT NOW!
IT'S CALLED "OBSEQUIES..." AND IT CONTA-
INS THREE BRUTAL TRAX WITH GOOD SOUND...
IT CAN BE ORDERED BY SENDING 25 Skr   or
6 US $ INCLUDING P&P. WRITE TO:

NICKLAS LILJA
ANISSTIGEN 12
611 45 NYKÖPING
SWEDEN

JIMMY KARLSSON
REKTORSV. 11
613 00 OXELÖSUND
SWEDEN

'ZINES SEND BLANK TAPE + IRC FOR OUR MA-
TERIAL. FOR INFO ETC. SEND IRC (SWEDEN :
2.80 KR STAMP) IF YOU WANT A SURE REPLY.

Gorement flyer

Gravity: Magic Doom *demo*

Guidance of Sin flyer

Guillotine

Harmageddon: Rather be Dead

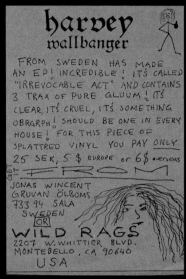

Harvey Wallbanger ultra-primitive flyer

Hasty Death: *Subterranean Corrosion*

Hasty Death flyer

*Hexenhaus/Mezzrow/Rosicrucian/
Tribulation gig poster*

Ice Age: Demo '88

Ileus: Demo '91

Immersed in Blood merchandise

Impious flyer

Incardine: Moment of Connection

Infernal Gates: In Sadness... *demo*

Infester flyer

Insision release poster

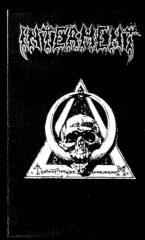

Interment: Where Death Will Increase

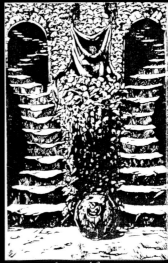

Inverted flyer

Hello!
"Doomsday celebration III" comp is out now. It is 60 minutes and feautering groups like INTERNAL DECAY, ENCINED, ADVERSARY, WOMBBATH, DAWN, SOLILOQUY, DERANGED, FULMINATION and LUBRICANT. Don't miss this chance to check the swedish and the finnish scene for 20 skr + postage or 5us europe, 6 us the world. You will also have some infos and stuff. You can also buy D.C. I and II for 15 skr + postage, 4 us europe or 5 us the world. The prices are for each tape. They includes groups like DARKIFIED, SUFFER, NECROPHOBIC, HOUSE OF USHER and many more. Write to Erik Gøtborn, Önsbo 850, S-810 65 Skärplinge, Sweden. Of course I need your death metal demo to next tape. Free ex av the tape to you then.

Interment: Forward to the Unknown

Internal Decay flyer

INVERTED

THE SWEDISH METALACT INVERTED ARE OUT
WITH THEIR SECOND DEMO TITLED "HEAVEN
DEFIED". IT CONTAINS 3SONGS AND A
INSTRUMENTAL PIECE. PACKED WITH PRINTED
COVER AND BAND PHOTO.
PRICE: 6usS (world) or 30skr (sweden)
or international moneyorder
ZINES CAN SENDBLANKTAPE AND 2IRCs.
for info and order contact:
DAN BENGTSSON   KRISTIAN HASSELHUHN
PL2373   PL2287
S-441 96 ALINGSÅS   S-44196 ALINGSÅS
     SWEDEN   SWEDEN

Intoxicate: Monomania

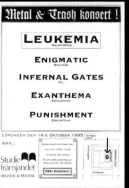

*Leukemia/Enigmatic/Infernal Gates
Exanthema/Punishment gig poster*

Leukemia logo

Lobotomy flyer

Mastication demo

Megaslaughter flyer

Melissa: A Flight to Insanity 7"

Memorium flyer

Merciless/Entombed gig flyer

Mezzrow artwork

Classic gig poster

Midas Touch flyer

THE A–Z OF SWEDISH DEATH METAL BANDS—GALLERY

MOONDARK - Demo #1

FOR CONTACT:

Kenneth Englund
Kolgillaregatan 8A
774 34 AVESTA
SWEDEN

Mattias Norrman
Skillingsgränd 16
774 35 AVESTA

SHADOWS PATH
INSIDE THE CRYPT
THE DAWN FOR OUR RACE
DIMENSION OF DARKNESS
TRESPASSING INTO...
...THE ABYSS
CONCEALING THE DAYLIGHT
WORLD DEVASTATOR

KENNETH.E..........GUITAR
MATTIAS.N..........GUITAR
MATS.B.............BASS/VOX
JOHAN.J.............DRUMS

PRODUCED & MIXED BY PER
SAMUELSSON AND MOONDARK
IN STUDIO SOUNDLINE 27-29
AUG, 2 SEP 1993. ALL MUSIC BY
MOONDARK. LYRICS BY MATS
& JOHAN.

ETERNAL GREETINGS TO:

Per Samuelsson, Jonas P, ABF, All...

Moondark: Demo #1

Morbid Fear: Darkest Age demo

MORPHEUS

BIOGRAPHY

MORPHEUS was formed in the dawn of January 1991 by
David Brink (Vocals), Sebastian Ramstedt (Lead Guitar)
and Johan Bergebäck (Bass), and we must not forget
Markus Rüden (Drums) who actually was the main
reason for the bands existence.
In March they went into a studio in Stockholm, to
record the first half of their demo.
But due to circumstances it never got finished.
Later they got an offer to do a 12" on Opinionate! Records,
so in July they went into the studio to record four songs
for their debut vinyl, "In The Arms Of..."
Just after recording of their vinyl, they were joined by
Janne Rudberg (Rhytm Guitar), who in the past had
played with some of them in another band.
The line-up became then as present:

David Brink - Vocals
Sebastian Ramstedt - Lead guitar
Janne Rudberg - Rhytm Guitar
Johan Bergebäck - Bass
Markus Rüden - Drums

They perform a fusionized way of technical and straight Death Metal.

For Contact: MORPHEUS
c/o David Brink
Skarpnäcks Allé 27
122 53 ENSKEDE
SWEDEN

OPINIONATE!
Box 3019
750 03 UPPSALA
SWEDEN

(Please include 2 IRC´s for reply)

Morpheus biography

Mortality: The Prophecy demo

Mourning Sign: Last Chamber

Mucky Pup/Merciless/
Filthy Christians flyer

Necrony demo inlay

Necrony flyer

Nihilist compilation CD

Necrony: Mucu-Purulent Miscarriage *7"*

Necrophobic/Sorg/Vinterkrig gig poster

No Remorse: Wake Up or Die *demo*

Obscura: In Agony *demo*

Early Opeth gig poster with Asphyx

Ophthalamia flyer

Pagan Rites flyer

Pexilated: A New Beginning *of* Unfaithful Life *demo*

Misery flyer

Regurgitate (Avesta): Trials of Life *demo*

SPLIT CD
OUT NOW!
DON'T HESITATE TO
ORDER A COPY
OF THIS PIECE OF
TRUE GRUESOME
S I C K N E S S

10 US$ WORLD
FROM:
REGURGITATE
C/O RIKARD JANSSON
FISKARNAS GATA 170
136 62 HANINGE
S W E D E N

Regurgitate (Stockholm)/Dead flyer

Repugnance flyer

Repugnance: Covetous Divinity *demo*

Rosicrucian: Initiation into Nothingness *demo*

Sacrium: Somnus es Morti Similis

Sadistic Gang Rape: Massdevastation

Scurvy demo tape

Thrash Bash 11

Serpent Obscene: Massacre *demo*

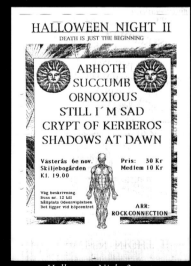

Halloween Night 2 poster

A wonderful flyer

Slow Death: Mystery of Tales

Society Gang Rape: More Dead Than Alive

Soils of Fate flyer

Suffer flyer

Suffer/Kazjurol/Deranged gig poster

Temperance flyer

THE DARKSEND

- ANOTHER FIERCE ATTACK IS LAUNCHED UPON MANKIND!

THE DARKSEND
"The Luciferian Whisper" 7"EP
(X-TR EP 001/ NEKRO 001)

-OUT NOW!!!

-It includes the title track, a fierce composition, with lyrics based on the satanic aspects of the Hammer films classic "The Satanic Rites Of Dracula"!
- No romanticized vampire nonsense here!
-Plus a re-recorded version of the demo track "A Flaming Red Dawn"!
-These songs won't be available elsewhere!

-Comes in a great RED/ BLACK cover, limited to 500 handnumbered copies!

PRICE: 40 KR(SVERIGE)!
8 US$(WORLD)!

order from:

X-TREME RECORDS
P.O.BOX 11238
S-404 25 GOTHENBURG
SWEDEN

NEKROLOGIUM PRODUCTIONS
P.O.BOX 9048
S-250 09 HELSINGBORG
SWEDEN

-KEEP THE CULT ALIVE! SUPPORT VINYL!

The Darksend flyer

Classic "Mosh not Pop" concert

Tiamat biography

Therion logo

Toxaemia EP

Tiamat: A Winter Shadow (insert)

"THE PROCESS OF RAPING A RANCID CADAVER"

4 trax Debut Demo out now!
BRUTAL SICK DEATHMETAL

Trade the tape:
J.Larsson
Industrig.11 NB
595 00 MJÖLBY
SWEDEN

Tele.0142/10161

Totte Martini
Edlundsg.8E
595 00 MJÖLBY
SWEDEN

Tele.0142/11729

Lyric sheet included!
5 $US or 20 Skr (everywhere)
For Info IRC=answer

Traumatic flyer

Tribulation: Void of Compassion

out now on: no fashion records

unanimated

debut album out now!

"in the forest of the dreaming dead"
11 tracks of dark and misty
swedish black/death metal.

cd: 18 $ sek: 100.
lp: 15 $ sek: 90.

send order to:

no fashion records
P.o.box 217
strängnäs   645 23
sweden

Unanimated flyer

Uncanny: Transportation
to the Uncanny *demo*

Uncurbed: The Strike of Mankind

DISCHANGE
TIMES SQUARE
PREACHERS
UNCURBED
+ Ev. GÄSTER

D-TAKTS MANGEL I
AVESTA FOLKETS HUS
LÖRDAGEN 15/5
KLOCKAN 20:00
INTRÄDE 40 Kr/MEDL.30 Kr

Dischange/Uncurbed/TSP poster

Demo 92 Out Now
Containing 7 tracks of Grind/Death
Price: 30 s kr or 6 $

Order From

Mathias Adamsson
Dalgatan 2 A
570 23 Anneberg
Sweden

or

Moses Shtieh
Smedjegatan 1
570 23 Anneberg
Sweden

Vermin flyer

Virgin Sin: Make 'Em Die Slowly *EP*

Wombbath: Several Shapes 7"

- MERCHANDISE -

Design A   Design B

Both shirts come w/ Abnormally-looking
back prints! * Printed on high quality
DARK shirts!

QUANTITY	DESCRIPTION	SIZE	L	XL	EACH	TOTAL
	T-Shirt A				$15.00	
	T-Shirt B				$15.00	
	Button with logo				$ 1.00	
	"But Life Goes On" tape				$ 5.00	
					TOTAL	

All prices include P & P.
Mail Cash or I.M.O.'s to:

CBR RECORDS
BOX 6038
126 06 HÄGERSTEN
SWEDEN
TEL: + 46 8 708 95 00
FAX: + 46 8 708 90 60

Sorry for the high t-shirt prices -
we've got 40% tax on shirts in Sweden.

© NICKE '90

21 LUCIFERS

Deadly grindcore band formed in Falun in 2002 by ex-Without Grief members Nicklas Lindh, Tobias Ols, and Ola Berg. Very brutal and quite good!
Line-Up Erik Skoglund: Vocals, Nicklas Lindh: Guitar/Vocals, Tobias Ols: Guitar, Ola Berg: Bass, Björn Åström: Drums
Deathography
Retaliation, Demo (2002)
Hope Fades, Demo (2004)
In the Name of..., CD (JMT Music, 2005)

9TH PLAGUE

Anti-Christian death metal combo formed in Helsingborg in 2000. Members of note include ex-Nominon and Obscene (Jönköping) man Tobias Hellman, and ex-Darksend vocalist Tony Richter, who also edited *Nekrologium* 'zine.
Line-Up Tony Richter: Vocals, Johan Lindberg: Guitar, Kristofer Örstadius: Guitar, Rafael Andersson: Drums, Tobias Hellman: Bass Past Members Stefan Stigert: Guitar
Deathography
Spreading the Satanic Gospel, EP (2002)
United in Real Brutality, Split (2003)
Age of Satanic Enlightenment, Demo (2004)

A-BOMB

Some kind of industrial death metal band that formed in Hällekil in 2004.
Line-Up Erik Gärdefors: Vocals/Guitar, Daniel Blomberg: Bass/Vocals, Simon Blomberg: Drums, Ulf Blomberg: Samples
Deathography
In a Moment of Aberration, Demo (2004)

A CANOROUS QUINTET

Formed in 1991 as A Canorous Quartet, after some line-up changes they ended up a Quintet. Their music is mainstream death metal, with a fair share of melodic touches. The most interesting aspect is listening to the mediocre drummer desperately trying to catch up with the other guys. This actually generates a feeling similar to the one achieved on Bathory's *Blood Fire Death*, where the drummer had the same problem! Linus is also editor of *Spellbound Mag.* A Canorous Quintet split up in 1999, but rumors state they have started again.
Line-Up Mårten Hansen: Vocals (1993-), Linus Nibrant: Guitar, Leo Pignon: Guitar, Jesper Löfgren: Bass, Fredrik Andersson: Drums
Deathography
The Time of Autumn, Demo (1994)
As Tears, MCD (Chaos, 1995)
Silence of the World Beyond, CD (No Fashion, 1996)
The Only Pure Hate, CD (No Fashion, 1998)

A MIND CONFUSED

A Mind Confused started out in Haninge in the beginning of 1993, heavily inspired by the mighty Gothenburg duo of Dissection and At the Gates (the vocals sound extremely like Thomas Lindberg), but

they don't have the power or originality of those bands at all. It's decent, but they should speed things up and cut some melodies to feed my taste. The band split up in 1998, after which Johan, Thomas, and Konstantin created the much better band Kaamos. Johan has also played with Serpent Obscene.
Line-Up Johan Thörngren: Vocals (1995-), Richard Wyöni: Guitar, Konstantin Papavassiliou: Guitar, Thomas: Drums (initially also Vocals) Past Members Anders: Bass (1995), Mattias Forsmark: Drums (1993), José: Bass (session only)
Deathography
Demo (1995)
Poems of a Darker Soul, Demo (1996)
Out of Chaos Spawn, 7" (Near Dark, 1996)
Anarchos, CD (Near dark, 1997)

ABEMAL

From the endless row of Swedish death metal projects in the 90's, this one is from Åtvidaberg. The members also played in Algaion, Pain, Nephenzy, Hypocrisy, The Abyss, and—well, a lot!
Line-Up Mathias Kamijo: Guitar, Mårten Björkman: Vocals, Yngve Liljebäck: Guitar, Martin Gärdeman: Drums, Kenneth Johansson: Bass
Deathography
Demo 1994, Demo (1994)

ABHOTH

Formed in Västerås back in 1989, and then known as Morbid Salvation Army, originally Abhoth played grindcore, but their style mellowed considerably over time. They only stayed together long enough to record one 7", the somewhat doomy *The Tide*. They continued as Chimera, releasing a demo as late as 1999. The high-pitched vocals of original singer Joakim Bröms were probably considered too "wimpy" in the early stage of Swedish death metal— the band never made it, even after his departure. Bröms joined the great Afflicted after deepening his vocals, while guitarist Kristensen and drummer Blyckert have worked with Suffer.
Line-Up Jörgen Kristensen: Guitar, Anfinn Skulevold: Guitar, Thomas Krzyzowski: Vocals (1991-), Jens Klövegård: Drums (1993-), Claes Ramberg: Bass (1993-) Past Members Anders Ekman: Vocals (1990-91), Joakim Bröms: Vocals (1989-90), Mats Blyckert: Drums (1989-93), Dag Nesbö: Bass (1989-93), Carl-Åke Johansson: Drums...and a lot of others.
Deathography
A Matter of Splatter, Demo (1990)
Instrumental Rehearsal, Demo (1990)
Forever to be Vanished There in, Demo (1991)
The Tide, 7" (Corpsegrinder, 1993)
Divine Orphan, Demo (1994)

ABLAZE MY SORROW

Started in 1993 in Falkenberg, this is standard melodic death metal with thrashy touches, heavily inspired At the Gates and In Flames. By the early band photos, I guess they initially wanted to be black metal. Though professional, the main problem with

Ablaze My Sorrow is that they don't really do justice to their inspirations, especially where songwriting is concerned. But if you're into melodic death metal, they are definitely worth checking out.
Line-Up Fredrik Arnesson: Vocals, Magnus Carlsson: Guitar, Anders Brorsson: Bass/Vocals, Alex Bengtsson: Drums (1994-), Dennis Linden: Guitar/Vocals (1996-), Kristian Lönnsjö: Vocals **Past Members** Fredrik Arnesson: Vocals , Martin Qvist: Vocals, Fredrik Wenzel: Drums (1993-94), Roger Johansson: Guitar (1993-96), Anders Lundin: Guitar
Deathography
For Bereavement We Cried, Demo (1994)
Demo 95, Demo (1995)
If emotions Still Burn, CD (No Fashion, 1996)
The Plague, CD (No Fashion, 1998)
Anger, Hate and Fury, CD (No Fashion, 2002)

ABNORMITY
An obscure death metal band of the early 90's. Apart from the demo, I haven't heard a thing about these guys. Vowdén went on to join Expulsion.
Line-Up Linus Johansson: Drums/Vocals, Christopher Vowdén: Guitar, Per Wannerheim: Bass
Deathography
Demo 1991, Demo (1991)

ABOMINATE
Gore-grind of the 2000's from Strömstad. Not the best band, but they sure sound fresh in these days of stereotypical retro thrash. It wouldn't hurt to put some more touches of death metal in the music, though.
Deathography
Abominate, Demo (2003)

ABOMINATION—see Tiamat

ABRANIA
Melodic death metal band that formed in Västerås in 1999 and is apparently on hold.
Line-Up Jho Abrai: Vocals, Peter Strömberg: Guitar, Jerry Engström: Guitar, Andreas Silfver: Bass, Martin Lindqvist: Drums **Past Members** Niklas: Guitar, Maria Forsberg: Vocals, Daniel Andersson: Guitar, Daniel Rejment: Bass, Linn de Wilde: Vocals, Daniel Forssten: Drums, Simon: Drums
Deathography
Calling My Name, Demo (2001)
Dyin' Screams, Demo (2005)

ABRUPTUM
Not really a death metal band at all, but rather one of the most original and strange black metal groups ever. It's actually hard to label the music of Abruptum, everything is just weird—slow, doomy and atmospheric beyond imagination. Their image is of course 100% satanic. Since their first demos in 1990, Abruptum has been hailed within the black metal scene for their cold sounds of "pure evil." Whether you like them or not, they definitely create morbid structures of creeping terror. When "It"

and "All" vanished from the scene in the late 90's, Morgan continued this project alone. But it was all laid to rest in 2005, and Morgan is now totally dedicated to his main creation Marduk. Evil Genius is a compilation CD, and Meleficent is a re-release of that compilation minus the song "Calibus Frontem Tumeo Acidus Abcessus."
Line-Up Morgan "Evil" Håkansson: Guitar/Sounds/Piano/Darkness **Past Members** Tony "It" Särkkä: Cries/Screams/Guitar/Violin/Drums/Torture, Jim "All" Berger: Vocals, "Ext": Bass (first demo only)
Deathography
Hextum Galaem Zelog, Demo (1990)
The Satanist Tunes, Demo (1990)
Evil, 7" (Psychoslaughter, 1991)
Orchestra of Dark, Demo (1991)
Obscuritatem Advoco Amplectere Me, CD (Deathlike Silence, 1993)
In Umbra Malitae Ambulado, In Aeternum in Triumpho Tenebrarum, CD (Deathlike Silence, 1994)
Evil Genius, CD (Hellspawn, 1995)
Vi Sonas Veris Nigrae Maliteaes, CD (Head Not Found, 1997)
De Profundis Mors Vas Cousumet, EP (Blooddawn Productions, 2000)
Casus Luciferi, CD (Blooddawn Productions, 2004)
Maleficent, CD (Blooddawn, 2005)

ABSINTH
Absinth is a mid-90's death metal band I've barely heard about. Anybody know anything?
Deathography
The Requiem, Demo (1994)

ABSORPTION
Mora band formed in 1990, and probably vanished the same year. I have heard nothing about them since. My guess is that these guys are the same bunch of lunatics that later formed Disenterment.
Deathography
Invocations to Eternal Darkness, Demo (1990)

ABSURD
One of these early 90's bands who just came and went. Brutal stuff. Christopher Vowdén was also in the band Abnormity around the same time, and later got a bit more attention with Expulsion.
Line-Up Daniel: Bass, Christopher Vowdén: Guitar/Vocals, Micke: Guitar, Mårten: Drums
Deathography
Storm of Malevolence, Demo (1991)
Drained of Body Chemicals, 7" (Seraphic Decay, 1991)

ABSURDEITY
Thrashy death metal band from Hultsfred, formed in 2002. The most absurd thing about this band is the name, but who can blame them since all cool English words were already taken?
Line-Up Johan Andersson: Vocals, Robert Johansson: Guitar, Lars Broddesson: Drums **Past**

Members Marcus Fahleryd: Bass/Vocals, Benny
Åkesson: Bass/Vocals, Gabriel Jensen: Guitar
Deathography
Onslaught of the Undead, Demo (2002)
Enter Necrosis, Demo (2003)
Absurdeity, Demo (2005)

ABSURDUM

Brutal death metal from Staffanstorp. This band
formed in 1993, but never caused any impact at all.
Line-Up Stefan Larsson: Guitar
Deathography
The Erotic Eclipse, Demo (1996)

ABYSSAL CHAOS—see Dead Awaken

ABYSSOS

Melodic black metal band with touches of death
metal, hailing from Sundsvall in the north of Sweden.
Abyssos formed in 1996, and still continue their
mission of vampirism, occultism, and satanism.
Line-Up Rehn: Vocals/Guitar, Meidal: Bass, Andreas
Söderlund: Drums
Deathography
Wherever Witches Fly, Demo (1996)
*Together We Summon the Dark, CD (Cacophonous,
1997)*
Fhinsthanian Nightbreed, CD (Cacophonous, 1999)

ACHROMASIA

This band started in Skärholmen in 1990. I guess they
wanted to be part of the death metal scene, but nothing
can hide that their sole demo is stereotypical and boring
thrash metal. The inverted cross and the pentagram in
the logo don't help one bit.
Line-Up Artur Pacheco: Guitar/Vocals, Sonny
Falk: Guitar, Danne Cummerow: Bass, Andreas
Palmkvist: Drums
Deathography
Chanting for Immortal Race, Demo (1991)

ADVERSARY

Good and pure death metal from Sandviken. This
band kicked off in 1990 and really had some good
stuff. Sadly, they disappeared before catching any
wider attention. Like many other great Swedish
death metal bands of the early 90's, they are
forgotten today. Matti Kärki (Dismember, Carnage,
Carbonized, General Surgery, Therion...now that's
a list of qualifications!) supplied guest vocals on the
second demo. When black metal became the new
fashion, David left Adversary to form the ridiculous
demo-only band Behemoth. Luckily he matured, and
transformed that band into In Aeternum.
Line-Up David Larsson: Bass, Jörgen: Vocals, Per:
Guitar/Keyboards, Jocke: Guitar, Henka: Drums
Deathography
Beyond Death, Demo (1991)
Human Reality, Demo (1992)
Remains of an Art Forgotten, Demo (1992)

AEON

Aeon formed in Östersund in 1999, basically a
continuation of Defaced Creation. They deliver well-
played anti-Christian death metal. The band has
been pretty successful, and is now part of Unique
Leader's crafty roster.
Line-Up Tommy Dahlström: Vocals, Daniel Dlimi:
Guitar, Zeb Nilsson: Guitar, Johan Hjelm: Bass,
Nils Fjellström: Drums *Past Members* Morgan
Nordbakk: Guitar (1999-2001), Arttu Malkki:
Drums (1999-2002)
Deathography
Demo #1, Demo (1999)
Dark Order, EP (Necropolis, 2001)
Bleeding the False, CD (Unique Leader, 2005)

AEONIC

Since the name Aeon was already taken when they
formed in 2004, I guess these guys from Hultsfred
settled for Aeonic. Thrash metal with some hints at
death. Nothing special.
Line-Up Gabriel Jensen: Guitar, Rickard Olausson:
Drums, Anders Håkansson: Bass, Mattias Svensson:
Vocals
Deathography
Hollow Masquerade, Demo (2005)

AFFLICTED

This heavyweight band was formed way back in
1988 by a bunch of beer-drinking teenagers. In the
early days they were called Afflicted Convulsion,
but shortened the name when singer Joakim Bröms
(ex-Abhoth) joined in 1990. Initially they played a
furious and strange mix of grind and death metal,
but the group gradually changed their style towards
80's heavy metal. Their later material can almost be
described as a deadly Iron Maiden. Afflicted is surely
one of the most original Swedish death metal bands,
worthy of all the respect in the world.
Line-Up Jesper Thorsson: Guitar, Joacim Carlsson:
Guitar (1989-1994), Yasin Hillborg: Drums (1989),
Michael van de Graaf: Vocals (1992-), Philip von
Segebaden: Bass (1991-) *Past Members* Fredrik
Ling: Bass (1988-1991), Joakim Bröms: Vocals
(1990-1992), Martin Holm: Vocals (1988-1990),
Mats Nordrup: Drums, Mikael Lindvall: Guitar
Deathography
Toxic Existence, Demo (1989—as Afflicted
Convulsion)
Rehearsal (1989—as Afflicted Convulsion)
Psychedelic grindcore, Demo (1989—as Afflicted
Convulsion)
Beyond Redemption, Demo (1990—as Afflicted
Convulsion)
The Odious Reflection, Demo (1990)
In Years to Come, EP (Relapse, 1990)
Wanderland, Demo (1991)
Ingrained, 7" (Thrash, 1991)
Astray, 7" (Relapse, 1992)
Rising to the Sun, 7" (Nuclear Blast, 1992)
Prodigal Sun, LP/CD (Nuclear Blast, 1992)
Demo 1993, Demo (1993)
Dawn of Glory, CD (Massacre, 1995)

AFFLICTED CONVULSION—see Afflicted

AGONI—see Agony

AGONY

A Stockholm (Solna, actually) act founded in August 1984, originally as the pure crust punk band Agoni. The group steadily went in a thrash metal direction following the addition of drummer Moberg and guitarist Sjölin. They stuck to their punk roots for a while, touring as Agoni with Swedish crust gods Anti Cimex across the U.K in 1986. After that it was all thrash, and the band secured a deal with Music for Nations in 1987 after their second demo. Although their album *The First Defiance* was recorded with two guitarists, Pelle Ström was fired before Christmas 1987. He later joined The Krixjälters/Omnitron and Comecon. After Agony broke up, Moberg joined Rubbermen. At their best moments, Agony actually echoed the mighty Slayer, and they were surely one of Sweden's best thrash metal bands.

Line-Up Peter Lundström: Vocals, Magnus Sjölin: Guitar, Nappe Benchemsi: Bass, Tommy Moberg: Drums **Past Members** Conny Wigström: Guitar, Pelle Ström: Guitar

Deathography

Stockholmsmangel, Comp-Tape (1985—as Agoni)

The Future is Ours, Demo (1985—as Agoni)

Execution of Mankind, Demo (1986)

The First Defiance, LP (Music for Nations, 1988)

AGRETATOR

Formed as Demise in Helsingborg in 1990. Two years later they switched their name to Agretator and started to make progress. Not very much though, since most of the members soon abandoned ship to form the far more successful Darkane.

Line-Up Pierre Richter: Vocals/Guitar, Christopher Malmström: Guitar, Jörgen Löfberg: Bass, Peter Wildoer: Drums **Past Members** Tony Richter: Vocals, Jesper Granath: Bass

Deathography

Delusions, LP (Crypta Rec, 1994)

Distorted Logic, EP (1996)

AGROTH

Early 90's death metal from the very northern town of Luleå. Actually a pretty good band, but probably sounded too much like Carbonized for their own good. And they are nowhere near the quality of that band, no offence. Sandorf also played with Gates of Ishtar and The Duskfall.

Line-Up Anders Ekström, Mikael Sandorf: Vocals/Guitar

Deathography

Travel, Demo (1993)

Vaginal Travel, Demo (1993)

Demo 1993, Demo (1993)

ALLEGIANCE

This Söderköping band started out playing old school thrash metal in 1989. With radical line-up changes Allegiance's music turned much more brutal, and by the mid-90's they had invented a genre—together with some other bands like the mighty Enslaved

from Norway—called Viking war metal. The band really sounds like a less satanic version of the black metal titans Marduk. This comes as no surprise, since Allegiance's most prominent members Roger Svensson and Fredrik Andersson also played in Marduk during their most brilliant period.

Line-Up Roger "Bogge" Svensson: Vocals/Guitar, Fredrik Andersson: Drums, Pär Thornell: Guitar, Mikael Almgren: Bass, Magnus "Devo" Andersson: Vocals

Deathography

Sick World, Demo (1989)

Eternal Hate, Demo (1990)

The Beginning Was the End, Demo (1991)

Odin Åge Er Alle, Demo (1993)

Höfdingadrapa, Demo (1994)

Hymn Till Hangagud, CD (No Fashion, 1996)

Blodörnsoffer, CD (No Fashion, 1997)

Vrede, CD (No Fashion, 1998)

ALTAR

Begun as Epidemic in the small town of Kumla in 1988, the next year they changed their name to Wortox, and in September 1990 finally settled for Altar. Initially they played thrash metal, but soon developed into brutal death metal. Though this band was pretty good, they never really made it. Original drummer Karlsson left for Suffer. Bülow joined on guitar towards the end of their career, and Nasum's Mieszko Talarczyk got in on vocals shortly after. Altar seems to have been damned: original bass player Magnus died in a motorcycle accident shortly after quitting the band, and Mieszko was killed in the Tsunami catastrophe in Thailand in 2004. May they rest in peace.

Line-Up Magnus Carlsson: Bass/Vocals, Jimmy Lundmark: Guitar, Fredrik Johansson: Drums (1990-) **Past Members** Johan Bülow: Guitar (1993), Mieszko Talarczyk: Vocals (1993-), Mattias O: Guitar (1988-1991), Per Karlsson: Drums (1989-1990), Magnus E: Bass (1988-1989), Dan Swanö: Keyboards/Vocals (session only)

Deathography

The Unknown, Demo (1989—as Wortox)

No Flesh Shall be Spared, Demo (1991)

Ex Oblivione, Altar/Cartilage Split LP (Drowned Products, 1993)

Promodemo 93, Demo (1993)

ALVSVART

This band emerged when old Gothenburg death metal band Decay decided to start rehearsing again in 2001. As you might guess by the name (the Swedish word for Goblins, or whatever, in *Lord of the Rings*), this is more of a trollish black metal band.

Line-Up Peter Wigeborn, Sebastian Petersson, Dennis Nilsson, Peter Merdén: Vocals **Past Members** Kristoffer Åberg: Vocals, Oskar Fredén: Guitar

Deathography

When Damnation Takes its Course, Demo (2003)

AMARAN

Formed in 2000 by Kari (ex-Mourning Sign) and

Robin (ex-Gorement). After initially having a fairly deadly style, the music soon transformed into power metal. Among the notable members that have played in the band at some point are Siebenbürgen's Niklas Sandin and Centinex's Ronnie Bergerståhl.
Line-Up *Ronnie Backlund: Guitar, Gunnar Hammar: Guitar, Niklas "Nille" Sandin: Bass, Robin Bergh: Drums* **Past Members** *Kari Kainulainen: Guitar, Mikael Andersson: Bass, Ronnie Bergerståhl: Bass, Johanna Depierre: Vocals, Pär Hjulström: Drums*
Deathography
Promo 2001, Demo (2001)
A World Depraved, CD (Listenable, 2002)
Pristine in Bondage, CD (Listenable, 2004)

AMARATH
Two members of Hypocrite trying to be Paradise Lost. Professional, but unoriginal and boring.
Line-Up *Henrik Hedborg: Guitar* **Deathography**
Demo 98, Demo (1998)

AMAROK—see Omnius Deathcult

AMENOPHIS
Formed in Norrköping in 1989 by Pettersson, Eriksson, and Hylen. After two demos and a few gigs (the first had Marduk as openers!) the band split. For a short while, Pettersson teamed with Gustafsson in Darkified, but soon enough Darkified folded, too.
Line-Up *Tim Pettersson: Guitar/Vocals, Esa Sorsa: Guitar, Robert Hylen: Bass, Mikael Eriksson: Drums, Martin Gustafsson: Vocals (1992-)*
Deathography
Amenophis, Demo (1991)
The Twelfth Hour, Demo (1992)

AMENTIA
Early 90's death/thrash from Hedemora. Amentia was a short-lived band with only one demo, and not a very exciting one at that. Basically this is stereotypical and dated thrash, spiced up with some attempted death metal vocals. Still, it's pretty tight and well played. But if you compare Amentia to pioneering townmates Hatred, they sound very weak.
Line-Up *Matte Kärvemo: Vocals/Keyboards, Nestor Hallengren: Guitar, Magnus Myrzell: Guitar, Micke Numelin: Bass, Johnny Eriksson: Drums*
Deathography
Demo 1, Demo (1992)

AMON AMARTH
Basically a standard mid-tempo death metal band with many melodic touches, and a kind of "Viking" image on top of it all. They began as Scum back in 1988 in Tumba, a small (and boring—death metal was probably the only way out!) suburb of Stockholm. The name changed to Amon Amarth in 1992, and their career has been extremely successful ever since, with many international tours and massive sales. They are the Manowar of death metal.
Line-Up *Fredrik Andersson: Drums, Johan Hägg: Vocals, Ted Lundström: Bass, Olavi Mikkonen: Guitar, Johan Söderberg: Guitar* **Past Members**
Martin Lopez: Drums, Anders Hansson: Guitar, Nico Kaukinen: Drums, Ted Lundström: Bass
Deathography
Demo 1, Demo (1992—as Scum)
Thor's Rise, Demo (1993)
The Arrival of Fimbul Winter, Demo (1993)
The Arrival of the Fimbul Winter, EP (Pulverized, 1994)
Sorrow throughout the Nine Worlds, MCD (Pulverized, 1996)
Once Sent from the Golden Hall, CD (Metal Blade, 1998)
The Avenger, CD (Metal Blade, 2000)
The Crusher, CD (Metal Blade, 2001)
Versus the World, CD (Metal Blade, 2002)
Fate of Norns Release Show, Split (Metal Blade, 2004)
Fate of Norns, CD (Metal Blade, 2004)

AMSVARTNER
Started as a black metal band in Umeå in 1994, but as trends changed they moved towards melodic Gothenburg-style death metal. I guess you can imagine the originality and quality here. I don't know about you, but I think the "The Trollish Mirror" might be one of the nerdiest titles of all time.
Line-Up *Jonathan Holmgren: Guitar, Albin Johansson: Bass, Alfred Johansson: Drums, Marcus Johansson: Vocals, Daniel Nygaard: Guitar*
Deathography
Demo 1, Demo (1995)
Underneath the Thousand Years Gate, Demo (1996)
Towards the Skullthrone of Satan/The Trollish Mirror, Enthroned/Amsvartner-Split (Blackend, 1997)
The Trollish Mirror, EP (Blackend, 1997)
Dreams, CD (Blackend, 1999)
Theatrical Lunacy, Demo (2002)

ANACHRONAEON
A melodic death metal band that started out as Human Failure in Västerås in 2003.
Line-Up *Andreas Åkerlind: Drums, Patrik Carlsson: Guitar/Vocals, Carl Ullbrandt: Bass, Marcus Wadstein: Guitar/Keyboards*
Deathography
As the Last Human Spot in Me Dies, Demo (2004)

ANAEMIA
Doomy band that got going in 1994, and has stuck around without making any impact at all.
Line-Up *Kim Stranne: Vocals, Tobias Ogenblad: Drums, Krister Sundqvist: Guitar, Martin Svensson: Bass*
Deathography
The Second Incarnation, CD (Endtime Productions, 2001)

ANATA
Formed by Fredrik Schälin in the small town of Varberg back in 1993, in the beginning Anata played crossover/thrash, but they soon developed a

somewhat deadlier sound. The quality of the band is undeniable, and in 2003 they earned a deal with the world's best-known death metal label, Earache. Still, they tend to mix in a bit too much into their songs—thrash, death, black...you name it. The results are confusing rather than good, at least to my damaged ears. They are awesome musicians, though. Original drummer Peterson used to edit *Fearless Mag*. All the current members of Anata also play in the side project Rotinjected.
Line-Up Fredrik Schälin: *Guitar/Vocals, Andreas Allenmark: Guitar (1997-), Henrik Drake: Bass (1996-), Conny Petersson: Drums (2001-)* **Past Members** *Robert Petersson: Drums (1993-2001), Matthias Svensson: Guitar (1993-1996), Martin Sjöstrand: Bass (1993-1996)*
Deathography
Burn Forever the Garden of Lie, Demo (1996)
Vast Lands of My Infernal Dominion, Demo (1997)
The Infernal Depths of Hatred, CD (Seasons of Mist, 1998)
War Volume III: Anata vs. Bethzaida, MCD (Seasons of Mist, 1999)
Dreams of Death and Dismay, CD (Seasons of Mist, 2001)
Under a Stone With no Inscription, CD (Earache/Wicked World, 2004)

ANATHEMA—see Eructation

ANCIENT
One of many small metal bands from Umeå, and among the first as they started out in September 1992. They produced slow death/goth in the vein of Tiamat, and the results weren't very exciting. Norman went on to form Bewitched.
Line-Up Marcus Norman: Guitar/Vocals, Anders Nilsson: Drums, Fredrik: Bass (1993-) **Past Members** *Ulf: Bass (1992-1993)*
Deathography
In the Eye of the Serpent, Demo (1993)

ANCIENT WINDS
Typical melodic black/death metal from the mid-90's. This band's from Visby. Svegsjö later continued in Thyrfing and Construcdead. As I remember, Ancient Winds was originally called Wind of Ancient, but I really hope that I am wrong.
Line-Up Henrik Svegsjö: Everything
Deathography
Reach My Journey's End, Demo (1995)

ANCIENT WISDOM
This Umeå-based group started in the early 90's, simply as Ancient. In 1993 they added Wisdom to their name, and continued their melodic death metal task. This group should probably be seen as a side project of Bewitched (Norman) and Naglfar (Nilsson and Rydén). Bass player Jacobsson had previously been in Throne of Ahaz. Like Bewitched, Ancient Wisdom has used Nocturnal Rites drummer Ulf Andersson during live performances. Their titles make me believe that this is actually some kind of a

joke—maybe Marcus Norman's own joke since he seems to be the only member left.
Line-Up Marcus Norman: Vocals/Guitar **Past Members** *Andreas Nilsson: Guitar, Fredrik Jacobsson:Bass, Jens Rydén: Keyboards (session only)*
Deathography
In the Eye of the Serpent, Demo (1993—as Ancient)
Through Rivers of the Eternal Blackness, Demo (1994)
For the Snow Covered the Northland, CD (Avantgarde, 1996)
The Calling, CD (Avantgarde, 1997)
And the Physical Shape of Light Bled, CD (Avantgarde, 2000)
Cometh Doom Cometh Death, CD (Avantgarde, 2004)

ANCIENT'S REBIRTH
A black/death group from Falkenberg that started out in July 1992 as Desert Ritual. When the youngsters were told the meaning of their band name, they changed it to Infernus Ritual, then settled for Ancient's Rebirth. A band from the times when fat death metal was out and primitive black metal was in. Corpse paint, no live shows (well, they played a couple gigs in 1992 before they got really evil!), Satan, and pseudonyms like Goatnecro and Nuncorpse—do you dare listen to them? The evil nature of this band led to a lot of line-up changes. Martin Qvist and Anders Brorson went on to Ablaze my Sorrow.
Line-Up Henrik Bengtsson: Guitar, Oskar Frankki: Drums, Dennis Widén: Vocals/Guitar **Past Members** *Patrik Bergström: Drums, Anders Brorsson: Bass, Martin Qvist: Bass, Thomas Hedlund: Drums, Anders Dahnberg: Bass, Fredrik: Drums, Henke: Guitar, Jesper Larsson: Drums ...well, I guess about every teenager from Falkenberg has played with them at some point in the early 90's.*
Deathography
Twisted Tales of the Crucified, Demo (1992)
Culte del Diablos, Rehearsal (1993)
Below the Nocturnal Skies, Demo (1994)
Of Wrath, Demo (1994)
Drain the Portal in Blood, CD (Necromantic Gallery, 1996)
Damnation Hell's Arrival, CD (Necropolis, 1998)

ANGEL GOAT
An obscure, occult death metal band that started out in Angered during 1990. I don't know if they ever found a regular singer or recorded anything officially, but I remember song titles like "Black Mass" and "Damnation". Korhonen was also in Monkey Mush, and edited the *Slimy Scum* 'zine.
Line-Up Tommy Korhonen: Bass, Miika Salmela: Guitar, Juvonen: Drums, A Juurika: Guitar/Vocals

ANGELS OF FALL
A minor melodic metal band that still hasn't gotten outside the field of demos.
Line-Up Jessica Andersson-Skäär: Vocals, Johannes Ohlsson: Drums, Daniel Augustsson: Bass, Martin

Bryngelsson: Guitar, Mikael Carlsson: Guitar
Past Members Leonard Johnels: Vocals, Tomas
Blomstrand: Bass
Deathography
Cry Out, Demo (1999)
Nocturnal Tears, Demo (1999)
As Raindrops Fled Demo, (2005)

ANNIHILATION
Kiruna is surely a fucked-up place in the very very
very (I mean very, it's above the polar circle) north of
Sweden (two pubs, no fun, eternal winter, and nothing
to do). This short-lived death/thrash project must be
one of the few extreme acts ever to crawl out of that
hellhole. They emerged in 1999. Both members are
currently in the band Deadlock. Isn't Das Übergay a
wonderful nickname? For what I know it might be his
actual name, they are mad up there!
Line-Up Phan: Bass/Vocals, Das Übergay: Guitar
Deathography
Murder Industry, Demo (2000)
Analsex66, Demo (2003)

ANTI BOFORS—see Disfear

APATHY
Mid-90's catchy death metal from Umeå. A bit similar
to Tiamat, but with none of their originality.
Line-Up Johan Eklund
Deathography
Dark Shattered Death, Demo (1994)

APOLLGON
An early 90's death/black metal band from Karlskrona.
The list of past members indicates that there has been
turbulence within the band, or maybe nobody ever
cared to stay. Both main members used to be in
Midvinter.
Line-Up Damien Midwinter: All instrumental
arrangements, Vlad Morbius: Vocals **Past Members**
Jag: Bass, Mikel: Vocals, Sogatha: Guitar, Mankik:
Guitar, Maniek: Guitar, Korona: Drums, Krol:
Drums, Hans: Vocals
Deathography
End, Demo (1994)

ARCH ENEMY
Started in 1995 as a kind of "all-star" project,
members include such well-known death metallers
as Johan Liiva-Axelsson (Carnage, Furbowl), Mike
Amott (Carnage, Carcass), Daniel Erlandsson
(Eucharist, In Flames), and Amott's younger brother
Christopher (Armageddon). Among later members
are Sharlee D'Angelo from Mercyful Fate...what a
line-up! Their music could be described as muscular,
melodic death metal with a lot of thrash touches.
Arch Enemy has quickly built a great reputation, and
has toured all around the world. Since 2000, this has
been one of very few death metal bands with a female
vocalist, or a female member at all!
Line-Up Angela Nathalie Gossow: Vocals
(2000), Michael Amott: Guitar, Sharlee D'Angelo
(Charles Peter Andreason): Bass (1998-), Daniel

Erlandsson: Drums, Fredrik Åkesson: Guitar (2005)
Past Members Johan Liiva-Axelsson: Vocals/Bass
(1995-2000), Martin Bengtsson: Bass (1997-1998),
Peter Wildoer: Drums, Christopher Amott: Guitar
(1995-2005), Gus G: Guitar (session only)
Deathography
Demo, Demo (1996)
Black Earth, CD (Wrong Again, 1996)
Stigmata, CD (Century Media, 1998)
Burning Bridges, CD (Century Media, 1999)
Burning Japan Live 1999, CD (Toys Factory, 2000)
Wages of Sin, CD, (Century Media, 2001)
Burning Angel, Single (Century Media, 2002)
Anthems of Rebellion, CD (Century Media, 2003)
*Dead Eyes See No Future, EP (Century Media,
2004)*
Doomsday Machine, CD (Century Media, 2005)

ARISE
Retro thrash band from Alingsås that started in
1994. They have been somewhat successful, even
though they sound pretty average to my ears.
Line-Up Erik Ljungqvist: Vocals/Guitar, Daniel
Bugno: Drums, L-G Jonasson: Guitar, Patrik
Skoglöw: Bass **Past Members** Jörgen Sjölander:
Vocals (1994-1995), Björn Andvik: Vocals (1995-
1996)
Deathography
Abducted Intelligence, Demo (1997)
Arise, Demo (1998)
Statues, Demo (1999)
Resurrection, Demo (1999)
Hell's Retribution, Demo (2000)
Abducted Intelligence, Demo (2000)
The Godly Work of Art, CD (Spinefarm, 2001)
*Kings of a Cloned Generation, CD (Spinefarm,
2003)*
The Beautiful New World, CD (Spinefarm, 2005)

ARMAGEDDON
Pretty powerful death metal project formed in
Halmstad 1997 by some members from Arch Enemy,
Darkane, and In thy Dreams. Perhaps this is how
those bands would sound if they had guts! Still,
beware of unhealthy doses of boring melodies and
ghastly hints at power metal.
Line-Up Christopher Amott: Guitar/Vocals
(1997-), Tobias Gustafsson: Bass (2001-), Daniel
Erlandsson: Drums (1997/2000-) **Past Members**
Rickard Bengtsson: Vocals (2000-2001), Jonas
Nyrén: Vocals (1997), Michael Amott: Guitar,
Kari Lönn: Keyboards, Dick Lövgren: Bass (2000-
2001), Martin Bengtsson: Bass (1997-2000), Peter
Wildoer: Drums (1997-2000)
Deathography
Crossing the Rubicon, CD (War Music, 1997)
Embrace the Mystery, CD (Toy Factory, 2000)
Three, CD (Toy Factory, 2002)

ARSEDESTROYER
Stockholm act, one of the wildest and coolest Swedish
grindcore bands ever. Starting in the winter of 1991,
they were totally unrelenting. Unlike most other

Swedish grindcore acts of the 90's, Arsedestroyer actually gained recognition. Not like the response their later colleagues Nasum received, but still... Endless line-up changes make it difficult to know who is in the band now, or if they even still exist. Band leader Terje (who has played with Regurgitate) is perhaps most known for his ultra-short answers to interviewers. He rarely says more than "yes," "no," or "I don't fucking care." Hilarious!
Line-Up Terje Andersson: Vocals/Guitar, Thorbjörn Gräslund: Guitar, Peter Hirseland: Bass, Kenneth Andersson: Drums *Past Members* Linus, Brandt & many others.
Deathography
Arsedestroyer/Noise Slaughter, Split 7" (Psychomania, 1994)
Arsedestroyer/Confusion, Split 7" (Distortion, 1994)
Mother of All Chaotic Noisecore, CD (Distortion, 1995)
Live Aboard the M.S. Stubnitz (split with Abstain), LP (In League Wit' Satan, 1998)
Arsedestroyer/Gore Beyond Necropsy, Split 7" (Devour, 2000)
Teenass Revolt, LP/CD (Devour, 2001)

ASHES

Hold your horses, another Finspång project! This one started in 1996 to play a kind of death/black metal. Mikael and Jonas are also in Facebreaker. Andreas is ex-Pan-thy-Monium, Marduk, and Edge of Sanity.
Line-Up Andreas: Guitar, Jonas: Bass/Vocals, Mourning: Guitar, Mikael: Drums, Timo H: Drums
Deathography
Death has Made its Call, CD (Necropolis, 1998)
And the Angels Wept, EP (Necropolis, 2000)

ASMODEUS (Eskilstuna)

Formed July 1987 out of the ashes of Death Ripper. With Torro as chief composer they created good brutal death metal, but sadly never left the deepest underground. After a few rehearsal tapes and a single gig at Fredrik Karlén of Merciless' twentieth birthday in 1991, the band folded in May 1994. Thinking back, it's stunning that two such legendary metalheads as SOD Jocke and Glenning were ever in the same band—even more amazing are session musicians Fredrik Karlén (Merciless), John Forsberg (Interment), and Mattias Kennhed (Macrodex)! The old school was the best school. The CD compiles various rehearsals.
Line-Up Ntarogan (Cleas Glenning): Drums, Torro: Guitar, SOD Jocke: Vocals *Past Members* Fredrik Karlén: Bass (session member only), John Forsberg (session member only): Guitar, Gamen: Guitar, Mattias Kennhed: Guitar (session member only), Stefan Källarsson: Bass (session member only)
Deathography
Brought Forth from the Depths, CD

ASMODEUS (Helsingborg)—see Gardens of Obscurity

ASMODEUS (Rönninge)

Melodic and melancholic death metal of the mid-90's from Rönninge. But why those keyboards? Not to be confused with the band Asmodeus that transformed into Gardens of Obscurity. Envall is more known from his work in Kaamos.
Line-Up Kalle Envall: Bass, Eric Hellman: Guitar/Vocals, Jonny Mogren: Guitar, Björn Ahlström: Guitar, Fredrik Sundqvist: Drums, Kristian Martti: Keyboards
Deathography
Demo (1996)

ASPHYXIATION

A band from Falun that started in 1997, but still hasn't made it beyond demos, not for lack of trying. Asphyxiation originally contained all the members from Ceremonial Death, so I guess it's basically the same band. Other members can also be found in Shock Wave, Waxwork, and Dementia 13. As you might guess, Falun is not the most exciting town.
Line-Up Daniel Silfver: Vocals, Niklas Olsson: Guitar/Vocals, Gene Zeder: Drums *Past Members* Andreas Nyman: Guitar (session only, 2002-2004), Fredrik Sundfors: Bass (session only, 2004), Magnus Rosén: Drums/Guitar, Per Rosén: Bass
Deathography
Moving Target, Demo (1997)
Towards Death, Demo (1999)
Lifeless Through Suffocation, Demo (2002)
Shades of Infinity, Demo (2004)

ASTRAL CARNEVAL

Formed in Eskilstuna 2001, another act in the endless row of modern thrash/death metal acts.
Line-Up Per Humbla: Vocals, Kenneth Nielsen: Guitar, Magnus Vitén: Guitar, Ivan Jovanovix: Bass, Jane: Drums *Past Members* Göte: Drums
Deathography
Astral Carneval, Demo (2003)
Chaos, Demo (2006)

ASTRAY—see Mindcollapse

ASYLUM

A 2000's death/thrash band. That's all I know.
Line-Up Andreas Runfors: Vocals, Fredrik Lundell: Guitar/Vocals
Michael Nasenius: Guitar, Mikaela Åkesson: Bass, Joel Axelsson: Drums
Deathography
Asylum, Demo (2004)

AT THE GATES

At the Gates was formed in 1990 when drummer Adrian Erlandsson and twin brothers Anders (guitar) and Jonas Björler (bass) invaded the remains of cult band Grotesque. Initially Alf Svensson was the creative force, but he left and the talented Björler brothers took command. The music developed into an aggressive mix of thrash and death metal with a lot of mood and feeling. At the Gates is just fantastic, one of the best metal bands in the world

ever, in my opinion. Their music has been copied by countless bands, but none has ever come close to the qualities of At the Gates. All their albums are classic masterpieces. After At the Gates split in late 1996, Anders and Jonas continued their musical mission in the brilliant retro thrash band The Haunted.
Line-Up Tomas Lindberg: Vocals (1990-), Anders Björler: Guitar (1990-), Bass (1990), Jonas Björler: Bass (1990-1992, 1992-1996), Drums (1990), Adrian Erlandsson: Drums (1990-), Martin Larsson: Guitar (1993-) **Past Members** Alf Svensson, Guitar (1990-1993), Tony Andersson: Bass (1992), Hans Nilsson: Drums (1990), Kristian Wåhlin: Guitar (1990)
Deathography
Gardens of Grief, Demo (1991, though I'm not sure this was ever released as a demo)
Gardens of Grief, EP (Dolores, 1991)
The Red in the Sky is Ours, CD/LP (Peaceville, 1992)
With Fear I Kiss the Burning Darkness, CD/LP (Peaceville, 1993)
Terminal Spirit Disease, CD/LP (Peaceville, 1994)
Gardens of Grief, 7" (Peaceville, 1994)
Slaughter of the Soul, CD/LP (Earache, 1995)

ATHELA
Progressive death/doom band that started in Stockholm in 1999. Note the amazing number of members in its few years of existence (including Dennis Ekdahl, better known from Raise Hell).
Line-Up Pär Hjulström: Drums, Alexander Nordquist: Guitar, Jacob Alm: Vocals/Guitar, Elin Lavonen: Bass **Past Members** Tomas Bjernedahl: Drums, Patrik Andersson: Bass, Patrik Pira: Guitar, Adam Hobr: Drums, Per Wenström: Guitar, Patrik Karlsson: Guitar, Johan Andrén: Guitar, Dennis Ekdahl: Drums
Deathography
Unspoken Wish, Demo (2000)
Spectral, Demo (2002)
Reliance, Demo (2003)

ATOM & EVIL
A death/thrash band that started in 2002.
Line-Up Jimmy Larsén: Vocals/Guitar, Benny Andersson: Drums, Robert Hylén: Bass, Devo Andersson: Guitar **Past Members** Varg Stening: Guitar
Deathography
Atom & Evil, Demo (2002)
Neutralize Me, Demo (2003)
Fist Through You, Demo (2004)
Nemesis, Demo (2005)

ATROCIOUS REEK—see Repugnance

ATROCITY
Late 80's thrash metal from Västerås—actually they started in Sala, but moved to Västerås later. Some inspiration comes from bands like Testament and Heathen, but their heavy metal touches are too apparent to make them extreme in any way. I remember this band clearly, as one of my old punk bands (Roof Rats, if anyone cares) opened for them in Sala in 1988. For me they were rock stars—just seeing a Swedish thrash metal band made a huge impact. As we know, things soon changed, and within two years the thrash metal genre was erased. Atrocity folded in 1989, and transformed into Rosicrucian.
Line-Up Glyn Grimwade: Vocals/Guitar, Magnus Söderman: Guitar, Fredrik Jacobsen: Bass, Johan: Drums (1988-) **Past Members** Ronny Bengtsson: Vocals (-1989), Fredrik Andersson: Drums (-1988)
Deathography
Atrocious Destruction, Demo (1988)
Atrocity/Damien/Gravity/Tribulation Split 7"(Is This Heavy or What Records, 1988)
To Be...or Not To Be, Demo (1989)

ATROX
An obscure band that blended speed and black metal influences into a deadly mess. Early line-up changes probably killed the band.
Line-Up Stephan Hermansson: Bass, Isti: Drums, Nicke Eriksson: Vocals (1992-), Johan Gärdestedt: Guitar (1992-), Johan Dahlström: Guitar (1992-) **Past Members** Tobbe Johansson: Vocals/Guitar (-1992), Johan Larsson: Guitar (-1992), Pelle Nilsson: Guitar (-1992)
Deathography
Land of Silence, 7" (PLC, 1992)
Plague of Nature, Demo (1993)

AUBERON
This Umeå-based band began with the name Oberon as a school project back in 1988. When they secured a deal with Black Mark in the mid-90's, the name changed to Auberon since their original name was already taken. The music is melodic and thrashy metal, with clear hints at death. As usual with bands from smaller towns, many of the massive amount of members passing though have also been active in similar bands such as Bewitched (Degerström), Naglfar (Degerström, Lie), Nocturnal Rites (Norberg), and Amsvartner (Holmgren). Fredrik Degerström also used to edit Arqtique Zine.
Line-Up Jonathan Holmgren: Guitar (2000), Christer Bergqvist: Guitar (2003-), Andreas Nilsson: Bass (2004), Morgan Lie: Drums (1993-) **Past Members** Fredrik Degerström: Vocals/Guitar, Richard Nilsson Jokela: Bass (2003-2004), Johan Asplund: Guitar, Magnus Lindblom: Guitar, Johan Westerlund: Guitar, Pekka "Power" Kiviaho: Bass, Andreas: Guitar, Jon Andersson: Guitar, Nils Norberg: Guitar, Andreas Johansson: Guitar
Deathography
Follow the Blind, Demo (1994—as Oberon)
Insane, Demo (1995—as Oberon)
The Tale of Black, CD (Black Mark Production 1998)
Crossworld, CD (Black Mark Production, 2001)
Scum of the Earth, Demo (2003)

AUTHOR OF PAIN
Mediocre mid-90's death metal band, just recently

claiming to be playing black metal. Since they are from Strömstad, it's not very hard to guess some of the members' actual names. By the title of their second demo you'll find that this is probably just one of these hilarious joke projects.
Line-Up Satanas: Vocals, Corpse: Guitar, The Baron: Guitar, Butcher: Bass, Helltor: Drums
Deathography
Suicidal Thoughts, Demo (1996)
1998/3=666, Demo (1998)

AUTHORIZE
Death/thrash band from Söderhamn started out as Morbid Fear in the autumn of 1988. Originally they were mainly a thrash metal band, but developed a much deadlier style over the first years. Well played and intense. I liked this band a lot back then.
Line-Up Micke Swed: Drums, Jörgen Paulsson: Guitar, Lars Johansson: Guitar/Vocals, Patrik Leander: Bass, Tomas Ek: Vocals (1990-)
Deathography
Darkest Age, Demo (1990—as Morbid Fear)
The Source of Dominion, CD (Putrefaction, 1992)

AUTOPSY TORMENT
Notorious underground band formed back in 1989 in Uddevalla, originally as madman Tomas Karlsson's solo project. At first they almost played grindcore, but soon developed towards death metal. Tomas Karlsson and Karl Vincent went on to form Pagan Rites. Karlsson also later became the singer for Tristitia. After ten years of silence, three releases suddenly came to light in 2002. You should never give up on the dead! Note that an early line-up featured the infamous Bajsmannen ("The Shit Man", aka "Onkel") on guitar. One of Sweden's most notorious sleazebags, he has gained a like-minded following over the years. The band's image is hilarious, with blood, gore, and upside-down crosses to the limit. I'm uncertain about the actual existence of some of their demos, but possibly they have made even more that I'm not aware of.
Line-Up Daniel Nilssen: Guitar, The Demon: Bass, Thomas Hedlund: Drums, Thomas Karlsson (Unholy Pope): Vocals Past Members Karl Vincent (Sexual Goat Licker): Drums, Onkel: Guitar, Harri: Guitar (1989-1994)
Deathography
Jason Lives, Rehearsal (1989)
Splattered, Rehearsal (1989)
Satanic Sadist, Demo (1991)
Darkest Rituals, Demo (1991)
Adv. tape, Demo (1992)
Nocturnal Blasphemy, Demo (1992)
7th Soul of Hell, Demo (1992)
Moon Fog, EP (Slaughter Records, 1992)
Orgy With the Dead, EP (Miriquidi/City of the Dead, 2002)
Darkest Ritual, 7" picture disc (Miriquidi, 2002)
Tormentorium, CD (Painkiller, 2002)
Premature Torture, Split (2003)
Graveyard Creatures, CD (Painkiller, 2005)

AUTUMN DWELLER
This band that began in Västerås in 1998 as a Joakim Jonsson (Dust, The Mist of Avalon, Mornaland, Skyfire, Skinfected) solo project. The music is some kind of ambient mix between thrash and death.
Line-Up Joakim Jonsson: All instruments, Henrik Wenngren: Vocals, Andreas Johansson: Lyrics
Past Members John Grahn: Vocals/Lyrics, Tommy Öberg: Lyrics
Deathography
A Level Beyond, EP (Riddle Records, 1998)

AVATAR
This band formed in Gothenburg in 2001. You guessed it! Yet more melodic In Flames clones!
Line-Up Johannes Eckerström: Vocals, John Alfredsson: Drums, Jonas Jarlsby: Guitar/Vocals, Henrik Sandelin: Bass, Simon Andersson: Guitar
Past Members Christian Rimmi: Vocals, Albin Dahlquist: Bass, Kim Egerbo: Guitar
Deathography
Personal Observations, Demo (2003)
4 Reasons to Die, Demo (2004)
My Shining Star, Single (Blood Stained Art, 2005)
And I Bid You Farewell, Single (Blood Stained Art, 2005)
Thoughts of No Tomorrow, CD (GAIN Music Entertainment, 2006)

AXIS POWERS
Formed in the Gothenburg area (Uddevalla) in 1998, it sounds like this should be another melodic thrash/death band—but what do you know, it's an old school death metal band! Refreshing. Most members also play in Suicidal Winds, more of a black/thrash band. (There's a world of a difference you know).
Line-Up Mathias Johansson: Vocals, Peter Haglund: Guitar, Karl Nilsson: Guitar, Fredrik Andersson: Bass, Christoffer Larsson: Drums Past Members Karl Nilsson: Guitar
Deathography
Evil Warriors, EP (2000)
Born for War, EP (2002)
Fresh Human Flesh, Axis Powers/Ill-Natured- Split (Deathstrike Records, 2004)
Tribute to I-17, Axis Powers/Bestial Mockery-Split (Agonia Records, 2005)
Pure Slaughter, CD (Iron Fist, 2005)

AZATOTH
Cool death metal band formed by Carl Birath (ex-Ophedia) and Raza Anjam (ex-Sonic Slayer) in the depressing Stockholm suburb of Tensta/Hjulsta in 1992. At the end of 1993 the band found a steady line-up, and started to rehearse for the demo *The Dawn*, released the following year. After a dozen gigs in the western suburbs of Stockholm and a second demo in 1995, the band folded in the end of 1996. Carl Birath pursued even more brutal death metal as he joined Insision in 1999.
Line-Up Carl Birath: Vocals, Raza Anjam: Guitar, Andreas Holking: Guitar, Vladik Lindström: Drums, Daniel Rhör: Bass

Deathography
The Dawn, Demo (1994)
Through the Halls of Hatred, Demo (1995)

AZEAZERON
Death/black metal band formed in Uddevalla/Ljungskile in 1996. Though Azeazeron has been inactive for a while, they are apparently looking for new members and a new dawn.
Line-Up Harold: Vocals, Nojjman: Guitar, Emil: Guitar, Torbjörn: Bass, Jonas: Drums, Johan: Keyboards
Deathography
Funeral of Samirith, Demo (1996)
Diabolical Angels (Destruction Of Eden), CD (Loud N' Proud, 2000)

AZHUBHAM HAANI—see Dysentery

AZURE
Typical mid-90's (formed in 1995) melodic black/death band from Lindesberg. Melodies and no power, forget them. I guess mainly a project of Relentless man Robert Kanto. Listen to them instead.
Line-Up Robert Kanto: Guitar/Bass/Vocals, Mattias Holmgren: Drums/Keyboards/Vocals Past Members Velvet: Drums (1995-1998), Enormous: Bass (1995-1998)
Deathography
Dark & Mysterious, Demo (1996)
Demo 1 '96, Demo (1996)
Demo 2 '96, Demo (1996)
The Erotican, Demo (1997)
A Vicious Age Lasting..., MCD (Pentheselia Records, 1998)
Moonlight Legend, CD (Solistitium Records, 1998)
Shadows in Midark, Demo (2000)
King of Stars—Bearer of Dark, Demo (2004)
King of Stars—Bearer of Dark, CD (Solistitium Records, 2005)

BACON WARRIORS—see Dethronement

BAROPHOBIA
Short-lived thrash metal band from Domsjö in the north of Sweden that existed around 1990. Their music resembles Testament, and every riff is delivered tight and clear. Believe me, this band delivered plenty of riffs in true thrash fashion! The bell had already tolled for this kind of music in 1990 though, and they never got anywhere. Haake left to join Meshuggah in 1990, and Hagström followed in 1994. Since then they have dominated the world.
Line-Up Mårten Hagström: Guitar/Vocals, Niclas Nordin: Bass, Håkan Östman: Drums Past Members Tomas Haake: Drums
Deathography
Demo, Demo (1990)
Labyrinth of the Mind, Demo (1990)

BATHORY
Mainly the one-man project of the mysterious Quorthon (Tomas Forsberg), his creation is one of the most legendary of all metal bands. Started

in Stockholm back in 1983, Bathory quickly stood out as one of the most extreme bands ever. The satanic lyrics and lack of band photos on albums increased the bands notoriety. The aura of mystique surrounding the band was further thickened because they never played live—apart from some early shows, before the band's style was settled. For a few years in the mid-80's, Bathory ruled black metal together with Mercyful Fate, Venom, and Celtic Frost. Their importance simply cannot be overestimated, and the whole black metal scene of the 90's probably wouldn't have happened without them. The band's early efforts still stand as the rawest and most original black metal ever produced. One of the musicians Quorthon used, drummer Jonas Åkerlund, is today hailed as one of the world's greatest music video directors, with works for Madonna, Metallica, and Prodigy on his conscience (you know, flashy speculative videos with loads of annoying cuts and nudity). Sadly, Quorthon passed away way too early—due to heart failure—on July 6, 2004. His legacy will go on forever.
Line-Up Quorthon: Vocals/Guitar/Bass/Drums/Programming Past Members Vvornth (Pålle): Drums, Kothaar: Bass, Rickard Bergman: Bass, Stefan Larsson: Drums, Jonas Åkerlund: Drums, Fredrick: Bass ...and a bunch of other anonymous guys. I guess more than one of them hid behind the name "Kothaar".
Deathography
Bathory, LP/CD (Tyfon/Black Mark, 1984)
The Return, LP/CD (Tyfon/Black Mark, 1985)
Under the Sign of the Black Mark, LP (Under One Flag/Black Mark, 1986)
Blood Fire Death, LP/CD (Under One Flag/Black Mark, 1988)
The Sword, Promo EP (Black Mark, 1988)
Hammerheart, LP/CD (Noise, 1990)
Twilight of the Gods, LP/CD (Black Mark, 1991)
Twilight of the Gods, Promo EP (Black Mark, 1991)
Jubileum Volume 1, CD (Black Mark, 1992)
Jubileum Volume 2, CD (Black Mark, 1993)
Requiem, CD (Black Mark, 1994)
Octagon, CD (Black Mark, 1995)
Blood on Ice, CD (Black Mark, 1996)
Destroyer of Worlds, CD (Black Mark, 2001)
Nordland 1, CD (Black Mark, 2002)
Nordland 2, CD (Black Mark, 2003)
In Memory of Quorthon, Box-Set (Black Mark, 2006)

BATTLELUST
Started in 1996 as a side project of Necronomicon member Henrik Åberg. Originally he called the band Ondska (Swedish for "Evil"), but the name was soon changed to Battlestorm and ultimately Battlelust. After a brief period in Gates of Ishtar, Åberg quit Necronomicon to put all his efforts into Battlelust. Following some line-up changes, Satariel's singer Micke Grankvist and Darkest Season's guitarist Markus Terramäki completed the line-up. The music? Fast black/death of dubious quality.
Line-Up Henrik Åberg: Guitar/Bass/Drums, Micke Grankvist: Vocals, Markus Terramäki: Guitar

Past Members *Patrick Törnkvist*
Deathography
The Eclipse of the Dying Sun, Demo (1996)
*Of Battle and Ancient Warcraft, CD
(Hammerheart, 1997)*

BATTLESTORM—see Battlelust

BEHEMOTH—see In Aeternum

BELSEBUB
Death metal from Linköping/Mjölby. A Swedish
band from the early 90's that disappeared after one
EP. The coolest thing about Belsebub was how they
used two lead vocalists. Original and effective!
Line-Up *Mika Savimäki: Vocals/Bass, Peter
Blomman: Guitar, Johnny Fagerström: Vocals/
Drums*
Deathography
Lord of Locust, Demo#1, Demo (1990)
Disembowelled, Demo#2, Demo (1991)
Elohim, Single (1992)
Chemical Warfare, EP (Drowned, 1992)

BENIGHTED (Forserum)
Early 90's band from Forserum that started out as
Sickness in November 1991. After a couple demos
they changed their name to Benighted, but never got
much attention. Originally very brutal death/grind of
decent quality, they soon mellowed out to harmless
and melodic death/thrash. Engqvist was also the
editor of *Undead Mag.*
Line-Up *Kristian Enqvist: Drums, Martin Edwertz:
Guitar, Stefan Englund: Bass/Vocals, Sven Karlsson
Guitar (1993-), Mats Nordborg: Vocals* **Past
Members** *Johan Edwertz: Vocals (1992)*
Deathography
Demo 92, Demo (1992—as Sickness)
Eternal Horizon, Demo (1993—as Sickness)
The Master of Darkness, Demo (1993)
We Don't Care, Demo (1997)

BENIGHTED (Linköping)—see Spiteful

THE BEREAVED
Melodic death metal band from Åsbro, started out in
1998. Originally known as Clone, but the name was
soon changed.
Line-Up *Mikael Nilsson: Bass, Tobbias Ljung:
Drums, Henrik Tranemyr: Guitar, Jonny Westerback:
Vocals/Guitar, Tony Thorén: Keyboards* **Past
Members** *Jimmy Johansson: Vocals*
Deathography
Inverted Icons, Demo (2002)
*Darkened Silhouette, CD (Black Lotus Records,
2004)*

BERSERK
Short-lived death metal project formed during 1993
in Stockholm. Obviously they made a demo, but I
have never seen it. Among members of note is Martin
Persson—now in Dismember and formerly of Mörk
Gryning, Sins of Omission, and Thyrfing.

Line-Up *Martin Persson: Guitar/Vocals, Pelle
Söderberg: Bass, Markel Månson: Drums*
Deathography
Demo (?)

BESEECH
Melodic goth/heavy/death metal from Borås. Like
most bands from that city, they mix a lot of styles.
The results aren't that convincing, though they sure
are professional. A lot of line-up changes have held
the band back, but they've struggled on since 1992.
Line-Up *Erik Molarin: Vocals, Lotta Höglin: Vocals,
Robert Vintervind: Guitar/Programming, Daniel
Elofsson: Bass, Mikael Back: Keyboards, Jonas
Strömberg: Drums, Manne Engström: Guitar* **Past
Members** *Morgan Gredåker: Drums (1994-1998),
Andreas Wiik: Bass (1994-1998), Anna Andersson:
Vocals (session only, 1998), Jörgen Sjöberg: Vocals
(1994-2001), Klas Bohlin: Guitar/Vocals (1994 -
2003)*
Deathography
A Lesser Kind of Evil, Demo (1993)
Last Chapter, Demo (1994)
Tears, Demo (1995)
From a Bleeding Heart, CD (Metal Blade, 1998)
Black emotions, CD (Pavement Music, 2000)
Beyond the Skies, Demo (2001)
Souls Highway, CD (Napalm, 2002)
Drama, CD (Napalm, 2004)
Sunless Days, CD (Napalm, 2005)

BESTIAL MOCKERY
Hilariously brutal black/speed metal act, emerged
from Uddevalla in 1995. These guys mean business,
old school style! The lyrics and image are totally
callous, and you just can't help loving these guys.
Note the immense problems with bass players.
Members have also played in Sons of Satan, Sadistic
Grimness, Zyclone System, Psychomantum, Kill, and
wonderfully-named Bestial Destructive Blasphemy.
Line-Up *C. Warslaughter: Drums, Master Motorsåg:
Vocals, Micke Doomfanger: Guitar, Ted Bundy:
Guitar, Devil Pig: Bass* **Past Members** *Sir Torment:
Bass, Fjant Sodomizer: Bass, Anti-Fred-Rik: Bass,
Jocke Christcrusher: Bass*
Deathography
Battle Promo, Demo (1996)
Christcrushing Hammerchainsaw, Demo (1997)
Chainsaw Demons Return, Demo (1998)
*Live for Violence, Bestial Mockery/Lust-split
(Impaler of Trendies, 1999)*
*Nuclear Goat/Joyful Dying, Bestial Mockery/Social
Winds-split (2000)*
War: The Final Solution, Demo (2000)
Chainsaw Execution, CD (Sombre, 2001)
*A Sign of Satanic Victory, EP (Warlord Records,
2002)*
*Christcrushing Hammerchainsaw, CD (Metal
Blood Music, 2002)*
*Evoke the Desecrator, CD (Osmose Productions,
2003)*
*Tribute to I-17, Bestial Mockery/Axis Powers-split
(Agoni Recordings, 2004)*

*Outbreak of Evil, Bestial Mockery/Nocturnal/
Vomitor/Toxic Holocaust-split (Witching Metal
Reckords, 2004)*
*Eve of the Bestial Massacre, Bestial Mockery/
Unholy Massacre-split (Deathstrike Records, 2005)*
*Gospel of the Insane, CD (Osmose Productions,
2006)*

BEYOND (Avesta)

This competent quartet was the first of many great
death metal bands from the small town of Avesta.
Beyond started back in 1988, since Johan Jansson
wanted to express himself way more violently than
he was allowed in his brilliant thrash metal group
Hatred. Beyond only recorded one rare demo tape,
Birth of the Dead, a blasting primitive work of sonic
mayhem recorded in their rehearsal room. The grim
atmosphere, crude sound, and harmonized vocals
are hard to resist. The guitar sound is sooo much
Hellhammer! Afterwards Beyond transformed into
the incredible Interment.
*Line-Up Johan Jansson: Guitar/Vocals (occasionally
also drums), John Forsberg: Guitar, Micke
Gunnarsson: Bass (1989-), Sonny Svedlund: Drums*
*Past Members Dan Larsson: Vocals (1988-1990),
Tomas Änstgård: Bass (1988-1989)*
Deathography
Birth of the Dead, Demo (1990)

BEYOND (Holmsund)—see Embracing

BIRDFLESH

Tight grindcore orchestra from Växjö, started back
in 1992. Unlike some political bands of this genre
they seem to have a great sense of humor, evident in
a title like "Burgers of the Fucking Dead." Almost
sounds like an S.O.D song, doesn't it? Birdflesh has
been pretty successful lately, and has toured far off
places like Japan. Note that the band's original bass
player quit this furious band to play in Melody Club,
an 80's style pop band!
*Line-Up Alex: Vocals/Guitar, Magnus: Vocals/Bass,
Andreas: Vocals/Drums*
Deathography
The Butcherbitchtape, Demo (1994)
Demo of Hell, Demo (1995)
Fishfucked, Demo (1997)
*We Were 7 Who 8 Our Neighbours on a Plate,
Demo (1998)*
The Hungry Vagina, 7" (Burning Death, 1998)
*Birdflesh/Carcass grinder, split 7" (Underground
Warder Productions, 1999)*
*Morbid Jesus/Wo-man, Birdflesh/Squash Bowels-
split (Fudgeworthy Records, 1999)*
*Trip to the Grave, EP (Nuclear Barbecue Party
Records, 1999)*
Birdflesh/The Dead, Split (Nocturnal Music, 2001)
Alive Autopsy, CD (Leather Rebel, 2001)
*Carnage on the Fields of Rice, EP (Nuclear
Barbecue Records, 2002)*
Live in Japan, Live album (2002)
*Night of the Ultimate Mosh, CD (Razorback
Records, 2002)*

*Birdflesh/The Kill Split EP, Split (Regurgitated
Semen Records, 2003)*
Killing Rosenkeller, Demo (2004)
*My Flesh Creeps at Insects/Death Metal Karaoke,
Birdflesh/Embalming Theatre-split (From Life,
2004)*
*Time to Face Extinction, Birdflesh/Catheter-split
(Civilisation Rec, 2004)*
*Live @ Giants of Grind, Live album (Power It Up
Records, 2005)*

THE BLACK

Cool black metal project founded in 1991 by a trio
of youngsters wanting to play truly evil music. These
guys were in fact Jon Nödtveidt (Dissection), Marcus
Pedersen (Crypt of Kerberos), and Markus Pesonen
(Eternal Darkness). The music is pretty raw, and
the band photos are great! With the new line-up,
Bragman and Jonsson are both from Tyrant and ex-
Vinterland.
*Line-Up Daniel Bragman: Vocals/Strings, Adde
Jonsson: Guitar, Markus Pesonen (aka The Black):
Drums/Keyboards*
*Past Members Jon Nödtveidt (aka Rietas):
Vocals/Guitar/Keyboards, Marcus Pedersen (aka
Leviathan): Bass*
Deathography
Black Blood, Demo (1992)
The Priest of Satan, CD (Necropolis, 1994)
Alongside Death (Hell's Cargo, 2008)

BLACK SATAN

Totally hilarious band of pure evil noise that started
out in Stockholm in 1988, reportedly with another
line-up. They spread (well, not really) their message
in songs like "Return of Satan" and "Rape the Kids"
before they folded in 1991. Petrov is perhaps a bit
more known for his work with Entombed.
*Line-Up Tommy Gurell: Vocals/Guitar, Lars-Göran
Petrov: Drums, Rikard: Bass*
Deathography
Rehearsal (1990)

BLACKLIGHT

Death metal band formed in Mellösa (ever heard
about it?) in 1996. After one EP, they split up.
*Line-Up Richard Karlsson: Vocals, Jan Iso-Aho:
Guitar, Patric Hedberg: Guitar, Kaj Ukura: Bass,
Patrick Nygren: Drums*
Deathography
Blacklight, EP (1997)

BLAZING SKIES

Formed as the death metal band Defective Decay
in Bollnäs during 1994, the style gradually became
melodic. As they mellowed out, the name changed to
Blazing Skies. Soon the band was your regular At the
Gates rip-off, but nowhere near the quality even of
weaker retro thrash bands like Arise or Ablaze My
Sorrow. Blazing Skies has apparently recorded two
full-length albums, both shelved from release due to
problems with labels Loud N' Proud and Plasmatica.
Line-Up Henke Westin: Vocals, Tomas Hedlund:

Guitar, Lars Larsson: Guitar, Rickard Harryson: Bass, Krille Nyman: Drums **Past Members** Krille Hed: Bass, Niklas Brodd: Guitar, Johan Wadelius: Bass/Vocals, Damian: Bass, Antonio Fix: Drums, Peter Andersson: Drums
Deathography
The Thriving Thorns of November, Demo (1997)
Debris, Demo (1998)
Neo-Delusional, EP (2003)

BLESSED
Blessed began as a technical death metal band in Gothenburg in 1996. The style gradually got more melodic and simple, and the big change came in 2004 when they decided to change their name to Openwide (since people thought they were Christians!) and their style to become a kind of doom metal. Johan Olsson also played in Inverted.
Line-Up Mikael Ungell: Guitar, Magnus Ohlsson: Drums, Johan Ohlsson: Guitar **Past Members** Joakim Unger: Drums
Deathography
Promo 1999, Demo (1999)
Consume 3000, Demo (2000)
Last Breath Before the Flesh, EP (2002)
Openwide, EP (2005—as Openwide)

BLINDED COLONY
This band began their melodic journey as Stigmata in 2000. Two years later they became Blinded Colony, but the music was still the same melodic mess.
Line-Up Roy Erlandsson: Bass, Staffan Franzen: Drums, Tobias Olsson: Guitar, Johan Blomström: Guitar, Johan Schuster: Vocals **Past Members** Niklas Svensson: Vocals, Christoffer: Bass
Deathography
Painreceiver, Demo (2000—as Stigmata)
Tribute to Chaos, Demo (2002—as Stigmata)
Blinded Colony—Tribute to Chaos, Demo (2002)
Divine, CD (Scarlet, 2003)
Promo 2005, Demo (2005)

BLITZKRIEG—see Therion

BLOODBATH
Kind of a death metal "all-star" project with Dan Swanö (Edge of Sanity), Mikael Åkerfeldt (Opeth), Anders Nyström (Katatonia), and Jonas Renske (Katatonia) that began in 1999. And they sound so good! Pure old school violent death metal in the vein of early Entombed, it will make your ears bleed. I wish they would all just quit their other bands and go full speed ahead with Bloodbath. In 2003 Åkerfeldt was replaced by Peter Tägtgren (Hypocrisy, etc). Martin Axenrot (Witchery, Satanic Slaughter) took over the drums when Swanö decided to play guitar. It still sounds like an all-star band, although the absence of Åkerfeldt was slightly felt until his return in 2008.
Line-Up Dan Swanö: Guitar (2003-), Drums (1999-2003), Anders Nyström: Guitar, Jonas Renske: Bass, Martin Axenrot: Drums (2003-) **Past Members** Peter Tägtgren: Vocals (2003-2005), Mikael Åkerfeldt:

Vocals (1999-2003)
Deathography
Breeding Death, EP (Century Media, 2000)
Resurrection Through Carnage, CD (Century Media, 2002)
Nightmares Made Flesh, CD (Century Media, 2004)
Unblessing the Purity, EP (Peaceville, 2008)

BLOODLUST
Old school death/thrash metal from Fjälkinge in the north of the south of Sweden—the middle of nowhere in other words! One demo is all I have seen.
Line-Up C Lindell
Deathography Demo 1, Demo (2004)

BLOODSHED
Stockholm's Bloodshed has delivered fast and furious black metal since 1997, with mechanical precision that makes them sound pretty death metal at times. In recent years they have also used Insision's drummer Marcus Jonsson for an extra deadly touch.
Line-Up Tommy: Guitar/Vocals, Robin: Bass/Vocals, Wall: Vocals, Mats Nehl: Guitar **Past Members** Markus Jonsson: Drums (session drummer only), Stange: Vocals, Joel: Guitar, Mikael: Drums, Glenn: Vocals, Johannes Pedro: Guitar
Deathography
Laughter of Destruction, Demo (1999)
Skullcrusher, EP (Ledo Takas Records, 2001)
Inhabitants of Dis, CD (Code 666, 2002)
Blade Eleventh, Demo (2004)
Blade Eleventh, EP (Cursed Division, 2005)

BLOODSTONE
Hellish death metal group, formed in Stockholm in 1991. Five years later it was all over, but what a fun time it was! Samuelsson is also known from Cauterizer and Bifrost (which also included Wikberg).
Line-Up Damien Hess: Vocals, Michael Samuelsson: Guitar, Svante Friberg: Bass, Mats Wikberg: Drums
Deathography
Branded at the Threshold of the Damned, Demo (1994)
Hour of the Gate, CD (Burn Records, 1996)

BLOT MINE
Project featuring three Setherial members, formed in Sundsvall in 1995. It is a miracle they still exist, since the climate for black metal with death tendencies might not be what it once was. You might suspect their riffs are leftovers from other bands, though—and in the north of Sweden, everybody seems to play in at least three.
Line-Up Athel W: Guitar, Steril Vwreede: Vocals, Thunaraz: Guitar, Thorn: Bass, Zathanel: Drums
Deathography
Kill for Inner Peace, Demo (1996)
Porphyrogenesis, CD (Near Dark, 1998)
Ashcloud, CD (Near Dark, 2005)

BLOTSERAPH
Late 90's band from Hudiksvall. Their music is some kind of black metal with death metal vocals. Not

very original or good.
Deathography
Terminal Autumn, Demo (1999)
Beheaded Screams, Demo (2000)

BODY CORE
Death metal constellation formed in Hässleholm in 1997. The congas and flute on the instrumental side give me the impression that this is mainly a joke band.
Line-Up Dan Hejman: Vocals/Congas, Markus Wallén: Guitar, Nicklas Wallén: Bass/Flute, Håkan Johansson: Drums/Percussion, Jakob G Löfdahl: Guitar Past Members Daniel Larsson: Guitar, William Ekeberg: Guitar
Deathography
I Kill You in My Dreams, Demo (2000)
Welcome to our Dying World, Demo (2002)
Idle Mind Amputation, Demo (2003)
Blunt Force Trauma, CD (2004)
Rancid Cerebral Lobotomy, Demo (2005)

BONESAW—see Murder Squad

BORN OF FIRE
Some members of Entombed, Unleashed, Dismember, etc, decided to play thrash/death in this project during 2001. It's uncertain they'll ever play again, but what a line-up!
Line-Up Mr. Dim: Vocals/Guitar, Fredrik Lindgren: Guitar, Richard Cabeza: Bass, Peter Stjärnvind: Drums
Deathography
Chosen by the Gods, EP (Primitive Art, 2001)

BORN OF SIN
A band from Trollhättan that began in 2001.
Line-Up Jerker Backelin: Vocals, Kristoffer Hjelm: Guitar, Robert Green: Guitar, Blaad: Bass, Henning Nielsen: Drums
Deathography
The Beheader, Demo (2002)
Hell Will Walk the Earth, Demo (2004)

BRAIN CANCER—see Leukemia

BREJNDEDD
Funny crossover band that made the streets of Finspång unsafe during 1988-1990. The line-up consisted of a bunch of rebellious teenagers, among them Dan Swanö (Edge of Sanity, Bloodbath, etc) and Tony Särkkä (Abruptum, War, etc). Brejndedd's four demos can be regarded as historical documents in the world of death metal, but the music is not actually very original or exciting. Also check out Incision for more teenage mayhem by these guys.
Line-Up Dan Swanö: Drums/Vocals, Michael Bohlin: Guitar/Bass, Tony Särkkä: Vocals, Christer Bröms: Bass Past Members Anders Måreby
Deathography
The First Demo, Demo (1988)
Ugly Tape, Demo (1988)
Born Ugly, Demo (1989)
The Ugly Family, Demo (1990)

BRIMSTONE—see Havoc

BULLET PROOF—see Disowned

BUTCHERY
Ultra-brutal and meaty death metal from the forgotten city of Karlskoga. These guys started in the end of 1999 with just one goal: to be brutal as fuck. They are. In small doses, this band will shake your foundations. Do not overdose, though, since heavy consumption proves to erase the initial effect. The band eventually transformed into Strangulation (see separate entry).
Line-Up Christer Elgh: Vocals, Robert Lundgren: Bass, Tobias Israelsson: Drums, Martin Jansson: Guitar Past Members Juha Helttunen: Guitar, Jonathan Gonzales: Guitar
Deathography
The Coming, Demo (2000)
Repulsive Christ Curse, Demo (2002)

CABAL
Absolutely standard early 90's death metal from Mölndal. Slow and evil, but not very good. Munoz later started "true" black metal band Thornium.
Line-Up Daniel Munoz: Vocals, Mikael Uimonen: Drums, Pascov: Guitar, Malle: Bass
Deathography
Midian, Live-Demo (1991)
Satanic Rites, Demo (1991)
Incantations from Beyond, Demo (1992)

CAEDES
Standard early 90's death metal from Gothenburg.
Deathography
Demo (199?)
Unworthy Existence, Demo (1992)

CANDLEMASS
Since their start in Stockholm in 1984, Candlemass has been the best doom metal band in the world. At least that's my opinion. In fact, you might say they kind of invented the genre out of Black Sabbath's groundbreaking riff style. Their success also helped kickstart the Swedish death metal movement. I for sure started learning the guitar after hearing their monumental debut album. One of the best bands in the world. Enough said.
Line-Up Messiah Marcolin: Vocals, Lars Johansson: Guitar, Mappe Björkman: Guitar, Leif Edling: Bass (in the very early days, also vocals), Jan Lindh: Drums Past Members Johan Langquist: Vocals (1986), Thomas Vikström: Vocals (1991-1992), Björn Flodkvist: Vocals (1997-1999), Christian Weberyd: Guitar (1984-1985), Klas Bergwall: Guitar (1986), Mike Wead: Guitar (1987), Patrik Instedt: Guitar (1997-1998), Michael Amott: Guitar (1997-1998), Mats Ståhl: Guitar (1998-1999), Matz Ekström: Drums (1984-1986), Jejo Perkovic: Drums (1997-1999), Carl Westholm: Keyboards (1998)
Deathography
Witchcraft, Demo (1984)
Second 1984 Demo, Demo (1984)

Epicus Doomicus Metallicus, LP/CD (Black Dragon, 1986)
Demo with Marcolin, Demo (1987)
Nightfall, LP/CD (Active Records, 1987)
Samarithan, Single (Axis Records, 1988)
At the Gallows End, EP (MFN, 1988)
Ancient Dreams, LP/CD (Active Records, 1988)
Tales of Creation Demo, Demo (1988)
Tales of Creation, LP/CD (Music for Nations, 1989)
Candlemass—Live, Live album (Metal Blade, 1990)
Chapter VI, LP/CD (Music for Nations, 1992)
Sjunger Sigge Fürst, EP (Megarock, 1993)
The Best Of Candlemass: As it is, As it was, CD (Music for Nations, 1994)
Dactylis Glomerata, CD (Music for Nations, 1998)
From the 13th Sun, CD (Music for Nations, 1999)
Nimis, Single (Trust Noone Recordings, 2001)
The Black Heart of Candlemass/Leif Edling Demos & Outtakes '83-99, CD (Powerline, 2002)
Doomed for Live, Live CD (Powerline Records/GMR, 2003)
Diamonds of Doom, CD (GMR, 2003)
Essential Doom, CD (Powerline/GMR, 2004)
Solitude/Crystal ball, Single (Vinyl Maniacs, 2005)
At the Gallows End/Samarithan, Single (Vinyl Maniacs, 2005)
Mirror, Mirror/Bells of Acheron, Single (Vinyl Maniacs, 2005)
Dark Reflections/Into the Unfathomed Tower, Single (Vinyl Maniacs, 2005)
Candlemass, CD (Nuclear Blast, 2005)

CANOPY

Melodic death metal band that started in Södertälje in 2001. The most striking thing about them is that Dan Swanö appeared on one of their recordings.
Line-Up Fredrik Huldtgren: *Vocals, Jonatan Hedlin: Guitar, Daniel Ahlm: Bass, Erik Björkman: Guitar, Peter Lindqvist: Drums*
Deathography
During Day One, EP (2004)
Will and Perception, EP (2005)

CAPTOR

Good old thrash metal from Katrineholm. This band can be traced back to 1987, and before that the core of the group had launched a Slayer/Possessed cover band in 1985. But not until 1991 was their first demo *Memento Mori* released, after massive line-up changes. Like so many other thrash metal bands, Captor was erased by the death metal movement. Any success was next to impossible once black metal came around, since they had political lyrics. Still, they just kept on going. Respect.
Line-Up Fredrik Olofsson: *Guitar (1990-), Angelo Mikai: Drums (1991-), Magnus Faust: Vocals (1995-), Christoffer Andersson: Bass (1995-), Jonnie Carlsson: Guitar* Past Members *Jacob Nordangård: Vocals/Bass (1987-1995), Tommy Strömberg: Drums, Petri Airaksinen: Drums, Lars-Ingvar Eriksson: Drums, Robert Gren: Guitar, Juha Mäyre: Bass, Christer Johansson: Drums/Guitar, Niklas*

Kullström: Guitar
Deathography
Memento Mori, Demo (1991)
Domination, Demo (1992)
Refused to Die, EP (Dolphin Productions, 1995)
Lay it to Rest, CD (Euro, 1995)
Drowned, CD (Progress, 1996)
Dogface, CD (Die Hard, 1998)
Alien Six, CD (Die Hard, 2001)

CARBONIZED

This brutal band was among the pioneers of Swedish death metal (well, sort of death metal, anyway). Carbonized was formed in Spånga back in November 1988 by Lars Rosenberg, later in Entombed and Therion. During the band's first years they suffered from lots of line-up changes. Among the defectors were Matti Kärki (later in Carnage and Dismember); and Stefan Ekström and Markus Rüdén, who left to form Morpheus. Real problems came when Rosenberg joined Entombed in 1991, followed the next year by the departure of drummer Piotr Wawrzeniuk for Therion. Despite all these problems, the band managed to release a couple of albums during the first half of the 90's. After that, Carbonized seems to have vanished. The music was very original death metal, with a lot of weird stuff incorporated (Voivod, anybody?). They are surely missed.
Line-Up Jonas Derouche: *Vocals/Guitar, Lars Rosenberg: Bass/Vocals, Piotr Wawrzeniuk: Drums* Past Members *Matti Kärki: Vocals, Richard Cabeza: Bass, Markus Rüdén: Drums, Christoffer Johnsson: Guitar/Vocals, Stefan Ekström: Guitar, Per Ax: Drums, Henrik "Hempa" Brynolfsson: Guitar ...well, I guess about everybody in the Stockholm region went in and out of the band...never mind.*
Deathography
Au-To-Dafe, Demo (1989)
No Canonization, 7" (Thrash, 1990)
Recarbonized, Demo (1990)
For the Security, LP (Thrash, 1991)
Chronology of Death, Split (Black Out/Thrash Your Brain, 1991)
Disharmonisation, LP/CD (Foundations 2000, 1993)
Screaming Machines, LP/CD (Foundations 2000, 1996)

CARBUNCLE—see Deranged

CARCAROHT

Mid-90's band from Mjölby, originally called Dominus. They offer fast death/grind with beast-like vocals à la Glen Benton of Deicide. Remarkably, they stuck to the roots of death metal when black metal surrounded us in the mid-90's. The members are all local "celebrities" from bands like Traumatic and Funeral Feast.
Line-Up Micke Andersson: *Guitar, Jocke Pettersson: Drums, Andreas Karlsson: Vocals (1994-), Jonas Albrektsson: Bass (1994-)* Past Members *Lars Thorsén: Bass/Vocals, Henke Forss: Vocals (session only, in Dominus)*

Deathography
Demo (1993—as Dominus)
Dragons Dawn, Demo (1994)
Promo 94, Demo (1994)

CARDINAL SIN
All-star project formed in Gothenburg in 1995. All members are known from bands such as Marduk, Darkified, Decameron, and Dissection. Their style was typical mid-90's death/thrash.
Line-Up Magnus "Devo" Andersson: Guitar, Jocke Göthberg: Drums, Alex Losbäck: Bass, Dan-Ola Persson: Vocals, John Zwetsloot: Guitar
Deathography
Spiteful Intents, EP (Wrong Again, 1996)

CARNAGE
The short existence of Carnage is indeed interesting. The band crawled out of small town Växjö in October 1988, originally as Global Carnage and playing grindcore. After one demo they recruited drummer Fred Estby from the moribund Dismember, and after another demo they also got Dismember's guitarist David Blomqvist. In between time, Carnage also added Matti Kärki (ex-Therion, later of Dismember). In 1989, the band became the first Swedish death metal band after Merciless and Entombed to secure a recording deal, signing with Necrosis. But after one album and only three live gigs, Carnage split up. Most of the members soon reformed Dismember. The others joined Carcass (Mike Amott) and Entombed (Johnny Dordevic), while original guitarist Liiva-Axelsson formed Furbowl. Carnage plays pure good-old Swedish death metal in all its massive glory, very similar to Dismember (of course) and Entombed. A classic band.
Line-Up Matti Kärki: Vocals (1990-), Mike Amott: Guitar, Fred Estby: Drums, Johnny Dordevic: Bass (originally Guitar), David Blomqvist: Guitar (1990)
Past Members Johan Liiva-Axelsson: Vocals/Guitar (1988-1990), Ramon: Bass (1989-1990), Jeppe Larsson: Drums
Deathography
The Day Man Lost, Demo (1989)
Infestation of Evil, Demo (1989)
Live EP, 7" (Distorted Harmony, 1989)
Torn Apart, 7" (Distorted Harmony, 1989)
Dark Recollections, LP (Necrosis, 1990)

CARNAL FORGE
Hyper-fast modern thrash metal, built around the technical riffs of Kuusisto (In Thy Dreams) and the majestic voice of Kjellgren (Dellamorte). Since their start in 1997, the band has gone from strength to strength. The only drawback for Carnal Forge is that they can sound like a hyperspeed At the Gates/The Haunted cover band. Problems occurred when Kjellgren left in 2004, and time will tell if Mortensen can fill his position well.
Line-Up Jari Kuusisto: Guitar, Stefan Westberg: Drums, Petri Kuusisto: Guitar, Lars Linden: Bass, Jens C. Mortensen: Vocals Past Members Jonas Kjellgren: Vocals, Johan Magnusson: Guitar (1997-

2001), Dennis Vestman: Bass (1997-1998)
Deathography
Who's Gonna Burn?, CD (Wrong Again, 1998)
Firedemon, CD (Century Media, 2000)
Please... Die!, CD (Century Media, 2001)
Deathblow, Single (Century Media, 2003)
The More You Suffer, CD (Century Media, 2003)
Aren't You Dead Yet?, CD (Century Media, 2004)

CARNAL GRIEF
As melodic death metal took over the streets of Sweden, these boys from Arboga jumped on the bandwagon in 1997. After a row of demos they finally made it to CD in 2004.
Line-Up Per Magnus Andersson: Guitar, Aaron Henrik Brander: Drums, Per Jonas Carlsson: Vocals, David, Johan Olsen: Bass, Bernhard Johan Lindgren: Guitar Past Members Johan Larsson: Guitar
Deathography
Embraced by the Light, Demo (1997)
Cradlesongs, Demo (1998)
Wastelands, Demo (1999)
Out of Crippled Seeds, CD (Trinity Records, 2004)

CARNEOUS
A very new death metal band from Gällivare in the far north of Sweden. Since their start in 2004 they have produced two demos. I guess the future will tell if they cause any impact.
Line-Up Tobias: Guitar/Vocals, Henke: Guitar, Simon: Bass, Mr. Vanha: Drums
Deathography
Wave of Sickness, Demo (2005)
Promo 2005, Demo (2005)

CARNEUS
Like the similarly-named Carneous from Gällivare, this is a new death metal band. This one is from Osby, however, and began in 2003. Judging by the names of these bands it seems like Swedish death metal is running out of ideas...
Line-Up Jonas: Vocals/Bass, Viktor: Guitar, Mange: Guitar, Arvid: Drums
Deathography
Heaven is Painted in Gore, Demo (2004)
Hate Incarnated, Demo (2005)

CARRION CARNAGE
Brutal band that kicked off in Linköping during 2001. Considering the number of members changed during their short existence, you'd expect that their rehearsal space is a zone of sheer turbulence.
Line-Up Daniel: Vocals/Guitar, Stefan: Guitar, Cyrus: Bass, Jakob: Drums Past Members Ulf Ståhl: Vocals/Bass, Johan Dyyk: Guitar, Nicklas Karlsson: Drums, Johan Heril: Bass/Guitar, Kristofer Stäke: Vocals
Deathography
Mass Murder Rampage, Demo (2003)
Evil, Single (2003)
Awaiting Salvation of Death, Demo (2004)

CARVE
This Gamleby (ever heard of it?) band formed out of

the ashes of Paganizer at the end of 2001. (Maybe the same band under a new name?) Their straightforward death metal sounds so much like Vader they almost seem a cover band. Still, it's good! However, after a couple of demos and CDs it was all over for Carve.
Line-Up Matthias Fiebig: Drums, Rogga Johansson: Vocals/Guitar, Emil Koverot: Guitar, C. Nyhlén Bass Past Members Oskar Nilsson: Bass
Deathography
Hunters Rise from Turmoil, Demo (2001)
Promo 2002, Demo (2002)
Stillborn Revelations, CD (Black Hole Prod, 2002)
Revel in Human Filth, CD (Black Hole Prod,2004)

CAULDRAN
Formed in Sundsvall in 2001, made a demo, and then disappeared.
Line-Up Krille: Vocals, Simon: Guitar, Nicklas: Guitar, Jacob: Bass, Fredrik: Drums
Deathography
Chaos, Demo (2002)

CAUTERIZER
Early 90's death metal from Stenhamra/Färentuna. They started in the fall of 1989 as joke band Living Guts, but with time got more serious. Or not? Initially more hardcore and grind, like so many others in the early 90's, they gradually discovered the power of death metal. Good deep vocals, and some nice music, too. Too bad they split up in 1996. Pelle Ekegren also played in Grave and Coercion. Frisk used to be editor of *Formless Klump Mag* (later *Necropolitan Zine*).
Line-Up Jesper Bood: Guitar (initially drums), PG Berglind: Vocals, Andreas Frisk: Bass, Mikael Samuelsson: Guitar (1991-), Pelle Ekegren: Drums (1991-) Past Members Iman: Drums (session only)
Deathography
The Summer Rehearsal, Rehearsal (1991)
...And Then the Snow Fell, Demo (1992)

CAVEVOMIT
Modern industrial grind/death from Sundsvall. Cavevomit formed in 2001, and seem to be a side project of Diabolical and My Own Grave.
Line-Up Mikael Aronsson: Vocals, Jonny Petterson: Guitar/SFX/Drum programming, Magnus Ödling: Bass Past Members Joel Viklund: Drums, Toffe: Vocals
Deathography
Never Trust A P.I.G, Demo (2002)
Shitstorms, Demo (2003)

CELEBORN
In 1989, two death metal bands formed in the northern town Östersund: Harassed and Celeborn. Celeborn had a rehearsal space in the center of town, while Harassed had to take a ferry, so Celeborn soon lured superior drummer Robert Eriksson into their ranks. Original drummer Niklas Gidlund could do nothing but join Harassed—oh, the shame! And the music? This band produced rather confused and slow death metal of decent quality. They included weird Malmsteen-solos and female vocals to no good effect.

After three demos, Celeborn called it quits. Eriksson went on to form The Hellacopters with Nicke Andersson of Entombed, while Magnus Sahlgren played with Tiamat and joined Dismember. Guitarist Klingberg went on with successful pop bands Whale and Docenterna. He is also a pretty well-known rock journalist, and is in fact working on a book about Swedish metal together with Ika Johannesson.
Line-Up Magnus Sahlgren: Guitar, Jörgen Bylander: Bass/Vocals, Robert Eriksson: Drums (1990-) Past Members Jon J Klingberg: Guitar (1992), Niklas Gidlund: Drums (1989-1990)
Deathography
Demo 90, Demo (1990)
Etherial, Demo (1992)
Fall, Demo (1993)

CELEPHAIS
Mid-90's Uttran-based death metal in the Florida vein, and pretty good. Worth checking out for sure!
Line-Up Joni Mäensivu
Deathography
Human Failure, Demo (1994)

CELESTIAL PAIN
Deadly speed/heavy metal of the mid-90's, harkens back to Sodom, Kreator and Tankard. Only lasted for two demos, both released on a limited 500-copies CD in 2004. Micke Jansson is ex-Unanimated.
Line-Up Benkr (Benke Borgwall): Bass, Mike Metalhead (Micke Jansson): Drums/Vocals, John Blackwar (Johan Sandberg): Guitar/Vocals, Vic Anders (Victor Andersson): Guitar
Deathography
Hatred, Demo (1995)
Aggression, Demo (1996)
Aggression, CD (Sway Records, 2004)

CEMETARY
Borås-based band formed back in 1989. Heavy death metal with groovy vocals. Not bad. The group fell apart in 1997 when Lodmalm put his efforts into Sundawn. They never made it, so he "reincarnated" Cemetary on his own as Cemetary 1213. Josefsson and Saarinen were also in the great Evocation, and Iwers' resumé includes contributions to Tiamat, Desecrator, In Flames, and Ceremonial Oath.
Line-Up Anders Iwers: Guitar, Tomas Josefsson: Bass, Mathias Lodmalm: Vocals/Guitar/Keyboards, Markus Nordberg: Drums Past Members Zriuko Culjak: Bass (1989-1993), Juha Sievers: Drums (1989-1993), Morgan Gredåker: Drums (1989), Christian Saarinen: Guitar (1989-1992), Anton Hedberg: Guitar (1992-1993)
Deathography
Incarnation of Morbidity, Demo (1990)
Articulus Mortis, Demo (1991)
An Evil Shade of Grey, LP/CD (Black Mark, 1992)
Godless Beauty, LP/CD (Black Mark, 1993)
Black Vanity, CD (Black Mark, 1994)
Sundown, CD (Black Mark, 1996)
Last Confessions, CD (Black Mark, 1997)
Phantasma, CD (Black Mark, 2005)

CEMETARY 1213
Basically Matthias Lodmalm's "solo reunion" of Cemetary, but a lot more progressive and a lot less deathly than the former constellation. In 2005 Lodmalm left the scene for good, so we probably won't hear much from him in the future.
Line-Up Mathias Lodmalm: Vocals/Guitar, Manne Engström: Guitar/Vocals, Vesa K: Bass, Christian Silver: Drums
Deathography
The Beast Devine, CD (Century Media, 2000)

CENTINEX
This band started in the small town of Hedemora back in 1990, originally as some kind of hardcore/death band with two vocalists. (Sounds like Uncurbed, doesn't it?) Their style soon went into pure death territory, later settling somewhere between the Swedish and American sounds. Their quality seemed paralyzed, but luckily Centinex has evolved constantly for the better during their career. A major change took place in 1999 when Centinex recruited no less than three members of Dellamorte: Johan (vocals, guitar in Dellamorte), Jonas (guitar, vocals in Dellamorte), and Kenneth (drums). During their career Centinex had many problems with labels, and also had a hard time in the scene due to some inferior releases. The line-up changes brought further problems. For long periods they were actually using a drum machine (called Kalimaa). Even though Centinex has never really made it, their neverending explorations have slowly gained a steady following around the world. The only original member, Martin Schulman, must be given all the credit for his constant battle in the name of death metal. As I am writing, Schulman tells me Centinex has split up. However, Jansson (now on guitar), Schulman, and Bergerståhl will continue as Demonical. Personally I don't understand why they decided to change their name now—they never bothered before when the band has been restructured!
Line-Up Martin Schulman: Bass, Johan Jansson: Vocals (1999-), Jonas Kjellgren: Guitar (1999-), Johan Ahlberg: Guitar (2003-), Ronny Bergerståhl: Drums (2003-) *Past Members* Daniel Fagnefors: Guitar (1993), Kenneth Englund: Drums (1999-2003), Kenneth Wiklund: Guitar (1990-2001), Mattias Lamppu: Vocals (1990-1998), Andreas Evaldsson: Guitar (1990-1998), Joakim Gustafsson: Drums (1992-1993), Erik Lamppu: Vocals (1992), Fred Estby: Drums (session only)
Deathography
Demo (1990)
End of Life, Demo (1991)
Subconscious Lobotomy, LP (Underground, 1992)
Under the Blackened Sky, MC (Wild Rag, 1993)
Transcend the Dark Chaos, Demo (1994)
Transcend the Dark Chaos, EP (Sphinx, 1994)
Malleus Malefaction, CD (Wild Rags, 1995)
Sorrow of Burning Wasteland (split w/Inverted) 7" (1996)
Reflections, CD (Die Hard, 1997)
Shadowland, Single (Oskorei Productions, 1998)

Reborn Through Flames, CD (Repulse, 1998)
Bloodhunt, CD (Repulse, 1999)
Apocalyptic Armageddon, 7" (DAP, 2000)
Hellbrigade, CD (Repulse, 2001)
Enchanted Land (split with Nunslaughter), 7" (Painkiller, 2001)
Diabolical Desolation, CD (Candlelight, 2002)
Hail Germania, Split (Painkiller/Hell's Headbangers, 2003)
Deathlike Recollections, Single (Sword and Sorcery Records, 2003)
Decadence—Prophecies Of Cosmic Chaos, CD (Candlelight, 2004)
Live Devastation, EP (Swedmetal, 2004)
World Declension, CD (Cold Records, 2005)

CERBERUS
Death/black band formed in Mjölby in 1992. After just one demo, they regrouped as the Viking/folk metal band Mitothyn (see separate entry).
Line-Up Christian Schütz: Vocals/Bass/Drums/Keyboards, Stefan Weinerhall: Guitar/Bass, Johan: Guitar
Deathography
Cursed Flesh, Demo (1992)

CEREBRAL DEATH
What would it sound like if some teenage kids from a boring suburb of Stockholm wanted to make some kind of deadly version of heavy metal in the late-90's? The answer is Cerebral Death.
Deathography
To a Better World, Demo (1998)

CEREMONIAL EXECUTION
Anti-religious/pro-gore death metal band formed in Mjölby in 2001.
Line-Up Robert "Gorebert" Kardell: Vocals, Mattias "Flesh" Frisk: Guitar/Vocals, Jimmy "Dollar" Johansson: Guitar, Björn Ahlqvist: Bass, David Andersson: Drums *Past Members* Jonas Albrektsson: Bass, Tommy "Tomby Zombie": Bass
Deathography
Demo 2003, Demo (2003)
Ceremonial Execution/Borigor Split, Split (Erode Records, 2004)
Death Shall Set Us Free, CD (2005)

CEREMONIAL OATH
Gothenburg band formed way back in 1989 (originally as heavy metal band Desecrator) by Anders Iwers, Mikael Andersson (ex-Forsaken), Jesper Strömblad, and Oscar Dronjak (ex-Crystal Age). Their music soon radically transformed via thrash to melodic death metal, and they also changed their name. Ceremonial Oath was a Swedish death metal band that never really made it. They were held up by serious member circulation. Many ex-members have subsequently made it big time, though. Dronjak and Strömblad started power metal flagship Hammerfall, and Strömblad made it even bigger via In Flames. Iwers is now in Tiamat, and has also been successful in Cemetary and

briefly In Flames. At one point, Ceremonial Oath even contained In Flames' singer Anders Fridén and Grotesque/At the Gates' Tomas Lindberg. In retrospect, Ceremonial Oath was like a plant nursery for future Swedish rock stars.
Line-Up Anders Iwers: Guitar, Mikael Andersson: Guitar, Thomas Johansson: Bass (1991-), Markus Nordberg: Drums, Anders Fridén: Vocals (1991-) **Past Members** Oscar Dronjak: Vocals/Guitar (1989-1991), Jesper Strömblad: Bass (1989-1991), Tomas Lindberg: Guitar
Deathography
Black Sermons, Demo (1990—as Desecrator)
Promo 1991, Demo (1991)
Lost Name of God, EP (CGR, 1992)
The Book of Truth, CD (Modern Primitive, 1993)
Carpet, CD (Black Sun, 1995)

CHAOSYS
Socially-aware ("life metal", as the Norwegian black metal scene would label it) death/thrash band formed in Södertälje 2002.
Line-Up Stefan: Vocals, Tomas: Guitar, Holger: Guitar, Johan: Bass, Tommy: Drums
Deathography
Demo 2003.02.23, Demo (2003)
The Imperfection is Yours, Demo (2004)
Development of the Human Mind, Demo (2005)

CHASTISEMENT
Melodic death metal band, apparently started in Östersund as early as 1993, though no signs of life came until 1999. Most members are also in a similar band, Souldrainer, and busy drummer Fjellström is in Aeon, In Battle, Odhinn, Sanctification—and probably a bunch of others I don't know of.
Line-Up Johan Klitkou: Vocals, Marcus Edvardsson: Guitar, Tommy Larsson: Guitar, Nicklas Linnes: Bass, Nils Fjellström: Drums **Past Members** Fredrik Magnusson: Guitar, Per Gabrielsson: Bass
Deathography
...But Lost We Are, CD (1999)
Alleviation of Pain, CD (2002)
Live at Gamla Tingshuset, Östersund, CD (2003)

CHILDREN OF WAR
This is indeed a strange band, formed in Västerås in 2001. Their music? Jazz-fusion death metal.
Line-Up Andreas Helsing: Vocals, Nicklas Hovberg: Instruments
Deathography
La Nigiro, Demo (2005)

THE CHOIR OF VENGEANCE
This death metal band formed in Mjölby in 1995. I guess it's basically a project by some members from Mithotyn, Dawn, and Falconer. Their sole recording, an EP from 1996, isn't that impressive.
Line-Up Karsten Larsson: Drums, Magnus Linhardt: Bass, Rickard Martinsson: Guitar/Vocals, Lars Tängmark: Guitar/Vocals
Deathography
The Choir of Vengeance, EP (1996)

CHOROZON
Death metal act started in Jönköping during 1990. They produced some thrashy death metal before they folded in 1993. Some of the members went on to form the great Nominon.
Line-Up Juha Sulasami: Guitar, Andreas Risberg: Drums, Robert Ericsson: Bass, Marcus Tegnér: Guitar (1991-)
Deathography
The Hierophant, Demo (1991)
Demo (Recorded 1992, but never released)
Deamon 1, Demo (1993)
Deamon 2, Demo (1993)

CHRONIC DECAY
Originating from the city of Eskilstuna in 1985, during its early years Chronic Decay made a demo and a split 7", but in 1991 the band folded—only to be resurrected the next year. This is rather thrashy death metal, and actually quite good. But they never made it. The peak of their career was participating on the C.B.R. compilation album *Projections of a Stained Mind* alongside Entombed, Mayhem, Grave, Unleashed, Dismember, Therion, Grotesque, and Merciless. Jocke Hammar and Micke Sjöstrand are probably more known from the crust band Dischange. Later, Sjöstrand committed suicide and Dischange continued as Meanwhile (their original name). Micke Sjöstrand was one of the nicest and best persons I ever met in the Swedish death metal scene, and we all miss him badly. Rest in peace.
Line-Up Jocke Hammar: Guitar/Vocals, Micke Sjöstrand: Drums (1992-), Guitar (1985-1991), Roger Petterson: Guitar **Past Members** Gunnar Norgren: Bass/Vocals (1992-1993), Guitar/Bass (1985-1991), Micke Karlsson: Drums (1987-1991)
Deathography
Death Revenge, Demo (1986)
Ecstasy in Pain, EP (Studiofrämjandet, 1989)
Chronic Decay/Exanthema Split CD (Studiofrämjandet, 1993)

CHRONIC TORMENT—see Sacretomia

CICAFRICATION—see Uncanny

CIPHER SYSTEM
Originally formed as Eternal Grief around the year 2000, they soon became Cipher System, purveyors of modern thrash/death in the vein of At the Gates, spiced up (down?) with a keyboard. Well-played and tight, but oh-so-boring—like a Z-grade version of Children of Bodom.
Line-Up Magnus Öhlander: Guitar, Johan Eskilsson: Guitar, Pontus Andersson: Drums, Peter Engström: Electronics **Past Members** Daniel Schöldström: Vocals, Henric Carlsson: Bass
Deathography
Path of Delight, Demo (1998—as Eternal Grief)
Raped by Chaos, Demo (1999—as Eternal Grief)
Awakening of Shadows, Demo (2000—as Eternal Grief)
Eyecon, Demo (2002—as Eternal Grief)

Promo 2002, Demo (2002)
Promo 2003, Single (2003)
Split CD, Split (Lifeforce Records, 2004)
Central Tunnel 8, CD (Lifeforce Records, 2004)

CLONAEON

This band formed in Gothenburg in 2002, but what do you know—they actually play decent death metal! So far they have only made one demo, but let's hope they will continue. Most of the members can also be found in Slaughtercult, a somewhat more black metal-oriented orchestra.
Line-Up Andreas Frizell: Guitar, Johan Huldtgren: Vocals, Mattias Nilsson: Bass, Jonas Wickstrand: Drums Past Members Mikael Härsjö: Drums, Anders Ahlbäck: Guitar
Deathography
Strike the Root, Demo (2004)

CLONE—see Bereaved

COERCION

This band formed back in 1992 on the classic death metal soil of Skärholmen/Stockholm, home of Entombed and many others. They took a while to have any impact, probably due to numerous line-up changes and problems with record labels. Once they got it together, they produced very high-quality death metal. Brutal, sick, awesome. Though usually inactive, they occasionally play live. Pelle Ekegren has also played with Grave, Mastication, and Cauterizer, and Dag Nesbö is known from Abhoth.
Line-Up Pelle Ekegren: Drums, Dag Nesbö: Bass, Kenneth Nyman: Vocals/Guitar, Rickard Thulin: Guitar Past Members Ola Eklöf: Bass, Pelle Liljenberg: Bass, Tor Frykholm: Drums, Gordon Johnston: Drums , Lasse "Malte" Ortega: Guitar, Stefan Persson: Guitar, Stefan Söderberg: Guitar
Deathography
Headway, Demo (1993)
Human Failure, Demo (1994)
Forever Dead, CD (Perverted Taste, 1997)
Delete, CD (Perverted Taste, 1999)
Lifework, EP (Animate Records, 2003)

COLD EXISTENCE

This band from Gothenburg claims to play death metal, but seeing pictures of them, I am skeptical…
Line-Up Jan Sallander: Guitar/Vocals, Jan Hellenberg: Guitar, Björn Eriksson: Drums, Peter Laustsen: Bass Past Members Patrik Syk: Bass/Vocals
Deathography
Demo I, Demo (2002)
Second Demo, Demo (2003)
Beyond Comprehension, MCD (Khaosmaster Productions, 2005)

COMANDATORY

Someone told me this band started out in Västerås in 1992, and they play death metal. Well, is she right?
Deathography
Comandatory, CD (Garden of Grief Prod., 1998)

COMECON

Death metal project initiated in 1989 by Pelle Ström and Rasmus Ekman from the metalcore act Omnitron, previously known as the hardcore band Krixhjälters. One of their ideas was to have a new singer on each recording. Consequently, L.G. Petrov (Entombed) handled the microphone on their first record, Martin van Drunen (Asphyx) on the second, and Marc Grewe (Morgoth) on the third. Decent stuff, but rather confusing. I suspect that all the drummers listed are in fact just guys who posed for photos; my hunch is they consistently used a drum machine—but I might be wrong.
Line-Up Pelle Ström: Guitar/Bass/Keyboards, Rasmus Ekman: Guitar/Bass/Keyboards Past Members Marc Grewe: Vocals, Martin Van Drunen: Vocals (1993), L.G. Petrov: Vocals (1991), Fredrik Pålsson: Drums, Anders Green: Drums, Jonas Fredriksson: Drums
Deathography
Merciless/Comecon, Split (CBR, 1991)
Megatrends in Brutality, CD/LP (Century Media, 1991)
Converging Conspiracies, CD (Century Media, 1993)
Fable Frolic, CD (Century Media, 1995)

COMPOS MENTIS

If anybody knows anything about these guys, let me know!

CONCEALED

Mid-90's black/death from Södertälje. They had a cool unreadable logo—just forget about the rest.
Line-Up Holger Thorsin: Guitar, Johan: Bass/Vocals, Hugo: Drums
Deathography
Dance of Dying Dreams, Demo (1995)

CONCRETE SLEEP

These guys from Vällingby (Stockholm) started out in 1991, made a demo in 1992, and then disappeared. They played some thrashy death metal.
Line-Up Andreas Wahl: Bass/Vocals, Daniel Berglund: Guitar, Patrik: Guitar, Patrik: Drums
Deathography
As I Fly Away, Demo (1992)

CONDEMNED

This is basically thrash metal from Skoghall that started in 1989. Like most thrash metal bands, they disappeared in the wake of death metal.
Line-Up Arne Elmlund
Deathography
Demo 1, Demo (1992)

CONQUEST—see Grotesque

CONSTRUCDEAD

This 2000's band from Enskede in Stockholm is a mixture of everything brutal in metal, but basically it's retro thrash. Some of their material is good, but some is not. Band leader and guitar equilibrist

Ericsson joined the brutal death metal band Insision on their Scandinavian tour 2004-2005, but decided to continue with Construcdead after the tour despite all the line-up problems within his own band. Respect.
Line-Up Christian Ericson: Guitar, Rickard Dahlberg: Guitar, Erik Thyselius: Drums, Jens Broman: Vocals (session only), Viktor Hemgren: Bass (session only) Past Members Henrik Svegsjö: Vocals, Jonas Sandberg: Vocals, Daniel Regefelt: Vocals, Joakim Harju: Bass, Johan Magnusson: Bass, Peter Tuthill: Vocals
Deathography
The New Constitution, Demo (1999)
Turn, Demo (2000)
A Time Bleeds, Demo (2000)
God After Me, Demo (2001)
God After Me, MCD (2001)
Repent, CD (Cold, 2002)
Violadead, CD (Black Lodge, 2004)
Woundead, EP (Black Lodge, 2005)
The Grand Machinery, CD (Black Lodge, 2005)

CONTRA
Stockholm's Contra was one of Sweden's original thrash bands in the late 80's. These guys were obviously inspired by Voivod, and they sounded quite good. Pretty cool, but nowhere near the quality of Hatred, Agony, or Hasty Death. Patrick and Glenn continued as Skull (see separate entry) for a short while with Jens from the legendary Morbid.
Line-Up Patrick Lindqvist: Vocals/Guitar, Jocke Strid: Guitar, Glenn Sundell: Drums
Deathography
Revolution, Demo (1989)
Contradiction, Demo (1989)

CORPORATION 187
Pretty good death/thrash band that started in Linköping in 1998. They attracted some attention, and signed to Earache sub-label Wicked World. Lately I haven't heard much, but hope they are still active. Both Carlsson and Eng are ex-Satanic Slaughter.
Line-Up Filip Carlsson: Vocals, Olof Knutsson: Guitar, Magnus Pettersson: Guitar, Robert Eng: Drums, Viktor Klint: Bass Past Members Pelle Severin: Vocals, Johan Ekström: Bass
Deathography
Subliminal Fear, CD (Wicked World, 2000)
Perfection in Pain, CD (Wicked World, 2002)

CORPSE—see Grave

CORPSIFIED
Brutal mid-90's death metal in the vein of Cannibal Corpse and Suffocation. I wish these guys could have had greater impact on the Swedish scene.
Deathography
Demo 95, Demo (1995)

CORPUS CHRISTI—see Seraph Profane

CORRUPT
This raging old school style thrash metal band from

Arvika began as Corrupted in November 2002 with just Micke and Joseph. They completed the line-up the next year, and in 2004 shortened their name to Corrupt since other bands were already called Corrupted. (Do we dare mention there are also a few Corrupts out there?) A cool band that keeps thrash the way it was supposed to be, and much more brutal than any death/thrash band could ever hope to be.
Line-Up Joseph Toll: Guitar/Vocals, Mikael Wennbom: Drums, Olof Wikstrand: Guitar, Tobias Lindquist: Bass
Deathography
Lethal Anger, Demo (2003—as Corrupted)
Shotgun Death, Demo (2003—as Corrupted)
Destroyed Beyond Recognition, Demo (2003—as Corrupted)
Born of Greed, Demo (2004—as Corrupted)
Curse of the Subconscious, Corrupt/Necrovation Split CD (Blood Harvest, 2005)

CORRUPTED—see Corrupt

CRAB PHOBIA—see Traumatic

CRANIUM
Formed in 1985 by brothers Philip and Gustaf von Segebaden, the band changed their name to Legion in 1986, but broke up after one demo. Ten years later, Philip reformed the band as Cranium. They signed to Necropolis, and I guess that gives you an idea what they sounded like. (Their album titles all contain the term "Speed Metal".) The band dissolved after drummer Johan Hallberg committed suicide in 2001, may the speed be with him. Philip is probably more known for his work with Afflicted and Dawn.
Line-Up Philip von Segebaden: Vocals, Fredrik Söderberg: Guitar Past Members Gustaf von Segebaden: Guitar, Johan Hallberg: Drums, Fredrik Enquist: Drums (1985-86), Jocke Pettersson: Drums (1996-98)
Deathography
The Dawn, Demo (1986—as Legion)
Speed Metal Satan, CD (Necropolis, 1997)
Speed Metal Slaughter, CD (Necropolis, 1998)
Speed Metal Sentence, CD (Necropolis, 1999)

CRAWL
All I know about this band is that they made a demo in 1992. Judging by their name, it's not a wild guess to say it probably sounded a lot like Entombed.
Deathography
After Grace, Demo (1992)

CREMATORY
This classic band started in the summer of 1989 in the southern Stockholm suburb Haninge. Their gore-infected style takes grind/death to the very limit, and sounds so good! Around 1990, Crematory played with Entombed, Unleashed, Therion, and Carnage. Sadly, they never had any of the success of those bands. A couple years later they folded, and are truly missed. The vocals on their first demo are delivered by Therion's Christoffer Johnsson. Crematory stand tall

among the great old Swedish death metal acts, just a brilliant band. Most of the members went on to form the relentless grindcore act Regurgitate. Urban Skytt also joined Nasum shortly before they folded.
Line-Up Stefan Harwik: Vocals (1989-), Urban Skytt: Guitar (1989-), Johan Hansson: Bass, Mats Nordrup: Drums **Past Members** *Mikael Lindevall: Guitar, Christoffer Johnsson: Vocals (1989)*
Deathography
Mortal Torment, Demo (1989)
The Exordium, Demo (1990)
Wrath from the Unknown, Demo (1991)
Netherworlds of the Mind, Demo (1992)
Into Celephaes, EP (MBR, 1992)
Denial, EP (MBR, 1992)

CRESTFALLEN
A mid-90's doom metal project of Västerås-bound Tommy Carlsson (Succumb). Depressive and majestic, too bad about the mediocre vocals.
Line-Up Tommy Carlsson: Everything
Deathography
Sorrows, Demo (1993)

CRETORIA
Death metal band formed in 2000. One demo is all they have produced so far.
Line-Up Kristian Laimaa: Vocals/Guitar, Peter Huss: Guitar, Kristoffer Andersson: Drums, Jimmy Karlsson: Bass
Deathography
Cretoria 2002, Demo (2002)

CRIPPLE
Early 90's band from Örebro that basically played thrash metal, with some death metal inspiration shining through. A bit like Sepultura, actually. Later in their career they turned stranger, and smelled like Voivod. Yeah, this is actually pretty good shit!
Line-Up Anton Renborg: Guitar, Daniel Ruud: Guitar/Vocals, Mattias "Lurgo" Fransson: Bass, Daniel Berg: Drums
Deathography
No More Living, Demo (1990)
Independent Luminary, Demo (1991)
Green Pillow, LP (Inline Music, 1993)
Promo 94, Demo (1994)

CRITICAL STATE—see Internal Decay

CROMB—see Genocrush Ferox

CROMLECH
Formed as Delirium in Varberg back in 1994. Not much happened for the band, even though their last demo was made into a mini-album in 2001. The band split, and turned into Divine Souls. Cromlech played some brutal shit for sure, in the vein of Carcass.
Line-Up Fredrik Arnesson: Vocals, Jonas Eckerström: Guitar, Henrik Meijner: Guitar, Dick Löfgren: Bass, Mattias Back: Drums **Past Members** *Anders Lundin: Bass (1995-1999)*
Deathography

And Darkness Fell, Demo (1996)
Promo 99 Demo, 1999
The Vulture Tones, Demo (2000)
The Vulture Tones, MCD (Beyond Productions, 2001)

CROWLEY
A band from Täby that formed in 1991, made a demo, and then disappeared.
Deathography
The Gate, Demo (1991)

THE CROWN
This continuation of Crown of Thorns changed its name in 1997 when an American AOR act with the same name threatened to take legal action. The band has been pretty successful, with lots of gigs and a deal with Metal Blade. This is more thrash and less death than Crown of Thorns. Tomas Lindberg (ex-At the Gates) and Mika (Impaled Nazarene) supply guest vocals on *Deathrace King*, and Lindberg became the actual singer on the following CD. They had a lot going for them, but the band folded in 2004.
Line-Up Johan Lindstrand: Vocals, Marcus Sunesson: Guitar, Marko Trevonen: Guitar, Magnus Osfelt: Bass, Janne Saarenpaa: Drums
Deathography
Hell is Here, CD (Metal Blade, 1998)
Deathrace King, CD (Metal Blade, 2000)
Crowned in Terror, CD (Metal Blade, 2002)
Possessed 13, CD (Metal Blade, 2003)
Crowned Unholy, CD (Metal Blade, 2004)
14 Years of No Tomorrow, CD (Metal Blade, 2005)

CROWN OF THORNS
Founded in Trollhättan in October 1991 by singer Johan Lindstrand, Crown of Thorns got a lot of attention after their debut demo, and appeared at major gigs like Sweden's biggest rock festival in Hultsfred in 1993. This was one of the first bands that played pure death/thrash, initially more death than thrash. In 1997 they became The Crown, and have since become rather successful.
Line-Up Johan Lindstrand: Vocals, Marcus Sunesson: Guitar, Marko Trevonen: Guitar, Magnus Osfelt: Bass, Janne Saarenpaa: Drums
Past Members *Robert Österberg: Guitar (1991-93)*
Deathography
Forever Heaven Gone, Demo (1993)
Forget the Light, Demo (1994)
The Burning, CD (Black Sun, 1995)
Eternal Death, CD (Black Sun, 1997)

CRYPT OF KERBEROS
A great Eskilstuna band that rose from the ashes of Macrodex in 1990. One of my personal favorites among minor Swedish bands, with a very dark and doomy kind of death metal. Highly original and cool as hell! Pettersson/Bjärgö also formed the highly respected electronic act Arcana, played bass in the crust band Meanwhile, and in 2006 started Tyrant. The sick bastard has also made music for a porn film. A CD of older material was released in 2005. Get it!
Line-Up Daniel Gildenlöw: Vocals, Peter Pettersson/

Bjärgö: *Guitar, Stefan Karlsson: Bass, Peter Jansson: Keyboards (1993-), Johan Hallgren: Guitar (1993), Mattias Borgh: Drums (1991-)* **Past Members** *Christian Eriksson: Vocals, Marcus Pedersén: Bass, Jessica Strandell: Keyboards (1992-1993), Jonas Strandell: Guitar (1990-1993), Johan Lönnroth: Guitar (1990-91), Mikael Sjöberg: Drums (1990-91)*
Deathography
Demo 91, Demo (1991)
Promo 91, Demo (1991)
Visions Beyond Darkness, 7" (Sunabel, 1991)
Cyclone of Insanity, 7" (Adipocere, 1992)
World of Myths, CD (Adipocere, 1993)
The Macrodex of War, CD (Bleed Records, 2005)

CRYPTIC ART
Tullinge/Stockholm band formed in March 1994. A lot of gothic stuff sneaks into their death, and the singer switches between growls and clean vocals. Don't confuse this band with the pure gothic band Cryptic Art which started in Stockholm around the same time that these guys split up. (But it's a cool idea, one band dissolves and you steal their name and style—you get an audience from scratch!)
*Line-Up Tomas Hodosi: Guitar, Johan: Vocals, Dimman: Drums **Past Members** Gandhi Isaksson: Vocals/Guitar/Bass, Jonas Alin: Guitar, Karin: Vocals, Dagna Plebaneck: Vocals, Melissa Nordell: Bass, Danne: Vocals, Wire McQuaid: Guitar, Jonas Kimbrell: Bass*
Deathography
In the Fog of Frustration, Demo (1996)
Thorns of Passion, Demo (1998)

CRYSTAL AGE
Mid-90's Gothenburg band that disappeared after the completely unexpected mega-success of Dronjak and Larsson's joke-project Hammerfall. The music? To quote my mother, *"they can play really well...but it's nothing I would listen to,"* as she always says about my bands. Like most bands from Gothenburg, they played melodic and technical death metal in the vein of, once again, At the Gates and In Flames. Note this was one of few old bands from Gothenburg whose drummer had long hair.
Line-Up Oscar Dronjac: Vocals/Guitar, Jonathan Elfström: Guitar, Fredrik Larsson: Bass, Hans Nilsson: Drums
Deathography
Promo 94, Demo (1994)
Far Beyond Devine, CD (Vic, 1995)

CURRICULUM MORTIS
This is a 2000's project of Amon Amarth's drummer Fredrik Andersson, helped out by Mattias Leinikka (Guidance of Sin, Sanguinary) and Linus Nirbrandt (ex-A Canarious Quintet). The result is pretty good. Like a better version of Amon Amarth.
Line-Up Fredrik Andersson: Drums, Mattias Leinikka: Vocals, Linus Nirbrandt: Guitar/Bass
Deathography
Into Death, Demo (2003)

CURSE
This band started back in 1986 in Spånga, and kept it going long enough to make two demos in the late 80's. Their music wasn't that developed, but you've got to start somewhere. Karlsson-Hård and Johansson have also played in Sorcery.
Line-Up Ishtar: Guitar/Vocals/Effects, Raffe (Magnus Karlsson-Mård): Bass, Brajan (Patrik L. Johansson): Drums
Deathography
Ad Futuron de Memoriam, Demo (1989)
Integumenton de Tenebrae, Demo (1989)

CYANIDE
Stockholm band from the 2000's influenced by better Swedish west coast bands like At the Gates and Eucharist, but nowhere near as good.
Deathography
Promo 2001, Demo (2001)

CYPHORIA
Melodic death metal act formed in Uddevalla in 2003.
Line-Up Ali Horuz: Vocals/Guitar, Christian Bernhall: Guitar, Fredrik Carlsson: Bass, Lena Hjalmarson: Keyboards, Alexander Weding: Drums
Past Members Andreas Backlund: Guitar
Deathography
Contradiction Conundrum Deprived, Demo (2004)

DAEMONIC
Uninspired and boring mix between heavy metal and mid-90's death metal. About their origin and line-up, I don't know a fuck.
Deathography
Daemonic, Demo (1996)

DAMIEN
One of Sweden's first thrash metal bands, Damien roamed the streets of Uppsala from 1982-1988, and was actually quite good and brutal. Then death metal came, and it was all over for these guys. Agrippa and Palm later played in the better-known but far worse-sounding Hexenhaus.
Line-Up Tommie Agrippa: Vocals, Laurence West: Guitar, Marre Martini: Bass, Mike Thorn: Drums
Past Members Andreas "Adde" Palm (Rick Meister): Guitar, Mick Coren: Guitar
Deathography
Hammer of the Gods, Demo (1986)
Onslaught Without Mercy, Demo (1986)
Chapter I, Demo (1987)
Chapter II, Demo (1987)
Damien/Atrocity/Gravity/Tribulation Split 7" (Is this Heavy or What Records, 1988)
Requiem for the Dead, EP (Gothic Rec, 1988)

DAMNATION
Black/death band from Stockholm that started as early as 1989, but never really got serious since its members were occupied with far bigger bands like Dismember (Rickard) and Unanimated (Peter and Rickard). Too bad, this was intense stuff. Have you ever heard

a more blasphemous title than "Insulter of Jesus Christ"? (Well, besides Black Sabbath's "Disturbing the Priest"?) Hilarious! Strangely, the band became more productive after Stjärnvind joined Merciless, and later Entombed. Get all their stuff! Be raw and brutal!

Line-Up Björn Gramell: Bass, Rikard Cabeza: Guitar, Peter Stjärnvind: Drums **Past Members** Micke Janson: Vocals (1989-1994)

Deathography
Divine Darkness, Demo (1995)
Divine Darkness, 7" (Iron Fist, 2004)
Insulter of Jesus Christ, 7" (Iron Fist, 2004)
Desctructo Evangelia, CD (Threeman Recording, 2004)

DAMNATIONS PRIDE

Malmö band active during 1988-90, with Daniel Vala from the folded Obscurity. He was only a minor force here—that might be why they never got anywhere.

Line-Up Micke: Vocals, Marcus Freij: Guitar, Daniel Vala: Bass, Peter: Drums

Deathography
Demo (1988)

DARK ABBEY—see Epitaph (Sollentuna)

DARK FUNERAL

As Lord Ahriman and Blackmoon turned their evil minds to blasphemic music in 1993, this was the last band to get on the black metal bandwagon with any credibility. Dark Funeral had a lot of quality, though that quality decreased somewhat after the departure of riff master Parland. Still, they have been immensely successful throughout their career. And boy, is Matte Modin fast behind the drums. Since Blackmoon left, Dark Funeral has mainly been a duo consisting of Ahriman and Emperor Magus Caligula. Together they have run through an incredible amount of musicians, all from pretty good bands themselves.

Line-Up Emperor Magus Caligula (Masse Broberg): Vocals, Lord Ahriman (Micke Svanberg): Guitar, Chaq Mol: Guitar, Nils Fjällström: Drums, Gustaf Hielm: Bass **Past Members** B-Force: Bass (session only), Draugen: Drums (1993-1994), Equimanthorn (Peter): Drums (1994-1995), Alzazmon (Tomas Asklund): Drums (1996-1998), Gaahnfaust, Robert Lundin : Drums (1998-2000), Matte Modin: Drums (2001-2007) Themgoroth (Paul): Vocals (1993-1995), Blackmoon (David Parland): Guitar (1993-1996), Typhos (Henrik Ekeroth): Guitar (1996-1998) , Dominion (Matti Mäkelä): Guitar (1998-2002), Richard Cabeza: Bass (session only), Lord K (Kent Philipson): Bass (session only)

Deathography
Dark Funeral EP (Hellspawn, 1994)
The Secrets of the Black Arts, CD (No Fashion, 1996)
Vobiscum Satanas, CD (No Fashion, 1998)
Teach Children to Worship Satan, EP (No Fashion, 2000)
In the Sign..., EP (No Fashion, 2000)
Diabolis Interium, CD (No Fashion, 2001)

Under Wings of Hell, Split (Hammerheart, 2002)
Dark Funeral—Live In Sundsvall, CD (No Fashion, 2002)
De Profundis Clamavi ad te Domine, CD (Regain, 2004)
Devil Pigs, Split (The End Records, 2004)
Attera Totus Sanctus, CD (Regain, 2005)

DARK STONE

Formed in 1999, they sing about ancient wars, the dark ages, and fantasy. They claim to play death metal, but sound more like they have played too many rounds of Dungeons and Dragons in their mother's basement.

Line-Up Darkstone: Guitar, Redemptor: Bass, Revenant: Drums

Deathography
La Matanza, Demo (2001)
Blood Vengeance, Demo (2003)
Metalrelegion, Demo (2004)

DARK TERROR—see Hypocrite

DARK TRANQUILLITY

Kicked off as pretty brutal act Septic Boiler in 1989 but soon renamed Dark Tranquillity, the band's music has drifted far away from an initial Kreator-like assault (the Trail of Life Decayed demo remains their best work). They tried to do something similar to At the Gates, with dubious results. Today, they aren't really metal at all. To me, this is one of the more unexciting Swedish death metal-linked bands that ever made it big. But I guess they have qualities outside the field of Metal, as their latest albums have shown. Note that Stanne and Sundin helped create the "love-em or-hate-em" power metal act Hammerfall. Sadly for Stanne, he left prior to their gigantic success to concentrate completely on Dark Tranquillity. I guess he has regretted that more than once, perhaps only in terms of cash flow. Original singer Fridén left for Ceremonial Oath, and later joined In Flames.

Line-Up Mikael Stanne: Vocals (1993-), Guitar (1989-1993), Anders Jivarp: Drums, Martin Henriksson: Guitar (1998-), Bass (1989-1998), Niklas Sundin: Guitar, Michael Nicklasson: Bass, Martin Brändström: Electronics **Past Members** Fredrik Johansson: Guitar (1993-1998), Anders Fridén: Vocals (1989-1993), Robin Engström: Drums (session only 2001)

Deathography
Enfeebled Earth, Demo (1990—as Septic Broiler)
Trail of Life Decayed, Demo (1991)
Rehearsal oct-92, Demo (1992)
Trail of Life Decayed, EP (Guttural, 1992)
A Moonclad Reflection, 7" (Slaughter Records, 1992)
Skydancer, CD (Spinefarm, 1993)
Of Chaos and Eternal Night, MCD (Spinefarm, 1995)
Enter Suicidal Angels, MCD (Osmose, 1995)
The Gallery, CD (Osmose, 1995)
Skydancer + Chaos and Eternal Light, CD (Spinefarm, 1996)

The Mind's I, CD (Osmose, 1997)
Projector, CD (Century Media, 1999)
Haven, CD (Century Media, 2000)
Damage Done, CD (Century Media, 2002)
Exposures—In Retrospect and Denial, CD
(Century Media, 2004)
Lost to Apathy, EP (Century Media, 2004)
Character, CD (Century Media, 2005)

DARKANE
Familiar death/thrash band formed in Helsingborg
in 1998. Though not really my kind of music, I tend
to like this band more than others in the modern
thrash/death genre. Several members were previously
in Agretator.
Line-Up Klas Ideberg: Guitar, Jörgen Löfberg: Bass,
Christofer Malmström: Guitar, Andreas Sydow:
Vocals, Peter Wildoer: Drums *Past Members*
Lawrence Mackrory: Vocals, Björn "Speed" Strid:
Vocals
Deathography
Rusted Angel, CD (War, 1998)
Insanity, CD (Nuclear Blast, 2001)
Expanding Senses, CD (Nuclear Blast, 2002)
Layers of Lies, CD (Nuclear Blast, 2005)

DARKEND
Death/thrash of the 2000's. A Darkane cover band?
Line-Up Johan Bergqvist: Vocals/Guitar, Kim
Lindstén: Guitar, Christian Johansson: Drums
Deathography
Together We Shall Rise, Demo (1999)
Death Inside, Demo (2000)
Vengeance, Demo (2001)

DARKIFIED
Obscure black/death metal band from Finspång/
Söderköping, formed in February 1991. Pretty intense
stuff with deep guttural vocals. The band was never
anything more than a project, and disagreements
within the group made it short-lived. When Entombed
sacked L.G. Petrov, they brought in the singer from
this band to audition for the the job since they loved
Darkified's demo. But when he turned up, they were
shocked how young he was and just could not even
consider him for that reason—even though Entombed
themselves were teens! They basically gave him a bag
of candy, and put him on a bus back home. Drummer
Göthberg has also played in Marduk, and Karlsson used
to sing for Pan-Thy-Monium and Edge of Sanity. Ahx
was kicked out of the band in 1993, after which it all
faded. He went on to join Amenophis, while Göthberg
concentrated on Marduk, though he was soon sacked.
Ahx also edited Abnormalcy 'zine. Repulse released a
compilation of all Darkified's material in 1995.
Line-Up Martin Gustafsson: Vocals, Joakim
Göthberg: Drums, Robert Karlsson: Bass/Vocals
Past Members Martin Ahx: Guitar, Jonas Amundin:
Acoustic Guitar, Tim Pettersson: Guitar, Alex
Bathory: Vocals *Deathography*
Dark, Demo (1991)
Sleep Forever, 7" (Drowned, 1992)
A Dance on the Grave, CD (Repulse, 1995)

THE DARKSEND
Apparently formed as early as 1991 in Helsingborg,
their style is basically black metal with hints at
deadlier stuff. The Darksend made a couple CDs
later in their career, but never got much attention.
They had a lot of trouble with the line-up, especially
drummers. Richter and Stigert went on to form 9th
Plague, and Tony also edits the *Nekrologium Zine*
(still alive on the Internet).
Line-Up Mikael Bergman: Guitar, Anders Stigert:
Bass, Stefan Stigert: Guitar, Tony Richter: Vocals
Past Members Per Christoffersson: Drums, Tau
Jacobsen: Guitar, Mihalj Stefko: Bass, Martin
Thorsén: Drums, Magnus Hoff: Drums, Christian
Andersson: Drums
Deathography
Unsunned, CD (Head Not Found, 1996)
The Luciferian Whisper, EP (X-Treme Records,
1997)
Antichrist in Excelsis, CD (X-Treme Records,
2000)

DAS ÜBER ELVIS—see Necrovation

DAWN
Mjölby-based band formed by guitarists Fullmestad
and Söderberg in 1991. They got pretty inspired by
the black metal trend after a while, which made their
music pretty unoriginal and dull—and caused some
hilarious corpse paint photo sessions. Henrik Forss
also edited the 'zines *Brutal Mag* and *Dis-organ-
ized*. Later he co-edited the classic *Septic Zine*, and
sang on In Flames' first mini-CD! Other members
have a history in Dissection, Dark Funeral, Afflicted,
Mithotyn, and Regurgitate. It's busy here in Sweden!
Line-Up Tomas Asklund: Drums, Henke Forss:
Vocals, Stefan Lundgren: Guitar, Fredrik Söderberg:
Guitar, Philip Von Segebaden: Bass *Past Members*
Andreas Fullmestad: Guitar, Dennis Karlsson: Bass,
Karsten Larsson: Drums, Jocke Pettersson: Drums,
Lars Tängmark: Bass
Deathography
Demo 1, Demo (1992)
Apparition, Demo (1993)
Promo 93, Demo (1993)
The Eternal Forest EP (split with Pyphomgertum),
7" (Bellphegot, 1993)
Naer Solen Gar Niber vor Evogher, CD
(Necropolis, 1995)
Sorgh pa Svarte Vingar Flogh, EP (Necropolis,
1996)
Slaughtersun (Crown of the Triarchy), CD
(Necropolis, 1998)

DAWN OF DECAY
In 1989 a couple of teenagers in Forshaga decided to
form the band Purgatory. Initially they played thrash
metal, but they soon discovered death metal and
changed their name and style. They grew far better,
with a lot of Florida influences as well as slower parts
à la Paradise Lost. Despite their quality, they always
had to stand in the shadow of townmates Vomitory.
Johan and Tomas are also in Moaning Wind.

Line-Up Johan Carlsson: Bass/Vocals, Micke Birgersson: Drums, Tomas Bergstrand: Guitar (1993-) **Past Members** Matthias Ekelund: Guitar (1995-1996), Rickard Löfgren: Vocals/Guitar (1992-1995)
Deathography
Grief, Demo (1992)
Promo 1993, Demo (1993)
Into the Realm of Dreams, EP (1994)
Hell Raising Hell, Demo (1996)
New Hell, CD (Voices of Death, 1998)

DCLXVI
This band formed in Stockholm 2002, made a demo and an EP, and then split up.
Line-Up Seb: Vocals, Alle: Bass/Vocals, Billy: Guitar, Ossi: Guitar, Marcus: Drums, Jonas: Vocals
Deathography
10 Minutes to the End, Demo (2003)
Chainsaw, EP (2003)

DE INFERNALI
Solo project of Jon Nödtveidt (Dissection), also featuring Dan Swanö (Edge of Sanity, Unisound, etc.) on vocals for one song. Then again, what project doesn't involve Dan Swanö?
Line-Up Jon Nödtveidt: Basically everything
Deathography
Symphonia de Infernali, CD
(Nuclear Blast, 1997)

THE DEAD
In the early 2000's, the Stockholm trio of Nirbrandt (A Canorous Quintet, Guidance of Sin), Sillman (Guidance of Sin, Vicious Art), and Andersson (A Canorous Quintet, Amon Amarth, Guidance of Sin) started a pure death metal project with big chunks of grind. I would like to see more bands like this.
Line-Up Linus Nirbrandt (aka Dr. Jones): Guitar, Tobbe Sillman (aka Necrobarber): Bass, Fredrik Andersson: Drums
Deathography
The Dead/Birdflesh, Split CD (Nocturnal Music, 2001)
Real Zombies Never Die, EP (Nocturnal Music, 2003)

DEAD AWAKEN
Melodic thrash/death metal slightly inspired by the likes of Slayer and Vader. This band formed in Västerås 2002, and has recently developed into Abyssal Chaos.
Line-Up Jörgen Kristensen: Guitar/Vocals, Andreas Backström: Guitar, Andreas Morén: Bass/Vocals, Joakim Edlund: Drums
Deathography
Death Before Dishonour, Demo (2002)
Instrument of War, Demo (2003)
..Tomorrow We Die.., Demo (2004)

DEAD END
Death/thrash band that formed in 1989, made a few demos, and then vanished.
Deathography

2 Minute Warning, Demo (1991)
Infinite, Demo (1992)

DEAD ON ARRIVAL
Formed 2002 in the very northern town Gällivare.
Line-Up Kristian Hjelm: Vocals, Tommy Norlin: Guitar, Christoffer Hansson: Guitar, Kjell Norman: Bass/Vocals, Mattias Johansson: Drums **Past Members** Kristoffer Johansson: Vocals, Salomon Nutti: Vocals, Joakim Aukea: Guitar
Deathography
D.O.A., Demo (2004)

DEAD SILENT SLUMBER
Solo project of Naglfar's Jens Rydén. Symphonic and not very extreme.
Line-Up Jens Rydén: Everything
Deathography
Entombed in the Midnight Hour, CD (Hammerheart, 1999)

DEATH BREATH
After nearly a decade of absence from the death metal field, Nicke Andersson (ex-Nihilist/Entombed) formed this project in 2005. With partner in crime Robert Pehrsson (Runemagick, Deathwitch, Masticator), they set out to create the dirtiest and sickest death metal this side of Death's Scream Bloody Gore. They may well have succeeded, and let's hope the project survives. To hear Andersson play the drums again is a blessing.
Line-Up Nicke Andersson: Guitar/Drums, Robert Pehrsson: Guitar/Vocals, Mange Hedquist: Bass **Past Members** Markus Karlsson: Vocals (session only), Jörgen Sandström: Vocals (session only), Scott Carlson: Vocals/Bass (session only)
Deathography
Death Breath, 7" (Black Lodge, 2006)
Stinking Up the Night, CD (Black Lodge, 2006)

DEATH DESTRUCTION
Project initiated in Gothenburg during 2004 by Henrik and Jonas of Evergray, who wanted to play something a bit more extreme.
Line-Up Henrik Danhage: Guitar, Jonas Ekdahl: Drums, Fredrik Larsson: Bass, Jimmie Strimell: Vocals
Deathography
Demo, Demo (2004)

DEATH RIPPER
Completely forgotten and clandestine band from Eskilstuna that made noise from early 1985 until late 1986. Death Ripper played extreme thrash/black with necro vocals and corpse paint. They actually had some good ideas, though they were sloppy and not too competent. One of their rehearsals is preserved on video, a perfect document of how early extreme bands looked in the mid-80's—short hair, weird poses, ghastly makeup, and a broken drum kit from hell. After four gigs the band called it quits. Brian, Ron, and Bille formed Oxygene, and legendary metalhead Glenning went on to Asmodeus.

Line-Up Randy Natas (Cleas Glenning): Drums, Brian Witchsword: Bass (initially Bass & Vocals), Horny Bloodsucker: Vocals, Ron Gambler: Guitar, Bille: Guitar Past Members Dennis: Drums (1985)
Deathography
Rehearsalroom Live at Balsta, Video (1985)
Deciples of Violence, Rehearsal (1986)

DEATHWITCH
Old school death/thrash/black mixture begun in Gothenburg in 1995, the brainchild of Niklas Rudolfsson of Runemagick, Sacramentum, and Swordmaster. After several years on Necropolis, they turned to Earache's imprint Wicked World in 2003. Cool and dirty metal.
Line-Up Slade Doom: Guitar, Dan Slaughter: Drums, Niklas "Terror" Rudolfsson: Vocals/Bass/Guitar **Past Members** Peter "Carnivore" Palmdahl: Bass, Corpse: Drums, Doomentor: Guitar, Reaper: Vocals, Fredrik "Af Necrohell" Johnsson: Guitar, Emma "Lady Death" Karlsson: Bass, Morbid Juttu: Drums
Deathography
Triumphant Devastation, CD (Necropolis, 1996)
Dawn of Armageddon, CD (Necropolis, 1997)
The Ultimate Death, CD (Necropolis, 1998)
Monumental Mutilations, CD (Necropolis, 1999)
Deathfuck Rituals, CD (Hellspawn, 2002)
Violence Blasphemy Sodomy, CD (Earache/Wicked World, 2004)

DECADENCE
Melodic death metal band formed in Stockholm in 2003. Note that they have already changed almost all their members, so their future seems uncertain.
Line-Up Kitty Saric: Vocals, Kenneth Lantz: Guitar, Daniel Green: Guitar, Joakim Antman: Bass, Erik Röjås: Drums Past Members Peter Lindqvist: Drums, Niclas Rådberg: Guitar, Christian Lindholm: Guitar, Roberto Vacchi Segerlund: Bass, Mikael Sjölund: Guitar, Patrik Frögéli: Drums
Deathography
Land of Despair, Demo (2004)
Decadence, CD (2005)

DECAMERON
Mainly the creation of brothers Alex and Johannes Losbäck, who started their deadly mission during 1991 in Hunnebrostrand, originally as Nocrophobic. Initially they seemed obsessed with black metal cosmetics, and used corpse paint. But they soon created cool and melodic death/black metal with a lot of good arrangements and ideas. The band had a lot of line-up problems, and both Norrman and Kjellgren eventually left for the mighty Dissection. Decameron was actually a very good and technical band that deserved more attention than they got.
Line-Up Alex Losbäck: Vocals/Bass, Johannes Losbäck: Guitar/Vocals, Johnny Lehto: Guitar, Peter Gustavsson: Guitar, Magnus Werndell: Drums **Past Members** Christoffer Hermansson: Guitar, Jonny Lehto: Guitar, Tomas Backelin: Guitar, Johan Norman: Guitar, Tobias Kellgren: Drums, Adrian

Erlandsson: Drums
Deathography
My Grave is Calling, Demo (1992)
Mockery of the Holy, 7" (Corpsegrinder, 1993)
My Shadow, CD (No Fashion, 1996)

DECAY—see Alvsvart

DECHAINED
Death/thrash band formed in Gällivare in 2002. A lot of bands seem to have popped up there lately, is there a scene going on or something?
Line-Up Kristian Hjelm: Vocals, Tommy Norlin: Guitar, Christoffer Hansson: Guitar, Kjell Norman: Bass, Mattias Johansson: Drums
Deathography
Demo 2004, Demo (2004)
The Dying Sun, Demo (2005)

DECOLLATION
Early 90's project created by Kristian Wåhlin (Grotesque, Liers in Wait, later in Diabolique) and Johan Österberg (now in Diabolique), joined by Tomas Johansson (Ceremonial Oath, later Diabolique).
Line-Up Johan Österberg: Vocals/Guitar, "John Jeremiah": Guitar, "Nick Shields": Keyboards, Tomas Johansson: Bass, Kristian Wåhlin: Drums **Past Members** Lars Johansson: Drums
Deathography
Cursed Lands, EP (Listenable, 1992)

DECORTICATION
Death metal group from Luleå started in 1990 as Torture. The name soon changed to Gilgamosh, and after a couple of demos, Decortication. Originally they played Kreator-style thrash metal, but later incorporated influences from Florida death metal bands like Morbid Angel and Deicide. Initially they were also tempted by the black metal thing, taking photos in corpse paint. They came to their senses, but kept the screaming vocals, which doesn't help.
Line-Up Pierre Törnkvist: Guitar/Vocals, Niklas Svensson: Bass, Oskar Karlsson: Drums **Past Members** Mats Granström: Bass, Torbjörn Fält: Drums, Patrik Törnkvist: Guitar
Deathography
They Shall All be Sent To..., Demo (1991 - as Gilgamosh)
Funeral Rites, Demo (1992—as Gilgamosh)
Lucichrist—The Third God, Demo (1993)
Promotape-94, Demo (1994)

DEFACED CREATION
Straightforward death metal band formed in Östersund in 1993 as Unorthodox. They were soon forced to change their name since an established group already used it. The original guitarist was sentenced for arson and grave desecration in 1994 and eventually sent to a mental institution, so the band had to regroup. Defaced Creation has been pretty successful since, touring Europe with such great bands as Dying Fetus and Deranged. After splitting, most of the members went on to form Aeon.

Line-Up Thomas Dahlström: Vocals, Jörgen Bylander: Guitar, Arrtu Malkku: Drums (1997-), Johan Hjelm: Bass (1998-), Zeb Nilsson: Bass *Past Members* Stefan Dahlberg: Guitar (1993-1994), Jocke Wassberg: Bass (1997-1998)
Deathography
Santeria, Demo (1994)
Defaced Creation, Demo (1995)
Resurrection, EP (Paranoya Syndrome, 1996)
Fall (split w/Aeternum), EP (Paranoya Syndrome, 1997)
Infernal (split w/Standing Out), EP (Rockaway, 1998)
Serenity in Chaos, CD (Vod, 2000)

DEFECTIVE DECAY—see Blazing Skies

DEFILER
2000's death metal with war lyrics, based in the southern city of Malmö. Brutal and straightforward, but pretty average.
Deathography
Random Detonation, Demo (2002)

DEFLESHED
This deadly thrash platoon started in Uppsala in 1991, originally playing death metal. Karlsson left in 1994 to focus on Gates of Ishtar, replaced by Matte Modin. With this incredible fast madman on the drums (he became drummer of Dark Funeral in 2000), Defleshed soon emerged as one of the most intense thrash acts on the planet. The band played their last gig on Christmas Day 2005—since I was there, I can confirm that they went out in style.
Line-Up Lars Löfven: Vocals/Guitar, Matte Modin: Drums (1995-), Gustaf Jorde: Bass/Vocals (1992-) *Past Members* Kristoffer Griedl: Guitar (1991-1995), Oskar Karlsson: Drums (1991-1994), Johan Hedman: Vocals (session only), Robin Dolkh: Vocals (1991-1992)
Deathography
Defleshed, Demo (1992)
Abrah Kadavrah, Demo (1993)
Body Art, Demo (1993)
Obsculum Obscenum, 7" (Miscarriage, 1993)
Ma Belle Scalpelle, CD (Invasion, 1994)
Abrah Kadavrah, CD (Invasion, 1995)
Under the Blade, CD (Invasion, 1997)
Death...the High Cost of Living, CD (War Music, 1999)
Fast Forward, CD (War Music, 1999)
Royal Straight Flesh, CD (Regain, 2002)
Reclaim the Beat, CD (Regain, 2005)

DEFORMED (Floda)
Mid-90's band from Floda. (Are they "Floda death metal"?) Their first demo is good old death metal in the vein of Entombed and Grave. I've heard they changed their music towards black metal later, that's probably why I haven't heard about them since.
Line-Up Micke Nordin
Deathography

Obsessed by the Past, Demo (1994)
Shades from a Missing Epoch, Demo (1995)

DEFORMED (Växjö)
Death/black band formed in the 2000's. Not to be confused with the older Deformed from Floda. Both Segerback and Nilsson are also in Mindcollapse.
Line-Up Rob: Bass/Vocals, Olle Segerback: Guitar, Mathias "Matte" Nilsson: Guitar, Chrille: Drums
Deathography
Infuriate, Demo (2003)

DEFORMITY
From one of the most boring places on earth: Märsta. Formed in 1991 to play standard mid-tempo death metal with keyboards, cheesy melodies, and bad vocals. Sounds like pure shit doesn't it? I shouldn't be too hard on these guys, there are actually a few good riffs in there. A few. The band never made it, but Harry and Micke went on to form Vörgus.
Line-Up Tommie Jansson: Vocals/Guitar, Kenneth Nyholm: Bass/Vocals, Micke Nyholm: Drums, Harry Virtanen: Guitar
Deathography
Demo (1991)
Repulsions of War, Demo (1992)
Sickly Obsessed, Demo (1992)
Deformity, Demo (1994)

DEGIAL OF EMBOS
A great group of old school-loving youngsters who long for the time when death metal was pure and raw. Degial of Embos formed in Uppsala 2004, and I wish them all luck. Their band photos are great, it looks like 1989 again! Eriksson is also in the other extremely young old school death band from Uppsala, Katalysator. Around 2006, they shortened their name to Degial.
Line-Up Hampus Eriksson: Guitar/Vocals, Rickard Höggren: Guitar, Per Östergren: Bass, Emil Svensson: Drums *Past Members* Johan Petterson: Bass, Johan Östman: Vocals
Deathography
Blood God, Demo (2004)
Death Will Arise, Demo (2005)
Live Demo, Demo (2005)
Awakening From Darkness, Demo (2006—as Degial)

DEGRADE
Great and brutal gorc/death metal band formed in Linköping in 2001. Aggressive, fast, and well-played. A hope for the future.
Line-Up Manne: Vocals, Victor: Guitar, Söder: Guitar, Kristian: Bass, Berto: Drums
Deathography
Feasting on Bloody Chunks, Demo (2003)
Hanged and Disembowelled, EP (Permeated Records, 2005)

DELIRIUM—see Cromlech

DELLAMORTE

From the ruins of Uncanny and Interment, Dellamorte started their deadly mission in 1994 in the small town of Avesta. Death metal in the vein of Entombed (in fact, very much like Entombed), though maybe a little more punk-oriented. The band hasn't officially split up, as Johan insists they will record at least once more, but Dellamorte has been totally inactive since 2001. All the members have been heavily involved in the following significant groups: Insision (Daniel), Centinex (Johan, Kenneth, Jonas), Carnal Forge (Jonas), and Katatonia (Mattias). Johan and, eh, me (Daniel) have also been very active in the crust bands Uncurbed and Diskonto respectively. Since I was in this band myself I really can't judge the quality clearly. Listen and decide for yourselves.

Line-Up Johan Jansson: Guitar/Vocals, Jonas Kjellgren: Vocals (...and everything else he could get his hands on!), Daniel Ekeroth: Bass/Vocals, Mattias Norrman: Guitar, Kenneth Englund: Drums (1994-1998, 2000-) *Past Members* Sonny Svedlund: Drums (1998-2000)

Deathography
Drunk in the Abyss, Demo (1995)
Everything You Hate, CD (Finn Records, 1996)
Dirty, Dellamorte/Corned Beef Split 7" (Yellow Dog, 1996)
Uglier & More Disgusting, LP/CD (Osmose, 1997)
Home Sweet Hell, CD (Osmose, 1999)
Fuck Me Satan, 7" (Elderberry, 2000)

DELUSIVE

Melodic death/thrash formed in Stockholm in 2000.
Line-Up Robin "Reaf" Niklasson: Vocals, Tommy Lindström: Drums, Adam Olsen: Guitar, Robin Sandström: Bass, Niclas Rådberg: Guitar *Past Members* Ragain: Vocals
Deathography
The Dark Chronicle, Demo (2004)
Regret, EP (2005)

DELVE—see Verminous

DEMENTIA 13

Brutal death metal, formed in Nyköping in 2004. Silfver and Olsson are also in Asphyxiation, Shock Wave, and Ceremonial Death. Busy guys.
Line-Up Daniel Silfver: Vocals, Niklas Olsson: Guitar/Bass, Emil Norlander: Drums
Deathography
In Blood We Drown, Demo (2004)

DEMISE—see Agretator

DEMON SEED

Progressive death metal band formed in Nyköping during 2004. According to their nicknames, I guess this is mainly a joke—the pseudonym "Gamblore" is taken from a *Simpsons* episode!
Line-Up Fredde (Slobo): Vocals, Håkan (Demonhead): Guitar, Mattias (Gamblore): Guitar, Damien (Neid): Bass, Andreas (Tappadifarstun): Drums

Deathography
[DEMO]N SEED, Demo (2005)

DEMONOID

Basically a side project of Therion, initiated in 2004. I guess the guys longed for the old times when they actually played metal. Better than the latest Therion albums, worse than the first ones.
Line-Up Kristian Niemann: Guitar, Johan Niemann: Bass, Christofer Johnsson: Vocals, Rickard Evensand: Drums
Deathography
Riders of the Apocalypse, CD (Nuclear Blast, 2004)

DENATA

Death/thrash formed in Linköping by Tomas Andersson after the break-up of Skullcrusher in 1998. They got attention, but split after a few albums.
Line-Up Tomas Andersson: Vocals/Guitar, Åke Danielsson: Drums, Roger Blomberg: Bass *Past Members* Pontus Sjösten: Vocals/Drums
Deathography
Necro Erection, EP (Ghoul Records, 1999)
Departed to Hell, CD (Ghoul Records, 2000)
Deathtrain, CD (Arctic, 2002)
Art of the Insane, CD (Arctic, 2003)

DEPRAVED

Death metal band formed in Norrtälje in 2004.
Line-Up Robin Joelsson: Vocals, Jonatan Thunell: Guitar, Anders Berndtsson: Guitar, Tobias Rydsheim: Bass, Jonas Holmström: Drums
Deathography
Glimpse of Death, Demo (2004)
Pieces of You..., Demo (2004)

DEPRIVED

Melodic death metal formed in Blekinge in 2004.
Line-Up Mattias Svensson: Vocals, Christian "Jacke" Sonesson: Guitar, Joakim "Jocke" Pettersson: Drums, Victor Dahlgren: Bass , Jonas Martinsson: Guitar *Past Members* Lennie Persson: Vocals, Henrik Olausson: Guitar
Deathography
A Deceptive Soul, Demo (2004)
Demo, Demo (2004)
This Last Hollow Dance, Demo (2005)

DERANGED

This incredibly brutal band started in the southern city of Malmö (actually Hjärup, but even I don't know where the fuck that is) way back in 1989, under the name Carbuncle. Seemingly, their intention was to out-gross all other bands of the genre. With a minimal style and gore-drenched lyrics, they pretty much succeeded. In 1991 they became Deranged, and recorded their first demo the following year. Deranged's pure brutality was very different from the black metal wave of the times, and they fought against all trends with furious gore-grind. Especially *High on Blood* is a masterpiece of deranged and depraved death metal in its most extreme and compressed form. Their lack of variation might get a bit boring when listening to a whole album—but in smaller doses they surely tear your soul apart! Axelsson also works at the mighty Berno studio recording bands like Seance, The Haunted, Defleshed, Vomitory, Insision, and Kaamos. Note that both Wermén (*Cerebral Zine*) and Gyllenbäck (*Helter Skelter*) edited 'zines in the early days of Swedish death metal. As this band has faced an incredible amount of line-up turbulence, respect them for never giving up!

Line-Up Johan Axelsson: *Guitar (1990-), Rikard Wermén: Drums, Calle Feldt: Bass/Vocals* **Past Members** *Andreas Deblén: Vocals/Drums, Dan Bengtsson: Bass, Per Gyllenbäck: Vocals, Fredrik Sandberg: Vocals, Jean-Paul Asenov: Bass (1990-1995), Johan Anderberg: Vocals/Bass, Mikael Bergman: Bass (1995)*

Deathography
Confessions of a Necrophile, Demo (1992)
...The Confession Continues, 7" (1993)
Orgy of Infanticide Exposed Corpses (Part II), 7" (Obliteration, 1993)
Architects of Perversion, CD (Repulse, 1994)
Internal Vaginal Bleeding, EP (Repulse, 1995)
Rated X, CD (Repulse, 1995)
Sculpture of the Dead, EP (Repulse, 1996)
High on Blood, CD (Regain, 1999)
III, CD (Listenable, 1999)
Abscess/Deranged, Split (Listenable, 2001)
Deranged, CD (Listenable, 2001)
Plainfield Cemetery, CD (Listenable, 2002)

DESCENDING
Death/black band formed in Fjällbacka in 2003, and reportedly on hold at the moment.
Line-Up Stefan Eliasson: *Guitar, Carl Nordblom: Drums, Kaj Palm: Bass/Vocals*
Deathography
A World Shaped to Die, Demo (2004)

DESECRATED
Brutal death metal, formed in Stockholm in 2003.
Line-Up Billy: *Guitar, Enar: Bass, Marcus: Drums, Totte: Vocals* **Past Members** *Sebb: Vocals*
Deathography
Awakened Fury Demo, Demo (2004)

DESECRATOR—see Ceremonial Oath

DESERT RITUAL—see Ancients Rebirth

DESTRUCTO
Black/death metal, formed in 2003 under the coolest minimalistic and gruesome pseudonyms!
Line-Up E: *Drums/Vocals, O: Guitar, W: Bass*
Deathography
Sanguis Draconis, Demo (2004)

DESULTORY
Rönninge/Södertälje act that began in 1989 with thrash-inspired death metal. More Bay Area than Tampa, like a thrash metal band with death metal vocals. Though they never impressed me, they were pretty successful in the early 90's. *Forever Gone* is a compilation of their two demos. After Desultory split up, the members continued as Zebulon in a similar style to Desultory's last recording.
Line-Up Klas Morberg: *Guitar/Vocals, Thomas Johnson: Drums, Håkan Morberg: Bass (1995-)* **Past Members** *Stefan Pöge: Guitar (1989-1995), Jens Almgren: Bass (1989-1992)*
Deathography
From Beyond, Demo (1990)
Death Unfolds, Demo (1991)
Visions, Demo (1991)
Forever Gone, LP (HOK, 1992)
Into Eternity, CD (Metal Blade, 1993)
Bitterness, CD (Metal Blade, 1994)
Swallow the Snake, CD (Metal Blade, 1996)

DETHRONEMENT
This Växjö orchestra was formed as the messy project Bacon Warriors by Jonasson and Örnhem in 1993. Eventually they developed into the death metal band Dethronement in the summer of 1996. Among the members should be noted notorious grind freak Andreas Mitroulis, known from superior bands like Birdflesh, General Surgery, and Sayyadina.
Line-Up Johan Jonasson: *Guitar, Andreas Mitroulis: Drums, Jörgen Örnhem: Bass/Vocals, Robert Lilja: Guitar* **Past Members** *Johan Orre: Guitar, Kristoffer Svensson: Vocals*
Deathography
Astral Serenity, Demo (1997)
Breeding the Demonseed, Demo (1998)
Survival of the Sickest, CD (Loud N' Proud, 1999)
World of Disgust, Unreleased CD (2000)
Steel Manufactured Death, CD (2003)

DEUS EX MACHINA
One of countless melodic death metal bands that popped up after In Flames' incredible success.
Line-Up Alex Holmstedt: *Vocals, John Lidén: Guitar, Joseph Astorga: Drums, Robin Strömberg: Bass, Vincent Andrén: Guitar*
Deathography
Recreation, Demo (2004)

DEVASTATED
Melodic death metal that started in Värnamo in 1995, made a demo in 1996, and then vanished.
Line-Up Kosta Christoforidis: *Vocals/Guitar, Dado Hrnic: Drums/Keyboard, Liz-Marie Johansson: Vocals, Mattias Lilja: Bass, Pawel Budzisz: Guitar*
Deathography
Devastated, Demo (1996)

DEVIANT
Blasting gore-grind act formed in Uppsala in 2002 by guitarists and twin brothers Johan and Magnus. Their style changed a lot towards brutal death metal since, much more tight and powerful. Once this band figures out how to write songs with better structure, they will be unstoppable. Both EB and Fredrik are ex-Inception. Erik is also in Penile Suffocation.
Line-Up Alex: *Vocals, Johan: Guitar, Magnus: Guitar, EB: Drums, Fredrik: Bass* **Past Members:**

Erik: Bass (2004)
Deathography
Deviant, Demo (2003)
Tools of Termination, EP (Nuclear Winter, 2004)
Larvaeon, CD (Spew Records, 2005)

DEVOUR

Early summer 1997, two teenagers Fredrik and Jan decided to start a brutal death metal band. The result is Devour. Fredrik is also the head of Army of the Northstar—Enslaved's Swedish Fan Club!
Line-Up Fredrik: Bass, Jari S: Vocals, Patrick: Guitar/Vocals (2001-), Jimmy: Drums (2001-)

DEVOURED

Started out during 1989 in the Stockholm suburb of Hägersten. They blended all kinds of styles into their death metal, and the results were confusing. Some problems with the line-up also held back the band. I can't remember if they made any official demos.
Line-Up Victor: Drums, Matte: Vocals, Stefan: Guitar (1992-), Micke: Bass (initially Guitar)

DHRAUG

Formed in Uppsala in 2003, mixing influences from thrash, death, and black metal.
Line-Up Dhraug: Vocals, Nerothos: Guitar, Morigmus: Bass, Sky: Drums *Past Members* Lord Xzar: Guitar
Deathography
Early Morning Slaughter, Demo (2003)
Live at Genomfarten, Live CD (2004)

DIABOLICAL

This guitar solo and melody-obsessed death/thrash band from Sundsvall formed in 1996. Diabolical has faced numerous line-up changes and survived, probably through determination to tour under any conditions. Mörk Gryning's Jonas Berndt and Hectorite's Roger Bergsten have joined for tours. Carlsson is also in the better-known band In Battle.
Line-Up M. Ödling: Vocals, Carl Stjärnlöf: Drums, Vidar W: Guitar/Vocals, H. Carlsson: Guitar, Rickard Persson: Bass *Past Members* H. Carlsson: Guitar, Kim Thalén: Drums, Fredrik Hast: Bass, Jens Blomdal: Bass, L. Söderberg: Drums, Henrik Ohlsson: Drums, Jonas Berndt: Bass (session only, 2001-2002), Roger Bergsten: Bass (session only)
Deathography
Deserts of Desolation, EP (Cadla, 2000)
Synergy, CD (Scarlet, 2001)
A Thousand Deaths, CD (Scarlet, 2002)

DIABOLIQUE

Doomy band started in Gothenburg in 1995, mainly the creation of Kristian Wåhlin, ever-productive founder of Grotesque and Liers in Wait. Österberg previously played in Decollation, and Nilsson has played with Liers in Wait and Dimension Zero. Carlsson was in Seance, and original members Svensson and Erlandsson originate from At the Gates and Eucharist. Wåhlin is also famous for cover artwork under his pseudonym "Necrolord." Despite

the pedigree, their music is totally non-aggressive. Professional of course, but not very metal.
Line-Up Kristian Wåhlin: Vocals/Guitar, Johan Österberg: Guitar, Bino Carlsson: Bass (1996-), Hans Nilsson: Drums (1996-) *Past Members* Daniel Erlandsson: Drums (1995-1996), Alf Svensson: Guitar (1995-1996)
Deathography
The Diabolique, EP (Listenable, 1996)
Wedding the Grotesque, CD (Black Sun, 1997)
The Black Flower, CD (Black Sun, 1999)
Butterflies, EP (Necropolis, 2000)
The Green Goddess, CD (Necropolis, 2001)

DIMENSION ZERO

Hobby band initiated in Gothenburg 1995 by well-known musicians Jocke Göthberg (ex-Marduk, Darkified, Cardinal Sin), Hans Nilsson (ex-Crystal Age, Diabolique, Luciferion, Liers in Wait), Jesper Strömblad (In Flames, ex-Hammerfall), and Glenn Ljungström (ex-In Flames, ex-Hammerfall). Far better than In Flames, far worse than Marduk. Worth checking out anyway.
Line-Up Jocke Göthberg: Vocals, Hans Nilsson: Drums, Jesper Strömblad: Bass, Daniel Antonsson: Guitar (2000-) *Past Members* Fredrik Johansson: Guitar (1996-1998), Glenn Ljungström: Guitar (1996-2003)
Deathography
Screams from the Forest, Demo (1996)
Penetrations from the Lost World, EP (War, 1998)
Silent Night Fever, CD (Regain, 2002)
This is Hell, CD (Regain, 2003)

DIMNESS

Mid-90's black/death from Järfälla.
Line-Up Linus Ekström
Deathography
The Seventh Gate to Infinity, Demo (1996)

DINLOYD—see Megaslaughter

DION FORTUNE

Doom/death band from Jönköping, founded in 1993. I suspect these guys liked Tiamat a lot. Listen to the demo and you will understand. Slow and atmospheric music of decent quality. Holstenson, Sulasalmi, and Hellman all played with Nominon at some point.
Line-Up Mattias Berger: Guitar, Niklas Holstenson: Vocals, Juha Sulasalmi: Guitar, Martin Perdin: Drums, Mattias Andreasson: Bass *Past Members* Tobias Hellman: Bass
Deathography
Tales of Pain, Demo (1993)
Black Ode, Demo (1994)

DIRTY JIHAD

Reportedly some kind of death metal band that started in Örebro during 2001. Their name, along with the band pictures, make me suspect that these guys really haven't understood the concept of death metal—or are they just fucking with us?
Line-Up Ludvig Martell: Drums, Master Taisto

Blomerus: Guitar, Charlotta "Greven" Gredenborn: Bass, Andrej Wicklund: Vocals, Christian Schill: Guitar
Deathography
The War has Begun, Demo (2004)
Second Stage 2005, Demo (2005)

DISENTERMENT
Early-90's black/death metal band from Mora. A decent group that formed in 1992, made one demo, gigged a bit, then split up. Johan Lager was previously in the ultra-classic Grotesque, and later formed the trollish laughfest Arckanum, which also included Sataros for a while.
Line-Up Johan Lager (aka Shamaatae): Drums, Sataros: Bass/Vocals, Basse: Guitar
Deathography
Metapsychosis, Demo (1993)

DISFEAR
Crustcore band launched as Anti-Bofors in 1989. After using the famous Sunlight studio, their sound turned more towards death metal. Whether fat production makes Disfear sound like primitive death metal or super-produced punk is up to you. They were metal enough to convince both Osmose Productions and Relapse to release their albums. The connection to death metal is intensified by Tomas Lindberg (Grotesque, At the Gates), their current singer. Further, Entombed's Uffe Cederlund joined as second guitarist for several shows in 2003—and eventually quit Entombed and joined this band.
Line-Up Björn Pettersson: Guitar, Henke Frykman: Bass, Tomas Lindberg: Vocals, Marcus Andersson: Drums, Ulf Cederlund: Guitar (2003-) Past Members Robin Wiberg: Drums, Jeppe: Vocals, Jallo Lehto: Drums
Deathography
Anti Bofors, 7" (No Records, 1991—as Anti Bofors)
Disfear, 7" (No Records, 1992)
A Brutal Sight of War, CD (Lost and Found, 1993)
Disfear/Uncurbed, Split 7" (Lost N Found, 1995)
Soul Scars, CD (Distortion, 1995)
Everyday Slaughter, CD (Osmose, 1997)
Misanthropic Generation, CD (Relapse, 2002)

DISFIGURED VICTIMS
Death/thrash from Sundsvall which has struggled since starting in 1998, not yet passing the demo stage. Since the line-up includes two percussionists and one guy on didgeridoo (!) you may understand why.
Line-Up Jonny Pettersson: Guitar/Bass/Vocals, John Henriksson: Drums, Olle Groth: Percussion David Mårdstam: Percussion, Ayla Yavazalp: Didgeridoo
Deathography
Fist of Death, Demo (1999)
Theory of Death, Demo (2000)
Inhuman Celebration, Demo (2001)
Blood of the Gods, Demo (2002)
Human Damnation, Demo (2003)

DISGORGE
Obscure Swedish death metal band which I think started in 1992. I know they made one brutal demo, but not much else.
Line-Up Jonas Davidsson: Drums, Fredrik Lakss: Guitar, Martin Petersson: Guitar, Florin Suhoschi: Vocals, Anders Verter: Bass
Deathography
Epousal Bleeding, Demo (1994)

DISGRACE
Short-lived band from Sala which formed and made a demo in 1990. Samuelsson went on with the somewhat longer-lasting Wombbath.
Line-Up Daniel Samuelsson: Vocals, Thomas Mejstedt: Guitar, Sammy Holm: Guitar, Mikael Alm: Bass/Vocals, Thomas Hammarstedt: Drums
Deathography
The Last Sign of Existence, Demo (1990)

DISMEMBER
One of the most typical and best original Swedish death metal bands, Dismember was formed in May 1988 by Robert Sennebäck (vocals/bass), David Blomqvist (guitar), and Fred Estby (drums). The original Dismember only lasted until October 1989, releasing two legendary demos. Estby and Blomqvist (also in Entombed for a while) joined Mike Amott's band Carnage, and Sennebäck started out with Unleashed. But Carnage only lasted one album, after which Estby, Kärki and Blomqvist reformed Dismember in April 1990. Sennebäck soon came back, too, leaving Unleashed. Bassist Robert Cabeza (Carbonized) joined, and Dismember recorded their masterful debut *Like an Ever Flowing Stream*. The band has never come near the same brutal impact, but they have delivered relentless old school death metal over the years. Though a bit inactive at times (we shared rehearsal space with them some years ago, and they were hardly ever there) and undergoing some line-up problems, they are still going strong. At their best, Dismember was the greatest example of classic old school Swedish death metal. They remain the only original band that never lost touch with the original style. Today Dismember, and perhaps the reborn Unleashed, are the only classic bands of the genre that still deliver pure death metal—though some Iron Maiden-esque melodies have infected their music increasingly over the years.
Line-Up David Blomqvist: Guitar, Matti Kärki: Vocals, Martin Persson: Guitar, Tobias Christiansson: Bass (2005-), Tomas Daun, Drums (2007-) Past Members Richard Cabeza: Bass, Sharlee D'Angelo: Bass, Magnus Sahlgren: Guitar, Robert Sennebäck: Vocals/Bass/Guitar, Erik Gustafsson: Bass, Johan Bergebäck: Bass, Fred Estby: Drums (1988-2007)
Deathography
Dismembered, Demo (1988)
Last Blasphemies, Demo (1989)
Rehearsal Demo 1989, Demo (1989)
Reborn in Blasphemy, Demo (1990)
Like an Ever Flowing Stream, LP/CD (Nuclear Blast, 1991)
Skin Her Alive, MCD (Nuclear Blast, 1991)
Pieces, 12"/MCD (Nuclear Blast, 1992)

Indecent and Obscene, CD *(Nuclear Blast, 1993)*
Massive Killing Capacity, CD *(Nuclear Blast, 1995)*
Casket Garden, MCD *(Nuclear Blast, 1995)*
Death Metal, CD *(Nuclear Blast, 1997)*
Misanthropic, MCD *(Nuclear Blast, 1997)*
Hate Campaign, CD *(Nuclear Blast, 2000)*
Where Ironcrosses Grow, CD *(Karmageddon Media, 2004)*
Complete Demos, CD *(Regain, 2005)*
The God that Never Was, CD *(Regain, 2006)*
Dismember, CD *(Regain, 2008)*

DISORGE
1992 band from Umeå, playing standard death metal with porno lyrics. Rather stupid and boring. Later they turned a bit hardcore, the fashion of their hometown.
Line-Up Marcus Johansson: Vocals, Christer Bergqvist: Guitar, Johan Moritz: Drums, Anders Nyberg: Guitar/Keyboards, Fredrik Jakobsson: Bass/Vocals
Deathography
Demo 92, Demo (1992)
Sleeping Prophecies, Demo (1993)
Promo 94, Demo (1994)
Contemporary Oppression, CD (1997)

DISOWNED
Started out playing black/death in Forshaga in the late 90's, first as Bullet Proof, then as Soulless, later as Disowned (I think). Over time they have become pure thrash metal. Most members used to be in Into the Unknown. The name changes have puzzled me when it comes to figuring out the discography—maybe I fucked it up big time.
Line-Up Eric Ekelund: Vocals, Markus Thimberg: Vocals, Daniel Johanson: Guitar, Andreas Norlén: Guitar, Markus Norlén: Drums, Thomas Öberg: Bass *Past Members* Fredrik Sefton: Guitar (2000-2003)
Deathography
Sacrificed Souls, Demo (2000—as Soulless)
Neverending Sorrow, Demo (2002—as Soulless)
Spawn of Evil, Demo (2000)
Soulless, Demo (2002)
Progressive Death, Demo (2004)

DISPATCHED
Dispatched started in tiny Stockholm suburb Gnesta at the very end of 1991. After nothing but trouble with the line-up, they folded in 1995 (as they should, they were not the best band), but founding member Daniel Lundberg reformed the band the next year. As I'm writing this, they are still going, strong or not. Dispatched's first demo is in my opinion one of the very worst death metal demos ever, definitely worth checking out for kicks! Lundberg and Kimberg also edited *Nocuous Zine* in the early 90's.
Line-Up Fredrik Karlsson: Vocals/Keyboards, Emil Larsson: Guitar, Daniel Lundberg: Guitar/Keyboards, Mattias Hellman: Bass, Dennis Nilsson: Drums *Past Members* Krister: Vocals, Fredrik Larsson: Bass, Micke: Guitar (1992), Jonas Kimberg: Bass, Fredrik: Drums (1991-1992), Emanuel Åström: Drums (1992)
Deathography

Dispatched into External, Demo (1992)
Promo 93, Demo (1993)
Promo 2, Demo (1993)
Blue Fire, MCD (Exhumed, 1995)
Promo 1997, Demo (1997)
Motherwar, CD (MFN, 2000)
Terrorizer, CD (Khaosmaster, 2003)

DISPIRITED
Death metal band started in Forshaga 1999.
Line-Up Peter Östlund: Guitar, Erik Gustafsson: Guitar, Fredrik Thörnesson: Bass, Lowe Wikman-Åbom: Drums *Past Members* Pontus Nordqvist: Drums (1999), Mikael Sundin: Bass (1999-2002), Henric Ivarsson: Vocals (1999-2004), Roger Larsson: Drums
Deathography
Suicide Angel, Demo (2000)
Violent Forms of hatred, Demo (2002)

DISRUPTION
Death metal band formed in Ronneby in 1999. Their demos didn't impress me, but they might have improved. Jonas is also in the extremely technical band Spawn of Possession.
Line-Up Danny: Bass, Jonas: Vocals, Jonte: Drums, Mike: Guitar, Pete: Guitar *Past Members* Tom Persson: Guitar (1999-2001)
Deathography
A Soul Full of Hate, Demo (1999)
Bitch on the Cross, Demo (2000)
Behind the Trigger, Demo (2001)
Get Down-Reload-Attack, Demo (2002)
Promo, Demo (2003)
Face the Wall, CD (Copro, 2005)

DISSECTION
The mighty Dissection was created in February 1990 in Strömstad by Jon Nödtveidt (ex-Rabbit's Carrot, later in Ophthalamia, The Black) and Peter Palmdahl. Their first song, "Inhumanity Deformed," was Napalm Death-inspired grind, but they soon developed their own melancholic and atmospheric death metal style. Dissection is one of the most original bands from Sweden, and their uniqueness attracted both the black metal and death metal audiences of the mid-90's. Just as they were about to take on the world, everything came to a halt in late 1997. Nödtveidt was accused and later imprisoned for assisting a murder. A personal and musical loss, for everyone involved. After Nödtveidt was released in 2003, he created a new version of the band. After extensive touring over Europe and a new album, Jon decided to cancel it all for good in the summer of 2006. Shortly after, he shot his brains out in his apartment and effectively ended Dissection's macabre career forever. In their prime, Dissection was one of the best Swedish bands ever.
Line-Up Jon Nödtveidt: Vocals/Guitar, Set Teitan: Guitar, Haakon Forwald: Bass, Tomas Asklund: Drums *Past Members* Erik Danielsson: Bass (session only), Peter Palmdahl: Bass (1989-1997), Johan Norman: Guitar (1994-1997), John Zwetsloot:

Guitar (1991-1994), Tobias Kjellgren: Drums (1995-1997), Ole Öhman: Drums (1990-1995), Mattias Johansson: Guitar (session only 1990-1991), Emil Nödtveidt: Bass (session only 1997), Brice Leclerc: Bass (2004-2005), Bård Eitun: Drums
Deathography
Rehearsal (1990)
The Grief Prophecy, Demo (1990)
Into Infinite Obscurity, 7" (Corpsegrinder, 1990)
The Somberlain, Promo (1992)
Promo 93, Demo (1993)
The Somberlain, CD (No Fashion, 1993)
Storm of the Light's Bane, CD (Nuclear Blast, 1995)
Where Dead Angels Lie, EP (Nuclear Blast, 1996)
The Past is Alive (The Early Mischief), CD (Necropolis, 1996)
Live Legacy, CD (Nuclear Blast, 2003)
Maha Kali, Single (Nuclear Blast, 2004)
Reinkaos, CD (Nuclear Blast, 2006)

DISSECTUM—see The Shattered

DISSOLVED
Melodic death (well, not very) metal from Gällivare. This mid-90's band might have been a joke, if you ever see the cover of their demo you will understand why.
Line-Up Mats Ömalm
Deathography
Bä, Demo (1997)

DIVINE
Black/death metal act began in Gothenburg, 2001.
Line-Up Mikael Klaening: Bass, Edvard Höcke: Guitar, Patrik Berglund: Guitar, Christian Bronewicz: Keyboards, Fredrik Fällström: Drums, Emil Wallberg: Vocals *Past Members* Thomas van Loo: Drums, Johan Harald: Drums, Jonathan Ängdahl: Guitar, Kasper Lörne: Guitar
Deathography
Divine, Demo (2005)

DIVINE SIN
Thrash/death act from Söderhamn that began in 1990. Originally raw and technical, they soon mellowed into power metal territory. The vocals remind me of King Diamond, which of course is cool. But there is just one king. Lundberg has also been active in Lefay.
Line-Up Fredrik Lundberg: Vocals, Micke Andersson: Guitar, Martin Unoson: Guitar, Martin Knutar: Drums, Bobby Goude: Bass *Past Members* Peter Halvarsson: Guitar
Deathography
Dying to Live, Demo (1990)
Years of Sorrow, Demo (1991)
Resurrection (1993)
Winterland, CD (Black Mark, 1995)
Thirteen Souls, CD (Black Mark, 1997)

DIVINE SOULS
Melodic death metal, formed in Kramfors in 1997. After a row of demos and two CDs it was all over in 2004, as main man Mikael Lindgren got fed up.

Line-Up Stefan Högberg: Guitar, Mattias Lilja: Vocals, Daniel Sjölund: Drums *Past Members* Daniel Lindgren: Bass, Mikael Lindgren: Guitar
Deathography
Demo 97, Demo (1997)
Astraea, Demo (1998)
Devil's Fortress, Demo (1999)
Perished, Demo (2000)
Erase the Burden, Demo (2000)
Embodiment, CD (Scarlet, 2001)
The Bitter Self Caged Man, CD (Scarlet, 2002)

DOG FACED GODS
Formed by Ebony Tears members Wranning and Jonsson in 1997, all the other members of Ebony Tears were soon also involved. More thrash than death metal, and not so special even if well-played.
Line-Up Conny Jonsson: Guitar, Peter Tuthill: Bass, Richard Evensand: Drums *Past Members* Johnny Wranning: Vocals, Peter Kahm: Bass, Iman Zolgharnian: Drums
Deathography
Demo 1997, Demo (1997)
Random Chaos Theory in Action, CD (GNW, 1998)
Demo 1999, Demo (1999)
Demo 2000, Demo (2000)

DOMINION CALIGULA
Basically Mats Broberg from Dark Funeral, backed by Vicious Art. The project was initiated in 1998, and as with most projects, it is hard to tell if they will ever produce anything more than their one CD. The music is okay, but surprisingly melodic and slow.
Line-Up Lars Johansson: Guitar, Matti Mäkelä (Dominion): Guitar, Joakim Widfeldt: Bass, Masse Broberg (Emperor Magus Caligula): Vocals, Robert Lundin (Gaahnfaust): Drums
Deathography
A New Era Rises, CD (No Fashion, 2000)

DOMINUS—see Carcaroht

DORMITORY
Death metal band formed in Helsingborg during 1993. They never had much impact, and eventually changed their name to Ripstich.
Line-Up Stefan Asanin: Bass/Vocals, Jesper Leidbring: Drums, Armin Pendek: Guitar/Vocals, Björn Svensson: Guitar/Vocals
Deathography
Amend (Demo 3), Demo (1996)

DRACENA
All-female heavy/death Gothenburg group begun in 1994. Not very deadly—or good for that matter.
Line-Up Mia: Vocals, Lotta: Guitar, Åsa: Bass, Mojjo: Drums *Past Members* Emma Karlsson: Guitar
Deathography
Demo 97, Demo (1997)
Demonic Women, Demo (1999)
Demonic Women, 7" (Bloodstone Entertainment,

1999)
Labyrinth of Darkness, Demo (2001)
Infernal Damnation, CD (Hellbound Recs., 2004)

DRACONIAN

Melodic death/goth/doom act formed as Kerberos in Sattle in 1994. After a few months, the name changed to Draconian, and their gloomy mission began. Actually quite a good band, resembling a deadlier My Dying Bride.
Line-Up Anders Jacobsson: Vocals, Lisa Johansson: Vocals, Daniel Arvidsson: Guitar, Johan Ericson: Guitar/Vocals (initially drums), Jesper Stolpe: Bass/Vocals, Andreas Karlsson: Keyboards, Jerry Torstensson: Drums **Past Members** Andy Hindenäs: Guitar (1994-2000), Susanne Arvidsson: Vocals/ Keyboards (1995-2000), Magnus Bergström: Guitar
Deathography
Shades of a Lost Moon, Demo (1996)
In Glorious Victory, Demo (1997)
The Closed Eyes of Paradise, Demo (1999)
Frozen Features, EP (2000)
Dark Oceans We Cry, Demo (2002)
Where Lovers Mourn, CD (Napalm, 2003)
Arcane Rain Fell, CD (Napalm, 2005)

DRAIND OF EMPATHY

Recently-launched death metal band from Falun. So far they have made one demo.
Line-Up Fredrik Råsäter, Samuel Ahnberg, David Janstaff, Patrik Blomström
Deathography
Under a Blackened Sky, Demo (2004)

THE DUSKFALL

Started as Soulash in the frozen town Luleå in 1999, after one demo the name changed to The Duskfall. They got a bit of success playing melodic death metal. Their commercial style eventually led to a deal with Nuclear Blast. Mikael, Oskar, and Urban are all ex-Gates of Ishtar.
Line-Up Kai Jaakola: Vocals, Mikael Sandorf: Guitar, Oskar Karlsson: Drums, Antti Lindholm: Guitar, Marco Eronen: Bass **Past Members** Joachim Lindbäck: Guitar, Glenn Svensson: Guitar, Pär Johansson: Vocals, Jonny Ahlgren: Guitar, Tommi Konu: Bass, Urban Carlsson: Drums, Kaj Molin: Bass
Deathography
Tears are Soulash, Demo (2000—as Soulash)
Deliverance, Demo (2001)
Frailty, CD (Black Lotus, 2002)
Source, CD (Black Lotus, 2003)
Lifetime Supply of Guilt, CD (Nuclear Blast, 2005)

DYSENTERY

Linus Åkerlund started this one-man band in Alunda outside Uppsala back in 1989, playing ultra-primitive and doomy metal. He could barely play in the beginning, some of the songs just sound like jokes. Soon, inspired by the new trend, he converted to black metal. The name was changed to Azhubham Haani to fit the new style. "Sadly," the band disappeared when sole member Åkerlund got sentenced to four years in prison after stabbing a man repeatedly in the throat after a drunken party in Finspång with some guys from Abruptum and Dissection (reportedly Åkerlund was sober, though).
Line-Up Linus Åkerlund: Everything
Deathography
Black Fucking Metal, Demo (1991)
Crawling in Blood, Demo (1991)
Rehearsal-92, Rehearsal (1992)
De Vermis Mysteriis/Azhubham Haani, Split (1992 —as Azhubham Haani)
On a Snowy Winternight, Demo (1992—as Azhubham Haani)
Total Evil, Demo (1992—as Azhubham Haani)
Rehearsal 20/09/1992, Demo (1992—as Azhubham Haani)

DYSPLASIA

Death/thrash band that started out in Tyresö in 2003. Kristoffer Hell is also in Sanctfication.
Line-Up Kristoffer Hell: Bass/Vocals, Fredrik Jansson: Guitar, Andreas Kender: Drums
Deathography
Subconscious Voices of Anger, Demo (2004)

EBONY TEARS

Melodic thrash/death band that began in Stockholm in 1996. After three records they split up, but all the members continued in Dog Faced Gods.
Line-Up Richard Evensand: Drums, Conny Jonsson: Guitar, Peter Kahm: Bass, Johnny Wranning: Vocals **Past Members** Thomas Thun: Bass, Iman Zolgharnian: Drums
Deathography
Demo, Demo (1996)
Tortura Insomniae, CD (Black Sun, 1997)
A Handful of Nothing, CD (Black Sun, 1999)
Evil as Hell, CD (Black Sun, 2001)

ECTOMIA

Started in 1997, made two demos, disappeared.
Deathography
Feasting on Human Skulls, Demo (1998)
Penetrating into Euphoria, Demo (2000)

EDGE OF SANITY

Edge of Sanity is the main vehicle of one of the most important persons of the Swedish death metal scene, Dan Swanö. He is also well-known for his studio Gorysound/Unisound, plus loads of other bands including Pan-Thy-Monium, Unicorn, Nightingale, Bloodbath, etc. Edge of Sanity kicked off in Finspång in September 1989, and soon attracted attention from labels and listeners with melancholic, intense and catchy death metal. Together with Swanö's powerful voice and Larsson's incredibly tight drumming, this proved a winning recipe. After signing to Black Mark in 1990, the band released an impressive 7 records in the 6 years between 1991-97. After the initial style of traditional death metal (best heard on *Unorthodox*), Swanö gradually forged the band to explore more symphonic and bizarre structures. The most striking result is *Crimson*, which contains just one song...over 40 minutes long! After Swanö's departure in 1997, the band quickly faded. This could have been one of the biggest death metal bands in the world if they landed a label that pushed them a little more. Swanö should probably also have laid down his other projects to focus on the real deal—like guitarist Axelsson did when he quit as singer for Marduk. As irony would have it, Marduk turned out far more successful in the end. Swanö will apparently continue Edge of Sanity as a solo project now. It's a strange world...

Line-Up Dan Swanö: Vocals (1989-1997), Everything: (2003-) *Past Members* Andreas Axelsson: Guitar (1989-2000), Sami Norberg: Guitar (1989-2000), Benny Larsson: Drums (1989-2000), Anders Lundberg: Bass (1989-2000), Robert Karlsson: Vocals (1997-2000)

Deathography
Euthanasia, Demo (1989)
Immortal Souls, Rehearsal (1989)
Kur-Nu-Gi-A, Demo (1990)
The Dead, Demo (1990)
The Immortal Rehearsals, Demo (1990)
Nothing but Death Remains, CD (Black Mark, 1991)
Unorthodox, CD (Black Mark, 1992)
The Spectral Sorrows, CD (Black Mark, 1993)
Until Eternity Ends, MCD (Black Mark, 1994)
Sacrificed, Promo MCD (Black Mark, 1994)
Purgatory Afterglow, CD (Black Mark, 1994)
Crimson, CD (Black Mark, 1996)
Infernal, CD (Black Mark, 1996)
Cryptic, CD (Black Mark, 1997)
Evolution, CD (Black Mark, 2000)
Infernal Demos, Demo (2003)
Crimson II, CD (Black Mark, 2003)

EDICIUS
Södertälje band apparently active in the mid-90's. All I know is their 1994 demo, a 4-track porta-recording—this was a short-lived combo.

Line-Up Havila: Vocals, Björn Glasare: Guitar, Andreas Sollen: Guitar, Johan Lag: Bass, Mattias Johansson: Drums

Deathography
Pleasant Pain, Demo (1994)

EGREGORI
Black/death metal duo from Sundsvall active in 1993 and 1994. The project was cancelled when both members joined Setherial.

Line-Up Kraath: Vocals, Thorn: Bass

Deathography
Angel of the Black Abyss, Demo (1994)

EIDOMANTUM
Black/death metal formed in Linköping in 1998 from the ashes of pure black metal act Lukemborg. The vocalist's pseudonym must be one of the most ridiculous ever, second only to "Ace Gestapo Necrosleazer and Vaginal Commands" of Blasphemy. The CD compiles their old recordings.

Line-Up Sexual Death: Vocals, S:t Erben:

Guitar/Bass, Ace Tormenta: Drums/Guitar

Deathography
From the Tomb of All Evil, Demo (2000)
The Death, EP (Sombre, 2001)
Old Blood, Demo (2003)
At War with Eidomantum, CD (Witchammer Records, 2004)

ELOHIM
Formed 2001, absolutely standard melodic Gothenburg-sound death metal that only makes me long for pure brutal death metal...

Line-Up Joakim Karlsson: Vocals/Guitar, Martin Svensson: Guitar, Johan Hermansson: Guitar, Henrik Green: Bass, Tommy Magnusson: Drums, Kim Petersson: Keyboards

Deathography
Yet Unnamed, Demo (2002)
Modest Memoirs, Demo (2003)
Modest Epilogue, Demo (2003)

EMBALMED
One of the first death metal bands from Uppsala, these guys started in autumn 1989 as Necrotism. After line-up changes, they became Embalmed in March 1990. Their style sure was brutal, but they never gained wide attention. Fredrik Wallenberg went on to greater things with Sarcasm, and later the highly successful crust punk band Skitsystem (with ex-At the Gates singer Tomas Lindberg). Stefan Petterson also went on to a crust career in Diskonto and Uncurbed. Embalmed was also the first band of Matte Modin, later of Defleshed, Dark Funeral, and Sportlov (with Petterson).

Line-Up Peter Åhke: Bass, Fredrik Wallenberg: Guitar, Stefan Petterson: Vocals, Matte Modin: Drums

Deathography
Decomposed Desires, Demo (1990)

EMBRACED
Standard black/death. Julius C. later started melodic black/death band Misteltein. Håkansson and Karlsson later joined the awful Evergray, but Karlsson soon quit to join the better Soilwork. *Amorous Anathema* is a re-release of their demo. The band split in 2000, but reportedly started playing again in 2004.

Line-Up Kalle Johansen: Vocals, Michael Håkansson: Vocals/Bass, Davor Tepic: Guitar, Peter Mardklint: Guitar, Julius Chmielewski: Keyboards, Tomas Lejon: Drums *Past Members* Andreas Albin: Drums, Daniel Lindberg: Drums, Sven Karlsson: Keyboards (-2000)

Deathography
A Journey into Melancholy, Demo (1997)
Within, CD (Regain, 2000)
Amorous Anathema, CD (Regain, 2000)

EMBRACING
Mid-90's band from Holmsund who produced melodic death metal. Started in 1993 under the name Beyond (and later Mishrak), they eventually transformed into Embracing. Initially pure death metal, they soon mellowed a lot. Decent, but no real thrills. The lyrics are about magic and heroes—you really need to hear

them to believe it! "Hero Metal"? Adolescents, they never stop. Holmgren is ex-Naglfar. Westerlund left to concentrate on Auberon. Member turbulence is the style of the underground! The band made a couple CDs in the late 90's, then went straight back to demos.
Line-Up *Ronnie Björnström: Guitar, Matthias Holmgren: Vocals/Drums/Keyboards, Mikael Widlöf: Bass, Ulph Johansson: Guitar* **Past Members** *Ola Andersson: Bass, Markus Lindström: Guitar/Bass, Peter Lundberg: Bass, Rickard Magnusson: Guitar, André Nylund: Guitar/Bass, Henrik Nygren: Vocals, Johan Westerlund: Guitar, Nicklas Holmgren: Drums*
Deathography
Of Beauty Found in Deep Caverns, Demo (1993— as Mishrak)
Winterburn, Demo (1996)
I Bear the Burden of Time, CD (Invasion, 1996)
Dreams Left Behind, CD (Invasion, 1998)
Inside You, Demo (1998)
Rift, Demo (1999)
The Dragon Reborn, Demo (2003)

EMBRYO
Death metal band from Strängnäs that started in 1989 as Tantalize, but soon changed that awful name to Embryo. Pretty intense, but oh-so-bad. Their demo must be one of the worst releases during the early phase of Swedish death metal. Luckily they stopped after that. Matthias Borgh joined the mighty Crypt of Kerberos. Odd and Peter formed Harmony (that later became Torment, and still later Maze of Torment), and Jocke started Xenophanes. All these bands are far superior to Embryo.
Line-Up *Matthias Borgh: Drums, Peter: Bass, Odd: Vocals (initially also Bass), Jocke Hasth: Guitar* **Past Members** *Olle: Bass, Znorre: Vocals, Chrille: Vocals*
Deathography
Damnatory Cacophony, Demo (1991)

ENCINED
Apparently started in 1990, and made two demos in 1991. Honestly, that's all I know about them!
Deathography
Funeral Rites, Demo (1991)
Midian, Demo (1991)

END
Mid-90's death metal from Lund, split in 1997 when Westesson and Ahlgren formed Pandemonium.
Line-Up *David Tanentzapf: Vocals, Jonas Helgertz: Drums, Oskar Westesson: Guitar, Thomas Ahlgren: Guitar, Ulf Nordström: Bass*

THE END
Varberg act started in 1994, stayed together long enough to make one EP. All the members used to play in Eucharist, so you should be able to guess what it sounds like.
Line-Up *Matti Almsenius: Guitar, Tobias Gustafsson: Bass/Vocals, Daniel Erlandsson: Drums*
Deathography

The End, EP (House of Kicks, 1996)

ENEMY IS US
One of countless death/thrash bands that flooded the market after The Haunted. This one formed in Uppsala around 2000. Mackrory is ex-Darkane and has also played in Sportlov and F.K.Ü.
Line-Up *Ronnie Nyman: Vocals, Staffan Winroth: Guitar, Peter Lindholm: Guitar, Lawrence Mackrory: Bass, Magnus Ingels: Drums*
Deathography
Ashes of the World, Demo (2003)
We Have Seen the Enemy... And the Enemy is Us, CD (Rising Realm Records, 2004)

ENGRAVED
Mid-90's death metal, made two demos in 1994.
Deathography
Before the Tales, Demo (1994)
Promo '94, Demo (1994)

ENIGMATIC
Originally named Limited Knowledge, death-tinged doom metal from the mid-90's who haunted Bollnäs —a small and worthless town, what did you think?
Line-Up *Tommie Ericsson: Bass, Peter Jonsson: Guitar, Stefan Karlsson: Vocals/Guitar, Magnus Lövgren: Drums, Per Ryberg: Guitar*
Deathography
Two Days of April, EP (LR, 1993)
Demo 94 (1994)
The Tranquilled Icy Water, MCD (LR, 1996)

ENSEMBLE NOCTURNE
Melodic death metal from Hedared, they made one demo in 1995 and then disappeared.
Line-Up *Mats Lyborg: Vocals/Guitar, Edvard Gustafsson: Guitar/Keyboards, Kristian Benia: Bass, Martin Johansson: Drums/Percussion*
Deathography
Crimson Sky, Demo (1995)

ENSHRINED
Malmö band formed in 2002. Nauclér is ex-Misteltein and Cirera is ex-Ominous.
Line-Up *Anders Nauclér: Bass/Vocals, Dejan Milenkovits: Guitar/Vocals, Thomas Frisk: Guitar, Joël Cirera: Drums*
Deathography
Abyssimal, Demo (2003)
Spawn of Apathy, Demo (2005)

ENTANGLED—see Regurgitate (Avesta)

ENTHRALLED
Vänersborg band started in 1996. Though they never crawled out of a demo tape phase, this is good thrashy music with touches of U.S. death metal. Nielsen is also in Lord Belial. Peterson and Norén are ex-Impious.
Line-Up *Robert Gréen: Vocals, Hjalmar Nielsen: Guitar/Vocals, Hannes Berggren: Guitar, Erik Peterson: Bass* **Past Members** *Martin Restin: Drums (1996-1999), Mikael Norén: Drums (2000-2003)*

Deathography
First Chapter, Demo (1996)
Forever Gone, Demo (1997)
Accession, Demo (1998)
Death is Breeding, Demo (2001)
Anthropomorphous, Demo (2002)

ENTHRONE—see Teatre

ENTITY
Falkenberg band created by Tomas Gustafsson in April 1991. He aimed to produce dark and sad doom metal, but seemed too preoccupied with finding new members. The band never had any impact. Gustafsson was also editor of *Falken Zine*. Oh!—this band promoted the fact that they didn't use distortion on their guitars!
Line-Up Danne Persson: Vocals (1993-), Jimmy Svensson: Guitar (1992-), Tomas Gustafsson: Bass/Keyboards, Tomas Hedlund: Drums (1993-), Ola Hugosson: Keyboards (1993-), Bass (1992) *Past Members* Chris Wallin: Vocals (1992), Jeppe: Drums (1992-1993)
Deathography
The Sad Fate, Rehearsal (1993)
The, Demo (1993)
Demo #1 1994, Demo (1994)
The Lasting Scar, 7" (Megagrind, 1994)
The Payment, 7" (Megagrind, 1995)

ENTOMBED
What more can I possibly say about Entombed? Probably the most influential and important Swedish death metal band, they are also one of the best bands of any kind Sweden has ever offered. Entombed was born of the band Nihilist in Skärholmen back in 1989. The band took over the deal intended for Nihilist by Earache, went into the Sunlight studio, and delivered the goods. The debut *Left Hand Path* set new standards for death metal. Never before (or since...?) have crushing guitars, raw vocals, catchy songs, and incredible drumming combined in a more devastating way. This is the real deal! After the masterful debut, Entombed developed death metal into more traditional rock structures, always creating something fresh and wonderful—except for the somewhat weak *Same Difference* following founder Nicke Andersson's departure. Entombed has also sorted out dramatic line-up turbulence. After early problems around L.G. Petrov were solved, he has constantly been the singer. Further, Rosenberg was successfully replaced by Jörgen Sandström (ex-Grave), when he left to focus on Therion in 1995. Sandström was later replaced with Nico from Terra Firma. Most difficult was replacing founding member and main songwriter Nicke Andersson who quit in 1997 to focus on his successful punk/rock group The Hellacopters. Peter Stjärnvind (Merciless, Unanimated) has gradually filled Nicke's extremely large shoes in style. Recently Entombed faced yet another crisis, as founding member Uffe Cederlund decided to leave. Things got even worse as Stjärnvind left in May 2006, but the others carry on with a new drummer as a four piece. During 1989-1994, Entombed was one of the best bands in the world.
Line-Up Alex Hellid: Guitar, L.G. Petrov: Vocals (1989-1991, 1992-), Nico Elgstrand: Bass (2004-), Olle Dahlstedt: Drums (2006-) *Past Members* Peter Stjärnvind: Drums (1997-2006), Uffe Cederlund: Guitar (1989-2005), Nicke Andersson: Drums (1989-1997), Jörgen Sandström: Bass (1995-2004), Lars Rosenberg: Bass (1990-1995), Orvar Säfström: Vocals (1991, session only), Johnny Dordevic: Vocals (1991-1992), David Blomqvist: Bass (1989)
Deathography
But Life Goes On, Demo (1989)
Left Hand Path, LP (Earache, 1990)
Crawl, 12" (Earache, 1991)
Clandestine, LP (Earache, 1991)
Stranger Aeons, 12" (Earache, 1992)
Hollowman, EP (Earache, 1993)
Wolverine Blues, LP/CD (Earache, 1993)
State of Emergency, Entombed/Teddybears/Doll Squad Split 7" (King Kong, 1993)
Out of Hand, EP (Earache, 1994)
Night of the Vampire, Entombed/New Bomb Turks Split 7" (Earache, 1995)
To Ride, Shoot Straight and Speak the Truth, LP/CD (Music for Nations, 1997)
Wreckage, EP (Earache, 1997)
Same Difference, CD (1998)
Monkey Puss—Live in London, CD (Earache, 1999)
Black Juju EP, EP (Man's Ruin, 1999)
Uprising, CD (Metal Is, 2000)
Morning Star, CD (Music For Nations, 2001)
Inferno CD (Music For Nations, 2003)
Unreal Estate, Live CD (Plastic Head, 2005)

ENTRAILS
An early band from the minor death metal center Avesta. They did one demo, and a few memorable gigs. (Joel must be one of the sloppiest, most exciting drummers ever, watching him play was a spectacle!) Mabbe went on to Fulmination, Henka went to Uncurbed. Sohlström briefly ran the small label Sunable, releasing a Crypt of Kerberos 7".
Line-Up Joel: Drums, Mabbe: Bass, Henka: Vocals, Stefan Sohlström: Guitar, Leif Forsell: Guitar
Deathography
Rehearsal, Demo (1991)

ENVILED
2000's retro death metal from Bollnäs that sounds a lot like old Crematory, which can't fail! They should grind more, though, to obtain even greater power.
Line-Up Anders Ljung
Deathography
Malevolent Execution, Demo (2002)

EPHEMERAL
Melodic black/death. From Lindesberg. Mid-90's. Does that sound interesting? It isn't. Kanto has also played with the much better Relentless.
Line-Up Robert Kanto
Deathography

...As Life Ends, Demo (1996)
Awaiting the Winter Frost, Demo (1997)

EPIDEMIC—see Altar

EPITAPH (Sollentuna)
Death metal from Sollentuna, formed in summer 1989 by a trio of 15-year old metalheads, and originally called Dark Abbey. They produced strange music somewhat similar to Disharmonic Orchestra. Early gigs happened with well-known bands like Grave, Therion, and Desultory. Don't mistake this band for the dreadful thrash/doom band from Västerås.
Line-Up Manne Svensson: Guitar, Nicke Hagen: Guitar/Bass, Johan Enochsson: Drums/Vocals
Deathography
Blasphemy, Demo (1990—as Dark Abbey)
Disorientation, Demo (1991)
Epitaph/Excruciate, Split LP (Infest, 1991)
Seeming Salvation, LP (Thrash, 1993)

EPITAPH (Västerås)
A late 90's band from Västerås dreadfully attempting some kind of doomy metal. The vocals are among the worst I have ever heard. Their pseudonyms make me think these guys were not very coordinated.
Line-Up Magnus "The Oak": Vocals/Guitar, Carl "HYB": Bass, Johan "Keso" Burman: Drums, Peter "Satan": Guitar/Vocals
Deathography
Demo, Demo (1990)

ERODEAD
A new groovy death band from Norrköping. The future will tell if they last.
Line-Up Jake: Vocals, Jocke: Guitar, Vladi: Guitar, Rogga: Bass, Gadde: Drums
Deathography
Demo #1, Demo (2005)

EROTTICA
Death metal from Ljungby, begun in 1999. Charming band name, huh?
Line-Up David Gabrielsson: Vocals, Torgny Johansson: Guitar, Henrik Petersson: Drums, Torbjörn Skogh: Bass
Deathography
Erottica, Demo (1999)
Inside a Blackened Heart, Demo (2001)
Erotticism, CD (Swedmetal Records, 2005)

ERUCTATION
Thrash/death act from Alafors formed in 1988, initially under a bunch of other names such as Neon Death and Anathema. The music contains some hints at Morbid Angel, but is pretty poorly performed.
Line-Up Tobias Sannerstig: Drums, Mattias Stenborg: Guitar, Anders Melander: Vocals (1989-), Tobias Karlsson: Bass (1990-) *Past Members* Daniel: Bass (1988-1990)
Deathography
Day of Confusion, Demo (1992)
Demo (1993)

ERUPTION—see Opeth

ETERNAL AUTUMN
Metallic black/death metal act started in 1993 in Töreboda/Mariestad; mainly a solo project of guitarist/vocalist John. Not very impressive. Try to imagine Manowar playing black metal and you'll have an inkling how this sounds. Folded in 2001.
Line-Up John Carlson: Vocals/Guitar, Thomas Ahlgren: Guitar, Sami Nieminen: Bass, Ola Sundström: Drums *Past Members* Daniel: Vocals, Tobias Vipeklev: Bass, Andreas Tullson: Drums
Deathography
Demo 1, Demo (1994)
Promo 96, Demo (1996)
Moonscape, Demo (1996)
The Storm, CD (Black Diamond, 1998)
From the Eastern Forest, CD (Head Mechanic, 2000)

ETERNAL DARKNESS
Started in Eskilstuna in 1990 as Necropsy, but soon settled for Eternal Darkness. Slow, crushing death metal, like a deadly Candlemass with ultra-brutal vocals. Things started well; they played gigs with Impaled Nazarene in Finland. After that, Eternal Darkness disappeared. Shamefully, their album was never released. The band deserved much more attention. Markus later formed early black metal band The Black with Jon Nödtveidt (Dissection), and Jonas played with the excellent Crypt of Kerberos. Jarmo Kuurola was killed in 1995—rest in peace.
Line-Up Danne: Guitar, Manner: Guitar, Tero Viljanen: Bass, Markus Pesonen: Drums, Janne: Vocals *Past Members* Jarmo Kuurola: Guitar, Jonas Strandell: Guitar
Deathography
Demo 1, Demo (1991)
Suffering, Demo (1991)
Doomed, 7" (Distorted Harmony, 1992)
Twilight in the Wilderness (Unreleased CD, 1993)

ETERNAL GRIEF—see Cipher System

ETERNAL LIES
Melodic death metal, formed in Varberg in 1998. Musically a bit similar to Eucharist, which comes as no surprise since original member Martin used to play with them. Most of the members also play in Trendkill. Conny can also be found in Anata.
Line-Up Björn Johansson: Guitar, Conny Pettersson: Drums, Erik Månsson: Bass, Marcus Wesslén: Bass *Past Members* Tommy Grönberg: Vocals, Martin Karlsson: Bass
Deathography
Demo, Demo (2000)
Spiritual Deception, CD (Arctic Music Group, 2002)

ETERNAL MIND
Mid-90's death metal from Gothenburg. Don't run yet, this is not your average melodic At the Gates rip-off! In fact, their approach is more old school, containing some doomy parts à la Paradise Lost.

Deathography
Demo 1 (1995)
Season of the Frozen, Demo (1996)

ETERNAL OATH
Symphonic death metal begun in Stockholm in 1991. Melodic and catchy, but not very interesting. Peter Nagy has also played with Hypocrite and Mörk Gryning. Ted Lundström is now in Amon Amarth.
Line-Up Joni Mäensivu: Vocals, Peter Nagy: Guitar, Petri Tarvainen: Guitar, Stefan Norgren: Keyboard, Peter Wendin: Bass, Ted Jonsson: Drums Past Members Pelle Almquist: Keyboard, Ted Lundström: Bass (1991-1993), Daniel Dziuba: Guitar (1991-1993), Martin Wiklander: Bass (1993-1996)
Deathography
Art of Darkness, Demo (1994)
So Silent, MCD (Wrapped Media, 1996)
Promo 97, Demo (1997)
Through the Eyes of Hatred, CD (Pulverised, 2000)
Righteous, CD (Greater Art, 2002)
Wither, CD (Black Lodge, 2005)

ETERNAL TORMENTOR
Hilarious and maybe 100% unserious Uppsala band formed as early as 1988. Their song titles tell the story: "Il Sadico Dentistico," "Schweinehund," and "Have a Nice Death." Their contact address was care of "Satanic Brotherhood of ET". The music? I don't know, I've never heard them. But they've been described as "U.S. grindcore," "noise," or simply just crap. So I guess it's good!
Line-Up Stefan Pettersson: Vocals, Patric Nadalutti, Johan Olausson, Tobias Petterson
Deathography
E.T is not a Nice Guy, Demo (1988)
Even Never and Definitely More Fucking Demo/E.T Lost in the Land of Shadows & Extreme Distortion, Demo (1991)

ETHEREAL
A death metal band that formed in 2001.
Line-Up Mikael Åkerström: Vocals/Guitar, Simon Exner: Guitar, Alexander Persson: Bass, Martin Latvala: Drums
Deathography
Diseased Existence, Demo (2004)
Vol 2: Another Failure, Demo (2005)

ETHNOCIDE
Early-90's death/thrash from Huddinge. Pretty good stuff.
Line-Up Staffan Skoglund
Deathography
Tearful, Demo (1993)

EUCHARIST
Pioneers in combining death metal and melody, Eucharist are one of the inventors of the "Gothenburg sound." They started summer 1989 in Veddinge near Gothenburg. The initial years saw some line-up turbulence. The guys were about 14 years old, so I guess the band wasn't very serious. They released their great first demo in 1992, but split up during the recording of their first album due to personal disagreements. Though they started up again some years later, it was too late for them at that point. Daniel Erlandsson (brother of Adrian, drummer of At the Gates/The Haunted/Cradle of Filth) went on to join the more successful Arch Enemy, In Flames, Liers in Wait, and Diabolique. Eucharist never gained the recognition they rightly deserved. Together with Dissection and At the Gates they are the only brilliant bands in the "Gothenburg style." Hailed in the underground, they were just everywhere back in the early 90's. This band could have become big if they got it together, as they were much better than the likes of In Flames and Dark Tranquillity.
Line-Up Daniel Erlandsson: Drums, Markus Johansson: Vocals/Guitar, Henrik Meijner: Guitar Past Members Thomas Einarsson: Guitar, Tobias Gustafsson: Bass, Matti Almsenius: Guitar, Martin Karlsson: Bass, Niklas Gustafsson: Vocals/Bass
Deathography
Rehearsal (1991)
Demo 1, Demo (1992)
Greeting Immortality, 7" (Obscure Plasma, 1993)
A Velvet Creation, Demo (1993)
A Velvet Creation, CD (Wrong Again, 1993)
Mirror Worlds, CD (War, 1998)

EUPHORIA
From Uppsala—that's all I know!
Deathography
Demo 1997, Demo (1997)

EVENTIDE
Another one of those melodic death metal bands.
Line-Up Jacob Magnusson: Vocals/Guitar, Max Seppälä: Drums/Percussion, Jonas Sjölin: Guitar, Andreas Kronqvist: Keyboards, Niclas Linde: Bass Past Members Åke Wallebom: Guitar
Deathography
Caress the Abstract, Demo (1999)
Promo 2000, Demo (2000)
No Place Darker, Demo (2005)

THE EVERDAWN
Black/death from Luleå created by Oskar Karlsson and Niclas Svensson from Gates of Ishtar in 1993. Released an EP and a CD, but I've heard nothing since. They were mediocre, so I hope they split up.
Line-Up Pierre Törnkvist: Vocals/Guitar/Bass, Patrik Törnkvist: Guitar, Niklas Svensson: Bass, Oskar Karlsson: Drums
Deathography
Opera of the Damned EP, EP (Black Diamond, 1996)
Poems—Burn the Past, CD (Invasion, 1997)

EVOCATION
This Borås outfit is a great Swedish death metal band that never made it. They started in Sept. 1991 out of the ashes of Morbid Death, Harrassmentation, Forsaken Grief, and Decomposed. From the start they delivered high class Sunlight death to the bone!

They may have been a little late with their classic death metal as black metal swept over the country, but I assure you Evocation can crush almost any black metal band any day! Great stuff! Saarinen and Josefsson were also in Cemetary, and Wacker and Karvola started crust punk band Raioitus in 1993 Apparently Evocation is playing again recently, and their demos have been released on CD. Get it!
Line-Up Thomas Josefsson: Vocals (initially bass), Vesa Kenttäkumpu: Guitar, Janne Kenttäkumpu: Drums, Marko Wacker (now Palmén): Guitar, Christian Saarinen: Bass (1992-) **Past Members** *Jani Karvola: Vocals (1991)*
Deathography
Ancient Gate, Demo (1992)
Promo 92, Demo (1992)
Evocation, CD (Breath of Night, 2004)

EVOKED CURSE
One-man project from Angered which produced one demo during the early 90's. The music is a chaotic mix between grindcore and death metal, old school style! If you can get hold of their demos, grab them! In the late 90's the band moved to Lahti in Finland, and released some ultra-obscure demos.
Line-Up Harri Juvonen
Deathography
Transmigration, Demo (1990)
Demo (?)

EXANTHEMA
Started in Eskilstuna in 1990. They sounded pretty standard even then, but they had moments. The best thing about them was the deep, beastly vocals of Kristoffer Svensson. Some of the countless members in Exanthema were in Tears of Grief back in the day.
Line-Up Kristoffer Svensson: Vocals, Mattias Björklund: Guitar, Janne Röök: Guitar, Mattias Arreflod: Bass, Adam Grembowski: Drums **Past Members** *Jacek Kedzierski: Guitar, Oliver Mets: Bass/Vocals/Guitar, Ricardo Videla: Guitar, Adam Krembowski: Drums, Jörgen "Jögge" Persson: Bass, Fredrik Carlsson: Guitar, Tero Viljanen: Bass/Vocals*
Deathography
The Dead Shall Rise, Demo (1992)
Follow the Path, Demo (1992)
Exanthema/Chronic Decay, Split CD (Studiefrämjandet, 1993)
Lunacy, Demo (1994)
Dream World, Demo (1995)

EXCRETION
Created in Rönninge/Stockholm during spring 1990, they deliver brutal grinding death metal with some touches of melody and guttural vocals. Pretty good, but also pretty standard.
Line-Up Thomas Wahlström: Vocals/Bass, Anders Hanser: Guitar, Christoffer Holm: Guitar, Seppo Santala: Drums **Past Members** *Tommy Ottemark: Drums*
Deathography
The Dream of Blood, Demo (1992)

Suicide Silence, Demo (1993)
Exanthema/Chronic Decay Split CD (1993)
Voice of Harmony, CD (Wrong Again, 1996)

EXCRUCIATE
This Upplands Väsby band began in Sept. 1989 as a trio—guitarists Hempa Brynolfsson and Johan Melander, and drummer Per Ax—playing pretty intense death metal with deep growling vocals. The band had line-up problems, and folded shortly after their 1993 album *Passages of Life*. Both Levin and Rudberg previously played with Mastication. They reformed briefly in 2001, and managed a demo. Older material has subsequently been released on CD.
Line-Up Hempa Brynolfsson: Guitar, Per Ax: Drums, Fredrik Isaksson: Bass (1990-), Janne Rudberg: Guitar (1992-), Lars Levin: Vocals (1991-) **Past Members** *Johan Melander: Guitar (1989-1992), Christian Carlsson: Vocals (1990-1991)*
Deathography
Mutilation of the Past, Demo (1990)
Excruciate/Epitaph Split LP (Infest, 1991)
Hymns of Mortality, Demo (1991)
Passages of Life, CD (Thrash, 1993)
Excruciate, Demo (2001)
Beyond the Circle, CD (Konqueror, 2003)

EXECRATORY
Gore/death metal band formed in 1999—that's all I know! I haven't even seen a demo, but I know they are out there!
Line-Up Grinder: Drums, Zombieflesh: Vocals/Guitar, Evil D: Bass

EXEMPT
Formed in Angered in October 1990, playing thrashy death metal of good quality. Andersson also formed the great Immersed in Blood, joined Inverted, and also Nominon. The guy arranged a lot of true death metal gigs and deserves all the respect in the world.
Line-Up Joel Andersson: Bass, Daniel Berlin: Guitar (1992-), Raimo Koskimies: Drums, Rune Foss: Guitar, Magnus Arvidsson: Vocals **Past Members** *Jani Pietäle: Guitar (1990-1992)*
Deathography
Tomorrow's Exemption, Rehearsal (1990)
Wake Up, Demo (1991)
Ill Health, Demo (1992)

EXHALE
Death/grind band formed in 2004. Going by the name, I guess they are pretty inspired by Nasum.
Line-Up Johan F: Bass, Uffe: Vocals, Gurra: Drums, Johan Y: Guitar/Vocals
Deathography
Die Inside, Demo (2004)

EXHUMED
Brutal band formed in Stockholm back in 1989. Exhumed soon folded, afterwards Ramstedt and Brink formed Morpheus with Markus Rüden and Stefan Ekström from Carbonized.
Line-Up David Brink: Vocals, Sebastian Ramstedt:

Guitar, Johan Bergebäck: Bass, Janne Rudberg: Drums
Deathography
Obscurity, Demo (1990)

EXILE
Obscure band from Falkenberg/Halmstad that got going around 1985. The band's evil Celtic Frost vibe is definitely worth tracking down for collectors of obscure Swedish metal. One member, Paulo Staver, later started the label Primitive Art.
Deathography
Rehearsal (1985)
Final Breath, Demo (1986)

EXPOSITORY
One of many mid-90's bands of Västerås boys Tommy Carlsson and Jens Klovegård. Formed in 1990 as a Thrash band, after numerous line-up changes they ended up death metal. Their melodic and frenzied death metal is somewhat similar to Unanimated. Never made it out of the deep underground.
Line-Up *Jens Klovegård: Guitar, Tommy Carlsson: Drums (1991-), Johan Åström: Guitar (1993-), Tony Sundqvist: Vocals (1992-)*
Deathography
Rehearsal (1992)

EXPULSION
Ready for a long story? Stockholm's Expulsion was started as River's Edge in early 1988 by Stefan Lagergren and Anders Holmberg. A certain Johan Edlund supplied some early vocals. Lagergren, Holmberg, and Edlund soon formed Treblinka, and River's Edge entered a state of chaos. But simultaneous to Treblinka, Lagergren and Holmberg continued River's Edge as Expulsion. After two decent demos that sounded like a thrashier Treblinka, the band went on hold when Holmberg joined Tranquillity. Lagergren and Fransson reformed Expulsion in 1991 after leaving Treblinka/Tiamat, together with vocalist Fredrik Thörnqvist and bassist Chelsea Krook. Holmberg later returned and replaced Krook in time for the debut 7". Tiamat's singer Johan Edlund sings guest vocals on Expulsion's first full length. In summary: The Stockholm band River's Edge divided into Expulsion and Treblinka in 1988. Both contained Stefan Lagergren and Anders Holmberg and sounded pretty similar.
Line-Up *Stefan Lagergren: Guitar, Calle Fransson: Drums, Anders Holmberg: Vocals/Bass (1989-1990, 1992-), Christopher Vowdén: Guitar (1992-), Fredrik Thörnqvist: Vocals* **Past Members** *Chelsea Krook: Bass (1991-1992), Magnus Krants: Guitar, Johan Edlund: Vocals (session only)*
Deathography
Mind the Edge, Demo (1988—as River's Edge)
Cerebral Cessation, Demo (1989)
Veiled in the Mist of Mystery, Demo (1989)
A Bitter Twist of Fate, 7" (Dödsmetallfirma Expulsion, 1993)
Overflow, CD (Godhead, 1994)
Man Against, CD (Godhead, 1996)

EXPURGATE
This death metal act formed in 1990, made a demo in 1991, then vanished. A story similar to many...
Deathography
Forbidden Ruler, Demo (1991)

EXTINCTION
Thrash metal band with death influences that started out in Uddevalla in 2002.
Line-Up *Andreas Karlsén: Guitar/Vocals, Niklas Hero: Bass, Janne Rimmerfors: Drums*
Deathography
Sworn to Extinction, Demo (2005)

EYECULT
A duo that began producing melodic black/death metal in Västerås during 2004. Good luck guys.
Line-Up *Patrik Carlsson: Vocals/Guitar/Bass/Synthesizer, Andreas Åkerlind: Drums*
Deathography
Eyecult, Demo (2004)

EYETRAP
Melodic death metal band started in Stockholm in the year 2000. Wranning is ex-Ebony Tears, Miscreant, Dog Faced Gods, and Månegarm.
Line-Up *Johnny Wranning: Vocals, Joakim Rhodin: Bass, Jan Karlsson: Drums, Fredrik Rhodin: Guitar*
Deathography
Folkmagic, CD (Black Sun, 2003)

FACE DOWN
Originally named Machine God, Face Down was formed by ex-Afflicted/Proboscis/General Surgery guy Joakim Carlsson in Hägersten in 1993. Their brutal death/thrash proved pretty successful on Roadrunner and later Nuclear Blast. Things looked good until Stjärnvind left for Entombed and Aro split for The Haunted. Face Down was in ruins, and finally broke up in 1999. In 2004 the band reunited after Aro quit The Haunted. The future suddenly seems brighter than the past for Face Down!
Line-Up *Marco Aro: Vocals, Joacim Carlsson: Guitar, Joakim (Harju) Hedestedt: Bass, Erik Thyselius: Drums* **Past Members** *Richard Bång: Drums (1993-95), Alex Linder: Guitar (1993-94), Niklas Ekstrand: Guitar (1994-95), Håkan Ericsson: Drums (1997-99), Peter Stjärnvind: Drums (1995-97)*
Deathography
Demo 1, Demo (1994)
Demo 2, Demo (1995)
Demo 3, Demo (1995)
Mindfield, CD (Roadrunner, 1995)
Demo 4, Demo (1996)
Demo 5, Demo (1998)
The Twisted Rule the Wicked, CD (Nuclear Blast, 1998)
Promo Demo 2004, Demo (2004)
The Will to Power, CD (Black Lodge, 2005)

FACEBREAKER
Good thrash metal with a deadly touch, started in

Finspång in 1999. Jonas and Mikael also play in Ashes, and Robban has been in great bands like Edge of Sanity, Darkified, and Pan-Thy-Monium.
Line-Up Robban: *Vocals, Janne: Guitar, Mika: Guitar/Vocals, Jonas: Bass/Vocals, Mikael: Drums*
Deathography
Use Your Fist, Demo (2000)
Hate & Anger, Single (Rage of Achilles, 2003)
Bloodred Hell, CD (Rage of Achilles, 2004)

FACING DEATH
Recent project by Ola of Subcyde and Fredrik of Canopy.
Line-Up Fredrik "Reaper of Souls" Huldtgren: *Vocals, Ola "Collector of Bones" Englund: Guitar/Vocals, Jim Kekonius: Bass, Fredrik Widigs: Drums*
Deathography
Facing Death, Demo (2005)

FALLEN ANGEL
Classic early Swedish thrash metal band started in Örebro in 1984, although they didn't use the name Fallen Angel (then Fallen Angels) until 1986. Lots of line-up changes didn't stop them from going strong into the 90's. But they were soon overshadowed by the death metal movement, and folded in 1993. Some members tried to continue with Micke Sved (Authorize) as Under the Sun, but nothing really came of it.
Line-Up Johan Bülow: *Vocals/Guitar (1987-), Joacim Persson: Guitar/Vocals (1988-), Fredrik Lindén: Drums, Matte Hedenborg: Bass (1990-)* **Past Members** *Gustaf Ljungström: Bass/Vocals (1984-1990), Fredrik Hahnel: Vocals/Guitar (1984-1989), Kent Engström: Guitar (1988)*
Deathography
Demo 1, Demo (1988)
Hang-Over, Demo (1989)
Fallen Angel/Nirvana 2002/Authorize/Appendix-split, 7" (Opinionate, 1990)
Fallen Angel, 7" (1990)
Fallen Angel, mini-LP (1991, UNI)
Faith Fails, LP (Massacre Records, 1992)

FALLEN ANGELS
Melodic and very silly-looking band from Falkenberg has produced three demos and changed about a thousand members since starting in 2000. Recently they changed their name to Sonic Syndicate and released an album called *Eden Fire*, which is divided into three pretentious chapters. Now very successful on Nuclear Blast, but an abyssmal band.
Line-Up Richard Sjunnesson: *Vocals, Roger Sjunnesson: Guitar, Robin Sjunnesson: Guitar, Andreas Mårtensson: Keyboards, Karin Axlesson: Bass, Kristoffer Bäcklund: Drums* **Past Members** *David Blennskog: Bass (2000), Fredrik Wellsfält: Guitar/Vocals (2000-2001), Dan Land: Guitar (2000-2001), Daniel Bengtsson: Bass/Vocals (2001), Andreas Andersson: Guitar (2002), Jacob Strand: Drums (2001-2002), Mikael Hauglund: Bass (2002), Magnus Svensson: Bass (2002-2004)*
Deathography
Fall from Heaven, Demo (2003)

Black Lotus, Demo (2003)
Extinction, Demo (2004)
Eden Fire, CD (Pivotal Rockordings, 2005—as Sonic Syndicate)

FANTASMAGORIA
Bollnäs band formed in the early 90's. Initially they rather deadly, they soon turned into some kind of Pantera clones. Almost all the members also played in Morgana Lefay.
Line-Up Peter Grehn: *Guitar, Robin Engström: Drums, Fredrik Lundberg: Bass/Vocals* **Past Members** *Mikael "Micke" Åsentorp: Bass, Rickard Harrysson: Guitar*
Deathography
Inconceivable Future, Demo (1991)
Fantasmagoria, Demo (1997)
Fuck You All, CD (Trudani, 1998)

FATAL EMBRACE
Your typical Swedish mid-90's death/thrash with a screaming vocalist, formed in Varberg 1992. Totally unoriginal and average, and still they managed to secure a deal with Candlelight. Damn you At the Gates! In 1998 the band apparently recorded the album *Hail Down Deep*, but to my knowledge it never saw the light of day. Herman Engström also played in Beseech, Cemetary 1313, and Sundown.
Line-Up Tommy Grönberg: *Vocals/Guitar, Herman Engström: Vocals/Guitar, Henrik Serholt: Drums/Vocals, Andreas Johansson: Guitar* **Past Members** *Andreas Johansson: Keyboards/Flute*
Deathography
Scars in Dismal Icons, Demo (1996)
Shadowsouls Garden, CD (Candlelight, 1997)

FEARED CREATION
Massive-sounding death/thrash band, I guess from Malmö, since members are local "celebrities" from Deranged (Fäldt), The Forsaken (Sjöholm), and Misteltein (Gillberg). The group is fairly new, so the future will tell if they can have any impact.
Line-Up Anders Sjöholm: *Vocals, Calle Fäldt: Guitar, John Huldt: Guitar, Magnus Gillberg: Bass, Sebastian Westberg: Drums*
Deathography
Five Reasons to Hate, Demo (2004)

FEMICIDE
A joke band from the 2000's which focused on misogynist lyrics. Sure stupid as hell, but the music is pretty good Obituary-style death metal.
Deathography
Promo 2002, Demo (2002)

FENRIA
Fairly new act from the forgotten town of Härnösand. Reportedly they have switched their style from black/thrash to death/thrash. May I suggest pure death?
Line-Up Jonas Helander: *Guitar/Vocals, Johan Jansson: Vocals, Pelle Sjölander: Guitar, Claes Svedin: Bass, Jesper Bodin: Drums* **Past Members** *Pelle: Guitar*

Deathography
Fleshless, Demo (2004)

FESTER PLAGUE

Technical thrash metal from Sunne. This early-90's (formed in 1988) band didn't have much to offer in the heyday of death metal. Apparently some members started to play together as early as 1986 as Voodoo, and I guess the original Metallica influences never left them. It all ended in 1993 after one traditional Sunlight-produced demo—which, in spite of the name, was not completed until January 2, 1992.
Line-Up Rino E Rotevatn: Vocals, Kjell Elmlund: Drums, Ulf Jansson: Bass, Jan Janson: Guitar/Vocals Past Members Larsa: Drums (in Voodoo)
Deathography
Demo 91, Demo (1992)

FILTHY CHRISTIANS

Insane grindcore band from Falun formed in 1985. Their story is a cool one. These guys went on a crazed train journey over Europe in 1986, met Earache boss Digby Pearson in the UK, and kept in touch. When they played in the UK the next year, he offered them a deal if they could show a decent demo. They sent him their third demo, and within a flash became the first Swedish band signed to Earache. For some reason, Filthy Christians played on national Swedish television in 1989 (I think it had something to do with an interview with Fredda Holmgren of the label CBR). I remember being happily shocked seeing them on an otherwise ultra-boring live program called "Svepet." I guess regular viewers choked on their crisps that night as Filthy Christians grinded away insanely! We loved them back in the day, but today they sound very dated. Nevertheless, one of the coolest grindcore bands Sweden ever produced. Nowadays, Thunell and Hammare play in the hardcore band Bruce Banner.
Line-Up Daniel Hammare: Guitar, Ola Strålin: Drums, Per Thunell: Vocals, Lasse Larsson: Guitar (1990-), Pelle Sörensen: Bass (1992-) Past Members Greger Brennström: Bass (-1990), Patrick Forsberg: Bass/Guitar (-1992)
Deathography
Demo (1987)
Demo (1987)
Demo (1988)
Filthy Christians/G-Anx Split 7" (1989)
Mean, LP (Earache, 1990)
Demo 1992, Demo (1992)
Nailed, Single (We Bite, 1994)

FISSION

Melodic thrash/death duo which began in 2002. The result? Well, it's mediocre. Andreas Hedlund is also in Borknagar, Otyg, and Havayoth.
Line-Up Vintersorg (Andreas Hedlund): Vocals/ Keyboards, Benny Hägglund: Drums/Guitar/Bass
Deathography
Crater, CD (Napalm, 2004)

FLAGELLATION

Pretty good death metal act founded in Stockholm in 1997. Their journey was short, though. Lindström and Cannerfelt went off to In Grey, and Brynedal joined Insision. To close the circle, Jonsson joined Insision at the same time Brynedal left in 2004.
Line-Up Per Lindström: Vocals/Bass, Daniel Cannerfelt: Guitar, Marcus Jonsson: Drums Past Members Toob Brynedal: Guitar (session only)
Deathography
Spineless Regression, Demo (1998)

FLEGMA

Pure hardcore act founded in Malmö during 1987. Influenced by thrash metal, things soon got crossover. Not even the addition of Obscurity's Jörgen Lindhe in 1993 got the band into brutality. In the end, they flirted with goth, toured Italy, and soon folded. In 1995, Flegma split for good, dividing into two bands: Tenebre and Redrvm. Neither played death metal. Nowadays Kalle Metz is on the staff at the successful booking agency The Agency Group.
Line-Up Kalle Metz: Vocals, Olvar: Guitar, Richard Lion: Bass, Joel: Drums, Jörgen Lindhe: Guitar Past Members Martin Olsson: Guitar, Ola Püschel: Guitar, Rother: Vocals, Martin Brorsson: Drums
Deathography
Hippiehardcore, Demo (1987)
Demo II, Demo (1988)
Eine Kleine Schlachtmusik, 7" (Insane, 1990)
Blind Acceptance, LP (Black Rose, 1992)
Flesh to Dust, CD (Black Rose, 1994)

FLESH

There seems to be a revival of old school death metal in Sweden, and Flesh is one of the newest to embrace the old-time ways. Actually, this "band" is a one-man project featuring Pete Flesh (ex-Maze of Torment, Deceiver).
Line-Up Pete Flesh: Vocals/Guitar/Bass, Flingan: Drums (session only)
Deathography
Dödsångest, CD (Iron Fist, 2005)

FORCE MAJUERE—see Infanticide (Piteå)

FORESKIN FESTER

A bunch of crazy guys started this project in 2002 in Karlskrona, using the death metal formula to make jokes about sexually transmittable diseases. As with most bands of this kind, eventually only the master joke-maker still finds it amusing. So now he's alone.
Line-Up Fjalar: Drums/Vocals Past Members Necrowizard: Vocals (session only), Onkel Herpes: Vocals (session only), Joel Broskfölje: Keyboards (session only), Max: Vocals/Bass (2002-2005), Wibbe: Guitar (2002-2005)
Deathography
Rehearsing with Pung, Demo (2002)
Destruction of the Penis, Demo (2003)

FORLORN

Doom metal from Gävle, formed by Daniel Bryntse

(Withered Beauty, Sorcerer) in 1991. The endless stream of demos apparently led nowhere, and after about ten years the band folded. They survive in some form as Isole. As often happens, the old demos were released on CD after the break-up. Bryntse has also been in Windwalker.

Line-Up Daniel Bryntse: Vocals/Drums, Christer Olsson: Guitar, Henrik Lindenmo: Bass **Past Members** *Kim Molin: Drums (1991), Magnus Helin: Guitar (1991-92), Jan Larsson: Bass (1991-95), Magnus Björk: Guitar/Vocals (1992-96), Per Sandgren: Guitar*

Deathography
Vivere non Necesse Est, Demo (1992)
Tired, Demo (1993)
Promo '95, Demo (1995)
Waves of Sorrow, Demo (1995)
Promo '96, Demo (1996)
Autumn Leaves, Demo (2001)
Autumn Promos, CD (2005)

FORMICIDE
Early 90's Bay Area-influenced thrash from the northern suburbs of Stockholm. On the second demo they tried a deadlier sound in Sunlight Studios, but the vocals ruined it. Andreas Wahl went on to heavier stuff in Concrete Sleep, Serpent, and Therion.

Line-Up Fredrik Petersson: Vocals, Andreas Wahl: Bass, Magnus Barthelson: Guitar/Keyboards, Daniel Berglund: Guitar, Patrick: Drums

Deathography
Demented, Demo (1990)
Comatose, Demo (1991)

FORSAKEN
This band formed in 1991, made a demo in 1992, and then... Well, they are gone.

Deathography
Departed Souls, Demo (1992)

THE FORSAKEN
Formed as Septic Breed in Landskrona in 1997, the name soon changed to The Forsaken. They deliver powerful death/thrash metal. Good stuff, and the band has rightly been successful. Old bass player Håkansson left to focus on Evergray and Embraced. Do not confuse with the early 90's Forsaken.

Line-Up Anders Sjöholm: Vocals, Stefan Holm: Guitar, Patrik Persson: Guitar, Stefan Berg: Bass, Nicke Grabowski: Drums **Past Members** *Roine Strandberg: Bass (1997-1999), Mikael Håkansson: Bass (1999-2001)*

Deathography
Patterns of Delusive Design, Demo (1998)
Reaper-99, Demo (1999)
Manifest of Hate, CD (Century Media, 2001)
Arts of Desolation, CD (Century Media, 2002)
Traces of the Past, CD (Century Media, 2003)

FORSAKEN GRIEF
This short-lived band from Borås formed in 1990, and stayed together long enough to make one demo. Odhuis went on with Lake of Tears, and Josefsson joined Evocation and Cemetary.

Line-Up Thomas Josefsson: Guitar/Vocals, Johan Oudhuis: Drums, Patrik Lundberg: Guitar, Tony Splatt: Bass

Deathography
Promo 92, Demo (1992)

FULMINATION
One of the great death metal acts from Avesta, born from the ruins of Entrails in the early 90's. Brutal yet catchy and groovy death metal the way it should sound—and similar to Bolt Thrower in a way. Norrman also played in Uncanny, and is today one of the forces behind Katatonia. It's a shame none of the great bands from Avesta ever made it. Interment, Uncanny, and Fulmination deserved so much more than they got.

Line-Up Mats Berggren: Bass/Vocals, Mats Forsell: Guitar, Johan Jansson: Guitar (1994-), Christer Enström: Drums **Past Members** *Fredrik Norrman: Guitar (-1994)*

Deathography
Demo 92, Demo (1992)
Through Fire, Demo (1992)
Promo 93, Demo (1993)

FUNERAL FEAST
Early 90's death/grind band from Mjölby, formed in 1991. More project than band, since Forss soon concentrated on Dawn, and Manuel focused on Traumatic. Gore & grind—you know what you get.

Line-Up Henrik Forss: Vocals, Manuel: Guitar/Vocals, Jocke Larsson: Bass/Vocals (& later some terrible drums) **Past Members** *Ola: Drums (-1992)*

Deathography
Rehearsal (1991)
Emanuating Mucous Semen, Demo (1992)

FURBOWL
Death/goth band started in Växjö in 1991 by ex-Carnage man Johan Liiva-Axelsson and former Jesus Exercise drummer Max Thornell. First demo features a guest appearance by Mike Amott (Carnage/Carcass/Arch Enemy). Their death metal soon transformed into death rock, predating the Entombed style of the mid-90's. Later they played psychedelic rock. The band has since become Wonderflow, having nothing more to do with death metal. Johan Liiva-Axelsson left his creation in 1993, and became involved with Mike Amott's acclaimed Arch Enemy for a while.

Line-Up Nicke Stenemo: Guitar/Keyboards, Max Thornell: Drums, Per Jungberger: Guitar (1993-) **Past Members** *Johan Liiva-Axelsson: Guitar/Vocals/Bass (1991-1993)*

Deathography
The Nightfall of Your Heart, Demo (1991)
Demo 2, Demo (1992)
Those Shredded Dreams, LP/CD (Step One, 1992)
Promo 93, Demo (1993)
Rehearsal (1993)
7" (Cenotaph, 1993—unreleased?)
The Autumn Years, CD (Black Mark, 1994)

FURIA

Stockholm band that emerged around 2000, obviously very inspired by At the Gates, but with a black metal touch. Decent.

Line-Up *Micke Broman*
Deathography
Sagor, Demo (2000)

GADGET

Started as a solo project of William Blackmon in 1997, he kept it alive long enough to make one demo. In late 1999 he resurrected the project, and with guitarist Rikard Olsson created intense grind/death in the vein of Nasum. Soon they had a complete band. Eventually they ended up on Relapse, and as Nasum has vanished Gadget are now probably Sweden's leading grind band. Rightly so—they are great, apart from a few annoying emo touches. William Blackmon is also in Withered Beauty, Rikard Olsson is also in Diskonto (the bass position I once held) and Fredrik Nygren is known from previous work with Sorcery, Ashram, and "legendary" punk band Dross.

Line-Up *William Blackmon: Guitar/Drums/Vocals, Rikard Olsson: Guitar, Emil Englund: Vocals, Fredrik Nygren: Bass*
Deathography
Promo 00, Demo (2000)
Promo December 00, Demo (2000)
Exhumed/Gadget-split, EP (Relapse, 2001)
Remote, CD (Relapse, 2004)
The Funeral March, CD (Relapse, 2006)

GARDENIAN

Straight-to-CD Gothenburg band that began in 1996 playing typical melodic "death metal." After two mediocre albums they split up.

Line-Up *Niclas Englin: Guitar, Thym Blom: Drums, Robert Hakemo: Bass, Apollo Papathanasio: Vocals*
Past Members *Håkan Skoger: Bass, Jim Kjell: Vocals, Kriss Albertsson: Bass*
Deathography
Two Feet Stand, CD (Listenable, 1997)
Soulburner, CD (Nuclear Blast, 1999)
Sindustries, CD (Nuclear Blast, 2000)

GARDENS OF OBSCURITY

Began as grindcore combo Slavestate in Helsingborg in 1991. After a few rehearsals, the name changed to Asmodeus, and their style to doomy death. After a demo the name became Gardens of Obscurity, but they soon folded since no labels were interested. Some of the guys concentrated on the band Darksend. Many members are known from other bands, but none has a more impressive resumé than Peter Wildoer (Agretator, Arch Enemy, Armageddon, Darkane, Dawn of Oblivion, Electrocution 250, Honey Hush, Majestic, Silver Seraph, Time Requiem, ZanineZ).

Line-Up *Tony Richter: Vocals, Mathias Teikari: Guitar, Mikael Bergman: Bass, Peter Wildoer: Drums* **Past Members** *Martin Thorsén: Drums, William Fetty: Guitar, Joakim Persson: Guitar*
Deathography
The Lamentation, Demo (1993)

GATES OF ISHTAR

Created in the northern Swedish city of Luleå in 1992 by ex-Decoration members Oskar Karlsson and Niclas Svensson. After initial success, the duo left to form The Everdawn. Gates of Ishtar's second album, *The Dawn of Flames*, turned out to be the last thing recorded in the famous Unisound studio. The music? Melodic death metal in the vein of Dissection, but not nearly as good.

Line-Up *Mikael Sandorf: Guitar/Bass/Vocals, Urban Carlsson: Guitar, Oskar Karlsson: Drums*
Past Members *Andreas Johanson: Drums, Stefan Nilsson: Guitar, Thomas Jutenfäldt: Guitar, Harald Åberg: Bass, Daniel Röhr: Bass (session only)*
Deathography
Best Demo of 95, Demo (1995)
Promo 95 Live, Demo (1995)
Seasons of Frost, Demo (1995)
A Blood Red Path, CD (Spinefarm, 1996)
The Dawn of Flames, CD (Invasion, 1997)
At Dusk and Forever, CD (Invasion, 1998)

GEHENNAH

Forshaga's Gehennah started their primitive music in 1990 as Gehenna. Not really death metal at all, rather a retro band that sounds very much like Venom. They are cool, but not actually good. Still the band attracted Osmose Productions in the mid-90's, signing to their sub-label Kron-H together with a bunch of other Swedish death/punk hybrids like Disfear, Dellamorte, and Driller Killer. They never gained any real success, but were hailed in the underground for a brief period. Ronnie used to be in Vomitory in the old days, and Hellcop played in Dawn of Decay.

Line-Up *Mr Violence: Vocals, Rob Stringburner: Guitar, Ronnie Ripper: Bass, Hellcop: Drums*
Past Members *Captain Cannibal: Drums*
Deathography
Kill, Demo (1992)
Brilliant Load Overlords of Destruction, Demo (1993)
Hardrocker, CD (Primitive Arts, 1995)
No Fucking Christmas, 7" (Primitive Arts, 1995)
King of the Sidewalk, CD (Osmose, 1996)
Headbangers Against Disco vol. 1, Split 7" (Primitive Arts, 1997)
Decibel Rebel, CD (Osmose, 1997)
Gehennah/Rise and Shine, Split 7" (Primitive Arts, 1998)
10 Years of Fucked Up Behaviour, EP (Bad Taste Entertainment HQ, 2003)

GENERAL SURGERY

Cool side project founded in 1989 by Matti Kärki (Carbonized, Dismember) and Grant McWilliams. The duo was soon joined by Joacim Carlsson (Afflicted Convulsion) and Mats Nordrup (Crematory), and in the beginning vocals were handled by Richard Cabeza (Unanimated, Dismember). Initially a pure Carcass rip-off, they soon tried to be somewhat more original. Several members passed through the line-up since the start, and none of the initial members lasted very long (understandably, since virtually all were busy in successful bands). With any line-up, they delivered ultra-brutal and primitive death metal to the limit! After eleven years of inactivity, the band is now kicking again. Of course they have a new line-up, which has most definitely changed again since I wrote this! A great fucking band.

*Line-Up Joacim Carlsson: Guitar, Adde Mitroulis: Drums, Johan Wallin: Guitar, Micke van Tuominen: Bass, Erik Sahlström: Vocals **Past Members** Glenn Sykes: Bass, Richard Cabeza: Vocals, Grant McWilliams: Vocals, Jonas Derouche: Guitar, Andreas Eriksson: Bass, Matti Kärki: Bass, Mats Nordrup: Bass, Erik Thyselius: Drums (session only), Christofer Barkensjö: Drums (in theory only, he never rehearsed with the band), Anders Jakobsson: Drums (even more theoretically, he quit before even meeting the guys)*

Deathography
Erosive Offals, Demo (1990)
Pestiferous Antrhopophagia, Demo (1990)
Internecine Prurience, Demo (1990)
Necrology EP, 7" (Relapse, 1991)
Necrology, MCD (Nuclear Blast, 1994)
General Surgery/County Medical Examiners, Split CD (Razorback Records, 2003)
General Surgery/County Medical Examiners, Split LP (Yellow Dog, 2003)
General Surgery/Filth, Split (Bones Brigade, 2004)
Demos, 7" (Nuclear Abominations, 2004)
General Surgery/Machetazo, Split (Escorbuto Recordings, 2004)
Left Hand Pathology, CD/LP (Listenable/Power-It-Up, 2006)

GENETIC MUTATION

Mid-90's death metal joke project from Mjölby, with Stefan and Karsten from Mithotyn. Some melody and half-screamed vocals remind us this was made in the heyday of black metal and melodic death metal, but they keep themselves pretty brutal throughout. A demo from 1995 called *Future Vision* appears in some discographies, but simply does not exist.

Line-Up Karsten: Drums, Stefan Weinerhall: Everything else
Deathography
Promo 93, Demo (1993)
Promo , Demo (1994)

GENOCRUSH FEROX

In the godforsaken town of Borlänge these death metal freaks started out as Cromb in 1997. Soon they transformed into the brutal old school Death machine Genocrush Ferox. Old guitarist Olsson had a huge influence in the band, his idea was to play "like seagulls, backwards." This is fucking awesome, brutal, catchy, and sick as hell. Toob's vocals are among the best, just bone-chilling. After a few years it was all over. Toob joined Insision in 2000, but left in 2004. Oddly enough, Jonsson joined Insision one week later on drums. Both Genocrush Ferox and Kromb's demos have subsequently been released on CD—get it all!

*Line-Up Toob Brynedal: Vocals/Guitar, Per: Guitar, Marcus Jonsson: Bass, Henke: Drums **Past Members***

Dan Olsson: Guitar (until 2000)
Deathography
The Sepulchre Devastation, Demo (1998)
Glory Glory Strangulation, Demo (2000)
The Sepulchre Strangulation, CD (Escorbuto Recordings, 2003)
Demo, Demo (2003—as Cromb)
4 Tormenting Ways to Death, Split CD (Gruft Production, 2005—as Cromb)

GHAMOREAN

Death/black band formed in Umeå in 1997. I haven't seen any demos, but someone released a CD by them recently.

Line-Up Henrik Sundström: Vocals, Andreas Båtsman: Guitar, Niklas Gandal: Bass, Jimmy Borgström: Drums
Deathography
Plaguempire, CD (Kharmageddon, 2005)

GILGAMOSH—see Decortication

GOD—see GOD B.C.

GOD AMONG INSECTS

Formed in Stockholm 2003, the latest in the endless projects led by the tireless (and, sometimes, tiresome) Kentha Philipson (eh, Lord K). This is probably the best stuff he has ever done, thanks to Dark Funeral's Masse Broberg (eh, Emperor Magus Caligula) and Vomitory's Tobias Gustafsson.

Line-Up Emperor Magus Caligula: Vocals, Lord K Philipson: Guitar, Tomas Elofsson: Bass, Tobias Gustafsson: Drums
Deathography
World Wide Death, CD (Threeman Recordings, 2004)

GOD B.C.

Thrash metal from Helsingborg, started out simply as God in 1986. They had small success after switching names to God B.C., releasing an album on Wild Rags. The band never got much attention, and split up shortly after the album. Granath and Richter went on to Agretator. Hallbäck joined Hyste'riah, which then became Hyste'riah G.B.C. Note that Tom Hallbäck edited *At Dawn They Read*, one of Sweden's first fanzines that cared for extreme Metal.

*Line-Up Joakim Warneryd: Vocals, Magnus Nilsson: Guitar, Jesper Granath: Bass, Tom Hallbäck: Drums **Past Members** Fredrik Elander: Vocals, Pierre Richter: Guitar*
Deathography
Four Wise Men, Demo (1988)
Eargasms in Eden, LP (Wild Rags, 1989)

GOD MACABRE

In 1991, Karlstad's Macabre End wanted to get rid of their bass player, so—like Nihilist a couple of years earlier—they disbanded, only to start up again soon after under a new name without telling the unwelcome bandmate. As God Macabre they continued with dark and intense death metal, incorporating some

daring and progressive elements such as a Mellotron. Though quite big in the underground for some time, they never really made it. One reason was that their sole record wasn't released until two years after it was recorded. In 1993 they called it a day. Stålhammar went on to join Utumno. In retrospect, they probably should have kept their old name to keep their audience. Still, a prime example of true Swedish death metal. God Macabre's sole album was re-mixed, re-edited and re-released by Re-lapse in 2002. (The CD also includes Macabre End's demo).
Line-Up Per Boder: Vocals, Jonas Stålhammar: Guitar/Bass/Mellotron, Ola Sjöberg: Guitar *Past Members* Niklas Nilsson: Drums
Deathography
The Winterlong, MLP (MBR, 1993)
The Winterlong, CD (Relapse, 2002)

GODBLENDER
Death metal from Härnösand, moved to Stockholm to play *nu*-metal in the late 90's. Forget it.
Line-Up Håkan Eriksson
Deathography
Demo 95, Demo (1995)

GODDEFIED
Early death metal from Karlskoga formed in 1990. Cool band in the vein of Dismember and Entombed, but not as original (or good). They split in 1995, but reportedly began again in 2004. Note that their name is misspelled as "Goddified" on the 7" because the label manager misread the band logo! True!
Line-Up Jonas Aneheim: Guitar, Matthias Pettersson: Drums, Richard Eriksson: Bass, Jan Arvidsson: Guitar/Vocals *Past Members* Micke Persson: Guitar
Deathography
Assembly of the Damned, Demo (1991)
Abysmal Grief, Demo (1992)
Abysmal Grief, 7" (Wild Rags, 1993)

GODGORY
Good melodic death metal from Karlstad, founded in 1992. Unlike many others, Godgory combines melody and brutality nicely. When the band became a duo and signed to Nuclear Blast, the quality faded.
Line-Up Erik Andersson: Drums, Matte Andersson: Vocals *Past Members* Mikael Dahlqvist: Guitar (1994-1996), Fredric Danielsson: Bass (1994-1996), Stefan Grundel: Guitar (1994-1996), Thomas Heder: Keyboards (1996)
Deathography
Demo 94, Demo (1994)
Sea of Dreams, CD (Invasion, 1995)
Shadow's Dance, CD (Invasion, 1996)
Resurrection, CD (Nuclear Blast, 1999)
Way Beyond, CD (Nuclear Blast, 2001)

GODHATE
When Throneaeon got fed up with their old name (no one could ever remember it, and they were going nowhere) they became Godhate. No bullshit, just straightforward death metal in the vein of Deicide. The band is apparently unsigned at the moment, so if

you have a label—sign them!
Line-Up Tony Fred: Vocals/Guitar, Jens Klovengård: Guitar, Claes Ramberg: Bass Roger Sundquist: Drums
Deathography
Anguish, EP (2005)

GODS OF OBSCURITY
I don't know shit about this band except that they have obviously made a demo. Fitting name.
Deathography
Abyss of Coloured Tears, Demo (1994)

GOREFLESH
Death metal from Värnamo, made a demo in 1994.
Line-Up Kosta Christoforidis: Vocals, Andreas Andersson: Drums, Michael Palm: Guitar, Daniel Ögren: Bass
Deathography
Stoned, Demo (1994)

GOREGOAT 3007
Micke Samuelsson of Keks, Bloodstone, and Cauterizer made a doomy solo demo in 1991 under the charming name Goregoat 3007. He also had a similar solo band called "Xyt-Thul" or something like that, I really can't remember.
Line-Up Micke Samuelsson: Everything
Deathography
Aliens on Acid, Demo (1991)

GOREMENT
Nyköping band, started as a thrash metal combo in 1989, but soon changed radically into an extremely brutal death metal platoon with guttural, low-pitched vocals. Gorement was hailed in the early 90's underground, but never got anywhere. It's a shame, because this is the real stuff. One of Sweden's most brutal bands. Fucking great! Their old material has recently been released on CD—get it or be a wimp. Most of the members continued in Piper's Dawn, but that band had nothing to do with death metal, and mercifully split up after a sole demo. Note that Gorement had the same logo as Gorefest, and that one of their demos had the same cover as Morbid Angel's *Blessed are the Sick* (the same Delville painting already used by Hexenhaus on their debut album).
Line-Up Jimmy Karlsson: Vocals (1991-), Patrik Fernlund: Guitar, Daniel Eriksson: Guitar, Nicklas Lilja: Bass, Mattias Berglund: Drums *Past Members* Mikael Bergström: Vocals (1991), Evil-Jeppe: Vocals (1989-1991), Tobbe: Drums (1989-1991)
Deathography
Human Relic, Demo (1991)
Obsequies, Demo (1992)
Obsequies, 7" (After World, 1992)
Into Shadows/The Memorial, 7" (Poserslaughter, 1992)
The Ending Quest, CD (Crypta, 1994)
Promo 95, Demo (1995)
Darkness of the Dead, CD (Necroharmonic/Morbid Wrath, 2004)

GRAVE

Brilliant original death metal from the island of Gotland. Grave is definitely a pioneer of Swedish death metal. Jörgen claims they started to play heavy metal back in 1984 under names like Destroyer, Anguish, and Rising Power, and became extreme in the end of 1986. Initially they called themselves Corpse, but in 1988 changed to Grave and the music turned from Germanic speed to Swedish death. Their debut album *Into the Grave* remains one of the best Swedish death metal albums of all. They produced high quality music as long as Sandström was in the band, but after he left in 1995 they lost some of the original power. Lindgren has gradually become a better singer, though.
Line-Up Ola Lindgren: Guitar/Vocals, Jonas Torndal: Guitar (initially bass), Fredrik Isaksson: Bass, Ronnie Bergerståhl: Drums **Past Members** Jörgen Sandström: Guitar/Bass/Vocals, Jens Paulsson: Drums, Pelle Ekegren: Drums, Christofer Barkensjö: Drums
Deathography
Black Dawn, Demo (1987—as Corpse)
Sick Disgust Eternal, Demo (1988)
Sexual Mutilation, Demo (1989)
Anatomia Corporis Humani, Demo (1989)
Tremendous Pain, 7" (Century Media, 1991)
Grave/Devolution, Split LP (Prophecy Records, 1991)
Anatomia Corporis Humani, MLP (MBR, 1991)
Into the Grave, LP/CD (Century Media, 1991)
You'll Never See, CD (Century Media, 1992)
And Here I Die...Satisfied, MCD (Century Media, 1993)
Soulless, CD (Century Media, 1994)
Hating Life, CD (Century Media, 1996)
Extremely Rotten Live, CD (Century Media, 1997)
Back From the Grave, CD (Century Media, 2002)
Morbid Ways To Die, Box (Century Media, 2003)
Fiendish Regression, CD (Century Media, 2004)
As Rapture Comes, CD (Century Media, 2006)

GRAVITY

Raw thrash band started in Motala in the late 80's. They appeared on a split 7" before falling into nothingness in the wake of death metal. Too bad, since this was an intense band of great quality.
Line-Up Flammex: Vocals/Guitar, Rosco: Bass/Vocals, Mike: Drums
Deathography
Magic Doom, Demo (1988)
Gravity/Damien/Atrocity/Tribulation Split 7"(Is this Heavy or What Records, 1988)

GREEDKICK—see Regurgitate (Avesta)

GREFFWE

Extremely obscure thrash/black/death solo project apparently initiated in 1985. Everything went on hold in 1992 after two neglected demos, but I've heard the project was revived in 2001. Still no new signs of life. They might even be a myth for all I know.
Line-Up Nechrochristcrusher: Guitar/Bass/Drums/Vocals, Jimmie: Drums (2001-)

Deathography
Bloodhunting, Demo (1986)
The Burning of Priests, Demo (1989)

GRIEF OF EMERALD

Decent black/death band from Uddevalla formed during 1990-92 (I guess some kind of building period), but they only really got going in 1995. Johnny Lehto also used to play in Decameron.
Line-Up Anders Tång: Bass, Johnny Lehto: Vocals/Guitar, Jonas Blom: Drums, Jimmy Karlsson: Guitar, Lena Hjalmarsson: Keyboards, Anders Hedström: Guitar/Vocals **Past Members** Fredrik Helgesson: Drums (1997-1998), Dennis Karlsson: Drums (1996-1997), Robert Bengtsson: Keyboards (1994-2003)
Deathography
The Beginning... , Demo (1995)
...The Beginning, EP (Spellcast/Deviation Records, 1997)
Signs From a Stormy Past, CD (1997)
Nightspawn, CD (Listenable, 1998)
Malformed Seed, CD (Listenable, 2000)
Christian Termination, CD (Listenable, 2002)

GRIMORIUM

Death metal project of Söderköping's Joakim Göthberg (later in Marduk), started in 1989. Some slow death/black of dubious quality. Guest vocals by Andreas Axelsson (Edge of Sanity, Marduk) on the demo, after which the project folded.
Line-Up Joakim Göthberg: Everything
Deathography
Dead Tales, Demo (1991)

GRINDNECKS

Some kind of project/joke band I guess, initiated by a bunch of Gothenburg dudes in 2003 (most of them involved with the band Slaughtercult). Standard thrash/death with stupid lyrics. The band is currently on hold.
Line-Up Mikael Eriksson: Guitar, Mattias Nilsson: Bass, Joakim Proos: Vocals, Daniel Moilanen: Drums, Jonas Larsson: Guitar **Past Members** Johan Lundin: Guitar, Thim Blom: Drums
Deathography
Terror Rising, Demo (2004)
460 from Hell, Demo (2005)

GROTESQUE

When this incredible band crawled out of the remains of Conquest in Gothenburg in late 1988, they were one of the very first Swedish death metal bands. They remain one of the best and most brutal Swedish bands of all time, and their style has never been successfully copied. Though truly great, Grotesque had a short life, after which Lindberg and Svensson teamed up with the talented Björler brothers to form the fantastic At the Gates. Meanwhile Wåhlin created Liers in Wait—both are among the best bands Sweden has ever produced. Wåhlin is of course also known as the artist Necrolord, painting loads of album covers for bands like Emperor and Dissection. Original drummer Johan Lager is also known from

weird black metal acts Arckanum and Sorhin.
Line-Up Kristian Wåhlin: Guitar, Tomas Lindberg: Vocals (on occasions, he has also played bass and drums!), Alf Svensson: Guitar (1989-), Thomas Eriksson: Drums (1989-) **Past Members** *Johan Lager: Drums (1988-1989) David Hultén: Bass/Guitar (1988-1989), Per Nordkvist: Bass (1988), Jesper Jarold: Bass (1989)*
Deathography
Ripped From the Cross, Rehearsal (1988)
Ascension of the Dead, Rehearsal (1988)
4/7/89, Rehearsal (1989)
Blood Run From the Altar (aka The Black Gate is Closed), Rehearsal (1989)
Fall Into Decay, Rehearsal (1989)
In the Embrace of Evil, Demo (1989)
Incantation, MLP (Dolores, 1991)
In the Embrace of Evil, CD (Black Sun, 1996)

GRUEL
Brand new death metal act whose demo debuted in 2005. The future will tell if they have any impact.
Line-Up Jocke: Vocals/Guitar, Victor: Vocals/Guitar, Peo: Bass, Andreas: Drums
Deathography
Gruel, Demo (2005)

GUIDANCE OF SIN
Originally a side project with Jeppe Löfgren and Linus Nirbrandt from A Canorous Quintet, started in 1994 in Kungsängen. Guidance of Sin sounds a bit like Paradise Lost, but their compositions fail to impress greatly. They split up in 2001.
Line-Up Mattias Leinikka: Vocals, Jeppe Löfgren: Guitar (initially also Bass), Linus Nirbrandt: Guitar, L.E Simnell: Bass (1998-), Tobbe Sillman: Drums (1999-) **ast Members** *Fredrik Andersson: Drums (1996-1998)*
Deathography
Soul Disparity, Demo (1997)
Souls Seducer, CD (Mighty Music, 1999)
Acts, 7" (Nocturnal Music, 2000)
6106, CD (Mighty Music, 2000)

GUILLOTINE
Very Germanic mid-90's thrash metal from Umeå, formed in 1995. Basically a project involving some Nocturnal Rites members.
Line-Up Nils "Snake" Eriksson: Bass, Fredrik Mannberg: Guitar/Vocals, Cobra: Drums **Past Members** *Insane: Drums, Fredrik "Spider" Degerström: Guitar/Vocals*
Deathography
Under the Guillotine, Demo (1996)
Under the Guillotine, CD (Necropolis, 1997)

HARASSED
Quintet of death metal kids, started in Östersund around 1989. After losing original drummer Robert Eriksson to town "mates" Celeborn, I guess they always were number two locally. After producing three decent demos they called it quits. The most memorable fact about Harassed is the numerous

spelling errors on their demos—the guys were so ashamed they actually produced loads of small stickers to glue over the errors (such as: "explaning" instead of "exploring." Hilarious!) Note that Robert Eriksson later formed The Hellacopters together with Nicke Andersson of Entombed.
Line-Up Daniel Hedblom: Guitar, Jocke Bylander: Guitar, Martin Hoväng: Bass, Niklas Gidlund: Drums (1990-), Thomas Johansson: Vocals **Past Members** *Robert Eriksson: Drums (1989-1990)*
Deathography
Mindly Disorder, Demo (1991)
Desire of Exploring the Afterlife, Demo (1992)
Blessed by Suffering, Demo (1993)

HARMAGEDDON
I think from Uppsala, but I know nothing else.
Line-Up Andreas Öman: Vocals/Guitar, Christer Lundström: Drums/Samples, Micke Holmgren: Bass
Deathography
Rather be Dead, Demo (1994)

HARMONY
Formed from the ashes of Embryo in Strängnäs in 1992, soon transformed into Torment (see separate entry) after the release of the split EP in 1995. Decent death metal with some thrashier elements. Their old recordings have recently been released on CD.
Line-Up Pehr Larsson: Vocals/Bass (1994-), Peter Karlsson: Guitar, Kjell Enblom: Drums **Past Members** *Odd Larsson: Vocals/Bass/Keyboards (1992-1994), Crille Lundin: Bass (1992-1994), Thomas Fyrebo: Guitar (1992-1994), Ingela Ehrenström: Vocals*
Deathography
Blood Angels, Demo (1992)
Until I Dream, Demo (1993)
The Radice from a Star, Demo (1994)
The Radice from a Star EP, Harmony/Serenade Split EP (Sere, 1995)
Summoning the Past, CD (Konqueror Records, 2004)

HARVEY WALLBANGER
Amateurish thrashcore band started out in Sala in 1989. Though this sounds crappy as hell today, it represents the sounds of the late 80's pretty well as a time when everything fairly extreme was accepted in the name of uniting the forces of underground music. Of course this band could never make it far into the 90's, and in 1993 they folded. Sören went on to join Tribulation before they folded as well.
Line-Up Daniel Sören: Guitar/Vocals, Johan Feldtmann: Bass/Vocals, Fritz Quasthoff: Vocals, Jonas Wincent: Drums/Vocals, Magnus Hansson: Guitar
Deathography
Abominations of the Universe, Demo (1990)
Have a Nice Day, Demo (1991)
Irrevocable Act, 7" (Active Music, 1992)
Sick Jar of Jam, LP (Frisk Fisk Records, 1992)

HASTY DEATH
This cool thrash metal band formed in Falun/Orsa in 1988, delivering some Slayer/Celtic Frost-inspired thrash metal. Especially the vocals sound very much like Tom Warrior. I wish the retro thrash bands of today would sound at least a bit like this. Great, groovy, and raw. For me, this is classic stuff! Note that Tomas Olsson later joined Unleashed.
Line-Up Micke Jarvegård: Bass/Vocals, Mange Starbrink: Drums, Tomas Olsson: Guitar/Vocals, Johan Hinders: Guitar (1989-)
Deathography
Deadly Illusion, Demo (1989)
Subterranean Corrosion, Demo (1990)

HATRED
Aggressive thrash metal band of superior quality formed in Hedemora, 1987. Great, but they never got anywhere after appearing on a compilation LP released by classic Swedish metal radio show Rockbox. Vocalist Lundin left for Hexenhaus, an inferior but more successful group. The others went to good death metal bands like Interment (Svedlund & Jansson), Centinex (Wiklund & Jansson), and Dellamorte (Jansson & Svedlund). Anderson and Berggren are known from the pioneering crust band Asocial (as is Jansson, though later). This is, in my opinion, the best thrash metal band Sweden ever produced. Do whatever it takes to get their demos.
Line-Up Thomas Lundin: Vocals, Johan Jansson: Guitar, Kenneth Wiklund: Guitar, Thomas Anderson: Bass, Sonny Svedlund: Drums *Past Members* Tommy "T.B" Berggren: Vocals/Bass, Jan Björke: Guitar
Deathography
Winds of Doom, Demo (1987)
Welcome to Reality, Demo (1989)
The Forthcoming Fall, Demo (1990)

THE HAUNTED
The Haunted was formed by ex-Seance guitarist Patrik Jensen in 1996, together with At the Gates drummer Adrian Erlandsson. When At the Gates split, Anders and Jonas Björler joined as well. The Haunted basically continued At the Gates' contract on Earache, and developed their music into pure thrash territory, becoming probably the best retro thrash band of the 90's. Both Jensen and Anders Björler are masters of effective riffs. Erlandsson left for Cradle of Filth after the first record, replaced by the incredible Per Möller Jensen from Danish groups Invocator and Konkhra. Singer Dolving also left after the debut, replaced by Marco Aro of Face Down. However, in 2004 Dolving returned to his old flock. Anders quit for a while to focus on his studies, during that time the group seemed unable to produce anything at all. On his return, he wrote the main part of *One Kill Wonder* and the band was back on the move. The Haunted has rightly been very successful, even winning two Swedish Grammies for Best Metal Album—one of the few true metal bands to ever win. At the Gates had been nominated after *Slaughter of the Soul*, but the prize ludicrously went to emo-pop band Fireside.

Line-Up Patrik Jensen: Guitar, Anders Björler: Guitar, Jonas Björler: Bass, Per Möller Jensen: Drums (1998-), Peter Dolving: Vocals (1996-1998, 2004-) *Past Members* Marco Aro: Vocals (1998-2003), Adrian Erlandsson: Drums (1996-1998), John Zweetsloot: Guitar (1996)
Deathography
Demo 97, Demo (1997)
The Haunted, CD (Earache, 1998)
The Haunted Made Me Do It, CD/LP (Earache, 2000)
Live Rounds in Tokyo, CD (Earache, 2001)
One Kill Wonder, CD/LP (Earache, 2003)
rEVOLVEr, CD/LP (Century Media, 2004)
The Dead Eye, CD (Century Media, 2006)

HAVOC
Mid-90's death/black metal from Kristinehamn. Later changed their name to Brimstone, and started playing some kind of deadly heavy metal instead.
Deathography
Nightfrost, Demo (1996)
Feel Our Flames Caress, Demo (1997—as Brimstone)

HEADLESS
Of all death metal bands from Avesta around 1990, this was probably the least successful. They possessed a certain raw and primitive feeling, but weren't really musically skilled. As I remember, live they sounded a bit like early Sodom. Guitarist Jonny Lejonberg tragically passed away after their split. He will be remembered by the ones who knew him as the crazed metalhead he was.
Line-Up Jonny Lejonberg: Guitar, Leif Forsell: Vocals/Bass, Stefan Sohlström: Guitar, Staffan Dickfors: Drums

HEADLESS CORPSE
Brutal death metal from Mölndal. This 2000's band plays in the vein of Mortician, and also uses a drum machine. Though somewhat second-rate, it is nice to hear music this brutal coming from the west coast. The second demo is much better than the first.
Deathography
Support Violence!, Demo (2002)
Seconddemon, Demo (2003)

HEARSE
In 2001 ex-Furbowl members Johan Liiva-Axelsson (fresh from Arch Enemy) and Max Thornell decided to play death metal again. They went pretty much back to the roots, resuming their old mission of death/rock with some melodic touches.
Line-Up Johan Liiva-Axelsson: Vocals/Strings, Mattias Ljung: Strings/Vocals, Max Thornell: Drums/Strings
Deathography
Hearse, Demo (2002)
Torch, EP (Hammerheart, 2002)
Dominion Reptilian, CD (Hammerheart, 2003)
Armageddon, Mon Amour, CD (Candlelight, 2004)
Cambodia, EP (Karmageddon, 2005)
The Last Ordeal, CD (Karmageddon, 2005)

HECTORITE

Interested in yet another death/thrash band of the 2000's? If so, here's a band for you.
Line-Up Peter Strömqvist: Guitar, Roger Bergsten: Guitar, Olle Groth: Drums, Niklas Sundström: Bass, Klas Wiklund: Vocals
Deathography
Insano Technimetal, Demo (2001)
Nocturnal Metempsychosis, Demo (2002)
Subliminal Torment, Demo (2003)

HELLICON

Melodic death/thrash started in Haninge in 2001. The band has potential, but has yet to focus on a particular style. My advice: drop the clean vocals—the screaming sounds so much better!
Line-Up Pehr Hägg: Vocals, Joakim Antman: Guitar, Mattias Frånberg: Guitar, Johannes Borg: Bass, Robert Wernström: Drums
Deathography
Helliconia, Demo (2002)
A New Beginning, Demo (2004)

HELLMASKER

Once upon a time (1998) in the frozen town of Luleå, singer "Hellviz" gathered some members from Deathbound to play death metal. It resulted in the demo *Probably the Best Band in the World*—but nothing happened, so they probably weren't. (Or the world just wasn't ready for them.) "Zoid" must be one of few drummers in Luleå as he also plays in Game Over, Necromicon, Deathbound, Morthirim, Zmegma, The Hippos, Satariel, Cide, and Bootpunk.
Line-Up Hellviz: Vocals, Good Old Nick: Guitar, Mr Moshbaron: Guitar, Tommi "Hellkuntz" Konu: Bass, Zoid: Drums
Deathography
Probably the Best Band in the World, Demo (1998)

HELLMASTER—see Incardine

HELLPATROL

Retro thrash from Borlänge, formed in 2003.
Line-Up Micke Brander: Vocals, Jimi Wallin: Guitar/ Vocals, Linus Bergquist: Guitar, Stefan Eriksson: Bass Past Members Olle Mårthans: Drums (session only)
Deathography
Rot the Fuck Up, Demo (2003)
At the Depths of Despair, Demo (2004)
At the Crypt, Demo (2005)

HELLSPELL

Black/death duo from Kristianstad formed as Infernal in 1997, becoming Hellspell in 1999. The same year brought a demo and a CD, but then the band evaporated. Both members also play in Supreme Majesty and Non Sereviam. Chrille is also previously known from Mortum and Darksend.
Line-Up Chrille Andersson: Vocals/Drums, Daniel Andersson: Bass/Guitar/Vocals
Deathography

Evil Gathering, Demo (1997—as Infernal)
Warlust, Demo (1999)
Devil's Might, CD (Invasion, 1999)

HELLTRAIN

In 2002 some ex-members of Decortication/The Everdawn, Gates of Ishtar, Defleshed, The Duskfall, and Scheitan formed Helltrain in Luleå. They play commercialized death/rock attractive to Nuclear Blast, who signed them.
Line-Up Pierre Törnkvist: Vocals/Guitar, Patrik Törnkvist: Guitar/Organ/Piano/Bass, Oskar Karlsson: Drums/Guitar
Deathography
The 666 EP, EP (Heathendoom, 2003)
Route 666, CD (Nuclear Blast, 2004)

HELOTRY

Halmstad-born doom/black/death early 90's project. Brainchild of Tomas Karlsson, known from Autopsy Torment, Devil Lee Rot, Tristitia, and Pagan Rites.
Line-Up Tomas Karlsson, Luis B Galvez
Deathography
Demo January-93, Demo (1993)

HELVETICA—see Incarnated

HERESY

New death metal band of two members from Insult. They are probably too young to realize the band name was already taken by a classic band from the UK.
Line-Up Erik Gärdefors: Vocals/Guitar, Karl Wahllöf: Drums, Robert Granli: Bass
Deathography
Perdition, Demo (2004)

HETSHEADS

Formed Johanneshov, August 1988, as the wonderfully named hardcore group Hetsheads with Hetsfaces and the Fuckfaces of Death. Now that is a name! The music gradually transformed into death metal, and their name shortened to just Hetsheads. Later, they changed their name to Blackshine and started playing punkish rock n' roll. Strokirk is probably more known from Necrophobic (or even Mykorrhiza).
Line-Up Anders Strokirk: Vocals/Guitar, Stabel: Guitar, Fredda: Bass, Freimann: Drums
Deathography
Remonstrating the Preserver, Demo (1991)
We Hail the Possessed, CD (Repulse, 1994)

HEXENHAUS

Hexenhaus formed in Stockholm in 1987, and was probably Sweden's most successful thrash metal band in the 80's. Originally called Maninnya, the continuation of metal band Maninnya Blade. The name soon changed, as did many members, as Hexenhaus sought the perfect thrash line-up. They "stole" members from the superior bands Mezzrow, Hatred, and Damien. But this process held them back, and they never got everything together. Eventually it was too late for thrash metal—Hexenhaus vanished when death metal took over. Notably, they had

different vocalists on each album, but even stranger none ever sounded very good. Their last singer Tomas Lundin did a much better job in Hatred, a much better band. Later, Mike Wead briefly joined King Diamond's band, by far the best thing he ever did.
Line-Up Mike Wead (Mikael Vikström): Guitar, Marty Marteen: Bass, Marco A Nicosia: Guitar, John Billerhag: Drums, Thomas Lundin: Vocals *Past Members* Thomas Jaeger: Vocals, Nicklas Johansson: Vocals, Andreas Palm: Guitar, Mårten Sandberg: Bass, Ralph Rydén: Drums, Jan Blomqvist: Bass, Conny Welén: Bass, Martin Eriksson: Drums
Deathography
Demo (1987—as Maninnya)
A Tribute to Insanity, LP (Active, 1988)
The Edge of Eternity, LP (Active, 1990)
Awakening, LP (Active, 1991)
Deja Voodoo, CD (Black Mark, 1997)

HOLOCAUST
No-bullshit death metal from Lidköping which began in 1994 and stayed together long enough for two demos and a MCD. There are some hints at black metal in there as well, and it all sounds pretty good. Great name as well—too bad they split up.
Line-Up Metalwarrior (Andreas Söderlund): Guitar/ Vocals, Gutsfucker (Kristian Carlin): Bass, Berto Hjert: Drums
Deathography
Eternized Death, Demo (1996)
Gloom, Demo (1998)
Hellfire Holocaust, EP (Sound Riot, 2000)

HORNED
Thrash/death act from Skoghall, formed in 2000. Average music, but Björn Larsson possesses good growling vocals. During three years they produced no less than five demos, plus a "best of" compilation!
Line-Up Björn Larsson: Vocals/Bass, Kim Jardemark: Guitar, Henrik Kihlgren: Guitar, Johan Rudberg: Drums
Deathography
Dark Society, Demo (2000)
Three Ways to Kill, Demo (2001)
Sun City Compilation Vol 4, Split CD (Studiofrämjandet, 2002)
Live at Metal Clüb, Demo (2002)
Revenge, Demo (2002)
Unholy Anthology, Best of/Compilation (2003)
Halo of the Flesh, Demo (2003)

HÖST
Heavy metal band desperately trying to be a bit death metal; does that make them old school black metal? Formed in Linköping in 1994, and basically the solo project of Filip Carlsson (Corporation 187, ex-Satanic Slaughter). Among session musicians was Andreas Deblén, once of Deranged and Satanic Slaughter.
Line-Up Filip Carlsson: Guitar/Bass *Past Members* Robban Eng: Drums (session only), Andreas Deblén: Vocals (session only), Pehr Severin: Vocals (session only)
Deathography

Demo 95, Demo (1995)
Demo 96, Demo (1996)
Demo 97, Demo (1997)

HOUSE OF USHER
When Eskilstuna's metal flagship Macrodex split up in 1990, Kennhed, Martin, and Jani started House of Usher (the others became Crypt of Kerberos). Slow and cool death metal that really deserved attention, they were featured on the classic compilation LP *Projections of a Stained Mind* with Entombed, Grotesque, Merciless, and Mayhem. Kennhed used to play guitar in fantastic crust band No Security, and went on to be drummer of Dischange/Meanwhile (while No Security's drummer Jallo Lehto became the guitarist). Kenth Philipson went on with endless projects (Leukemia, Project Hate, God Among Insects etc.), and has also played with Dark Funeral. Probably most notably, Martin Larsson played in At the Gates for a while after the split of House of Usher. Man, this little piece almost turned into a history lesson in extreme Swedish music!
Line-Up Stefan Källarsson: Vocals/Bass, Mattias Kennhed: Guitar, Martin Larsson: Guitar, Kenth Philipson: Drums *Past Members* Jani Ruhala: Vocals, Jani Mylläringen: Drums
Deathography
On the Very Verge, 7" (Obscure Plasma, 1991)
When Being Fucked With, Demo (1993)
Promo #2, Demo (1993)
HUMAN FAILURE—see Anachronaeon

HYDRA
Melodic black/death metal from Stockholm whose lyrics refer to Greek mythology. Formed by "Titan" in 1995, they didn't really complete the line-up and get going until 1999. Initially the style was down-tuned death metal, but later the guys were attracted to melodies and black metal.
Line-Up Flame: Guitar/Bass, Titan: Guitar, Thunder: Drums *Past Members* Tornado: Drums, Maugrim: Bass, Erebus: Vocals
Deathography
Polemos, Demo (1999)
Cursed Battlegrounds, Demo (2000)
To Aima emon, Demo (2000)
Phaedra, CD (Heretic Sound, 2003)
Head of Medusa, Demo (2004)

HYPNOSIA
At the Gates-smelling band formed in Växjö in 1995. Not exactly original, but they have moments of fast and furious thrash metal. Hypnosia had some line-up problems, especially with bass players—including Johnny Dordevic, known from Entombed, Carnage, and Spiritual Beggars. The band split up in 2002.
Line-Up Lenny Blade: Bass, Mikael Castervall: Vocals/Guitar, Hampus Klang: Guitar, Michael Sjöstrand: Drums *Past Members* Carl-Petter Berg: Guitar, Johnny Dordevic: Bass, Klas Gunnarsson: Bass/Vocals, Johan Orre: Guitar, Mange Roos: Bass/Vocals

Deathography

Crushed Existence, Demo (1996)
The Storms, Demo (1997)
Violent Intensity, MCD (Iron Fist, 1999)
Extreme Hatred, CD (Hammerheart, 2000)

HYPOCRISY

Formed in 1990 as Seditious by the mighty man from the woods of Pärlbyn: Peter Tägtgren. He and drummer Lars Szöke played heavy metal since 1984 in Conquest. Before Hypocrisy, Peter spent some time in the U.S., where he attempted to join Malevolent Creation and Meltdown. But his Swedish roots brought him back, and during the 90's he became one of the most important persons of the Swedish death metal scene—not only the driving force of Hypocrisy, but also soundmaster of The Abyss studio. Hypocrisy has released a row of successful albums on Nuclear Blast. Their initial brutal death metal gradually turned more melodic and atmospheric, and the changes have garnered more followers around the world. Peter also created the successful electronic group Pain, and toured with Marduk as session guitarist. He has participated in more projects than I can list, notably War and The Abyss. He also helped start Lock Up (from the pieces of a Terrorizer reunion!), but couldn't find time to continue. Horgh used to be drummer of Immortal, and original singer Mats Broberg is now in Dark Funeral.
Line-Up Peter Tägtgren: *Guitar/Vocals, Mikael Hedlund: Bass, Horgh: Drums (2004-), Andreas Holma: Guitar* *Past Members Lars Szöke: Drums (1990-2003), Jonas Österberg: Guitar (1992), Mats Broberg: Vocals (1992-1993), Mattias Kamijo: Guitar (session only)*

Deathography

Rest in Pain, Demo (1992)
Penetralia, LP/CD (Nuclear Blast, 1992)
Pleasure of Molestation, MCD (Relapse, 1993)
Obsculum Obscenum, LP/CD (Nuclear Blast, 1993)
Inferior Devoties, MCD (Nuclear Blast, 1994)
The Fourth Dimension, CD (Nuclear Blast, 1994)
Abducted, CD (Nuclear Blast, 1996)
Carved Up/Beginning of the End, 7" (Relapse, 1996)
Hypocrisy/Meshuggah, Split 7" (Nuclear Blast, 1996)
Maximum Abduction, MCD (Nuclear Blast, 1996)
The Final Chapter, CD (Nuclear Blast, 1998)
Hypocrisy Destroys Wacken, CD (Nuclear Blast, 1999)
Hypocrisy, CD (Nuclear Blast, 1999)
Into the Abyss, CD (Nuclear Blast, 2000)
10 Years of Chaos and Confusion, CD (Nuclear Blast, 2001)
Catch 22, CD (Nuclear Blast, 2002)
The Arrival, CD (Nuclear Blast, 2004)
Virus Radio EP, EP (Nuclear Blast, 2005)
Virus, CD (Nuclear Blast, 2005)

HYPOCRITE

Standard death metal band started in Stockholm during 1989 as Dark Terror. Initially inspired by Merciless, they lacked originality and good songs. Later they looked to At the Gates for inspiration, with similar results. Peter Nagy is probably more known in Mörk Gryning. Note that Swedish death metal singer supreme, Lars-Göran Petrov, was once in this band (for kicks I guess). Six years since Hypocrite recorded anything, they are reportedly still active.
Line-Up Johan Haller: Vocals/Bass, Peter Nagy: Drums (1990-), Henrik Hedborg: Guitar (1992-)
Past Members Niklas Åberg: Guitar (1989-1995), Jim: Guitar (1990-1991), Dennis: Drums (1989-1990), L.G. Petrov: Vocals

Deathography

Ruler of the Dark, Demo (1989)
Welcome to Abaddon, Demo (1991)
Dead Symbols, Demo (1994)
Heaven's Tears, Hypocrite/Electrocution Split 7" (Molten Metal, 1994)
Edge of Existence, CD (Offworld, 1996)
Into the Halls of the Blind, CD (No Fashion, 1999)

HYSTE'RIAH

Thrash metal from Landskrona, started late 80's, probably under the influence of their pals God B.C. (or is it the other way around?) Fast and intense metal in the vein of Destruction and Exodus, but never a success. Joined in 1989 by God B.C. drummer Tom Hallbäck, they morphed into Hyste'riah G.B.C.
Line-Up Jerry "Krown" Kronqvist: Vocals/Bass/Drums, Klas Ideberg: Vocals/Guitar/Bass *Past Members Håkan Lindén: Bass, Ray Grönlund: Vocals, Joachim Leksell: Vocals, T. Seehagen: Drums*

Deathography

Attempt the Life, Demo (1987)
Jeremiad of the Living, Demo (1988)
Demo, Demo (1989)

HYSTE'RIAH G.B.C.

Continuation of Hyste'riah, with God B.C.'s Tom Hallbäck on drums. The guys released an album in 1991 (already two years old by that time), before they were wiped away by death metal. Klas Ideberg went on to Darkane, The Defaced, and Terror 2000.
Line-Up Jerry "Krown" Kronqvist: Vocals/Bass, Klas Ideberg: Vocals/Guitar, Tom Hallbäck: Drums

Deathography

Snakeworld, LP (Hellhound, 1991)

IGNATUM

Death/thrash band that started in Malmö 2002.
Line-Up Thomas Hulteberg: Vocals, Martin Eklöv: Guitar/Vocals, Martin "Germ" Bermheden: Guitar/Vocals, Alex Hassel: Bass, Fredrik "Natas" Illes: Drums

Deathography

Ward 13, Demo (2005)

ILEUS

Eskilstuna/Kungsör act formed in late 1990. Peter is also known from Crypt of Kerberos, the crust band Meanwhile, and industrial synth duo Arcana.
Line-Up Peter Pettersson: Drums (1991-), Vocals

(1991), B.S: Bass, Jari Manner: Guitar, Tero Viljanen: Vocals (1991-), Dan Jonsson: Guitar **Past Members** Tero (another one...): Vocals (1990-1991), Johan Syversen: Vocals
Deathography
Demo 91, Demo (1991)
Demo 92, Demo (1992)

IMMEMOREAL
Formed in Alingsås in 1993, they claim to play black metal but are clearly also inspired by death metal. Among the members are ex-Prophanity men Christer Olsson, Anders Malmström, and Christian Aho. Martin Qvist from Ablaze My Sorrow and Ancient's Rebirth also spent time here. Now the band is on hold, searching for a new singer and a bass player.
Line-Up Grendel (Christer Olsson): Guitar, Blash: Guitar, Wouthan (Anders Malmström): Drums/Keyboards **Past Members** Tyr: Guitar (1993-1994), Lord Asael: Vocals (1994-1995), Christian Aho: Bass/Vocals, GoatN. (Martin Qvist): Vocals
Deathography
Winterbreeze, Demo (1995)
The Age Nocturne, Demo (1998)
Towards 1347, Demo (1999)
Temple of Retribution, CD (Blackend Records, 2001)

IMMERSED IN BLOOD
Gothenburg band Immersed in Blood rose from the ashes of Inverted in 1998, created by the active Joel Andersson (also in Exempt and Nominon, and organizer of loads of gigs). This is the shit! Brutal death metal to the limit, the way it should be done. Truly one of the best bands from Gothenburg ever.
Line-Up Joel Andersson: Bass, Johan Ohlsson: Guitar, Jonny Bogren: Drums, Christian Strömblad: Guitar, Fredric Johnsson: Vocals **Past Members** Jocke Unger: Drums, Stefan Lundberg: Vocals, Robert Tyborn Axt: Guitar
Deathography
Eine Kleine Deathmusik, Demo (1999)
Sweets for My Sweet/Chapter 1, Split (Lowlife Records, 2000)
Relentless Retaliation, EP (Downfall Records, 2001)
Killing Season, CD (Arctic Music Group, 2003)

IMMERSION
New, melodic death metal from Värnersborg. The title of their only demo is not very original, neither is their music.
Line-Up Linus Johansson: Vocals, Marcus Hesselbom: Guitar, Jon Sannum: Bass, Anders Brusing: Guitar, Erik Johansson: Drums
Deathography
Death Is Just the Beginning, Demo (2004)

IMMORTAL DEATH—see Iniuria

IMPERIAL DOMAIN
Standard melodic death metal, formed in Uppsala back in 1994.

Line-Up Philip Borg: Guitar, Tobias V. Heideman: Vocals, Peter Laitinen: Guitar, Alvaro Romero: Drums **Past Members** Anders Eklöf: Guitar, Kalle Wallin: Drums, Erik Wargloo: Bass
Deathography
The Final Chapter, Demo (1995)
In the Ashes of the Fallen, Demo (1996)
In the Ashes of the Fallen, CD (Pulverised Recs., 1998)
The Ordeal, CD (Konqueror Records, 2003)

IMPERIOUS
Pure death metal band formed under the name Obscura in Nynäshamn, 1997. Changed to Imperious in the early 2000's, and the band continued on their deadly path. Chris is an insanely good drummer.
Line-Up Johan: Vocals/Guitar, Chris: Drums, Rickard Thulin: Bass, Adam Skogvard: Vocals/Guitar **Past Members** Emil: Vocals/Guitar
Deathography
Demo 99, Demo (1999—as Obscura)
In Agony, Demo (2000—as Obscura)
In Splendour, CD (Retribute Records, 2003)

IMPIOUS (Sundsvall)
Doomy mid-90's death metal from Sundsvall. Not the deadlier Impious from Trollhättan.
Line-Up Roger Lagerlund
Deathography
Let there be Darkness, Demo (1996)
Winter Goddess, Demo (1997)

IMPIOUS (Trollhättan)
Fairly aggressive death metal from Trollhättan (so they're trollish?), formed in 1994. They quickly made five demos, none spectacular, before recording a row of equally non-spectacular albums for Black Sun, Hammerheart, Konqueror, and even Metal Blade! I can't understand how they got their deals. This band should not to be confused with the doomier Impious from Sundsvall. Note that Impious has had its problems with drummers—two of them left for The Crown.
Line-Up Valle Daniel Adzic: Guitar, Martin Åkesson: Vocals, Mikael Norén: Drums (2002-), Erik Peterson: Bass, Robin Sörqvist: Guitar **Past Members** Johan Lindstrand: Drums (1994-1996), Marko Tervonen: Drums (1996), Ulf "Wolf" Johansson: Drums (1996-2002)
Deathography
Infernal Predomination, Demo (1995)
The Suffering, Demo (1996)
Promo 97, Demo (1997)
Evilized, CD (Black Sun, 1998)
Promo 99, Demo (1999)
Terror Succeeds, CD (Black Sun, 2000)
The Killer, CD (Hammerheart, 2002)
The Deathsquad, EP (Hammerheart, 2002)
Fate of Norns Release Shows, Split CD (Metal Blade, 2004)
Hellucinate, CD (Metal Blade, 2004)
Born to Suffer, CD (Karmageddon Media, 2004)

IN AETERNUM

Stubborn black/thrash/death metal band from Sandviken. Starting in 1992 as Behemoth, this band has seen an amazing number of members, most from other bands such as Infernal, War, Nominon, Suffer, Serpent, Sorcery, Funeral Mist, and Watain. A good band, but not good enough to rise above the majority of Swedish metal bands. Maybe they try to mix too many styles. Still pretty successful, they have toured the U.S. and appeared at Wacken Open Air.
Line-Up David Larsson: Guitar/Vocals, Perra Karlsson: Drums, Clabbe Ramberg: Bass, Erik Kumpulainen: Guitar Past Members Daniel Nilsson-Sahlin: Guitar, Demogorgon: Vocals (1992-1994), The Dying: Drums (1992-1994), Andreas Vaple: Bass (1994-2003), Paul Johansson: Guitar (1997-2001), Joacim Olofsson: Drums (1997-2001), Tore Stjerna: Drums (2002-2004), Robert: Bass (2003-2004)
Deathography
Domini Inferi, Demo (1992)
The Ancient Kingdom, Demo (1993)
The Pale Black Death, Demo (1996)
And Darkness Came, MCD (1997)
Demon Possession, Pic-7"(Metal Supremacy, 1999)
Forever Blasphemy, CD/LP (Necropolis, 1999)
The Pestilent Plague, CD/LP (Necropolis, 2000)
Past and Present Sins, CD/LP (Necropolis, 2001)
Nuclear Armageddon, CD (Agonia, 2003)
Beast of the Pentagram, 10" (Agonia, 2003)
Covered In Hell, Picture-7" (Bloodstone Entertainment, 2004)
No Salvation, MCD (Agonia, 2004)
The Pestilent Plague, Pic-LP (2005)
Dawn of a New Aeon, CD (Agonia, 2005)

IN BATTLE

Sundsvall-based war metal project launched in 1996. The initial black metal style was abandoned, and by 2004 they were a brutal death metal act in the vein of Morbid Angel. Frankly, their music nowadays depends too much on ultra-fast and tight drumming (courtesy of machine-man Nils Fjällström, who also hammers in Aeon, Chastisement, Odhinn, Sanctification, and Souldrainer). The fills, riffs, and song structures are too blunt and stereotypical to really excite. It feels more like a project than a band, since there simply are no dynamics. But hell, what a fast drummer! In Battle's latest album was recorded by Eric Rutan (Hate Eternal, ex-Morbid Angel), who also plays a guitar solo on one song.
Line-Up Nils Fjällström: Drums, John Frölén: Bass, Hasse Karlsson: Guitar, John Odhinn Sandin: Vocals, Tomas Elofsson: Guitar Past Members Håkan Sjödin: Guitar/Bass, Chastaintment: Bass, Otto Wiklund: Drums, Marcus Edvardsson: Bass (session only)
Deathography
In Battle, CD (Napalm, 1997)
The Rage of the Northmen, CD (Napalm, 1998)
Soul Metamorphosis, EP (Imperial Dawn, 2004)
Welcome to the Battlefield, CD (Metal Blade, 2004)

IN COLD BLOOD—see Raise Hell

IN FLAMES

In Flames ingnited in 1990, but changed many members before making a demo three years later. They picked up the melodic style of death metal that made At the Gates so great, and streamlined the concept. (Amazingly, In Flames were first a Bad News cover band—the UK rock comedy act!) To my ears they sound disturbingly commercial and calculated, but I'll admit it has worked beyond anyone's expectations. Today they are one of Sweden's biggest bands of any kind, with gigantic tours everywhere and insane record sales. They don't have much to do with death metal anymore. Note that Fridén originally was singer of Dark Tranquillity, while Dark Tranquillity's singer Mikael Stanne was the original singer of In Flames! Among other old members are ex-members of Marduk, Tiamat, Hammerfall, Arch Enemy, Eucharist, Dawn, Cemetary, etc.
Line-Up Anders Fridén: Vocals, Jesper Strömblad: Guitar, Björn Gelotte: Guitar (initially Drums), Peter Iwers: Bass, Daniel Svensson: Drums Past Members Johan Larsson: Bass (1990-1997), Anders Jivarp: Drums (1995), Daniel Erlandsson: Drums (1995),Glenn Ljungström: Guitar (1990-1997), Niclas Engelin: Guitar (1997-1998), Anders Iwers: Guitar (1990-1992), Carl Näslund: Guitar (1993-1994), Mikael Stanne: Vocals (1993-1994), Joakim Göthberg: Vocals (1995)
Deathography
Promo Demo '93, Demo (1993)
Lunar Strain, CD (Wrong Again, 1994)
Subterranean, EP (Wrong Again, 1994)
The Jester Race, CD (Nuclear Blast, 1995)
Scorn/Resin, Single (Nuclear Blast, 1997)
Whoracle, CD (Nuclear Blast, 1997)
Black Ash Inheritance, EP (Nuclear Blast, 1997)
Colony, CD (Nuclear Blast, 1999)
Clayman, CD (Nuclear Blast, 1999)
The Tokyo Showdown, CD (Nuclear Blast, 2001)
Reroute to Remain, CD (Nuclear Blast, 2002)
Cloud Connected, Single (Nuclear Blast, 2002)
Trigger, EP (Nuclear Blast, 2003)
The Quiet Place, Single (Nuclear Blast, 2004)
Soundtrack to Your Escape, CD (Nuclear Blast, 2004)
Come Clarity, CD (Nuclear Blast, 2006)
A Sense of Purpose, CD (Nuclear Blast, 2008)

IN PAIN

Traditional death metal from Anderslöv/Trelleborg that got going during the early 90's.
Deathography
Demo (1994)

IN THY DREAMS

Mid-90's band from Sala (formed in 1996) that sounds so ridiculously like At the Gates it is embarrassing. Later, some members formed Carnal Forge with Dellamorte's vocalist Jonas Kjellgren, after which In Thy Dreams soon split up. (By the way, Carnal Forge sounds ridiculously like The Haunted!) Still, In Thy Dreams was one of the very best At the Gates rip-

off bands (and Carnal Forge is great at cloning The Haunted). Both Stuvemark and Lindfors used to play in the pure death metal band Wombbath.
Line-Up Jari Kuusisto: Guitar, Petri Kuusisto: Bass, Håkan Stuvemark: Guitar, Stefan Westerberg: Drums **Past Members** *Fredrik Ericsson: Bass, Thomas Lindfors: Vocals, Jonas Nyren: Vocals*
Deathography
Stream of Dispraised Souls, EP (Wrong Again, 1997)
The Gate of Pleasure, CD (WAR, 1999)
Highest Beauty, CD (WAR, 2001)

INCAPACITY
Thrashy death metal, formed in Skövde in 2002. Pretty good stuff—no surprise as the members come from Edge of Sanity, Marduk, and Unmoored. Incapacity was formed when Cold Records label manager Omer Akay asked Anders Edlund of Solar Dawn to create a death/thrash band. So the manufactured boy band method seems to have snuck into the death metal world as well.
Line-Up Andreas Axelsson: Vocals, Robert Ivarsson: Guitar, Christian Älvestam: Guitar, Anders Edlund: Bass, Henrik Schönström: Drums **Past Members** *Kalle Johansson: Drums, Robert Karlsson: Vocals*
Deathography
Chaos Complete, CD (Cold Records, 2003)
9ᵗʰ Order Extinct, CD (Cold Records, 2004)

INCARDINE
Skärholmen/Vikarbyn band started in late October 1991 as Hellmaster. After initially playing Slayer and Entombed covers, they changed their name to Incardine and produced their own material. Good old death metal with thrash hints, or thrash with death metal vocals if you prefer. A CD was to be released in 1993, but the band split up instead.
Line-Up David Ahlberg: Vocals, Daniel Wallner: Guitar, Fredrik Folkare: Guitar/Bass, Jonas Tyskhagen: Drums **Past Members** *Rickard Arvidsson: Bass (1991-1992)*
Deathography
Moment of Connection, Demo (1992)
Demo 2, Demo (1992)

INCARNATED
Pure death metal from Bollnäs, formed in 1991 as Helvetica. Pretty good. A lot of problems with different labels (Voice of Death, Wild Rags) plagued their releases. Multiple line-up changes also held up the band. (Three Tony's have been in the group, and three drummers named Peter!) Former members joined Morgana Lefay, Divine Sin, and Carbunate.
Line-Up Henrik Andersson: Vocals, Fredde: Guitar, Peter "Kråkan" Jonsson: Guitar, Fredrik Lundberg: Bass, Peter Andersson: Drums **Past Members** *...I guess about every youngster in Bollnäs that knew the right end of a guitar.*
Deathography
Wool Gathering, Demo (1993)
Choirs of the Dead, Demo (1997)
Drown in Blood, MCD (unreleased, 1998)

INCENDIARY
This band started in 1998, and made a demo in 2002. They may still be going. If so, I guess beer-drinking holds them aloft, judging from band photos.
Line-Up Pontus Arvidson: Vocals/Guitar, Tobbe: Bass, Lalle: Drums **Past Members** *David: Vocals, Jens: Guitar*
Deathography
Incineration, Demo (2002)

INCEPTION
Avant garde death metal band formed in Uppsala in 2000. Problems occurred when two members left to focus on the much more extreme Deviant, but Inception remains active.
Line-Up Sebbe: Guitar, Simon: Guitar, Victor: Drums **Past Members** *Fredde: Bass, Tobbe: Vocals, EB: Drums, Fritz: Drums, Kenneth Valdek: Guitar*
Deathography
Awaken the Hordes, Demo (2002)
Before a Kneeling God, Demo (2003)
In Plethora, Demo (2005)

INCINERATOR
Thrash metal formed in 1995 in the ultra-Christian town of Jönköping. (To be really rebellious, shouldn't they be playing black metal?) Unlike so many At the Gates clones, this is pure old school thrash in the rough German style. So dusty, but it still sounds fresh! I prefer this to the likes of Arise and Terror 2000. The band has changed so many members I can't keep a record, but who cares? This is just good fun!
Line-Up Lenny Blade: Bass/Vocals, Andreas Nilzon: Drums, Jonas Mattson: Guitar **Past Members** *Lomm: Drums Wikstén: Guitar, Mikael "Cab" Casterval: Guitar, Mikael Granqvist, Magnus Alakangas, Fredrik Andersson, Jonas Larsson, Henrik Åberg*
Deathography
Order of Chaos, Demo (1996)
Thrash Attack, Demo (1998)
Thrash Attack, EP (Sound Riot, 2000)
Hellavator Musick, CD (Mourningstar Records, 2002)
World Incinerator, Demo (2003)
Disciples of Sodom, Demo (2003)
The Cocoon of Asphyx, Split Demo (Nihilistic Holocaust, 2005)

INCISION
One of Dan Swanö's (Edge of Sanity, etc) projects in the early 90's. The sole other member was Tony "It" Särkkä (Abruptum, etc). Pure death metal drenched in gore, death, and perversions! Don't mistake this for the later Stockholm band Insision.
Line-Up It (Tony Särkkä): Vocals (he might have provided some drums as well), Dan Swanö: All instruments
Deathography
Infest Incest, EP (1991—unreleased)
Perverted Possession, Demo (1991)

INCURSION
One of many obscure death metal bands from Stockholm that started in 1990. Their demo is one of

the few I couldn't find during work on this book, so I can't really describe what they sounded like.
Line-Up Joel Andersson: Guitar/Vocals
Deathography Demo (1990)

INDUNGEON
Mjölby-based project started in 1996 by Mithotyn member Wienerhall and Thy Primordial members Andersson and Albrektsson. Later Wienerhall formed the power metal act Falconer. Indungeon's thrash/death meets reasonable standards. No more, no less.
Line-Up Stefan Wienerhall: Bass/Guitar, Karl Beckman: Drums/Vocals, Michael Andersson: Vocals, Jonas Albrektsson: Bass
Deathography
Machinegunnery of Doom, Demo (1996)
Machinegunnery of Doom, CD (Full Moon Productions, 1997)
The Misanthropocalypse, CD (Invasion, 1998)

INEVITABLE END
Another new thrash/death band, this one from Nässjö, formed in 2003.
Line-Up Andreaz Hansen: Vocals, Emil Westerdahl: Bass, Joakim Malmborg: Guitar, Christoffer Johansson: Drums *Past Members* Joakim Bergquist: Vocals/Bass, Jonas Arvidson: Guitar, Magnus Semerson: Vocals
Deathography
Inevitable End, Demo (2004)

INFANTICIDE (Gävle)
New and pretty cool death/grind from Gävle, formed in 2002. Not the old thrash band from Piteå.
Line-Up Simon Frid: Vocals (initially also bass), Johan Malm: Guitar, Kristoffer Lövgren: Drums, Olle: Bass
Deathography
Global Death Sentence, Demo (2003)
Ultra Violence Propaganda, Demo (2003)
Promo 2005, Demo (2005)

INFANTICIDE (Piteå)
Standard early 90's thrash from Piteå, started out as Force Majeure in 1990, but soon changed their name. This is decent but something is definitely missing. Oh, it reminds me of... Kazjurol. Don't mistake this band for the newer grind band from Gävle.
Line-Up Andreas Fors: Guitar, Micke: Guitar (1992), Niklas: Guitar (1990-1992), Öberg
Deathography
Disharmony, Demo (1991—as Force Majeure)
Obtain and Devour, Demo (1992)
Obtain and Devour, 7"(Hit It, 1992)
Infanticidemo, Demo (1993)

INFERIOR BREED—see Soilwork

INFERNAL (Kristianstad)—see Hellspell

INFERNAL (Stockholm)
David Parland left Dark Funeral in 1996, and formed this intense band. Hellish, brutal black metal delivered with super precision. All past and present members come from high-caliber bands like Dark Funeral, Necrophobic, Funeral Mist, War, Dissection, Dawn, Defleshed, In Aeternum, and Sportlov.
Line-Up Typhos (Henrik Ekeroth): Vocals/Guitar, Blackmoon (David Parland): Guitar/Bass, Alzazmon (Tomas Asklund): Drums *Past Members* Matte Modin: Drums, Themgoroth: Vocals
Deathography
Infernal, EP (Hellspawn, 1999)
Under Wings of Hell, Split (Hammerheart, 2002)
Summon Forth the Beast, EP (Hammerheart, 2002)

INFERNAL GATES
Kil/Forshaga act formed 1992. Originally blasted death metal (they called it black metal), but developed to ultra heavy and slow doom metal.
Line-Up Stefan Sundholm: Vocals/Keyboards, Anders Hagerborn: Bass, Jonas Gustafsson: Drums, Johan Hedman: Guitar, Jan-Åke Österberg: Guitar
Deathography
In Sadness..., Demo (1993)
The Gathering of Tears, Demo (1994)
From the Mist of Dark Waters, CD (X-Treme, 1997)
When Angels Fell, EP (1999)

INFERNAL WINTER—see Serpent Obscene

INFERNUS RITUAL—see Ancients Rebirth

INFESTATION
Brutal band started in Hovås in February 1990 by soon-to-be famous brothers Anders and Jonas Björler, together with the already-known Tomas Lindberg. Band vanished when the trio chose to concentrate on the fantastic At the Gates.
Line-Up Björn Mankner: Guitar, Jonas Björler: Drums, Anders Björler: Guitar, Tomas Lindberg: Bass/Vocals *Past Members* Jan-Erik: Bass
Deathography
When Sanity Ends, Demo (1990)
Fears, Demo (1990)

INFESTDEAD
One of countless projects by Finspång's Dan Swanö, this time with Andreas Axelsson (both from the great Edge of Sanity). Blasphemous stuff!
Line-Up Dan Swanö: Basically Everything, Andreas Axelsson: Vocals
Deathography
Kill Christ EP, EP (Invasion, 1996)
Hellfuck, CD (Invasion, 1997)
Jesusatan, CD (Invasion, 1999)
Hellfuck & Killing Christ, CD (Hammerheart, 2000)

INFESTER
Early 90's death metal from Eskilstuna. Like House of Usher and Crypt of Kerberos, they formed from the ashes of Macrodex in 1991. Infester only lasted about a year, though.
Line-Up Johan Hallgren: Guitar, Marcus Pedersen:

Bass, Roger Pettersson: Vocals/Guitar, Janne Vårbeck: Drums
Deathography
Demo 1, Demo (1992)

INFURIATION
Short-lived project by Utte Cederlund and Lars-Göran Petrov somewhere around the break-up of Nihilist. The few who heard this all say it was great.
Line-Up Ulf Cederlund, Lars-Göran Petrov

INIURIA
Örebro band known as Immortal Death until 1993. Doomy and thrashy death metal, for sure—but I wouldn't call it immortal. I guess they were right to change their name. Mid-tempos, melodies, and bad vocals are what they are all about.
Line-Up Fredrik Johannessen: Vocals, Henrik Dahlberg: Guitar, Stefan Karlsson: Guitar, Johan Landhäll: Bass, Patrik Pelander: Drums **Past Members** Jenny: Keyboards (session only)
Deathography
Beyond Darkness, Demo (1991)
When All is Lost, Demo (1992)
Forgiveness, Demo (1993)
All the Leaves Has Fallen EP, EP (1995)
Promo 96, Demo (1996)

INNERFLESH
This band meant to play punk when they started in Uppsala in 2003, but the members loved metal so much that it turned into some thrashy death metal instead.
Line-Up Markus Luotomäki: Vocals/Guitar, Peter Wiström: Guitar, Johan Björkenstam: Bass, Gustaf Hedlund: Drums **Past Members** Henrik Myrberg: Vocals, Magnus Hakkala: Bass
Deathography
The Flesh Unleashed, Demo (2005)

INSALUBRIOUS
Good, though clearly copyist, death metal band formed in Sundsvall/Sundsbruk in 1993. Insalubrius virtually ceased to exist in 1996, as three members concentrated on Abyssos instead. When guitarist Niklas Johansson committed suicide in 2002, I guess it was all over. Rest in peace.
Line-Up Niklas Johansson: Guitar, Daniel Meidal: Guitar, Niklas Nilson: Vocals, Andreas Söderlund: Drums, Pär Eriksson: Bass **Past Members** Christian Rehn: Bass, Vincent Dahlquist: Vocals
Deathography
Le Culte des Morts, CD (Spiritual Winter Productions, 1994)
Pieces of a Dream, Demo (1994)
She Only Flies at Night, EP (Spiritual Winter Productions, 1995)
Lament of the Wolves, CD (Spiritual Winter Productions, 1995)
Bringer of the Northern Plague, EP (Spiritual Winter Productions, 2002)

INSANE OBSESSION
New and raw death metal band from Kalmar.

Line-Up Erik Bengtsson: Bass/Vocals, Tobias Berqvist: Drums, Martin Nilsson: Bass, Andreas Eriksson: Guitar
Deathography
Welcome to the Maniacs Hall of Fame, Demo (2002)

INSANITY—see Shagidiel

INSISION
Started in Stockholm in 1997, and soon recognized for their very "un-Swedish" brutality. Very extreme and technical stuff that sounds far more like Cannibal Corpse and Suffocation than Dismember or At the Gates. Their technical style has led to massive line-up changes, since members have had a hard time keeping up with the complex songs. (Today there are no original members left—just like Napalm Death!) When I myself joined in 1999, I had to really learn how to play the bass to keep up with Roger Johansson's unorthodox musical ideas. Insision's lyrical content changed dramatically from gore towards satanism when Carl Birath joined forces in 2000. Together with Johansson's complex riffs, this made Insision a completely new band. This reconfigured band gained the attraction of Earache, and secured a deal in 2001. As an underground band, Insision has toured extensively with the likes of Suffocation and The Haunted, and was the first Western death metal band ever to play in Thailand in 2005. But are we good? Well, I hope so. (But we're probably nerds—I'm writing books for fuck's sake!)
Line-Up Roger Johansson: Guitar (1997-), Daniel Ekeroth: Bass (1999-), Carl Birath: Vocals (2000-), Marcus Jonsson: Drums (2004-) **Past Members** Johan Thornberg: Vocals (1997-1999), Tomas Daun: Drums (1997-2004), Toob Brynedal: Guitar (2001-2004), Joonas Aahonen: Guitar (1997-1998), Danne Sommerfeldt: Bass (1998), Patrik Muhr: Guitar (1997-1998), Christian Ericsson: Guitar (session only, 2004-2005), Janne Hyttiä: Bass (session only)
Deathography
Meant to Suffer, Demo (1997)
Live Like a Worm, Demo (1998)
The Dead Live On, MCD (Heathendoom, 1999)
Promo 2000, Demo (2000)
Revelation of the Sadogod, Demo (2001)
Insision/Inveracity, Split 10" (Nuclear Winter, 2001)
Beneath the Folds of Flesh, CD (Earache/Wicked World, 2002)
Revealed and Worshipped, CD (Earache/Wicked World, 2004)
Ikon, CD (Dental Records, 2007)

INSULT
Brand new death metal band formed in Hällekil in 2004. Two members also play in Heresy.
Line-Up Erik Gärdefors: Guitar/Vocals, Karl Wahllöf: Drums, Johan Thorstensson: Bass, Johan Svensson: Vocals
Deathography
Decree, Demo (2005)

INTERMENT

Avesta band that rose from the ashes of the primitive Beyond around 1990. Their style is pure Swedish death metal the way it should be done. All the musicians are great, and the songwriting is even better. Oh fucking yes, this is what death metal is all about! It's a shame these guys never made it, because they were so incredibly good. One of the best Swedish death metal bands ever. Brutal as fuck. Jansson and Englund continued their deadly mission in Dellamorte and Centinex. Englund was also in the great Uncanny. During the 2000's Interment has rehearsed some, and a new demo has recently been recorded. You better make damn sure you get it!
Line-Up Johan Jansson: Guitar/Vocals, John Forsberg: Guitar, Micke Gunnarsson: Bass, Kennet Englund: Drums (1992-) Past Members Sonny Svedlund: Drums (1990-1992), Jens Törnros: Vocals
Deathography
...Where Death Will Increase, Demo (1991)
Forward to the Unknown, Demo (1992)
Shall Evil Unfold, Demo (1994)
The Final Chapter, Demo (1994)
Demo (2006)

INTERNAL DECAY

Formed in Märsta back in 1987, using the name Critical State, then Subliminal Fear, before settling on Internal Decay for their 1991 demo. Over time they transformed from heavy metal to grind and thrash to melodic death. Line-up changes and disagreements probably held them back. Finally in 1994, Internal Decay broke up. In their prime they opened for prominent bands including Obituary, Tiamat, and Edge of Sanity.
Line-Up Kim Blomquist: Vocals, Micke Jakobsson: Guitar, Kenny: Bass (1990-), Karim Elomary: Keyboards (1993-), Thomas Sjöholm: Drums, Hempa Brynolfsson: Guitar (1993-) Past Members Danne: Guitar (1987-1991), Pontus: Vocals (1987-1989), Willy Maturna: Guitar (1991-1993), Kim: Bass (1987-1990), Dave: Drums (1987-1990)
Deathography
Demo (1991)
A Forgotten Dream, CD (Euro Records, 1993)

INTOXICATE

Speed metal from Gothenburg, started during summer 1988. Decent songs, catchy riffs, and an overall good feel. However, they were probably a bit too thrash-oriented for the early 90's. Also, the joke intro of their first demo might have erased any possibility of future credibility.
Line-Up Grytting: Vocals, Tommy Carlsson: Guitar, Pasi: Drums, Tomas: Guitar, Martin: Bass
Deathography
Monomania, Demo (1989)
Tango of Nietzsche, Demo (1990)
Into Hiberation, Demo (1991)

INVADER

Melodic symphonic death metal band (what the hell is that?) formed in Umeå in 1997. They have made three demos so far, and I have avoided all of them.
Line-Up Axel Sebbfolk: Bass, Choffe: Guitar, Peppe: Guitar, Barre: Vocals, Robert Wiberg: Drums, Gustav Svensson: Keyboards Past Members Jonas Eriksson: Drums, Tonie Rombin: Vocals
Deathography
Furial, Demo (1998)
Negative Dimension, Demo (2003)
Equilibrium, Demo (2005)

INVERTED

Death metal act formed in Alingsås, February 1991. The originators were Mats Blomberg and Kristian Hasselhuhn, previously together in Inverted Cross. Pretty brutal stuff with lots of grind parts and a German speed metal feeling. For many years they struggled to rise from the underground, but never made it. After breaking up, some members created the great band Immersed in Blood. Dan Bengtsson joined Deranged for a while, and is now in Crowpath.
Line-Up Patrik Svensson: Vocals, Johan Ohlsson: Guitar, Joel Andersson: Bass, Kristian Hasselhuhn: Drums Past Members Henric Heed: Vocals, Larsen Svensson: Guitar, Dan Bengtsson: Bass, Joakim Almgren: Vocals, Mats Blomberg: Guitar, Anders Malmström
Deathography
Tales of Estaban, Demo (1991)
Heaven Defied, Demo (1992)
Empire of Darkness, 7" (Regress Records, 1994)
Revocation of the Beast, MCD (Wild Rag, 1994)
Shadowland, CD (Shiver Records, 1995)
Inverted/Centinex Split 7" (Voice of Death, 1995)
There Can Only Be One, CD (1998)

INVIDIOUS—see Katalysator

JARAWYNJA—see Solar Dawn

JIGSORE TERROR

Gore-grind act formed in 2001—good to see such a nice genre still alive! This is great music in the vein of Repulsion, Terrorizer, and Carcass. Hell yes! Two members also play in Birdflesh, and at least one was also in General Surgery. I guess this is mainly a project, but what quality grind band isn't?
Line-Up Tobbe Ander: Guitar, Adde Mitroulis: Drums/Vocals, Hampus Klang: Bass Past Members Tobbe Eng: Vocals
Deathography
World End Carnage, CD (Listenable, 2004)

JULIE LAUGHS NOMORE

Melodic death metal formed in Ljusdal in 1995. The band made some records, but never really made it. Ronnie Bergerståhl is now in Grave.
Line-Up Danne Carlsson: Vocals, Benny Halvarsson: Guitar/Vocals, Thomas Nilsson: Guitar, Thomas Olsson: Bass/Vocals, Ronnie Bergerståhl: Drums/Vocals
Deathography
Julie Laughs Nomore, EP (1996)

Live in Studio 1996, Demo (1996)
De Tveksamma/Julie Laughs No More, Split (Humla Productions, 1997)
When Only Darkness Remains, CD (Serious Entertainment, 1999)
From the Mist of the Ruins, CD (Vile, 2001)

KAAMOS

Stockholm's Kaamos started when A Mind Confused split in 1998, and Johan, Thomas, and Konstantin wanted to create something more brutal. Like Repugnant, Kaamos takes it back to the roots of the early 90's Swedish scene. Edge of Sanity comes to mind when you listen to *Lucifer Rising*, though I'm sure they would never admit to that. Kaamos just sound so fucking good, and are great live as well. Thörngren and Nicke used to be members of Serpent Obscene, and Christopher also played with them plus Repugnant and Grave—is he an old school-o-holic or what? If I were to decide, this band would rule the Swedish charts. Still, Kaamos have misunderstood one thing about the old scene: the key role of humor. Kaamos take themselves dead seriously, so they are actually more connected spiritually to early 90's black metal than late 80's death metal. Sadly, I was informed that Kaamos decided to throw in the towel in May 2006. They will not be forgotten.
Line-Up Karl Envall: Vocals/Bass, Konstantin Papavassiliou: Guitar, Nicke: Guitar, Christofer Barkensjö: Drums Past Members Thomas Åberg: Drums (1998-2000), Johan Thörngren: Vocals/Bass (1998-1999)
Deathography
Promo 1999, Demo (1999)
Kaamos, 7" (Dauthus, 1999)
Curse of Aeons, Demo (2000)
Kaamos, CD (Candlelight, 2002)
Lucifer Rising, CD (Candlelight, 2005)

KARNARIUM

Death metal from Gothenburg, formed in 1998. A couple demos and a single didn't go anywhere, so most of the members left. In 2005 a CD of old material emerged. We'll see if that makes a difference.
Line-Up Funeral Whore: Guitar/Vocals, Jim Voltage: Drums/Bass Past Members Gurra: Guitar, Redjet: Bass, Aho: Bass, Saigittarius: Drums
Deathography
Breaking the Manakles of Malkuth, Demo (2000)
Demo #1, Demo (2000)
Split Tape, Split (Into the Warzone, 2004)
Karnarium, Single (Nuclear Abominations Records, 2004)
Tänk På Döden, CD (Embrace My Funeral Records, 2005)

KATALEPTIK

Death metal project (one member also plays in a band inspired by Poison and Ratt, so don't expect too much) that produced two demos during 2000. Since then, nothing has been heard about it.
Line-Up Henke: Guitar, Micke: Vocals Past Members Björn

Deathography
Built To Destroy, Demo (2000)
Haunted by Disaster, Demo (2000)

KATALYSATOR

Fantastic old school death metal from Uppsala that must have started very recently. When I saw them at Uppsala Deathfest in 2005 their average age was reportedly under 14, but they sounded good! They looked like Nihilist, sounded like Grotesque, and had the most death metal attitude at the festival. They poured beer into themselves after the gig. Their only demo so far is fucking evil-sounding and feels like 1989 again. It was recorded in the Åhman brothers' garage! Let's hope these boys never grow old. They changed their name to Invidious in 2007, but good luck getting hardcore fans to call them anything but Katalysator! Probably Sweden's best band today.
Line-Up Hampus Eriksson: Guitar, Pelle Åhman: Vocals, Adde Mat: Guitar, Adde B Bollben: Drums, Gotte Åhman: Bass
Deathography
Zombie Destruction, Demo (2005)
Mass Genocide Ritual, Demo (2007)

KATATONIA

This highly original band started in Stockholm as a duo back in 1987 (originally called Melancholium) with Anders Nyström and Jonas Renske. These two have remained the creative force of the band. After their 1992 demo *JHVA Elohin Meth*, things started to happen. Though they never actually played black metal (only their early rehearsals can be described as black metal—fuck, were they ahead of their time in 1988!), Katatonia quickly got associated with that genre since it was the reigning trend of the times. They used black metal trademarks: corpse paint, pseudonyms like "Blackheim" and "Lord Seth," and for a long time even had a pentagram in their logo. The music was initially dark and atmospheric death/goth, but they gradually changed their style towards metallic emo-pop. The major turning point came when Renske decided to sing with a clean voice on *Discouraged Ones*, a drastic move for someone used to screaming his guts out. The change in style also brought lots of line-up changes. Among recent recruits are the Norrman brothers Fredrik (ex-Uncanny) and Mattias (ex-Dellamorte). Several session musicians have included Dan Swanö (Edge of Sanity etc.) and Micke Åkerfeldt (Opeth), who provided drums and vocals respectively for *Brave Murder Day*. Whatever you think of Katatonia, they undoubtedly possess a unique style. Their early releases are minor classics of moody and atmospheric metal.
Line-Up Anders Nyström: Guitar, Jonas Renske: Vocals (and Drums initially), Fredrik Norrman: Guitar, Mattias Norrman: Bass, Daniel Liljekvist: Drums Past Members Mikael Åkerfeldt: Vocals (session only), Israphel Wing: Bass, Dan Swanö: Drums (session only), Mikael Oretoft: Bass (session only)
Deathography
Rehearsal (1988)

Jhva Elohin Meth, Demo (1992)
Jhva Elohin Meth...the Revival, EP (Vic Recs 1992)
Dance of December Souls, CD (No Fashion, 1993)
For Funerals To Come, EP (Avantgarde, 1995)
Scarlet Heavens EP, Katatonia/Primordial Split 7"
(Misanthropy, 1996)
Brave Murder Day, CD (Avantgarde, 1996)
Sounds of Decay, MCD (Avantgarde, 1997)
Saw You Drown, MCD (Avantgarde, 1997)
Discouraged Ones, CD (Avantgarde, 1998)
Tonight's Decision, CD
Teargas EP, MCD (Peaceville, 2001)
Last Fair Deal Gone Down, CD (Peaceville, 2001)
Tonight's Music, EP (Peaceville, 2001)
Ghost of the Sun, Single (Peaceville, 2003)
Viva Emptiness, CD (Peaceville, 2003)
Brave Yester Days, CD (Peaceville, 2004)
The Black Sessions, CD (Peaceville, 2005)
The Great Cold Distance, CD (Peaceville, 2006)

KAZJUROL

Attempting to start a Swedish thrash metal band, some punk kids from gloomy industrial Fagersta (home of classic Swedish death metal venue Rockborgen) created Kazjurol in 1986. Though their first demos were decent, the band failed miserably. It's impossible to understand how they ever got a record deal—they are so unbelievably mediocre. I guess it helped that they were close friends with Peter Ahlqvist, who organized massive amounts of extreme shows in Sweden and ran the small label Uproar. The poor-sounding Kazjurol died quickly as death metal took over. Ahlquist abandoned the scene as his new label Burning Heart, which once featured Kazjurol, started to grow. He has since made a fortune on pop/punk bands like Millencollin and The Hives.
Line-Up Pontus: Guitar, T-ban: Guitar, Håkan: Bass, Uffe: Drums, Henrik Ahlberg: Vocals/Bass
Past Members Tomas Bengtsson: Vocals, Kjelle: Vocals, Bäs: Vocals, Andy: Bass, Bonden: Drums
Deathography
Breaking the Silence, Kazjurol/Homo Picnic/Instigators/Quod Massacre Split 7" (1986)
The Earlslaughter, Demo (1987)
Messengers of Death, 7" (Uproar, 1987)
A Lesson in Love, Demo (1988)
Dance Tarantella, LP (Active, 1990)
Bodyslam EP, 7" (Burning Heart, 1991)
Concealed Hallucinations, EP (Burning Heart, 1991)
Toothcombing Reality's Surroundings, EP (Burning Heart, 1991)

KEKS

Early death metal band that existed from 1989 to 1991. They made one demo, and basically consisted of Michael Samuelsson (Cauterizer) on vocals and bass. According to Samuelsson the band rehearsed only once, made one gig, and recorded a demo—with no bass, though he is listed as bass player.
Line-Up Michael Samuelsson: Vocals/Bass
Deathography
Darkness, Demo (1991)

KENTIK BROSK

One of countless hobby projects that the guys from Tribulation concocted during drunken days in Surahammar in the late 80's. This band is a furious mix between hardcore and death metal, and is by far the best music Forsberg ever produced.
Line-Up Magnus Forsberg ...and probably the rest of Tribulation.
Deathography
Demo (1988)

KERBEROS—see Draconian

KILL

Satanic death/black metal from Gothenburg, started in 1998. Many members with funny nicknames have passed since; read them for an idea how this sounds.
Line-Up Getaz: Drums, Gorgorium: Bass/Guitar, DD Executioner: Guitar Past Members Carl Warslaughter: Vocals, Assassmon: Bass, Black Curse: Guitar, Hellthrasher: Bass, Havoc: Vocals, Killhailer (Jens Pedersen): Vocals
Deathography
Nocturnal Death, Demo (1999)
Necro, EP (Evil Never Dies, 2001)
Morbid Curse, Demo (2003)
Horned Holocaust, CD (Invictus Productions, 2003)
Live for Satan, CD (Satanic Propaganda, 2004)
Morbid Curse, EP (Apocalyptor/Pentagram Warfare, 2005)

KILLAMAN

When Murder Corporation's singer left, Deranged men Rickard and Johan made this new project with Reclusion's Rune. Initially grindy, crusty death metal with punk touches, later it got more thrash-oriented. Nothing special, like most projects. Insision's Roger Johansson joined after teaming up with Axelsson for the recording of *Beneath the Folds of Flesh*.
Line-Up Johan Axelsson: Guitar, Rune Foss: Vocals, Roger Johansson: Guitar, Rikard Wermén: Drums, Kaspar Larsen: Bass
Deathography
Killaman, Demo (2002)
Killaman, CD (Displeased, 2003)

KNIFE IN CHRIST

Death metal band founded in Umeå in 2002. The fact that this group hasn't made a demo, and instead keeps putting MP3s on the Internet makes me want to puke. Get your shit together and do a proper tape!
Line-Up Henrik Boman Mannberg: Vocals, Ronnie Björnström: Guitar, Ludvig Johansson: Guitar, David Ekevärn: Drums

KOMOTIO

Deadly metalcore begun in Falun during 2000. First two demos are recorded in the famous Abyss studio.
Line-Up Sonny: Vocals, Daniel: Guitar, Sodomizer: Drums, Jansson: Guitar, Pär: Bass
Deathography
Coma Delirium, Demo (2001)
A Document of...., Demo (2002)

La Divina Slakthus, Demo (2003)

KÖTTBULLAR

Ultra-obscure band apparently lurking in Gothenburg during the late 80's. A split demo is all that remains. Note that their name means "meatballs" in Swedish, so maybe this wasn't a very serious band.
Deathography
Köttbullar/Meatgrinder-split, Demo (1988)

KREMATORIUM

Yet another new death/thrash act from Gothenburg. In 2004 they apparently changed their name to Seminarium, and then quit because Björn was about to start studying the cello. Metal?
Line-Up Kim Söderström: Vocals (initially Guitar), Leo Berglund: Bass, Björn Risberg: Guitar, Jocke Nordanståhl: Drums Past Members Andreas Henriksson: Vocals
Deathography
Demo II, Demo (2003)
Seminarium, Demo (2004)

KRIXHJÄLTERS

Good hardcore/crossover of the 80's from Stockholm. They eventually developed into the thrashier—but far worse—Omnitron. This is not death metal in any way, but worth checking out if you feel adventurous!
Line-Up Pontus Lindqvist: Vocals/Bass, Pelle Ström: Guitar, Rasmus Ekman: Guitar, Stefan Källfors: Drums
Deathography
Krixhjalters, 12" EP (Rosa Honung, 1984)
Hjälter Skelter, EP (CBR, 1988)
Evilution, MLP (CBR, 1989)
A Krixmas Carol, EP (CBR, 1990)

KRUX

Pure doom metal project formed in 2002 by Peter Stjärnvind and Jörgen Sandström of Entombed, and Leif Edling of Candlemass. Good stuff indeed, but you kind of suspect that the songs are made from riffs that weren't good enough for Candlemass or Entombed.
Line-Up Jörgen Sandström: Guitar, Peter Stjärnvind: Drums, Leif Edling: Bass, Mats Levén: Vocals
Deathography
Krux, CD (Mascot Records, 2003)

LACRIMAS—see Rapture (Alingsås)

LAETHORA

Gothenburg's Laethora is the new band since 2005 of Dark Tranquillity guitarist Niklas Sundin. Their style is supposed to be death metal, but I can't swear on it since I haven't heard them.
Line-Up Jonatan Nordenstam: Vocals/Bass, Joakim Rosen: Guitar, Niklas Sundin: Guitar, Joel Lindell: Drums
Deathography
Promo (2005)

LAKE OF TEARS

Lake of Tears was created from the ashes of Carnal Eruption and Forsaken Grief in the obscure town of Borås in May 1992. Initially their music had metal touches and growling vocals, but all the heavy aspects quickly vanished. In fact, this is probably one of the least metallic bands in this book. The music could be described as gothic pop/melancholic rock. I personally never cared much for this band, but they must have a following, since they are the second best-selling band on Black Mark after the mighty Bathory. However, in 2003 the band left their old label in favor of classic German thrash label Noise. Interestingly, Quorthon's sister Jennie Tebler liked them a lot, and sings backing vocals on their albums.
Line-Up Daniel Brennare: Vocals/Guitar, Mikael Larsson: Bass, Johan Odhuis: Drums, Magnus Sahlgren: Guitar Past Members Christian Saarinen: Keyboards, Jonas Eriksson: Guitar, Ronny Lahti: Keyboards/Guitar, Ulrik Lindblom: Guitar, Jennie Tebler: Vocals (session only)
Deathography
Demo 1, Demo (1993)
Greater Art, CD (Black Mark, 1994)
Headstones, CD (Black Mark, 1995)
A Crimson Cosmos, CD (Black Mark, 1997)
Lady Rosenred, MCD (Black Mark, 1997)
Forever Autumn, CD (Black Mark, 2000)
Sorcerers/Natalie and the Fireflies, Single (Black Mark, 2002)
The Neonai, CD (Black Mark, 2002)
Greatest Tears Vol. 1, CD (Black Mark, 2004)
Greatest Tears Vol. 2, CD (Black Mark, 2004)
Black Brick Road, CD (Noise, 2004)

LAST RITES—see Phobos

LEAVE SCARS

Mediocre death/thrash from Lund, started in 1988 as Macabre. (Guess why they changed the name?)
Line-Up Jonas Regnéll: Guitar/Vocals, Marcus Freij: Guitar, Daniel Preisler: Drums/Vocals
Deathography
Demo (as Macabre, 1988)
The Terminal Suffer, Demo (1992)

LEFT HAND SOLUTION

Formed in the northern town of Sundsvall in 1991. One of the better Swedish doom metal acts—distinguished by their clean female vocals. For a brief period they attracted the attention of Nuclear Blast, who re-released the *Fevered* album in 1997. However, sales failed and they soon found themselves back on their old label. Original singer Kristina Höijertz later joined melodic black metal act Siebenbürgen. (At the very start the band had a male singer, the mighty Jörgen Fahlberg of hardcore gods Totalitär and insanely funny The Kristet Utseende.)
Line-Up Erik Barthold: Drums (1992-), Marina Holmberg: Vocals (1994-), Janne Wiklund: Guitar (1997-), Robert Bergius: Bass Past Members Peter Selin: Bass, Jocke Mårdstam: Guitar (1991-1997), Kristina Höijertz: Vocals (1992-1994), Jörgen Fahlberg: Vocals/Bass (1991-1992), Liljan Liljekvist: Drums (1991-1992), Henrik Svensson: Bass (session only)

Deathography
Dwell, Demo (1992)
Falling, Demo (1993)
Shadowdance, MCD (Massproduktion, 1994)
Demo 95, Demo (1995)
Fevered, CD (Massproduktion, 1996)
Missionary Man, MCD (Massproduktion, 1999)
Black in Grace, CD (Massproduktion, 1999)
Light Shines Black, CD (Massproduktion, 2001)

LEGION—see Cranium

LEPRA
Melodic death metal band formed in 2001. Since then they have produced three ignored demos.
Line-Up Benny Hallman: Vocals, Thomas Dahlman: Guitar, Aad Andersson: Bass, Christoffer Andersson: Drums Past Members Krille: Guitar
Deathography
The Doomsday Shadow, Demo (2001)
Bleeding, Demo (2003)
Quick, Easy & Painful, Demo (2003)

LEPRECHAUN
Frankly, I don't know anything about this band, but in 1998 they released a demo of brutal death metal.
Deathography
Blasphymon, Demo (1998)

LEPROSY
Ultra-obscure Helsingborg band that formed in 1987, changed a member, and made two pretty intense demos. It's a shame they weren't noticed.
Line-Up Patrik "Peo" Olofsson: Vocals, Patrik "Svarre" Svärd: Guitar, Magnus "Mange" Liljetoft: Guitar, Miko Mattson: Bass, Niclas "Snille" Olsson: Drums Past Members Christian "Damen" Carlsson: Bass
Deathography
Death to This World, Demo (1988)
Full of Hate, Demo (1990)

LEUKEMIA
This project of Kentha Philipson (editor of *Hypnosia* and founder of countless projects) began as Braincancer in October 1989. Previously, Jocke and Jimmy had a straight rock band called Purpose, but after seeing Filthy Christians on national television they went for the brutal stuff. The next year they started calling themselves Misery, but on December 4, 1990 they changed the name to Leukemia. The group has used lots of session musicians, such as Lars-Göran Petrov (Entombed), Jörgen Sandström (Grave/ Entombed), and Mattias Kennhed (Meanwhile). Still, their hardcore-flavored death metal fails miserably— the vocals are especially terrible. The band apparently changed its name to Lame later on. Very suitable. Philipson continued with better The Project Hate (with Jörgen Sandström) and God Among Insects. He has also lately played bass with Dark Funeral. In my opinion he should start *Hypnosia* again, the best thing he has ever done.
Line-Up Kentha Philipson: Drums, Jocke Granlund:

Vocals, Tobias: Guitar Past Members Jimmy: Guitar (1989-1990), Jörgen: Bass (1989-1990)
Deathography
Morbid Imaginations, Reh. (1989—as Braincancer)
Antiqued Future, Demo (1990—as Braincancer)
Visions From Within, Demo (1991)
Innocence Is Bliss, Demo (1992)
Suck My Heaven, CD (Black Mark, 1993)
Grey Flannel Souled, CD (Step One, 1994)

LEVIATHAN—see Ophthalamia

LIERS IN WAIT
When Grotesque split in 1990, Tomas and Alf started At the Gates, while Kristian Wåhlin formed Liers in Wait. The sound and style is a continuation of Grotesque, in which Wåhlin practically did all of the material, but sadly they never really made it. Though the band was pretty successful at first (they made a video in 1992 and toured with Vader in 1993), it fell apart after a couple years. This probably had to do with serious line-up problems, as members constantly went on to other things. (Check the impressive list of past members.) Drummer Nilsson later joined Luciferion, and with guitarist Wåhlin he founded Diabolique in 1995. Wåhlin is probably best known for CD and T-shirt artwork. Under the name "Necrolord" he has worked for Emperor, King Diamond, Tiamat, Therion, Entombed, etc. For their first album, Liers in Wait hired Therion's Christoffer Jonsson for vocal duties. An ultra-brutal band of a kind that you don't hear anymore. For me, this is the very essence of brutality.
Line-Up Kristian Wåhlin: Guitar, Matthias Gustafsson: Bass, Hans Nilsson: Drums Past Members Anders Björler: Guitar, Jörgen Johansson: Guitar, Christoffer Johnsson: Vocals/Guitar/ Keyboards (session only), Tomas Lindberg: Vocals, Mattias Lindeblad: Bass, Mats: Drums, Moses: Guitar, Alf Svensson: Guitar, Daniel Erlandsson: Drums
Deathography
Spiritually Uncontrolled Art, MLP (Dolores, 1991)
Immersie Obscura, Demo (1992)
Deserts of Rebirth, LP (well, this one was never released to my knowledge)

LIFELESS—see Project Genocide

LIGAMENT
Standard early 90's death metal from Holmsund/ Umeå, I guess some kind of joke band featuring members from Nocturnal Rites. Ironically, Nocturnal Rites sounds much more like a joke.
Line-Up Mattias Lönnback, Mats Björklund: Vocals
Deathography
Demo 92, Demo (1992)
Demo (1993)

LIVING GUTS—see Cauterizer

LOBOTOMY
In January 1989 the band Rapture emerged from the

boring Stockholm suburb of Kista. That October, they changed their name to Lobotomy and got serious. Their style was grind at first, but they soon became more death metal. After problems with labels and line-up, they ended up on No Fashion in 1996. They never gained any real success, though. Listening to them, you kind of understand why. Don't get me wrong, they aren't bad. But in a music scene of such quality as Swedish death metal, this lot couldn't compete. And their earlier efforts are far more interesting than the later material. In 2000, the guys gave up for good. Bandleader Strachal used to edit *Ruptured Zine*. Today he runs Dental Records (with Birdflesh, Hearse, and Insision on its roster). *Line-Up* Max Collin: Vocals, Etienne Belmar: Guitar, Lars Jelleryd: Guitar (initially bass), Patric Carsana: Bass, Daniel Strachal: Drums *Past Members* Fredrik Ekstrand: Guitar, Jonas: Vocals (1989), Leffe: Guitar (1989)
Deathography
When Death Draws Near, Demo (1990)
Against the Gods, Demo (1992)
Nailed in Misery, Demo (1992)
Hymn, 7" (Rising Realm, 1993)
Lobotomy, CD (Chaos, 1995)
Nailed in Misery—Against the Gods, CD (Thrash Corner, 1995)
Kill, CD (No Fashion, 1997)
Born in Hell, CD (No Fashion, 1999)
Holy Shit, EP (No Fashion, 2000)

LOCK UP
Fueled by ever-intense Peter Tägtgren, this international project began as a reunion of Los Angeles legends Terrorizer. When those plans fell apart, Lock Up was created. The line-up included the late Jesse Pintado (Napalm Death, ex Terrorizer), Shane Embury (Napalm Death), Peter Tägtgren (Hypocrisy), and Nick Barker (Dimmu Borgir, ex-Cradle of Filth). Tägtgren was later replaced by Tomas Lindberg (Skitsystem, Disfear, ex-At the Gates). Lock Up delivers hyper-fast and intense grindcore, produced to an almost clinical level. I guess you can hardly describe this as a Swedish band, but I'm including it anyway.
Line-Up Jesse Pintado: Guitar, Shane Embury: Bass, Nick Barker: Drums, Tomas Lindberg: Vocals (2000-) *Past Members* Peter Tägtgren: Vocals (-2000)
Deathography
Pleasures Pave Sewers, CD (Nuclear Blast, 1999)
Hate Breeds Suffering, CD (Nuclear Blast, 2002)
Live in Japan, CD (Nuclear Blast, 2005)

LOGIC SEVERED
A new, experimental death metal band, started in Hässleholm in 2004. Look at the amazing number of people already involved for an idea how experimental it is. Rumored to be a project by members of Body Core, Verminous, and Infernal Hellfire.
Line-Up John Doe: Vocals/Samples/Congas/Didgeridoo, Jane Doe: Guitar, Missing: Drums/V-drums/Percussion, Lost: Bass, Withheld: Guitar *Past Members* Mjölner: Drums, Behemoth: Vocals, Gandalf: Bass, Vlad: Guitar, Pan: Guitar,

Necrophallus: Vocals
Deathography
Complete Maggotry EP, EP (Dustbin, 2004)
Fraction of a Vile Existence, CD (Dustbin, 2004)

LORD BELIAL
Trollhättan band started out in December 1992. They obviously wanted to fit into the black metal movement, but their music was probably a bit too slow and death metal-inspired to gain any great recognition. Still, they secured a deal with No Fashion early on, and have since progressed over a row of decent records. After some trouble when No Fashion refused to release the fascist song "Purify Sweden," Lord Belial ended up on Regain Records. Though their image is extreme, the music is pretty mellow—which figures if you consider that they have used five flute players in the band.
Line-Up Thomas Backelin: Vocals/Guitar, Anders Backelin: Bass, Mickael Backelin: Drums, Hjalmar Nielsen: Guitar *Past Members* Daniel Moilanen: Drums, Vassago (Niclas Andersson): Guitar (1992-2000, 2001-2003), Plague (Fredrik Wester): Guitar (2000, 2002), Lilith: Flute (1993-1999), Jenny Andersson: Flute (session only), Cecilia Sander: Flute (session only), Catharina Jacobsson: Flute (session only), Annelie Jacobsson: Flute (session only), Jelena Almvide: Cello (session only)
Deathography
The Art of Dying, Demo (1993)
Into the Frozen Shadows, Demo (1994)
Kiss the Goat, CD (No Fashion, 1995)
Enter the Moonlight Gate, CD (No Fashion, 1997)
Unholy Crusade, CD (No Fashion, 1999)
Angelgrinder, CD (No Fashion, 2002)
Doomed by Death, Lord Belial/Runemagick- Split (Aftermath, 2002)
Purify Sweden, picture 7" (Metal Fortress, 2003)
Scythe of Death, EP (Metal Fortress, 2003)
The Seal of Belial, CD (Regain, 2004)
Nocturnal Beast, CD (Regain, 2005)

LOSS
Death metal, launched in Karlstad in 2000. Mainly a project by Mental Crypt's Janson and Jansson.
Line-Up Matte Andersson: Vocals, Kjell Elmlund: Drums, Sven Erik Fritiofsson: Guitar, Jan Janson: Guitar, Ulf Jansson: Bass *Past Members* Hugo Bryngfors: Vocals
Deathography
Human Decay, Demo (2000)
Verdict of Posterity, CD (Scarlet Records, 2001)
Promo 2002, Demo (2002)
No Sanity Left, Demo (2004)

LOTHLORIEN
Varberg band that released an album on Black Mark in 1998 and split up in 2002. They claimed to play death metal. Listen and decide for yourself. Most of them then joined the very un-death band Frequency.
Line-Up Henrik Serholt: Vocals, Tobias Birgersson: Guitar, Linus Wisdom: Guitar, Tobias Johansson: Bass, Daniel Hannendahl: Drums/Percussion, Nils-

Petter Svensson: Keyboards (session only)
Deathography
In the Depth of Thee Mourning, Demo (1996)
The Primal Event, CD (Black Mark, 1998)

LOUD PIPES
A project launched in Stockholm during the early 90's, Loud Pipes is basically a bunch of death metal maniacs playing dirty, fast punk. Roster included Peter Stjärnvind (Entombed, Merciless), Fredrik Lindgren (Terra Firma, Unleashed), Fredrik Karlén (Merciless), and notorious madman Nandor Condor. Hearing the result, it's pretty obvious that the members spent more time drinking beer than trying to create interesting riffs. The energy is there, but not much else. Still, Loud Pipes got a deal when French label Osmose focused on Swedish crust/metal in the mid-90's (signing Dellamorte, Driller Killer, and Disfear). Stjärnvind's drumming is inferior to all his other work. I bet he was drunk during the recording. Listen to Uncurbed instead.
Line-Up Peter Stjärvind: Drums, Fredrik Lindgren: Guitar, Fredrik Karlén: Bass, Nandor Condor: Vocals
Deathography
Drunk Forever, Demo (1995)
Loud Pipes/Essoasso split 7" (1995)
The Downhill Blues, CD (Osmose, 1997)

LUCIFER
Lucifer formed from the ashes of Salvation in Mjölby in 1990, mainly to pick up a recording deal Salvation had been offered shortly before its demise. They made a couple demos and a 7" single. Then they made an album for Mexican label Bellphegoth Records, but for some reason never sent the master tape. The band split up, and the album is lost. Mikael has also played in Atryxion, Carcaroht, Indungeon, Thy Primordial, and Metroz (which also included Jonny).
Line-Up Mikael Andersson: Guitar (initially also bass), Jonny Fagerström: Drums/Vocals, Michael Fast: Bass (1992-) Past Members Lars Thorsén: Guitar (1992), Mika Savimäki: Guitar (1993)
Deathography
The Ritual, Demo (1991)
Darkness, Demo (1991)
The Dark Christ, Single (1992)
Promo, Demo (1993)

LUCIFERION
Gothenburg band founded in 1993 by Peter Weiner Andersson and Sarcazm's Mikael Nicklasson—also in the equally brutal Liers in Wait at the time. Peter soon left, and Liers in Wait's Hans Nilsson entered to complete the brutality. They released an album and appeared on a couple compilation CDs, but never really made it. Nilsson formed Diabolique in 1996 when Luciferion split up. Like many other early 90's bands, Luciferion's early recordings have been released on CD in the 2000's. Get it and be brutal.
Line-Up Wojtek Lisicki: Vocals/Guitar, Mikael Nicklasson: Guitar, Hans Nilsson: Drums, Martin Furängen: Bass Past Members Peter Weiner

Andersson: Drums, Johan Lund: Keyboards
Deathography
DT, Demo (1994)
Demonication (The Manifest), CD (Listenable, 1994)
The Apostate, CD (Listenable, 2003)

LYKANTROP
New band inspired by black/death metal, with Nazi lyrics. I don't know if it's for shock value, or for real, but reportedly the band includes members from the white power band Heysel.
Deathography
Violent Behavior, CD (Resistance, 2003)

MACABRE—see Leave Scars

MACABRE END
This good old death metal band in pure Swedish style started in December 1988 in Vålberg, under another name that I have forgotten. The initial grindcore style changed towards death metal during 1989, and in February 1990 they became Macabre End. They recorded a 7" and planned to record an EP called *Nothing Remains Forever* for Relapse, but nothing came of it. In late 1991 Johansson (who edited *Suppuration Zine*) left the band, and the others continued as God Macabre (see separate entry). Raw and pure death metal of good quality.
Line-Up Per Boder: Vocals, Jonas Stålhammar: Guitar (1990-), Ola Sjöberg: Guitar, Thomas Johansson: Bass, Niklas Nilsson: Drums
Deathography
Consumed by Darkness, Demo (1990)
Consumed by Darkness, 7" (Corpse grinder, 1991)

MACHINE GOD—see Face Down

MACRODEX
Eskilstuna band which kicked off in 1987 as the hardcore band Cruelty. (Note that two members, Jani and Jari, continued with an early version of notorious white power band Pluton Svea...unbelievable). Soon Cruelty became the fast and furious death/thrash band Macrodex. In 1989 they were among the elite of Swedish death metal, but always seemed one step behind bands like Entombed, Grave, and Merciless. After a couple thrashy death demos they mellowed out, and started writing slower stuff. Due to musical disagreements, the group soon dissolved, splitting into Crypt of Kerberos and House of Usher. Harri Mänty is now in Kent, Sweden's biggest Pop band!
Line-Up Roger Pettersson: Guitar/Vocals, Peter Pettersson: Guitar, Christian Eriksson: Vocals, Martin Larsson: Bass, Micke Sjöberg: Drums Past Members Jocke: Guitar, Mattias Kennhed: Guitar, Jani Myllärinen: Drums, Stefan Karlsson: Bass, Jari "Roiten" Riutanheimo: Bass, Harri Mänty: Vocals (session only, in Cruelty)
Deathography
Who Cares, Demo (1988—as Cruelty)
Disgorged to Carrion, Demo (1989)
Infernal Excess, Demo (1989)
Remains of a Lost Life, Demo (1990)

MADRIGAL
Melodic Gothenburg act launched in 1998, influenced by death metal as well as goth. Like many others, Madrigal signed to Nuclear Blast for one album, and were dropped when it failed commercially.
Line-Up *Martin Karlsson: Vocals/Guitar, Linda Emanuelsson: Piano/Keyboards, Kristoffer Sundberg: Guitar, Lukas Gren: Bass* **Past Members** *Marcus Bergman: Drums*
Deathography
Enticed, Demo (1998)
I Die, You Soar, CD (Nuclear Blast, 2001)

MALEDICTUM
Melodic black/death band from Stockholm that formed, released a demo, and split up (to my knowledge) all during 2000. They are not missed. The members' other bands include Hydra, Nocturnal Damnation, and Siebenbürgen, so you might guess the lack of brutality.
Line-Up *Dennis (Death's Poet): Vocals, Linda: Guitar, M. Ehlin: Guitar/Vocals/Programming, Jessica: Bass* **Past Members** *Berge: Guitar, Kim: Drums*
Deathography
Into the Darkness, Demo #1, Demo (2000)

MALEFICIO
Lerum band reportedly formed as early as 1990. Maleficto tried mixing everything metallic into their music, along with very un-metal things such as flutes and violins. The result is a confused mess of death/black/thrash/folk and heavy metal. They must hold the world record for demo tapes released without getting a record deal, having made eighteen attempts. In fact, their sole CD is self-financed, and of demo quality! I guess some people don't understand when to call it quits, or are they just misunderstood? Get one of the demos and find out for yourself.
Line-Up *Daniel Johannesson: Guitar/Vocals, Mikael Fredriksson: Guitar, Ebion: Bass, Peter Derenius: Drums/Keyboards* **Past Members** *Martin Söderqvist: Bass/Vocals (1995-1996), Charlotte: Vocals (1996), Fredrik Ramqvist: Bass (1996), Hanna: Violin (1996), Heiki: Flute (1996), Rickard Yxelflod: Vocals (1996), Jimmy Hiltula: Guitar/Vocals, Erik Gustafson: Bass/Vocals*
Deathography
Eyes of Darkness, Demo (1991)
Go to Hell, Demo (1991)
Hail You the Beast, Demo (1991)
I Killed Jesus, Demo (1992)
Silence, Demo (1995)
Bockfot, Demo (1995)
Liar on the Cross, Demo (1996)
The Truth, Demo (1996)
Burn, Demo (1997)
Thy Morbid Fear, Demo (1997)
Winterschlacht 97, Demo (1997)
Under the Black Veil, Demo (1998)
Wings of Malice, Demo (1998)
Winterschlacht 99, Demo (1999)
Malediction Lecture, Demo (2000)

Army of Forgotten, CD (2001)
Human Remains, Demo (2003)
Entwined in Mysteries, Demo (2004)

MALUM
Death metal band formed in Landskrona in 2001. Later moved to Sireköpinge—none of the persons I asked has a clue where that is. The title of their first demo is great, learn Swedish to understand it!
Line-Up *Dahrum: Bass/Vocals, Chrisum: Guitar, Smaluml: Drums/Vocals* **Past Members** *Jocke: Guitar*
Deathography
Åt Helvete Med Skiten, Demo (2002)
Angel Descending, Demo (2005)

MANIFREST
One of countless Swedish bands that never got anywhere, Manifrest formed in Örebro in 1992. They made a demo, then vanished. Their music was actually quite good, with a heavy Deicide influence. They definitely had unique qualities, and incorporated thrashier elements into the mix. Their demo also has pretty good sound, courtesy of Dan Swanö and Gorysound studio. Daniel Andersson was also a member of the better-known Necrony. Note this band is sometimes listed as Manifest, but Manifrest seems to be the correct spelling.
Line-Up *Björn: Guitar/Vocals, Mikael: Guitar, Daniel Andersson: Bass, Mattias Borg: Drums*
Deathography
Mind, Demo (1992)

MANINNYA BLADE
Began as Fair Warning in Boden back in 1980, and after a name change to Maninnya Blade they became one of Sweden's first speed metal bands (or at least they played dirty heavy metal). One of the first Swedish bands with any degree of extremity to release an album. However, by 1987 it was all over for these guys. Some members continued as Maninnya, soon becoming the better-known Hexenhaus. During the 2000's Maninnya Blade has reactivated, playing a few gigs and releasing old material on CD. Note that ex-drummer Martin Eriksson today is a huge techno star in Europe under the name E-Type. The band has reputedly recorded about ten early demos which I have never seen or heard.
Line-Up *Leif Eriksson: Vocals (initially guitar), Andreas "RIck Meister" Pahlm: Guitar, Nicke "Ripper" Johansson: Guitar, Jan "Blomman" Blomqvist: Bass, Ingemar Lundeberg: Drums* **Past Members** *Martin Eriksson: Drums, Mikael "Mike Wead" Wikström: Guitar, Jerry Rutström: Guitar*
Deathography
Demo (1982—as Fair Warning)
The Barbarian/Ripper Attack, 7" (Platina, 1984)
Demo 85, Demo (1985)
Merchants in Metal, LP (Killerwatt, 1986)
Tribal Warfare, Demo (1987)
A Demonic Mistress From the Past, CD (Marquee Records, 2001)

MARAMON

Melodic black metal band which transformed into melodic death metal. They started in Lindesberg in 2001, and have since churned through more members than interesting riffs.

Line-Up Peter Ristiharju: Vocals, Christer Karlsson: Guitar, Stefan Andersson: Bass, Christian Muhr: Drums Past Members Tommie Dahlberg: Keyboards, Tommy Bruhn: Keyboards, Tobias Matsson: Bass, Kalle Jansson: Drums, Christian Persson: Keyboards, Rickard Källqwist: Guitar/Bass, Ola Högblom: Guitar, Pär Hjulström: Drums, Rickard Källqwist: Guitar (session only), Martin Jacobsson: Drums (session only)

Deathography
Hednaland, EP (2002)
Sömn, Demo (2002)
Dödens Rike, Demo (2003)
Me, Myself, I, CD (Karmageddon Media, 2005)

THE MARBLE ICON

Doom/death band from Gnesta that emerged in July in 1994. Somewhat similar to My Dying Bride, though deadlier, less melodic, and less professional. Jonas Kimbrell is ex-Dispatched.

Line-Up Jonas Kimbrell: Bass, Oskar: Guitar (initially also vocals), Mattias: Drums, Erik Sahlström: Vocals (1995-), Jimmi: Guitar

Deathography
Queen Damager, Demo (1995)
Sombre Epigraph, Demo (1996)

MARDUK

Formed by guitarist Morgan Håkansson (Abruptum) in the end of 1990, this was one of the first Swedish post-Bathory black metal bands. From the beginning, they aimed to create the most brutal kind of metal ever. You've got to admit they came close. Their unique violent music developed constantly over the years, perfected on the *Panzer Division Marduk* album in 1999. Though the majority of their work is awesome, this is their brutal masterpiece. Precision, speed and violence to the limit. Marduk is one of few bands hailed by the majority of death metal fans and black metal fans alike. In my opinion this is the best that the Swedish black metal scene of the 90's produced. In fact, since Dissection and Abruptum really aren't traditional black metal bands, Marduk might be the only pure and original Swedish band of the genre after Bathory. (Even a later band like Dark Funeral drew from a more established tradition).

Line-Up Morgan "Steinmeyer" Håkansson: Guitar, Emil Dragutinovic: Drums (2002-), Magnus "Devo" Andersson: Bass (2004-), Guitar (1992-1995), Mortuus: Vocals (2003-) Past Members Roger "B War" Svensson: Bass (1992-2004), Fredrik Andersson: Drums (1994-2002), Erik "Legion" Hagstedt: Vocals (1995-2003), Joakim Göthberg: Drums (1990-1993), Vocals (1993-1995), Andreas Axelsson: Vocals (1990-1993), Rikard Kalm: Bass (1990-1992), Kim Osara: Guitar (1995-1996)

Deathography
Demo #1, Demo (1991)

Fuck Me Jesus, Demo (1991)
Here's No Peace, 7" (Slaughter, 1991)
Dark Endless, CD/LP (No Fashion, 1992)
Those of the Unlight, CD/LP (Osmose, 1993)
Opus Nocturne, CD/LP (Osmose, 1994)
Fuck Me Jesus (91 Demo), MCD (Osmose, 1995)
Heaven Shall Burn...When we are Gathered, CD/LP (Osmose, 1996)
Glorification, CD (Osmose, 1996)
Live in Germania, CD/LP (Osmose, 1997)
Nightwings, CD/LP (Osmose, 1998)
Panzer Division Marduk, CD/LP (Osmose, 1999)
Infernal Eternal, CD (Blooddawn, 2000)
Obedience, EP (Blooddawn, 2000)
La Grande Danse Macabre, CD (Blooddawn, 2001)
Slay the Nazarene, Single (Blooddawn, 2002)
Blackcrowned, Box (Blooddawn, 2002)
Hearse, Single (Blooddawn, 2003)
World Funeral, CD (Blooddawn, 2003)
Plague Angel, CD (Blooddawn, 2004)
Deathmarch, EP (Blooddawn, 2004)
Warschau, CD (Regain, 2005)

MASTICATE

This Finspång/Örebro platoon is one of Dan Swanö's countless projects of the early 90's. Basically a two-man band formed on October 5, 1990, when Swanö teamed up with Jakobsson (Necrony, later Nasum) to create brutality. Definitely one of Swanö's better projects. Cool and intense death metal with grind parts and ultra-low-pitched vocals.

Line-Up Dan Swanö: Guitar/Bass/Vocals, Anders Jakobsson: Drums/Vocals

Deathography
Desecration, Demo (1990)

MASTICATION

Death metal from Upplands Väsby, formed in 1990. Amazingly, they played live with Crematory, Candlemass, and Dismember before their first demo—makes me wish it was 1990! Young bands lived for metal then, unlike the quality-reducing "straight to album" mentality of today (or maybe I'm just old). The members are known from Grave, Unanimated, Coercion, Excruciate, Morpheus, Mykorrhiza, and Cauterizer. Good stuff, as you might guess.

Line-Up Janne Rudberg: Guitar, Daniel Lofthagen: Bass/Guitar, Lars Levin: Vocals, Per Ekegren: Drums

Deathography
Demo 1991, Demo (1991)
Demo #2, Demo (1991)
Mastication, Demo (1991)

MASTICATOR

An early Swedish death metal band which made three demos in 1991. The singer later turned to black metal with Vintersorg (and Otyg, Borknagar, Fission, Havayoth, and Cosmic Death).

Line-Up Vintersorg: Vocals/Guitar, Daniel O: Guitar, Mattias Marklund: Bass, Benny Hägglund: Drums

Deathography

Demo, Demo (1991)
Demo (Title Unknown), Demo (1991)
Dismembered Corpse, Demo (1991)

MASUGN
Black/thrash/death metal band, formed in Gothenburg in 2005. I guess this is a joke band.
Line-Up Frid: Guitar, M.K Stenvold: Guitar, Noc: Drums, Eytzinger: Bass/Vocals
Deathography
Damballah, Demo (2005)
A Scent of Decreation (2005)

MAUSOLEUM
Melodic death metal band from Arboga formed in 2002. Apparently they replaced a couple members and changed their name to Soulbreach. Dino, Magnus, and Timo all play in Septic Breed. Magnus also used to be in Throneaeon.
Line-Up Per Fransson: Guitar, Dino Medanhodzic: Guitar, Magnus Wall: Bass, Henrik Brander: Drums *Past Members* Timo Kumpumäki: Vocals, Peter Svensson: Bass
Deathography
Demo 2003, Demo (2003)
Fluctuating Senses, Demo (2003)

MAZE OF TORMENT
Strängnäs band initially known as Torment (see separate entry), became Maze of Torment for the 1996 debut album and are still going. An average band with brilliant moments. Chrille Lundin and Peter Karlsson are known from Deceiver, and Peter Jansson used to play in Crypt of Kerberos.
Line-Up Kjell Enblom: Drums, Erik Sahlström: Vocals, Magnus Lindvall: Guitar, Rickard Dahlin: Guitar, Cloffe Caspersson: Bass *Past Members* Pehr Larsson: Vocals/Bass (1994-1998), Peter Jansson: Bass (1997-1999), Kalle Sjödin: Bass, Viktor Hemgren: Guitar
Deathography
The Force, CD (Corrosion, 1996)
Faster Disaster, CD (Iron Fist Productions, 1999)
Death Strikes, CD (Necropolis, 2000)
Maze Bloody Maze, Single (Merciless, 2002)
The Unmarked Graves, CD (Hellspawn, 2003)
Brave the Blizzard, Single (TPL records, 2004)
Hammers of Mayhem, CD (Black Lodge, 2005)

MEADOW IN SILENCE
Death/doom/heavy metal act started in Vikingstad during 1995. They apparently saw themselves as black metal, but I don't think they qualify. They have likely changed some members, but I can't tell you for sure. I don't think they exist anymore.
Line-Up Weinherhall: Vocals/Guitar, Karl: Vocals/Guitar/Keys, Karsten: Drums, Schutz: Bass/Vocals
Deathography
Rehearsal (1995)
Rehearsal 2 (1995)
From Beyond the Stars, Demo (1995)
Promo 96, Demo (1996)
Through the Tides of Time and Space, CD (Violent Nature, 1996)

MEADOWS END
Melodic death metal band formed in Örnsköldsvik in 1993. Apparently they are still going since they self-financed a mini-CD some years ago, but they aren't talked about in the scene.
Line-Up Henrik Näslund: Keyboards, Jan Dahlberg: Guitar, Daniel Tiger: Drums, Mats Helli: Bass, Anders Rödin: Vocals
Deathography
Beyond Tranquil Dreams, Demo (1998)
Self-Forsaken, Demo (1999)
Everlasting, Demo (2000)
Soulslain, Demo (2002)
Somber Nation's Fall, EP (2004)

MEASURELESS
Brutal, grinding death metal from Säffle. They may not be the best band, but you've got to admire a band that just fucked the black metal trend of 1993 and went for the deadlier stuff!
Line-Up Henrik Persson: Drums/Vocals, Christer: Guitar, Mats Bergqvist: Guitar, Daniel: Bass/Vocals
Deathography
Abandoned to Die, Demo (1993)
Demo 2, Demo (1994)

MEFISTO
One of the very first brutal Swedish bands to follow the path laid out by Bathory, their cult status is firmly cemented. They started in Stockholm as Torment in 1984, but soon changed the name. As Mefisto they created evil-sounding death/black metal to the limit. They were probably the first underground band in Sweden that got some attention, and they even had a manager to take care of their career. It obviously didn't work, since they never played live and only recorded two demos before vanishing. These demos have been released on CD by Blooddawn/Regain, and you better get their stuff if you want to know your history. A cult band if there ever was one.
Line-Up Omar Ahmed: Guitar, Sandro Cajander: Bass/Vocals, Roberto Granath: Drums
Deathography
Megalomania, Demo (1986)
The Puzzle, Demo (1986)
The Truth, LP/CD (Blooddawn/Regain, 1999)

MEGASLAUGHTER
Early minor band formed in Gothenburg in 1986 as Dinloyd. Later music is a confused blend of Cannibal Corpse and Metallica. That particular mix doesn't work so well. After some demos and an album, the band folded in 1992. Lilic later surfaced in the project Murder Corporation with members of Deranged. He and the Räfling brothers formed the traditional heavy metal band Jaggernaut in 2001. Patrik Räfling was also drummer of the immensely successful, but hideous, Hammerfall during 1997-1999.
Line-Up Jens Johansson: Vocals, Emil Lilic: Vocals, Kenneth Arnestedt: Guitar, Alex Räfling: Bass, Patrik Räfling: Drums
Deathography
Death Remains, Demo (1989)

Demo, Demo (1991)
Calls from the Beyond, LP (Thrash, 1991)

MEGATHERION—see Therion

MELANCHOLIUM—see Katatonia

MELISSA
Starting in 1986 in Bjärnum playing hardcore/grind, at the end of the 80's they turned towards some kind of technical thrash. They didn't survive the hard competition of early 90's Swedish death metal. I had forgotten about them myself until I started work on this book (and I never knew much to start with).
Line-Up Schizo: Drums (initially Vocals), Paranoya: Guitar/Vocals (1988-, initially Bass), Trauma: Bass (1989-), Stezzo: Guitar (1989-) Past Members Necro: Bass (1988-1989)
Deathography
Demo (1986)
Garagedemo 1, Demo (1988)
Garagedemo 2, Demo (1988)
Welcome, Demo (1989)
A Flight to Insanity, 7" (Underground Records, 1989)

MEMORIA
Melodic death metal band formed in Nässjö in 1999. They released a demo CD in 2000, but since then I haven't heard anything. Probably for the better.
Line-Up Ludvig: Vocals, Johan: Drums, Josef: Guitar, Martin: Bass, Patrik: Keyboards
Deathography
Memoria, MCD (2000)

MEMORIUM
A band from Horred that formed in 1992. They tried to stand out from the crowded death metal scene by using a keyboard player and a drum machine. Well, this band is living proof that "original" doesn't necessarily mean "interesting." Does anyone remember them? Daniel Andersson was also the editor of *Recension Mag.*
Line-Up Daniel Andersson: Keyboards, Fredrik: Vocals, Joel, Markus Past Members Dennis
Deathography
The Oak of Memories, Rehearsal (1992)
Enlightment, Demo (1992)
At the Graveyard, Rehearsal (1993)
Deepest Woods, Demo (1993)
Memorium, EP (1994)

MENTAL CRYPT
Karlstad band formed in 1993. Death metal in the old school vein of Dismember and Interment, with a tendency to mix in other influences like Pantera, Sepultura, and Slayer. A bit confused, but okay. Originally a side project of some members from Loss. Mental Crypt are reportedly still active, but nothing has been heard from them for years.
Line-Up Hugo Brygfors: Vocals, Kjell "Kjelle" Elmlund: Drums, Sven Erik Fritiofsson: Guitar, Jan Janson: Guitar, Ulf Jansson: Bass Past Members Blappan: Bass/Vocals
Deathography

Black Hole, Demo (1993)
Aimless, Demo (1994)
Sects of Doom, Demo (1996)
Extreme Unction, CD (Black Mark, 1998)
Ground Zero, Demo (1999)

MEPHITIC
Heavy death/thrash from Nordmaling, on the scene in the early 90's. The only thing I have heard by them is pretty sloppy and unconvincing.
Line-Up Patrik Jonsson
Deathography
The Sweet Suffering, Demo (1992)
Demo (1993)

MERCILESS
One of the first, and most original, death metal bands from Sweden. Formed during 1986 in the small town of Strängnäs, they set out to create brutal and ultra-fast thrash metal in the vein of Sodom. Their extreme, unrelenting style attracted Norwegian black metal icon Euronymous, and Merciless' debut album became the first release on his Deathlike Silence label. In the late 80's and early 90's, they played virtually every show in Sweden, including memorable gigs with Sodom and Sepultura. After Karlsson left for highly successful punk group Dia Psalma in 1992, Merciless recruited talented drummer Peter Stjärnvind (Unanimated, Face Down, Entombed). Still, the band never got the attention they deserved. Though completely inactive for long periods (in the late 90's they didn't even exist), Merciless still play their personal mix of thrash and death metal. In 2004, original drummer Stefan Karlsson returned, since Stjärnvind's obligations in Entombed took too much of his time (frankly, Karlsson's drumming fits Merciless better). In my opinion, Merciless is one of the best bands Sweden has produced. In particular, their second demo, *Realm of the Dark*, and debut album, *The Awakening*, are masterpieces.
Line-Up Fredrik Karlén: Bass, Erik Wallin: Guitar, Roger Pettersson: Vocals (1987-), Stefan "Stipen" Karlsson: Drums (1986-1991, 2004-), Kalle: Vocals (1986-1987) Past Members Peter Stjärnvind: Drums (1991-2004)
Deathography
Behind the Black Door, Demo (1987)
Realm of the Dark, Demo (1988)
The Awakening, LP (Deathlike Silence, 1990)
Branded by Sunlight, Merciless/Comecon Split 7" (CBR, 1992)
The Treasures Within, LP/CD (Active, 1992)
Unbound, LP/CD (No Fashion, 1994)
Merciless, CD (VME, 2003)

MESENTERY
Early 90's death metal from Mjölby that mainly consists of grinding drums and deep growls. The members are of course from other Mjölby bands.
Line-Up Lars Tängmark, Janne Martinsson, Rickard Martinsson, Karsten Larsson, Magnus Linhardt
Deathography

Demo 1, Demo (1992)
Demo 2, Demo (1993)

MESHUGGAH

Unbelievably experimental thrash, formed in the boring northern town Umeå way back in 1987. Their initial style was heavily influenced by Metallica (their original name was Metallien), but gradually they transformed into an incomparable hyper-technical riff machine. These guys are insanely skilled, and Jens' vocals are awesome. Just when Meshuggah was about to break big, they faced immense problems as some members injured themselves badly. First guitarist Thorendal cut off the top off a finger, then drummer Haake trapped his hand in a lathe. Still, Meshuggah continued their manic mission. As the guitarists kept adding strings to their guitars, their music became stranger with each record. Along with Dismember and Afflicted, the only great Swedish band Nuclear Blast ever signed. (Okay, Dischange was cool too!) A unique and brilliant band which everybody should check out. Their connection to death metal? Oh, fuck it! Meshuggah belong in every book about extreme metal.
Line-Up Jens Kidman: Vocals (initially also guitar), Fredrik Thorendal: Guitar, Tomas Haake: Drums, Martin Hagström: Guitar, Dick Lövgren: Bass *Past Members* Peter Nordin: Bass, Niklas Lundgren: Drums, Gustav Hielm: Bass
Deathography
Ejaculation of Salvation, Demo (1989)
Psykisk Testbild, EP (Garageland, 1989)
Promo 1991, Demo (1991)
Contradictions Collapse, LP/CD (Nuclear Blast, 1991)
None, EP (Nuclear Blast, 1994)
Destroy Erase Improve, CD (Nuclear Blast, 1995)
Selfcaged, MCD (Nuclear Blast, 1995)
Hypocrisy/Meshuggah, Split (Nuclear Blast, 1996)
The True Human Design, MCD (Nuclear Blast, 1997)
Chaosphere, CD (Nuclear Blast, 1998)
Rare Trax, CD (Nuclear Blast, 2001)
Nothing, CD (Nuclear Blast, 2002)
I, EP (Nuclear Blast, 2004)
Catch 33, CD (Nuclear Blast, 2005)

MESQET

Mid-90's melodic death metal of poor quality.
Deathography
Dreamless, Demo (1996)

METALLIEN—see Meshuggah

METEMPSYCHOSIS—see Mournful

METROZ

Primitive death/thrash band from Motala, formed in 1989. Stevo left to join Toxaemia, after which Mikael and Jonny went on to form Lucifer.
Line-Up Mikael Andersson: Bass, Tommy: Guitar, Jonny: Drums *Past Members* Stevo Bolgakoff: Vocals

Deathography
Brain Explosion, Demo (1989)
Demo (1990)

MEZZROW

One of Sweden's original thrash metal bands when they started in Nyköping in 1988, Mezzrow really caused a buzz in the underground with their demos, and played live a lot. I saw them at least three times in 1989. But after the release of their album, death metal swept away Mezzrow with all other thrash metal bands in Sweden. But for a few years, they were among the leading bands in the Swedish scene.
Line-Up Staffe Karlsson: Guitar/Vocals, Zebba Karlsson: Guitar/Vocals, Uffe Pettersson: Vocals/Bass, Steffe Karlsson: Drums *Past Members* Conny Welén: Bass, Nicke Andersson: Bass
Deathography
Frozen Soul, Demo (1988)
The Cross of Tormention, Demo (1989)
Then Came the Killing, LP (Active, 1990)
Demo 91, Demo (1991)

MIDAS TOUCH

Technical speed metal started in Uppsala as early as 1985. They secured a deal with Noise Records, then disappeared in the death metal boom of the early 90's. Patrick Wirén and Patrick Sporrong continued with the highly successful industrial group Misery Loves Company, with a couple records on Earache.
Line-Up Patrick Wirén: Vocals, Lasse Gustavsson: Guitar, Thomas Forslund: Guitar, Patrick Sporrong: Bass, Bosse Lundström: Drums *Past Members* Rickard Sporrong: Guitar
Deathography
Ground Zero, Demo (1987)
Presage of Disaster, LP (Noise Records, 1989)

MIDIAM

One-man early 90's project from Mjölby by Jocke Pettersson, who created some furious grindcore with elements of both hardcore and death metal.
Line-Up Jocke Pettersson
Deathography
Demo (1992)

MIDVINTER

Black/death project from the north of Sweden. The band has apparently had a lot of line-ups, and received session help from prominent musicians like Jon Nödtveidt (Dissection) and Alf Svensson (At the Gates). Nothing helped a lot, though, since their songs are absolutely standard and bland.
Line-Up "Kheeroth": Vocals, "Damien": Guitar/Bass, "Zathanel": Drums *Past Members* Björn: Vocals, Krille: Drums
Deathography
Midvinternatt, Demo
At the Sight of the Apocalypse Dragon, CD (Black Diamond, 1997)

MIGUL

Short-lived black/death band from Falun. They made

a demo in 2000, but that's about it.
Line-Up Jocke Olsson: Guitar/Vocals, Olof Henriks: Guitar/Vocals, Johan Bengs: Bass/Vocals, Gustav, Bergqvist: Drums
Deathography
Hymns of Migul, Demo (2000)

MINDCOLLAPSE
Death/thrash band started as early as 1989 in Växjö. Originally called Astray, but changed to Mindcollapse in the early 90's. They finally found a label in 2001, then split up two years later.
Line-Up Johan Kaiser: Vocals, Mathias Nilsson: Guitar, Eddie Partos: Guitar, Olle Segerback: Bass, Jonas Hallberg: Drums
Deathography
Lifeless, CD (1996)
Vampires Dawn, CD (VOD, 2001)

MINDFALL
Death/thrash band from Gothenburg which began in 2001. So far they have released one demo.
Line-Up Alexander Avenningson: Drums, Axel Widén: Vocals, Erik Ward: Bass, Thommy Thorin: Guitar/Vocals
Deathography
From the Barren, Demo (2003)

MINDSLIP
Death/thrash band formed in Stockholm 1999.
Line-Up Daniel Lundh: Vocals, Johan Adamsson: Guitar, Janek Hellqvist: Guitar, Andreas Lundin: Bass, Jaanus Kalli: Drums
Deathography
Dissident, Demo (2000)
No Allegiance, Demo (2001)
Dead Silence, Demo (2004)

MINDSNARE—see Relevant Few

MISCREANT
Slow and melodic death metal from Västerås, started in 1993. Their first demo was recorded in Rosicrucian's rehearsal room, and sounds terrible. Marduk's Joakim Göthberg supplied vocals on the second demo, recorded in Unisound. At this point they sounded a bit like At the Gates. Next they made a decent CD for Wrong Again, then quickly disappeared. Johnny Wranning also played in Ebony Tears, Dog Faced Gods, Eyetrap, and Månegarm.
Line-Up Johnny Wranning: Vocals, Peter Kim: Guitar, Peter Johansson: Guitar, Magnus Ek: Bass/Keyboards, Johan Burman: Drums/Percussion Past Members Pontus Jansson: Drums
Deathography
Ashes, Demo (1993)
Promo 93, Demo (1993)
Dreaming Ice, CD (Wrong Again, 1995)

MISHARK—see Embracing

MIST
Late in 2002, four guys from Kristinehamn and

Björneborg formed a death metal band. They did one gig and a demo (recorded live in the rehearsal room) before quitting and reforming as the much more melodic Porkrind.
Line-Up Andreas Henningsson: Vocals/Bass, Kent Andersson: Drums, Andreas Gottschalk: Guitar, Josef Laében Rosén: Guitar
Deathography
Mist of Darkness, Demo (2003)

MISTWEAVER
Melodic death metal band with progressive ambitions, formed in Täby in 1998. After five years and four demos they realized no one would ever sign them, and made the wise decision to quit.
Line-Up Sebastian Olsson: Guitar, Tobias Gustafsson: Drums, Pamela Saarelainen: Synthesizers, Oskar Tell: Vocals/Bass Past Members Petter Högsander: Vocals, Herman Nygren: Bass
Deathography
Visions & Dreams, Demo (1999)
Denomination, Demo (2000)
Time Breeds Insanity, Demo (2001)
Demo 2003, Demo (2003)

MITHOTYN
Mid-90's Viking metal with raw vocals, hailing from Mjölby. Not my cup of tea (even with vodka in it), but I guess one of the better bands of this type. After four demos (one called *In the Dead of Night* is occasionally listed, but does not exist) they landed a deal with Invasion, but their time was already done. After three neglected CDs they split. They probably deserved more. Originally they were called Cerberus (see seperate entry), and sucked big time. Most members are known from other bands such as The Choir of Vengeance, Falconer, Indungeon, and Dawn.
Line-Up Rickard Martinsson: Vocals/Bass, Stefan Weinerhall: Guitar, Karl Beckmann: Guitar/Keyboards, Karsten Larsson: Drums Past Members Helene Blad: Vocals, Christian Schütz: Vocals/Bass, Johan: Guitar
Deathography
Behold the Shields of Gold, Demo (1993)
Meadow in Silence, Demo (1994)
Nidhogg, Demo (1995)
Promo'96, Demo (1996)
In the Sign of the Ravens, CD (Invasion, 1997)
King of the Distant Forest, CD (Invasion, 1998)
Gathered Around the Oaken Table, CD (Invasion, 1999)

MNEMONIC
Death metal band from Gothenburg formed in 1994. The following years saw the release of two demos, but the band soon vanished.
Line-Up Mikael Nordin: Guitar/Vocals, Pär Romvall: Bass, Mikael Fredriksson: Guitar, Boss Dr Rhythm: Drums (well, sounds like a drum machine to me) Past Members Michael Jungestrand: Drums
Deathography
Shades From a Missing Epoch, Demo (1995)
While We Dream, Demo (1996)

THE MOANING

Melodic death/black (more black than death to be honest) from Luleå/Boden that got together in 1994. They secured a deal with No Fashion about a year later. One album was all they managed, and honestly not very good. Svensson is also in Gates of Ishtar (and used to be in Throne of Ahaz).
Line-Up Pierre Törnkvist: Vocals, Mikael Granqvist: Guitar, Patrik Törnkvist: Guitar, Niklas Svensson: Bass, Andreas Nilzon: Drums
Deathography
Promo Okt 94, Demo (1994)
Blood from Stone, CD (No Fashion, 1996)

MOANING WIND

Minor death metal act from Karlstad, around in the mid-90's. Maybe not death—rather a kind of gothic metal. Their first demo was recorded in the rehearsal room, but still sounds pretty good. Johan and Tomas could also be found in the deadlier Dawn of Decay. Moaning Wind apparently changed its name to Capricorn in 1997, but I don't know what happened after that. Martin Björn also edited *Möffa Zine*.
Line-Up Johan Carlsson: Vocals/Bass, Tomas Bergstrand: Guitar, Magnus Eronen: Guitar, Martin Bjöörn: Drums **Past Members** Anders Karlsson: Bass
Deathography
In Thy Forest, Demo (1994)
Demo 2, Demo (1994)
Demo 3, Demo (1995)
Visions in Fire, CD (Corrosion, 1996)
Demo 1997, Demo (1997—as Capricorn)

MOMENT MANIACS

Brutal crust/death metal project by two Marduk members and three from Wolfpack/Wolfbrigade. I was in The Abyss studio when they recorded this, so I know they played Motörhead's *Overnight Sensation* and Dellamorte's *Uglier & More Disgusting* albums constantly to get in the mood. Obviously it worked—this is pretty intense. They also drank a lot. In fact, the vocals had to be recorded later due to the fact that Jonsson (a true maniac, known from crust pioneers Anti Cimex) was so fucked up, he passed out during a take in front of our very eyes.
Line-Up Bogge: Bass, Fredrik: Drums, Jonsson: Vocals, Alho: Guitar, Jocke: Guitar
Deathography
Two Fucking Pieces, CD (Distortion, 1998)

MONKEY MUSH

Drum machine grindcore from Angered. Started as Splort, but changed names Oct. 4, 1989. Monkey Mush was indeed sick, and obsessed with porn and gore. The band featured one of Sweden's most notorious characters, Patrik Andersson, alias "Onkel," alias "the Shit man." Grotesque for sure, but not all that good. Korhonen was in primitive death metal act Angel Goat for a bit. This busy guy also edited the great *Slimy Scum* 'zine in the good old days.
Line-Up Harri Juvonen: Guitar/Bass/Vocals,

Tommi Korhonen: Bass/Vocals, Patrik Andersson: Vocals/Guitar
Deathography
Demo 90, Demo (1990)

MOONDARK

An impressive band from Avesta that got going in 1993. Their music was heavily inspired by Crypt of Kerberos, and they delivered an ultra-slow and down-tuned version of the deadliest metal. Eventually they transformed into the better-known Dellamorte.
Line-Up Kennet Englund: Guitar, Johan Jansson: Drums, Mattias Norrman: Bass, Mats Berggren: Bass/Vocals
Deathography
Demo #1, Demo (1993)

MOONSTRUCK

Melodic and technical death metal from Bjärred, initiated in 1993. The band seemed to work in three year lapses. A demo came in 1996 and a CD in 1999. Nothing came in 2002, so I guess the band split up.
Line-Up Fredrik Sandberg: Vocals/Guitar, Jonas Forsen: Guitar, Magnus Persson: Bass/Keyboards, Per Telg: Drums
Deathography
Under Her Burning Wings, Demo (1996)
First Light, CD (Dragonheart, 1999)

MOORGATE

Black/death band formed in Lund in 2001.
Line-Up Joakim Holst: Vocals, Magnus Åberg: Guitar, Fredrik Svensson: Guitar, Simon Lundh: Bass, Erland Olsson: Drums
Deathography
Drawn From Life, Demo (2003)
I Am the Abyss When You Fall, Demo (2004)

MORAL DECAY

Formed in Umeå at the end of 1990. Initially they faced serious line-up changes—like most Swedish bands of the period, they were restless teenagers. Before long, they faded away. Thrashy death metal of mediocre quality, especially in the vocal department.
Line-Up Matte: Guitar, Hampus Stigbrand: Guitar, Rogga: Drums, Janne: Bass/Vocals
Deathography
Aeons of Iniquity, Demo (1991)

MORBID

Formed in Stockholm in early 1987, Morbid became one of the biggest Swedish cult bands. Their horror-themed image was striking, and the music was very raw and aggressive for the time. The band faded when Per Yngve "Dead" Ohlin moved to Norway to join notorious black metal act Mayhem. L.G. Petrov and Uffe Cederlund continued with Nihilist/Entombed, and Jens Näsström went on with Contras and Skull. TG, who wrote most of *December Moon*, was also in the punk band The Sun. The cult status of Morbid went sky high when Per Yngve Ohlin shot himself in 1991, and their demos (plus some rehearsals) have been re-released on different labels.

Line-Up Lars-Göran "Drutten" Petrov: Drums, Uffe "Napoleon Pukes" Cederlund: Guitar, Jens "Dr Schitz" Näsström: Bass, Zoran: Guitar (1988-), Johan Scarisbrick: Vocals (1988-) *Past Members* Per Yngve "Dead" Ohlin: Vocals (-1988), John "John Lennart" Hagström (aka "Gehenna"): Guitar (-1988), "Slator": Bass, "TG": Guitar, "Klacke": Guitar
Deathography
Live From the Past, Rehearsal (1987)
Dark Execution, Rehearsal (1987)
December Moon, Demo (1987)
Last Supper, Demo (1988)
December Moon, 12" (Reaper records, 1994)
A Tribute to the Black Emperors, CD (Bootleg, 1994)
Death Execution (Bootleg, 1996)
Death Executions II, LP (Bootleg, Holycaust records, 1997)
Live From the Past (Bootleg, 1997)
Defiants of the Church, MC (Bootleg, DEAD Productions, 1998)
My Dark Subconscious, flexi-6" (Russian pressing, 2000)
Death Execution III, 7" (Reaper Records, 2001)
Live in Stockholm, LP (Reaper Records, 2002)

MORBID FEAR—see Authorize

MORBID GRIN
Death metal band from Tingsryd, formed in 2001.
Line-Up Rune: Vocals, Alex: Guitar. Sjögren: Drums
Past Members Robban: Bass
Deathography
Demo (2003)

MORBID INSULTER
Crude metal project initiated in Hönö during 2004. Originally into thrash, influences from death metal snuck into their music. As they are inspired by bands like Bathory, Nifelheim and Vulcano, it's rather useless to speak in terms of death, black or thrash. This is simply filthy extreme metal, old school style!
Line-Up Erik: Guitar/Bass/Vocals, Alex: Drums
Past Members Daniel: Vocals
Deathography
Strike from the Grave, Demo (2005)
Endless Funeral, Demo (2005—unreleased to my knowledge)

MORBID LUST
Obscure band from Lund/Staffanstorp, existed briefly in 1986. Morbid Lust did a few gigs and one rehearsal, before members of the mighty Obscurity put an end to their saga. They thought it was a waste that such a good drummer as 16-year old Valentin was stuck in a sloppy band like this, so they stole him! Then after he left, Rother started Flegma.
Line-Up Micke "Muh" Jönsson: Vocals, Rother: Guitar/Vocals, Anders Hansson: Guitar
Folkesson: Bass, Valentin: Drums
Deathography
Rehearsal (1986)

MORBIDITY
This is probably a project, led by Satanic Slaughter's Stefan Karlsson. I assume the band began in 1988, and their sole demo is from 1989. The music? Raw and unpolished speed metal, what did you think?
Line-Up Stefan Karlsson: Guitar
Deathography
Demo #1, Demo (1989)

MORDANT
Dals Långed is a small town in the middle of nowhere that is known for basically one thing: Nifelheim. So as these guys from the same hellhole grew up, that was probably their greatest source of inspiration when they started this black/death constellation in 1997. You know what to expect.
Line-Up Bitchfire: Vocals, Carnage: Bass, Necrophiliac: Drums
Past Members Leatherdemon: Guitar
Deathography
DIE!!!!, Demo (2001)
Suicide Slaughter, Demo (2002)
Suicide Slaughter, EP (Agonia, 2002)
Momento Mori, CD (Agonia, 2004)

MORGH
Forgotten band from Piteå. They only did one demo, and I'm not exactly positive when it was released.
Deathography
Ashes of Disgrace, Demo (1992)

MORGUE
Pretty standard death/thrash started in Linköping in 1990. Led by Satanic Slaughter's main man Stefan Karlsson, all the other members of Morgue have played with them as well. Other credits on the guys' merit lists include Deranged, Nephenzy, Bloodbath, Nifelheim, Witchery, Seance, and Spiteful. Metalheads to the bone, even though they only did one demo. They have been talking about a full-length called *Mission to Eradicate* for a long time, but to my knowledge it hasn't been released.
Line-Up Andreas Deblèn: Vocals, Stefan "Ztephan Dark" Karlsson: Guitar, Stefan Johansson: Guitar, Kecke Ljungberg: Bass, Martin "Axe" Axenrot: Drums *Past Members* Imse: Drums (1990-1996), Halle: Vocals (1991-1996), Jalle: Guitar (1991), Esa: Bass (1991), Andreas Fullmestad: Guitar (1991-1992), Rille: Bass (1994-1996)
Deathography
Gospel of Gore, Demo (1992)

MORIBUND (Gothenburg)
Gothenburg band formed in 2002. They use the death metal formula and incorporate left-wing political lyrics. Dreadful. Luckily they have split up.
Line-Up Niklas: Vocals, Mathias: Guitar, Jimmy: Guitar, Robin: Drums, Peter: Bass/Vocals
Deathography
Moribund, Demo (2003)
Annihilation, Demo (2005)

MORIBUND (Söderhamn)
Early 90's death metal from Söderhamn, this is good stuff. Competent, tight and original. Still, they fell in the shadow of townmates Authorize (who never really made it, either). Check them out if you can. But for Hell's sake, don't mistake them for the new Gothenburg band of the same name!
Line-Up Martin Ståhl
Deathography
Into Depths of Illusion, Demo (1991)

MÖRK GRYNING
A typical black metal band that popped up in the mid-90's heyday of black metal. Based in Stockholm, they have succeeded pretty well since starting in late 1993. But bands like this sound pretty lame compared to leading Swedish black metal bands such as Marduk or Dark Funeral. Still decent and competent, and their later death metal-inspired records are far superior. They probably could have been great continuing as a pure death metal band, but instead they quit in early 2005 (main member Peter Nagy had left about a year earlier, and they probably needed his ideas). Jonas Berndt is also known from Wyvern, Diabolical and Mortifer, and Peter Nagy has a past in Hypocrite, Wyvern, Eternal Oath, and Defender.
Line-Up Goth Gorgon (Jonas Berndt): Guitar/Bass/Vocals/Keyboards, Johan Larsson: Keyboards *Past Members* Avatar (Mattias Eklund): Guitar/Vocals, Draakh Kimera (Peter Nagy): Vocals/Guitar/Drums/Percussion/Keyboards
Deathography
Demo 1, Demo (1993)
Demo 2, Demo (1994)
1000 År Har Gått, CD (No Fashion, 1995)
Return Fire, CD (No Fashion, 1997)
Maelstorm Chaos, CD (No Fashion, 2001)
Pieces of Primal Expressionism, CD (No Fashion, 2003)
2005 Demo, Demo (2005)
Mörk Gryning, CD (Black Lodge, 2005)

MORNALAND
Black/death metal band from Västerås that got going in 1995. Apart from a split single, these guys never went beyond demos. Since 2000 nothing has been heard from them.
Line-Up Jacob Alm: Bass, Joakim Jonsson: Drums, Tommy Öberg: Guitar, Henrik Wenngren: Vocals
Deathography
Origin Land, Demo (1996)
The Journey, Demo (1996)
Prelude to World Funeral..., Split (Near Dark, 1997)
In Dead Skies..., Demo (1998)
Promo 1999, Demo (1999)
Feathers of Rapture, Demo (2000)

MORPHEUS
One of countless good Swedish death metal bands of the early 90's that remained underground despite great music. Stockholm's Morpheus is basically the continuation of Exhumed, with the addition of ex-Carbonized members Rudén and Ekström. They never

got wind under their wings, and faded after a few active years. Rudberg left prior to the album to form Excruciate (he was also in Mastication). Both Ramstedt and Bergebäck are now in Nifelheim and Necrophobic. Great stuff, check them out.
Line-Up David Brink: Vocals, Stefan Ekström: Guitar, Sebastian Ramstedt: Guitar, Johan Bergebäck: Bass, Markus Rudén: Drums *Past Members* Janne Rudberg: Guitar
Deathography
Obscurity, Demo (1990)
In the Arms of Morpheus, 7" (Opinionate, 1991)
Son of Hypnos, CD (Step One, 1993)

MORSUS
Ah, these nice youngsters from Surahammar really bring back some life to my old bones. The very fact that they decided to start a gore/death band in 2004 must be hailed, since we are drowning in melodic In Flames clones today. I hope they will continue on this brutal path. Some members are also in the black metal band Dark Obsession.
Line-Up Tobias Johansson: Vocals, Alexander Söderstedt: Guitar, Simon Hyytiäinen: Guitar, Fredrik Ekström: Drums, Emelie Svenman: Bass
Deathography
Zombie Terror 04, Demo (2004)
Sledgehammer Holocaust, Demo (2005)

MORTAL ABUSE
Fairly anonymous thrash metal from Växjö, played during 1987 and 1988. They were young teenagers simply looking for kicks, and couldn't handle their instruments very well. They recorded a demo that was never released, and played a couple gigs at youth centers. Why am I telling you about them? Among the members were none other than Johnny Dordevic (later in Carnage and Entombed) and Johan Liiva-Axelsson (later in Carnage and Furbowl)! Their tape is a treasure for collectors of rare Swedish underground metal—and great in all its messy violence!
Line-Up Johan Liiva-Axelsson: Drums, Johnny Dordevic: Guitar, "Mr Sodom": Bass/Vocals
Deathography
Demo (1988)

MORTALITY
Nyköping/Tystberga thrash metal act that came in 1987, a bit too late to make it (as if any original Swedish thrash band ever made it, unless you count Meshuggah). Pure Bay Area stuff with mosh parts and endless riffs in the vein of Metallica and Testament. The peak of their career was the *Rockbox* compilation album. Compared to that album's other thrash metal band, Hatred, you can tell why they never made it. (But I can't tell why the great Hatred *didn't*). Not bad, but not good enough.
Line-Up Danne Andersson: Vocals/Guitar, Peter Rosén: Guitar, Tobbe Pettersson: Drums, Sammy Wendelius: Bass
Deathography
Demo 1, Demo (1989)
The Prophecy, Demo (1990)

When Barbarity Reigns, Demo (1991)

MORTELLEZ
Black/death metal from Gävle, founded in 2000. The lyrics are Swedish, and the overall feeling is more black than death.
*Line-Up Eki: Guitar, Patrik: Vocals, Forsberg: Drums, Robert: Bass, Krisha: Guitar **Past Members** Dennis: Guitar, Andreas: Drums*
Deathography
Oskuldens Ängel, Demo (2001)
De Dödas Dal, Demo (2001)
De Dödas Dal, EP (2002)
Pesten, Demo (2002)
Sorg, Demo (2003)

MORTIFER
Melodic black/death metal act started in Tyresö in 1994, basically the solo project of Mörk Gryning's Jonas Berndt. Actually, Mortifer started before Mörk Gryning. They were active for years, but nothing much came of it—probably because the music is average. They recorded the *Masters of the Universe* album for release in 1998, but it never came out. After another demo, they faced reality and gave up.
*Line-Up Jonas Berndt: Bass/Keyboards, Danny Eideholm: "Insane Art", Dennis Ekdahl: Drums **Past Members** Peter Wendin: Guitar (session only), Daniel: Vocals (session only), Jonas Nilsson: Guitar*
Deathography
Promo, Demo (1993)
Battle of the Tyrants, Demo (1996)
Running out of Time, Demo (1997)
Harbringer of Horror, Demo (1999)

MORTUARY
Death metal from Bagarmossen, they released a demo in 2000. Since then, nothing has been heard.
Line-Up Martin Fernström: Vocals/Bass, Magnus Lundkvist: Drums, Fredrik Palmqvist: Guitar/Vocals
Deathography
Enter the Mortuary, Demo (2000)

MORTUM
Kristianstad bunch started as a death metal band of some sort in 1997, but before long turned to medieval black metal. The title of their CD makes me think this band would be a good opener for Spinal Tap. When Mortum split up, Rille, Bartek and Chrille formed Supreme Majesty. Håkansson is also known from Embraced, Evergray and The Forsaken.
Line-Up Chrille Andersson: Vocals/Guitar, Tina Carlsdotter: Vocals, Michael Håkansson: Bass, Bartek Nalezinski: Drums, Rille Svensson: Guitar
Deathography
The Goddess of Dawn, Demo (1997)
Promo 98, Demo (1998)
The Druid Ceremony, CD (Invasion, 1998)

MORTUUS
Blackish death metal project that lasted for one 7".
Deathography
Mortuus, 7" (The Anja Offensive, 2005)

MOURNFUL
Death metal band started in the early 90's as Metempsychosis. After one demo the name changed, and the band did a couple gigs with Berserk. After the second demo the band quickly vanished. Some members are also known from Wyvern, Sins of Omission, Mörk Gryning, and Raise Hell.
Line-Up Toni Kocmut: Guitar/Vocals, Joy Deb: Guitar, Marco Deb: Bass, Dennis Ekdahl: Drums
Deathography
Demo (as Metempsychosis)
2nd Demo

MOURNING SIGN
Early 90's (formed 1992) Hallstahammar band which has remained unnoticed despite a couple decent albums. Fast, well-played death metal worth checking out.
*Line-Up Kari Kainulainen: Guitar, Robert Pörschke: Vocals, Henrik Persson: Drums, Petri Aho: Guitar/Bass **Past Members** Tomas Gårdh: Bass*
Deathography
Last Chamber, Demo (1992)
Alienator, EP (Godhead, 1995)
Mourning Sign, CD (Godhead, 1995)
Multiverse, CD (Godhead, 1996)

MURDER CORPORATION
Project formed in Malmö in 1995, basically Deranged plus vocalist Emil Lilic (ex-Megaslaughter). Much lighter than Deranged's mayhem, with more thrash metal. In 2002 it ended, but the Deranged guys soon started the similar project Killaman. In my opinion, they should focus on Deranged. Sweden desperately needs ultra-brutal death metal to counterbalance all the melodic and thrashy bands out there.
*Line-Up Johan Axelsson: Guitar, Rikard Wermén: Drums, Johan Anderberg: Vocals/Bass **Past Members** Dan Bengtsson: Bass, Jens Johansson: Vocals, Emil Lilic: Vocals*
Deathography
Blood Revolution 2050, MCD (Repulse, 1996)
Kill, MCD (Planet End, 1998)
Retract the Hostile, 7" (Stormbringer, 1998)
Murder Corporation/Vomitory Split 7" (Hangnail, 1999)
Murder Corporation, CD (Regain, 1999)
Santa Is Satan, Deranged/grind Buto Split CD (Psychic Scream, 2000)
Santa Is Satan, CD (Psychic Scream, 2000)
Whole Lotta Murder Going On, CD (Psychic Scream, 2000)
Tagged and Bagged, CD (Displeased, 2001)

MURDER SQUAD
Uffe Cederlund of Entombed, Peter Stjärnvind of Merciless (later in Entombed), and Richard Cabeza and Matti Kärki of Dismember had one thing in common—the belief Autopsy was the best band in the world. What to do? Well, they got together in 1993 and started this project. Initially an all-out cover band called Bonesaw, they quickly changed their name and started writing their own tunes. Murder Squad still sounds so much like their inspiration it

is almost ridiculous. Only because Autopsy might be the best in the world can they get away with this. Perfection came when Mr. Autopsy himself, Chris Reifert, offered some vocals for the second album.
Line-Up Uffe Cederlund: Guitar, Peter Stjärnvind: Drums, Rickard Cabeza: Bass, Matti Kärki: Vocals Past Members Chris Reifert: Vocals (session only)
Deathography
Unsane, Insane and Mentally Deranged, CD (Pavement, 2001)
Ravenous, Murderous, CD (Threeman Recording, 2003)

MUTANT
Industrial black/death metal of reasonable quality. Founded in 1998, basically a project of Henrik Ohlsson (Scar Symmetry, Altered Aeon, Theory in Practice, ex-Diabolical, ex-Thrawn). The only other musician is Peter Sjöberg, who used to be in Sorcery.
Line-Up Henrik Ohlsson: Vocals/Drum Programming, Peter Sjöberg: Guitar
Deathography
Eden Burnt to Ashes, Demo (1998)
The Aeonic Majesty, CD (Listenable, 2001)

MUTILATED UNDEAD
A U.S.-smelling Death band from the southern town of Åhus. They formed around 2000, but that's about all I know.
Line-Up Mongoblaster: Vocals/Guitar/Bass, GG Zillah: Drums
Deathography
Death, Demo (2001)

MUTILATOR
Obscure death metal from Alingsås, made a demo and then vanished (probably into other bands).
Deathography
Demo, Demo (1990)

MY OWN GRAVE
Melodic death/thrash from Sundsvall, begun in 2001. Consistent demos finally led to a recording deal, and they will probably be around a while.
Line-Up Mikael Aronsson: Vocals, Anders Härén: Guitar, Stefan Khilgren: Guitar, Max Bergman: Bass, John Henriksson: Drums Past Members Ramin Farhadian: Vocals
Deathography
New Path/Same Path, Demo (2001)
Dissection of a Mind, Demo (2002)
Blood and Ashes, Demo (2003)
Progression Through Deterioration, Demo (2004)
Unleash, CD (New Aeon Media, 2005)

MY SANCTUARY OF HATE
Melodic heavy metal with death metal influences, started out in Uppsala in 2003.
Line-Up Mattias: Guitar, David: Bass, Irfan: Vocals, Edvin: Drums, Anders: Guitar Past Members Nicklas, Gustav
Deathography
Hatelist, Demo (2004)

Marks of Violence, Demo (2004)

MYKORRHIZA
Death metal band from Stockholm, founded 2001, mainly the solo project of ex-Excruciate member Henrik Brynolfsson. Vocals have been provided by a number of singers, most notably Anders Strokirk (ex-Necrophobic, Blackshine) and Lars Levin (ex-Excruciate, Mastication).
Line-Up Henrik "Hempa" Brynolfsson: Guitar/Bass, Martin Karlsson: Drums Past Members Anders Strokirk: Vocals (session only), Lars Levin: Vocals (session only), Tor Adolfsson: Vocals (session only), Matilda Karlsson: Vocals (session only), Siri Hagerfors: Vocals (session only)
Deathography
Mykorrhiza, EP (Konqueror Records, 2002)
Shattered Dreams, CD (Konqueror Records, 2003)

MYNJUN
Melodic death metal band formed in Stockholm 2002 by Imperious men Skagvard and Thulin (also in Coercion) together with Bergerstähl (Centinex, World Below, ex-Amaran). Pretty good, but I guess the other bands are the main focus and this project is fading.
Line-Up Adam Skogvard: Guitar/Vocals, Ronnie Bergerstähl: Drums, Rickard Thulin: Bass Past Members Daniel Josefsson: Guitar
Deathography
Commencement, Demo (2003)
Receding Strengths, Demo (2005)

NAGLFAR
Umeå act formed in 1992. Though they never called themselves black metal, they are a mainstreamed carbon copy of the reigning trend of the time, only lacking satanic lyrics. Though pretty unoriginal, they have had international success. Over the years they have become better, faster, and more brutal. I smell a lot of Marduk in them now, and some death metal tendencies. Problems came when leading man and vocalist Jens Rydén quit in early 2005, but the others are apparently determined to continue. Members are known from other local bands Bewitched, Setherial, Midvinter, Havayoth, Ancient Wisdom, Guillotine, Throne of Ahaz, Embracing, and Auberon.
Line-Up Kristoffer Olivius: Vocals/Bass, Marcus Norman: Guitar, Andreas Nilsson: Guitar, Mattias Grahn: Drums, Peter Morgan Lie: Bass (Drums 1995-1997) Past Members Fredrik Degerström: Guitar (1993-1994), Morgan Hansson: Guitar (1993-2000), Ulf Andersson: Drums (1992–1994), Mattias Holmgren: Drums (1995), Jens Rydén: Vocals (1992-2005)
Deathography
Stellae Trajectio, Demo (1994)
We are Naglfar—Fuck You, Demo (1995)
Vittra, CD (Wrong Again, 1995)
Maiden Slaughter, Demo (1996)
When Autumn Storms Come, 7" (War, 1997)
Diabolical, CD (War, 1998)
Ex Inferis, MCD (Century Media, 2001)
Sheol, CD (New Haven/Century Media, 2003)
Pariah, CD (Century Media, 2005)

NASUM

Highly successful grind group from Örebro, started in 1992 as a side project by Necrony members Alriksson and Jakobsson. Mieszko Talarczyk came a year later, and after Alriksson left the band he ran Nasum as a duo with Jakobsson for long periods. Nasum quickly built a reputation for intensity, and a long row of singles proved their strength. With the addition of Liveröd (ex-Burst) things really started to happen. Lots of tours followed, one with Per Karlsson from Suffer, In Aeternum etc. on drums. In 2004 Nasum received a Swedish P3 Guld award for Best Metal/Rock Album. Their music is basically grindcore. At their best they sound a bit like early Carcass, but sometimes Nasum drifts into monotony so common with grind bands. Still, they are definitely a great band, maybe the best modern grind act of all. Since Mieszko took possession of Dan Swanö's equipment from the classic Gorysound/Unisound studios and started his own Studio Soundlab, the releases of Nasum have sounded very impressive. The creative Mieszko also worked with bands like Insision and Nine with great results. This band sure had a bright future, but it was all over in the end of 2004 when Mieszko Talarczyk was killed in a Tsunami disaster while on holiday in Thailand. He is badly missed.

Line-Up Anders Jakobsson: Drums (originally guitar and bass), Mieszko Talarczyk: Vocals/Guitar (1993-2004), Urban Skytt: Guitar, Jon Lindqvist: Bass Past Members Jesper Liveröd: Bass, Rickard Alriksson: Drums/Vocals, Per Karlsson: Drums (session only), Jari Lehto: Drums (one rehearsal only!)

Deathography
Blind World, Nasum/Agathocles Split 7"
(Poserslaughter, 1993)
Really Fast, EP (Really Fast, 1993)
Domedagen, Demo (1994)
Grindwork, Split (Grindwork Productions, 1994)
Smile When You're Dead, Nasum/Psycho Split 7"
(Ax/ction, 1994)
Industrislaven, MCD (Poserslaughter, 1995)
The Black Illusions, Nasum/Abstain Split 7"
(Yellow Dog, 1996)
World in Turmoil, 7" (Blurred, 1996)
Regressive Hostility, EP (Hostile Regression, 1997)
Nasum/Warhate Campaign, Split 7" (Relapse, 1999)
Inhale/Exhale, CD (Relapse, 1998)
Human 2.0, CD (Relapse, 2000)
Nasum/Asterisk, Split 7" (Busted Heads, 2001)
Nasum/Skitsystem, Split 7" (No Tolerance, 2002)
Helvete, CD (Relapse, 2003)
Shift, CD (Relapse, 2004)
Grind Finale, CD (Relapse, 2005)

NAUSEA—see Omnius Deathcult

NECROCIDE

Nordanstig/Hudiksvall act, formed 1996 by members from all over Sweden. Attempts at U.S.-influenced death metal were not good—the songs are rudimentary and unexciting. Standard gore-grind of the 2000's, nothing more, nothing less. Brandt also plays bass for successful crust band Totalt Jävla Mörker.

Line-Up Victor Brandt: Vocals, Tommy Holmer: Drums, Per Söderlund: Bass, Pär Swing: Guitar, Roberth Svensson: Guitar Past Members Richard: Bass, Daniel Westerberg: Vocals, Roberth Svensson: Bass, Erland

Deathography
Necrocide, Demo (2000)
The Second Killing, Demo (2002)
Declaration of Gore, Demo (2003)

NECROGAY

Started in Vetlanda in 2001 with the aim of creating gore-grind/old school death metal. And that is exactly what they have done, for better and worse.

Line-Up Viktor Berggren: Drums, Erik Nystrand: Guitar, Emil Forstner: Bass, Emil Palm: Vocals Past Members Carl-Oskar Andersson: Vocals, Henrik Gustafsson: Bass, Andreas Holmsten: Vocals

Deathography
Necrogay, Demo (2004)

NECROMICON

Decent black/death group from Luleå, emerged in 1993. Pretty aggressive, but not pure death metal due to weak symphonic elements. Compared to the real stuff, this is a bit lame. They apparently changed names to Cimmeran Dome in 2003. The most impressive aspect is the members' incredible list of other bands: Dissection, Dark Funeral, Hellmasker, Deathbound, Dawn, Blackmoon, The Duskfall, Morthirim, Satariel, Battlelust, Infernal, Them, and Sobre Nocturne!

Line-Up Stefan Lundgren: Guitar, Nicklas Sundkvist: Guitar, Patrick Sundkvist: Bass, Kai Jaakola: Vocals Past Members Daniel Björkman: Vocals, Jonas Mejfeldt: Bass/Guitar, Roger Johansson: Keyboards, Sara Näslund: Vocals, Robert "Zoid" Sundelin: Drums/Vocals, Tomas "Alzazmon" Asklund: Drums, Henrik Åberg: Guitar

Deathography
When the Sun Turns Black, Demo (1994)
Through the Gates of Grief, Demo (1994)
Realm of Silence, CD (Impure Creations, 1996)
Sightveiler, CD (Hammerheart, 1998)
Peccata Mundi, CD (Hammerheart, 2000)

NECRONOMIC—see Nocturnal Rites

NECRONY

Insane gore/death from Örebro, started summer 1990 as Necrotomy. After a short period with another name I can't remember, they settled for Necrony and blasted away. Insanely brutal, with lyrics that make you laugh in disgust. Obviously their inspiration was Carcass, Carcass, and only Carcass. Let's face it, they sounded exactly like Carcass (and thus just like General Surgery). Being so unoriginal, they failed to impress me back then. I thought their best release was the cover album *Necronycism: Distorting the Originals* (featuring a guest spot by Dan Swanö). Listening back today, they actually sound pretty good! Jakobsson had reportedly never held a guitar before starting Necrony! He later returned to his main instrument, drums, and

started successful grind group Nasum with Alriksson, who soon left. Further, Jakobsson also edited the great 'zine *Hymen* during the 90's. Note that they changed their lyrical content from "gore" to "pathological" early on—there's a world of difference, you know.
Line-Up Anders Jakobsson: Guitar/Bass, Rickard Alriksson: Vocals/Drums **Past Members** Dan Wall: Guitar, Daniel Andersson: Bass, Jimmy: Guitar (in theory, but he never actually played with the band)
Deathography
Severe Malignant Pustule, Demo (1991)
Mucu-Purulent Miscarriage, 7" (Poserslaughter, 1991)
Pathological Performances, CD (Poserslaughter, 1993)
Promo Tapes 93-94, Demo (1994)
Necronycism: Distorting the Originals, CD (Poserslaughter, 1995)
Under the Black Soil, pic-7" (2000)
Poserslaughter Classic Remasters, CD (Poserslaughter, 2005—not authorized by band)

NECROPHOBIC
Death metal from Stockholm, originated way back in 1988 under another name, originally led by riff-master David Parland. Necrophobic has continued with brutal death metal over the years without wide attention. They have been hampered by a lot of line-up trouble, and by signing to Black Mark (who has never broken any band but Bathory). Further, they were sadly obscured by the black metal movement when they finally got some albums out. When Parland left for Dark Funeral they suffered a lot—as Dark Funeral did when he later left them. Still very well worth checking out. In their best moments they are one of the best bands playing Swedish death metal. Most of the members have also been involved with great acts like Dismember, Crematory, Morpheus, Nifelheim, and Therion.
Line-Up Joakim Sterner: Drums, Tobias Sidegård: Bass (1991-), Sebastian Ramstedt: Guitar (1996-), Johan Bergebäck: Guitar (2001-) **Past Members** David Parland: Guitar (1989-1996, 2000), Martin Halfdahn: Guitar (1997-2000), Anders Strokirk: Vocals (1992-), Stefan Harrvik: Vocals (1991-1992), Jocke Stabel: Bass (1991) ...originally the band also contained a "Christian homo-poser", according to Parland (Funeral Zine #2)
Deathography
Rehearsal (1989)
Slow Asphyxiation, Demo (1990)
Unholy Prophecies, Demo (1991)
The Call, 7" (Wild Rags, 1993)
The Nocturnal Silence, CD (Black Mark, 1993)
Spawned by Evil, EP (Black Mark, 1996)
Darkside, CD (Black Mark, 1996)
The Third Antichrist, CD (Black Mark, 2000)
Bloodhymns, CD (Hammerheart, 2002)
Tour EP 2003, EP (Hammerheart, 2003)
Hrimthumsum, CD (Regain, 2006)

NECROPIA
Formed in 1996, split up in 1998. I don't think they

even did a demo in those two years. Svärd has since appeared in Terror 2000, and Orstadius played in 9th Plague and Sacrificial Thorns.
Line-Up Riad Haddouche: Vocals/Bass, Niklas Svärd: Guitar, Kristofer Orstadius: Guitar, Jonas Gagner: Drums

NECROPSY—see Eternal Darkness

NECROTISM—see Embalmed

NECROTOMY—see Necrony

NECROVATION
Death metal act formed in Everöd in 2002, originally with the wonderful name Das Über Elvis. When they chose the more "serious"-sounding Necrovation, they got into pure old school death metal. Really good stuff.
Line-Up Seb: Vocals/Guitar, Cliff: Bass, Biinger: Drums, Robert: Guitar
Deathography
Bratwürst Terror, Demo (2002—as Das Über Elvis)
Chants of Grim Death, EP (Blood Harvest, 2004)
Necrovation, Demo (2004)
Ovations to Putrefaction, Demo (2004)
Curse of the Subconscious, Necrovation/Corrupt Split CD (Blood Harvest, 2005)

NEFARIOUS
Brutal early 90's grind from Mjölby. Basically Henke Forss (Dawn, etc.) and a drum machine. A short-lived project. When you hear it, you'll understand why.
Line-Up Henrik Forss: Vocals, Lasse
Deathography
Demo
Necrorgasm Convulsions, Demo (1992)

NEON DEATH—see Eructation

NEPHENZY—see Nephenzy Chaos Order

NEPHENZY CHAOS ORDER
Formed as Nephenzy in Linköping during 1995, they played good quality death metal in the vein of At the Gates and released a couple of demos, an EP, and a CD. But in 1999 they changed their name to Nephenzy Chaos Order, and became more modern. Well, it didn't work, and the band split up after one CD. Kamijo is familiar from Hypocrisy, Pain, The Abyss, and Algaion. Martin Axenrot's resumé is even more impressive, including Witchery, Bloodbath, Nifelheim, Triumphator, Morgue, and Satanic Slaughter.
Line-Up Martin Hallin: Vocals, Mathias Kamijo: Guitar, Tobbe Leffle: Guitar, Simon Axenrot: Bass, Martin Axenrot: Drums **Past Members** Kim Arnell: Drums (1998-2000), Mattias Fredriksson: Bass (1998-2000), Adrian Kanebäck: Guitar (1998-2000)
Deathography
Stolen Blessing, Demo (1996—as Nephenzy)
Worshipped by the Mass, Demo (1997—as Nephenzy)
In Anguish and Furious Pain, 7" (Loud N' Proud,

1998—as Nephenzy)
Where Death Becomes Art, CD (Black Diamond,
1998—as Nephenzy)
The Right to Remain Violent, Demo (2000)
Pure Black Disease, CD (Black Diamond, 2003)

NEZGAROTH
Doom metal, started in Karlstad during winter
1992. The band disappeared when Dalgren decided
to focus on the much deadlier Vomitory, which also
included Bergqvist for a while.
Line-Up Fredrik Danielsson: Drums, Thomas
Bergqvist: Bass, Bengt Sund: Guitar, Ulf Dalgren:
Guitar *Past Members* Rikard Löfgren: Vocals
(session only), Robert Fjälleby: Lyrics
Deathography
Demo 1, Demo (1993)
Demo 2, Demo (1994)

NIDVERK
Black/death metal act formed in Gällivare in 2002.
Line-Up Ante: Vocals/Bass, Simon: Guitar, Hellfire:
Guitar, Robert: Drums
Deathography
Nattens Hälsning, Demo (2005)

NIFELHEIM
Nifelheim formed in 1990 in Dals Långed, and
Sweden was never to be the same. This hilarious
black metal band is the creation of fascinating twin
brothers Erik and Per Gustavsson, determined to
make the purest black metal possible. Pushing spikes
and image to the extreme, influences come mainly
from South American and Eastern European bands
and Satan himself. Evil, funny, crazy, and hilarious!
The brothers became famous even for average Swedes
when a national television documentary profiled their
obsession with Iron Maiden. They are indeed the most
die-hard Iron Maiden fans in the world. Later clips of
the twins were used in TV commercials for an insurance
company. Still, Nifelheim symbolizes everything black.
If you don't hail them, you can fuck off. Note that
former member "Demon" is actually a drummer—but
played guitar on every album he appeared on!
Line-Up Tyrant (Erik Gustavsson): Guitar/Bass,
Hellbutcher (Per Gustavsson): Vocals, Vengeance
From Beyond (Sebastian Ramstedt): Guitar, Sadist:
Guitar, Peter Stjärnvind: Drums *Past Members* Goat
(Per Alexandersson): Vocals (1996), Jon Zwetsloot:
Guitar, Morbid Slaughter: Guitar (1991-1993),
Demon: Guitar, Battalion: Guitar, Devastator
(Martin Axenrot): Drums
Deathography
Unholy Death, Demo (1993)
Nifelheim, CD (Necropolis, 1995)
Headbangers Against Disco Vol. 1, Split (Primitive
Art, 1997)
Devil's Force, CD (Necropolis, 1998)
Servants of Darkness, CD (Black Sun, 2000)
Unholy Death, Single (Primitive Art, 2000)
13 Years, CD (I Hate Records, 2003)
Envoy of Lucifer (Regain, 2006)

NIGHTCHANT
Formed in Linghem in 1993, basically a melodic
death/black metal band with two screaming vocalists.
Sounds like a project, and of course it is. Nightchant
is basically three guys from Thornclad blasting away,
with two guys from Forlorn screaming on top. Their
sole demo is standard and unmemorable.
Line-Up Viktor Klint: Guitar/Bass/Keyboards,
Jonas Remne: Guitar, Adrian Hörnquist: Drums
Past Members Daniel Bryntse: Vocals (session only),
Magnus Björk: Vocals (session only)
Deathography
Peacebleed, Demo (1996)

NIGHTSHADE
Melodic death/black act from Kungsbacka, formed
in 1996.
Line-Up Daniel Kvist: Vocals, Snake Stevens:
Guitar, Daniel Hjelm: Guitar, Christer Pedersen:
Bass, Daniel Larson: Keyboards, Kristo Napalm:
Drums *Past Members* Daniel Hjelm: Guitar, Sebbe:
Bass, Birdie: Bass, Peter: Bass, Daniel Boström:
Drums, Adam: Vocals
Deathography
Benighted, Demo (1997)
Devil, Demo (1998)
Astoreth, Demo (1999)
Wielding the Scythe, CD (Scarlet, 2001)

NIHILIST
Legendary band that transformed into the mighty
Entombed. In my opinion, this was the first 100%
death metal band in Sweden. Nihilist was created in
1987 by restless teenagers Nicke Andersson—from
the depressing Stockholm suburb Skärholmen; and
Alex Hellid and Leif Cuzner—both from the equally-
depressing Kista. Their music was supercharged
with brutality and high-quality riffs courtesy of
Andersson, and they were destined for greatness.
Everybody in Sweden could feel it—at least everybody
in the scene, then only a couple hundred people at
most. Disagreements between the principal members
and bass player Johnny Hedlund caused Nihilist
to fold in August 1989—the others didn't dare fire
their slightly older friend! Hedlund then started the
mighty Unleashed, and the others regrouped after a
few days to form you-know-who. Miraculously, the
early Nihilist demos were finally re-released on CD
in 2005—bloody well the best CD of that year! This
is archetypical Swedish death metal. Together with
Bathory, Nihilist/Entombed is probably the most
influential Swedish metal band. Obey. Leif Cuzner
tragically passed away during work with this book—
may he always be remembered as the creator of the
fat Swedish death metal guitar sound.
Line-Up Nicke Andersson: Drums, Alex Hellid:
Guitar, Lars-Göran Petrov: Vocals (1988-), Johnny
Hedlund: Bass (1988-), Uffe Cederlund: Guitar
(1987-1988, 1989-), Vocals (1987) *Past Members*
Leif Cuzner: Guitar (1988)/Bass (1987-1988),
Mattias (aka "Buffla"): Vocals (1987-1988, well he
posed for photos anyway)
Deathography

Premature Autopsy, Demo (1988)
Only Shreds Remain, Demo (1988)
Drowned, Demo (1989)
Drowned, 7" (Bloody Rude Defect records, 1989)
1987-1989, CD (Threeman Recordings, 2005)

NINE

Obviously inspired by Entombed's deadly rock attack on *Wolverine Blues*, Nine was formed in Linköping in 1994. This band feels pretty calculated, and they went straight to records without developing in the underground via demos. Musically they are pretty standard. The songs are rudimentary and feel made up in the studio, but of course they sound professional. Nine has been pretty successful, and is now on big Swedish hardcore label Burning Heart.
Line-Up Johan Lindqvist: *Vocals*, Benjamin Vallé: *Guitar/Vocals*, Robert Karlsson: *Bass*, Tor Castensson: *Drums* **Past Members** Oskar Eriksson: *Bass*
Deathography
To the Bottom, EP (No Looking Back Records, 1995)
Listen, CD (Sidekicks, 1997)
Kissed by the Misanthrope, CD (Sidekicks, 1998)
Lights Out, CD (Burning Heart, 2001)
Killing Angels, CD (Burning Heart, 2003)

NINNUAM

Black/death band from Katrineholm formed under the name Yxa ("axe" in Swedish) in 2001. The name was soon changed, and they have made a CD.
Line-Up Mattias *"Matte Hellcore"* Johansson: *Vocals*, Kim Laakso: *Guitar*, Robert Gustafsson: *Guitar*, Thord Brännkärr: *Drums*, Måns Jaktlund: *Bass*, Robert Johansson: *Keyboards* **Past Members** Andreas Jennische (Lenny): *Bass (2001-2002)*
Deathography
Scar Salvation, Demo (2002)
Process of Life Separation, CD (Low Frequency Records, 2004)

NIRVANA 2002

Four of the very best Swedish death metal bands never made an album: Interment from Avesta, Evocation from Borås, Crematory from Stockholm, and this band—Nirvana 2002 from Edsbyn. These guys started their deadly mission early, in 1988, putting them among the very first Swedish death metal bands. Initially known as Prophet 2002, they renamed themselves Nirvana in 1989. But since some inferior group from Seattle apparently had the same name, they tagged on the old 2002 to their new name. Säfström later helped Entombed with vocal duties for a short time, appearing on their *Crawl* EP. Sadly, Nirvana 2002 never got anywhere. Their departure is a big loss for everyone the least bit interested in old Swedish death metal. Killer riffs, powerful sound, heavy groove, and superb screaming vocals—it's all there. I still play their demos a lot. Until recently Säfström hosted the biggest Swedish cinema program on national television. I wish him all the best in life, on one condition: start a band again,

you multi-talented bastard! Säfström and Quick were also editors of the cool *Hang 'Em High* 'zine.
Line-Up Orvar Säfström: *Vocals/Guitar*, Erik Qvick: *Drums*, Lars Henriksson: *Bass* **Past Members** Robert Eriksson: *Drums (session only, 2007)*
Deathography
Truth & Beauty, Rehearsal (1989)
Watch the River Flow, Rehearsal (1989)
Excursion in 2002 (No Dimension), Rehearsal (1989)
Mourning, Demo (1990)
Rehearsal (1990)
Disembodied Spirits, Demo (1990)
Nirvana 2002/Appendix/Authorize/Fallen Angel, Split EP (Opinionate Records, 1990)
Promo 91, Demo (1991)

NO FUCKING GOD

Mid-90's death metal with touches of Motörhead rock and thrash. Originally named No Fucking Way, luckily they changed that (not that the name got much better). Good brutal stuff from the death center of Finspång. Sadly, they never got anywhere.
Line-Up Janne: *Drums*, Rob: *Vocals*, Tompa: *Guitar*, Robert Ivarsson: *Bass/Guitar*
Deathography
Demo (1996)

NO REMORSE

Thrash metal from Växjö which started in November 1988. Unlike many other thrash bands, they were never influenced by the growing death metal scene. Instead, they included touches of power metal. This is just not aggressive enough to catch my interest. Later they developed into the somewhat deadlier Temperance (see separate entry). Possibly they just changed their name so not to be confused with the brutal Nazi band called No Remorse.
Line-Up Fredrik Ernerot: *Guitar/Vocals*, Johan Ernerot: *Drums*, Magnus Magnusson: *Bass* **Past Members** Tor: *Bass*
Deathography
Wake Up or Die, Demo (1990)

NOCROPHOBIC—see Decameron

NOCTURNAL DAMNATION

Old school death metal project started in Stockholm in 2004, originally as Nocturnal Domination. For some reason the name was soon changed to the very similar Nocturnal Damnation (the line-up was also edited). Some members are known from bands such as Hydra, Dispatched, and Maledictum.
Line-Up Death's Poet (Dennis): *Vocals*, Danne: *Bass*, Dimman: *Drums* **Past Members** Micke: *Guitar*, Berge: *Guitar*, Kimpa: *Bass*
Deathography
The Harvester, Demo (2005—as Nocturnal Domination)
When Life has Lost all Meaning, Demo (2005)

NOCTURNAL DOMINATION—see Nocturnal Damnation

NOCTURNAL RITES

Metal from the northern town of Umeå. Nocturnal Rites began in 1990 as Necronomic, and got some attention in the early 90's though they never made an album. In the old days of death metal, they never succeeded in impressing me and my drunken friends in Avesta with their standard riffs. They have now switched to power metal, proving we were right all along. Just look at the album titles and you get the idea. As a power metal group they have been very successful. Personally, I think they suck big time. Give me Katalysator any day!

Line-Up Jonny Lindkvist: Vocals, Nils Norberg: Guitar, Fredrik Mannberg: Guitar, Nils Eriksson: Bass, Owe Lingvall: Drums **Past Members** *Mattias Bernhardsson: Keyboards, Anders Zackrisson: Vocals, Ulf Andersson: Drums, Mikael Söderström: Guitar*

Deathography
Obscure, Demo (1991)
Promodemo, Demo (1992)
In a Time of Blood and Fire, CD (Megarock, 1995)
Tales of Mystery and Imagination, CD (Century Media, 1997)
The Sacred Talisman, CD (Century Media, 1999)
Afterlife, CD (Century Media, 2000)
Shadowland, CD (Century Media, 2002)
New World Messiah, CD (Century Media, 2004)
Lost in Time: The Early Years of Nocturnal Rites, CD (Century Media, 2005)
Nocturnal Rites/Falconer, Split (Swedmetal Records, 2005)
Grand Illusion, CD (Century Media, 2005)

NOMINON

Great Jönköping band that rose from the ashes of Chorozon (see separate entry) as Nilsson and Sulaslami got busy in 1993. The brutal style predates the new rise of Swedish death metal (Soils of Fate, Spawn of Possession, Insision, Visceral Bleeding, etc.), even though their first efforts aren't that impressive. They were inactive for a time, when both Nilsson and Sulasalmi joined Dion Fortune. But Nominon was soon resurrected, only to hit a patch of line-up turbulence that has continued ever since. Really good death metal, so track them down! Drummer Dragutinovic left for black metal titans Marduk in 2001, but Nominon recruited Perra Karlsson (ex-Serpent, In Aeternum). I think (and hope) this band will go on forever. All past and present members are known from too many other bands to list.

Line-Up Daniel Garptoft: Vocals, Juha Sulasalmi: Guitar/Vocals, Joel Anderson: Bass, Perra Karlsson: Drums, Kristian Strömblad: Guitar **Past Members** *Peter Nilsson: Vocals, Nicke Holstensson: Vocals, Jonas Mattsson: Vocals/Guitar, Christian Cederborg: Guitar, Lenny Blade: Bass, Tobias Hellman: Bass, David Svartz: Bass, Emil Dragutinovic: Drums*

Deathography
My Flesh, Demo (1996)
Demo II 96, Demo (1996)
Promo 97, Demo (1997)
Diabolical Bloodshed, CD (X-treme, 2001)

Blaspheming the Dead, EP (Nuclear Winter, 2003)
Fafner/Nominon: Daemons of the Past, Split CD (Northern Silence, 2004)
The True Face of Death, EP (Nuclear Winter, 2004)
Blaspheming the Dead, 7" (Nuclear Winter, 2005)
Recremation, CD (Konqueror/Blood Harvest, 2005)

NON SERVIAM

Black/death metal band from Kristianstad founded in 1995. They made a couple of records, but never attracted any wider attention. Since 2000 nothing has happened, but they are apparently still active.

Line-Up Rikard Nilsson: Vocals, Anders Nylander: Guitar, Daniel Andersson: Guitar/Vocals, Christian Andersson: Bass/Drums/Vocals **Past Members** *Magnus Emilsson: Drums (1995-1998), Johannes Andersson: Guitar (1996-1997)*

Deathography
The Witches Sabbath, Demo (1995)
The Witches Sabbath—The Second Vision, Demo (1996)
Between Light and Darkness, CD (Invasion, 1997)
Necrotical, CD (Invasion, 1998)
Play God, Single (Aftermath, 2000)
The Witches Sabbath, CD (Aftermath, 2000)

NONEXIST

Melodic death metal project that featured Johan Liiva-Axelsson (Arch Enemy, Furbowl, Carnage), Matte Modin (Defleshed, Dark Funeral, Infernal), and Johan Reinholdz (Andromeda, Opus Atlantica, Skyfire). I guess it all ended when Liiva-Axelsson got tired of it, so their sole CD is the only thing we will ever hear.

Line-Up Johan Reinholdz: Guitar/Bass, Matte Modin: Drums **Past Members** *Johan Liiva-Axelsson: Vocals*

Deathography
Deus Deceptor, CD (New Haven, 2002)

NOSFERATU

Death metal band formed in Strömstad in August 1989. Originally played thrash metal, but soon went for deadlier stuff. Brutal and simple. Guitarist Mathias went on to start Rabbit's Carrot with Jon Nödtveidt and Ole Öhman, who in turn went on to form Dissection.

Line-Up Jocke: Guitar/Vocals, Mäbe: Drums (1990-), Bass (1989-1990), Martin: Bass (1990-) **Past Members** *Mathias: Guitar (1989-1990), Frykholm: Drums (1989-1990)*

Deathography
Decadence Remains, Demo (1990)

NUGATORY

Started in winter 1990/1991 in intensely depressing and worthless Hallsberg (a town most Swedes have passed through by train, but never set foot in). Originally called Wild Youth, as they grew older they wanted something less wimpy and settled for Nugatory in 1992. Their music is furious death metal, with something definitely lacking. Quality?

Line-Up Jocke Olsson: Bass/Vocals, Mogge

Johansson: Guitar, Veikko Heikkinen: Drums, Fredrik Gahm: Guitar, Knutis: Vocals (1996-)
Deathography
Mongoloized, Demo
Nugatory, MCD (Playwood, 1995)
Promo 1997, Demo (1997)

NUMANTHIA
Södertälje band started in 1993. Originally they played primitive death metal, but transformed into black metal as that genre grew bigger. Later they tried being more original, but by then it was too late.
Line-Up James Göransson: Keyboard, Tommy Rundblad: Bass, Fredrik Börjesson: Guitar, Fredrik Pira: Vocals, Pontus Wedenlid: Drums Past Members Albin Wall: Guitar (1993-1995)
Deathography
And Then the Water Came, Demo (1994)

OBDURACY
Formed in 2000, death metal from the classic soil of Finspång. They still have a long way to go to live up to the high standards of local death metal history. Daniel and Tomas are also in Suicidal Seduction.
Line-Up Daniel Persson: Bass/Vocals, Mikael Silander: Guitar, Niklas Persson: Drums, Tomas Lagrén: Guitar/Vocals
Deathography
Death by Dawn, Demo (2002)

OBERON—See Auberon

OBLIGATORISK TORTYR
Another unorthodox signing by French label Osmose Productions. In Sweden, nobody knew this death/grind band from Uddevalla/Gothenburg, who apparently started in 1998. They made one CD for the Frenchies and are now quietly active. The name means "mandatory torture" in Swedish, by the way.
Line-Up Jens Kjerrström: Guitar/Vocals, Viktor: Bass/Vocals, Fredrik: Drums
Deathography
Obligatorisk Tortyr, CD (Osmose Productions, 2000)

OBNOXIOUS—see Skinfected

OBSCENE (Eskilstuna)
Obscure death metal from Eskilstuna, made one demo back in 1990.
Line-Up Jani: Guitar/Vocals, Stefan: Guitar/Vocals, Sami: Drums, Tobbe: Bass
Deathography
Grotesque Experience, Demo (1990)

OBSCENE (Jönköping)
Brutal death metal band launched in Jönköping in the 2000's. Original bass player Hellman is now in 9th Plague, and has a history in Nominon and Dion Fortune. Don't mistake this band with the older band from Eskilstuna of the same name.
Line-Up Henrik Olin: Vocals, Mikael Wedin: Guitar/Vocals, Olaf Landen: Drums, Alexander Andersson:

Bass *Past Members Tobbe Hellman: Bass*
Deathography
Rehearsal '01, Demo (2001)
Demo '02, Demo (2002)
Laceration of the Unborn, Demo (2003)
Laceration of the Unborn, Obscene/Bestial Devastation, Split (Redrum Records, 2005)

OBSCURA—see Imperious

OBSCURE DIVINITY
Death metal act from Gislaved. They started in 1999, made a demo a few years later, and then split. Kemi has also been in Misteltein under the name Skorrgh—what kind of name is that?!
Line-Up Dan Sörensen: Guitar, Joakim Tapio: Bass, Ville Kemi (Skorrgh): Vocals, Tobias Lindman: Drums Past Members Robert Sveningsson: Vocals, Anders Lindsten: Bass
Deathography
Obscure Divinity, Demo (2002)

OBSCURE INFINITY
Formed 1991, death metal from Mariestad. Similar to early Gorefest, but why the keyboards? In 1994 they prepared a split album with the superior band Fulmination, but for some reason it never happened.
Line-Up Magnus Persson: Vocals, Jockalima: Guitar, Erik: Bass, Frank: Drums, Leif Eriksson: Keyboards
Deathography
Beyond the Gate, Demo (1992)
Requiem, Demo (1992)
Promo, Demo (1994)
Lycanthrope, Demo (1996—unreleased?)

OBSCURED
Fittingly, an absolutely obscure death metal act who made one demo and was never heard from again.
Deathography
Obscured, Demo (1994)

OBSCURITY (Järfälla)
Early 90's death metal from Järfälla, made an EP in 1992, then split up. Jocke, Matti, and Robert still play together, and are highly active in today's scene in Vicious Art. All have also played in Dominion Caligula. Robert and Matti have both been in Dark Funeral as well. In other words: Definitely check this out. Don't mistake them for the ultra-legendary Obscurity from Malmö, though.
Line-Up Jocke Widfeldt: Vocals/Guitar, Matti Mäkelä: Guitar/Vocals, Robert Lundin: Drums/Vocals, Martin Modig: Bass
Deathography
Wrapped in Plastic, EP (1992)

OBSCURITY (Malmö)
Very early extreme Swedish band from Malmö that released two demos in the mid-80's. Started in 1985, heavily influenced by Bathory, Sodom, and Destruction. As you might guess, they sounded awesome. Sadly, Obscurity never grew beyond the

underground. Looking into the origins of Swedish death metal, together with Mefisto and Bathory this is what you need to hear. Fucking great band of a kind that simply no longer exists. (At least until reading the first edition of this book, when the members felt the flame and started rehearsing again!)
Line-Up Daniel Vala: Bass/Vocals *(and initially Guitar)*, Jan Johansson: Guitar *(initially Drums)*, Jörgen Lindhe: Guitar *(1985-)*, Valentin: Drums *(1986-)*
Deathography
Ovations of Death, Demo (1985)
Damnations Pride, Demo (1986)
Ovations of Death, 7" (To the Death, 1998)
Damnations Pride, 7" (To the Death, 1998)
Damnations Pride, CD (Scarlet, 1998)

OCCRAH
Death metal combo formed in Storfors in 1996, originally as a joke. Not very good, to be honest.
Line-Up Hedman: Vocals, Chris: Guitar, Juha: Guitar, Eric: Drums
Deathography
Slaughter of the Innocent, Demo (1997)

OCTOBER TIDE
When Katatonia's future was uncertain in 1995, Renske and Norrman created this project. Since Katatonia is now back in full force, this very similar-sounding group has effectively ceased to exist.
Line-Up Jonas Renske: Vocals/Drums, Fredrik Norrman: Guitar/Bass, Mårten Hansen: Vocals
Deathography
Promo Tape, Demo (1995)
Rain Without End, CD (Vic, 1997)
Grey Dawn, CD (Avantgarde, 1999)

OFERMOD
Unholy death metal project initiated in 1996 by black metal kids known from bands like Malign, Teitanblood, Dödfödd, Nefandus, Funeral Mist, etc. The Stockholm/Norrköping collective was inactive for many years, but reportedly got back together in 2004.
Line-Up Leviathan (Nebiros/Nord): Vocals, Moloch: Vocals, Atum: Guitar, Michayah (Belfagor): Guitar, J. Kvarnbrink (Tehom): Bass, Shiva (Necromorbus): Drums *Past Members* Mist: Bass
Deathography
Mystérion Tés Anomias, 7" (Pounding Metal, 1998)
Mystérion Tés Anomias, EP (Evangelium Diaboli, 2005)

OMINOUS
Powerful death/thrash from Malmö, started as early as 1991. It took a long time to get in shape, but in 2000 they finally released an album. Previous singer Sjöholm is also known from The Forsaken and Feared Creation. Nowadays, Sandved can be found in S.K.U.R.K with Obscurity's Jörgen Lindhe.
Line-Up Joel Cirera: Drums, Johan Linden: Bass, Sören Sandved: Guitar, Johan Saxin: Guitar *Past Members* Mårten: Drums *(1994-1997)*, Pontus: Vocals *(1993-1996)*, Björn: Bass *(1995-1997)*,

Thomas Lejon: Drums *(1998)*, Dan Johansson: Bass *(2000-2001)*, Anders Sjöholm: Vocals, Jocke: Bass
Deathography
Demo 1994, Demo (1994)
Sinister Avocation, Demo (1995)
Promo 97, Demo (1997)
The Spectral Manifest, CD (Holy Records, 2000)
Void of Infinity, CD (Holy Records, 2002)

OMNITRON
As the 80's became the 90's, classic hardcore group Krixhjälters changed its name to Omnitron and went for a more serious thrash metal style. Billing them as "harder than Slayer," "heavier than Prong," "more original then [sic!] Red Hot Chili Peppers," and "Sweden's greatest Power Thrash band," CBR released the album and waited for Omnitron to take on the world. They failed. The guitarists continued in the somewhat deadlier project Comecon.
Line-Up Stefan Kälfors: Drums/Vocals, Pontus Lindqvist: Vocals/Bass, Pelle Ström: Guitar/Vocals, Rasmus Ekman: Guitar/Vocals
Deathography
Omnitron, LP (CBR, 1990)

OMNIUS DEATHCULT
According to themselves, these Norrköping guys play extreme metal. Formed in 2002 as Nausea, they changed their name to Amarok in 2004, then finally [for now?] became Omnius Deathcult in 2005. More black than death, and not very exciting.
Line-Up Hrym: Guitar, Selvmord: Bass, Mictian: Drums/Vocals *Past Members* Mean: Guitar *(session only)*, Norðurljós: Guitar
Deathography
Demo 1, Demo (2004—as Nasuea)
Promo 2005, Demo (2005—as Amarok)
Amarok, Demo (2005)
Demo #2, Demo (2005)

ONDSKA—see Battlelust

ONE MAN ARMY AND THE UNDEAD QUARTET
When The Crown split up in 2004, Johan Lindstrand formed this band. One demo later, the Trollhättan-quintet secured a deal with Nuclear Blast. Basically the same kind of death/thrash as The Crown, though a bit more relaxed and catchy. Johan is also in Impious, and Pekka can be found in Reclusion.
Line-Up Johan Lindstrand: Vocals, Valle Adzic: Bass, Mikael Lagerblad: Guitar, Pekka Kiviaho: Guitar, Marek, Dobrowolski: Drums
Deathography
When Hatred Comes to Life, Demo (2005)
21st Century Killing Machine, CD (Nuclear Blast, 2006)

OPENWIDE—see Blessed

OPETH
Back in 1987, young teenagers Mikael Åkerfeldt and Anders Nordin played in Eruption in their hometown

of Stockholm. Simultaneously, their friend David Isberg split up his group Opet to form Crowley. Since neither of the young groups worked very well, the core members soon regrouped under the refined name Opeth. Originally the band was a bit obsessed with the black metal trend, but gradually they transformed towards more strange and progressive fields. The band's big troubles with line-ups only seem to have made them more powerful. Their commercial and critical success has been beyond imagination. Though I personally don't like the band's music at all, I surely respect them. Åkerfeldt in particular is an extremely talented singer and musician.
Line-Up Mikael Åkerfeldt: Guitar/Vocals, Peter Lindgren: Guitar, Martin Lopez: Drums, Martin Mendez: Bass, Per Wiberg: Keyboards **Past Members** Mattias Ander: Bass (1992), Johan DeFarfalla: Bass (1991, 1994-1996), Nick Döring: Bass (1990-1991), Stefan Guteklint: Bass (1992-1993), David Isberg: Vocals (1990-1992), Anders Nordin: Drums (1990-1997), Kim Pettersson: Guitar (1991), Andreas Dimeo: Guitar (1991)
Deathography
Promo, Demo (1994)
Orchid, CD (Candlelight, 1995)
Morning Rise, CD (Candlelight, 1996)
My Arms Your Hearse, CD (Candlelight, 1998)
Still Life, CD (Peaceville, 1999)
The Drapeny Falls, Single (Koch Records, 2001)
Blackwater Park, CD (Peaceville, 2001)
Deliverance, CD (Music for Nations, 2002)
Still Day Beneath the Sun, Single (Music for Nations, 2003)
Damnation, CD (Music for Nations, 2003)
The Grand Conjuration, Single (Roadrunner, 2005)
Ghost Reveries, CD (Roadrunner, 2005)

OPHTHALAMIA
Deadly act from death metal center Finspång, created under the name Leviathan in 1989 by Tony Särkkä—the famous "It" from strange black metal groups Abruptum, Vondur, and War. Their form of black/death metal is okay, but the most notable thing is how many influential musicians have passed through the band's line-up. Vocals have been supplied by Jon Nödtveidt of Dissection, Erik "Legion" Hagstedt (later of Marduk), and finally Jim "All" Berger from Abruptum. Drums were handled by the super-talented Benny Larsson (Edge of Sanity) and the bass player was Swordmaster/Deathstars' Emil Nödtveidt (younger brother of Jon—he later moved to guitar). Because the core members were focused on other bands, Ophthalamia never really made it, and today are almost forgotten.
Line-Up Tony Särkkä (It): Guitar, Emil Nödtveidt: Guitar/Vocals (initially bass), Jim Berger (All): Vocals, Ole Öhman: Drums, Mikael Schelin: Bass **Past Members** Benny Larsson: Drums (1989-1996), Robert Ivarsson: Bass (1994), Erik Hagstedt: Vocals (1994-1995), Jon Nödtveidt: Vocals (guest vocals really)
Deathography
A Long Journey, Demo (1991)
A Journey in Darkness, CD (Avantgarde, 1994)

Via Dolorosa, CD (Avantgarde, 1995)
To Elisha, CD (Necropolis, 1997)
Dominion, CD (No Fashion, 1998)
A Long Journey, CD (Necropolis, 1998)

ORAL
Basically a crust band with a few deadly tendencies, active during 1984-1989 in their hometown of Gothenburg. The band is of historic interest mainly since guitarist Alf Svensson later joined Grotesque, and then At the Gates. In 1994 the band briefly reunited to make their sole recording.
Line-Up Pedda: Bass, Uno: Vocals, Niklas: Drums, Alf Svensson: Guitar
Deathography
Slagen i Blod, EP (Fairytale Records, 1994)

ORCHARDS OF ODENWRATH
Some kind of Viking/death duo from Stockholm.
Line-Up Lord Zacharias Z.: Vocals/Guitar, Emil Holmgren: Vocals/Bass/Drums
Deathography
Orchards of Odenwrath, Demo (2002)

ORCHRISTE
Early doom/thrash from Linköping, formed by Patrik Jensen in October 1987. Their style gradually grew deadlier, and the 1989 demo can be described as doom/death. After folding in 1990, Jensen and Larsson formed the better-known Seance with guys from Total Death. Afterwards Jensen forged ahead with Satanic Slaughter (briefly), Witchery, and The Haunted.
Line-Up Johan Larsson: Vocals, Patrik Jensen: Guitar, Matthias Carlsson: Bass, Johan Imselius: Drums, Jörgen Johansson: Guitar
Deathography
Necronomicon, Demo (1989)

ORIGIN BLOOD
New death/thrash band—can we take another one?
Line-Up Rob: Vocals/Guitar, Robin: Guitar, Simon: Bass, Brian: Drums
Deathography
Mr. Jakker Daw, CD (RAHW Production, 2004)

ORION
Melodic death metal act formed in Varberg in 2004.
Line-Up Lisa Hultgren: Vocals, Joakim Rydberg: Guitar, Conrad Ohlsson: Bass, Jonas Karlsson: Drums **Past Members** Anton Honkonen: Guitar (2004-2005), Jonathan Serey Araya: Vocals (2004), Christoffer: Bass (2004)
Deathography
Stars of Orion, Demo (2004)
Angels Never Die, Demo (2005)

OVERFLASH
Death metal project of Magnus "Devo" Andersson (Cardinal Sin, Marduk), started in Norrköping in 1992. The one other member is ever-present Swanö on drums. Don't you just love the title of the demo?
Line-Up Magnus "Devo" Andersson: Vocals/Bass/

Guitar, Dan Swanö: Drums
Deathography
Sodomizing Songs of Pure Radiation, Demo (1992)
Threshold to Reality, CD (MNW, 1993)
Silent Universe, CD (MNW Zone, 1996)

OVERLORD
Minor death metal band from Stockholm. Overlord started as early as 1997, but the only demos I have seen are from 2002. Currently on hold, probably due to lack of members.
Line-Up Victor: Guitar, Tobbe: Drums *Past Members* Wall: Vocals, Jocke: Bass
Deathography
Bloodstained Demo III, Demo (2002)
Demo 2002, Demo (2002)

OVERLORD INDUSTRIES
Gällivare, in the very frozen north of Sweden, is one of the most depressing places I have been in my life. I guess the only way to survive there is to form a death metal band, which these guys did in 2004. The demo titles reveal that this is a joke band, created mainly for kicks.
Line-Up Peter Strandgårdh: Vocals/Bass, Patrik Ylmefors: Vocals/Guitar, Olle Dyrander: Drums
Deathography
Die Konspiracy of the Midi Drum Translator, Demo (2004)
Superunderground Vehicle, Demo (2004)
Wissen, Kreativität und Macht, Demo (2004)
Pissingonanazi.com, Demo (2005)

OXIPLEGATZ
Solo band from Gothenburg featuring Alf Svensson (At the Gates, Grotesque) playing a kind of electronic "Space Metal." Starting in 1993, the strange and highly original project produced three CDs before vanishing in 1999. The name Oxiplegatz comes from a Donald Duck comic, by the way.
Line-Up Alf Svensson: Guitar/Vocals/Bass/Keyboards /Drum Programming, Sara Svensson: Vocals (session only)
Deathography
Fairytales, CD (Fairytale, 1995)
Worlds and Worlds, CD (Adipocere, 1997)
Sidereal Journey, CD (Season of Mist, 1999)

PAGAN RITES
The town of Halmstad proudly offers this amusingly unserious black/heavy/death attack. Born in 1992, the band has seen a massive circulation of members. Since all use funny [or not?] nicknames, it's hard to tell who has been in the group. Karlsson and Letelier are ex-Autopsy Torment, and others have been in Nifelheim, Devil Lee Rot, Tristitia, and Ancient's Rebirth. Fun? Maybe. Good? Find out for yourself...
Line-Up Harri Juvonen: Guitar (initially also Drums), Thomas Karlsson (Unholy Pope): Vocals *Past Members* Adrian Letelier (Black Agony): Bass, Dennis Widén (Angerbodor): Guitar, Karl Vincent (Sexual Goat Licker): Drums, Lord of the Deeps: Bass, Luis B Galvez: Guitar, Hellbutcher: Drums, Tyrant: Bass

Deathography
Pagan Rites, Demo (1992)
Through the Gates of Hell, Demo (1992)
Frost, Demo (1992)
Promo, Demo (1993)
Pagan Metal, Demo (1993)
Flames of the Third Antichrist, 7" (Stemra, 1993)
Hail Victory!, 7" (Molon Lave, 1993)
Sodomy in Heaven, EP (1994)
Pagan Rites, CD (Warmaster, 1996)
Live Smedjan 14/9/00, Demo (2000)
Bloodlust and Devastation, LP (Primitive Art, 2001)
Hell Has Come to Mother Earth, Demo (2002)
Mark of the Devil, CD (Primitive Art, 2002)
Rites of the Pagan Warriors, CD (Iron Pegasus, 2003)
Dancing Souls, Single (Monster Nation, 2005)

PAGANDOM
Together with Intoxicate, one of the original thrash acts from Gothenburg, formed in 1987. Tight, catchy and quite good.
Line-Up Christian Jansson: Vocals, Rickard Ligander: Drums, Martin Carlsson: Guitar, Jens Florén: Bass
Deathography
Demo
Hear Your Naked Skin Say Ashes to Ashes, Demo (1990)
Crushtime, CD (Crypta, 1994)

PAGANIZER
Thrashy death metal, formed in Gamleby/ Gothenburg in 1998. They reportedly transformed into Carve in 2000, but they also continued to make albums as Paganizer. The members are also involved in Ribspreader, Blodsrit, Portal, and Primitive Symphony. Active guys.
Line-Up Roger Johansson: Vocals/Guitar, Matthias Fiebig: Drums, Patrik Halvarsson: Bass *Past Members* Andreas (Dea) Carlsson: Guitar, Oskar Nilsson: Bass, Jocke Ringdahl: Drums, Diener: Bass
Deathography
Stormfire, Demo (1998)
Into Glory's Arms We Will Fall, Paganizer/Abbatoir Split CD (Psychic Scream, 1999)
Deadbanger, CD (Psychic Scream, 1999)
Promoting Total Death, CD (Forever Underground, 2001)
Dead Unburied, CD (Forever Underground, 2002)
Murder Death Kill, CD (Xtreem Music, 2003)
Death Forever "The Pest of Paganizer", CD (Xtreem Music, 2004)
No Divine Rapture, CD (Xtreem Music, 2004)

PAN-THY-MONIUM
One of many bands of Edge of Sanity's main man Dan Swanö, this is definitely one of the better. Formed in summer 1990, they were soon recognized for a unique style of atmospheric death metal. Among the other members are Benny Larsson (Edge of Sanity, Ophthalamia, etc.) and Robert Karlsson (Darkified, replaced Dan Swanö in Edge of Sanity in 1997). High

quality progressive death metal, Finspång-style!
Line-Up Dan Swanö: *Guitar/Bass/Keyboards/ Effects, Benny Larsson: Drums, Robert Karlsson: Vocals, Robert Ivarsson: Guitar, Dag Swanö: Guitar/Organ/Saxophone*
Deathography
...Dawn, Demo (1990)
Dream II, 7" (Obscure Plasma, 1991)
Dawn of Dreams, LP/CD (Osmose, 1992)
Khaoohs, LP/CD (Osmose, 1993)
Khaoohs and Kon-Fus-Ion, CD (Relapse, 1996)

PANDEMONIC
Great thrash metal from Upplands Väsby that came to being in 1998. Good stuff, way better than most boring retro thrash acts. Drummer Marcus used to play bass in the deadlier Genocide Ferox, and in 2004 he joined the even deadlier Insision just before their tour with Suffocation.
Line-Up Micke Ullenius: *Vocals, Micke Jakobsson: Guitar, Linus Ekström: Bass, Marcus Jonsson: Drums* **Past Members** *Eric Gjerdrum: Guitar, Nicke Karlsson: Drums, Harry Virtanen: Bass*
Deathography
Suburban Metal, Split (Denim Records, 1999)
Lycanthropy, Demo (1999)
The Authors of Nightfear, CD (WWM, 2000)
Ravenous, Demo (2002)
The Art of Hunting, Demo (2004)

PANDEMONIUM
When Lund-based death metal band End split up in 1997, guitarists Westesson and Ahlgren decided to pursue doom metal with Pandemonium. Since then they have progressed from a demo and independent EPs to a record deal and CDs. Even though they spell their name differently, do not mistake this band with the far superior Pan-Thy-Monium from Finspång.
Line-Up Erik Olsson: *Keyboard/Vocals, Jacob Blecher: Drums/Vocals, Johan Sånesson: Bass, Kalle Wallin: Vocals, Oskar Westesson: Guitar/Vocals, Thomas Ahlgren: Guitar/Vocals* **Past Members** *David Länne: Keyboards, Erik Odsell: Keyboards, Patrik Magnusson: Drums*
Deathography
emotions from the Deep, Demo (1998)
...To Apeiron, EP (1998)
Twilight Symphony, EP (2000)
Insomnia, CD (JCM, 2002)
The Autumn Enigma, CD (JCM, 2005)

PANTHEON
Standard black/death metal from Tyresö, formed in 1995. Since all the members also started the more successful Thyrfing the same year, Pantheon quickly faded, disappearing completely after two demos.
Line-Up Jocke Kristensson: *Guitar/Keyboards/ Vocals, Patrik Lindgren: Bass, Thomas Väänänen: Drums*
Deathography
By the Mist of Nightfall, Demo (1996)
Only Chaos Reigns, Demo (1997)

PANTOKRATOR
Progressive death metal band known for one thing—pro-Christian biblical lyrics. They have released a row of demos and a CD since their start in 1996. But all I have ever heard by them has been weak and uninspired, as one might suspect. I'm just waiting for a gospel choir with overly satanic lyrics to counterbalance this ludicrous genre manipulation.
Line-Up Karl Walfridsson: *Vocals, Mattias Johansson: Guitar, Jonas Wallinder: Bass, Rickard Gustafsson: Drums, Jonathan Steele: Guitar/Vocals*
Deathography
Ancient Path/Unclean Plants, Demo (1997)
Even Unto the Ends of the Earth, Demo (1998)
Allhärskare, Demo (2000)
1997-2000, CD (2001)
In the Bleak Midwinter/Songs of Solomon, Split (CLC Music, 2001)
Songs of Solomon, EP (2001)
Blod, CD (Rivel Records, 2003)

PATHOLOG
Death metal band completely unknown to me. They made one demo in 1995—that's all I know.
Deathography
Demo 1995, Demo (1995)

PATHOLOGY
Obscure band I know nothing about, apart from the sole demo. They might be the same as Patholog, but that's a wild guess from a guy completely at a loss.
Deathography
Exasperating Slow Dissection, Demo (1992)

PENTAGRAM—see Tribulation (Surahammar)

PERGAMON—see Taketh

PERGOLOS
Kicking death metal from Falun. They have made two demos this far, now we'll see if they survive.
Line-Up Jocke Olson: *Guitar, Linus Bergqvist: Guitar, Christer Björklund: Bass, Olle Ekman: Drums, Olof Henriks: Vocals*
Deathography
Dawn of Recreation, Demo (2003)
Century Warcult, Demo (2004)

PEXILATED
Early 90's experimental thrash metal from Avesta. This is actually very good. Jonas Kjellgren sings like a god, and many of the riffs are great. The incredible vocalist/guitarist continued with Dellamorte, Carnal Forge, Centinex, and Scar Symmetry.
Line-Up Jonas Kjellgren: *Vocals/Guitar, Johan Engström: Guitar, Peter Sundmark: Bass, Johan Tillenius: Drums*
Deathography
A New Beginning of Unfaithful Life, Demo (1994)

PHOBOS
Death metal from Hallsberg/Kumla, formed back in 1997. For a long time they were known as Last Rites,

but in the 2000's they decided to call themselves Phobos instead. Nothing happened, and the band quit after just two demos.
Line-Up Joel Fornbrant: Vocals/Guitar, Kari Kallunki: Guitar, Martin: Bass, Appi: Drums **Past Members** Gabbe: Bass, Tobbe: Drums/Vocals
Deathography
Last Rites, Demo (2000—as Last Rites)
Essential Agony, Demo (2002)

PLAGUE DIVINE
Death/grind from Stockholm, going since 1997. So far they only made three demos, but let's hope they go further. The world needs more deadly blast beats!
Line-Up Nico Åsbrink: Guitar, Jacob Andersson: Bass, Johan Husgavel: Vocals **Past Members** Peter Emanuelsson: Vocals, Chris Konstandinos: Guitar, Juan Araya: Drums
Deathography
Demo 1999, Demo (1999)
Conceived to Perish, Demo (2002)
Promo, Demo (2004)

PLEDGE SIN AND THE PAINFUL
New-ish doom/death metal project.
Line-Up Firesteel: Guitar/Vocals, Moonsorrow: Vocals
Deathography
Demo, Demo (2004)

POEM
Melodic death/thrash band around since 2002.
Line-Up Alex Widén: Vocals, Martin Meyerman: Guitar, Staffan Persson: Bass **Past Members** Mike: Drums, Ufuk Demir: Drums
Deathography
Virginity, Demo (2003)
Angelmaker, Demo (2004)

POLTERKRIST
Satanic death metal from the northern town of Luleå. Since 2000 they have made one demo a year, and they are about to record their first CD.
Line-Up Stefan Granlund: Drums, Martin Åberg: Guitar, Andreas Pelli: Bass, Johan Sinkkonen: Guitar, Mats Asplund: Vocals **Past Members** Erik Lejon: Guitar (2000-2002), Johan Dahlberg: Bass (2000)
Deathography
Cold Lazarus, Demo (2000)
Killed With Domination, Demo (2001)
Stabs You in the Back, Demo (2002)
The Death Cell, Demo (2003)
Force of Evil, Demo (2004)

PORPHYRIA
Obscure death/black metal project formed in 1993 in Eskilstuna, they made one demo four years later.
Line-Up A. Berglund: Guitar, Andreas Svensson
Deathography
Demo, Demo (1997)

PORTAL
Emil and Mattias from Blodsrit/Carve launched this band in 1996. I guess it's basically a project, since they have made one album but no demos.
Line-Up Kristian Kaunissaar: Guitar/Vocals, Stefan Johansson: Guitar/Vocals, Emil Koverot: Bass, Mattias Fiebig: Drums
Deathography
Forthcoming, CD (Cadla Productions, 2001)

POSEIDON
Melodic death metal band formed in Helsingborg in 1998. The overpopulated market for this kind of music has kept them relegated to demos—or maybe they just haven't got what it takes?
Line-Up Andreas Weis: Guitar/Vocals, Jocke Petterson: Guitar/Vocals, Emil Sandin: Bass/Vocals, Robban Bengtsson: Vocals, Jesper Sunnhagen: Drums **Past Members** Sebastian Rydell: Bass, Daniel Pålsson: Drums
Deathography
My Last Kingdom, Demo (2000)
The Counting, Demo (2001)
Crucified, Demo (2003)
Error, Demo (2003)
Unplugged, Demo (2003)

PRIMITIVE SYMPHONY
Death metal from Västervik, formed 1992. Decent Deicide-inspired music with terrible vocals. Jimmie and Patrik are also in Blodsrit, and Patrik plays in Paganizer.
Line-Up Patrik Halvarsson: Bass, Björn Jonsson: Drums, Christian Nordh: Guitar, Jimmie Nyhlen: Vocals, Rasmus Ström: Guitar/Keyboards
Deathography
Obscene Sadist, Demo (1995)
Of Satan's Breed, Primitive Symphony/Bluttaufe Split CD (Psychic Scream, 2001)

PROBOSCIS
Highly technical, strange death metal with elements of hardcore and funk—like a deadlier Primus! Created in the Stockholm suburb of Vällingby by vocalist Magnus Liljendahl in 1991. Original guitarist Joacim Carlsson (Afflicted, General Surgery, Face Down) left in 1995 to join Facedown, replaced by ex-Crematory man Mikael Lindevall.
Line-Up Magnus Liljendahl: Vocals, Andreas Eriksson: Bass, Mikael Lindevall: Guitar (1995-), Björn Viitanen: Drums (1995-) **Past Members** Joacim Carlsson: Guitar (1991-1995), Linus Bladh: Drums (1991-1995)
Deathography
Demo 1992, Demo (1992)
Slap Psycho Metal Core, Demo (1993)
Fall in Line, 7" (Amigo, 1995)
Stalemate, CD (Diehard, 1997)

PROCREATION
Basically a project of Therion's Christoffer Jonsson, with help from David Isberg (known from Opeth). Formed in 1989, they lasted long enough to make a demo and play some live shows. Then Therion got big, and this project went on ice.

Line-Up *Christoffer Jonsson: Drums/Guitar, David Isberg: Vocals* **Past Members** *Erik Gustafson: Guitar (1989, session only), Peter Hansson: Guitar (1991, session only)*
Deathography
Enter the Land of the Dark Forgotten Souls of Eternity, Demo (1990)

PROJECT GENOCIDE
From the frosty northern town of Boden, originally they called themselves Lifeless and played metalcore, but soon went (a bit) deadlier as Project Genocide. I doubt that they will ever progress beyond demos.
Line-Up Lasse: Vocals, Nicke: Guitar, Hellish: Guitar, Micke: Bass, Ante: Drums
Deathography
Arise to Obey, Demo (2002)
Promo 2003, Demo (2003)

THE PROJECT HATE
Örebro project by the ever-active Kenth Philipson (House of Usher, Leukemia, Odyssey, Dark Funeral, God Among Insects). Started in 1998, and Philipson's main sidekick soon became Jörgen Sandström (Entombed, ex-Grave). The line-up might impress, but the lame industrial death metal music fails. Now Philipson is mainly occupied with God Among Insects, but The Project Hate still seems to be active.
Line-Up Kenth Philipson (aka Lord K): Guitar/ Keyboards/Programming, Jörgen Sandström: Vocals/Bass, Petter S. Freed: Guitar, Jo Enckell: Jo Enckell, Michael Håkansson: Bass **Past Members** *L.G. Petrov: Vocals, Magnus Johansson: Bass (session only), Mia Ståhl: Vocals*
Deathography
Deadmarch: Initiation of Blasphemy, CD (1998)
1999 Demo, Demo (1999)
Cyber Sonic Super Christ, CD (Massacre/ Pavement, 2000)
When We Are Done, Your Flesh Will Be Ours, CD (Massacre/Pavement, 2001)
Killing Hellsinki, CD (Horns Up Records, 2002)
Hate, Dominate, Congregate, Eliminate, CD (Threeman Recordings, 2003)
Armageddon March Eternal (Symphonies of Slit Wrists), CD (Threeman Recordings, 2005)

PROPHANITY
Alingsås' Prophanity was an early Swedish attempt at black metal, began in 1991 under some names I can't recall. The band never got wind under their wings, and the album didn't appear until 1998. By then it was much too late. Prophanity has always suffered due to line-up turmoil. Their unnoticed demos are only recommended for fans of unproduced black metal with screamed vocals. The more deathly album might attract more people, but I doubt it. Christer, Anders, and Christian have also been in the superior Immemoreal. Anders also used to play in Inverted.
Line-Up Christer "Grendel" Olsson: Guitar, Anders "Woutan": Drums, Nicklas Magnusson: Guitar, Patrick "Patsy" Johansson: Vocals/Bass **Past Members** *Mathias "Ferbaute" Järrebring:*

Vocals (1991-1999), Christian Aho: Bass, Carl-Johan Sörman: Vocals, Robert Lindmark: Bass (1996-1999), "Nauthis" (Mats)
Deathography
Demo 1, Demo (1994)
Messenger of the Northern Warrior Host—Demo 2, Demo (1994)
I Vargens Tecken, 7" (Voice of Death/Sorrowmoon, 1995)
Battleroar, Demo (1997)
Stronger than Steel, CD (Blackend, 1998)

PROPHECY
Unknown death/thrash band that made one demo.
Deathography
Remission of Sins, Demo (1992)

PROPHET 2002—see Nirvana 2002

PURGAMENTUM
Death metal from Linköping, formed 2002. After a demo, two members left and the band went on hold.
Line-Up Linus Fredriksson: Guitar, Johan Larsson: Bass/Vocals **Past Members** *Jonas Lundberg: Guitar/ Vocals, Jakob Selbing: Drums*
Deathography
Deathenchanté, Demo (2003)

PURGATORY—see Dawn of Decay

PUTREFACTION
These guys from Visby are in fact Grave. This side project started around 1989. When it vanished the songs were roped into the mighty Grave repertoire. Ola Lindgren has confessed that this band was formed from pure love for Carcass (like General Surgery, Necrony, and most bands from Mjölby), as Sweden fell head over heels for *Symphonies of Sickness*.
Line-Up Well...the line-up of Grave (1989)
Deathography
Painful Death, Demo (1989)

RABBIT'S CARROT
Insanely-named (and obviously very young) thrash metal from Strömstad, memorable for one thing—as early outlet for future Dissection men Jon Nödtveidt and Ole Öhman. I don't know who the other guys in this band were, but they tried to continue after Jon and Ole left to form Dissection, even gigging with Dissection in 1991. They didn't make it very far.
Line-Up A bunch of guys **Past Members** *Jon Nödtveidt: Guitar, Ole Öhman: Drums*
Deathography
A Question of Pain, Demo (1989)
Demo 1990, Demo (1990)

RAISE HELL
Raise Hell started in Stockholm in 1995 as In Cold Blood (and were also called Frost, Frozen in Time, and Forlorn). After their demo, labels fought to sign the band, and they landed on Nuclear Blast. All this is a mystery to me, since their music is substandard retro thrash. I think the labels were attracted because

the members were so very young (around 15) when the demo was released. Nuclear Blast lost faith as these guys grew older, and they now find themselves on local label Black Lodge.
Line-Up Dennis Ekdahl: Drums, Jimmy Fjällendahl: Vocals, Jonas Nilsson: Guitar/Vocals, Niklas Sjöström: Bass/Vocals **Past Members** *Henrik Åkerlund: Drums (1995-1996), Johan Lindquist: Drums, Torstein Wickberg: Guitar*
Deathography
Nailed, Demo (1997—as In Cold Blood)
Holy Target, CD (Nuclear Blast, 1998)
Not Dead Yet..., CD (Nuclear Blast, 2000)
Nuclear Blast Festivals 2000, Split (Nuclear Blast, 2001)
Wicked Is My Game, CD (Nuclear Blast, 2002)
To the Gallows, EP (Black Lodge, 2005)
City of the Damned, CD (Black Lodge, 2006)

RAPTURE (Alingsås)
Melodic band formed in 1996 as Lacrimas. As Rapture, a demo came out in 1999. Since then I haven't heard a thing. Olof and Elias are also in Dragonland, and Patrick is known from Prophanity.
Line-Up Patrick Johansson: Vocals, Olof Morck: Guitar, Niklas Örnfelt: Guitar, Johnny Johansson: Bass, Elias Holmlid: Drums
Deathography
Sphere of Sorrow, Demo (1999)

RAPTURE (Kista)—see Lobotomy

RAVAGED
Visby on the island of Gotland hasn't seen a lot of death metal activity since the old days of Grave, but in 2001 these guys tried to change that. Unsuccessfully, though—Ravaged folded after two demos.
Line-Up Joon Svedelius Lindström: Vocals, Marcus Persson: Guitar, Johan Olofsson: Drums, Pelle Andersson: Guitar **Past Members** *Anton Randahl: Bass, Jenz Ekedahl: Bass*
Deathography
Embrace the Sound of Death, Demo (2002)
Funeral Parade, Demo (2003)

REAPER—see Soulreaper

REGURGITATE (Avesta)
Obscure death metal from Avesta that emerged in January 1991 under the name Entangled. Originally they played death metal in the vein of Disharmonic Orchestra and Pungent Stench (with some hints of Voivod), but their style got stranger and less Metal with time. Later they changed their name to Greedkick, after which they disappeared. Not to be confused with Regurgitate from Stockholm. David Bock was also the editor of *Ugly Logo Zine*.
Line-Up David Bock: Guitar/Vocals, Fredrik Palm: Bass/Vocals, Thomas: Drums
Deathography
Trials of Life, Demo (1992)
Promo 93, Demo (1993—as Greedkick)

REGURGITATE (Stockholm)
Brutal grindcore from Stockholm which emerged in 1990, mainly as Rikard Jansson's one-man creation. For a while Peter Stjärnvind (Merciless, Entombed) was involved, but his obligations to other bands made that time brief. He has made comeback appearances, though, and his drum work in Regurgitate is among the best he ever delivered. Other members have equally impressive resumés in bands like Crematory, Afflicted, Dawn, and General Surgery. Regurgitate can be seen as the pure grindcore equivalent to the deadlier Crematory. Gore lyrics, noisy grind, insane vocals—what more could you want? This is great! Note the massive list of split records this band has produced, in pure grind fashion. Avesta's main man of death metal, Johan Jansson, joined in 2006.
Line-Up Rikard Jansson: Vocals, Urban Skytt: Guitar, Jocke Pettersson: Drums, Johan Jansson: Bass (2006-) **Past Members** *Glenn Sykes: Bass Peter Stjärnvind: Drums, Johan Hanson: Bass, Mats Nordrup: Guitar/Drums, Terje: Bass (session only), Anders Jakobsson: Drums (session only)*
Deathography
Demo 1, Demo (1991)
Regurgitate/Vaginal Massacre, Split 7" (Poserslaughter, 1992)
Brainscrambler, Regurgitate/Psychotic Noise, Split 7" (Glued Stamps, 1993)
Concrete Human Torture, Demo (1994)
Regurgitate, CD (Poserslaughter, 1994)
Regurgitate/Grudge, Split 7" (Obsession, 1994)
Regurgitate/Dead, Split MCD (Poserslaughter, 1994)
Effortless Regurgitation of Bright Red Blood, CD (Lowland, 1994)
Fleshmangler, Regurgitate/Intestinal Infection, Split 7" (Noise Variations, 1996)
Promo 1999, Demo (1999)
Regurgitate/Filth, Split 7" (Painiac, 2000)
Carnivorous Erection, CD (Relapse, 2001)
Regurgitate/Gore Beyond Necropsy, Split 7" (No Weak Shit, 2001)
Regurgitate/Realized, Split 7" (Stuhlgang, 2001)
Sodomy and Carnal Assault, Split (2001)
Cripple Bastards/Regurgitate, Split (2002)
Hatefilled Vengeance, EP (2002)
Regurgitate/Entrails Massacre, Split (2003)
Regurgitate/Noisear, Split (2003)
3-Way Grindcore Knockout, Round 1, Split (2003)
Bonesplice/Baltic Thrash Corps, Split (2003)
Deviant, CD (Relapse, 2003)
Regurgitate/Suppository, Split (2004)
Sickening Bliss, CD/LP (Relapse, 2006)

RELENTLESS
U.S.-inspired death metal band from Örebro/Lindesberg, started in 1997. Originally they played old school death metal, but soon developed a more complex and modern style. The thing that works against them is their unimpressive songs, but it's still a good band. I guess all the problems with the line-up held them back, but I hope they will keep it going. Robert Kanto used to be the editor of *Serenity Zine*.

Line-Up *Matte Andersson: Vocals/Guitar (for some time, bass), Pär Svensson: Drums, Oscar Pålsson: Bass (2003-)* **Past Members** *Gabbe: Guitar (1999-2001), Robert Kanto: Bass (2000-2001, 2001-2002), Guitar (1997-1999, 2001), Fredrik: Guitar (2002-2003)*
Deathography
Pestilence of the Undead, Demo (1999)
Experiment in Excrement, Demo (2000)
Relentless, Demo (2001)
Tempest of Torment, CD (Crash Music, 2004)

RELEVANT FEW
Began as Mindsnare around the year 2000. Something unusual here: a Gothenburg band playing grind/death metal in the vein of Napalm Death.
Line-Up *Christian Lampela: Guitar, Henke Svensson: Vocals, Robert Hakemo: Bass, Daniel Moilanen: Drums* **Past Members** *Johan Carlsson: ocals, Johan Nilsson: Guitar*
Deathography
Demo (as Mindsnare)
Who Are Those of Leadership, CD (No Tolerance, 2002)
The Art of Today, CD (No Tolerance, 2003)

REMAINS OF THE GROTESQUE
Black/death group from Kalmar formed in 2003.
Line-Up *Lars Bakken, Oskar Öberg* **Past Members** *Oskar Jacobsson*
Deathography
The Black Moon Rises, Demo (2005)

REMASCULATE
Grind/death metal from Vårby with a punk feeling, formed in 2004. I guess this is mainly a project, with drums handled by Insision's Marcus Jonsson.
Line Up *Micke Strömberg: Guitar/Vocals, Marcus Jonsson: Drums, Johan Bladlund: Bass, Ludde Engellau: Vocals*
Deathography
Til the Stench Do Us Part, Demo (2004)
Blend in and Juice Them, CD (Evigt Lidande Productions, 2005)

REPUGNANCE
Saxdalen band formed in February 1990, originally as Atrocious Reek. Probably one of the first death/thrash bands with harsh screaming vocals (instead of growls) since Grotesque. They never got anywhere. Maybe they were ahead of their time, but probably they were just way too bad.
Line-Up *Micke Timonen: Guitar/Vocals, Mattias Timonen: Drums, Hedlund: Bass*
Deathography
Rehearsal (1990—as Atrocious Reek)
Covetous Divinity, Demo (1990)

REPUGNANT
Starting in 1998 in Norsborg, a small suburb of Stockholm, their aim was to make utterly old school death metal and they really succeeded. The songs, the vocals, the sound—all there! Repugnant fully understood the major part that humor played in the old death metal scene. Just look at their stage names: Mary Goore, Roy Morbidson, Side E Burns, and Chris Piss! After a few gigs with the legendary Macabre, Ahonen and Barkensjö left the band. In came Tomas Daun of Insision and Gustaf Lindström. The band folded after a shaky tour in Finland with Centinex in 2004. The album they recorded in 2002 was long-delayed, and turned out to be best album of 2006! To me, the best retro death metal band Sweden ever saw. Get all their stuff. Note that Ahonen was an original guitarist of Insision—he joined this band when Insision got too complicated for him.
Line-Up *Tobias "Mary Goore" Forge: Vocals/Guitar, Johan "Sid E Burns" Wallin: Guitar, Gustaf "Carlos Sathanas" Lindström: Bass (2000-), Tomas "Tom Bones" Daun: Drums (2000-)* **Past Members** *Joonas "Roy Morbidson" Ahonen: Bass (1999-2000), Christofer "Chris Piss" Barkensjö: Drums (1998-2000), Karl Envall: Bass (1998-1999)*
Deathography
Spawn of Pure Malevolence, Demo (1999)
Hecatomb, 7" (To The Death, 1999)
Hecatomb, MCD (Unveiling the Wicked, 2000)
Draped in Cerecloth, Demo (2001)
Dunkel Besatthet, Repugnant/Pentacle, Split (To the Death, 2002)
Repugnant/Kaamos, Split Live Demo (2003)
Premature Burial, EP (Soulseller Recs, 2004)
Epitome of Darkness, CD (Soulseller Records, 2006)

RETALIATION
Unrelenting death/grind band started in Mjölby in 1993 by the ever-creative Henrik Forss (Dawn, ex-Nefarious), who also edited *Brutal Mag* and *Dis-Organized Zine*. Originally the band used a drum machine, but soon recruited drummer Petersson and guitarist Albrektsson. They produced a number of records over the years, but strangely only once played live, with Thy Primordial and Dawn in 1994. If Traumatic, Funeral Feast, Retaliation, Nefarious, and Carcaroht were compressed into one single band, I think Mjölby would have ruled eternally. As it is, we have to make due with a bunch of good ones.
Line-Up *Henrik Forss: Guitar/Vocals, Andreas Carlsson: Vocals, Jonas Albrektsson: Guitar (1994-), Jocke Petersson: Drums (1994-), Jon: Bass/Vocals*
Deathography
Acrid Genital Spew, Demo (1993)
Devastating Doctrine Dismemberment, Demo (1994)
The Misanthrope, Retaliation/Gut Split 7" (Regurgitated Semen, 1994)
Grindwork, Retaliation/Nasum/Vivisection/CSSO Split 7" (Grindwork Productions, 1995)
Pray for War, Retaliation/Exhumed Split 7" (Headfucker, 1998)
The Execution, CD (Headfucker, 1999)
Suicidal Disease, Retaliation/The Kill Split 7" (Mortville, 2000)
Boredom and Frustration, EP (Blood Harvest/Sounds of Betr, 2001)
Violence Spreads its Drape, CD (Putrid Filth Conspiracy, 2002)

RETRIBUTION

Death metal band from Piteå, active since 2002 and responsible for a row of demos.

Line-Up Fredrik Nyman: Vocals, Joel Öhman: Guitar, Rickard Karlsson: Guitar, Hans Sunnebjer: Drums **Past Members** Daniel Nordh: *Various Instruments (session only), Kristofer Bäckström: Bass, Erik Flodin: Drums/Bass*

Deathography
Archaic Warfare, Demo (2002)
Carnage of Autumn, Demo (2003)
Ahead the Days of Reprisal, Demo (2004)
Vol. 4, Demo (2005)

REVOCATION

Good death metal band from Stockholm, formed in 1998. Probably on hold or split up, since I haven't heard anything for a long time. Some members are also busy with the successful Kaamos. Note that Repugnant's Tobias Forge was in this band.

Line-Up Drunkschwein: Bass/Vocals, Fred Hellbelly: Drums, Jonny Putrid: Guitar **Past Members** Erik Hellman: Guitar, Tobias Forge: Guitar

Deathography
Reincarnated Souls of Hell, Demo (1999)
Reincarnated Souls of Hell, EP (Nuclear Winter, 2004)

RIBSPREADER

Death metal project formed in Gamleby in 2003, lasting long enough to release two albums. Basically this is a Johansson (Carve, Paganizer) solo act, but the most prominent member is definitely Dan Swanö.

Line-Up Roger Johansson: Guitar/Vocals, Mattias Fiebig: Drums, Patrik Halvarsson: Bass **Past Members** Andreas Karlsson: Guitar/Bass, Dan Swanö: Guitar, Johan Berglund: Drums

Deathography
Bolted to the Cross, CD (New Aeon/Karmageddon Media, 2004)
Congregating the Sick, CD (New Aeon/Karmageddon Media, 2005)

RIPSTICH—see Dormitory

RIVER'S EDGE—see Expulsion

ROSICRUCIAN

Västerås-based band originally called Atrocity (see separate entry), but changed name and some members in 1989 to begin a somewhat deadlier mission. They kept some moshy riffs and Bay Area vocals, which turned off a lot of people in the early 90's. Lots of line-up problems led to a premature end. Linden, Söderman, and Jacobsen then formed Slapdash.

Line-Up Magnus Söderman: Guitar, Johan Wiegal: Keyboards, Fredrik Jakobsson: Bass, Lars Linden: Vocals/Guitar (1990-), Andreas Wallström: Drums (1994-) **Past Members** Glyn Grimwade: Vocals (1989-1993) Ulf Peterson: Vocals, Patrik Marchente: Drums (1992-1994), Kentha Philipson: Drums (1989-1992)

Deathography

ROTINJECTED

Death metal band formed in Varberg in 2000. In reality, this is Anata appearing under another name. But why? Conny and Björn also play in Eternal Lies.

Line-Up Fredrik Schälin: Vocals, Björn Johansson: Guitar, Andreas Allenmark: Guitar, Henrik Drake: Bass, Conny Pettersson: Drums

Deathography
Demo 2001, Demo (2001)

ROTTING FLESH

Death metal from Angered, played for six months in 1990-1991 before folding. Vocalist Jouni and Tommy formed Chronic Torment (later Sacretomia), and the guitarists started Angel Goat. Why does the town of Angered have so many crazed Finnish metalheads?

Line-Up Ari Juurikka: Guitar, Jouni Parkkonen: Vocals, Tommy Parkkonen: Drums, Harri J: Guitar, Mikka V: Bass

Deathography
Rehearsal (1991)

ROUTE NINE

Active from 1991-1994, another of Swanö's endless side projects—can we handle them all? He is helped on drums by Jacobsson of Necrony/Nasum (recreating the line-up of Masticate, in other words). The album collects old demos. A progressive Örebro/Finspång alliance you might want to check out.

Line-Up Dan Swanö: Vocals/Guitar/Bass/Keyboards, Anders Jacobsson: Drums

Deathography
Demo 92, Demo (1992)
Before I Close my Eyes Forever, EP (Inorganic, 1993)
The Works, MCD (Spam, 2001)

RUNEMAGICK

Side project of Nicklas Rudolfsson (Swordmaster, Sacramentum, Deathwitch), founded in Gothenburg in 1990. At early gigs he was helped by Norman (Dissection) and Losbäck (Decameron). The band went on hold in 1993, but was resurrected in 1997 with some new members, notably bass player Palmdahl (ex-Dissection). Further line-up changes followed, and I don't know if anybody knows who is in the band anymore. The music is some kind of death metal with a doomy gothic feel, even though they originally labelled themselves black metal and used corpse paint. Since reuniting they have produced an insane stream of releases of varying quality. Early member Pehrsson formed Death Breath with Nicke Andersson.

Line-Up Niklas Rudolfsson: Vocals/Guitar, Daniel Moilanen: Drums (1999-), Emma Karlsson: Bass (1999-) **Past Members** Jonas Blom: Drums (session only, 1998-1999), Nils Karlén: Bass (1990-1992), Johan Norman: Guitar (1992-1993), Robert Persson: Vocals/Guitar (1991-1993), Alexander Losbäck: Bass (1992-1993), Johan Bäckman: Bass

(1993), Peter Palmdahl: Bass (1997-1998), Fredrik Johnsson: Guitar (1997-2003), Tomas Eriksson: Guitar
Deathography
Promo Demon, Demo (1991)
Alcoholic Rehearsal, Demo (1991)
Fullmoon Sodomy, Demo (1992)
Necro Live, Demo (1992)
Dark Magick Promo, Demo (1997)
The Supreme Force of Eternity, CD (Century Media, 1998)
Enter the Realm of Death, CD (Century Media, 1999)
Resurrection in Blood, CD (Century Media, 2000)
Ancient Incantations, 7" (Aftermath, 2001)
Sepulchral Realms, Demo (2001)
Dark Live Magick, LP (Bloodstone, 2001)
Worshippers of Death, Runemagick/Soulreaper split (2002)
Requiem of the Apocalypse, CD (Aftermath, 2002)
Moon of the Chaos Eclipse, CD (Aftermath, 2002)
Doomed by Death, Runemagick/Lord Belial split (Aftermath, 2002)
Darkness Death Doom/The Pentagram, CD (Aftermath, 2003)
Darkness Death Doom, CD (Aftermath, 2003)
On Funeral Wings, CD (Aftermath, 2004)
Envenom, CD (Aftermath, 2005)
Black Magick Sorceress, EP (Aftermath, 2005)
Invocation of Magick, CD (Aftermath, 2005)

SACRAMENTUM
Formed in Falköping in 1990 by Karlén as Tumulus. After numerous line-up changes they changed the name in 1993. As Sacramentum they've had a little success, but never completely made it. Rudolfsson was also in Runemagick and Swordmaster (before they transformed into the electro/pop/metal/goth band Deathstars). Decent, though I find these mixes between black and death metal unaggressive and unfocused.
Line-Up Anders Brolycke: Guitar, Nils Karlén: Vocals/Bass *Past Members* Nicklas Andersson: Guitar, Freddy Andersson: Bass, Mikael Rydén: Drums Nicklas Rudolfsson: Bass/Drums Thomas Backelin: Guitar, Tobias Kjellgren: Drums, Johan Norrman: Guitar, Micke: Drums
Deathography
Sedes Imporium, Demo (1993)
Finis Malorum, EP (Northern Production, 1994)
Far Away from the Sun, CD (Adipocere, 1996)
The Coming Chaos, CD (Century Media, 1997)
The Black Destiny, CD (Century Media, 1999)

SACRETOMIA
Formed in Angered, April 1991, originally as Chronic Torment. At first playing thrash metal, like many bands of the era they quickly became brutal. Good death metal in the vein of Deicide and Morbid Angel—one look at their demo's title tells you how it sounds. Too bad they didn't continue. The Parkkonen brothers were also in the short-lived Rotting Flesh.
Line-Up Mikael Vänhanen: Guitar Jouni Parkkonen: Guitar/Vocals, Tommy Parkkonen: Drums/Vocals,

Niclas: Bass *Past Members* Mirko Varis: Bass
Deathography
Altar of Sin, Demo (1992)

SACRILEGE
The only interesting thing to say is that Svensson joined In Flames on drums in 1998. Apparently the band still exists, but has made nothing since 1997.
Line-Up Daniel Dinsdale: Guitar, Richard Bergholz: Guitar, Daniel Kvist: Bass, Daniel Svensson: Drums/Vocals *Past Members* Michael Andersson: Vocals, Christian Frisk: Bass
Deathography
...and Autumn Failed, Demo (1996)
To Where the Light Can't Reach, Demo (1996)
Lost in the Beauty You Slay, CD (Black Sun, 1996)
The Fifth Season, CD (Black Sun, 1997)

SACRIUM
Early 90's band from Falun. Mainly slow death metal with deep vocals. Though far from bad, this is too standard and unexciting to impress. Granvik's next band, Without Grief, is far better.
Line-Up Jonas Granvik: Vocals, Dahlquist: Bass/Guitar, Lindh: Bass/Drums
Deathography
Somnus es Morti Similis, Demo (1992)

SADISTIC GANG RAPE
This wonderfully-named band was started in 1991 by three pissed-off girls in the small town of Avesta. Initially, local death metal lunatics Jansson (Dellamorte, Beyond, Interment, Hatred, Fulmination, Centinex, Uncurbed, Asocial, Regurgitate (Stockholm), Uncanny, Demonical—how about those credits!) and Törnros (Uncanny, Uncurbed) helped out with drums and vocals. Soon, Sussie and Marie-Louise took charge of the vocals themselves, to great effect. They found a permanent drummer in Kattis' boyfriend at the time, Christoffer Harborg. Unfortunately, the group drifted away from death metal roots and developed a crust punk style instead. Even worse, they changed their brilliant name to the lamer Society Gang Rape. Though their later material wasn't bad, it just wasn't the same. The mainly female Sadistic Gang Rape is indeed a rare and welcome find in the all too male-dominated death metal scene. In their brightest (darkest?) moments, they were the deadliest female group on Earth.
Line-Up Kattis Lammi: Guitar, Sussie Berger: Bass/Vocals, Marie-Louise Ehrs: Guitar/Vocals, Christoffer Harborg: Drums *Past Members* Johan Jansson: Drums/Vocals (1992), Jens Törnros: Vocals (1992)
Deathography
Massdevastation, Demo (1992)

SADISTIC GRIMNESS
Sadistic Grimness formed in Uddevalla/Stenungsund in 2000. Originally played pure black metal, but have lately incorporated more death metal structures. Members have also been involved in minor bands like Angst, Kill, Diabolicum, Conspiracy, Ill-Natured, and Mastema.

Line-Up DD Executioner: Vocals/Guitar, Kemper Lieath (aka Kevorkian): Drums, Fleshripper (Rikard): Bass **Past Members** Nocturnal Skullsodomizer: Guitar (session only), Robert Carnifex: BassMaster Motorsåg: Vocals (session only)
Deathography
From Heaven to the Abyss, Demo (2000)
Bleed for the Goat, Demo (2001)
Split Cunt of Virgin Mary, Sadistic Grimness/ Kerberos split (Ordealis Records, 2004)
Vicious Torture, CD (Infernus Rex, 2004)

SADO BASTARDOS

This book lists a lot of obscure and pointless bands, but this wayward lot from Uppsala is without a doubt one of the strangest, sickest, and most mind-blowing of all. This extreme grind outfit rehearsed regularly for two years in the mid-90's and, according to bassist Robin, a violent fight between band members broke out during every single rehearsal. Notably, when Robin came up with the idea of a song that included a non-grind part, he immediately got his nose broken by the vocalist! When Robin mentioned that he should probably go see a doctor, the vocalist (a forty-something homeless guy) calmly told him: *If you don't finish the rehearsal, I'll kill you.* Their first and only gig was a private party in the rough suburb Gottsunda with about 15 people in the "audience." It ended in tragedy—during their last song, the singer stagedived onto the concrete floor, broke his neck, and died on the spot. The band broke up. Shortly afterwards, the guitarist (the late vocalist's son!) was committed to a mental institution, the drummer went to prison for manslaughter, and Robin started living in an abandoned train car at Uppsala rail station. Apparently Sado Bastardos recorded a rehearsal tape, but unfortunately the only known copy was kept in a box with the rest of Robin's belongings at an ex-friend's place. Though he was offered a considerable amount of money for the tape by various local grind fanatics, he didn't have the guts to face the guy again. One can only suspect it's lost forever. Yes, this is really a band to check out for those into the bizarre and morbid, but I guess your chances to hear them or see them live are slim to none. The only thing left to do is probably just to write their name on your leather jacket. That will also be a problem since nobody knows what their logo looked like—but I sure hope it was Times New Roman with a hand-drawn pentagram in the background...
Line-Up Old, dead homeless guy: Vocals, Son of Old, dead homeless guy: Guitar, Robin: Bass, Some weirdo: Drums
Deathography:
Rehearsal (199?)

SALVATION

Death metal band from Mjölby. Formed in 1989, they stayed together long enough to make one demo. The members went on to Lucifer, Atryxion, Carcaroth, Indungeon, Thy Primordial, and Metroz.
Line-Up Mikael Andersson: Bass, Jonny Fagerström: Drums, Fredrik Åstrand: Guitar, Tommy: Guitar
Past Members Jonas Larsson: Vocals (session only)

Deathography
Carnage Remains, Demo (1990)

SANCTIFICA

Formed in 1996, they made a couple CDs before splitting in 2002. One of those bands that used melodic black/death metal to incorporate a Christian message. Weird. Bad, too. Jonathan is also in similar band Pantokrator. Some members have continued in As a Reminder, which I don't know anything about. I don't want to know, either.
Line-Up David: Vocals, Jonathan: Bass/Vocals, Hubertus: Guitar/Vocals, Henrik: Guitar/Vocals, Daniel: Drums, Aron: Keyboards
Deathography
In the Bleak Midwinter, Demo (1998)
Spirit of Purity, CD (Little Rose Productions, 2000)
In the Bleak Midwinter/Songs of Solomon, Sanctifica/Pantokrator Split (CLC Music, 2001)
Negative B, CD (Rivel Records, 2002)

SANCTIFICATION

Anti-Christian death metal formed in Östersund in 2001. Good-quality Americanized death metal well worth checking out. All members have been or still are active in quality groups including Divine Desecration, God Among Insects, In Battle, Aeon, Souldrainer, Deranged, and Defaced Creation.
Line-Up Mathias Mohlin: Vocals, Tomas Elofsson: Guitar, Nils Fjellström: Drums, Kristoffer Hell: Bass
Past Members Daniel Dlimi: Guitar, Peter Jönsson: Bass, Jörgen Bylander: Bass
Deathography
Demo 01-02, Demo (2002)
Misanthropic Salvation, CD (Remission Records, 2003)
Promo 2004, Demo (2004)

SANGUINARY

Melodic mid-90's death metal from Bro. Actually sounds more like early 90's, which is good!
Line-Up Mattias Lenikka: Guitar/Vocals, Raimo: Drums, Danne: Guitar, L-E: Bass **Past Members** Juppe: Bass
Deathography
Demo 1, Demo (1995)

SARCASM

High-quality atmospheric death metal from Uppsala, Sarcasm was founded in late 1990 by madman guitarist Fredrik Wallenberg and notorious metal legend Heval Bozarslan. (No one is more metal than he is. No one.) Before proper demos they produced a couple rehearsals that sounded like Autopsy, but soon developed a more original style. Melodic yet crushing riffs from Wallenberg and ghastly vocals by Bozarslan really made Sarcasm stand out, and the overall feeling was a lot like raw black metal—pretty much like Dissection, really. The future might have led to something, but Sarcasm started falling apart when Wallenberg left to form crust band Skitsystem with Tomas Lindberg (At the Gates) in 1994. They

never regained their strength. A band to check out.
Line-Up Heval Bozarslan: Vocals, Dave Janney: Bass, Henrik Forslund: Guitar (initially drums), Oscar Karlsson: Drums, Anders Eriksson: Guitar Past Members Fredrik Wallenberg: Guitar, Simon Winroth: Drums
Deathography
In Hate, Demo (1992)
Porta 1, Demo (1992)
Porta 2, Demo (1992)
Demo (1993, unreleased)
Dark, Demo (1993)
Demo 93, Demo (1993)
A Touch of the Burning Red Sunset, Demo (1994)
A Touch of the Burning Red Sunset, CD (Breath of Night, 1998)
Scattered Ashes, 7" (Danse Hypnotica, 1999)

SARCAZM
One of the countless Gothenburg bands that never got anywhere, Sarcazm started during summer 1990 playing thrashy metal in the vein of Slayer, Metallica, and Annihilator. Don't mistake them for Uppsala's far superior Sarcasm! Andersson and Engelin later formed Luciferion, and Engelin played guitar for In Flames during live gigs in 1997-1998.
Line-Up Krister Albertsson: Vocals/Guitar, Niclas Engelin: Guitar, Beppe Kurdali: Bass (1993-), Peter Andersson: Drums Past Members Bo Falk: Bass
Deathography
Snaildeath, Demo (1990)
Human Decadence, Demo (1991)
Jeremiads, Demo (1993)
Breathe Shit Exist, CD (Deathside, 1994)

SARGATANAS REIGN
Steady death metal that started out in Norrköping in 1997. Originally, vocals were handled by Devo (Marduk), who was in turn replaced by Jonas Mattson (Incinerator, ex-Nominon).
Line-Up Jonas Mattson: Vocals, Niklas Samuelsson: Bass, Stefan "Vrashtar" Kronqvist: Drums, Kristoffer "Ushatar" Andersson: Guitar, Marcus Lundberg: Guitar Past Members Johan Ericsson: Bass, Magnus "Devo" Andersson: Vocals
Deathography
Sargatanas, Demo (1998)
Satanic Hymns, Demo (1998)
The God Below, Demo (1998)
Hellucination, EP (I Hate Records, 2001)
Euthanasia... Last Resort, CD (I Hate Records, 2002)
Bloodwork: Techniques of Torture, CD (Blooddawn/Regain, 2005)

SARS
Death/grind band formed in Arvika in 2003. Lyrics are filled with perversion and humor, not a shock since members come from Tribulation (Arvika) and Guerilla. I guess this is basically just a project.
Line-Up Adam "Ma Sars" Zaars: Guitar/Vocals, Jonka "Pipen Doom Occulta" Andersson: Bass/Vocals, Jakob "Doom Krahft" Pungberg: Drums
Deathography
Night of the Living Sars, Demo (2003)

SARTINAS
Melodic Swedish death metal with screaming vocals—you guessed it, this band emerged after At the Gates' *Slaughter of the Soul*. They only existed long enough to make a couple of ignored demos.
Deathography
Sartinas, Demo (1996)
Demo CD '97, Demo (1997)

SATANIC SLAUGHTER
The life's work of Stefan "Ztephan Dark" Karlsson, you have to respect Satanic Slaughter. They started as early as 1985 (and BEFORE that they played as Evil Cunt!), and are surely one of the first extreme metal bands from Scandinavia (though the early style was more punk/thrash). The band was surrounded by problems from the start. Their original bass player was convicted for pyromania, and subsequently isolated in a mental institution. Further, main man Karlsson was charged with assault in 1989, and Satanic Slaughter was put on ice while he went to jail. The band resurrected in 1992, only to collapse again in 1997 due to musical disagreements and serious line-up problems. Stefan sacked everyone, so they went off and formed Witchery. He quickly found new members, but problems occurred once again when bassist Carlsson left to become vocalist of Corporation 187. However, Stefan continued—you really must give him credit. What about the music? Oh, it's a hybrid of black, speed, and death metal. The best comparisons would probably be Sodom and Destruction. It's cool, but hardly great. In the end, even Stefan couldn't keep it together, and the band split after immense line-up problems (running through at least 25 members!) and lack of success. I got a mail in 2006 from Stefan saying he had restarted the band—obviously in it for life! But sadly just four days before I was to interview him about the earliest phase of the Swedish death metal scene, Karlsson passed away due to a serious heart condition. He WAS in it for life. Rest in peace.
Line-Up Andreas Deblèn: Vocals (1995-), Ztephan Dark (Stefan Karlsson): Guitar (1985-), Stefan Johansson: Guitar (1999-), Simon Axenrot: Bass (2003-), Martin Axenrot: Drums (1998-) Past Members Toxine (Tony Kampner): Vocals (1987, 1994-1996), Mikki Fixx: Guitar (1985), Jörgen Sjöström: Guitar (1985), Patrik Strandberg: Guitar (1985), Jonas Hagberg: Guitar (1987-1989), Janne Karlsson: Guitar (1989), Patrik Jensen: Guitar (1995-1996), Richard Corpse: Guitar, Kecke Ljungberg: Guitar (1997-1999), Ron B. Goat: Bass (1985-1987), Patrik "Kulman": Bass (1987-1989), Peter Blomberg: Bass (1989), Filip Carlsson: Bass (1997-2003), Pontus Sjösten: Drums (1985), Peter Svedenhammar: Drums (1985-1987), Robert Falstedt: Drums (1987-1989), Evert Karlsson: Drums (1989), Gerry Malmström: Drums (1989), Mique (Mikael Kampner): Drums (1987, 1994-1997), Robert Eng: Drums (1997-1998)
Deathography
One Night in Hell, Demo (1988)
Satanic Slaughter, CD (Necropolis, 1995)

Land of the Unholy Souls, CD (Necropolis, 1997)
Afterlife Kingdom, CD (Loud 'n Proud, 2000)
The Early Years: Dawn of Darkness, CD (Necropolis, 2001)
Banished to the Underworld, CD (Black Sun, 2002)

SATANIZED
Death metal from Gothenburg, formed in 1991 and only existed long enough to record one rehearsal and play one gig. The members went on to form better-known bands including Dissection, Decameron, Nifelheim, Ophthalamia, Soulreaper, Runemagic, and Lord Belial. A band of massive historic interest!
Line-Up Per Alexandersson: Vocals, Jon Nödtveidt: Guitar, Johan Norman: Guitar, Tobias Kellgren: Drums, Thomas Backelin: Bass
Deathography
Demo, Demo (1991)

SATARIEL
Satariel started in 1993 from the remains of Beheaded and Dawn of Darkness. Due to a lot of problems with the line-up, Satariel has been inactive during lengthy periods. Their music is a mix between old school death, melodic guitars, and doom. For me, this doesn't work. Like other bands from the northern part of Sweden (Satariel hails from the very northern town Boden), they sound a bit unoriginal and fabricated. Go for pure stuff and you'll do better!
Line-Up Pär Johansson: Vocals, Magnus Alakangas: Guitar/Keyboards, Mikael Degerman: Bass, Robert Sundelin: Drums, Mikael Grankvist: Guitar Past Members Fredrik Andersson: Guitar, Andreas Nilsson: Drums, Mats Ömalm
Deathography
Thy Heaven's Fall, Demo (1993)
Desecration Black, Demo (1994)
Hellfuck, Demo (1995)
Promo 96, Demo (1996)
Lady Lust Lilith, CD (Pulverized, 1998)
Promo 2000, Demo (2000)
Phobos and Daimos, CD (Hammerheart, 2002)
Hydra, CD (Cold Records, 2005)

SATUREYE
Thrash metal formed at the very end of the 90's in Strängnäs. On the plus side are brilliant screaming vocals by Rogga (Merciless), and some groove that is badly missed in other retro thrash acts. Good stuff, but a far cry from the mighty Merciless.
Line-Up Rogga: Vocals, Norsken: Guitar, Jocke: Bass, Henke: Drums
Deathography
Silvery Souls, Demo (2001)
Satureye, Demo (2002)
Where Flesh and Divinity Collide, CD (Karmageddon Media, 2004)

SAWCHAIN
A new thrash/death band from Piteå.
Line-Up Jonathan Asplund: Drums, Johnny Johansson: Guitar, Joel Karlsson: Guitar, Andreas Nilsson: Bass, Fredrik Nyman: Vocals Past Members

Roland: Drums, Toni Sunnari: Guitar, Stefan Lundberg: Vocals
Deathography
Abra Cadaver, Demo (2002)
Monument of Hate, Demo 2002
Architecture of Evil, Demo (2004)

SCAR SYMMETRY
Avesta's main man of metal, Jonas Kjellgren, left Carnal Forge in 2004 and was immediately offered a deal by Cold Records to put together "a Soilwork-sounding group." (They ended up on Nuclear Blast, small surprise.) He gathered his favorite musicians, but instead of mimicking melodic death metal he did what he wanted. The result is a confusing mix of styles that doesn't really work. Listen to Centinex, Carnal Forge, Dellamorte, and Pexilated instead to grasp the brilliance of Kjellgren. Sorry dude, I would like to enjoy this more, but I just can't.
Line-Up Christian Älvestam: Vocals, Henrik Ohlsson: Drums, Jonas Kjellgren: Guitar, Per Nilsson: Guitar, Kenneth Seil: Bass
Deathography
Symmetric in Design, CD (Metal Blade, 2005)
Pitch Black Progress, CD (Nuclear Blast, 2006)

SCENTERIA
Death/thrash from Halmstad, formed in 2002. Still a long way to go to match town mates Arch Enemy.
Line-Up Niklas Pettersson: Guitar, Daniel Landin: Drums, Stefan Persson: Vocals/Guitar, Johan Andreasson: Bass
Deathography
Signs of Hypnotica, Demo (2002)
Descent from Darkness, Demo (2002)
Path of Silence, Demo (2003)
Art of Aggression, CD (Karmageddon Media, 2004)

SCHEITAN
From the northern town of Luleå, started in 1996 and immediately got a deal with Invasion. Like all bands going straight to albums without developing through demos, you should be careful. This usually means the music is commercialized crap. Well, Scheitan might not be crap, but the melodic music can't convince me. Pretty successful in the 90's, though, and ended up on Century Media. Since 1999 nothing has been heard, so maybe they split up. Does anyone keep a record of how many bands Törnkvist has been involved in?
Line-Up Oskar Karlsson: Guitar/Bass/Drums, Pierre Törnkvist: Guitar/Vocals/Bass, Lotta Högberg: Vocals, Göran Norman: Keyboards
Deathography
Travelling in Ancient Times, CD (Invasion, 1996)
Berzerk 2000, CD (Invasion, 1998)
Nemesis, CD (Century Media, 1999)

SCREAMS OVER NORTHLAND
One-man project from Linköping making atmospheric doom/death. An EP was released, that's all I know.
Line-Up Tomas Andersson: Everything
Deathography

Screams over Northland, EP (Ghoul Records, 1999)

SCUM—see Amon Amarth

SCURVY
Hilarious band from Upplands Väsby, formed in 1998. Scurvy sounds extremely similar to Macabre, so of course it's great! Wallin can now be found in General Surgery, and used to play in the mighty Repugnant (he also ran small label/distro Escorbuto). I liked this band a lot, and really hope they will record something more, though I suspect they have split up.
Line-Up Fredrik Andersson: Bass/Vocals, Johan Wallin: Guitar/Vocals, Martin "Curry" Persson: Drums
Deathography
Demotape, Demo (2000)
Scurvy/Death Reality, Split (Perverted Taste, 2001)
Tombstone Tales/Second Ejaculation, CD (Perverted Taste, 2002)
Funeral Fist Fucker, Scurvy/Morsgatt, Split (Noise Variations, 2002)

SCYPOZOA
Early 90's project from Finspång, playing crazed death/thrash that kicks some serious ass. No, this is not one of Dan Swanö's endless musical explorations. In fact, it may be one of few bands from this city that didn't include any members of Edge of Sanity, though Pan-Thy-Monium's Robert Karlsson is represented. (Wait, didn't he join Edge of Sanity in 1997? Argh!)
Line-Up Tomas Lindgren, Janne Ivarsson, Robert Karlsson
Deathography
Signs From the Erratic Past, Demo (1991)
Diary, Demo (1992)

SCYTHER
Death/black metal project started in Jönköping during 2002. Raw, cool and pretty good, old school style. Main man Martinsson might be more known for his work with Legion.
Line-Up Lars Martinsson: Vocals/Drums
Deathography
Tombgrinding Dead Metal, Demo (2003)
The Sick Curse of Scyther, Demo (2004)

SEANCE
In 1990 in Linköping, Seance rose from the ashes of Orchriste (Larsson and Jensen) and Total Death (Kampner, Pettersson, and Carlsson). Kampner and Pettersson were also previously in Satanic Slaughter. They started with a bang, and soon played their first gig, alongside Merciless. The 1991 demo sealed a deal with Black Mark. Seance was truly great, but didn't get much attention after their second album and gradually grew inactive. Most members went on to Satanic Slaughter, then left to found Witchery. Carlsson joined Diabolique. Jensen formed The Haunted, one of the most successful of all Swedish metal bands. Seance never folded, and has financed the recording of their own third album (titled

Awakening of the Gods, I think). They are looking for a label, so if you have one, sign them!
Line-Up Tony Kampner: Guitar (1990-), Rikard Rimfält: Guitar (1995-), Bass (1994-1995), Micke Pettersson: Drums (1990-), Jonne: Bass (1995-), Johan Larsson: Vocals (1990-) *Past Members* Christian "Bino" Carlsson: Bass (1990-1994), Patrik Jensen: Guitar (1990-1995)
Deathography
Levitised Spirit, Demo (1991)
Forever Laid to Rest, CD (Black Mark, 1992)
Saltrubbed Eyes, CD (Black Mark, 1993)

SEARING I
Death/thrash from Uppsala, formed in 1999. After a row of demos, they finally made an album in 2005.
Line-Up Marcus Olofsson: Guitar, Mattias Hultman: Bass, Andreas Engman: Drums, Anders Björk: Guitar, Andreas Öman: Vocals *Past Members* Andreas Hansson: Vocals
Deathography
Vol. 01, Demo (2002)
A Treacherous Ride, Demo (2003)
Vol. 02, Demo (2003)
Tons of Hate, Demo (2004)
Bloodshred, CD (Black Lotus Records, 2005)

SEDITIOUS—see Hypocrisy

SEGREGATION
Early 90's black/death metal from Gothenburg. Surprisingly brutal, but not very good. One demo is all they left the world.
Line-Up Mika Suolanko: Guitar/Vocals, Petteri: Bass/Vocals, Otto: Guitar, Branko: Drums
Deathography
Blessed, Demo (1992)

SEMINARIUM—see Krematorium

SEPTEMBER
Obscure doom/death metal band which made one demo in 1992, then vanished into the darkness.
Deathography
Time of Darkness, Demo (1992)

SEPTIC BREED (Landskrona)—see The Forsaken

SEPTIC BREED (Västerås)
New hope for Swedish death metal, this young band started in Västerås in early 2003, and sounds very promising! Most members also play in the inferior Mausoleum, but I hope they focus more on Septic Breed in the future. Note: The Forsaken was initially called Septic Breed, an entirely different band.
Line-Up Timo Kumpumäki: Vocals, Dino Medanhodzic: Guitar, Andreas Lagergren: Guitar, Magnus Wall: Bass, Erik Stenström: Drums
Deathography
Killorama, Demo (2003)

SEPTIC BROILER—see Dark Tranquillity

SEPTIC GRAVE

Brutal yet melodic death metal from Gällivare, started in 1994. Lindmark joined Prophanity in 1996.
Line-Up Daniel Engman: Vocals, Fredrik Hjärström: Guitar, Robert Lindmark: Bass, Jörgen Björnström: Drums
Deathography
Beyond the..., Demo (1994)
Caput Mortam, MCD (Midnight Sun, 1995)

SEPTIC SOUL

Black/death metal from Söderhamn, with three demos from 2003-2004. They might have split now, I'm not sure.
Line-Up Peter Lindblom: Keyboards, Lars Emil Fredlund: Bass, Nicklas Holmsten: Vocals, Jimmy Östlin: Guitar, Johan Erik Samuelsson: Guitar/ Vocals, Mattias Lars Sjögren: Drums Past Members Sonny Helström: Guitar/Vocals
Deathography
Demented Existence, Demo (2003)
Pure Hate, Demo (2003)
Grief Induced Hallucination, Demo (2004)

SERAPH PROFANE

Formed from the ashes of Salvator in Glommen/ Falkenberg in April 1991. Initially called Corpus Christi, they soon settled for Seraph Prophane. This is heavy and melodic death metal of decent quality, but not much more. Christofer (and original bassist Tomas) also played with doom band Entity.
Line-Up Niklas Sjöberg: Drums, Erik Frankki: Guitar, Christofer Wallin: Vocals, Håkan Johansson: Guitar (1991-), Pierre Gregersson: Bass (1991-) Past Members Tomas Gustafsson: Bass (1991)
Deathography
Incarcerated, Demo (1992)
Rehearsal (1993)

SERPENT (1993)

Originally founded in 1993 as a side project by bass players Lars Rosenberg of Entombed and Andreas Wahl of Therion. The line-up changed greatly, and in 1994 two former Suffer members Samuelsson and Karlsson joined. The most notorious change came later, when the departed guitarist Wahl returned to replace Rosenberg on bass—as Rosenberg took over Wahl's duties in Therion. It ended with Wahl leaving for good, and Piotr taking over the bass. Then the band folded. Serpent was indeed heavy and cool, but never attracted any wider attention.
Line-Up Piotr Wawrzeniuk: Vocals/Bass (initially also Drums), Johan Lundell: Guitar, Ulf Samuelsson: Guitar, Per Karlsson: Drums Past Members Andreas Wahl: Bass/Guitar, Lars Rosenberg: Bass
Deathography
In the Garden of Serpent, CD (Radiation, 1996)
Autumn Ride, CD (Heathendoom 1997)

SERPENT (2000)

Started in Stockholm during 2000, this is not to be confused with the band founded by Lars Rosenberg and Andreas Wahl seven years earlier. Basically old school death metal, spiced up a bit here and there with some thrash. They sneak in a bit of black metal, too, and use funny pseudonyms like Sin and Raven. Since Serpent use a drum machine, they also have an industrial edge. They have made five demos so far, but have yet to secure a record deal.
Line-Up J. "Tyr" Dyme: Guitar, K. "Sin" Alutoin: Vocals/Bass, M. "Raven" Säfstrand: Keyboards/ Vocals (2002-)
Deathography
Serpent, Demo (2001)
Art of War, Demo (2002)
Dominator, Demo (2003)
Dark Desires, Demo (2004)
Unleash the Fury, Demo (2005)

SERPENT OBSCENE

In 1993, Johan, Jonas and Niklas formed Infernal Winter. The Rönninge-based trio soon evolved into Serpent Obscene, and grew more serious. Their music is kind of simple death/thrash with a good feeling. Erik is ex-The Marble Icon, and he sang in Maze of Torment. Johan and Niklas also created (the much better) Kaamos in 1998 with current Serpent Obscene drummer Barkensjö. Now it seems both Kaamos and Serpent Obscene have folded. The winged skull design used in this book was original created by Erik Sahlström as a symbol for this band.
Line-Up Erik Sahlström: Vocals, Nicklas Eriksson: Guitar, Johan Thörngren: Guitar/Vocals, Christoffer Barkensjö: Drums, Rob Rocker: Bass Past Members Jonas Eriksson: Drums
Deathography
Behold the Beginning, Demo (1997)
Massacre, Demo (1999)
Serpent Obscene, CD (Necropolis, 2000)
Devestation, CD (Black Lodge, 2003)

SEVERED

Death/grind band that made a demo in 1990, then vanished without a trace.
Deathography
Rot, Demo (1990)

SGT. CARNAGE

War-obsessed death/thrash band from Kristianstad, started in 2001. The members are known from good bands such as Verminous, Non Serviam, Supreme Majesty, and Immersed in Blood.
Line-Up Mats Lyborg: Vocals, Pelle Melander: Guitar, Anders Nylander: Guitar, Simon Frödeberg: Bass, Jocke Unger: Drums Past Members Mattias Göransson: Guitar (2001-2003)
Deathography
Absolut Carnage, Demo (2004)

SHADOW CULT

Malmö band just might be the newest band in this book, as they came into being in 2005. Their music is reportedly some kind of *melodic death/grind*. Sounds strange to me—what is the world coming to?
Line-Up Karolina: Vocals, Mikael: Guitar, Andreas: Bass, Johan: Drums

Deathography
Transformation, Demo (2005)

SHADOWBUILDER
Another death/thrash band from Gothenburg, formed in 2001. More proof that no The Haunted/At the Gates clones will ever be as good as the originals.
Line-Up Henrik Blomqvist: Vocals, Oscar Albinsson: Guitar, Ufuk Demir: Drums, Thomas Broniewicz: Bass, Erik Johansson: Guitar **Past Members** Pontus Jordan: Drums, Christoffer Norén: Guitar, David Flood: Drums
Deathography
When God Created Light..., Demo (2002)
Bone Ritual, Demo (2003)
Pestilence, Demo (2004)

SHADOWS AT DAWN
Mid-90's black/death project from Västerås, basically made by the guys in Succumb, and sounding pretty similar to At the Gates.
Line-Up Tony Sundqvist
Deathography
The Cold and Beautiful, Demo (1993)

SHADOWSEEDS
Symphonic death metal from Stockholm, started in 1993 by Karlsson and Eriksson, then drummer of Therion. Karlsson is probably best-known as leader of dark magical cult Dragon Rouge, and was involved with creating many of the concepts of Therion. The music? Pretty lame, in my opinion. After many years of silence, Karlsson decided to continue the band as a solo project, releasing a demo in 2004.
Line-Up Daemon Deggial (Thomas Karlsson): Vocals/All Instruments **Past Members** Daemon Kajghal (Tommy Eriksson): Guitar/Bass/Drums, Petra Aho: Vocals (session only)
Deathography
Dream of Lilith, CD (Dark Age, 1995)
Der Mitternacht Löwe, Demo (2004)

SHAGIDIEL
Early 90's death metal from Örebro—pretty cool in its intense thrashiness. One of the first bands of Mieszko Talarczyk, before he joined Nasum and started famous studio Soundlab. This band existed as Insanity for many years before becoming Shagidiel, but during that time they didn't seem to know what kind of music they wanted to play—so let's just forget about that part of the story.
Line-Up Daniel Friberg: Vocals, Mieszko Talarczyk: Guitar, Jan Petterssen: Drums, Nico Torres: Bass
Deathography
Fall, Demo (1992)

SHAMHAROTH
Black/death metal from Stenhamra, they released a demo in 1995 and then disappeared.
Line-Up Jonas: Guitar, Acke: Drums, Micke: Bass/Vocals
Deathography
Spheres Ablaze, Demo (1995)

SHATTERED
Death/thrash from Dals Långed formed in 1996 after the success of At the Gates' *Slaughter of the Soul*. They tried mixing heavy metal and death metal in their music. To me, one of the better retro thrash bands, for what that's worth. The best band from Dals Långed will always be Nifelheim, anyway.
Line-Up Johan Karlsson: Drums, Jimi Andersson: Guitar, Erik Andersson: Vocals/Bass **Past Members** Lars Karlsson: Guitar
Deathography
Serenade of Sadism, Demo (2001)
Seductors Manual, Demo (2002)
Reckless Aggression, Demo (2003)
Wrapped in Plastic, CD (Black Mark, 2004)

THE SHATTERED
Formed in Karlskrona in 2001 as Dissectum. The name changed, but their furious pure death metal attack remained. Note the more familiar Visceral Bleeding "stole" this band's singer, so you can imagine that The Shattered had potential. The others are known from local acts Abused, Foreskin Fester, and Caustic Strike. Don't mistake them for Dals Långed's Shattered, an entirely different kind of group.
Line-Up Carle Jephson: Vocals, Andreas Wiberg: Guitar, Robin Holmberg: Guitar, Max Grahn: Drums **Past Members** Christoffer Renvaktar: Bass (session only), Martin Pedersen: Vocals (2001-2003), Björn Pettersson: Bass (2001-2004)
Deathography
Destined to Suffer, Demo (2002—as Dissectum)
Pale with Terror, Demo (2003—as Dissectum)
Dissectum, Demo (2004)
The shattering Begins, CD (Retribute, 2005)

SHIFTLIGHT
Melodic doom/death, began in 1997. Mattias is also known from Embraced, and Nicklas is in Sovereign.
Line-Up Mattias Lindström: Vocals/Bass, Andreas: Guitar, Nicklas: Drums **Past Members** Fredrik Nevander (session only)
Deathography
Life is a Dream, Demo (2000)
AM 25.807, Demo (2002)
Shiftlight, Demo (2003)
Demo 4, Demo (2003)

SHURIKEN
Melodic death duo formed in Gothenburg in 2000.
Line-Up Påhl Sundström: Vocals/Guitar/Bass, Erik Sundström: Drums
Deathography
Shuriken, Demo (2000)

SICK996
Progressive death metal started in the frozen town of Kiruna in 2001. Their sole CD is self-financed.
Line-Up Mick Syrmström: Guitar, V-Saäd Bashiti: Guitar, Anar Ström: Bass, Niklas Huru: Keys, Carl Andersson: Drums **Past Members** Max Chinile: Guitar
Deathography

Jerusalem Calling, CD (2004)

SICKNESS—see Benighted

SIDE EFFECTS—see Skinfected

SINS OF OMISSION
Stockholm group created from Berserk, Mournful, and Metempsychosis. Line-up has changed a lot since 1996, and various members also have credits with A Canorous Quintet, Mörk Gryning, Dismember, Thyrfing, Raise Hell, Wyvern, October Tide, and Crimson Moonlight. After just two CDs of melodic, riff-based music with death metal vocals (no demos to my knowledge), Sins of Omission split up.
Line-Up Mårten Hansen: *Vocals, Martin Persson: Guitar, Mattias Eklund: Guitar, Thomas Fällgren: Bass, Jani Stefanovic: Drums* **Past Members** *Dennis Ekdahl: Drums (1996-2002), Toni Kocmut: Vocals/ Guitar (1996-2000), Johan Paulsson: Guitar (1996), Marco Deb: Bass (1996), Jonas Nilsson: Guitar (1996-1997)*
Deathography
The Creation, CD (Black Sun, 1999)
Flesh on Your Bones, CD (Black Sun, 2001)

SIREN'S YELL
Thrash metal band started in Strömstad back in 1988. After one demo it was all over, but three members eventually formed the mighty Dissection. Know your history—get the Siren's Yell demo!
Line-Up Jon Nödtveidt: *Vocals/Guitar, Mattias "Mäbe" Johansson: Guitar, Peter Palmdahl: Bass, Ole Öhman: Drums*
Deathography
Demo, Demo (1988)

SKINFECTED
Formed in Västerås in 1989 as Obnoxious. During the early 90's they released three demo tapes without success, and in 1994 changed the name to Side Effects. Another name change followed, and in 1998 they released their first demo as Skinfected, *Addicted to Hate*. In 2001 the band finally released a mini-CD, but their time was over. The band is reportedly still active, though it has been very quiet for a while.
Line-Up Andreas Johansson: *Guitar, Daniel Johansson: Bass, Joakim Jonsson: Guitar (1994-), Andreas Edmark: Drums (1995-)* **Past Members** *Andreas Hermansson: Drums (1989-1997), Fredrik Petterson: Vocals (1989-2002)*
Deathography
A Brutal Act, Demo (1992—as Obnoxious)
Verdict of Futurity, Demo (1992—as Obnoxious)
In Silence, Demo (1993—as Obnoxious)
Addicted to Hate, Demo (1998)
Live 2000, Demo (2000)
Rehearsal, Demo (2000)
Blessed by Ignorance, MCD (King Size, 2001)

SKULL
Basically the continuation of Contra, with the addition of Morbid bassist Jens Näsström. As Skull, these thrashing Stockholm dudes appeared on classic death metal comp *Projections of a Stained Mind*, and were quite respected by the underground scene. They weren't death metal, though, and before long transformed into hardcore/pop band Teddybears, very successful in Sweden.
Line-Up Glenn Sundell: *Drums/Vocals, Patrik Lindqvist: Vocals/Guitar, Jens Näsström: Bass/ Vocals*
Deathography
You're Dead, Demo (1990)

SKULLCRUSHER
Death metal from Linköping with thrash touches. Formed and made a demo in 1997, then vanished.
Line-Up Tomas Andersson: *Guitar/Vocals, Viktor Westerberg: Guitar, Erik Anneborg: Bass, Fredrik Andersson: Drums*
Deathography
Tortured to Death, Demo (1997)

SLAKT
I don't have a clue about them, but they made a demo in 2005. According to the "names" and the title of the demo ("Love" in Swedish—the band name means "Slaughter"), I guess it's a joke. The guys are probably nerds.
Line-Up Lucy Bastard, Agent Fuckface, Lance Copkill, Åge Kreuger (aka Insekt) **Past Members** *Dirty Doris: Vocals*
Deathography
Kärlek, Demo (2005)

SLAUGHTERCULT
Death/black act formed in Gothenburg in 2003. All members also play in either Clonaeon, Grindnecks, or Stykkmord.
Line-Up Ronny Attergran: *Vocals, Andreas Frizell: Guitar, Robert Johansson: Vocals, Jonas Larsson: Guitar, Mattias Nilsson: Bass, Jonas Wickstrand: Drums* **Past Members** *Niklas Olsson: Drums, Mikael Eriksson: Guitar*
Deathography
To Gash the Skin, Demo (2004)
Suffer in Perversion, Demo (2005)

SLAVESTATE (Helsingborg)—see **Gardens of Obscurity**

SLAVESTATE (Varberg)
Melodic death metal band formed in Varberg in 2001, and since producing a steady stream of demos.
Line-Up Anton Hensner: *Drums, Jimmy Askelius: Vocals, Johan Persson: Guitar/Vocals, Julian Duniec: Bass, Fredrik Bastholm: Guitar/Vocals, Arek Trzaska: Vocals* **Past Members** *Oskar Nilsson: Bass*
Deathography
Thundereyes, Demo (2001)
Demo 3, Demo (2002)
Demo 4, Demo (2002)
Demo 5, Demo (2003)
Mordant Serenades, Demo (2004)

SOIL OF THE UNDEAD

2000's band from Älmhult, one of few newer bands with a real identity. They mix influences from old Swedish and American bands in a great way. Perhaps a hope for the future. Henke is also in Kataleptik and Springdusk.

Line-Up Slask: Vocals, Henke: Guitar/Bass, Chrille: Drums

Deathography

From Armageddon's Morbidity, Demo (2001)
Seduced by Mental Desecrations, Demo (2003)

SOILS OF FATE

Started as a duo by Crantz and Lindvall in Stockholm during 1995, their trademarks were ultra-guttural vocals and lots of groovy riffs. Initially an igniting force of the new wave of ultra-brutal Swedish death metal in the late 90's, they soon drifted from the core of the scene towards some kind of image with shorts, baseball caps, and hockey jerseys. They have brilliant moments though, and are great musicians. Note that Kevin Talley from famous U.S. bands Dying Fetus and Misery Index has been playing with them lately.

Line-Up Henke Crantz: Vocals/Bass, Magnus Lindvall: Guitar Past Members Kevin Talley: Drums (session only), Jocke: Drums, Nicke Karlsson: Drums, Henke Kolbjer: Guitar

Deathography

Pain...Has a Face, Demo (1997)
Blood Serology, EP (Empty Vein Music, 1998)
Sandstorm, CD (Retribute, 2001)
Crime Syndicate, CD (Forensick, 2003)
Highest in the Hierarchy of Blasting Sickness, CD (Forensick, 2005)

SOILWORK

Soilwork started in Gothenburg in 1996, briefly named Inferior Breed. They sound so much like In Flames it is almost ridiculous—Gothenburg retro thrash/death with tons of melody. After the immense success of In Flames, Soilwork got pretty successful as well. I think they are better than their more famous twin band, but that doesn't count for much in my book. Most members have impressive pasts in bands like Darkane, Embraced, Evergray, Aborted, Mortuary, and Terror 2000. The line-up has also faced a lot of turbulence—their current drummer is basically a session member.

Line-Up Björn Strid: Vocals, Ola Frenning: Guitar, Sven Karlsson: Keyboards, Ola Flink: Bass, Dirk Verbeuren: Drums Past Members Carl-Gustav Döös: Bass, Mattias Nilsson: Guitar, Ludvig Svartz: Guitar, Peter Wichers: Guitar, Jimmy Persson: Drums, Henry Ranta: Drums, Richard Evensand: Drums, Carlos del Olmo Holmberg: Keyboards

Deathography

In Dreams We Fall Into the Eternal Lake, Demo (1997)
Steel Bath Suicide, CD (Listenable, 1998)
The Chainheart Machine, CD (Listenable, 1999)
A Predator's Postcard, CD (Nuclear Blast, 2001)
Natural Born Chaos, CD (Nuclear Blast, 2002)
Light the Torch, Single (Nuclear Blast, 2003)
Figure Number Five, CD (Nuclear Blast, 2003)
Rejection Role, Single (Nuclear Blast, 2003)
The Early Chapters, EP (Nuclear Blast, 2004)
Stabbing the Drama, Single (Nuclear Blast, 2005)
Stabbing the Drama, CD (Nuclear Blast, 2005)
Stabbing the Drama, Sampler (Nuclear Blast, 2005)

SOLAR DAWN

Skövde band, began as Jarawynja in 1997. Pettersson (Dawn, Thy Primordial, Regurgitate) was borrowed to handle drums on the debut. It's all about melodic death metal. Edlund, Schönström, and Älvestam are members of Incapacity (the latter two are also in Torchbearer and Unmoored). Älvestam was recruited by Jonas Kjellgren (Carnal Forge, Dellamorte, Centinex) for the Scar Symmetry project.

Line-Up Anders Edlund: Guitar, Henrik Schönström: Drums, Christian Älvestam: Bass/Vocals, Robban Karlsson: Guitar Past Members Andreas Månsson: Guitar (1997-2002), Marcus Engström: Drums (1998-2000), Linus Abrahamsson: Bass (2000), Jocke Pettersson: Drums (session only)

Deathography

Festival of Fools, Demo (1998—as Jarawynja)
Desideratum, Demo (1999—as Jarawynja)
Frost-Work, MCD (Mighty, 2001)
Equinoctim, CD (Mighty, 2002)

SOLILOQUY

Early-90's death metal from Storvik. They didn't offer much to a crowded scene, so they soon split up.

Line-Up Allin: Vocals, Spålle: Guitar, Jocke: Drums, Leif Olsson: Guitar Past Members Jörgen: Bass (session only)

Deathography

Soliloquy, Demo (1992)
Nee, Demo (1992)

SOLITUDE

Yet another melodic death/thrash act, formed in 2001. Inactive since 2002, so let's hope they split up.

Line-Up Nina Nordgren: Bass, Andreas Johansson: Guitar, Henrik Unander: Keyboards, Johan Nordgren: Drums, Johan Kisro: Guitar, Mathias Öystilä: Vocals

Deathography

Evermore Alone, Demo (2001)
Inde Ira et Lacrimae, Demo (2002)

SOMNIUM

Melodic death metal of the mid-90's from Huddinge. Sounds lots like Without Grief, but not as good.

Line-Up Martin Erlandsson

Deathography

Timeless Grief, Demo (1997)

SONIC SYNDICATE—see Fallen Angels

SORCERY

Formed in Sandviken/Gävle as early as 1986, they got increasingly heavy as the years went by. Their final style was raw and brutal death metal like you don't hear any more. In their best moments they were brilliant, but somehow they never got it together. The band split in 1997 after many years in the shadows.

But during the late 80's, they were important in the Swedish death metal scene. Paul Johansson went on to join In Aeternum for a few years, and Nygren is now bassist in the great grind band Gadget.

Line-Up Ola Malmström: Vocals, Paul Johansson: Guitar/Drums, Peter Hedman: Guitar, Patrik Johansson: Drums **Past Members** Fredrik Nygren: Guitar (1986-1992), Magnus Karlsson-Mård: Bass/Guitar (1986-1992, 1993-1994), Patrik L. Johansson: Drums (1986-1987), Mikael Jansson: Bass (1988-1991), Erik Olsson: Bass (1992-1993), Peter Sjöberg: Guitar (1987), Joakim Hansson: Drums (1987-1988), Leif Nordlund: Guitar (1986)

Deathography
The Arrival, Demo (1987)
Ancient Creation, Demo (1988)
Unholy Crusade, Demo (1989)
Rivers of the Dead, 7" (Thrash, 1990)
Bloodchilling Tales, LP (Underground, 1991)

SORDID
Brutal metal platoon from Jönköping à la Soils of Fate and Thronaeon; their deadly journey began in 1999 as Sordid Death. In 2002, the name was shortened, but they continued their zombie death to the limit. The production on their 7" is just awful, but great!

Line-Up Samuel Johansson: Vocals/Guitar, Johan Ylenstrand: Guitar, Karl Hannus: Bass, David Wreland: Drums **Past Members** Gustav Karlsson: Drums

Deathography
Sordid Death, 7" (2001—as Sordid Death)
Demo CD-R, Demo (2002—as Sordid Death)
Armed to Their Grinning Teeth, CD (Forensick, 2004)

SORDID DEATH—see Sordid

SORG
Black/death metal band started in Sigtuna in 1995. They never got much attention, and folded after some demos. Many members have also been active in Maze of Torment, Soils of Fate, Deformity, Steel Prophet, Pandemonic, and Brain Damage. The title of their first demo (translates as "The Valley of My Dreams") must be one of the weakest and piss-awful ever!

Line-Up Victor Hemgren: Guitar/Vocals, Rickard Dahlin: Guitar, Micke Nyholm: Drums, Henke Kolbjer: Bass **Past Members** Petter Rosqvist: Drums (1995-1998), Nicke Karlsson: Drums (1999), Olle Bodin: Bass (1995-1998)

Deathography
Mina Drömmars Dal, Demo (1996)
Devestated Light, Demo (1997)
Demo III, Demo (1998)

SORHIN
Pure black metal from Borlänge, initially the one-man project of Micke "Nattfurst" Österberg. Clearly copying the trend of the mid-90's, their records are hardly amusing. Still, the first demo is great in its primitive nonsense. On early recordings, Peter Tägtgren (Hypocrisy, Abyss Studio) was hired to handle drums. Though not death metal in any

way, I felt compelled to include them since their first demo is so utterly bad and evil—a low-tech Swedish version of Burzum! Note that Johan Lager was original drummer of the ultra-classic Grotesque. The title of Sorhin's first 7" is so ridiculous, I feel too embarrassed to translate it for you.

Line-Up Micke "Nattfurst" Österberg: Vocals, Anders "Eparygon": Guitar/Bass **Past Members** Anders "Zathanel" Löfgren: Drums (1996-2000), Johan "Shamaatae" Lager: Drums (1993-1995)

Deathography
Svarta Själars Vandring, Demo (1993)
I Fullmånens Dystra Sken, Demo (1994)
Åt Fanders med Ljusets Skapelser, 7"
(Near Dark, 1996)
I det Glimrande Mörkrets Djup, CD
(Near Dark, 1996)
Skogsgriftens Rike, MCD (X-treme, 1996)
Döden MCMXCVIII, MCD (Near Dark, 1998)
Apocalypsens Ängel, CD/LP (Shadow, 2001)
Sorhin/Puissance Split 7" (Svartvintras, 2002)

SOULASH—see The Duskfall

SOULDEVOURER
I recently joined this band on bass. Who can refuse a band with Robban Sennebäck (ex-Dismember, ex-Unleashed) singing, playing guitar, and making all the songs? He is probably THE best death metal singer ever—and now he's back! The music is in the old-fashioned Swedish style (what did you think?) of his Dismember days, but with his killer vocals. He is the man. The others? Well, Sterner (Necrophobic) on drums and Ola Lindgren (Grave) on guitar.

Line-Up Robban Sennebäck: Vocals, Daniel Ekeroth: Bass, Sterner: Drums, Ola Lindgren: Guitar

SOULDRAINER
Melodic death metal from Östersund, formed in 2000. If you haven't been to Östersund, I can assure you it is very boring, so the members have stayed busy in Chastisement, Aeon, Divine Desecration, In Battle, Sanctification, Odhinn, and Defaced Creation.

Line-Up Johan Klitkou: Vocals, Daniel Dlimi: Guitar, Marcus Edvardsson: Guitar, Jocke Wassberg: Bass, Nils Fjellström: Drums

Deathography
Daemon II Daemon, Demo (2002)
Promo 2004, Demo (2004)
First Row in Hell, Single (2005)

SOULLESS—see Disowned

SOULREAPER
Brutal death metal group formed as Reaper in 1997 by ex-Dissection members Kjellgren and Norman (ex-Decameron). The name was changed due to copyright problems, and after a demo in the vein of Morbid Angel they earned a deal with Nuclear Blast. Apparently, Soulreaper has gone through a great deal of problems. They lost the contract with Nuclear Blast after one CD, and now are without a singer. I hope they sort things out and continue their deadly mission!

Line-Up Johan Norman: Guitar, Mikael Lang: Bass, Tobias Kjellgren: Drums, Stefan Karlsson: Guitar **Past Members** Christoffer Hjertén: Vocals, Mattias liasson: Guitar, Christoffer Hermansson: Guitar
Deathography
Written in Blood, CD (Nuclear Blast, 2000)
Worshippers of Death, Soulreaper/Rumemagick Split 7" (Bloodstone, 2002)
Son of the Dead, EP (Hammerheart, 2002)
Life Erazer, CD (Hammerheart, 2003)

SOURCE
Melodic death metal started in Herrljunga in 1998 by some very young teenagers. Most of them stuck together—and five years later they made an album.
Line-Up Jonathan Blomberg: Vocals, Pierre Andersson: Guitar, Niklas Fjärve: Guitar, Daniel Fjärve: Bass, John Gelotte: Drums **Past Members** Andreas Nilsson: Guitar (1998-2000), Per Korpås: Bass (1998-1999)
Deathography
Through The Skies of Destiny, Demo (1998)
Enslaved, Demo (1999)
Condemnation, Demo (2001)
Left Alone, CD (Goi Music, 2003)

SPAWN OF POSSESSION
Brutal death metal from Kalmar, formed back in 1997. Originally the band was a three-piece, consisting of Röndum, Karlsson, and Bryssling. During this time they did the right thing, rehearsing and perfecting their style. High-quality stuff indeed, very inspired by bands like Deeds of Flesh, Dying Fetus, and Cannibal Corpse. They take things to the limit, making everything as complex as possible. Their only disadvantage is not yet knowing how to write catchy songs. The music is more like a bunch of ultra-complex riffs sewn together. Still, they have been very successful, touring Europe and the U.S. very early in their career. Drummer Röndum and bassist Dewerud used to play in Visceral Bleeding (another great band) as vocalist and drummer. A leader of the new Swedish death metal scene until they sadly broke up in 2006.
Line-Up Dennis Röndum: Drums/Vocals, Jonas Karlsson: Guitar, Jonas Bryssling: Guitar, Niklas Dewerud: Bass (2001-) **Past Members** Jonas: Vocals (session only)
Deathography
The Forbidden, Demo (2000)
Church of Deviance, Demo (2001)
Cabinet, CD (Unique Leader, 2003)

SPAZMOSITY
Traditional death/black band formed in Stockholm in late 1994. Despite serious line-up changes, and though they have yet to record an album eleven years into their career, they are still going. Respect. Original singer Sistonen edited the 'zines Maelstorm and The Other Side. This is one of several bands hardworking drummer Marcus Jonsson (Insision, Pandemonic, Remasculate) helped during hard times.
Line-Up Peter Emanuelsson: Vocals, Björn Thelberg: Guitar, Mikael Lamming: Guitar, Micke Nordström:

Bass, Jesper Enander: Drums **Past Members** Acke Åkesson: Drums (1996-2000), Gurra Pellijeff: Bass (1995-1996), L-E Limnell: Bass (1996-1998), Mathias Sistonen: Vocals (1995-1996), Björn Vassuer: Drums (1994-1996), Tomas Örnsted: Bass (1994), Marcus Jonsson: Drums (session only)
Deathography
The Fading of Life, Demo (1997)
Brought Back From the Grave, Demo (1999)
Storm Metal, Demo (2003)

SPIRITUS SANCTI
Death/thrash band launched in Motala in 2000. These guys started with a CD, then moved to demos.
Line-Up Boris: Vocals, Hannes: Bass, TG: Guitar, Steve: Guitar, Westman: Drums **Past Members** Satan: Guitar
Deathography
Human Unknown, CD (Fullhouse Records, 2002)
Demo 2003, Demo (2003)
Rågersången, Demo (2004)

SPITEFUL
Linköping band formed as Benighted in 1992. After one demo the name changed to Spiteful, and the style turned a bit from death towards black. Andreas is probably better known from Deranged (and Satanic Slaughter), and Filip has gotten more attention for Corporation 187 (and Satanic Slaughter).
Line-Up Jocke: Bass/Guitar, Andreas: Drums/Vocals, Filip Carlsson: Guitar
Deathography
Demo 93, Demo (1993)
Demo #3, Demo (1994)

SPLATTER
Death/grind duo formed in Linköping in 2003. Grind on, you crazy diamonds.
Line-Up Stefan "Death Growler of Death" Hedström: Vocals, Anders "Gore" Carlborg: Guitar/Bass/Drum Programming/Vocals
Deathography
War Against the Living, Demo (2003)
An Ode, Demo (2004)

SPLATTERED MERMAIDS
New death/grind band from Malmö. They formed in 2005 and quickly produced a self-financed EP.
Line-Up Johan Bergström: Vocals, Johan Hallberg: Guitar, Martin Schönherr: Drums
Deathography
Bloodfreak, EP (2005)

SPLITTER
Death/grind from Stockholm, started in 2003. Pretty good stuff.
Line-Up Fredde: Vocals, Thimmy: Guitar, Niklas: Guitar, Oskar: Drums, Matte: Bass **Past Members** Thomas: Bass
Deathography
Stundens Chockerande Intryck, Demo (2004)
Vardagsångest, EP (2005)

SPLORT—see Monkey Mush

SPONTANEOUS COMBUSTION
Early 90's band from Vänersborg which played standard death metal. You'll find common inspirations to most Swedish bands of the time in here.
Line-Up Per Ståhlberg
Deathography
Spontaneous Combustion, Demo (1992)

SPORTLOV
The natural end result of the black metal movement. In 2000 some musicians from Uppsala heard about the German band Vintersemestre (which means "Winter Holiday" in Swedish), and decide the ridiculousness of black metal had gone too far. (What kind of name is that, anyway?) They decided to make some extreme black metal themselves, basing lyrics around winter sports to mock the genre's obsessions with snow, ice, trolls, etc. They succeeded beyond all expectations, and sound very good! This might come as no surprise, since members hail from supreme metal and crust acts like Defleshed, Dark Funeral, Diskonto, F.K.Ü, and Uncurbed. Highly recommended.
Line-Up Stefan "Count Wassberg" Pettersson: Vocals, Kaj "Dubbdäck Doom Occulta" Löfven (aka Lord Dubbdäck): Guitar, Lars "Hell Y Hansen" Löfven: Guitar, Matte "Fjällhammer" Modin: Drums, Lawrence "Thermoss" Mackory: Bass *Past Members* Daniel Ekeroth: Vocals (session only)
Deathography
Snöbollskrieg, MCD (Head Mechanic, 2002)
Offerblod i Vallabod, CD (Head Mechanic, 2003)

SPRINGDUSK
Solo project by Henke from Soil of the Undead and Kataleptik, in operation since 1999 producing doom/death. One demo is all he has accomplished yet, and that is probably for the better.
Line-Up Henke: Vocals/Guitar/Bass/Drums
Deathography
A Journey Through Misery, Demo (2002)

STABWOUND
2000's band from Gothenburg which really tried to be Dying Fetus and Deeds of Flesh. More gore-grind than actual death metal. During its short existence, Stabwound was pretty successful, and toured the U.S. But in 2005 it was all over, probably due to disagreements within the young band.
Line-Up Per Ahre: Guitar/Vocals, Viktor Linder: Drums/Vocals, Fredrik Linfjard: Guitar/Bass/Vocals, Mikka Häkki: Bass, Uffe Nylin: Vocals *Past Members* Ante: Guitar/Vocals, Oskar: Drums/Vocals, Henke Crantz: Vocals (session only)
Deathography
Stabwound, Demo (2001)
Malicious Addiction, Demo (2002)
Bloodsoaked Memories, EP (The Flood Records, 2002)
Human Boundaries, CD (Brutal Bands, 2004)

STIGMATA (1992)
One of countless bands that came from nowhere in the early 90's, made one demo, then disappeared. Don't confuse this pure death metal band with the newer melodic Stigmata—the one that changed its name in 2002 to Blinded Colony.
Deathography
Deceived Minds, Demo (1992)

STIGMATA (2000)—see Blinded Colony

STORMRIDER
War-obsessed black/death metal band from Bro (outside Stockholm), started in 1999. Four years into their battle, they released their first CD.
Line-Up YX: Vocals, Mikael Strandberg: Guitar, Henrik Larsén: Guitar, Morgan Ramstedt: Bass, Kristoffer Ahlberg: Drums
Deathography
Born of Chaos, Demo (1999)
God Is Dead, Demo (2000)
...Into Battle..., Demo (2001)
First Battle Won, CD (New Aeon Media, 2003)

STRANGULATION
Death metal from Karlskoga, emerged from the ashes of Butchery in 2001. Actually a quite good band in the vein of Cannibal Corpse, and the singer is just insane. Messy and meaty death metal like you don't hear as often as you wish. This might be a hope for the future. Note that busy Dennis Röndum (Spawn of Possession, Visceral Bleeding) was once in this band.
Line-Up Johnathan O. G (aka Gonzales): Vocals, Tobias Israelsson: Drums, Juha Helttunen: Guitar, John Carlsson: Bass *Past Members* L-E Limnell: Bass, Dennis Röndum: Vocals
Deathography
Carnage in Heaven, Demo (2002)
Withering Existence, Demo (2003)
Atrocious Retribution, CD (Retribute Records, 2004)

SUBLIMINAL FEAR—see Internal Decay

SUCCUMB
Early-90's melodic death metal from Västerås.
Line-Up Tony Sundquist
Deathography
Rehearsal 93, Rehearsal (1993)

SUFFER
This death/thrash hybrid rose from the small town of Fagersta in February 1988. Suffer was superior in all ways to town mates Kazjurol, and it's a shame they didn't get wider attention. After their only album, the band folded. Samuelsson and Karlsson (ex-Wortox) joined Serpent. Öhman has talked about a resurrection of Suffer with ex-Abhoth members Jörgen Kristensen and Mats Blyckert, but nothing has happened yet. Note that Per Karlsson also was editor of *Mould* mag, and short-time second guitarist Ronny Eide edited the classic *Morbid Mag*.
Line-Up Joakim Öhman: Guitar/Vocals, Patrik Andersson: Bass, Per Karlsson: Drums (1990-), Ulf

Samuelsson: Guitar (1991-) **Past Members** Ronny
Eide: Guitar (1990-1991), Conny Granqvist: Drums
(1988-1990)
Deathography
Cemetary Inhabitants, Demo (1989)
Manifestion of God, Demo (1991)
On Sour Ground, 7" (New Wave, 1993)
Global Warming, EP (Napalm, 1993)
Human Flesh (Live), 7" (Immortal Underground, 1993)
Structures, CD (Napalm, 1994)

SUICIDAL INSANE BASTARD

One-man project by ex-Throne of Pagan singer
Christoffer Richardsson, started in Gothenburg
during 1998. The goal was to show the town could
produce something intense. Well, drum machine
mayhem is what it is. After three demos I guess
Christoffer made his point, and the project folded.
Line-Up Christoffer Richardsson: Everything
Deathography
Psychotic Nightmare, Demo (1998)
Inside, Demo (1998)
Bastard, Demo (1999)

SUICIDAL SEDUCTION

Melodic death metal, formed in Finspång in 2000.
Their two EPs have a long way to go before rivalling
Finspång's majestic extreme metal history.
Line-Up Erik Dahlquist: Guitar, Samuel Öjring:
Drums, Tomas Lagrén: Vocals, Tomas Nilsson:
Guitar *Past Members* Daniel Persson: Bass
Deathography
Endless Suffering, EP (Black Moon Records, 2003)
Guilty on All Counts, EP (Ominous Recording, 2005

SUICIDAL WINDS

One of few bands from Uddevalla, Suicidal Winds
was formed by former Kristos Mortis members
Mathias and Peter in 1992. Line-up trouble delayed
their first demo until 1994. By the time they debuted
on CD in 1999, they already sounded dated. Further
problems arose in 2002, when Anders and Martin
left for Conspiracy. You should buy the records of
this band, simply because they need your support!
Line-Up Mathias Johansson: Vocals (initially also
Bass), Peter Haglund: Guitar, Emil Johansson:
Guitar (2002-), Fredrik Andersson: Bass (2002-),
Thomas Hedgren: Drums (2002-) *Past Members*
Andreas Ström: Guitar (1996-2002), Martin
Hogebrandt: Drums (1996-2002)
Deathography
The Road to..., Demo (1994)
Massacre, Demo (1996)
Aggression, Demo (1997)
Winds of Death, CD/LP (No Colours, 1999)
Joyful Dying, Suicidal Winds/Bestial Mockery Split 7" (2000)
Victims in Blood, CD/LP (No Colours, 2001)
Misanthropic Anger, 7" (Warlord, 2002)
Crush Us With Fire, EP (No Colours Recs., 2003)
Rarities, CD (Agonia Records, 2004)

Wrath of God, CD (Agonia Records, 2004)

SUNDOWN

Project featuring Johnny Hagel (ex-Tiamat/Sorcery)
and Mathias Lodmalm (Cemetary). They toured
with Paradise Lost in 1997, the year they formed,
but never really made an impact. When Hagel quit,
they were soon done. The music? Well, some kind of
progressive goth metal. Nothing special.
Line-Up Mathias Lodmalm: Vocals, Herman
Engström: Guitar, Andreas Karlsson: Bass, Christian
Silver: Drums *Past Members* Andreas Johansson:
Guitar, Johnny Hagel: Bass
Deathography
Design 19 Rough Mixes Promo, EP (Century Media, 1997)
Design 19, CD (Century Media, 1997)
Glimmer, CD (Century Media, 1999)
Halo, CD (Century Media, 1999)

DAN SWANÖ

Of course the man with a thousand bands would
eventually record something under his own name.
This happened in 1998, and though mainly it's
progressive music the vocals give a deadly feeling.
Line-Up Dan Swanö: Everything
Deathography
Moontower, CD (Black Mark, 1998)

SWEDISH MASSACRE

Death/thrash act formed in Kungsör in 2003. How
many of these bands can we take? And what about
the atrocious name? I really need some rest...
Line Up Jon Peterson: Guitar, Toni Åkerman: Bass,
Kristoffer Johansson: Drums *Past Members* Denny:
Vocals
Deathography
Eyes of Reflection, CD (2004)

SWORDMASTER

Started in 1993 in Gothenburg by Emil Nödtveidt,
brother of Jon from Dissection. Initially they seemed
obsessed with fitting into the black metal trend,
but as they matured they tossed the makeup and
turned into a pretty good thrash metal act. They
signed to Osmose Productions, and put out a couple
straightforward thrash albums. In 1997 they joined
the World Domination tour with Enslaved, Dark
Tranquillity, Dellamorte, Bewitched, and Demoniac.
Sadly, the band gave up everything in 2001, creating
an industrial project called Deathstars instead.
Rudolfsson refused to go along with this, and was
replaced by Ole Öhman (ex-Dissection). Note that
when original drummer Kjellgren left for Dissection
in 1995, he was also replaced briefly by Öhman.
Line-Up Andreas Bergh: Vocals, Emil Nödtveidt:
Guitar, Kenneth Gagfer: Bass, Niklas Rudolfsson:
Drums, Erik Halvorsen: Guitar *Past Members*
Tobias Kjellgren: Drums, Ole Öhman: Drums
Deathography
Demo, Demo (1994)
Rehearsal '94, Demo (1994)
Wrath of Times, EP (Full Moon Productions, 1995)
Wrath of Times, Swordmaster/Zyklon B Split CD

(Mystic Prod, 1996)
Postmortem Tales, CD (Osmose, 1997)
Deathrider, MCD (Osmose, 1998)
Moribund Transgoria, CD (Osmose, 1999)

SWORN
Yet another war-obsessed death metal band, this one from Ljungskile began in 2004.
Line-Up Dennis: Bass/Vocals, Peter: Guitar, Steff: Guitar, David: Drums **Past Members** Sebb: Vocals
Deathography
Global Demise, Demo (2005)

SYN:DROM
Melodic death metal, began in Sundsvall in 2003. Jonny Pettersson is also in Cavevomit.
Line-Up Jonny Pettersson: Vocals, David Karlsson: Guitar, Roger Bergsten: Guitar, Daniel Mikaelsson: Drums, Daniel Åsén: Bass
Deathography
Dead Silent Screaming, Demo (2004)
Promo 2005, Demo (2005)

SYSTEM SHOCK
Melodic death metal from Norrköping which started in 2003. Notably, George Kollias of the mighty U.S. titans Nile played drums with them at some point—that is just amazing.
Line-Up Lukas Bergis: Guitar, Dimitris Loakimogloul: Vocals, Markus Engström: Drums, Olle Sundfeldt: Bass, Slathis Cassios: Keyboards **Past Members** George Kollias: Drums
Deathography
Arctic Inside, CD (New Aeon Media, 2004)

T.A.R.
Stockholm band launched in 1993. Originally they were called Vulture King, that lasted about a year. T.A.R. never really had any impact, but they have played with bands like Dismember, Insision, and Face Down. In 1997 the crafty Per Karlsson (Serpent, ex-Suffer) joined on drums, but the band soon split nevertheless. The music can be described as deadly power metal. Check it out if you feel adventurous.
Line-Up Torbjörn Sandberg: Vocals, Juan Gauthier: Guitar, Östen Johansson: Bass (1994-), Stefan Sjöberg: Guitar (1995-), Per Karlsson: Drums (1997-) **Past Members** Tommi Sykes: Drums (1993-1996), Preston: Bass (1993-1994), Conny: Guitar (1994-1995)
Deathography
Baby Inferno, Demo (1994—as Vulture King)
Act II, Demo (1995—as Vulture King)
Are You Deaf, Demo (1996)
Fear of Life, CD (Heathendoom, 1997)
Tar and Feathers for the Millennium, MCD/7" (Heathendoom, 1998)

TAEDEAT
Death/black metal from Umeå with an impressive row of demos and a CD since forming in 2002.
Line-Up Mad Mathew: Bass, Mark Danneman: Drums, Azogh Martins: Vocals, Calvin Shroom:

Guitar **Past Members** Threat: Guitar
Deathography
Taedeat, Demo (2003)
The Hexagon Chronicles, Demo (2003)
Death Awaits You, Demo (2004)
Putrid, Demo (2004)
We Bring the Fourth, CD (Sulphur Community, 2004)
Quademortis, Demo (2005)

TAETRE
Melodic black/death act from—you guessed it—Gothenburg. Formed in 1993 and highly influenced by Dissection, with none of the quality. Originally called Enthrone, they later included more thrash and heavy influences in their music, but it didn't help. As I remember, drummer Pettersson used the ridiculous pseudonym "Graveyard Skeleton" for a while.
Line-Up Jonas Lindblood: Vocals/Guitar, Kalle Pettersson: Drums, Daniel Kvist: Bass/Vocals, Daniel Nilsson: Guitar (1995-2002, 2004-) **Past Members** Conny Vandling: Bass (1993-2001), Maggot: Guitar
Deathography
Demo, Demo (1995)
Eternal Eclipse, Demo (1996)
The Art, CD (Emanzipateon/Die Hard, 1997)
Out of Emotional Disorder, CD (Emanzipateon/Die Hard, 1998)
Divine Misanthropic Madness, CD (Mighty Music, 2002)

TAKETH
Just when you thought black metal had out-ridiculed itself with keyboards, trolls, forests, and fantasy, these Christian black/death bands started popping up. These guys started as Pergamon in 1996, but changed the name in 1999 after two demos. I can understand now why the new wave of black metal goes for suicide as its main lyrical theme. I would like to die, too, if I was associated with bands like this!
Line-Up David Dahl: Vocals, Mikael Lindqvist: Guitar, Atahan Tolunay: Guitar, Lars Walfridsson: Bass, Johan Dahl: Drums **Past Members** Emil: Guitar, Jonas: Bass
Deathography
Forgiven, Demo (2000—as Pergamon)
Breaking an Image, Demo (2001—as Pergamon)
His Majesty, Demo (2002)
Live Demo, Demo (2003)
Freakshow, CD (Fear Dark Productions, 2005)

TALION
Starting in Växjö in 1998, a high octane mix of speed/thrash and death metal. It sounds pretty cool, and it's a shame they haven't been more productive. Singer Martin Missy is known from his work with legendary German speed metal band Protector.
Line-Up Fredrik Lundquist: Guitar/Vocals, Martin Missy: Vocals, Magnus Karkea: Bass, Calle Sjöström: Drums **Past Members** Gustav Hjortsjö: Drums, Joakim Svensson: Bass, Erik Almström: Guitar

Deathography
Operation Massacre, Demo (2003)
Visions of Deterioration, CD (2003)

TANTALIZE—see Embryo

TEMPERANCE
Early thrash/death from Växjö, originally known as No Remorse (see separate entry). In 1991 they realized they did something wrong, and tried becoming a more brutal band with a new name. Temperance were featured in some 'zines in the early 90's, and they played in countries like Poland and Lithuania, but they never made it out of the underground. I guess their riff structures were still a bit too thrashy to compete with the pure death metal bands in Sweden, though they had intense super-fast moments. Note the flow of bass players—and I think they had yet another one whose name I can't remember.
Line-Up Fredrik Ernerot: Guitar/Vocals, B-Häng: Drums, Mange: Bass (1994-) **Past Members** Danne: Bass (1992-1993), Hasse: Bass (1993), Malena: Bass (1994-1995)
Deathography
Hypnoparatized, Demo (1992)
One Foot in the Grave, 7" (Shiver Records, 1993)
Temperance... Live!, Demo (1994)
Krapakalja, CD (Shiver Records, 1995)
Promo, Demo (1996)
7" EP, EP (Stormbringer Productions, 1999)

TENEBRE
Formed in Malmö during 1996, this is really a strange band that calls their music "evil metal." The creators were ex-Flegma members Metz and Lion. Tenebre has faced lots of member circulation, but kept going anyway. The album Mark ov the Beast features a guest appearance by Steve Sylvester from Italian cult band Death SS.
Line-Up Richard Lion: Guitar (initially bass), Fredrik Tack: Guitar, Andreas Albin: Drums, Ivana: Keyboards, Jenny T: Bass **Past Members** Peter Mårdklint: Guitar, Victor Fradera: Vocals, Julius: Keyboard, Joel Linder: Drums, Kalle Metz: Vocals, Lakas Sunesson: Guitar, Franco Bollo: Guitar, Martin Olsson: Guitar
Deathography
Halloween, EP (RH, 1997)
Cultleader, EP (RH, 1997)
Tombola Voodoo Master, EP (1997)
XIII, CD (RH, 1997)
Grim Ride, CD (1998)
Mark ov the Beast, CD (Regain, 2000)
Descend from Heaven, EP (Regain, 2002)
Electric Hellfire Kiss, CD (Regain, 2002)
Heart's Blood, CD (Regain, 2005)

TERMINAL FUNCTION
Pretentious progressive "death metal" band from Sandviken, began in 1998.
Line-Up Victor Larsson: Vocals, Mikael Almgren: Guitar, Stefan Aronsson: Guitar/Bass/Keyboards, Johan Wickholm: Bass, David Lindkvist: Drums/

Keyboards
Deathography
Time Bending Patterns, Demo (2002)
Time Bending Patterns 2003, Demo (2003)
The Brainshaped Mind, Demo (2004)

TERROR
Grind/death project which existed for a couple weeks during spring 1994 on the sleazy back streets of Gothenburg. Comprised of the core of At the Gates with vocals by Jon Nödtveidt of Dissection—what a fucking great line-up! If you get a chance to hear their demo, don't miss it. Intense, brilliant stuff.
Line-Up Jon Nödtveidt: Vocals, Anders Björler: Guitar, Jonas Björler: Bass, Adrian Erlandsson: Drums
Deathography
Terror Demo, Demo (1995)

TERROR 2000
Thrashy project involving Björn of Soilwork and Klas of Darkane. Founded in 1999, they have since put out a row of CDs and changed a couple members. Like most projects, it basically consists of clinically-produced leftover riffs, delivered without any soul. Still, in my humble opinion, it's slightly better than Soilwork or In Flames.
Line-Up Björn Strid: Vocals, Klas Ideberg: Guitar, Niklas Svärd: Guitar, Erik Tyselius: Drums (2001-), Dan Svensson: Drums **Past Members** Henry Ranta: Drums (1999-2001)
Deathography
Slaughterhouse Supremacy, CD (Scarlet, 2000)
Faster Disaster, CD (Scarlet, 2002)
Slaughter in Japan—Live 2003, CD (Scarlet, 2003)
Terror for Sale, CD (Nuclear Blast, 2005)

TERRORAMA
More retro thrash, this time from Norrköping. They try to flirt with black metal and crust punk, but this is basically just melodic modern thrash metal.
Line-Up Peter: Vocals, PP: Drums, Nilson: Guitar, Z: Bass **Past Members** Eric: Guitar
Deathography
Misanthropic Genius, Demo (2002)
Promoting the Orthodox, Demo (2003)
Horrid Efface, Demo (2004)
Horrid Efface, CD (Nuclear War Now! Productions, 2004)

TERRORTORY
Death/thrash from Skellefteå formed in 2000. If I lived in a forgotten hellhole like that, I would play far more extreme music than this.
Line-Up Johan Norström: Vocals, Peter Hägglund: Drums, Stefan Widmark: Guitar (initially bass), Michael Bergvall: Guitar, Olov Häggmark: Bass **Past Members** Anton Larsson, Marcus Carlsson
Deathography
2004 Demo, Demo (2004)
Demo 2005, Demo (2005)

THEORY IN PRACTICE

Technical death metal, formed in Sandviken, July 1995. Their first demo immediately got attention, leading to three acclaimed albums. While apparently on hold, drummer Ohlsson keeps himself busy in Scar Symmetry, Altered Aeon, and Mutant. (He has also been in Diabolical and Thrawn.)

Line-Up Mattias Engstrand: Bass/Keyboards, Peter Lake: Guitar, Henrik Ohlsson: Drums/Vocals **Past Members** *Johan Ekman: Guitar/Vocals, Patrick Sjöberg: Drums*

Deathography

Submissive, Demo (1995)

Third Eye Function, CD (Pulverised, 1997)

The Armageddon Theories, CD (Pulverised, 1999)

Colonizing the Sun, CD (Listenable, 2002)

THERION

This Upplands Väsby act was formed as thrash metal band Blitzkrieg in 1987 by Christoffer Johnsson and Peter Hansson. They became Megatherion in 1988, and soon after just Therion. Under that banner they emerged as one of Sweden's original death metal bands. Initially straightforward and high-quality, as the years passed their style grew stranger. Johnsson's blending of metal with classical music, opera, and choirs has changed the band a lot. His strange ideas also caused massive line-up changes, and I don't think anyone alive can keep the record straight. Among the prominent members are Lars Rosenberg (Entombed/Carbonized), Matti Kärki (Dismember), and Jonas Mellberg (Unanimated). However strange, Therion has been very successful. Since 1995 they have remained at the core of Nuclear Blast's commercially potent roster. If you feel adventurous, check out their latest records. But if you just want to bang your head to pure death metal, play their first mini-LP *Time Shall Tell* over and over.

Line-Up Christofer Johnsson: Vocals/Guitar/Keyboards, Kristian Niemann: Guitar, Johan Niemann: Bass, Petter Karlsson: Drums **Past Members** *Jonas Mellberg: Guitar/Keyboards, Peter Hansson: Guitar/Keyboards, Magnus Barthelson: Guitar, Erik Gustafsson: Bass, Fredrik Isaksson: Bass, Lars Rosenberg: Bass, Andreas Wallan Wahl: Bass, Piotr Wawrzeniuk: Drums, Oskar Forss: Drums, Sami Karpinnen: Drums, Matti Kärki: Vocals, Jan Kazda: Bass (session only), Tommy Eriksson: Guitar (also live drums, session only), Wolf Simon: Drums (session only), Richard Evensand: Drums (session only), Sarah Jezebel Deva (Sarah Jane Ferridge): Vocals (session only), Martina Astner (Hornbacher): Vocals (session only), Kimberly Goss: Keyboards/Vocals (session only), Mats Levén: Vocals (session only)*

Deathography

Paroxysmal Holocaust, Demo (1989)

Beyond the Darkest Veils of Inner Wickedness, Demo (1989)

Time Shall Tell, MLP (House of Kicks, 1990)

Of Darkness, CD (Deaf, 1991)

Beyond Sanctorium, CD (Active, 1992)

Symphony Masses/Ho Drakon Ho Megas, CD

(Megarock, 1993)

The Beauty in Black, EP (Nuclear Blast, 1995)

Lepaca Klifoth, CD (Nuclear Blast, 1995)

Siren of the Woods, MCD (Nuclear Blast, 1996)

Theli, CD (Nuclear Blast, 1996)

A'rab Zaraq Lucid Dreaming, CD (Nuclear Blast, 1997)

Vovin, CD (Nuclear Blast, 1998)

Crowning of Atlantis, CD (Nuclear Blast, 1999)

Deggial, CD (Nuclear Blast, 2000)

Secret of the Runes, CD (Nuclear Blast, 2001)

Bells of Doom, CD (Therion Fanclub, 2001)

Live in Midgard, CD (Nuclear Blast, 2002)

Lemuria, CD (Nuclear Blast, 2004)

Sirius B, CD (Nuclear Blast, 2004)

Atlantis Lucid Dreaming, CD (Nuclear Blast, 2005)

THIRD STORM

Definitely one of Sweden's first black metal bands, formed in Uppsala in 1986. The leader of the pack was vocalist Heval Bozarslan, who led the others into the extreme musical vein of Bathory, Sodom and Hellhammer. Third Storm's music was extremely brutal for its time, with blasting drums and violent guitars. The vocals of Bozarslan are among the craziest ever. Most of their riffs sucked, though. Sadly, the band never got anywhere. After a lot of member circulation, Bozarslan was the only one left in the end of 1988, and he was forced to fold the band. He made his return in the great band Sarcasm a few years later, however, and got at least a little attention. Jörgen Sigfridsson edited the fanzine *Heavy Rock*, and later started the Opinionate and Step One labels, releasing albums by Morpheus and Furbowl. He also promoted countless gigs back in the days, with bands like Deicide, Immolation, Candlemass, Master, Entombed, Therion, and Merciless. The name Third Storm is taken from a Hellhammer song. The title of their sole recording probably came from Hell.

Line-Up Heval Bozarslan: Vocals, Roland Esevik: Bass, Erik Forsström: Guitar (1987-), Drums (1986-1987), Jonas Holmgren: Drums (1987-) **Past Members** *Jimmy: Guitar (1986-1987), Jörgen Sigfridsson: Drums (1987)*

Deathography

Smell of Vomit in the Torture Hall, Rehearsal (1988)

THRASH AD

Death/thrash from Gothenburg which started in 1998, probably inspired by The Haunted. They made two demos, and split up in 2003.

Line-Up Anders Jönsson: Guitar, Tony Netterbrant: Drums, Patric Svärd: Guitar/Vocals, Jimmy Laj: Bass **Past Members** *Fredric Kuhlin: Drums*

Deathography

Century of Chaos, Demo (2000)

Escape the World, Demo (2002)

THRASHHOLES

Pure thrash metal founded in Växjö in 1985. They apparently made a couple demos, but I've only heard

Spooky Hour from 1990—pretty good thrash in the vein of Exodus and Testament that sounded dated in the early 90's. The band folded in 1995. Thrashholes eventually changed their name to Corrosive, and was about to release an LP on Bums, but like so many other bands, they got ripped off and the album never saw the light of day.
Line-Up Stefan Ström: *Vocals/Guitar, Anders Gyllensten: Guitar, Arild Karlsson: Bass, Magnus Georgsson: Drums*
Deathography
Braindamage in Botorp, Demo (1987)
The Pill, Demo (1988)
Spooky Hour, Demo (1990)
Gissa den Tredje?, Demo (1991)

THRAWN
Death/thrash band formed 2001, produced a demo, then transformed into pure thrash group Altered Aeon. Henrik Ohlsson is known from Scar Symmetry, Mutant, Theory in Practice, and Diabolical.
Line-Up Kjell Andersson: Vocals, Henrik Ohlsson: Guitar/Bass/Drums, Niklas Rehn: Guitar **Past Members** *Per Nilsson: Guitar (session only)*
Deathography
Light Creates Shadows, Demo (1997)

THREE DAYS IN DARKNESS
Death/thrash from Uppsala, started in 2004. The future will tell if they cause any impact.
Line-Up Erik Vieira: Vocals, Mattias Thalén: Guitar, Thomas Johansson: Guitar, David Ståhlberg: Bass, Johan Berggren: Drums
Deathography
Three Days in Darkness, Demo (2005)

THRONE OF AHAZ
Black-ish (in their words: *blood, spikes, corpse paint and black candles!*—Funeral Zine #2) death metal band from Umeå originating in 1991. After a demo, No Fashion offered them a deal. Their first album involved a lot of trouble, though, and the release was delayed until late 1994. By then, their time was over. They never got any wider attention or recognition for their mix of primitive riffs and melodic guitars.
Line-Up Fredrik Jocobsson: Vocals, Kalle Bondesson: Bass, Johan Mortiz: Drums, Marcus Norman: Guitar (1995-) **Past Members** *Nicklas Svensson: Guitar (1991-1995), Peter: Guitar (1991-1992)*
Deathography
At the Mountains of the Northern Storm, Demo (1992)
Nifelheim, CD (No Fashion, 1994)
On Twilight Enthroned, CD (No Fashion, 1996)

THRONE OF PAGAN
Gothic death metal started in Gothenburg during 1996. They claimed the influence of Deicide and Morbid Angel, but sounded absolutely nothing like either. Heavy stuff, with semi-satanic lyrics. Apart from two rehearsal tapes, they only appeared on one compilation CD before folding. Richardsson went on with the solo grind project Suicidal Insane Bastard.

Line-Up Christoffer Richardsson: Vocals, Christian Åkerberg: Bass, Niels Nankler: Drums, Niklas: Guitar (The others don't remember his last name! That's one difficulty with a project like this book!)
Deathography
In my Dreams, Rehearsal (1996)
Sacrifice Me, Rehearsal (1997)

THRONEAEON
Formed as early as 1991 in Västerås, they didn't use the name Throneaeon until 1995. Before that they suffered a lot of line-up circulation. Things didn't come easy for Throneaeon, though their demos got good reviews. A mini-CD finally saw the day of light in 1999, and two years later a full-length appeared. Throneaeon played technical and brutal death metal in the vein of Deicide (sometimes exactly like Deicide, with almost identical lyrics at some points). They are definitely among the better Swedish bands. In 2004 they changed their name to Godhate (see separate entry), since the older name never seemed to stick. If they fare better as Godhate, only time will tell. Still surely a great band—support them.
Line-Up Roger Sundqvist: Drums, Jens Klövegård: Guitar, Claes Ramberg: Bass, Tony Fred: Vocals/ Guitar **Past Members** *Andreas Dahlström: Bass, Göran Eriksson: Guitar, Magnus Wall: Bass*
Deathography
Demo 1, Demo (1995)
Carnage, Demo (1996)
With Sardonic Wrath, MCD (Helgrind, 1999)
Neither of Gods, CD/LP (Hammerheart, 2001)
Godhate, CD (2004)

THUS ABHOR
One-man black/death metal project from Linköping created in 1995. My suspicion is he mainly wanted a reason to wear makeup. After two demos the makeup washed away, and the project was dead.
Line-Up Abhorz: Guitar/Bass/Vocals
Deathography
Enchanted by Darkened Shadows, Demo (1997)
Dreadful Harmony—IV, Demo (1997)

THY PRIMORDIAL
After Lars Thorsén left Carcaroht, the other guys continued with this project. More black and less gore, know what I mean? After eleven years and six albums, the guys called it quits in 2005.
Line-Up Mikael Andersson: Guitar, Jonas Albrektsson: Bass, Jocke Pettersson: Drums, Nicke Holstensson: Vocals (2003-) **Past Members** *Andreas Karlsson: Vocals (-2003), Markus Nilsson: Guitar (-2000)*
Deathography
De Mörka Makters Alla, Demo (1994)
Svart Gryning, Demo (1995)
Signs of Leviathan, EP (Paranoia Syndrome, 1996)
Where Only the Seasons Mark the Paths of Time, CD/LP (Pulverised/Paranoia Syndrome, 1997)
Under Iskall Trollmåne, CD (Gothic Records, 1998)
At the World of Untrodden Wonder, CD

(Pulverised, 1999)
The Heresy of an Age of Reason, CD (Pulverised, 2000)
The Crowning Carnage, CD (Blackend Records, 2001)
Pestilence Upon Mankind, CD (Blackend Records, 2004)

THYRFING

Viking metallers from Stockholm who started in spring 1995. Though similar to Amon Amarth, Thyrfing distinguishes themselves with Swedish lyrics. But they rely way too much on keyboards to convince a traditional death metaller like me.
Line-Up Thomas Väänänen: Vocals, Patrik Lindgren: Guitar, Henrik Svegsjö: Guitar, Peter Lööf: Keyboards, Jimmy Sjölund: Bass, Joakim Kristensson: Drums *Past Members* Vintras: Guitar
Deathography
Solen Svartnar, Demo (1995)
Hednaland, Demo (1996)
Thyrfing, CD/LP (Hammerheart, 1998)
Valdr Galga, CD (Hammerheart, 1998)
Solen Svartnar, 7" (Grim Rune, 1998)
Hednaland, CD/LP (Unveiling the Wicked, 1999)
Urkraft, CD/LP (Hammerheart, 2000)
Vansinnesvisor, CD/LP (Hammerheart, 2002)
Farsotstider, CD (Regain, 2005)

TIAMAT

One of the original Swedish death metal bands, the first version of Tiamat was formed August 1988 by mastermind Johan Edlund. Initially called Treblinka, the teenaged Edlund soon realized the commercial limitations of that name, rechristened the group Tiamat (after a short stint as Abomination). Like Therion, Tiamat is basically a one-man project that has gone through constant line-up transformations (too many to mention). And as with Therion, the style has changed dramatically over the years. Initially very primitive and coarse black/death metal, they gradually drifted away from rawness. By the mid-90's there was hardly any metal left at all. The last deadly moments came with *Wildhoney* in 1994. Afterwards, Edlund started to create some kind of hybrid between progressive rock and psychedelic pop. Their success is beyond my comprehension, and they are probably the best-selling band ever on Century Media. They seem to have toured with everybody, including Black Sabbath and Type O Negative. In my opinion, their earliest recordings remain the best, but you have to give Edlund all the credit in the world for exploring his musical vision.
Line-Up Johan Edlund: Vocals/Guitar, Thomas Petersson: Guitar, Anders Iwers: Bass, Lars Skjöld: Drums *Past Members* Johnny Hagel: Bass (1990-1996) Jörgen Thullberg: Bass (1988-1992), Kenneth Roos: Keyboards (1992-1994), P.A. Danielsson: Keyboards, Magnus Sahlgren: Guitar, Stefan Lagergren: Guitar (1988-1990), Fredrik Åkesson: Guitar, Niklas Ekstrand: Drums (1990-1994), Anders Holmberg: Drums (1988-1990)
Deathography

Crawling in Vomits, Demo (1988—as Treblinka)
The Sign of the Pentagram, Demo (1989—as Treblinka)
Severe Abomination, 7" (Mould in Hell Records, 1989—as Treblinka)
A Winter Shadow, 7" (CBR, 1990)
Sumerian Cry, LP/CD (C.M.F.T, 1990)
The Astral Sleep, LP/CD (Century Media, 1991)
Clouds, CD (Century Media, 1992)
The Sleeping Beauty—Live in Israel, CD (1994)
Wildhoney, CD (Century Media, 1994)
A Musical History of Tiamat, CD (Century Media, 1995)
Gaia, EP (Century Media, 1997)
A Deeper Kind of Slumber, CD (Century Media, 1997)
Cold Seed, MCD (Century Media, 1997)
Brighter Than the Sun, MCD (Century Media, 1999)
Skeleton Skeletron, CD (Century Media, 1999)
For Her Pleasure, EP (Century Media, 1999)
Vote for Love, CD (Century Media, 2002)
Judas Christ, CD (Century Media, 2002)
Cain, Single (Century Media, 2003)
Prey, CD (Century Media, 2003)

TORCHBEARER

Death/thrash/black metal project started in 2003 by members of Satariel, Unmoored, Incapacity, Traumatized, Setherial, and Solar Dawn.
Line-Up Pär Johansson: Vocals, Christian Älvestam: Guitar, Göran Johansson: Guitar, Mikael Degerman: Bass, Henrik Schönström: Drums
Deathography
Yersinia Pestis, CD (Cold Records, 2004)

TORMENT (Stockholm)—see Mefisto

TORMENT (Strängnäs)

Mid-90's death metal from Strängnäs. First known as Harmony (see separate entry), Torment were obviously inspired by At the Gates, but like almost all other retro thrash bands they have none of the quality. Professional for sure, but with too much melody and annoying screaming vocals. They soon warped into Maze of Torment (see separate entry).
Line-Up Peter Karlsson: Guitar, Kjell Enblom: Drums, Pehr Larsson: Vocals/Bass
Deathography
Promo 95, Demo (1995)

TORTURE—see Decortication

TORTURE ETERNAL

Brutal death metal band formed in Upplands Väsby during 2003. I hope these guys go far, because this is true death metal.
Line-Up Linus Nylén: Drums, Rikard Bjernegård: Guitar/Vocals, Tobbe: Guitar, Ari: Bass *Past Members* Mathias: Bass, Ramis: Vocals, Jonas: Vocals, Christer, Peder
Deathography
Sickness and Dismembered Gutsorgasmus, Demo

(2003)
Mentally Killed Before the Birth, CD *(Sorrow Embraced Records, 2005)*

TOTAL DEATH
Started in Linköping in 1986, when brothers Micke and Tony left Satanic Slaughter. They rapidly got a following around Linköping, and went far in the national band competition Rock SM playing powerful thrash. However, they never really made it, and in 1990 the band folded. Tony, Micke and Christian teamed with Patrik Jensen and Johan Larsson from Orchriste to form the great Seance.
Line-Up Tony Kampner: Guitar, Micke Pettersson: Drums, Christian "Bino" Carlsson: Bass, Ponta: Vocals
Deathography
Rehearsal (1988/89)
Musik för Miljön, Comp LP (Studiefrämjandet, 1989)

TOTAL WAR—see War

TOXAEMIA
Brutal death metal from Motala, formed in January 1989. Their style is somewhere between the Swedish and American scenes, and they handle everything quite well. Anyway, the band never really made the grade during the competitive early 90's, and soon they were just gone like so many other good bands.
Line-Up Emil Norrman: Drums, Stevo Bolgakoff: Guitar/Vocals (1990-), Pontus Cervin: Bass Past Members Linus Olzon: Guitar (1989-1991), Brun: Vocals (1989), Holma: Vocals (1989-1990)
Deathography
Kaleidoscopic Lunacy, Demo (1989)
Toxaemia, 7" (Seraphic Decay, 1990)
Buried to Rot, Demo (1991)

TRAUMATIC
Crushing death metal from Mjölby which rose from the ashes of thrash band Crab Phobia in March 1990. Though lyrics are almost 100% Carcass-inspired gore-grind, the music is some fairly technical death metal. In 1992, problems started to occur, and Manuel went in and out of the group. The next year I think it all fell apart, but they didn't quit. Too bad they never made it, because this was a great band. Their old stuff sounds vital even today. The CD that turned up out of nowhere in 1996 isn't very death metal however—avoid it.
Line-Up Manuel: Guitar/Bass, Jonas Larsson: Vocals, Totte Martini: Drums Past Members Benny: Bass (in Crab Phobia), Matte: Guitar (in Crab Phobia), Lasse: Bass (session only)
Deathography
Crab Phobia Vol. 1, Rehearsal (1990—as Crab Phobia)
The Process of Raping a Rancid Cadaver, Demo (1990)
A Perfect Night to Masturbate, 7" (CBR, 1991)
The Morbid Act of a Sadistic Rape Incision, 7" (Distorted Harmony, 1991)
Spasmodic Climax, CD (Traumatic Ent., 1996)

TRAUMATIZED
Another death/thrash band, formed in 2000 in the southern town Trelleborg. One demo is their only sign of life. Schönström is also known from Unmoored, Solar Dawn, Torchbearer, and Incapacity.
Line-Up John Andersson: Vocals/Guitar, Andreas Hedberg: Guitar, Nicklas Leo: Bass Henrik Schönström: Drums
Deathography
The Mooring, Demo (2001)

TREBLINKA—see Tiamat

TRIBULATION (Arvika)
Started in Arvika in 2001, originally as a thrash band. Gradually they turned towards death metal, and by 2004 the change was complete (after some members were replaced). Even naming themselves Tribulation shows they didn't know anything about the old Swedish underground scene—or simply didn't care, since the name already belonged to the classic band from Surahammar. Don't mix these bands up, they sound very different. Nowadays Arvika's Tribulation is good and raw death metal, classic style. Violent.
Line-Up Johannes Andersson: Vocals/Bass, Jonathan Hultén: Guitar, Adam Zaars: Guitar, Jakob Johansson: Drums Past Members Joseph: Guitar, Jonas: Drums, Jimmie: Drums, Olof: Bass/Vocals
Deathography
Aggression Within, Demo (2001)
Agony Awaits, Demo (2004)
The Ascending Dead, Demo (2005)

TRIBULATION (Surahammar)
Weird thrash metal from Surahammar that gradually transformed into strange experimental Rock. These Swedish originators of thrash started back in 1986 as Pentagram, but in February 1987 they changed to Tribulation after the classic Possessed song. In 1990 they were at their peak, playing with bands like Carcass and Entombed. Afterwards it all went downhill. Death metal took over and Tribulation changed their style towards strange, experimental territory. The earlier stuff is much better than the later mess. I guess people abroad will have difficulty understanding how this band could be hailed in the Swedish underground back in the old days. Those were crazy days! After making their first member change ever (Daniel from Harvey Wallbanger replaced Stevo), the band quickly self-terminated and transformed into the punk/rock band Puffball. Drummer Magnus Forsberg was probably Sweden's most important tape trader during the 80's, and his influence on the scene should not be underestimated.
Line-Up Magnus Forsberg: Drums, Toza: Vocals/Guitar, Hojas: Bass, Daniel Sörén: Guitar (1993-), Stevo Neuman: Guitar (1986-1993)
Deathography
Infernal Return, Demo (1986—as Pentagram)
Pyretic Convulsions, Demo (1988)
Tribulation/Atrocity/Gravity/Damien Split 7"(Is This Heavy or What? Records, 1988)
Void of Compassion, Demo (1990)

Posers in Love, Demo (1991)
Clown of Thorns, LP (Black Mark, 1992)
Oil Up the Stud, Demo (1993)
Spicy, EP (Burning Heart, 1994)

TRISKELON
Trollhättan band known for using death metal to spread Nazi lyrics. Isn't it strange to choose a genre notorious for inaudible lyrics for such a purpose? Their music was pretty lame, though. Nazi bands should stick to stompy, untight oi music!
Deathography
Endast Mörker, CD (1997)
Vrede, CD (1998)

TRISTITIA
Doom/death from Halmstad, formed August 1992. Members are known from Pagan Rites—the infamous Tomas Karlsson is also known from Autopsy Torment and Devil Lee Rot. Not very deadly, though—check out the members' other bands instead.
Line-Up Thomas Karlsson: Vocals, Luiz Beethoven Galvez: Guitar/Bass/Keyboards **Past Members** Harri Juvonen: Bass, Bruno Nilsson: Drums, Adrian Letelier: Bass, Rickard Bengtsson: Vocals (session only), Alessio: Drums, Stefan Persson: Vocals
Deathography
Winds of Sacrifice, Demo (1993)
Reminiscences of the Mourner, Demo (1994)
One With Darkness, CD (Holy, 1995)
Crucidiction, CD (Holy, 1996)
The Last Grief, CD (Holy, 2002)
Garden of Darkness, CD (Holy, 2002)

TRIUMPHATOR
Basically a project of Marcus Tena, initiated in 1995 in Linköping. Fast and aggressive black metal with a deadly touch, Triumphator sound a lot like Marduk—no big surprise since most of the members were also in Marduk. Straightforward, with no bullshit. Tena used to run the store Shadow Records in Stockholm. After he was arrested for possession of drugs and weapons, the store and the band vanished.
Line-Up Marcus Tena: Bass, Arioch (Mortuus): Guitar/Vocals, Morgan S. Håkansson: Guitar, Fredrik Andersson: Drums **Past Members** Linus Köhl: Guitar/Vocals (1995-97), Martin Axenrot: Drums (1995-97)
Deathography
The Triumph of Satan, Demo (1996)
The Ultimate Sacrifice, 7" (The Mark of Sartan, 1999)
Wings of Antichrist, CD (Necropolis, 2000)
TUMULUS—see Sacramentum

TWILIGHT SYMPHONY
Doom/death band formed in Boden in 1994. They made one demo before falling apart.
Line-Up Henrik Stenqvist: Vocals/Guitar, Johan Ericsson: Guitar/Vocals, Benny Persson: Bass/Vocals, Henrik Leghissa: Drums
Deathography
At Dawn, Demo (1998)

TYRANT
In late 2006, Peter Bjärgö (ex-Crypt of Kerberos, ex-Macrodex, Meanwhile, Arcana) got fed up with well-produced music, and longed for the old times when everything was raw, simple, and ugly. So he created Tyrant. Soon came D.F Bragman (The Black, ex-Vinterland) and Andreas Jonsson (The Black, ex-Vinterland), and within 26 hours these guys wrote and recorded *Reclaim the Flame*. During the spring I (Daniel Ekeroth, Insision, ex-Dellamorte) joined on bass. After several offers we signed to Listenable and went on tour with Gorgoroth. Tyrant is all about raw, simple metal as dealt by Bathory, Celtic Frost, Venom, Motörhead, and Autopsy—nothing more, nothing less. It's strange what you can achive with three chords, a lot of distortion, and loads of beer!
Line Up: Peter Bjärgö: Guitar, D.F Bragman: Vocals, Andreas Jonsson: Drums, Daniel Ekeroth: Bass, Make Pesonen: Drums (session only)/Beer Mascot
Deathography:
Reclaim the Flame, LP/CD (Hell's Cargo/Listenable, 2007)

UNANIMATED
Blasting hybrid between black and death metal, spawned in the suburbs of Stockholm in 1989. Original line-up had Rickard Cabeza on vocals, but he soon left for Dismember—though he returned to play bass on the second album. The band split when Stjärnvind joined Face Down in 1996 (which he soon left for Entombed). Like Necrophobic, Unanimated was great, and deserved a far better fate.
Line-Up Peter Stjärnvind: Drums, Jonas Mellberg: Guitar, Richard Cabeza: Bass (1994-), Vocals (1989-90), Mikael Jansson: Vocals (1990-), Jonas Bohlin: Guitar (1991-), Jocke Westman: Keyboards **Past Members** Daniel Lofthagen: Bass (1991), Chris Alvarez: Guitar (1989-1991)
Deathography
Rehearsal, Demo (1990)
Fire Storm, Demo (1991)
In the Forest of the Dreaming Red, CD (No Fashion, 1993)
Ancient God of Evil, CD (No Fashion, 1995)

UNCANNY
In 1987, two pre-teen(!) children Fredrik Norrman (later in Katatonia) and Kennet Englund (later in Interment, Moondark, and Dellamorte) started playing music together. Some years later they launched Cicafracion, which led to the mighty Uncanny. They debuted some grind/death on the rare compilation tape *Avesta Mangel*, but soon got different ideas—crushing death metal, the right stuff! Fantastic songs, fat sound, brilliant drumming and devastating vocals. One of the most underrated Swedish death metal bands of all, in my opinion. The members have also appeared in Katatonia (Norrman), Dellamorte (Englund), Interment (Englund), Centinex (Englund), Sadistic Gang Rape (Harborg), Fulmination (Forsell), and Uncurbed (Törnros). Johan Jansson (guitar, Dellamorte, Interment, Uncurbed, Regurgitate, etc) and Mattias Norman (Dellamorte, Katatonia) joined

as session members for Uncanny's 2008 reunion gig.
Line-Up *Kennet Englund: Drums, Jens Törnros: Vocals, Fredrik Norrman: Guitar, Christoffer Harborg: Bass/Guitar, Mats Forsell: Guitar (1992-)*
Deathography
Transportation to the Uncanny, Demo (1991)
Nyktalgia, Demo (1992)
Uncanny/Ancient Rites Split LP (Warmaster, 1993)
Splenium for Nyktophobia, CD (Unisound, 1994)

UNCURBED
Avesta's Uncurbed is one of the deadliest crust bands Sweden has produced. Originally blasting noisy crust/grind in the vein of Extreme Noise Terror and Napalm Death, they gradually became a rocking crust act of immense destructive capacity. Since 1998, everything they've done has been of superior quality. Past and present members are known from the great bands Asocial, Uncanny, Interment, Dellamorte, Diskonto, Sportlov, Centinex, and Hatred.
Line-Up *Johan Jansson: Drums, Tommy "T.B" Berggren: Vocals (1994-), Kenneth Wiklund: Guitar (2000-), Bass (1999-2000), Mikael Gunnarsson: Guitar (2003-), Bass (1990-1999), Jimmy Lind: Bass (2000-)* **Past Members** *Steffe Pettersson: Vocals (2002-2005), Conny Enström: Guitar (1990-2003), Nico Knudsen: Guitar (1992-2002), Jens Törnroos: Vocals (1992-2002), Henrik Lindberg: Vocals (1992-1994)*
Deathography
The Strike of Mankind, Demo (1992)
The Strike of Mankind, CD (Lost & Found, 1993)
Uncurbed/Disfear, Split 7" (Lost & Found, 1993)
Mental Disorder, MCD (Lost & Found, 1994)
A Nightmare in Daylight, CD (Finn Records, 1995)
The Strike of Mankind/Mental Disorder, 2CD (Lost & Found, 1996)
Punk and Anger, CD (Finn Records, 1996)
Uncurbed/Society Gang Rape, Split 7" (Yellow Dog, 1996)
Peace, Love, Punk, Life...and Other Stories, CD/ LP (Sound Pollution, 1998)
Keeps the Banner High, CD/LP (Sound Pollution, 2000)
Punks on Parole, CD/LP (Sound Pollution, 2002)
Ackord för Frihet, MCD/10" (Sound Pollution, 2003)
Uncurbed/Autoritär, Split 7" (Yellow Dog, 2004)
Uncurbed/My Cold Embrace, Split 7" (Yellow Dog, 2005)
Welcome to Anarcho City, CD/LP (Sound Pollution, 2006)

UNGRACED
New death/black band from Stockholm.
Line-Up *O.Heiska: Vocals, T Jansson: Guitar/ Vocals, A Kuorilehto: Bass/Vocals*
Deathography
Demo 2005, Demo (2005)

UNHOLY
Decent death metal from Sundsvall, active during the 90's. Wiklund also played with Left Hand Solution.
Line-Up *Mattias Hagman: Vocals, Janne Wiklund:*

Guitar, Henke Svensson: Guitar, Johan Hamrin: Bass, Mårten Magnefors: Drums
Deathography
Abused, MCD (Massproduktion, 1994)

UNHOLY POPE
Obscure death/thrash band that made one demo in 1992 and then disappeared. Probably a project.
Deathography
Demo, Demo (1992)

UNLEASHED
Created by Johnny Hedlund (ex-Nihilist) and Robert Sennebäck (ex-Dismember) in Stockholm, December 1989, when their old bands fell apart. As you probably know, Sennebäck soon left Unleashed to reform Dismember after the break-up of Carnage. (Yes, it's hard to track the turbulent beginnings of death metal in Sweden.) Unleashed's devastating demos immediately secured them a deal with Century Media, and their debut *Where No Life Dwells* is among the pioneering masterpieces of Swedish death metal. They were rewarded with European and American tours with gods like Bolt Thrower, Sadus, Morbid Angel, and Cannibal Corpse, and their future seemed brighter than the sun. The two successive albums are also good—after that Unleashed's quality sank drastically. Too obsessed with heathen war history, and not enough interesting riffs. But Unleashed has recently gotten back on track with their great album *Sworn Allegiance*. They are as good as ever again!
Line-Up *Johnny Hedlund: Vocals/Bass, Thomas Olsson: Guitar, Anders Schultz: Drums, Fredrik: Guitar* **Past Members** *Fredrik Lindgren: Guitar (1989-1997), Robert Sennebäck: Vocals/Guitar (1989-1991)*
Deathography
The Utter Dark, Demo (1990)
Revenge, Demo (1990)
...Revenge, 7" (CBR, 1990)
Century Media Promo Tape, Demo (1990)
And the Laughter Has Died, 7" (Century Media, 1990)
Where No Life Dwells, LP/CD (Century Media, 1991)
Shadows in the Deep, LP/CD (Century Media, 1992)
Across the Open Sea, LP/CD (Century Media, 1993)
Live in Vienna '93, CD (Century Media, 1994)
Victory, CD (Century Media, 1995)
Eastern Blood—Hail to Poland, CD (Century Media, 1996)
Warrior, CD (Century media, 1997)
Hell's Unleashed, CD (Century Media, 2002)
Sworn Allegiance, CD (Century Media, 2004)
Midvinterblot, CD (SPY, 2006)

UNLEASHED SOUL
Death/thrash from Farsta, began in 2003. Note the amazing number of members already!
Line-Up *Magnus Grönberg: Vocals/Guitar, Joel Fernberg: Guitar, Krister Pilblad: Bass, Nils Åsén:*

Drums **Past Members** *Robin Bjelkendal: Vocals, Marie Nyström: Vocals, Eric Westerberg: Vocals, Victor Norberg: Guitar, Robin Lindlöf: Guitar, Hannes Wester: Drums*
Deathography
Theatre of Darkness, Demo (2004)
Asylum Dreams, Demo (2005)

UNMOORED
Started in Skövde in 1993. While without a drummer, they were helped out on their second album by Thy Primordial's Jocke Pettersson (Dawn, Cranium). Älvestrand and Schönström went on to form Solar Dawn (they also played together in Incapacity and Torchbearer). Unmoored's debut was apparently recorded in 1995, but not released for two years. Almost garage-like death metal with occasional flirts with doom and punk. They grew more progressive after that, but haven't gotten any wider attention.
Line-Up *Christian Älvestam: Guitar/Vocals, Thomas Johansson: Guitar, Henrik Schönström: Drums* **Past Members** *Rickard Larsson: Guitar, Torbjörn Öhrling: Bass, Jocke Pettersson: Drums, Niclas Wahlén: Drums*
Deathography
Shadow of the Obscure, Demo (1995)
More to the Story than Meets the Eye, Demo (1997)
Cimmerian, CD (Pulverised, 1999)
Kingdom of Greed, CD (Pulverised, 2000)
Indefinite Soul-Extension, CD (Code 666, 2003)

UNORTHODOX—see Defaced Creation

UNPURE
Death/black metal formed in Nynäshamn in 1991. Major line-up changes and somewhat unfocused music have kept them in the shadow of later black metal acts. Unpure has somehow continued to make albums all along, and they are pretty good.
Line-Up *"Kolgrim": Bass/Vocals, "Hräsvelg": Vocals/Guitar, "Jonathon": Drums* **Past Members** *Åberg: Guitar, Vic: Guitar, Johan Blackwar: Guitar*
Deathography
Demo 1, Demo (1992)
Demo 2, Demo (1993)
Demo 3, Demo (1994)
Unpure, CD (Napalm, 1995)
Coldland, CD (Napalm, 1996)
Headbangers Against Disco Vol. 1, Split 7" (1997)
Promo Tape 1998, Demo (1998)
Sabbatical Splittombstone, Sabbat/Unpure Split 7" (Iron Pegasus, 2001)
Trinity in Black, CD (Drakkar, 2001)
World Collapse, CD (Agonia Productions, 2004)

UPON THE CROSS
Forshaga band that got together in 1998, persevering long enough to make one demo.
Line-Up *Erik Hallstensson: Vocals, Kim Jadermark: Guitar, Joakim Sävman: Guitar, Johan Sundström: Drums*
Deathography
Point of No Return, Demo (1999)

UTUMNU
Västerås group started as Carnal Redemption in 1990. Initially death metal, they became inspired by the grunge movement and their music soon mellowed. Stålhammar was also a member of Macabre End/God Macabre. Johan Hallberg committed suicide in 2001, may he rest peacefully.
Line-Up *Jonas Stålhammar: Vocals, Staffan Johansson: Guitar, Dennis Lindahl: Guitar, Dan Öberg: Bass, Johan Hallberg: Drums (1992-)* **Past Members** *Pontus: Drums (1990-1991)*
Deathography
Twisted Emptiness, Demo (1990)
The Light of Day, 7" (Cenotaph, 1991)
Across the Horizon, CD (Cenotaph, 1994)

VALCYRIE
Thrash metal from Trollhättan, started in 1988. They never caused any buzz, and were soon eliminated by the death metal boom. They changed their name to Depict Pathos for a while before quitting. Some members later continued as Pathos.
Line-Up *Martin Sikström: Bass/Vocals, Esko Salow: Drums, Morgan Ruokolainen: Guitar, Lennart Specht: Guitar*
Deathography
Into the Questions of What, Demo (1990)

VARGAGRAV
One-man project started 1997 in Stockholm, playing experimental black/death. The sole demo by this ex-member of Hydra is not very exciting. But Vargagrav is one of the few palindromes of extreme Metal!
Line-Up *Maugrim: Everything*
Deathography
VargAgraV, Demo (2004)

VASSAGO
Project by Mikael and Niklas from Lord Belial, started in Gothenburg in 1994 (though they claim 1987). They deliver some kind of speed/thrash/black metal, far better than their regular band.
Line-Up *Nicklas Andersson: Vocals/Guitar, Mikael Backelin: Drums* **Past Members** *Janne Rimmerfors: Drums, Terje Eriksson: Bass, Suckdog: Guitar, Bloodlord: Bass, KK Kranium: Keyboards, Sadistic Sodomizer: Drums*
Deathography
Nattflykt, Demo (1995)
Hail War, Split LP w/Antichrist (Total War, 1996)
Knights from Hell, CD (No Fashion, 1999)

VERMIN
Founded in Nässjö in autumn 1991, initially they played pretty cool fast, brutal death metal. Unfortunately, they listened too much to Entombed's mid-90's albums. Later records turned into a bunch of Entombed rip-offs (some riffs are identical), and the vocals are just awful. As a result, the band lost its previous followers and folded. Fred Estby (Carnage, Dismember) appears on the second album. The first CD, compiling their demos, is easily the best release.
Line-Up *Jimmy Sjöstedt: Vocals/Guitar, Mathias*

Adamsson: Drums, David Melin: Guitar (1997-), Bass (1994-1997), Timmy Persson: Bass (1997-) **Past Members** Moses Shtich: Guitar (1991-1997), Johan Svensson: Bass (1991-1994)
Deathography
Demo 91, Rehearsal (1991)
Demo 92, Demo (1992)
Life Is Pain, Demo (1992)
Scum of the Earth, Demo (1994)
Obedience to Insanity, CD (Chaos, 1994)
Plunge Into Oblivion, CD (Chaos, 1995)
Millennium Ride, CD (No Fashion, 1998)
Filthy F***ing Vermin, CD (No Fashion, 2000)

VERMINOUS
Formed as Delve, but changed the name to Verminous in 2002. Fucking great old school death metal in the vein of Kaamos and Repugnant. Check them out!
Line-Up Linus Björklund: Guitar/Vocals, Andreas Johansson: Drums, Pelle Melander: Guitar, Simon Frödeberg: Bass
Deathography
Sentenced by the Unknown, Demo (2001—as Delve)
The Dead Amongst, EP (Nuclear Winter, 2002—as Delve)
Smell the Birth of Death, Demo (2003)
The Dead Amongst, Demo (2003)
Impious Sacrilege, CD (Xtreem Music, 2003)

VICIOUS
Death/thrash of the 2000's, formed in Västerås. Ex-drummer Adam Hobér is also known from Enthralled.
Line-Up Pontus Pettersson: Guitar, Simon Jarrolf: Guitar, Fredrik Eriksson: Drums/Vocals *Past Members* Adam Hobér: Drums, Erik Wallin: Drums, Henrik Wenngren: Vocals, Alexander Savander: Bass
Deathography
Pure Evil (Straight From Hell), Demo (2001)
Chains Won't Hold it Back, Demo (2002)
Vile, Vicious & Victorious, CD (Sound Riot, 2004)

VICIOUS ART
Great band formed in Stockholm in 2002. Powerful old school death metal, with nice black and thrash touches. The tight delivery is no surprise since the members are known from bands like Dark Funeral, Entombed, Grave, Obscurity (Järfälla), Guidance of Sin, and Dominion Caligula.
Line-Up Jocke Widfeldt: Vocals (initially also bass), Matti Mäkelä: Guitar, Tobbe Sillman: Guitar, Jörgen Sandström: Bass/Vocals, Robert Lundin: Drums
Deathography
Demo 2003, Demo (2003)
Fire Falls and the Waiting Waters, CD (Threeman Recordings, 2004)

VIRGIN SIN
Powerful thrash metal formed in Malmö as early as 1982, and miraculously still with us today. Initially they played raw thrash metal, but have mellowed into a hard heavy metal band. The band has been inactive for lengthy periods, while the band's leader has been

developing a stage show in the vein of Alice Cooper. Nothing of the kind has been seen yet, though. Drummer Martin has played in Deranged.
Line-Up Dagon: Vocals, SS66: Guitar, Schreck (Martin Schönherr): Drums, Zoak: Bass *Past Members* Mantus: Guitar, Fenris: Guitar, Terra: Bass, Euronymus: Bass, Rimmon: Bass, Gharon: Bass, Gorgo: Drums, Mr. Maniac: Drums
Deathography
Rehearsal (1985)
Demo 88, Demo (1988)
Suck for Salvation, Demo (1991)
Deep Red, Demo (1994)
Make 'Em Die Slowly, EP (To the Death, 1999)
Seduction of the Innocent, 10" EP (To the Death, 2003)

VISCERAL BLEEDING
Massive death metal from Kalmar formed by Peter and Niklas in 1999. Inspired by bands like Cannibal Corpse and Suffocation, they followed the path of Soils of Fate and Insision into technical brutality. Dennis quit in 2004 to concentrate on drumming in the equally good Spawn of Possession.
Line-Up Peter Persson: Guitar, Marcus Nilsson: Guitar, Calle Löfgren: Bass, Tobias Persson: Drums *Past Members* Martin Pedersen: Vocals (session only), Dennis Röndum: Vocals, Niklas Dewerud: Drums
Deathography
Internal Decomposition, Demo (2000)
State of Putrefaction, MCD (2001)
Remnants of Deprivation, CD (Retribution, 2002)
Transcend Into Ferocity, CD (Neurotic Records, 2004)
Remnants Revived, CD (Neurotic Records, 2005)

VITUPERATION
Death/thrash from Stockholm, began in 2004. With lyrics about violence, gore, and death, this band could become really brutal if they let themselves go.
Line-Up Sebbe Zingerman: Vocals/Guitar, Simon Zingerman: Bass, Tor Steinholtz: Guitar *Past Members* Jocke Wallgren: Drums
Deathography
Live at Bro, Demo (2005)

VOMINATION
Death/black band from Visby, started in late 2004. They seem to mean business, and the future will tell if they can match Grave's glorious past. Good luck!
Line-Up Joon Svedelius Lindström: Vocals, Pehr Andersson: Guitar/Bass, Johan Olofsson: Drums
Deathography
A Cold Wind of Sorrow, Demo (2004)
Yog-Sothoth, Demo (2005)
Four Ways of Brutality, Split CD (Magik Art Entertainment, 2005)

VOMITORY
Brutal death metal from Karlstad, got going in 1989. Basically a Venom and Sodom cover band at first—a good way to start! Together with Seance and Deranged, they presaged the uprising of brutal Swedish death metal

in the late 90's. Their music is full of grind parts, but the overall feeling is old school Swedish death. And it sounds good! Vomitory is living proof that by sticking to your beliefs, you will succeed. Initially they were outshined by bigger (and better) Swedish bands. When they released their first single, they were overshadowed by more popular (and worse) black metal acts. Some members left, but the Vomitory machine rolled ahead. Now among the biggest brutal Swedish death metal bands, they have a deal with Metal Blade. Respect.

Line-Up Urban Gustafsson: Guitar (initially also vocals), Tobias Gustafsson: Drums, Erik Rundqvist: Vocals/Bass (1997-), Peter Östlund: Guitar (2005-) **Past Members** Ulf Dalgren: Guitar (1991-2005), Thomas Bergkvist: Bass (1993-1996), Ronnie Olsson: Vocals (1989-1996, initially also bass), Bengt Sundh: Bass (1990-1993), Jussi Linna: Vocals (1996-1999)

Deathography
Nömefrgx, Demo (1991—unofficial release)
Promo 93, Demo (1993)
Moribound, 7" (Witchhunt, 1993)
Through Sepulchral Shadows, Demo (1994)
Raped in Their Own Blood, CD (Fadeless, 1996)
Redemption, CD (Fadeless, 1999)
Vomitory/Murder Corporation Split 7" (Hangnail Productions, 1999)
Anniversary Picture Disc, 7" (Vomitory, 1999)
Revelation Nausea, CD (Metal Blade, 2000)
Blood Rapture, CD (Metal Blade, 2002)
Primal Massacre, CD (Metal Blade, 2004)

VOODOO—see Fester Plague

VOTARY
Death metal from Spånga, made one demo in 1992, then vanished. Belmar and Collin had more success in Lobotomy. Belmar was also in Undercroft.
Line-Up Tore Öyen: Guitar, Etienne Belmar: Guitar, Max Collin: Bass, Micke Grip: Drums **Past Members** Nicko Karalis: Vocals (session only)
Deathography
Aimless Life, Demo (1992)

VOTUR
Stockholm act from the 2000's, heavily influenced by Gothenburg bands In Flames and Dark Tranquillity. Hansen is known from Sins of Omission, A Canorous Quintet, and October Tide.
Line-Up Jake Sandén: Guitar, Anden Englund: Guitar, Johan Majbäck: Bass, Erik Larsson: Drums, Mårten Hansen: Vocals
Deathography
Votur, Demo (2000)
Planet Cemetery, EP (Nocturnal Music, 2003)

VULCANIA
Ultra-obscure band which existed during 1983-84. During their short time they recorded one rehearsal, which I have never heard. Ola went on to Redrvm and Flegma. Lindhe joined the mighty Obscurity.
Line-Up Dennis "Anti": Vocals, Jörgen Lindhe: Guitar, Ola Püschel: Guitar, Kvidde: Drums

Deathography
Burn the Cross, Rehearsal (1984)

VULTURE KING—see T.A.R.

V.Ö.M.B.—see Walking Worm Colony

VÖRGUS
Chaotic death/thrash band started in Stockholm in 1994. Known for their true old school attitude, they have released a row of self-financed CDs during their drunken existence.
Line-Up Straight-G: Guitar/Vocals, Nenne Vörgus: Vocals/Bass, Mikke Killalot: Drums/Vocals **Past Members** Oppegaard: Vocals
Deathography
Vörgus is the Law, CD (2001)
The Evil Dominator, CD (2002)
Pure Perkele, CD (2003)
Vörgusized, CD (2004)

WALKING WORM COLONY
Messy death metal from Falun, originally called V.Ö.M.B. At first they sounded so old school that it was hard to imagine they could be from the 2000's. Pretty decent. The second demo is more thrash-oriented, and not half as good. When they changed their name to Walking Worm Colony they got more inspired by old Swedish death metal. Good.
Deathography
Right Foot Highway, Demo (2002—as V.Ö.M.B.)
Warcry, Demo (2002—as V.Ö.M.B.)
Demon 2003, Demo (2003)

WAR
Black metal project formed in 1997, consisting of leading members from Hypocrisy, Abruptum, and early Dark Funeral. Just hilariously-fast mayhem, played with such precision that it almost becomes death metal (like Marduk). The first mini-CD is by far the best effort, and the line-up on that one is their best. Good fun! The band apparently became Total War in 2001—since then nothing has been heard.
Line-Up Jim "All" Berger: Vocals, David "Blackmoon" Parland: Guitar, David "Impious" Larsson: Bass (1999-) **Past Members** Peter Tägtgren: Drums, Michael Hedlund: Bass, Tony "It" Särkkä: Guitar, Lars Szöke: Drums (session)
Deathography
Total War, MCD (Necropolis, 1998)
We Are War, CD (Necropolis, 1999)
We Are...Total War, CD (Hellspawn, 2001)

WAR EMPIRE
Death/black band from Kalix, started in 2001. They made a demo in 2002, and have been quiet since.
Line-Up Robert: Vocals, Rikard Ökvist: Guitar, Magnus: Guitar, Nisse: Bass, Alex: Drums **Past Members** Erik Forsgren: Drums
Deathography
End of Chapter Earth, Demo (2002)

WARMONGER

Late-90's doom/medieval/death metal from Nynäshamn. This sucks.
Line-Up Ulf Johansson
Deathography
Warmonger, Demo (1998)

WATAIN

Pure black metal, started in Uppsala in 1998. They later moved to Stockholm, as Uppsala was probably too small to host two bands as evil as Watain and Sportlov. Watain is by far the most successful new school black metal band in Sweden, probably because they sound and look so old school. If you are into classic black metal you will love this. But beware—these guys are evil on a metaphysical level!
Line-Up *Erik Danielsson: Vocals/Bass, H. Jonsson: Drums, P. Forsberg: Guitar, Sethlans Teitan: Guitar (live), A. (Alvaro Lillo): Bass (live)* **Past Members** *Y.: Bass, Tore Stjerna: Guitar (session only)*
Deathography
Go Fuck Your Jewish "God", Demo (1998)
Black Metal Sacrifice, Demo(1998)
The Essence of Black Purity, 7" (Grim Rune, 1999)
Rabid Death's Curse, Demo (2000)
The Ritual Macabre, Live Album (Sakreligious Warfare, 2000)
Rabid Death's Curse, CD/LP (Drakkar, 2000)
The Misanthropic Ceremonies, Split (Spikekult Rekords, 2001)
Promo 2002, Demo (2002)
Casus Luciferi, CD/LP (Drakkar, 2003)
Sworn to the Dark, CD (Season of Mist, 2007)

WELL OF TEARS

Melodic death metal, formed in Gävle in 2001.
Line-Up *Jonny Widén: Vocals, Kenneth Larsson: Guitar, Johan Sjöblom: Guitar, Andreas Melander: Bass* **Past Members** *Michael Rosendahl: Guitar, Jon Skoglund: Bass, Christian Wahlund: Drums*
Deathography
Well of Tears, Demo (2002)
Autumn Storms Has Come, Demo (2004)

WINDS

Basically a death metal side project by Thyrfing. Launched in 1998, they made one demo in 2001.
Line-Up *Henke Svegsjö: Guitar/Vocals, Kristoffer Dahl: Guitar, Jocke Kristensson: Bass, Thomas Vänäänen: Drums*
Deathography
Promo 2001, Demo (2001)

WITCHERY

In 1996, all the members of this band except the bass player were in Satanic Slaughter. They were fired en masse by bandleader Stefan Karlsson, and decided to form Witchery, with the addition of Sharlee D'Angelo. Their furious speed metal gained attention immediately, earning a deal with Necropolis. Jensen simultaneously started the immensely successful The Haunted, and Witchery has been overshadowed by them since. Problems with labels have held back the band, but they are still alive and kicking.
Line-Up *Tony "Toxine" Kampner: Vocals, Patrik Jensen: Guitar, Rikard "Richard Corpse" Rimfält: Guitar, Sharlee D'Angelo: Bass, Martin Axenrot: Drums* **Past Members** *Micke Pettersson: Drums*
Deathography
Restless & Dead, CD (Necropolis, 1998)
Witchburner, EP (Necropolis, 1999)
Dead, Hot and Ready, CD (Necropolis, 1999)
Symphony for the Devil, CD (Necropolis/MFN/ Toy's Factory, 2001)
Don't Fear the Reaper, CD (Century Media, 2006)

WITHERED BEAUTY

Doom/black/death metal act from Gävle created out of the deadlier Conspiracy during 1993. Bryntse was also a member of Sorcery (as well as Windwalker, Forlorn, and Morramon). This is pretty commercialized stuff—which explains the signing to Nuclear Blast. It obviously didn't work out, and nothing new has been heard in ages. Blackmon is now in the much, much better grind band Gadget.
Line-Up *Daniel Bryntse: Vocals/Guitar (initially also Drums), Tobias Björklund: Bass, William Blackmon: Guitar, Jonas Lindström: Drums* **Past Members** *Tobias Björklund: Bass/Vocals, Magnus Björk: Guitar*
Deathography
Screams From the Forest, Demo (1994)
Through Silent Skies, Demo (1995)
Withered Beauty, CD (Nuclear Blast, 1998)

WITHIN Y

Yet again, even more melodic death metal from Gothenburg—this band formed in 2002.
Line-Up *Andreas Solveström: Vocals, Mikael Nordin: Guitar, Niknam Moslehi: Guitar, Thim Blom: Drums, Matte Wänerstam: Bass* **Past Members** *Niklas Almen: Guitar*
Deathography
Feeble and Weak, Demo (2002)
Extended Mental Dimensions, CD (Karmageddon Media, 2004)

WITHOUT GRIEF

Formed November 1995 in Falun. For several years, singer Granvik edited the great 'zine *Metal Wire* (now he works for the big magazine *Close Up*). Drummer Patrik Johansson has also played with Yngwie J. Malmsteen over the years. And the music? Pretty standard Gothenburg-inspired melodic death metal, to my ears far better than Dark Tranquillity or In Flames. Special mention for the fantastic drumming and good deep vocals. Why do most melodic death bands use screaming black metal vocals? Growl!
Line-Up *Jonas Granvik: Vocals, Tobias Ols: Guitar, Daniel Thide: Guitar, Björn Tauman: Bass, Patrik Johansson: Drums* **Past Members** *Ola: Bass, Niclas Lindh: Guitar*
Deathography
Forever Closed, Demo (1996)
Promo 96, Demo (1996)

Deflower, CD (Serious Entertainment, 1997)
Absorbing the Ashes, CD (Serious Ent., 1999)

WOMBBATH

Sala band formed in August 1990. They produced pretty groovy death metal with deep grunted vocals. Not bad, but lacking the quality of bands from nearby Avesta. Uncanny, Interment, and Fulmination were always a notch above. They actually released an album, though it passed mostly unnoticed in the days of black metal. Lindfors went on to In Thy Dreams.
Line-Up Daniel Samuelsson: Vocals, Tobbe Holmgren: Guitar, Håkan Stuvemark: Guitar, Richard Lagberg: Bass, Roger Enestedt: Drums *Past Members* Boppe Andersson: Keyboards, Tomas Lindfors: Vocals
Deathography
Brutal Mights, Demo (1991)
Several Shapes, 7" (Thrash, 1992)
Internal Caustic Torments, CD (Thrash/Infest, 1993)
Lavatory, EP (Napalm, 1994)

WORTOX—see Altar

XENOPHANES

Formed June 1993 in Strängnäs, one of numerous Swedish bands playing melodic death/black with screamed vocals in the mid-90's. Quite good, but no thrills—as is usual with this kind of music. Lundin played in Harmony/Torment/Maze of Torment.
Line-Up Morgan Wiklund: Drums, Jocke Hasth: Guitar, Crille Lundin: Bass, Klabbe Alaphia: Vocals, Danne Sporrenstrand: Guitar *Past Members* P. Niva: Vocals, Marcus Öhrn: Vocals, Simon: Guitar
Deathography
In the Shadow of the Naked Trees, Demo (1996)
Promo 96, Demo (1996)
Xenofanes/Cranial Dust, Split (Cadla, 1997)

XYMONTHRA

Technical band from Jönköping, freely mixing doom, thrash, and death. Probably too strange for the mid-90's, but it certainly had some kind of quality. As I recall, their drummer only had one arm—if so, he is one of the fastest and best drummers in the world!
Line-Up Andreas Risberg
Deathography
Her Cherished Death, Demo (1993)

XZORIATH

Symphonic death metal ensemble from Linköping, founded 1999.
Line-Up Eva Heinaste: Vocals/Keyboards/Violin, Dzenan Kapidzic: Guitar, Rikard Johansson: Bass, Gustav Ladén: Keyboards, Jan Sigemyr: Bass, Joakim Svensson: Drums *Past Members* Emil Gustafson: Drums
Deathography
Laws of the Third Apocalypse, Demo (2002)
Redimensioned, Demo (2003)
Faces Reversed, Demo (2004)

ZAHRIM

Black/death metal from Falkenberg. Their first year they made a demo, but afterwards fell into silence. Lönnsjö is more known from Ablaze My Sorrow.
Line-Up Kristian Lönnsjö: Vocals, Carl Mörner: Guitar, Kristian Svensson: Guitar, Andreas Düring: Bass, Jens Wranning: Drums *Past Members* Henrik Möller: Guitar
Deathography
Within the Grey Shades, Demo (1997)

ZAVORASH

Black/death metal project created 1996 in Stockholm by the active Tore Stjerna (Necromorbus, Chaos Omen, In Aeternum, Funeral Feast, etc). On their first demo they sing using "the black speech of Mordor"—which I dare not utter here. Nerds.
Line-Up Tore Stjerna: Drums, Nil: Guitar, Totalscum: Vocals, Gideon: Bass *Pst Members* Zagzakel: Guitar, Zablogma
Deathography
Za Vorbashtar Raz Shapog, Demo (1997)
In Odium Veritas, Demo (1998)
In Odium Veritas 1996-2002, CD (Selbstmord Services, 2003)

ZINC ORGAN

Strange death/fusion band with gore and sex lyrics, started in Stockholm in 1998. Just insane stuff, but I don't know if it's good. Ponta and David are also known from Incendiary.
Line-Up David Segerbäck: Vocals, Ponta: Guitar, Johan Hallander: Bass, Anders Olsson: Drums *Past Members* Jocke: Guitar, Stefan: Guitar, David Lichter: Guitar
Deathography
Pleasure of Revenge, Demo (2000)
Alive With Worms, Demo (2001)

ZONARIA

These youngsters started as Seal Precious in Umeå in 2001. Initially they played power metal, but after the name change they turned towards melodic death metal—some kind of improvement, at least.
Line-Up Simon Berglund: Guitar/Vocals, Emil Nyström: Guitar, Karl Flodin: Bass, Emanuel Isaksson: Drums *Past Members* Christoffer Wikström: Bass, Mikael Hammarberg: Vocals, Claes-Göran Nydahl: Drums, Niklas Lindroth: Drums, Johan Aronsson: Keyboards, Simon Carlén: Drums, Gustav Svensson: Keyboards (session only)
Deathography
Evolution Overdose, Demo (2005)

Bibliography: Swedish Death Metal Fanzines

NOTE: A4 size= 8.3" × 11.7"
A5 size= 5.8" × 8.3"

ABNORMALCY (A5, in Swedish)

Started in 1991 in Finspång and edited by Martin Ahx, this is your typical Swedish 'zine of the early 90's: equally amounts of metal and punk, cut-and-paste layout, simple interviews with editors and bands, short uninformative reviews, and even a childish comic thrown in for good measure! Not very focused on the death metal scene, but since it's from the city of Finspång (known for the Gorysound/Unisound studio, Edge of Sanity, and lots of other deadly things) the death sneaks in all the time. Editor Ahx is also known from the band Darkified.

AGGRO CULTURE (A4, in Swedish)

Started around 1995 in Strängnäs and edited by Tomas Nyqvist, a pretty nice mid-90's fanzine that covers everything that is metal. Interviews are mainly with Swedish bands. On the downside is the dull (but clean) layout.

AKASHA MAGAZINE (A4, in Swedish)

Based in Järfäll and edited by Anki Sundelönn, this 'zine is curious since all the contributors are female. The contents are of a broad musical perspective, with everything from wimpy pop to brutal death metal. The layout is okay, and the whole 'zine struggles to be a professional magazine. Still, the abilities of the contributors are varied. Like many 'zines from the mid-90's, they tend to make jokes rather than being insightful. Though I usually like this approach, Akasha simply has too much of it. But who am I to judge? I bought the 'zine when it was distributed, so I guess it's alright! Contain loads of reviews, interviews, and articles on stupid topics like vampires.

AKASHA REVIEW (A4, in Swedish)

Based in Falkenberg and edited by Nils Larsson.

AMPUTATION (A4, in English)

Mikael Skala's 'zine is one of the last to emerge before the Internet swallowed all the 'zines. From his base in Stockholm, Skala did a good job covering the metal scene. This is a 'zine for extreme metal only, and a good one at that. If you can complain about anything it is the layout, which is boring. I really miss the times of cut-and-paste 'zines, they looked sooo good! Anyway, this is a great 'zine, and unlike so many others it really treats the music seriously. Further, Skala wrote everything himself. Everything! Now, that is true dedication. He seems especially concerned to cover the Swedish scene. I bow my head in respect...

AROTOSAEL (A5, in Swedish)

Started in 1995 in Umeå and edited by Markus Stenman and Peder Larsson, this is a very thick and good-looking 'zine of the mid-90's. Even though the black metal genre reigned at the time, the editors seem just as interested in death metal and doom metal. The attitude is straight and simple, with many in-jokes, just the way a classic 'zine should be. Pretty good stuff.

ARTIQUE 'zine (A4, in Swedish)

Started around 1993 in Umeå and edited by Fredrik Degerström, this is a messy and unserious death metal 'zine of the mid-90's. Focusing heavily on the local scene, some of the interviews turn out to be nothing but friendly chatting. Still, it's pretty fun to read.

AS 'zine (A5, in Swedish)
Started around 1991 in Forshaga by Steffe Mitander, here's a chaotic and primitive death metal fanzine. Well, the heart is in there but it's no masterpiece.

AT DAWN THEY READ (A5, in English)
Started around 1985 in Helsingborg and edited by Tom Hallbäck, this was one of the very first Swedish fanzines to notice extreme metal. Today the layout and the writing of the earliest issues feel pretty rudimentary, but they stand as documents of the time when thrash metal was taking over the world. Unlike other fanzines from the mid-80's, *At Dawn They Read* kept going well into the 90's. Editor Hallbäck is also known for his drum work in God B.C. and Hyste'Riah G.B.C.

ATHANOR 'zine (A4, in Swedish)
Started in 1999 in Umeå and edited by Daniel Lindholm, this 'zine definitely suffers from the poor computer layout. It looks sterile and boring. Further, the questions are unoriginal and dull. The 'zine also includes immature stuff like idiotic porn reviews. But fuck it—I still prefer 'zines like this over the moronic Internet shit we have to live with today!

AZZAZINE (A5, in Swedish)
Started around 1992 in Karlstad and edited by C.J. Larsgården and Daniel Magnusson, this messy and simple 'zine cared as much for punk as for metal.

BACKSTAGE (A4, in Swedish)
Started in 1988 in Dals Långed and edited by Lennart Larsson for many years. This magazine is unique in that it only deals with Swedish bands. Of course, this means the pages are filled with punk and rock acts as well as death metal. But it's all for the better! Decent layout, and lots and lots of reviews and interviews. This was once essential reading for any fan of aggressive Swedish music, and we could sure use a 'zine like this today.

BANG THAT HEAD (A5, in Swedish)
Sometime around 198/ in Halmstad, madman Tomas Karlsson released at least one issue of this cheap and poorly written 'zine. Later he continued with the 'zine *Splatter*, which was written in ultra-poor English. All good fun. Karlsson is probably more known from a bunch of west coast bands, such as Pagan Rites.

BARBARIC POETRY (A4, in English)
Started around 2000 in Gothenburg. Edited by Janne Huhta. This is one of the very few 'zines to emerge in the 2000's, and it's a good one! To begin with, it's exclusively dedicated to extreme metal, and Huhta knows what he is talking about. Just like all good 'zines, he covers a lot of gigs, reviews records, and makes interviews. It's essential for a true 'zine editor to be out there where it's happening. Is this all great? Well, no. The down aspect of *Barbaric Poetry*, like with all new 'zines, is the boring layout. I will curse computers until the day I die! It's still essential reading for every fan of 2000's extreme metal.

BATTLE OF BEWITCHMENT (A4, in English)
Started in 1993 in Uddevalla and edited by Robert Höög, this piece of paper was obviously made by someone who loved 'zines. (Höög interviewed other editors almost as often as bands!) Death metal and black metal are dissected without remorse through the pages. The questions are okay, and his English

is reasonable (like mine?). On the down side, there aren't many reviews in the 'zine, and the layout isn't very interesting. Still, this is a good one.

BESTIALISKT MANGEL (A4, in Swedish)
A wonderfully named 'zine made by one of the guys from *Metal Wire*. I've only seen the cover myself, but that was enough to convince me this must be great!

BLACKENED 'zine (A5)
Started around 1997 and based in Falkenberg.

BRUTAL MAG (A4, in English)
Started in 1991 in Mjölby and edited by Henrik Forss—now this is a 'zine I like. Ultra-cheap layout, complete with infantile drawings—great! Like every editor with good taste, Forss includes band logos as often as he can. The questions are almost moronic, as are the answers. The English is pretty bad. But it's all good fun! His views on music are also his very own; he even dared to make fun of Euronymous during a Mayhem interview in issue #2. Every great band you could wish for is interviewed, and most important demos are examined. I would give a lot to see a fanzine with this much intensity and energy today.

THE BURNING HEART (A4/A5, in Swedish)
Started around 1990 in Fagersta and edited by Peter Ahlqvist, the man behind countless brutal gigs during the late 80's and early 90's. He seems to be equally interested in punk and metal.

CADLA MAGAZINE (A5, in Swedish)
Started around 1995 in Sundsvall and edited by some guy, this boring and badly-written 'zine had a fucked-up layout to boot. Nothing good.

CANDOUR (A4, in English)
Edited by Martin Carlsson, this was the continuation of his previous 'zine *Megalomaniac*. Carlsson tried to incorporate more extreme stuff this time around, but it was still obvious he remained a thrash metal fan at heart.

CASCADE (A5/A4, in English)
Started in 1988 in Billdal/Gothenburg, this was one of the very first Swedish death metal 'zines, edited by none other than Tomas Lindberg of Grotesque (and At the Gates, Skitsystem, Disfear, Lock Up, and Great Deceiver) and Johan Österberg (later in Decollation, Diabolique and Great Deceiver). The layout is extremely messy and the texts are chaotic—to put it mildly—but this is the very essence of the early death metal scene. Totally full to the bone of teenage energy and madness. I enjoy this 'zine immensely still today, you should walk over corpses to get an issue! Don't spend too much time trying to find #2, it never came out—search instead for the pair's more punk/thrash-oriented previous 'zine effort, *Thrashin' Deluge*.

CEREBRAL 'zine (A4)
Started around 1992 in Hjärup, this cool piece of paper is the work of Deranged's main man Rikard Wermén. The content is mainly death metal, but refreshingly he can include some brutal crust punk bands that he likes as well.

CHAINSAW POETRY (A5, in Swedish)
Started in 1995 in Umeå and edited by Bo Sandberg, this mid-90's 'zine focused on death and black metal. The layout is pretty rudimentary, but not too bad. Decent, but nothing special. The first issue was a split-'zine with *Dusk Magazine*.

CHICKENSHIT (A5, in English)
Started in 1987 in Skärholmen, *Chickenshit* is the lost work of the most important man in Swedish death metal, Nicke Andersson (Nihilist/Entombed). Since he did the best artwork in the early Swedish scene, this 'zine would have looked so much cooler than anything else out there. But it was never published. I guess Nicke's bands took too much of his time. It's a loss for us all that he didn't continue with this 'zine.

CLOSE-UP MAGAZINE (A4, in Swedish)
Started in 1991 in Norrköping and later moved to Stockholm, this is the life achievement of the ultra-dedicated Robban Becirovic. What he originally made in his spare time on a zero budget eventually became the biggest and most massive metal magazine in Scandinavia. Sure, the original fire has died somewhat, and there isn't as much underground stuff in it anymore, but it's still good. Personally I miss the old days, when they covered small gigs and had film reviews instead of massive articles about big band such as Iron Maiden or Metallica. But you can't blame them—this has become their way of paying the bills,

so I guess they have to do it. It still contains articles and reviews of minor bands, and most importantly, it is probably the only 'zine left from the early 90's. Where are the rest of you? Respect.

CONFUSION (A5/A4)
Started around 1990 in Skärplinge and edited by Erik Gotborn, this 'zine was originally called *Gult Strykjärn*. Its focus is on death metal, even if they mix in some punk and other stuff. The quality improved with every issue, and around #4, when they started to do it in A4, it was actually quite good. But the last issues turned more mainstream and boring, and returned to the smaller A5 format. The final issue (#7) is very thin. I guess the editor just lost interest in the whole thing.

CONSPIRACY
Started in 1993 in Strängnäs, this short-lived 'zine was edited by Peter Karlsson, who went on to start the 'zine *Sadistic Bitch* in 1995.

CONSPIRACY MAGAZINE (A4, in English)
Started around 1996 in Bandhagen and edited by Klas Svensson, this nice black metal 'zine looks good. There is some death metal included as well. Unlike most followers of black metal these guys dare to show some sense of humor in their writing. Probably the best 'zine the "aristocratic" black metal generation of the mid-90's ever created (you know, guys that think they are renaissance men when they are just wimpy metal kids). Not to be confused with the earlier Swedish 'zine of the same name.

COWMAG FANZINE (A4, in Swedish)
Based in Fagersta and edited by Ted Dawidson, this mid-90's 'zine mixed metal and punk freely, though they tended to favor punk. They reviewed both recent releases and older personal favorites of the collaborators. Loads of interviews, almost entirely with Swedish bands. A 'zine by fans, just the way it should be. About the layout, they obviously tried to copy *Close-Up*, but it all looks very cheap. No masterpiece, but good anyway.

CRIMINAL TENDENCIES MAG
Started around 1991 in Gothenburg and edited by Mikael Uimonen.

CRITICAL MASS (A5, in Swedish)
Started in 1996 in Malmö and edited by Mr. Jernberg, this humorous and cool 'zine covered everything brutal about metal.

CURIOSITY 'zine (A4)
Started around 1993 in Nässjö by Peter Svensson, this pretty bad death metal 'zine had an atrocious layout. It's also very thin and really badly written.

DARK AGE MAGAZINE (A4, in Swedish)
Started in 1996 in Luleå and edited by Mr. Törnkvist, this is teenage black metal anger delivered in a furious, not very thought-through, manner. But hey, if it's black metal it should be like this!

DARK AWAKENING (A4, in English)
Started around 1988 in Stockholm, this rudimentary fanzine was edited by Alex Hellid of Entombed. His musical work is far better.

DARK DIMENSION (A4, originally in Swedish, but after #5 in English)
Based in Vällingby and edited by Jonas Berndt, this mid/late-90's 'zine was made by total fans of extreme music who didn't give a shit about reigning trends or anything. They just wrote about the bands they liked. You will find Gamma Ray and Scanner, as well as Marduk or Mayhem, and even some hardcore bands—though most of those got slaughtered in the reviews. These guys are metal! Highly personal texts and a hilarious no-budget layout. Yes, I know much of it is just childish and plain moronic (the first issue

will make you blush in shame). In fact, the earlier issues were just bad. But hey, this is a 'zine! What are you kids of today doing? Get off the moronic Internet and make something like *Dark Dimension*—now!

DARK DIVINITY (A5, in English)
Started around 1995 in Sundsvall and edited by "Jonas," this mid-90's 'zine looks pretty glossy, but it's not very amusingly written. Black metal is the overall taste, and things are spiced up a bit with articles about things like how to get high on mushrooms. Well, it's very fun to read if you're in the right mood.

DARK PAST 'zine (A4, in Swedish)
Started in 1996 in Kristianstad and edited by C. Andersson, this is chaotic black metal teenage confusion.

DAWN 'zine (A4, in Swedish)
Started around 1994 in Uddevalla, edited by Petrone and Tony—two guys who seem to love all metal. The layout is a bit boring, but the heart is there.

DEADBANGER 'zine (A5, in Swedish)
Started in 2005 in Västerås, and edited by Jesper Ahl. Isn't it great to see true death metal fanzines still emerging? This one is obsessed with the old school, and feels so fresh in this modern world of boring webzines. I surely hope this one will carry on.

DELICIOUS DISMEMBERMENT MAG (A4)
Started around 1991 in Halla and edited by Ronnie Olsson, this well-written 'zine had a nice look. No classic, though.

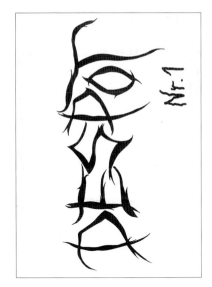

DESPOT (A5, in English)
Started in 1990 in Trollhättan and edited by Jari Kuusela, this is a classic example of a messy early 90's 'zine with death, grind, and thrash. Rudimentary writing and totally unserious overall.

DIS-ORGAN-IZED 'zine (A5, in English)
Based in Mjölby and edited by Henrik Forss, this looks absolutely cool in its messy 'zine style, and it's pretty well-written. Fanzines like this were a very important part of the Swedish death metal scene of the early 90's. Issue #3 is a split-'zine with the mighty *Septic 'zine*.

DOOMSDAY MAG (A5, in Swedish)
Started in 1996 in Kristinehamn and edited by Andreas Hedberg and Per Molin, this is a great 'zine from the late 90's with funny and ruthless writing and a chaotic punk-style layout. They focused on everything they liked, from garage punk to extreme death metal. Highly enjoyable.

DUSK MAGAZINE (A5, in Swedish)
Started in 1994 in Umeå and edited by Jens Rydén, this pretty good 'zine covers most aspects of the extreme metal scene—including bands, 'zines, and studios. The 'zine also includes original and cool stuff like logo analysis. A nice piece of work. Jens Rydén was also the singer in Naglfar until recently.

DWELLERS END (A5, in English)
Started around 1992 in Kumla and edited by Markus Rudahl, this is a pretty crammed 'zine dealing with everything from extreme metal and punk to splatter movies. There is loads of stuff, and it's pretty good. The layout is a bit messy, but still okay.

ELEGY (A4, in English)
Started around 1996 in Eskilstuna and edited by Elias Epstein, this mid-90's 'zine has a stereotypical and impersonal layout. But hey, this paper still delivers some good stuff. Nothing like the old days, but still pretty nice reading. Shame the groups covered aren't really interesting: Moonspell, Tiamat, Opeth...

ENDTIME (A5, in English)
Started around 1995 in Lidingö and edited by Eric Nordin, this pretty simple and thin 'zine focuses on doom metal. A 'zine without vision or energy.

EXPOSITORY MAG (A5, in Swedish)
Started in 1990 in Arboga and edited by Matte Pettersson, this is one of the pure old Swedish death metal 'zines. And what a good one! Funny and personal writing and a cool layout. Loads of reviews of demos, records, gigs, and 'zines (everything you need!), with amusing interviews to the limit. Especially the reviews section is outstanding, with every band logo reproduced to great effect. By the way, the 'zine's own logo is a rearrangement of Dismember's, and looks cool as hell! This is the real stuff—this is death metal.

FACT OR FICTION (A4, in Swedish)
Based in Finspång, this 'zine was entirely made by Åsa Jonsén, and sadly she only issued two numbers before she abandoned it—first to collaborate on *Close-Up* magazine, and then to become a mother (the father is the famous Dan Swanö, by the way). This 'zine is almost exclusively focused on Swedish death metal, and only contains interviews and demo reviews. Sure, the questions aren't very good and the layout kind of sucks, but I liked it anyway.

FALKEN 'zine (A4, in Swedish)
Started around 1996 in Falkenberg and edited by Tomas Gustafsson, this is a typical mid-90's 'zine, which mainly focuses on more "sad" metal groups.

It's decent, but the decline of the Swedish Metal scene can really be noticeably felt here.

FEAR MAGAZINE (A4, in Swedish)
Based in Klippan and edited by Michal Pogorzelski, this 'zine from the mid-90's is entirely focused on death metal. Good interviews with leading bands from all over the globe, and a lot of insightful reviews. The down part is the unexciting layout—damn those computers! A good 'zine with ambitions.

FEARLESS MAGAZINE (A5, in Swedish)
Started in 1997 in Varberg by Robert Petersson, this is something pretty rare—a death metal 'zine from the late 90's. The 'zine has a rather confused layout, and the editor's quirky decision to let two persons review each release leads to even more confusion. Some irrelevant and stupid articles weaken the whole thing—like one about tattoos, who the fuck cares! Still, this is decent reading.

FENRIR 'zine (A5, in Swedish)
Started around 1993 in Kumla by Mark Rudahl. When Rudahl got tired of writing in English in *Dwellers End*, he started this 'zine instead. A decent 'zine that covered the Swedish underground in a good way. I kind of liked *Dwellers End* more, but that's because I'm such an old-school-o-holic.

FENZINE (A5, in Swedish)
Started around 1990 in Saxdalen and edited by Micke Timonen, this is a pretty messy, but very cool, death metal 'zine. Since this 'zine started out before the invasion of black metal, there is a lot of punk as well. Besides coverage of the Swedish underground, a lot of foreign bands are included. All in all, a good old 'zine.

FILTHNOISE (A5, in Swedish)
Started around 1989 in Örebro and edited by Jimmy Johansson, this was a rude and brutal as fuck punk 'zine from hell. Metal bands appear very rarely. But it's great fun to read!

FLOTZILLA (A5, in Swedish)
Started in the late 80's in Skärpling and edited by Niklas Pettersson, this good old 'zine looked at everything metal or punk. Nice, messy layout with an overall good feeling. Apart from the standard interviews and reviews, this 'zine also offers some cool cartoons, courtesy of the immortal Jonas Lannergård. *Flotzilla* must hold the world record for spelling errors, and the primitive language skills make you wonder if Pettersson ever attended his English class in school. Anyway, this only adds to the anarchistic feeling. Fanzines like this just don't exist anymore, they are a thing of the past—like the silent movie and the typewriter.

FOAD (A5, in Swedish & English)
Started in 1991 in Ekerö and edited by Micke Samuelsson and Nille Carlsson, this very messy and primitive death metal 'zine sure delivered the goods. Among other great things, they interviewed a lot of very small and unknown bands. In this respect, *FOAD* is an important historical document today.

FORMLESS KLUMP MAG
Based in Stenhamra, and edited by Andreas Frisk, this fanzine covered death and punk, no more to say. Frisk also played in Cauterizer

FUNERAL 'zine (A5/A4, in Swedish)
Started around 1992 in Falkenberg by Anders Dahnberg, this typical early 90's 'zine had a messy cut-and-paste layout and loads of energy. Good coverage of the Swedish scene, plus interviews with foreign bands. The true rebellious teenage spirit is intensified by some gore-drenched film reviews, and cool pictures of demons and skeletons. Nice one!

THE GATHERING (A4, in English)
Started in 1993 in Lotorp by Erik Hagstedt, this 'zine grew obsessed with black metal after the atrocities in Norway. Much of the text is laughable today—the piece about why true black metal is superior to death metal or gore-grind is one of the most hilarious things I've ever read. Loads of spelling errors and an ultra-boring layout tops it all off. Like many black metallers of the early 90's, the editor thinks he's a renaissance man, though he is really a teenager who likes to drink beer and pick up girls. (Come on, we all were, even if we all failed!) But hey, this is great fun, I sure enjoyed reading it after all these years. Hagstedt is probably more known as the vocalist in Marduk (as "Legion").

GARYGOYLE MAGAZINE (A4)
Started around 1997 in Borlänge, this is a good death/black metal 'zine of the late 90's.

GIACOMINA (in Swedish)
Started in 1991 in Lidköping by Tobbe Sahl, this is a simple but good death metal fanzine.

GRAVEYARD MAGAZINE
Started around 1992 in Eskilstuna and edited by Make Pesonen, everything good about metal music

was featured in this fanzine—from Darkthrone to Running Wild. But the layout is a bit boring.

GRIMIORIUM DE OCCULTA (A5, in English)
Started around 1991 in Gothenburg and edited by Mikael Uimonen and Daniel Munoz, this messy 'zine revels in death metal. Both editors were members of Cabal, but this 'zine was way better than their band. Still, it's hardly among the best Swedish 'zines of the period. Previously, Uimonen edited *Criminal Tendencies Mag.*

GOETIA (A5, in Swedish)
Started in 1992 in Mörbylånga by Niclas Johansson, this 'zine popped up in the wake of the black metal frenzy. The editor despises everything that is brutal death, and hails everything that can be labelled as black metal—no matter how weak. It really is laughable to read this today. Still, the 'zine looks nice and is decently written. Too bad he used a font that is really annoying to read. The funniest things about this 'zine are the covers: one pictures a bunch of clouds (a photo from an airplane?), and another depicts of a bunch of trees (probably a photo from his garden). I suppose it's meant to look evil and dark—but it just looks stupid.

THE GOLDEN DAWN (A5, in Swedish)
Started in 1992 in Falkenberg and edited by Alex Bengtsson, only one issue was released.

GRAVEYARD SKELETON (A4, in English)
Make Pesonen is also known from the great black metal band The Black, the doomy death metal band Eternal Darkness, and he is involved with Tyrant.

GUTS MAG (in Swedish)
Started around 1991 in Örebro, this 'zine was edited by Magnus Asplund. Like *Hymen* from the same town, this 'zine mixes punk and metal freely. It is a far inferior publication, but still okay.

HAMMER (A4, in Swedish)

Based in Stockholm and edited by Johan Holm, this was the biggest Swedish metal magazine of the early 80's. As you might understand, this was before there was any death metal in the world. The magazine dealt with heavy metal, offering interesting and funny articles about new trends such as black metal—a great article from 1984, lumps together Angelwitch, Anvil, Witch, Oz, Venom, and Mercyful Fate under that banner! Everything is written in a rude and unserious way, and the 'zine had a cool layout. A nice mag to have grown up with.

HANG 'EM HIGH

NO 2. 1989

NIHILIST   THE KRIXHJÄLTERS   EXODUS
SAINT VITUS   NUCLEAR ASSAULT   CARNAGE
AND MUCH MORE!!

HANG 'EM HIGH (A5/A4, in English)

Started in 1988 in Edsbyn and edited by Orvar Säfström and Erik Qvick, this must be one of the first Swedish 'zines to focus on death metal—even if most of the contents cover thrash. It's pretty obvious this was made by a couple teenagers armed with a typewriter and a Xerox machine, but the heart is there to the limit. Highly enjoyable! Säfström and Quick were also the main forces behind the great band Nirvana 2002, and Säfström later joined Entombed for a short while as singer. Respect.

HARMONY (A5, in Swedish)

Started around 1997 in Mariestad and edited by Janne Jansson, this was mainly a crust 'zine, with some death metal in there as well. This just looks boring, and is badly written.

HEATHENDOOM (A5/A4, in Swedish)

Started in 1996 in Stockholm and edited by Petra Aho and Per Karlsson, this really fat and informative 'zine offers good layout, but is just a bit too computerized and impersonal. The editors also seem obsessed with the occult, and include a lot of articles about satanism, magic, hedonism, and other things that I personally don't give a shit about. Black and doom metal are favored genres, with just enough death metal to keep it interesting. These people should give up the pretentious crap and just be brutal! They really need to listen to some aggressive punk and realize how weak much of the stuff in this 'zine really is. Though it might sound like this 'zine is bad—it isn't. But much of it is just boring to read, and that can kill any 'zine.

HEAVY METAL MASSACRE (A4, in Swedish)

Started in 1983 in Dals Långed and edited by Lennart Larsson and Micke Jönsson, this was probably the first Swedish fanzine to explore the most violent aspects of metal. The four issues released before 1984 are priceless documents of the earliest phase of Swedish metal. Lennart Larsson went on to start the music magazine *Backstage*.

HEAVY ROCK 1 - 1987 Löpnr 2 Årgång 2 PRIS 5:-

Unika intervjuer!
Osannolika foton!!

Foto: J. Sigfridsson

LOOKER	EMPYRE	KEEL	DAMIEN
GARY MOORE	CRAIG GOLDY (DIO)		
STILETTO	GUNS 'N ROSES	MOGG	
MÖTLEY CRUE	FIRST CENTURY		
SURFACE	HITT MAN	PAGANINI	
TWISTED SISTER		BLACK JACK	
CATALEPSY		DEEPFREEZE	

HEAVY ROCK

Started in 1985 in Uppsala by Jörgen Sigfridsson, this crude-quality fanzine mainly covered heavy metal. Sigfridsson later became a prominent figure in the early death metal scene as a booker of gigs, and running the record labels Opinionate! and Step One.

HELLELUJA (STRANGE TASTE) (A4, in Swedish)

Based in Vällingby, this messy 'zine mixed together black metal, death metal, and some other things. A completely unserious and childish 'zine, but not without charm. Nothing to search for though.

HELTER SKELTER
Started around 1992 in Hjärup, this 'zine was edited
by Per Gyllenbäck, who runs Regain Records today.

HYMEN (A5, in Swedish)
Started in 1990 in Örebro, this legendary 'zine was
pumped out on a regular basis during the early 90's
by ever energetic Anders Jakobson (also of Necrony/
Nasum). Totally anarchistic and open-minded in his
views, he includes everything he likes—death, thrash,
punk, whatever. Apart from music, he has articles
about all kinds of topics, pretty much anything goes.
The 'zine is pretty well-written, and has a very nice
layout. He retained most of these qualities even after
switching to a computer layout with #7. Especially
the demo section looks fantastic, with reproductions
of almost every band's logo. Please Mr. Jakobson,
can't you start a 'zine like this again?

HYPNOSIA (A5, in English)
Started in 1990 in Malmköping, *Hypnosia* was
edited by Kentha Philipsson. The first issue was really
primitive, but the next few were actually pretty good.
It's pretty messy and looks cheap, but sure delivered
the stuff. Unlike many other Swedish 'zines, the focus
includes the international scene as much as Sweden.
Informative and fun to read, this is the best thing
Philipsson ever produced—forget Leukemia and his
many other bands!

IMMORTAL MAG (A4, in Swedish & English)
Started in 1993 in Uddevalla and edited by Peter
Haglund and Mathias Johansson, this nice 'zine
covered all kinds of black and death metal. Originally
mostly in Swedish, after issue #2 it was in English.
Nice interviews, loads of reviews (especially demos),
and a cool layout—exactly what a 'zine should be.

IMMORTAL UNDERGROUND (A4, in English)
Started around 1993 in Luleå, this computer- made

'zine was edited by Decortication's Pierre Thörnkvist. It's pretty well-written, and looks decent in spite of the computer style. The focus is almost entirely on Swedish death metal.

INSOMNIA 'zine (A5, in Swedish)
Based in Gällivare and edited by David Kareketo, this is a very boring 'zine—so boring in fact that it's painful to read.

IN THE CAVES (A5, in Swedish)
Started in 1994 in Umeå and edited by Patric Johnsson and Andreas Nilsson, this typical mid-90's 'zine covers melodic death and black metal. It's pretty

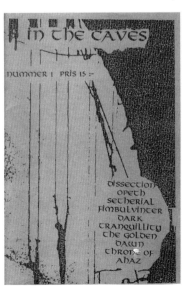

well written and has a nice layout, just like Umeå's other mid-90's 'zine *Dusk Mag* (their first issues were actually a split-'zine produced together).

INZINERATOR
Started in 1990 in Finspång/Norrköping, edited by Christian Carlquist and Dan Swanö. These guys only issued one volume before they quit to focus on bigger things: Swanö on Edge of Sanity and Unisound studio, and Carlquist on *Close-Up* magazine.

KABUTO (A5, in Swedish)
Started around 1992 in Norberg and edited by Torulf Lannergård, this funny 'zine mixes death metal with cartoons and other great stuff. Hilarious to read. Lannergård later committed suicide. R.I.P.

LEMONZINE (A5, in Swedish)
Based in Lund and edited by Staffan Snitting and Jesper Gunge, this is mainly a lame punk 'zine, but the editor seems to like a few death metal acts as well. Ultra-boring computer layout.

MAELSTORM (A4, in English)
Started around 1996 in Bro and edited by Mathias Sistonen, this good mid-90's 'zine focused on the underground of Swedish death metal. It looks very good, and the writing is above average. Informative, fun and just great!

MAGGOTY MAG (A5, in Swedish)
Starting around 1992 in Falkenberg, Anders Brorsson and Alex Bengtsson edited this primitive death metal 'zine with bad layout and rudimentary interviews.

MALARIA (A5, in Swedish)
Started around 1995 in Malmberget and edited by

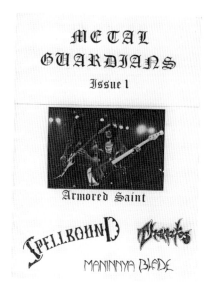

Mattias Lindmark, this pretty good 'zine included all kinds of brutal metal, as well as some progressive bands such as Änglagård. A prime example of a Swedish 'zine of the mid-90's.

MEGALOMANIAC (A4, in English)
Started in 1986 in Ystad, this was the early thrash metal fanzine of active Martin Carlsson, who later edited *Candour* and joined forces with *Close-Up* magazine. He is also a permanent contributor to the major Swedish tabloid *Expressen*. *Megalomaniac* was pretty crude, but the heart was there. A historical document of the times when Kreator and Destruction ruled the planet.

MEGA MAG (A5/A4, in English)
Started in 1989 in Strömstad and edited by the late Jon Nödtveidt before he formed Dissection. It's definitely a cool 'zine. The first issue was mainly occupied with thrash metal and hardcore, and had a crude layout. But #2 changed everything completely—it's one of the best Swedish fanzines ever. Death metal ruled every page, and in addition to international bands like Obituary and Sepultura, Jon swept Sweden for interesting acts. Furthermore, issue #2 had wonderful layout, good questions, gig reports, and funny and insightful reviews of demos, 'zines, and records—everything you might ask for. Though Jon was very young, his English was pretty good (better than many other 'zines, at least). It's also nice to see how cheerful and friendly the attitude was at the time, many light-years away from the black metal macho bullshit of years to come. To die for!

METAL DUCK MAG (A4, in Swedish)
Based in Waxholm and edited by Raffe Sjöström, this

decent death metal 'zine from the mid-90's mainly focused on the Swedish scene. The layout is a bit boring, as usual when computers enter the equation. But the content is good, so you can overlook that. Decent interviews, loads of reviews and gig reports, just like every good 'zine should have!

METAL GUARDIANS (A4 & A5, in English)
Started around 1986 in Gothenburg and edited by Edward Janson and Thomas Rosander, this heavy metal/thrash metal 'zine represents the time before death metal broke through. The layout is rudimentary, but it's pretty fun to read.

METAL WIRE (A4, in Swedish)

Started in 1997 in Falun and edited by Jonas Granvik, this fanzine was initiated by a guy named Patrik Andersson in Västerås, but before the first issue was complete Jonas Granvik started to take control. *Metal Wire* must be one of the best and greatest-looking Swedish metal magazines ever. Though the first issue is your regular Xeroxed 'zine, you could tell from the start that this was not your standard metal paper. Everything seemed a little bit more professional and interesting than usual. The editors made the very wise decision to hand out 1000 copies of their first issue for free, which immediately created a steady base of readers. The issues kept coming, and eventually *Metal Wire* became the glossiest and best Swedish metal magazine of all. Loads of great interviews, funny reviews, and original things like crosswords and quizzes. It's a loss for us all that Granvik folded his creation in 2004, to start contributing to *Close-Up* magazine—we needed them both.

MOTÖRMAG (A4, in Swedish)

Started in 1996 in Falkenberg and edited by Martin Qvist, this typical mid-90's 'zine focuses on black metal and melodic death metal. The layout is pretty dull, but the overall feeling is still okay.

MORBID MAGAZINE (A4, in English)

First based in Norway, later in Fagersta in Sweden, always edited by Ronny Eide. In the late 80's, this high-quality glossy death metal magazine ruled the fanzine scene along with Norway's *Slayer Mag*. I can't say anything bad about this superior paper, everything is just so good. Search it out at all costs.

MOULD MAGAZINE (A4, in English)

Started in 1990 by Per Karlsson, and originally based in Kumla, later in Lindesberg. This was a chaotic

and messy death metal 'zine—in the good old way. The first issue is almost moronic, with short stupid questions, and all bands get the same questions. Later issues are slightly more advanced, but I still really prefer the harsh style of that first issue! It reminds me of a lost wonderful time in death metal, and its primitive, childish energy. I really like this 'zine. A valuable document of past times.

MOURN MAG (A4, in Swedish)

Started in 1995 in Tranås and edited by Mattias Jackson, this is a decent Xeroxed 'zine of the mid-90's. Colored by the trends of the time, it tends to favor mediocre thrash/black bands instead of far superior death metal bands.

MYSTICISM MAGAZINE (A4, in English)

Based in Tyresö and edited by Thomas Väänänen and Patrik Lindgren, this 'zine covered the mid-90's black and death metal scene. It looked good, too.

MÖFFA (A5, in Swedish)

Started in 1992 in Karlstad and edited by Martin Björn, this 'zine focused on death metal. Despite a pretty messy layout, it's well-written and informative. Not one of the best Swedish 'zines of the period, but not too far behind. The editor also played drums in the doom band Moaning Wind.

NAZGUL MAG (A4, in Swedish)

Started in 1997 in Rönninge by Tommy Kuusela, this very simple and clean 'zine focused on black metal. I liked the underground feeling.

NEVER BELIEVE (A5, in English)
Started in 1990 in Surahammar by Magnus Forsberg, this great 'zine of the old days revels in all that is brutal in music. Great coverage of the scene and a "nice" punkish layout. I wish things could be like this today. Forsberg was also the drummer in Tribulation. Far more importantly, he was tape trader number one of the original Swedish death metal scene.

NITAD (A5, in Swedish)
Started around 1996 in Karlstad, and edited by Mattias Andersson. Basically a crust punk 'zine, the editor likes some death metal as well. Why shouldn't he? The two genres have many things in common.

NOCOUS 'zine (A5, in English)
Started around 1992 in Gnesta and edited by Daniel Lundberg and Jonas Kimbrell. This fat and informative 'zine is of a high caliber—even though its very messy layout seems to have been made in haste. Still much more interesting than the editors' band, Dispatched.

NOT (A4, in English)
Started in 1985, *NOT* was based in Malmö and edited by Johnny Christiansen, Richard Lion, and Kenneth Eintsen. A great old 'zine of a kind you don't see anymore, *NOT* ruled the southern part of Sweden in the late 80's, writing about all sorts of brutal music: hardcore, thrash, crossover, black, death, speed—you name it! Apart from interviews with bigger bands, the editors swept the underground in search of new sensations. I like the layout, which is filled with logos and pictures. A classic 'zine, get it if you ever see it.

THE OTHER SIDE (A5, in Swedish)
Started in 1995, based in Bro, and edited by Mattias Sistonen, this decent quality cut-and-paste-style 'zine is actually pretty well-written and very fun to read. Sistonen went on to start the 'zine *Maelstorm*.

OUTSHITTEN CUNT MAG (A5, in English)
Started around 1999 in Rönninge by Erik Sahlström, Tobias Forge and Karl Envall, this very good death metal 'zine contains all the energy of the early 90's. It's hard to believe it came out in 1999. Interviews explore legends like Possessed and Immolation, plus a lot of the rising bands in the Swedish underground. The 'zine also looks very good, with a perfect blend of computer work and classic cut-and-paste. The editors are known from bands such as Kaamos and Repugnant, and some material was supplied by Patric Cronberg of *To the Death*, so you might understand that these guys know what they are talking about!

PAINKILLER (A5, in Swedish)
Based in Mariestad and edited by Jan-Olof Jansson and Kalle Liljeberg, this mid-90's 'zine is basically a punk paper, but the editor doesn't hesitate to include some metal. Very amateurish layout, but it has a good feeling to it. The questions are very simple and childish, but effective! It's just great to read interviews

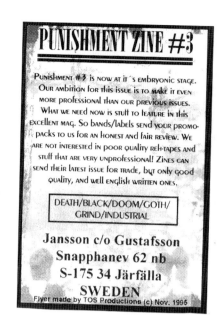

with bands such as Darkthrone being treated with no respect at all. This is the missing link between crust punk and black metal, two genres that emerged from the very same soil and eventually teamed up as buddies in the 2000's. Fun!

PEERLESS (A4/A5, in Swedish)
Started in 1993 in Västervik by Mikael Kalliomaa, this decent 'zine originally focused on death metal. Later the perspective broadened a bit, but it was still okay. The layout went totally awful when the editor got himself a computer, though.

PESTILENTIA (A5, in Swedish & English)
Started in 1997 in Linköping and edited by Joel Pälvärinne, this pretty standard 'zine of the late 90's was not great, but not bad either.

PIE MAG (A5, in Swedish)
Based in Västerås and edited by Calle Johansson, this long-lasting 'zine included all kinds of music inside its messy layout: Accept, Foetus, The Hellacopters, Entombed—you name it. However, death metal is not the favored taste of the editor. A good 'zine, but not great.

POLLUTION (A5, in Swedish & English)
Started in 2000 in Stockholm by Jonas Henrikson, this chaotic punk 'zine occasionally included some metal. Cool and original.

POSERKILL (A5, in English)
Started around 1988 in Täby by Stefan Lagergren, his fellow editor Johan Edlund is now perhaps better known for leading Treblinka and Tiamat. One issue is all they ever released, and that one is a treasure.

PRIMITIVE ART MAG (A5, in Swedish)
Started in 1993 in Halmstad and Motala by Paolo Staver and Joakim Knutsson, this 'zine nicely blends metal, punk and all kinds of stuff. Too bad the layout isn't very cool.

PROFITBLASKAN (A5/A4, in Swedish)
Started in 1984 by Mikael Sörling, who was originally based in Hällefors, later in Motala. This 'zine just kept on going until 1991. Sörling's main passion has always been punk, but he is one of those guys that can embrace a lot of metal, too. I love the layout of this 'zine, it's so damn crude and cool and messy and fucked up! Sörling went on to be a regular contributor to *Close-Up* magazine. He's a rare bird who has an equal passion for melodic pop punk and extreme black metal. Fuck yeah, this 'zine and its editor are insane—but great!

PUNISHMENT (A4, in English)
Based in Katrineholm and edited by Christian Jansson (later Gustafson), this mid-90's 'zine sure is massive! The loads of reviews and interviews are surprisingly well-written, with a lot more thought put into it than the usual death metal 'zine. The only down part is the layout, which is a bit messy and boring. Still one hell of a 'zine, with loads of stuff in it.

PURE DEATH 'zine (A5, in English)
Started in 2001 in Bohus by Carl Martinsson, this is one of very few death metal 'zines that emerged in the 2000's. Unfortunately, this one has a terrible computer layout made without the slightest finesse. It looks so fucking boring. But when you get down to reading, you will have a good time. It's not well-written, but it contains all the energy of the early

'zines of a decade before. These guys love pure death metal—bands like The Haunted are dismissed as pure crap! Yes, these guys are dedicated to the music they love, and nothing else. The scene definitely needs more 'zines like this.

PURE PASSION (A4, in English)
Started in 1997 in Vessigebro and edited by Therese Torstensson, this all-female 'zine from the late 90's focused on everything that is metal. Sadly, the magazine is poorly-written and has a terrible layout.

PUTREFACTION MAG (A4, in English)
Started in 1989 in Strängnäs, this was one of Sweden's first, best, and longest-lasting death metal 'zines, edited by Tomas Nyqvist and later Rogga Pettersson. It's all great. Nyqvist's English was wonderfully rudimentary in the first issues, but the layout looked right in a very primitive way! From 1990 to 1992, seven blistering issues saw the light of day. Then the 'zine was put on hold when Nyqvist focused on his record label No Fashion. Nyqvist eventually was ripped off, and lost his label, so he resurrected the 'zine in 1995 together with Merciless vocalist Rogga Pettersson. These later issues are better-written, but don't look as cool. Since this fanzine came out pretty often, you can really follow how the scene was developing through reading the interviews. In 1990, the term black metal wasn't even mentioned, and all the Norwegians who later claimed to always have been into black metal hailed the Swedish death metal scene (the soon-to-be hated Entombed seemed to have been a special favorite). Even in an interview with Per "Dead" Ohlin of Mayhem, he never uses the term black metal to describe their music! Ohlin also joked a lot in the answers, and the overall feeling is just friendly and nice. About a year later, in late 1990, when Dead was questioned again, he had become more nihilistic—and refers to their music as black/death. Sure, it's all laughable today, but as a historic document it's priceless. Get this 'zine, now!

READ ALL ABOUT IT (A4/A5)
Started around 1991 in Arboga by Magnus Brolin, this 'zine blends punk and death in a nice way.

RECENSION MAG (A4/A5, in Swedish)
Started around 1992 in Horred by Daniel Andersson, this decent early 90's 'zine embraced everything that was death or black metal. The layout is a bit boring, but it's still pretty nice reading.

R.S.S.S. (A5, in Swedish)
This cool 'zine was started around 1992 in Malmö by Johnny Christiansen and Patric Cronberg after dropping their pure metal fanzines *NOT* (Johnny) and *To the Death* (Patric). They focused on everything from electronic music to black metal. Pretty messy, but pretty good as well.

THE RUPTURED 'zine (A4, in English)
Founded in Kista by Daniel Strachal, this early 90's 'zine embraces everything in extreme metal. Pretty

adolescent, but very cool indeed. To bad the layout isn't very exciting. Still, this 'zine is fun to read even today. Editor Strachal was also the drummer of Lobotomy, and today he is running Dental Records.

SADISTIC BITCH
Started in 1995 in Strängnäs by Peter Karlsson.

SCENKROSS MAGASINET (A3, in Swedish)
Started in 1994 in Örebro by Jonny Deubler and Mieszko Talarczyk. This 'zine looks strange indeed, since it has the format of your average newspaper. Apparently editor Mieszko (known as the screamer/guitarist of Nasum and the man behind Soundlab Studio) found it was much cheaper to print a 'zine in this format, so here we go! The mag is filled with everything from melodic punk to extreme porno-grind. Loads of reviews, interviews, gig reports, and everything you want in a 'zine. The format makes it somewhat annoying to read, but you can live with it since it's so good.

SEPTIC 'zine (A5/A4, in Swedish)
Started around 1991 in Nyköping, and edited by

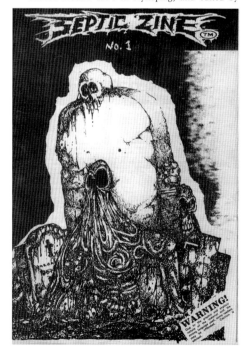

Dennis Tencic—later joined by Henke Forss. This is one of the best Swedish 'zines of the 90's. Great coverage of the Swedish scene, with nice interviews. This 'zine kept hailing death metal even after the black metal trend swept over the country, and treated all bands in the same critical way. *Septic* was one of the few 'zines that immediately realized what a trend the black metal scene was, and made good fun out of it—their guide to becoming a black metaller is just brilliant! The death metal roots are cemented by their original logo—a variation of the classic Earache label logo. This 'zine was the first to get an interview with the classic underground band Mefisto after they broke up in the mid-80's. Now, that was a scoop! If for no other reason, you should really learn Swedish just to be able to read this great paper.

SERENITY 'zine (A5, in Swedish)
Started around 1995 in Lindesberg by Robert Kanto, this 'zine originally looked pretty poor and messy (white text with pictures in the background is not recommended), but was a lot of fun to read. All the spelling errors just made it even more fun. In the second issue everything changed, and this became one of the glossiest 'zines ever released in Sweden. Sadly, it also became a bit more impersonal and boring. All in all, a good informative death and black metal 'zine.

SIKA ÄPERÄ (A5, in Swedish)
Based in Eskilstuna and edited by Jallo Lehto and Jari Juho, this utterly rude and chaotic punk 'zine came from the notorious duo behind Finn Records. They concentrated almost entirely on crust punk, but also featured their favorite metal bands like Entombed and Merciless. Definitely a personal favorite of mine. Original and hilarious to the limit, it spawned countless inferior copycats.

SIMULATIONS MUZIC MAG (A5)
Started around 1993 in Sala by Tony Zangelin.

SKOGSDUVAN (A4, in English)
Started in 1997 in Sundsvall by a guy named Klas. This 'zine wrote about all kinds of stuff—metal was just a small part. Well-written, but unfortunately not fun to read. A 'zine needs more rebellious energy than this!

SLAVESTATE MAGAZINE (A4, in Swedish)
Based in Gothenburg and edited by Ronnie Schmidt, this glossy 'zine competed with *Close-Up* for the throne of Scandinavian magazines in the 2000's. Well, it may not be as big or well-written, but I

sometimes prefer it to *Close-Up* these days. It actually reminds me more of how *Close-Up* used to be, with underground concert reviews and a lot of death metal. But as I have said, Slavestate really doesn't have any good writers.

SLIMY SCUM (A4, in Swedish)
Started around 1989 in Angered by Tommi Korhonen, this hilarious death metal 'zine was made back in the great old days. Totally ruthless and dirty, with a nice chaotic death metal layout. Interviews appear with bands from all over the world. Four issues were all they ever released—kill someone to get them!

SONIC RENDEZ-VOUS
Started in 1991 in Växjö by Johan Liiva-Axelsson, this is the great and highly personal 'zine by the former frontman of Carnage, Furbowl, and Arch Enemy. It looks great, too.

SORROW 'zine (A4, in English)
Started in 1992 in Västerås by Jonas Stålhammar, this decent, but pretty standard, early 90's 'zine is a bit messy, but looks cool anyway. It's obviously made in haste, but will give you a good time, anyway. The first issue was called *Ripping Slaughter*, so don't spend any time searching for *Sorrow* #1.

SPELLBOUND MAGAZINE (A5, in Swedish)
Started in 1996 in Bro, edited by Linus somebody.

SPLATTER 'zine (A5, in English)
Started around 1988 in Halmstad by Tomas Karlsson, this is the continuation of *Bang That Head*. Unlike the former 'zine, written in very bad Swedish, this is written in utterly bad English. Typical mid-80's thrash metal contents.

SUFFOZINE
Started around 1990 in Kumla by Marcus Rudahl, this messy and hopeless 'zine revelled in Swedish death metal. After four issues, Rudahl quit and started the better 'zine *Dwellers End*.

SUPPORATION 'zine
Based in Hägersten and edited by Ola Sjöberg, also in the mighty band Macabre End/God Macabre.

SUPREMACY 'zine (A5, in Swedish)
Started 1996 in Bjärred, edited by Erik Andersson.

SURLY 'zine (A4, in Swedish)
Based in Bromma and edited by Tina Knutar, this early 90's 'zine looks very cheap, but is cool as hell. The questions might be a bit standard and childish, but that was the way of those days. Some ridiculous articles about witches (and the Yeti!!) feel very silly today. Still, 'zines like this played an important part in the early days of Swedish death metal.

THRASHING HOLOCAUST (A5, in English)
Started around 1991 in Mörbylånga and edited by Niklas Johansson and Henrik Martinsson, this was a good quality death metal 'zine of the early 90's. Unlike all other Swedish 'zines, this one focused on foreign bands. After three issues, it folded in 1994. The 'zine was originally called *100% Pure Thrash*.

TORMENT MAG (A5, in Swedish)
Started in 2005 in Uppsala and edited by Pelle Åhman, this extremely crude cut-and-paste 'zine is welcome proof that pure death metal publications still emerge in paper form. The 14-year old editor and metal maniac Åhman also sings in the hilarious old-school band Katalysator. *Torment* is bad as hell and childish, with countless spelling errors—but it's just great anyway!

TORMENTOR MAGAZINE (A4, in Swedish)
Started around 1995 in Rönninge, this mid-90's 'zine was edited by Johan Thörngren, Nicklas Eriksson, Erik Sahlström and Jonas Kimbrell. They seemed obsessed with the black metal trend and various kinds of melodic metal. Later they proved to know everything about true death metal, through their bands Repugnant, Kaamos, and General Surgery.

TO THE DEATH (A5/A4, in English)
Started in 1986 in Ystad by Patric Cronberg, *To the Death* might very well be the first Swedish fanzine that truly attempted to be a death metal 'zine. Though it contained a lot of thrash and hardcore as well (like other contemporary 'zines like *NOT* and *Megalomaniac*), Cronberg sure covered more death metal than anyone else at the time. *To the Death* also developed a death metal look, courtesy of cool drawings by Nicke Andersson (Nihilist/Entombed). Too bad issue #4 was never released, because by then Sweden had developed into pure death territory. A fucking great 'zine. Patric Cronberg later contributed to *Close-Up* magazine.

TWILIGHT 'zine (A4, in Swedish)
Started around 1996 in Åhus by Magnus Emilsson.

UGLY LOGO 'zine (A4, in English)
Started around 1992 in Avesta by editor David Bock, this was a primitive and pretty amateurish death metal 'zine of the early 90's. The name says a lot about the content, but it's fun as hell to read. The layout is very messy—Bock seems to have used at least two typewriters as well as a computer.

ULV 'zine (A5, in Swedish)
Started around 1994 in Västervik by J. Wiberg, this 'zine really tries to be evil, exclusively writing about black metal and evil things like Elizabeth Bathory and the Black Plague.

UNDEAD MAG (A4)
Started in 1992 in Kinna by Kristian Engqvist.

UNICORN (A4)
Started in 1996 in Kalmar by Mattias Johansson, this standard 'zine of the mid-90's covered death metal and black metal—that's it.

VICTIM MAG (A4, in Swedish)
Based in Hägersten and edited by Maria Eriksson, this was a poorly-written and ugly 'zine of the mid-90's. Still, it's a relief that the contributors don't try to be funny and cool all the time. The 'zine features all kinds of music that is heavy and hard.

WRATH MAG (A4, in Swedish)
Started around 1992 in Hägersten and edited by Dennis Liljedahl, this is the very definition of a fanzine in all its glory. Okay, it may not be very well written, but it sure delivers tons of reviews, gig-reports, nice interviews, etc. The layout is a bit rough, but contains all the necessary stuff—such as the logos. A nice 'zine, filled with energy!

ZELOT 'zine (A4/A5, in Swedish)
Started around 1993, *Zelot* was originally based in Hägersten, later in Skogås. Edited by Stine Lundqvist, this was a very good-looking and well-written 'zine covering everything metal. A good 'zine, all in all.

ZINE OF SINS (A4, in English)
Started in 1991 in Enskede by Isabelle Larsson.

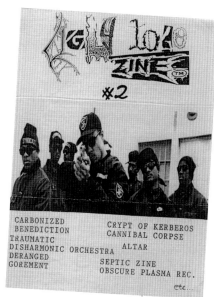

Issue # 1

ZYMPHONY 'zine (A4, in English)
Started around 1992 in Säffle by editor Max Thorén, this was one of countless Swedish death metal 'zines written in English that popped up around 1992-94. This is one of the better ones, with a nice exploration of the Swedish scene, as well as interviews with foreign bands.

Nu är den äntligen ute, universums enda och bästa döds zine... WRATH MAG #1. Den är tryckt i A4 format och är skriven på Svenska. Layouten är rent och proffsigt utförd. Innehåller utförliga intervjuer med: SUFFER, KATATONIA, LOBOTOMY, ROSI-CRUCIAN, DERANGED, TEMPERANCE, NECRONY, AFFLICTED, PAGAN RITES, GORYSOUND, LEUKEMIA, UNLEASHED, OBSCURE INFINITY, NOCTURNAL RITES och DEVOURED. Innehåller även artiklar med INTERNAL DECAY, LEAVE SCARS, EMBRYO, DROYS och DAWN OF DECAY. Självklart finns det oxå med Demo, Live och Zine recensioner. Allt det här kuliga kan du nu få direkt hem i din brevlåda för 15-20 Svenska pluringar (Ifall du skickar kronor, se till att de inte ramlar ur kuvertet. Tejpa fast dom!). Band som är intresserade av att vara med i #2 (Troligen på Engelska) kan skicka demos och annat kul till mig. All musik recenseras, och ifall jag tycker om musiken så skickar jag även en intervju. Vill någon skriva en artikel så är det bara att skicka den till mig så sätter jag in den, ifall den inte är väldigt dålig. Ni redaktörer som sitter och håller på massa tidningar (Engelska eller Svenska) kan skicka ett ex till mig så skickar jag mitt zine till er. Ja det var väl allt, hörs...

WRATH MAG
C/O Dennis Liljedahl
Utinivägen 3
126 54 HÄGERSTEN
SWEDEN

Johnny Hedlund:	Bass player of Nihilist and later the founder of Unleashed, which he leads to this day.
Åke Henriksson:	Legendary hardcore musician from Stockholm, mainly known for his band Mob 47.
Fredrik Holmgren:	Founder of Chickenbrain Records, the first label to distribute death metal records in Sweden. He also arranged gigs during the late 80's, and put out 7" singles and demos by Swedish death metal bands. A major character of the early death metal scene, today he is still in the record business.
Johan Jansson:	Avesta's death metal personality number one. He has been in countless bands—including Hatred, Asocial, Beyond, Interment, Dellamorte, Uncurbed, and Centinex—and can handle every instrument. Today he still plays in Uncurbed, a revitalized Interment, the newer band Demonical, and Regurgitate (Stockholm).
Patrik Jensen:	Founder and guitarist of Orchriste, Seance, Witchery, and The Haunted. He also played with Satanic Slaughter. The Haunted and Witchery are both still going strong today.
Jan Johansson:	Founder and guitarist of Obscurity.
Christoffer Jonsson:	Founder and undisputed leader of Therion. For some time a member of Carbonized, and he also has supplied guest vocals for Liers in Wait. Therion remains his main occupation.
Fredrik Karlén:	The madman of Swedish death metal. I couldn't imagine the scene without him. He showed us all how to behave, and taught us the important lesson of not caring at all about anything. On occasion he still keeps Merciless alive, together with the rest of its legendary line-up.
Mattias Kennhed:	Once the guitarist in the death metal bands Macrodex and House of Usher, as well as the hardcore band No Security. In the early 90's he left the death metal scene to focus on hardcore, and he has a become a central character of that scene.

Issue # 1

ZYMPHONY 'zine (A4, in English)
Started around 1992 in Säffle by editor Max Thorén,
this was one of countless Swedish death metal 'zines
written in English that popped up around 1992-94.
This is one of the better ones, with a nice exploration
of the Swedish scene, as well as interviews with
foreign bands.

Johnny Hedlund:	Bass player of Nihilist and later the founder of Unleashed, which he leads to this day.
Åke Henriksson:	Legendary hardcore musician from Stockholm, mainly known for his band Mob 47.
Fredrik Holmgren:	Founder of Chickenbrain Records, the first label to distribute death metal records in Sweden. He also arranged gigs during the late 80's, and put out 7" singles and demos by Swedish death metal bands. A major character of the early death metal scene, today he is still in the record business.
Johan Jansson:	Avesta's death metal personality number one. He has been in countless bands—including Hatred, Asocial, Beyond, Interment, Dellamorte, Uncurbed, and Centinex—and can handle every instrument. Today he still plays in Uncurbed, a revitalized Interment, the newer band Demonical, and Regurgitate (Stockholm).
Patrik Jensen:	Founder and guitarist of Orchriste, Seance, Witchery, and The Haunted. He also played with Satanic Slaughter. The Haunted and Witchery are both still going strong today.
Jan Johansson:	Founder and guitarist of Obscurity.
Christoffer Jonsson:	Founder and undisputed leader of Therion. For some time a member of Carbonized, and he also has supplied guest vocals for Liers in Wait. Therion remains his main occupation.
Fredrik Karlén:	The madman of Swedish death metal. I couldn't imagine the scene without him. He showed us all how to behave, and taught us the important lesson of not caring at all about anything. On occasion he still keeps Merciless alive, together with the rest of its legendary line-up.
Mattias Kennhed:	Once the guitarist in the death metal bands Macrodex and House of Usher, as well as the hardcore band No Security. In the early 90's he left the death metal scene to focus on hardcore, and he has a become a central character of that scene.

Totte Martini:	Drummer in Crab Phobia/Traumatic. Today he is mainly busy collecting rare horror movies.
Matti Kärki:	The original singer of Therion as well as Carbonized. Later he joined Carnage and Dismember. He was also an originator of General Surgery. Today, Kärki still screams his guts out in the tireless Dismember.
Lennart Larsson:	Creator of Sweden's first extreme metal magazine, *Heavy Metal Massacre*. Later the editor of *Backstage*, and organizer of the 2000 Decibel festival.
Tomas "Tompa" Lindberg:	The ghoulish voice of Grotesque and At the Gates. Long ago he edited the groundbreaking *Cascade* 'zine. Now Lindberg fronts the crust band Disfear and plays with Kristian Wåhlin in The Great Deceiver. He was also the second vocalist of Lock Up.
Ola Lindgren:	Guitarist and later vocalist of Grave, who are still going strong.
Jörgen Lindhe:	Guitarist in the cult band Obscurity.
Jon Nödtveidt:	Notorious leader of Dissection. Back in the days he had the bands Rabbit's Carrot and Satanized, cult act The Black, and edited the great 'zine *Mega Mag*. In 2006, he dissolved Dissection to focus on other things. Nothing came of it—he committed suicide in the summer of 2006.
Tomas Nyqvist:	Editor of the long-lasting fanzine *Putrefaction* and founder of No Fashion Records. Today he runs a new label, Iron Fist Productions.
Johan Österberg	In the old days he edited *Cascade* together with Tomas Lindberg. Later a member of Diabolique, Decollation, and The Great Deceiver.
Digby Pearson:	Founder of the classic Earache Records, which is still putting out death metal releases.
Lars-Göran "L.G." Petrov:	Drummer of Morbid, and later singer of Nihilist and Entombed. Almost single-handily he developed the

	typical growling style of Swedish death metal. He is still the frontman of Entombed.
Dennis Röndum:	Drummer of Spawn of Possession, he was previously the vocalist of Visceral Bleeding.
Lars Rosenberg:	Founder of Carbonized. Later he joined Entombed, as well as Therion.
Orvar Säfström:	Guitarist and vocalist in Nirvana 2002. He edited the fanzine *Hang 'Em High* during the late 80's, and was session vocalist in Entombed during 1991. Until 2006 he hosted the biggest Swedish film program on TV, and is now working on a textbook about cinema.
Jörgen Sandström:	Founder and singer/guitarist/bassist of Grave. Later he played bass in Entombed for many years. Nowadays he is the guitarist in Vicious Art.
Anders Schultz:	Drummer of Unleashed from the start to this day. Notorious metalhead. Heavy beer-drinker.
Jörgen Sigfridsson:	Organizer of many gigs with Therion, Deicide, Candlemass, Immolation, etc., and editor of *Heavy Rock*. He ran the record label Opinionate!/Step One Records. Now completely withdrawn from the scene.
Mats Svensson:	Guitarist in the legendary hardcore band Asocial. Today he is a dedicated fan of extreme death metal.
Roger Svensson:	Bass player in Marduk, and leader of Allegiance. Today he resides in Austin, TX, after a career of evil.
Dan Swanö:	Founder and mastermind of Edge of Sanity. He ran Gorysound/Unisound studio during the 90's. Apart from this, he has constantly been in involved in dozens of metal projects, notably Bloodbath, Incision, and Pan-Thy-Monium.
Peter Tägtgren:	Founder and mastermind behind Hypocrisy. He has participated in projects such as Bloodbath and Lock Up. His greatest achievement was probably The Abyss studio, though, which dominated the field of extreme metal recordings during the late 90's. He is still playing

in Hypocrisy, as well as the techno/metal group Pain.

Jesper Thorsson: Leader of Afflicted Convulsion/Afflicted and "scenester" extraordinaire. Today he has found a nice life for himself as A&R and label manager at Bonnier–Amigo, with classic labels such as Roadrunner under his command.

Daniel Vala: Bass player and vocalist in the legendary Obscurity.

Kristian Wåhlin: Mastermind behind Grotesque's complex songs. Later one of the forces behind Liers in Wait, Decollation and Diabolique. He is probably most known as the album cover artist "Necrolord," though. He has made a good life as a painter, and also plays guitar in Diabolique and The Great Deciever, both with Johan Österberg (and The Great Deceiver also features Thomas Lindberg).

Erik Wallin: Founder and riff-master of Merciless, which he still keeps alive, though on an irregular basis.